International Human Resource Management

International Human Resource Management

Managing people in a multinational context

FIFTH EDITION

Peter J. Dowling

Victoria University of Wellington,

New Zealand

Marion Festing

ESCP-EAP European School of Management,

Germany

Allen D. Engle, Sr

Eastern Kentucky University,

USA

THOMSON

SOUTH-WESTERN

Australia • Brazil • Canada • Mexico • Singapore • Spain • United Kingdom • United States

THOMSON
SOUTH-WESTERN

International Human Resource Management, Fifth Edition

Peter J. Dowling, Marion Festing & Allen D. Engle

VP/Editorial Director:
Jack W. Calhoun

VP/Editor-in-Chief:
Melissa Acuna

Executive Editor:
Joe Sabatino

Executive Marketing Manager:
Kimberly Kanakes

Technology Project Manager:
Kristen Meere

Manufacturing Coordinator:
Doug Wilke

Production House:
Thomson Learning

Printer:
Seng Lee Press, Singapore

Internal Designer:
Design Deluxe Ltd, Bath, UK

Cover Designer:
Design Deluxe Ltd, Bath, UK

Cover Image:
Dreamstime.com

COPYRIGHT © 2009

West Legal Studies in Business, an imprint of Thomson/South-Western. Thomson, the Star logo, and South-Western are trademarks used herein under license.

Printed in the United States of America
1 2 3 4 5 10 09 08 07

Student Edition
ISBN 13: 978-0-324-58034-1
ISBN 10: 0-324-58034-7

ALL RIGHTS RESERVED.
No part of this work covered by the copyright hereon may be reproduced or used in any form or by any means—graphic, electronic, or mechanical, including photocopying, recording, taping, Web distribution or information storage and retrieval systems, or in any other manner—without the written permission of the publisher.

For permission to use material from this text or product, submit a request online at
http://www.thomsonrights.com.

Library of Congress Control Number:
2007935784

For more information about our products, contact us at:
Thomson Learning Academic Resource Center
1-800-423-0563

Thomson Higher Education
5191 Natorp Boulevard
Mason, OH 45040
USA

Contents

CHAPTER 8   Re-entry and career issues 183

CHAPTER 9   IHRM in the host-country context 215

CHAPTER 10   International industrial relations 247

Preface

According to the 2006 *World Investment Report* issued by the United Nations, there are currently a total of 77 000 transnational corporations with over 770 000 foreign affiliates which employ 62 million workers worldwide. In 1990, when the first edition of this textbook was published, a total of 24 million workers were employed. This is merely one of many metrics that demonstrate the extent of the globalization of business. With this increase in scale, the role of human resource management in sustaining this increase in international business activity is a central theme of this Fifth Edition of our textbook. In writing this new edition we have retained much of the format that we developed for the Fourth Edition while including expanded coverage of the international business context in which international human resource management operates. A highlight of significant changes to the Fifth Edition includes the following:

- The explicit introduction of a research-based model of strategic HRM in a multinational enterprise in Chapter 1. This model is used as a heuristic point of reference throughout the text and is revisited in Chapter 12 to investigate trends and future challenges.

- All chapters have been reviewed and updated to incorporate the latest empirical research findings and richly detailed information from informed practitioners.

- The addition of a new chapter, Chapter 3, on the complex human resource challenges inherent in cross-border alliances and the growing internationalization of small and medium-sized enterprises.

- The addition or enhancement of a number of rapidly developing topic areas in HRM for multinational enterprises, including the following:
  - new strategic forms as they impact HRM capabilities and processes;
  - effectiveness in repatriation, transpatriation practices and strategic uses of global careers;
  - considering and calculating return on investment of expatriate assignments;
  - the complexities of standardizing and customizing HRM practices and activities across local environments;
  - the specific IHRM challenges of offshoring in India and China – currently the most popular offshoring locations;
  - challenges related to more sophisticated performance management activities across cultural, institutional and functional divides;
  - multinational family-owned firms;
  - nongovernmental organizations in the multinational context; and
  - safety and security issues and responsibilities in an age of global risk and uncertainty.

- A majority of the 'IHRM in Action' cases embedded throughout the chapters have been replaced or significantly updated. These changes will help students grasp the principles and models in the chapter and better apply these ideas to a range of settings or contexts.

- Three in-depth cases have been added at the end of the text to replace earlier cases. Two of these new cases have been written by the authors and their professional colleagues specifically for this text as a teaching aide to present issues of compensation, HR roles and systems across a wide range of operations, HR metrics and planning for international operations.

The challenge of this Fifth Edition has been to organize the complexities particular to HRM activities in multinational enterprises in such a way that provides teachers (of both undergraduate and graduate students) real choice as to how they will present the material. We have tried to find a balance that is meaningful and appropriate to the varying cultures represented by potential adopters and readers, and across educational traditions, institutions and forms, while accurately capturing the compelling realities facing HRM professionals practising in multinational enterprises. As always, we welcome your comments and suggestions for improvement in this task.

A significant change with this edition is a change in the author team following the decision of our colleague, Denice Welch, to withdraw from authorship of the book due to other commitments. We respect this decision and thank her for her considerable effort and contribution to earlier editions of the book. The new author team is an excellent example of collaborative work – across a great many time zones – in the new global context of the twenty-first century with tri-continental representation from the Asia Pacific, Europe and North America.

Acknowledgements

As with previous editions, we have received a great deal of assistance from numerous colleagues in various educational institutions and organizations across the globe. Particular thanks go to the following colleagues for their assistance with this edition of the book:

- John Boudreau; University of Southern California
- Chris Brewster; University of Reading
- Helen De Cieri; Monash University
- Barry Gerhart; University of Wisconsin-Madison
- Peter McLean; University of Wollongong
- Mark Mendenhall; University of Tennessee-Chattanooga
- Ali Niazi; IBM Australia
- Jozsef Poor; Mercer-Budapest and the University of Pécs
- Susanne Royer; University of Flensburg
- Hugh Scullion; National University of Ireland, Galway
- Günter Stahl; INSEAD

We also gratefully acknowledge the support of the following institutions:

Victoria University of Wellington

Peter Dowling thanks the Head of the School of Marketing and International Business, Associate Professor Val Lindsay, and Jacqui FitzGerald, Jessie Johnston and Margaret Boon for providing such a supportive environment for writing and research. He would also like to thank his colleagues in the International Business Discipline for welcoming him to VUW. The ongoing encouragement of his international business colleague, Elizabeth Rose, to complete this project is also gratefully acknowledged.

ESCP-EAP Berlin

Marion Festing thanks the Head of ESCP-EAP European School of Management in Berlin, Professor Herwig E. Haase and her colleagues for providing a supportive environment for writing and research. Special thanks go to the team of the Chair of Human Resource Management and Intercultural Leadership for outstanding support, especially to Judith Eidems, Ana Comas and Wibke Heidig.

Eastern Kentucky University

Allen Engle thanks the EKU Foundation Board as well as Robert Rogow, Dean of the College of Business and Technology for their ongoing financial support of research and travel. He would also like to acknowledge the longstanding technical and creative help of Ron Yoder, Director of Web Communications at EKU and Florencia Tosiani, an undergraduate and MBA student from Argentina.

The assistance from staff at Thomson Learning UK has been greatly appreciated. In particular, we thank our Publishing Editor, Jennifer Pegg, for her ongoing assistance and advice with this edition and Leandra Paoli and Lucy Mills for their work on the production of the book.

Finally, our personal thanks to the following individuals for their understanding, support and encouragement throughout the process of completing this Fifth Edition:

- Fiona Dowling
- Christian Daubenspeck, Janik and Annika
- Fred and Mary Engle, and Elizabeth Hoffman Engle

Peter J. Dowling,
Wellington

Marion Festing,
Berlin

Allen D. Engle, Sr,
Richmond, Kentucky

About the authors

Peter J. Dowling (PhD, The Flinders University of South Australia) is Professor of International Business in the School of Marketing & International Business at Victoria University of Wellington, New Zealand. Previous appointments include the University of Melbourne, Monash University, the University of Tasmania and University of Canberra. He has also held visiting appointments in the United States at Cornell University and Michigan State University and in Germany at the University of Paderborn and the University of Bayreuth. He has co-authored three books: *Strategic Management: Competitiveness and Globalisation – Pacific Rim Third Edition; Human Resource Management in Australia Second Edition;* and *People in Organizations: An Introduction to Organizational Behavior in Australia*. He has also written or co-authored over 70 journal articles and book chapters and serves on the editorial boards of *International Journal of Human Resource Management, Journal of International Business Studies, Journal of World Business, Management International Review, Journal of International Management, Journal of Management & Organization, ZfP-German Journal of Human Resource Research, Management Revue, Asia Pacific Journal of Human Resources* and *Thunderbird International Business Review.*

He is a past National Vice-President of the Australian Human Resources Institute, past Editor of *Asia Pacific Journal of Human Resources* (1987–96) and a Life Fellow of the Australian Human Resources Institute. Currently, he is a Vice-President of the Australia and New Zealand International Business Academy, President-Elect of the International Federation of Scholarly Associations of Management (IFSAM) and a Senior Research Affiliate of the Center for Advanced Human Resource Studies at Cornell University. Peter is also a past President of the Australian and New Zealand Academy of Management.

Marion Festing (PhD, University of Paderborn) is Professor of Human Resource Management and Intercultural Leadership at ESCP-EAP European School of Management in Berlin, Germany. Previous appointments include the University of Paderborn, Germany. Marion has gained educational, research and work experience in France, Australia, Tunisia, Taiwan and the USA. Her publications include a book on Strategic International Human Resource Management (*Strategisches Internationales Personalmanagement – Second Edition*), a co-authored text on International Human Resource Management (*Internationales Personalmanagement – Second Edition*) and she has guest-edited special issues of *Management International Review* on IHRM. She has also written or co-authored over 50 book chapters and journal articles and published in international journals such as *Management*

International Review, Economic and Industrial Demography, European Management Journal and *International Journal of Globalisation and Small Business*.

Marion serves on the editorial boards of *Career Development International, Journal of Management & Organization, International Journal of Globalisation and Small Business, ZfP-German Journal of Human Resource Research* and *Zeitschrift für Management*. She was co-organizer of the sixth conference on International Human Resource Management in Paderborn in 1998, and co-chair of the IHRM track at the International Federation of Scholarly Associations of Management (IFSAM) conference in Berlin in 2006. Her current research interests focus on transnational HRM strategies, global careers and global compensation.

Allen D. Engle, Sr. (DBA, University of Kentucky) is a Professor of Management in the College of Business and Technology at Eastern Kentucky University. He is a national and regional professional member of World at Work (formerly the American Compensation Association) and of the Society for Human Resource Management and a long time member of the US Academy of Management. While at Eastern, he has taught courses in management (undergraduate and graduate), a number of areas within human resource administration, organizational behavior, organizational theory and international management (undergraduate and graduate). He has been Visiting Lecturer at the FHS – Hochschule Für Technik, Wirtschaft und Soziale Arbeit, St Gallen in Switzerland and Visiting Professor of International Management at the University of Pécs in Hungary.

His research interests are in the topic areas of compensation theory and practices, leadership and organizational change, job analysis, managerial competencies and organizational design, particularly as they impact on multinational firms. He has published in regional, national and international academic journals, presenting academic papers on many of the topic areas presented above at conferences in the USA, Australia, Canada, Estonia, Germany, Hungary, Ireland, Slovenia, Spain and the United Kingdom. Allen has consulted for regional firms and presented professional seminars in the areas of performance appraisal systems, executive team building, strategically responsive compensation systems, intercultural management issues and organizational change.

Walk through tour

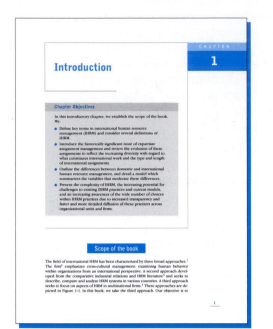

Chapter Objectives appear at the start of every chapter and help you monitor your understanding and progress through the chapter.

Figures give a visual representation of key concepts or data.

Tables help to order significant data and trends.

IHRM in Action cases provide real-life examples of the concepts and issues covered in the chapter.

Summary boxes at the end of each chapter provide a thorough re-cap of key issues and help you assess your understanding of key content.

Discussion Questions are provided at the end of each chapter and are designed to give a platform for classroom discussion.

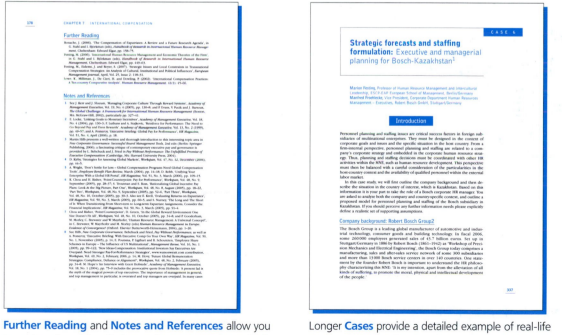

Further Reading and **Notes and References** allow you to explore the subject further and act as a starting point for projects and assignments.

Longer **Cases** provide a detailed example of real-life Human Resource situations. Some cases are accompanied by figures, tables and notes.

About the website

Visit the *International Human Resource Management – Fifth Edition* accompanying website at www.thomsonlearning.co.uk/dowling5 to find valuable further material including:

For students

- Case notes and answer notes relating to case studies and relevant chapters which will enhance your understanding of ideas within each chapter
- Related web links to direct you to further resources

For instructors

- Instructor's Manual consisting of teaching notes, how to use the text and answers to questions within the text
- Downloadable Powerpoint slides featuring diagrams and models from the book

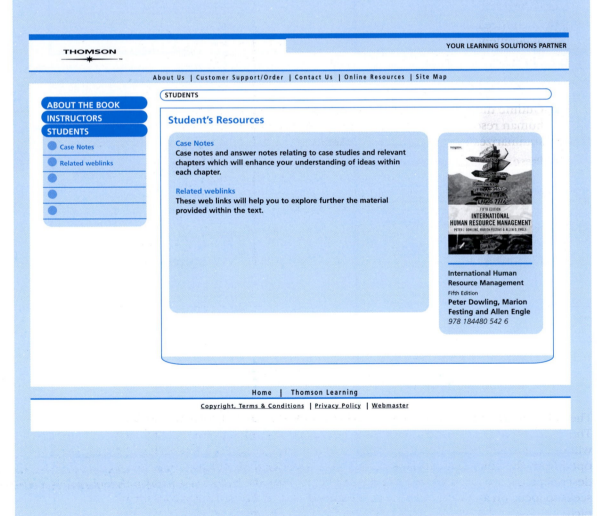

Introduction

Chapter Objectives

In this introductory chapter, we establish the scope of the book. We:

- Define key terms in international human resource management (IHRM) and consider several definitions of IHRM.
- Introduce the historically significant issue of expatriate assignment management and review the evolution of these assignments to reflect the increasing diversity with regard to what constitutes international work and the type and length of international assignments.
- Outline the differences between domestic and international human resource management, and detail a model which summarizes the variables that moderate these differences.
- Present the complexity of IHRM, the increasing potential for challenges to existing IHRM practices and current models, and an increasing awareness of the wide number of choices within IHRM practices due to increased transparency and faster and more detailed diffusion of these practices across organizational units and firms.

Scope of the book

The field of international HRM has been characterized by three broad approaches.[1] The first[2] emphasizes cross-cultural management: examining human behavior within organizations from an international perspective. A second approach developed from the comparative industrial relations and HRM literature[3] and seeks to describe, compare and analyze HRM systems in various countries. A third approach seeks to focus on aspects of HRM in multinational firms.[4] These approaches are depicted in Figure 1-1. In this book, we take the third approach. Our objective is to

| **Figure 1-1** | Inter-relationships between approaches to the field |

explore the implications that the process of internationalization has for the activities and policies of HRM. In particular, we are interested in how HRM is practiced in multinationals – hence the subtitle of this book 'Managing People in a Multinational Context'.

As Figure 1-1 demonstrates, there is an inevitable overlap between the three approaches when one is attempting to provide an accurate view of the global realities of operating in the international business environment. Obviously, cross-cultural management issues are important when dealing with the cultural aspects of foreign operations. Some of these aspects will be taken up in Chapter 9 where we deal with HRM in the host country context – indicated by (a) in Figure 1-1. Chapter 10 deals with industrial relations issues and draws on literature from the comparative IR field – (b) in the above figure. While the focus of much of this book is on the established multinational enterprise (MNE) – a firm which owns or controls business activities in more than one foreign country – we recognize that small, internationalizing firms which are yet to reach multinational firm status, and family-owned firms, also face international HRM issues.[5]

Defining international HRM

Before we can offer a definition of international HRM, we should first define the general field of HRM. Typically, HRM refers to those activities undertaken by an organization to effectively utilize its human resources. These activities would include at least the following:

1 Human resource planning
2 Staffing (recruitment, selection, placement)
3 Performance management
4 Training and development
5 Compensation (remuneration) and benefits
6 Industrial relations

The question is of course which activities change when HRM goes international. A model (shown in Figure 1-2) developed by Morgan[6] is helpful. He presents IHRM on three dimensions:

1 The broad human resource activities of procurement, allocation and utilization. (These three broad activities can be easily expanded into the six HR activities listed above.)

A model of IHRM   **Figure 1-2**

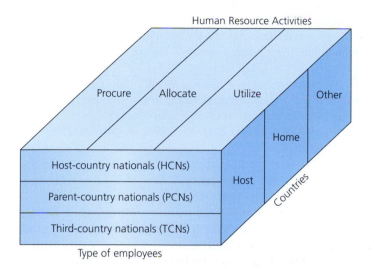

Source: Adapted from P.V. Morgan, 'International Human Resource Management: Fact or Fiction', *Personnel Administrator,* Vol. 31, No. 9 (1986), p. 44.

2   The national or country categories involved in international HRM activities:

   ● the host-country where a subsidiary may be located;
   ● the home-country where the firm is headquartered; and
   ● 'other' countries that may be the source of labor, finance and other inputs.

3   The three categories of employees of an international firm:

   ● host-country nationals (HCNs);
   ● parent-country nationals (PCNs); and
   ● third-country nationals (TCNs).

Thus, for example, the US multinational IBM employs Australian citizens in its Australian operations (HCNs), often sends US citizens (PCNs) to Asia-Pacific countries on assignment, and may send some of its Singaporean employees on an assignment to its Japanese operations (as TCNs). The nationality of the employee is a major factor in determining the person's 'category', which in turn is frequently a major driver of the employee's compensation.

Morgan defines international HRM as the interplay among these three dimensions in Figure 1-2 – human resource activities, type of employees and countries of operation. We can see that in broad terms IHRM involves the same activities as domestic HRM (e.g. procurement refers to HR planning and staffing). However, domestic HRM is involved with employees *within only one national boundary*. Increasingly, domestic HRM is taking on some of the flavor of IHRM as it deals more and more with a multicultural workforce. Thus, some of the current focus of domestic HRM on issues of managing workforce diversity may prove to be beneficial to the practice of IHRM. However, it must be remembered that the way in which diversity is managed within a single national context may not necessarily transfer to a multinational context without some modification.

What is an expatriate?

One obvious difference between domestic and international HRM is that staff are moved across national boundaries into various roles within the international firm's foreign operations – these employees have traditionally been called 'expatriates'. An expatriate is an employee who is working and temporarily residing in a foreign country. Some firms prefer to call such employees 'international assignees'. While it is clear in the literature that PCNs are always expatriates, it is often overlooked that TCNs are expatriates, as are HCNs who are transferred into parent country operations outside their home country.[7] Figure 1-3 illustrates how all three categories may become expatriates.

Lately, the term *inpatriate* has come into vogue to signify the transfer of subsidiary staff into the parent country (headquarters) operations.[8] Its use has added a level of confusion surrounding the definition of an expatriate. For example, the *International Human Resource Management Reference Guide,* published by the Institute for International Human Resources (a division of the US Society for Human Resource Management) defines an inpatriate as a 'foreign manager in the U.S.'. A 'foreign manager in the U.S.' is then defined as 'an expatriate in the U.S. where the U.S. is the host-country and the manager's home-country is outside of the U.S.'.[9] In other words, an inpatriate is also defined as an expatriate. A further indication of the confusion created by the use of the term 'inpatriate' is that some writers in international management define a HCN as an inpatriate. HCNs only become 'inpatriates' when they are transferred into the parent-country operations as expatriates, as illustrated in Figure 1-3.

Given the substantial amount of jargon in IHRM, it is questionable as to whether the term 'inpatriate' adds enough value to justify its use. However, companies now use the term. For example, the Finnish multinational Nokia uses 'expatriate' to signify staff who are transferred out of, and 'inpatriate' to signify staff transferred into, a particular country. These terms are regarded as a constant reminder to all managers that there are movements of staff that need to be managed, and not all are PCNs. For clarity, we will use the term *expatriate* throughout this text to refer to employees who are transferred out of their home base into some other area of the firm's international operations, unless we are directly quoting from another source. In doing so, we recognize that there is increasing diversity with regard to what constitutes international work and the type and length of international

---

Figure 1-3   International assignments create expatriates

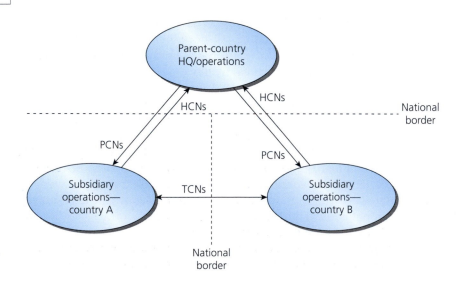

assignments and the increasingly strategic role of the HR function in many organizations, which in turn influences the nature of some expatriate roles.

Stahl and Björkman have recognized this expansion in the scope of the field of IHRM in their *Handbook of Research in International Human Resource Management* where they define the field of IHRM in the following way:

> We define the field of IHRM broadly to cover all issues related to the management of people in an international context. Hence our definition of IHRM covers a wide range of human resource issues facings MNCs in different parts of their organizations. Additionally, we include comparative analyzes of HRM in different countries.[10]

We will be examining the expanding scope of the IHRM field in this book and will return to the question of a definition of the field in the final chapter.

Differences between domestic and international HRM

In our view, the *complexity* of operating in different countries and employing different national categories of workers is a key variable that differentiates domestic and international HRM, rather than any major differences between the HRM activities performed. Dowling[11] argues that the complexity of international HR can be attributed to six factors:

1 More HR activities.
2 The need for a broader perspective.
3 More involvement in employees' personal lives.
4 Changes in emphasis as the workforce mix of expatriates and locals varies.
5 Risk exposure.
6 Broader external influences.

Each of these factors is now discussed in detail to illustrate its characteristics.

More HR activities

To operate in an international environment, a human resources department must engage in a number of activities that would not be necessary in a domestic environment: international taxation; international relocation and orientation; administrative services for expatriates; host-government relations; and language translation services.

Expatriates are subject to international taxation, and often have both domestic (i.e. home-country) and host-country tax liabilities. Therefore, tax equalization policies must be designed to ensure that there is no tax incentive or disincentive associated with any particular international assignment.[12] The administration of tax equalization policies is complicated by the wide variations in tax laws across host countries and by the possible time-lag between the completion of an expatriate assignment and the settlement of domestic and international tax liabilities. In recognition of these difficulties, many multinational firms retain the services of a major accounting firm for international taxation advice.

International relocation and orientation involves: arranging for predeparture training; providing immigration and travel details; providing housing, shopping, medical care, recreation and schooling information; and finalizing compensation details such as delivery of salary overseas, determination of various overseas allowances and taxation treatment. (The issue of expatriates returning to their home-country (repatriation) is covered in detail in Chapter 8.) Many of these factors may be a source of anxiety for the expatriate and require considerable time and attention to successfully resolve potential problems – certainly much more time than would be involved in a domestic transfer/relocation such as London to Glasgow, Frankfurt to Munich, New York to Dallas, Sydney to Melbourne, or Beijing to Shanghai.

An MNE also needs to provide administrative services for expatriates in the host countries in which it operates. Providing these can often be a time-consuming and complex activity because policies and procedures are not always clear-cut and may conflict with local conditions. Ethical questions can arise when a practice that is legal and accepted in the host country may be at best unethical and at worst illegal in the home country. For example, a situation may arise in which a host country requires an AIDS test for a work permit for an employee whose parent firm is headquartered in the USA, where employment-related AIDS testing remains a controversial issue. How does the corporate HR manager deal with the potential expatriate employee who refuses to meet this requirement for an AIDS test and the overseas affiliate which needs the services of a specialist expatriate from headquarters? These issues add to the complexity of providing administrative services to expatriates.

Host-government relations represent an important activity for a HR department, particularly in developing countries where work permits and other important certificates are often more easily obtained when a personal relationship exists between the relevant government officials and multinational managers. Maintaining such relationships helps resolve potential problems that can be caused by ambiguous eligibility and/or compliance criteria for documentation such as work permits. US-based multinationals, however, must be careful in how they deal with relevant government officials, as payment or payment-in-kind, such as dinners and gifts, may violate the US Foreign Corrupt Practices Act (FCPA).[13] Provision of language translation services for internal and external correspondence is an additional international activity for the HR department. Morgan[14] notes that if the HR department is the major user of language translation services, the role of this translation group is often expanded to provide translation services to all foreign operation departments within the multinational.

The need for a broader perspective

HR managers working in a domestic environment generally administer programs for a single national group of employees who are covered by a uniform compensation policy and taxed by one national government. Because HR managers working in an international environment face the problem of designing and administering programs for more than one national group of employees (e.g. PCN, HCN and TCN employees who may work together in Zurich at the European regional headquarters of a US-based multinational), they need to take a broader view of issues. For example, a broader, more international perspective on expatriate benefits would endorse the view that all expatriate employees, regardless of nationality, should receive a foreign service or expatriate premium when working in a foreign location. Yet some MNEs which routinely pay such premiums to their PCN employees on overseas assignment (even if the assignments are to desirable locations) are reluctant to pay premiums to foreign nationals assigned to the home country of the firm. Such a policy confirms the traditional perception of many HCN and TCN employees that PCN employees (particularly US and European PCNs) are given preferential treatment.[15] Complex equity issues arise when employees of various nationalities work together, and the resolution of these issues remains one of the major challenges in the IHRM field. (Equity issues with regard to compensation are discussed in Chapter 7.)

More involvement in employees' personal lives

A greater degree of involvement in employees' personal lives is necessary for the selection, training and effective management of both PCN and TCN employees. The HR department or HR professional needs to ensure that the expatriate employee understands housing arrangements, health care, and all aspects of the compensation package provided for the assignment (cost-of-living allowances, premiums, taxes and so on). Many multinationals have an 'International HR Services' section that coordinates administration of the above programs and provides services for PCNs and TCNs, such as handling their banking, investments, home rental while on assignment, coordinating home visits and final repatriation.

In the domestic setting, the HR department's involvement with an employee's family is limited. The firm may, for example, provide employee health insurance programs. Or, if a domestic transfer is involved, the HR department may provide some assistance in relocating the employee and family. In the international setting, however, the HR department must be much more involved in order to provide the level of support required and will need to know more about the employee's personal life. For example, some governments require the presentation of a marriage certificate before granting a visa to an accompanying spouse. Thus, marital status could become an aspect of the selection process, regardless of the best intentions of the firm to avoid using a potentially discriminatory selection criterion. In such a situation, the HR department should advise all candidates being considered for the position of the host country's visa requirements with regard to marital status and allow candidates to decide whether they wish to remain in the selection process. Apart from providing suitable housing and schooling in the assignment location, the HR department may also need to assist children left behind at boarding schools in the home country.[16] In more remote or less hospitable assignment locations, the HR department may be required to develop, and even run, recreational programs. For a domestic assignment, most of these matters either would not arise or would be primarily the responsibility of the employee rather than the HR department.

Changes in emphasis as the workforce mix of PCNs and HCNs varies

As foreign operations mature, the emphases put on various human resource activities change. For example, as the need for PCNs and TCNs declines and more trained locals become available, resources previously allocated to areas such as expatriate taxation, relocation and orientation are transferred to activities such as local staff selection, training and management development. The latter activity may require the establishment of a program to bring high-potential local staff to corporate headquarters for developmental assignments. The need to change emphasis in HR operations as a foreign subsidiary matures is clearly a factor that would broaden the responsibilities of local HR activities such as human resource planning, staffing, training and development and compensation.

Risk exposure

Frequently, the human and financial consequences of failure in the international arena are more severe than in domestic business. For example, while we discuss the topic in more detail in Chapter 5, expatriate failure (the premature return of an expatriate from an international assignment) and under-performance while on international assignment is a potentially high-cost problem for MNEs. The direct costs (salary, training costs and travel and relocation expenses) of failure to the parent firm may be as high as three times the domestic salary plus relocation expenses, depending on currency exchange rates and location of assignments. Indirect costs such as loss of foreign market share and damage to key host-country relationships may be considerable.

Another aspect of risk exposure that is relevant to IHRM is terrorism, particularly in the current political climate since the tragic 9/11 attack in New York in 2001. Most major multinationals must now consider political risk and terrorism when planning international meetings and assignments and spending on protection against terrorism is increasing. Terrorism has also clearly had an effect on the way in which employees assess potential international assignment locations.[17] The HR department may also need to devise emergency evacuation procedures for highly volatile assignment locations subject to political or terrorist violence, or major epidemic or pandemic crises such as severe acute respiratory syndrome (SARS) and avian influenza.[18] For a comprehensive analysis of the impact of SARS on human resource management in the Hong Kong service sector, see Lee and Warner.[19]

Broader external influences

The major external factors that influence IHRM are the type of government, the state of the economy and the generally accepted practices of doing business in each of the various host countries in which the multinational operates. A host government can, for example, dictate hiring procedures, as has been the case until recently in Malaysia. The Malaysian government during the 1970s introduced a requirement that foreign firms comply with an extensive set of affirmative action rules designed to provide additional employment opportunities for the indigenous Malays who constitute the majority of the population but tend to be under-represented in business and professional employment groups relative to Chinese Malays and Indian Malays. Various statistics showing employment levels of indigenous Malays throughout the firm were required to be forwarded to the relevant government department. Many foreign investors regarded these requirements as a major reason for complaints about bureaucracy and inflexibility in Malaysia and these complaints are one significant reason for the revision of these requirements.

In developed countries, labor is more expensive and better organized than in less-developed countries, and governments require compliance with guidelines on issues such as labor relations, taxation and health and safety. These factors shape the activities of the subsidiary HR manager to a considerable extent. In less-developed countries, labor tends to be cheaper and less organized, and government regulation is less pervasive, so these factors take less time. The subsidiary HR manager must spend more time, however, learning and interpreting the local ways of doing business and the general code of conduct regarding activities such as gift giving. It is also likely that the subsidiary HR manager will become more involved in administering benefits either provided or financed by the multinational, such as housing, education and other facilities not readily available in the local economy.

Variables that moderate differences between domestic and international HRM

Earlier in this chapter it was argued that the complexity involved in operating in different countries and employing different national categories of employees is a key variable that differentiates domestic and international HRM, rather than any major differences between the HRM activities performed. Many firms underestimate the complexities involved in international operations, and there has been consistent evidence to suggest that business failures in the international arena are often linked to poor management of human resources. In addition to complexity, there are four other variables that moderate (that is, either diminish or accentuate) differences between domestic and international HRM. These four additional moderators are:

● The cultural environment.
● The industry (or industries) with which the multinational is primarily involved.
● The extent of reliance of the multinational on its home-country domestic market.
● The attitudes of senior management.

Together with the complexity involved in operating in different countries, these five variables constitute a model that explains the differences between domestic and international HRM (see Figure 1-4).

The cultural environment

There are many definitions of *culture*, but the term is usually used to describe a shaping process over time. This process generates relative stability, reflecting a

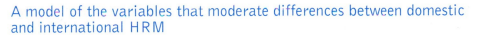

A model of the variables that moderate differences between domestic and international HRM

Figure 1-4

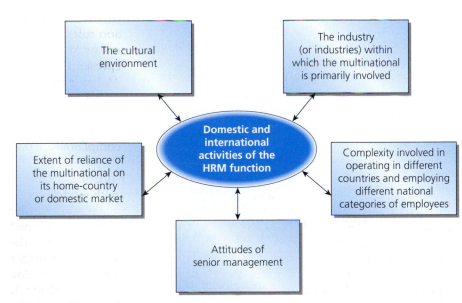

Source: P. J. Dowling, 'Completing the Puzzle: Issues in the Development of the Field of International Human Resource Management', (mir) *Management International Review,* Special Issue No. 3/99 (1999), p. 31.

shared knowledge structure that attenuates (i.e. reduces) variability in values, behavioral norms and patterns of behavior.[20] An important characteristic of culture is that it is so subtle a process that one is not always conscious of its effect on values, attitudes and behaviors. One usually has to be confronted with a different culture in order to fully appreciate this effect. Anyone traveling abroad, either as a tourist or on business, experiences situations that demonstrate cultural differences in language, food, dress, hygiene and attitude to time. While the traveler can perceive these differences as novel, even enjoyable, for people required to live and work in a new country, such differences can prove difficult. They may experience *culture shock* – a phenomenon experienced by people who move across cultures. The new environment requires many adjustments in a relatively short period of time, challenging people's frames of reference to such an extent that their sense of self, especially in terms of nationality, comes into question. People, in effect, experience a shock reaction to new cultural experiences that cause psychological disorientation because they misunderstand or do not recognize important cues. Culture shock can lead to negative feelings about the host country and its people and a longing to return home.[21]

Because international business involves the interaction and movement of people across national boundaries, an appreciation of cultural differences and when these differences are important is essential. Research into these aspects has assisted in furthering our understanding of the cultural environment as an important variable that moderates differences between domestic and international HRM. However, while cross-cultural and comparative research attempts to explore and explain similarities and differences, there are problems associated with such research. A major problem is that there is little agreement on either an exact definition of culture or on the operationalization of this concept. For many researchers, culture has become an omnibus variable, representing a range of social, historic, economic and political factors that are invoked *post hoc* to explain similarity or dissimilarity in the results of a study. As Bhagat and McQuaid[22] have noted, '*Culture* has often served simply as a synonym for *nation* without any further conceptual grounding. In effect, national differences found in the characteristics of organizations or their members have been interpreted as cultural differences.' To reduce these difficulties, culture needs to be defined a priori rather than *post hoc* and it should not be assumed that national differences necessarily represent cultural differences.

Another issue in cross-cultural research concerns the *emic-etic* distinction.[23] *Emic* refers to culture-specific aspects of concepts or behavior, and *etic* refers to culture-common aspects. These terms have been borrowed from linguistics: a phon*emic* system documents meaningful sounds specific to a given language, and a phon*etic* system organizes all sounds that have meaning in any language.[24] Both the emic and etic approaches are legitimate research orientations. A major problem may arise, however, if a researcher imposes an etic approach (that is, assumes universality across cultures) when there is little or no evidence for doing so. A well-known example of an imposed etic approach is the convergence hypothesis that dominated much of US and European management research in the 1950s and 1960s. This approach was based on two key assumptions.[25] The first assumption was that there were principles of sound management that held regardless of national environments. Thus, the existence of local or national practices that deviated from these principles simply indicated a need to change these local practices. The second assumption was that the universality of sound management practices would lead to societies becoming more and more alike in the future. Given that the USA was the leading industrial economy at that time, the point of convergence was the US model.

To use Kuhn's[26] terminology, the convergence hypothesis became an established paradigm that many researchers found difficult to give up, despite a growing body of evidence supporting a divergence hypothesis. In an important early paper which reviewed the convergence/divergence debate, Child[27] made the point that there is evidence for both convergence and divergence. The majority of the convergence studies, however, focus on macrolevel variables (for example, organizational structure and technology used by firms across cultures), and the majority of the divergence studies focus on microlevel variables (for example, the behavior of people within firms). His conclusion was that although firms in different countries are becoming more alike (an etic or convergence approach), the behavior of individuals within these firms is maintaining its cultural specificity (an emic or divergence approach). As noted above, both emic and etic approaches are legitimate research orientations, but methodological difficulties may arise if the distinction between these two approaches is ignored or if unwarranted universality assumptions are made.[28] The debate on assumptions of universality is not limited to the literature in international management as this issue has also become a topic of debate in the field of international relations and strategic studies where international management research is cited.[29] For a recent review of the convergence/divergence question, see Brewster.[30]

The importance of cultural awareness

Despite the methodological concerns about cross-cultural research, it is now generally recognized that culturally insensitive attitudes and behaviors stemming from ignorance or from misguided beliefs ('my way is best', or 'what works at home will work here') not only are inappropriate but often cause international business failure. Therefore, an awareness of cultural differences is essential for the HR manager at corporate headquarters as well as in the host location.[31] Activities such as hiring, promoting, rewarding and dismissal will be determined by the practices of the host country and often are based on a value system peculiar to that country's culture. A firm may decide to head up a new overseas operation with an expatriate general manager but appoint as the HR department manager a local, a person who is familiar with the host country's HR practices. This practice can assist in avoiding problems but can still lead to dilemmas for senior managers. For example, in a number of developing countries (Indonesia is one such example) local employees feel an obligation to employ their extended family if they are in a position to do so. This may lead to a situation where staff are hired who do not possess the required technical competence. While this could be seen as a successful example of adapting to local expectations and customs, from a Western perspective this practice would be seen as nepotism, a negative practice which is not in the best interests of the enterprise because the best people have not been hired for the job.

Wyatt[32] recounts a good example of the fallacy of assuming 'what works at home will work here' when dealing with work situations in another culture. HR department staff of a large firm in Papua New Guinea were concerned over a number of accidents involving operators of very large, expensive, earth-moving vehicles. The expatriate managers investigating the accidents found that local drivers involved in the accidents were chewing betel nut, a common habit for most of the coastal peoples of Papua New Guinea and other Pacific islands. Associating the betel nut with depressants such as alcohol, the expatriate managers banned the chewing of betel nut during work hours. In another move to reduce the number of accidents, free coffee was provided at loading points, and drivers were required to alight from their vehicles at these locations. What the managers did not realize was that betel nut, like their culturally acceptable coffee, is, in fact, a stimulant, though some of the drivers were chewing it to cover up the fact that they drank beer before commencing work. As Wyatt points out, many indigenous workers used betel nut as a pick-me-up in much the same way as the expatriates used coffee.

Coping with cultural differences, and recognizing how and when these differences are relevant, is a constant challenge for international firms. Helping to prepare staff and their families for working and living in a new cultural environment has become a key activity for HR departments in those multinationals that appreciate (or have been forced, through experience, to appreciate) the impact that the cultural environment can have on staff performance and well-being. We shall address key issues relating to cultural differences and staff preparation and adjustment in later chapters of this text.

Hofstede's framework of national culture

Before leaving the issue of culture and cultural differences, it is appropriate to acknowledge the important contribution to the international management literature of the cultural typologies proposed over 25 years ago by Hofstede in his classic book *Culture's Consequences: International Differences in Work-Related Values* which proposed that national culture can be set out as a measurable set of constructs.[33] While a more detailed discussion is beyond the scope of this chapter, a very considerable literature has been generated since the initial publication of Hofstede's book, much of it examining the methodological limitations of the cultural dimensions proposed by Hofstede (individualism/collectivism; power distance; masculinity/femininity; and uncertainty avoidance).[34] Part of this literature includes conceptual critiques of Hofstede's work with a relatively recent paper by McSweeney generating a considerable amount of debate.[35] For a broader review of the contribution of Hofstede's work to the field of international management, see Hoppe,[36] Gerhart and Fang[37] and Leung *et al.*[38]

Industry type

Porter[39] suggests that the industry (or industries if the firm is a conglomerate) in which a multinational firm is involved is of considerable importance because patterns of international competition vary widely from one industry to another. At one end of the continuum of international competition is the *multidomestic industry,* one in which competition in each country is essentially independent of competition in other countries. Traditional examples include retailing, distribution and insurance. At the other end of the continuum is the *global industry,* one in which a firm's competitive position in one country is significantly influenced by its position in other countries. Examples include commercial aircraft, semiconductors and copiers. The key distinction between a multidomestic industry and a global industry is described by Porter as follows:

> The global industry is not merely a collection of domestic industries but a series of linked domestic industries in which the rivals compete against each other on a truly worldwide basis. . . . In a multidomestic industry, then, international strategy collapses to a series of domestic strategies. The issues that are uniquely international revolve around how to do business abroad,

how to select good countries in which to compete (or assess country risk), and mechanisms to achieve the one-time transfer of know-how. These are questions that are relatively well developed in the literature. In a global industry, however, managing international activities like a portfolio will undermine the possibility of achieving competitive advantage. In a global industry, a firm must in some way integrate its activities on a worldwide basis to capture the linkages among countries.

The role of the HRM function in multidomestic and global industries can be analyzed using Porter's value-chain model.[40] In Porter's model, HRM is seen as one of four support activities for the five primary activities of the firm. Since human resources are involved in each of the primary and support activities, the HRM function is seen as cutting across the entire value chain of a firm. If the firm is in a multidomestic industry, the role of the HR department will most likely be more domestic in structure and orientation. At times there may be considerable demand for international services from the HRM function (for example, when a new plant or office is established in a foreign location and the need for expatriate employees arises), but these activities would not be pivotal – indeed, many of these services may be provided via consultants and/or temporary employees. The main role for the HRM function would be to support the primary activities of the firm in each domestic market to achieve a competitive advantage through either cost/efficiency or product/service differentiation. If the multinational is in a global industry, however, the 'imperative for coordination' described by Porter would require a HRM function structured to deliver the international support required by the primary activities of the multinational.

The need to develop coordination raises complex problems for any multinational. As Laurent[41] has noted:

> In order to build, maintain, and develop their corporate identity, multinational organizations need to strive for consistency in their ways of managing people on a worldwide basis. Yet, and in order to be effective locally, they also need to adapt those ways to the specific cultural requirements of different societies. While the global nature of the business may call for increased consistency, the variety of cultural environments may be calling for differentiation.

Laurent proposes that a truly international conception of human resource management would require the following steps:

1 An explicit recognition by the parent organization that its own peculiar ways of managing human resources reflect some assumptions and values of its home culture.

2 An explicit recognition by the parent organization that its peculiar ways are neither universally better nor worse than others but are different and likely to exhibit strengths and weaknesses, particularly abroad.

3 An explicit recognition by the parent organization that its foreign subsidiaries may have other preferred ways of managing people that are neither intrinsically better nor worse, but could possibly be more effective locally.

4 A willingness from headquarters to not only acknowledge cultural differences, but also to take active steps in order to make them discussable and therefore usable.

5 The building of a genuine belief by all parties involved that more creative and effective ways of managing people could be developed as a result of cross-cultural learning.

In offering this proposal, Laurent acknowledges that these are difficult steps that few firms have taken: 'They have more to do with states of mind and mindsets than with behaviors. As such, these processes can only be facilitated and this may represent a primary mission for executives in charge of international human resource management.'[42]

Implicit in Laurent's analysis is the idea that by taking the steps he describes, a multinational attempting to implement a global strategy via coordination of activities would be better able to work through the difficulties and complex trade-offs inherent in such a strategy. Increasingly, multinationals are taking a more strategic approach to the role of HRM and are using staff transfers and training programs to assist in coordination of activities. We discuss these issues in more detail in subsequent chapters of the book.

Reliance of the multinational on its home-country domestic market

A pervasive but often ignored factor which influences the behavior of multinationals and resultant HR practices is the extent of reliance of the multinational on its home-country domestic market. When for example, we look through lists of very large firms (such as those that appear in *Fortune* and other business magazines), it is frequently assumed that a global market perspective would be dominant in the firm's culture and thinking. However, size is not the only key variable when looking at a multinational – the extent of reliance of the multinational on its home-country domestic market is also very important. In fact, for many firms, a small home market is one of the key drivers for seeking new international markets.

The United Nations Conference on Trade and Development (UNCTAD) in its annual survey of foreign direct investment calculates what it refers to as an 'index of transnationality', which is an average of ratios of foreign assets to total assets; foreign sales to total sales; and foreign employment to total employment.[43] The 'top ten' multinationals are shown in Table 1-1. Based on this index of transnationality, the most foreign-oriented multinational is Thomson Corporation (Canada), with an average of 97 per cent of the three ratios (foreign assets to total assets, foreign sales to total sales and foreign employment to total employment) located outside of Canada.

The only US firm in the 30 multinationals ranked by the transnational index is the AES Corporation (electricity, gas and water) ranked 22nd. McDonald's Corporation is ranked 35th. The reason for this lower ranking of US firms in terms of the transnational index is as obvious as it is important – *the size of the domestic market* for US firms. A very large domestic market (for US firms this is in effect the North American Free Trade Agreement [NAFTA] market) influences all aspects of how a multinational organizes its activities. For example, it will be more likely to use an international division as the way it organizes its international activities (see Chapter 2) and even if it uses a global product structure, the importance of the domestic market will be pervasive. A large domestic market will also influence the attitudes of senior managers towards their international activities and will generate a large number of managers with an experience base of predominantly or even exclusively domestic market experience. Thus, multinationals from small advanced economies like Switzerland (population 7.5 million), Ireland (4 million),

Table 1-1

World top ten non-financial transnational corporations, ranked by transnational index

Transnational index	Ranking by foreign assets	Company name	Home economy	Industry
1	70	Thomson Corporation	Canada	Media
2	88	CRH Plc	Ireland	Lumber and other building material dealers
3	19	Nestlé SA	Switzerland	Food and beverages
4	2	Vodafone Group Plc	United Kingdom	Telecommunications
5	56	Alcan Inc	Canada	Metal and metal products
6	57	Koninklijke Ahold	USA/Netherlands	Retail
7	47	Philips Electronics	Netherlands	Electrical and electronic equipment
8	99	Nortel Networks	Canada	Telecommunications
9	38	Unilever	United Kingdom/ Netherlands	Diversified retail
10	5	British Petroleum Company Plc	United Kingdom	Petroleum

Source: The data in this table is based on the World Investment Report, 2006; *FDI from Developing and Transition Economies: Implications for Development,* United Nations Conference on Trade and Development (UNCTAD), 2006.

Australia (20 million) and The Netherlands (16.5 million) and medium-size advanced economies like Canada (33 million), the United Kingdom (60 million) and France (61 million) are in a quite different position compared to multinationals based in the USA which is the largest advanced economy in the world with a population of 300 million. US multinationals also enjoy the advantage of a dominant position in the NAFTA market (the USA, Canada and Mexico) which has a total market population of 439 million.

If the UNCTAD data is rank ordered only on the ratio of foreign assets to total assets the listing shown in Table 1-2 shows a number of changes, with four US firms listed and only two firms from the transnational index (the British companies Vodafone Group and British Petroleum) remaining. The removal of the other two ratios (foreign sales to total sales; foreign employment to total employment) from the transnational index significantly reinterprets the data which is presented in Table 1-1. It is worth keeping in mind that the frequent criticism of US companies, US senior managers and US business schools as inward-looking and ethnocentric may perhaps be true to some extent, *but it is equally true* that a focus on domestic US sales and revenue is also an entirely rational response to the overwhelming importance of the North American market for many of these businesses.

The demands of a large domestic market present a challenge to the globalization efforts of many US firms. As Cavusgil[44] has noted in an important book on

Table 1-2	World top ten non-financial transnational corporations, ranked only by foreign assets

Ranking by foreign assets	Transnational index	Company name	Home economy	Industry
1	68	General Electric	USA	Electrical and electronic equipment
2	4	Vodafone Group Plc	United Kingdom	Telecommunications
3	67	Ford Motors	USA	Motor vehicles
4	90	General Motors	USA	Motor vehicles
5	10	British Petroleum Company Plc	United Kingdom	Petroleum
6	38	Exxon Mobil	USA	Petroleum
7	25	Royal Dutch/ Shell Group	United Kingdom/ Netherlands	Petroleum
8	62	Toyota Motor Corporation	Japan	Motor vehicles
9	20	Total	France	Petroleum
10	10	France Telecom	France	Telecommunications

Source: The data in this Table is based on the World Investment Report, 2006; *FDI from Developing and Transition Economies: Implications for Development*, United Nations Conference on Trade and Development (UNCTAD), 2006.

internationalizing business education, the task of internationalizing business education in the USA is a large one. So too is the task facing many US firms in terms of developing global managers – an issue which we shall return to in Chapter 6.

Attitudes of senior management to international operations

The point made by Laurent earlier in this chapter that some of the changes required to truly internationalize the HR function 'have more to do with states of mind and mindsets than with behaviors' illustrates the importance of a final variable that may moderate differences between international and domestic HRM: the attitudes of senior management to international operations. It is likely that if senior management does not have a strong international orientation, the importance of international operations may be underemphasized (or possibly even ignored) in terms of corporate goals and objectives. In such situations, managers may tend to focus on domestic issues and minimize differences between international and domestic environments.

Not surprisingly, senior managers with little international experience (and successful careers built on domestic experience) may assume that there is a great deal of transferability between domestic and international HRM practices. This failure to recognize differences in managing human resources in foreign environments – regardless of whether it is because of ethnocentrism, inadequate information, or a lack of international perspective – frequently results in major difficulties in international operations. The challenge for the corporate HR manager who wishes to contribute to the internationalization of their firm is to work with top management in fostering the desired 'global mindset'. This goal requires, of course, a HR manager who is able to think globally and to formulate and implement HR policies that facilitate the development of globally oriented staff.[45]

Applying a strategic view of IHRM

Our discussion up to this point has suggested that a broader or more strategic view of IHRM is required to better explain the complexity and challenges of managing IHRM issues. An example of a theoretical framework that has been derived from a strategic approach using a multiple methodological approach is that of De Cieri and Dowling.[46] Their framework is depicted in Figure 1-5 and assumes that multinational firms operate in the context of worldwide conditions, including the external contexts of industry, nation, region, and inter-organizational networks and alliances. An example of the latter would be the impact of the removal of internal trade barriers and

A model of strategic HRM in multinational enterprises   Figure 1-5

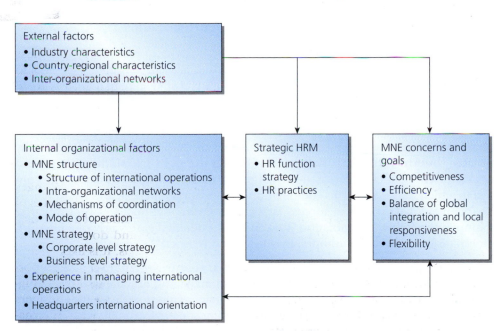

Source: Adapted from H. De Cieri and P.J. Dowling, 'Strategic Human Resource Management in Multinational Enterprises: Theoretical and Empirical Developments', in P.M. Wright *et al.* (eds), ***Research in Personnel and Human Resource Management: Strategic Human Resources in the 21st Century***, Supplement 4 (Stamford, CT, JAI Press 1999).

integration of national markets following the recent expansion of the membership of the European Union. These external factors exert direct influence on internal organizational factors, HRM strategy and practices, and multinational concerns and goals.

The internal organizational factors are shown in order of most 'tangible' to most 'intangible'. MNE structure refers to both the structure of international operations, intra-organizational networks and mechanisms of coordination that are discussed in more detail in Chapter 2. The life cycle stage of the firm and the industry in which it operates are important influences on HRM strategy and practices in multinationals, as are the various international modes of operation and levels of firm strategy. The most intangible organizational factors are experience in international business and headquarters international orientation. Following developments in the literature, such as that of Taylor, Beechler and Napier[47] who take an integration of resource dependence and resource-based perspective, the model suggests that there are reciprocal relationships between organizational factors, strategic HRM and multinational concerns and goals.

With regard to HR strategy and practices, reciprocal relationships between strategic issues and HRM strategy and practices have been highlighted by research taking a resource-based perspective.[48] In addition, several studies have shown that HR activities such as expatriate management are influenced by both external and internal factors.[49] A more strategic approach to HRM is expected to assist the firm in achieving its goals and objectives. This view is influenced by the emerging body of strategic HRM literature that examines the relationships between endogenous characteristics, HRM strategy and practices and firm performance or competitive advantage.[50] While some research has suggested that multinationals will gain by utilizing and integrating appropriate HRM strategy and practices, to enhance firm performance,[51] the evidence is inconclusive and important questions remain about the nature of this relationship.[52] The model offered by De Cieri and Dowling aims to assist in the cross-fertilization of ideas to further develop theory and empirical research in strategic HRM in multinational firms.

The enduring context of IHRM

As Figures 1-4 and 1-5 show, international firms compete in an increasingly complex environment where the level of challenge of doing business can be highly variable. Internationalizing firms rely on having the right people to manage and operate their businesses and good IHRM practices that are appropriate to the context in which they occur. This combination of appropriate people and HR practices has been a constant critical success factor in international business ventures. For example, the following quotation is taken from a detailed case study of a large US multinational, where the authors, Desatnick and Bennett[53] concluded:

> The primary causes of failure in multinational ventures stem from a lack of understanding of the essential differences in managing human resources, at all levels, in foreign environments. Certain management philosophies and techniques have proved successful in the domestic environment: their application in a foreign environment too often leads to frustration, failure and underachievement. These 'human' considerations are as important as the financial and marketing criteria upon which so many decisions to undertake multinational ventures depend.

This study was reported in 1978 but many international managers today would concur with the sentiments expressed in this quote. In this book we attempt to demonstrate some ways in which an appreciation of the international dimensions of HRM can assist in this process.

Summary

The purpose of this chapter has been to provide an overview of the emerging field of international HRM. We did this by:

- Defining key terms in IHRM and considering several definitions of IHRM.

- Introducing the historically significant issue of expatriate assignment management and reviewing the evolution of these assignments to reflect the increasing diversity with regard to what constitutes international work and the type and length of international assignments.

- Outlining the differences between domestic and international human resource management by looking at six factors which differentiate international and domestic HR (more HR activities; the need for a broader perspective; more involvement in employees' personal lives; changes in emphasis as the workforce mix of expatriates and locals varies; risk exposure; and more external influences) and detailing a model which summarizes the variables that moderate these differences.

- Presenting the complexity of IHRM, the increasing potential for challenges to existing IHRM practices and current models, and an increasing awareness of the wide number of choices within IHRM practices due to increased transparency and faster and more detailed diffusion of these practices across organizational units and firms.

We concluded that the complexity involved in operating in different countries and employing different national categories of employees is a key variable differentiating domestic and international HRM, rather than any major differences between the HR activities performed. We also discussed four other variables that moderate differences between domestic and international HRM: the *cultural environment*; the *industry (or industries) with which the multinational is primarily involved*; the *extent of reliance of the multinational on its home-country domestic market*; and the *attitudes of senior management*. These five variables are shown in Figure 1-4. Finally, we discussed a model of strategic HRM in multinational enterprises (Figure 1-5), which draws together a number of external environment and internal organizational factors which impact on IHRM strategy and practice and in turn on MNE goals.

In our discussion of the international dimensions of HRM in this book, we shall be drawing on the HRM literature. Subsequent chapters will examine the context for IHRM and the international dimensions of the major activities of HRM: HR planning and business operations, recruitment and selection, performance management, training and development, compensation and labor relations. We will provide comparative data on HRM practices in different countries, but our major emphasis is on the international dimensions of HRM confronting multinational firms, whether large or small, when facing the challenge of managing people in an international context.

Discussion Questions

1   What are the main similarities and differences between domestic and international HRM?

2   Define these terms: international HRM, PCN, HCN and TCN.

3   Discuss two HR activities in which a multinational firm must engage that would not be required in a domestic environment.

4   Why is a greater degree of involvement in employees' personal lives inevitable in many international HRM activities?

5   Discuss at least two of the variables that moderate differences between domestic and international HR practices.

Further Reading

Gerhart, B. and Fang, M. (2005). 'National Culture and Human Resource Management: Assumptions and Evidence', *International Journal of Human Resource Management,* 16(6): 971–86.

Leung, K., Bhagat, R., Buchan, N., Erez, M. and Gibson, C. (2005). 'Culture and International Business: Recent Advances and their Implications for Future Research', *Journal of International Business Studies,* 36(4): 357–78.

Stahl, G. and Björkman, I. (eds) (2006). *Handbook of Research in International Human Resource Management,* Cheltenham, UK: Edward Elgar.

Wright, P., Snell, S. and Dyer, L. (Guest Editors) (2005). *International Journal of Human Resource Management,* 16(6). Special issue on new models of strategic HRM in a global context.

Notes and References

1   H. De Cieri and P.J. Dowling, 'Strategic Human Resource Management in Multinational Enterprises: Theoretical and Empirical Developments', in P. Wright *et al.* (eds), *Research and Theory in SHRM: An agenda for the 21st century* (Greenwich, CT: JAI Press, 1999).

2   For examples of this approach, see N. Adler, *International Dimensions of Organizational Behavior,* 3rd edn (Cincinnatti, OH: South-Western, 1997) and A. Phatak, *International Management: Concept & Cases* (Cincinnati, OH: South-Western, 1997). See also the Special Issue on Asia-Pacific HRM, *International Journal of Human Resource Management,* Vol. 11, No. 2 (2000).

3   See for example, C. Brewster and A. Hegewisch, *Policy and Practice in European Human Resource Management – The Price Waterhouse Cranfield Survey* (London: Routledge, 1994).

4   See P. Dowling and R. Schuler, *International Dimensions of Human Resource Management,* 1st edn (Boston, MA: PWS-Kent, 1990); P. Dowling, R. Schuler and D. Welch, *International Dimensions of Human Resource Management,* 2nd edn (Belmont, CA: Wadsworth, 1994); P.J. Dowling, D.E. Welch and R.S. Schuler, *International Human Resource Management: Managing People in a Multinational Context*, 3rd edn (Cincinnati, OH: South-Western, 1998).

5   T.M. Welbourne and H. De Cieri, 'How New Venture Initial Public Offerings Benefit from International Operations', *International Journal of Human Resource Management,* Vol. 12, No. 4 (2001), pp. 652–68.

6   P. Morgan, 'International Human Resource Management: Fact or Fiction', *Personnel Administrator,* Vol. 31, No. 9 (1986), pp. 43–7.

7   See H. De Cieri, S.L. McGaughey and P.J. Dowling, 'Relocation' in M. Warner (ed.), *International Encyclopaedia of Business and Management,* Vol. 5 (London: Routledge, 1996), pp. 4300–10, for further discussion of this point.

8   For an example of the way in which the term is being used, see M.G. Harvey, M.M. Novicevic and C. Speier, 'Strategic Global Human Resource Management: The Role of Inpatriate Managers', *Human Resource Management Review*, Vol. 10, No. 2 (2000), pp. 153–75.

9   Curiously, the *Reference Guide* also states that the word inpatriate 'can also be used for U.S. expatriates returning to an assignment in the U.S.'. This is a contradiction of the first part of the definition of an inpatriate being a 'Foreign manager in the U.S.' and is illogical. US expatriates returning to the US are PCNs and cannot also be classed as 'Foreign managers in the U.S.' – perhaps they are 'repatriates', but they are not inpatriates. As defined, this term is only of use in the USA.

10   G. Stahl and I. Björkman (eds), *Handbook of Research in International Human Resource Management* (Cheltenham, UK: Edward Elgar, 2006), p. 1.

11   P.J. Dowling, 'International and Domestic Personnel/Human Resource Management: Similarities and Differences', in ed. R.S. Schuler, S.A. Youngblood and V.L. Huber (eds), *Readings in Personnel and Human Resource Management,* 3rd edn (St. Paul, MN: West Publishing, 1988).

12   See D.L. Pinney, 'Structuring an Expatriate Tax Reimbursement Program', *Personnel Administrator,* Vol. 27, No. 7 (1982), pp. 19–25; and M. Gajek and M.M. Sabo, 'The Bottom Line: What HR Managers Need to Know About the New Expatriate Regulations', *Personnel Administrator,* Vol. 31, No. 2 (1986), pp. 87–92.

13   For up-to-date information on the FCPA see the US Department of Justice website: www.usdoj.gov/criminal/fraud/fcpa.html.

14   P. Morgan, 'International Human Resource Management'.

15   R.D. Robinson, *International Business Management: A Guide to Decision Making,* 2nd edn (Hinsdale, IL: Dryden, 1978).

16   Although less common in the USA, the use of private boarding schools is common in countries (particularly European countries) which have a colonial tradition where both colonial administrators and business people would often undertake long assignments overseas and expect to leave their children at a boarding school in their home country. This is especially true of Britain which also has a strong cultural tradition of the middle and upper classes sending their children to private boarding schools (curiously described by the British as 'public' schools, even though they are all private institutions which charge fees) even if the parents were working in Britain.

17   See 'Terrorism', Chapter 4 in T.M. Gladwin and I. Walter, *Multinationals Under Fire: Lessons in the Management of Conflict* (New York: John Wiley, 1980); M. Harvey, 'A Survey of Corporate Programs for Managing Terrorist Threats', *Journal of International Business Studies,* Vol. 24, No. 3 (1993), pp. 465–78. For an excellent website on terrorism see the following site at Columbia University: www.columbia.edu/cu/lweb/indiv/lehman/guides/terrorism.html. Also see Chapter 12 of this text.

18   For the latest information on epidemic and pandemic crises see the World Health Organization web site at: www.who.int/csr/en/.

19   G. Lee and M. Warner, 'Epidemics, Labor Markets and Unemployment: The Impact of SARS on Human Resource Management in the Hong Kong Service Sector', *International Journal of Human Resource Management*, Vol. 16, No. 5 (2005), pp. 752–71.

20   M. Erez and P.C. Earley, *Culture, Self-Identity and Work* (Oxford: Oxford University Press, 1993).

21   J.E. Harris and R.T. Moran, *Managing Cultural Differences* (Houston, TX: Gulf, 1979).

22   R.S. Bhagat and S.J. McQuaid, 'Role of Subjective Culture in Organizations: A Review and Directions for Future Research', *Journal of Applied Psychology,* Vol. 67 (1982), pp. 653–85.

23   See J.W. Berry, 'Introduction to Methodology', in H.C. Triandis and J.W. Berry (eds), *Handbook of Cross-Cultural Psychology, Vol. 2: Methodology* (Boston, MA: Allyn and Bacon, 1980); H. De Cieri and P.J. Dowling, 'Cross-cultural Issues in Organizational Behavior', in C.L. Cooper and D.M. Rousseau (eds), *Trends in Organizational Behavior,* Vol. 2 (Chichester: John Wiley & Sons, 1995), pp.127–45; and M.B. Teagarden and M.A. Von Glinow, 'Human Resource Management in Cross-cultural Contexts: Emic Practices Versus Etic Philosophies', *Management International Review,* 37 (1 – Special Issue) (1997), pp. 7–20.

24   See H. Triandis and R. Brislin, 'Cross-Cultural Psychology', *American Psychologist,* Vol. 39 (1984), pp. 1006–16.

25   See G. Hofstede, 'The Cultural Relativity of Organizational Practices and Theories', *Journal of International Business Studies,* Vol. 14, No. 2 (1983), pp. 75–89.

26   T.S. Kuhn, *The Structure of Scientific Revolution,* 2nd edn (Chicago, IL: University of Chicago Press, 1962).

27   J.D. Child, 'Culture, Contingency and Capitalism in the Cross-National Study of Organizations', in L.L. Cummings and B.M. Staw (eds), *Research in Organizational Behavior,* Vol. 3 (Greenwich, CT: JAI Publishers, 1981).

28   See D.A. Ricks, *Blunders in International Business* (Cambridge, MA: Blackwell, 1993) for a comprehensive collection of mistakes made by multinational firms which paid insufficient attention to their cultural environment in their international business operations. For further literature on this topic see the following: P.S. Kirkbride and S.F.Y. Tang, 'From Kyoto to Kowloon: Cultural Barriers to the Transference of Quality Circles from Japan to Hong Kong', *Asia Pacific Journal of Human Resources,* 32, No. 2 (1994), pp. 100–11; M. Tayeb, 'Organizations and National Culture: Methodology Considered', *Organization Studies,* 15, No. 3 (1994), pp. 429–46; and P. Sparrow, R.S. Schuler and S.E. Jackson, 'Convergence or Divergence: Human Resource Practices and Policies for Competitive Advantage Worldwide', *International Journal of Human Resource*

Management, 5, No. 2 (1994), pp. 267–99; M. Morishima, 'Embedding HRM in a Social Context', *British Journal of Industrial Relations,* Vol. 33, No. 4 (1995), pp. 617–43; and J.E. Delery and D.H. Doty, 'Modes of Theorizing in Strategic Human Resource Management: Tests of Universalistic, Contingency, and Configurational Performance Predictions', *Academy of Management Journal,* Vol. 39 (1996), pp. 802–35.

29 S.P. Huntington, 'The West: Unique, Not Universal', *Foreign Affairs,* November/December (1996), pp. 28–46.

30 C. Brewster, 'Comparing HRM Policies and Practices Across Geographical Borders', in G. Stahl and I. Björkman (eds), *Handbook of Research in International Human Resource Management* (Cheltenham, UK: Edward Elgar, 2006), pp. 68–90.

31 R.L. Tung, 'Managing Cross-national and Intra-national Diversity', *Human Resource Management,* Vol. 32, No. 4 (1993), pp. 461–77.

32 T. Wyatt, 'Understanding Unfamiliar Personnel Problems in Cross-Cultural Work Encounters', *Asia Pacific HRM,* Vol. 27, No. 4 (1989), p. 5.

33 G. Hofstede, *Culture's Consequences: International Differences in Work-Related Values* (Newbury Park, CA: Sage, 1980).

34 There is a voluminous literature on Hofstede's work. An excellent website which summarizes some of this work can be found at: geert-hofstede.international-business-center.com/index.shtml. For a recent article on Hofstede's work see: F. Chiang, 'A Critical Examination of Hofstede's Thesis and its Application to International Reward Management', *International Journal of Human Resource Management,* Vol. 16, No. 9 (2005), pp. 1545–63.

35 B. McSweeney, 'Hofstede's Model of National Cultural Differences and Their Consequences: A Triumph of Faith – A Failure of Analysis', *Human Relations,* Vol. 55, No. 1 (2002), pp. 89–118.

36 M.H. Hoppe, 'Retrospective on Culture's Consequences', *Academy of Management Executive,* Vol. 18, No. 1 (2004), pp. 73–93.

37 B. Gerhart and M. Fang, 'National Culture and Human Resource Management: Assumptions and Evidence', *International Journal of Human Resource Management,* 16, No. 6 (2005), pp. 971–86.

38 K. Leung, R.S. Bhagat, N.R. Buchan, M. Erez and C.B. Gibson, 'Culture and International Business: Recent Advances and their Implications for Future Research', *Journal of International Business Studies,* Vol. 36, No. 4 (2005), pp. 357–78.

39 M.E. Porter, 'Changing Patterns of International Competition', *California Management Review,* Vol. 28, No. 2 (1986), pp. 9–40.

40 M.E. Porter, *Competitive Advantage: Creating and Sustaining Superior Performance* (New York: The Free Press, 1985).

41 A. Laurent, 'The Cross-Cultural Puzzle of International Human Resource Management', *Human Resource Management,* Vol. 25 (1986), pp. 91–102.

42 *Ibid.,* p. 100.

43 This section is based on the *World Investment Report, 2006: FDI from Developing and Transition Economies: Implications for Development,* United Nations Conference on Trade and Development (UNCTAD) (New York and Geneva: United Nations, 2006).

44 S. Tamer Cavusgil, *Internationalising Business Education: Meeting the Challenge* (East Lansing, MI: Michigan State University Press, 1993).

45 See C. Bartlett, S. Ghoshal and P. Beamish, *Transnational Management: Text, Cases, and Readings in Cross Border Management* (Boston, MA: McGraw-Hill/Irwin, 2008); and V. Pucik, 'Human Resources in the Future: An Obstacle or a Champion of Globalization?', *Human Resource Management*, Vol. 36 (1997), pp. 163–7.

46 H. De Cieri and P.J. Dowling, 'Strategic Human Resource Management in Multinational Enterprises: Theoretical and Empirical Developments', in P.M. Wright *et al*. (eds), *Research in Personnel and Human Resource Management: Strategic Human Resources in the 21st Century,* Supplement 4 (Stamford, CT: JAI Press, 1999).

47 S. Taylor, S. Beechler and N. Napier, 'Towards an Integrative Model of Strategic International Human Resource Management', *Academy of Management Review,* Vol. 21 (1996), pp. 959–85.

48 Taylor *et al., ibid.;* K. Kamoche, 'Knowledge Creation and Learning in International HRM', *International Journal of Human Resource Management,* Vol. 8 (1997), pp. 213–22.

49 D. Welch, 'Determinants of International Human Resource Management Approaches and Activities: A Suggested Framework', *Journal of Management Studies,* Vol. 31, No. 2 (1994), pp. 139–64; M. Harvey, M.M. Novicevis and C. Speier, 'An Innovative Global Management Staffing System: A Competency-based Perspective, *Human Resource Management,* Vol. 39, No. 4 (2000), pp. 381–94.

50   B. Becker and B. Gerhart, 'The Impact of Human Resource Management on Organizational Performance: Progress and Prospects', *Academy of Management Journal,* Vol. 39, No. 4 (1996), pp. 779–801; L. Dyer and T. Reeves, 'Human Resource Strategies and Firm Performance: What Do we Know and Where Do we Need to Go?', *International Journal of Human Resource Management,* Vol. 6, No. 3 (1995), pp. 656–70.

51   M. Festing, 'International Human Resource Management Strategies in Multinational Corporations: Theoretical Assumptions and Empirical Evidence from German Firms', *Management International Review,* Vol. 37, Special issue No. 1 (1997), pp. 43–63; and S.J. Kobrin, 'Is There a Relationship Between a Geocentric Mind-set and Multinational Strategy?', *Journal of International Business Studies,* Vol. 25 (1994), pp. 493–511.

52   P.M. Caligiuri and L.K. Stroh, 'Multinational Corporate Management Strategies and International Human Resource Practices: Bringing IHRM to the Bottom Line', *International Journal of Human Resource Management,* Vol. 6 (1995), pp. 494–507; R.B. Peterson, J. Sargent, N.K. Napier and W.S. Shim, 'Corporate Expatriate HRM Policies, Internationalization, and Performance in the World's Largest MNCs', *Management International Review,* Vol. 36 (1996), pp. 215–30; P. Sparrow, R.S. Schuler and S.E. Jackson, 'Convergence or Divergence: Human Resource Practices and Policies for Competitive Advantage Worldwide', *International Journal of Human Resource Management,* Vol. 5 (1994), pp. 267–99.

53   R.L. Desatnick and M.L. Bennett, *Human Resource Management in the Multinational Company* (New York: Nichols, 1978).

The organizational context

CHAPTER

2

Chapter Objectives

In this chapter, we examine how international growth places demands on management, and the factors that impact on how managers of internationalizing firms respond to these challenges. We start with the premise that the human resource (HR) function does not operate in a vacuum, and that HR activities are determined by, and influence, organizational factors. We cover the following areas:

- Structural responses to international growth.
- Control and coordination mechanisms, including cultural control.
- Effect of responses on human resource management approaches and activities.

This discussion builds upon material covered in Chapter 1 to provide a meaningful organizational context for drawing out the international dimension of human resource management – the central theme of this book.

Introduction

Human resource practices, policies and processes are imbedded in the strategic, structural and technological context of the MNE.[1] This 'administrative heritage' is particularly critical for global firms as the international organization will be called on to operate across a wide variety of competitive environments and yet somehow balance these diverse social, political and economic contexts with the requirements of the original home context.[2] In Chapter 1, we looked at the general global environment in which firms compete. Here we focus on internal responses as firms attempt to deal with global environment challenges. Figure 2-1 on the next page illustrates the major elements encountered as a result of international growth that place demands on management.

The various elements in Figure 2-1 are not mutually exclusive. For example, geographical dispersion affects firm size, creating pressure upon control mechanisms

Figure 2-1	Management demands of international growth

that, in turn, will influence structural change. Growth (size of the firm) will affect the flow and volume of information, which may reinforce a control response (such as what functions, systems and processes to centralize and what to decentralize). As we will examine in Chapter 3, mode of operation involved (such as international joint venture or mergers and aquisitions (M&As)) will affect the rate of geographical dispersion. Geographical dispersion will involve more encounters with national cultures and languages, thus affecting the flow and volume of information. The demands of the host country can influence the composition of the workforce (the mix of PCNs, HCNs and TCNs).

An in-depth examination of all these elements is beyond the scope of this book. Rather, the purpose of this chapter is to explore some of the managerial responses to these influences that concern HRM. Our focus remains on the connection between organizational factors, management decisions and HR consequences. To a certain extent, how the internationalizing firm copes with the HR demands of its various foreign operations determines its ability to execute its chosen expansion strategies. Indeed, early Finnish research suggests that personnel policies should lead rather than follow international operation decisions,[3] yet one could argue that most companies take the opposite approach – that is, follow market-driven strategies. We will now follow the path a domestic firm takes as it evolves into a global entity, and illustrate how the HRM function is affected by the way the internationalization process itself is managed.

The path to global status

Most firms pass through several stages of organizational development as the nature, and size, of their international activities grow. As they go through these evolutionary stages, their organizational structures[4] change, typically due to:

● The strain imposed by growth and geographical spread.

● The need for improved coordination and control across business units.

● The constraints imposed by host-government regulations on ownership and equity.

Multinationals are not born overnight; the evolution from a domestic to a truly global organization may involve a long and somewhat tortuous process with many and diverse steps, as illustrated in Figure 2-2. Although research into internationalization has revealed a common process, it must be stressed that this process is not exactly the same for all firms. As Figure 2-2 shows, some firms may use other operation modes such as licensing and subcontracting instead of, or as well as, establishing their own foreign production or service facilities.

Some firms go through the various steps rapidly while others evolve slowly over many years, although recent studies have identified a speeding up of the process. For example, some firms are able to accelerate the process through acquisitions, thus leapfrogging over intermediate steps (that is, move directly into foreign production through the purchase of a foreign firm, rather than initial exporting, followed by sales subsidiary, as per Figure 2-2 above). Nor do all firms follow the same sequence of stages as they internationalize – some firms can be driven by external factors such as host-government action (for example, forced into a joint venture), or an offer to buy a company. Others are formed expressly with the international market in mind – often referred to as *born globals*.[5] In other words, the number of steps, or stages, along the path to multinational status varies from firm to firm, as does the time frame involved.[6] However, the concept of an evolutionary process is useful in illustrating the organizational adjustments required of a firm moving along the path to multinational status. As mentioned earlier, linked to this evolutionary process are structural responses, control mechanisms and HRM policies, which we now examine.

Export

This typically is the initial stage for manufacturing firms entering international operations. As such, it rarely involves much organizational response until the level of export sales reaches a critical point. Of course, simple exporting may be difficult for service companies (such as legal firms) so that they may be forced to make an early step into foreign direct investment operations (via a branch office, or joint venture).[7]

Stages of internationalization   **Figure 2-2**

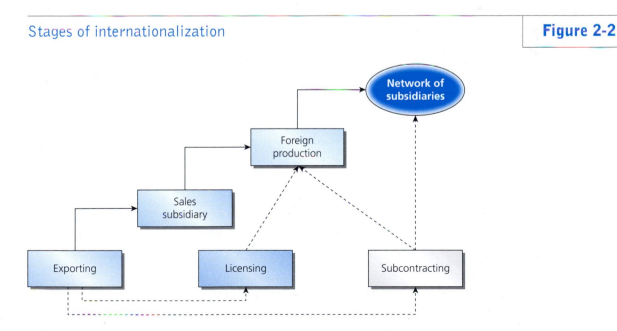

Exporting often tends to be handled by an intermediary (for example, a foreign agent or distributor) as local market knowledge is deemed critical. As export sales increase, however, an export manager may be appointed to control foreign sales and actively seek new markets. This person is commonly from the domestic operations. Further growth in exporting may lead to the establishment of an export department at the same level as the domestic sales department, as the firm becomes more committed to, or more dependent upon, its foreign export sales, as Figure 2-3 shows.

At this stage, exporting is controlled from the domestic-based home office, through a designated export manager. The role of the HR department is unclear, as indicated by the dotted arrow between these two functional areas in Figure 2-3. There is a paucity of empirical evidence about HR responses at this early internationalization stage, even though there are HR activities involved (such as the selection of export staff), and perhaps training of the foreign agency staff. As these activities are handled by the marketing department, or exporting staff, the HR department has little, if any, involvement with the development of policies and procedures surrounding the HR aspects of the firm's early international activities.[8]

Sales subsidiary

As the firm develops expertise in foreign markets, agents and distributors are often replaced by direct sales with the establishment of sales subsidiaries or branch offices in the foreign market countries. This stage may be prompted by problems with foreign agents, more confidence in the international sales activity, the desire to have greater control, and/or the decision to give greater support to the exporting activity, usually due to its increasing importance to the overall success of the organization. The export manager may be given the same authority as other functional managers, as illustrated in Figure 2-4.

Exporting is still controlled at corporate headquarters, but the firm must make a decision regarding the coordination of the sales subsidiary, including staffing. If it wishes to maintain direct control, reflecting an ethnocentric attitude, it opts to staff the sales subsidiary from its headquarters through the use of parent-country nationals (PCNs). If it regards country-specific factors – such as knowledge of the

| **Figure 2-3** | Export department structure |

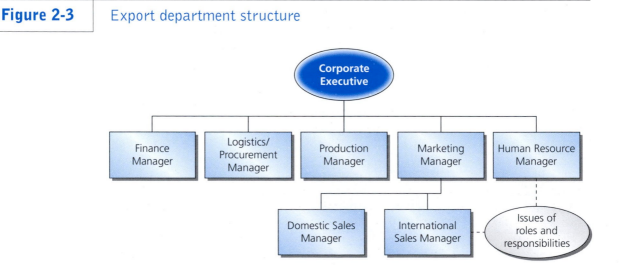

Sales subsidiary structure

Figure 2-4

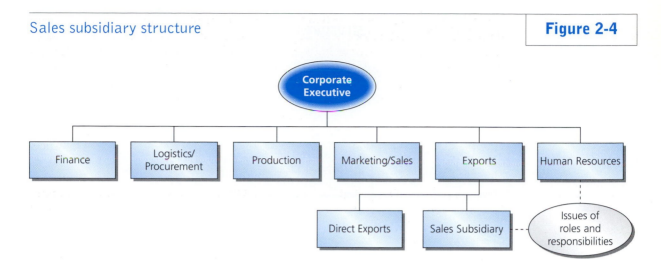

foreign market, language, sensitivity to host-country needs – as important, it may staff the subsidiary with host-country nationals (HCNs). However, it would appear that many firms use PCNs in key sales subsidiary positions.

The decision to use PCNs leads into expatriation management issues and activities. It may be that, at this point, the HR department becomes actively involved in the personnel aspects of the firm's international operations, though there is little empirical evidence as to when, and how, HR-designated staff become involved.

International division

For some firms, it is a short step from the establishment of a sales subsidiary to a foreign production or service facility. This step may be considered small if the firm is already assembling the product abroad to take advantage of cheap labor or to save shipping costs or tariffs, for example. Alternatively, the firm may have a well-established export and marketing program that enables it to take advantage of host-government incentives or counter host-government controls on foreign imports by establishing a foreign production facility. For some firms, though, the transition to foreign direct investment is a large step. However, having made the decision to produce overseas, the firm may establish its own foreign production facilities, or enter into a joint venture with a local firm, or buy a local firm. Regardless of the method of establishment, foreign production/service operations tend to trigger the creation of a separate international division in which all international activities are grouped, as Figure 2-5 demonstrates.

With the spread of international activities, typically the firm establishes what has been referred to as 'miniature replicas', as the foreign subsidiaries are structured to mirror that of the domestic organization. The subsidiary managers report to the head of the international division, and there may be some informal reporting directly to the various functional heads. For example, in reference to Figure 2-5, there may be contact between the HR managers in the two country subsidiaries, and the HR manager at corporate headquarters, regarding staffing issues.

Many firms at this stage of internationalization are concerned about maintaining control of the newly established subsidiary, and will place PCNs in all key positions in the subsidiary. However, some firms decide that local employment conditions require local handling and place a HCN in charge of the subsidiary HR function, thus

Figure 2-5	International division structure

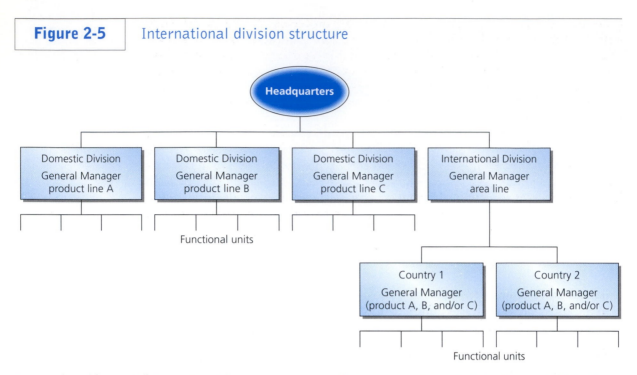

Source: Adapted from C. Hill, *International Business: Competing in the Global Marketplace,* 2nd edn (Chicago, IL: Richard Irwin, 1997).

making an exception to the overall ethnocentric approach. Others may place HCNs in several key positions, including HRM, either to comply with host-government directives or to emphasize the local orientation of the subsidiary.

The role of corporate HR staff is primarily concerned with expatriate management; though there will be some monitoring of the subsidiary HR function – formally through the head of the international division. Pucik[9] suggests that, initially, corporate HR activities are confined to supervising the selection of staff for the new international division and expatriate managers perform a major role in 'identifying employees who can direct the daily operations of the foreign subsidiaries, supervising transfer of managerial and technical know-how, communicating corporate policies, and keeping corporate HQ informed'. As the firm expands its foreign production or service facilities into other countries, increasing the size of its foreign workforce, accompanied by a growth in the number of expatriates, more formal HR policies become necessary. The capacity of corporate HR staff to design appropriate policies may depend on how institutionalized existing approaches to expatriate management concerns have become, especially policies for compensation and pre-departure training; and that the more isolated the corporate HR function has been from the preceding international activities, the more difficult the task is likely to be.[10] The export department (or its equivalent) may have been in charge of international staffing issues and instigated required personnel responses, and now considers it has the competence to manage expatriates.

Global product/area division

Over time, the firm moves from the early foreign production stage into a phase of growth through production, or service, standardization and diversification.

Consequently, the strain of sheer size may create problems. The international division becomes over-stretched making effective communication and efficiency of operation difficult. In some cases, corporate top managers may become concerned that the international division has enjoyed too much autonomy, acting so independently from the domestic operations to the extent that it operates as a separate unit – a situation that cannot be tolerated as the firm's international activities become strategically more important.

Typically, tensions will emerge between the parent company (headquarters) and its subsidiaries, stemming from the need for national responsiveness at the subsidiary unit and global integration imperatives at the parent headquarters. The demand for national responsiveness at the subsidiary unit develops because of factors such as differences in market structures, distribution channels, customer needs, local culture and pressure from the host government. The need for more centralized global integration by the headquarters comes from having multinational customers, global competitors and the increasingly rapid flow of information and technology, and from the quest for large volume for economies of scale.

As a result of these various forces for change, the multinational confronts two major issues of structure:

- The extent to which key decisions are to be made at the parent-country headquarters or at the subsidiary units (centralization versus decentralization).

- The type or form of control exerted by the parent over the subsidiary unit.

The structural response, at this stage of internationalization, can be either a product/service-based global structure (if the growth strategy is through product or service diversification) or an area-based structure (if the growth strategy is through geographical expansion); see Figures 2-6a and 2-6b.

As part of the process of accommodating subsidiary concerns through decentralization, the MNE strives to adapt its HRM activities to each host country's specific requirements. This naturally impacts on the corporate HRM function. As there is an increasing devolution of responsibility for local employee decisions to each subsidiary, with corporate HR staff performing a monitoring role, intervening in local affairs occurs less frequently. This HRM monitoring role reflects management's desire for central control of strategic planning; formulating, implementing and coordinating strategies for its worldwide markets. As well, the growth in foreign exposure combined with changes in the organizational structure of international operations results in an increase in the number of employees needed to oversee the activities between the parent firm and its foreign affiliates. Within the human resource function, the development of managers able to operate in international environments generally becomes a new imperative.[11]

As the MNE grows and the trend toward a global perspective accelerates, it increasingly confronts the 'think global, act local' paradox.[12] The increasingly complex international environment – characterized by global competitors, global customers, universal products, rapid technological change and world-scale factories – push the multinational toward global integration while, at the same time, host governments and other stakeholders (such as customers, suppliers and employees) push for local responsiveness. To facilitate the challenge of meeting these conflicting demands, the multinational will typically need to consider a more appropriate structure, and the choice appears to be either: the matrix; the mixed structure; the heterarchy; the transnational; or the multinational network. These options are now described and discussed.

Figure 2-6a	Global product division structure

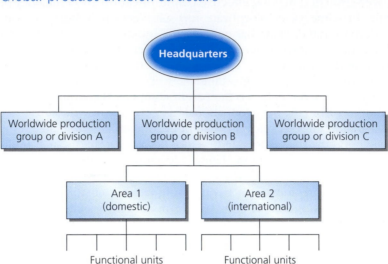

Source: Adapted from C. Hill, *International Business: Competing in the Global Marketplace,* 2nd edn (Chicago, IL: Richard Irwin, 1997).

Figure 2-6b	Global area division structure

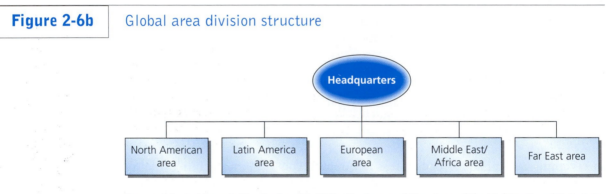

Source: Adapted from J. Stopford and L. Wells, *Strategy and Structure of the Multinational Enterprise* (New York: Basic Books, 1972).

The matrix

In the matrix structure, the multinational is attempting to integrate its operations across more than one dimension. As shown in Figure 2-7, the international or geographical division and the product division share joint authority. Advocates of this structural form see, as its advantages, that conflicts of interest are brought out into the open, and that each issue with priority in decision making has an executive champion to ensure it is not neglected. In other words, the matrix is considered to bring into the management system a philosophy of matching the structure to the decision-making process. Research on the matrix structure[13] indicates that the matrix 'continues to be the only organizational form which fits the strategy of simultaneous pursuit of multiple business dimensions, with each given equal priority. . . . [The] structural form succeeds because it fits the situation.' In practice, firms that have adopted the matrix structure have met with mixed success. One reason is that it is an expensive structural form in that it requires careful implementation and commitment (and often a great deal of time) on the part of top management to be successful.

Global matrix structure

Figure 2-7

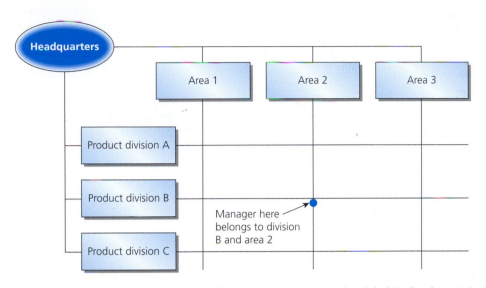

Source: Adapted from C. Hill, *International Business: Competing in the Global Marketplace,* 2nd edn (Chicago, IL: Richard Irwin, 1997).

In Figure 2-7, area managers are responsible for the performance of all products within the various countries that comprise their regions, while product managers are responsible for sales of their specific product ranges across the areas. For example, Product A Manager may be concerned with sales of product A in Europe, the Americas and in the Asia-Pacific area. Product managers typically report to a Vice President Global Products (or similar title) for matters pertaining to product, and to another Vice President (perhaps a VP International) who is responsible for geographical matters. There is a similar dual reporting line for functional staff, including HR staff. Country/Area HR managers may also be involved in staffing issues involving product division staff (reporting indirectly to Vice President Global Products). There may be additional reporting requirements to corporate HR at headquarters. One early and public supporter of the matrix organization was Percy Barnevik, former chief executive officer of Asea Brown Boveri (ABB), the European electrical systems and equipment manufacturer.[14] ABB's decade-long efforts at matrix control were very influential in the popular and academic press, intriguing executives at a number of global firms.

Overall, efforts to successfully implement the matrix solution have been problematic. Bartlett and Ghoshal[15] comment that, in practice, particularly in the international context, the matrix has proven to be all but unmanageable. They isolate four contributing factors:

1 Dual reporting, which leads to conflict and confusion.

2 The proliferation of communication channels which creates informational logjams.

3 Overlapping responsibilities, which produce turf battles and a loss of accountability.

4 The barriers of distance, language, time and culture, which often make it very difficult for managers to resolve conflicts and clarify confusion.

Bartlett and Ghoshal conclude that the most successful MNEs focus less on searching for the ideal structure, and more on developing the abilities, behavior and performance of individual managers. This assists in creating 'a matrix in the minds of managers', where individual capabilities are captured and the entire firm is motivated to respond cooperatively to a complicated and dynamic environment. It seems clear that if the MNE opts for a matrix structure, particular care must be taken with staffing. As Ronen[16] notes:

> It requires managers who know the business in general, who have good interpersonal skills, and who can deal with the ambiguities of responsibility and authority inherent in the matrix system. Training in such skills as planning procedures, the kinds of interpersonal skills necessary for the matrix, and the kind of analysis and orderly presentation of ideas essential to planning within a group is most important for supporting the matrix approach. Moreover, management development and human resource planning are even more necessary in the volatile environment of the matrix than in the traditional organizations.

Mixed structure

In an attempt to manage the growth of diverse operations, or because attempts to implement a matrix structure have been unsuccessful, some firms have opted for what can only be described as a mixed form. In an early survey conducted by Dowling[17] on this issue, more than one-third (35 per cent) of respondents indicated that they had mixed forms, and around 18 per cent had product or matrix structures. Galbraith and Kazanjian[18] also identify mixed structures that seem to have emerged in response to global pressures and trade-offs:

> For example, organizations that pursued area structures kept these geographical profit centres, but added worldwide product managers. Colgate-Palmolive has always had strong country managers. But, as they doubled the funding for product research, and as Colgate Dental Cream became a universal product, product managers were added at the corporate office to direct the R & D funding and coordinate marketing programs worldwide. Similarly, the product-divisionalized firms have been reintroducing the international division. At Motorola, the product groups had worldwide responsibility for their product lines. As they compete with the Japanese in Japan, an international group has been introduced to help coordinate across product lines.

Although all structural forms that result from the evolutionary development of international business are complex and difficult to manage effectively, given an MNE's developing capabilities and experience at each new stage, mixed structures appear even more complex and harder to explain and implement, as well as control. Thus, as our discussion of the matrix structure emphasized, it is important that all employees understand the mixed framework and that attention is also given to supporting mechanisms, such as corporate identity, interpersonal relationships, management attitudes and HR systems, particularly promotion and reward policies.

Beyond the matrix

Early studies of headquarter-subsidiary relationships tended to stress resources, people and information flows from headquarters to subsidiary, examining these relationships mainly in the context of control and coordination. However, in the large, mature, multinational, these flows are multidirectional: from headquarters to subsidiary; from subsidiary to subsidiary; and between subsidiaries. The result can be a complex network of inter-related activities and relationships and the multinational management literature identifies three descriptions of organizational structures – the heterarchy, the transnational and the network firm. Whilst they have been given different terms, each form recognizes that, at this stage of internationalization, the concept of a superior structure that neatly fits the corporate strategy becomes inappropriate. The proponents of these forms are in agreement that multinationals at this stage become less hierarchical. We shall take a brief look at each of these more decentralized, organic forms.

The heterarchy.   This structural form was proposed by Hedlund,[19] a distinguished Swedish international management researcher, and recognizes that a multinational may have a number of different kinds of centers apart from that traditionally referred to as 'headquarters'. Hedlund argued that competitive advantage does not necessarily reside in any one country (the parent country, for example). Rather, it may be found in many, so that each subsidiary center may be simultaneously a center and a global coordinator of discrete activities, thus performing a strategic role not just for itself, but for the MNE as a whole (the subsidiary labeled 'center' in Figure 2-8). For example, some multinationals may centralize research and development in a particular subsidiary. In a heterarchical MNE, control is less reliant on the top-to-bottom mechanisms of previous hierarchical modes and more on normative mechanisms, such as the corporate culture and a widely shared awareness of central goals and strategies.

From a HRM perspective, the heterarchy is interesting in that its success appears to rest solely on the ability of the multinational to formulate, implement and reinforce the required human resource elements. Hedlund recognized that the heterarchy demands skilful and experienced personnel as well as sophisticated reward and punishment systems in order to develop the normative control mechanisms necessary for effective performance. The use of staff as an informal control mechanism is important, which we shall explore later in this chapter.

The networked organization   **Figure 2-8**

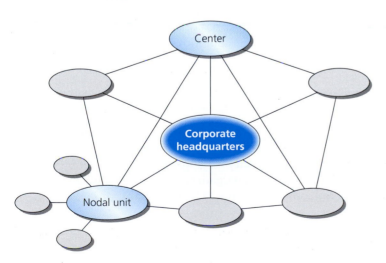

In a later article, Hedlund[20] proposed a structural model he termed the *N-form*. This model builds upon his heterarchy concept and integrates work from knowledge organization scholars. Hedlund argued that a new structural form is required to allow for knowledge management. His N-form takes away divisions, allows for temporary constellations and the use of project teams and places stress on lateral communication and dialogue between units and individuals. The top management role was presented as that of a catalyst, architect and protector of knowledge rather than a monitor and resource allocator. The use of mechanisms, such as cross-functional teams and empowerment of lower level employees was advocated to further support the N-form.

The transnational.

The term transnational has been coined to describe an organizational form that is characterized by an interdependence of resources and responsibilities across all business units regardless of national boundaries. The term has also become a descriptor of a particular type of multinational, that tries to cope with the large flows of components, products, resources, people and information among its subsidiaries, while simultaneously recognizing distributed specialized resources and capabilities. As such, the transnational demands a complex process of coordination and cooperation involving strong cross-unit integrating devices, a strong corporate identity, and a well-developed worldwide management perspective. In their study, Bartlett and Ghoshal[21] noted:

> Among the companies we studied, there were several that were in the process of developing such organizational capabilities. They had surpassed the classic capabilities of the *multinational* company that operates as decentralized federations of units able to sense and respond to diverse international needs and opportunities; and they had evolved beyond the abilities of the global company with its facility for managing operations on a tightly controlled worldwide basis through its centralized hub structure. They had developed what we termed *transnational* capabilities – the ability to manage across national boundaries, retaining local flexibility while achieving global integration. More than anything else this involved the ability to link local operations to each other and to the center in a flexible way, and in so doing, to leverage those local and central capabilities.

In fact, the matrix, the heterarchy and the transnational share a common theme regarding the human resource factor. Therefore, developing transnational managers or global leaders who can think and act across national and subsidiary boundaries emerges as an important task for top management introducing these complex organizational forms. Staff transfers play a critical role in integration and coordination.

The multinational as a network.

Some scholars are advocating viewing certain large and mature internationalized firms as a network, in situations where:

- Subsidiaries have developed into significant centers for investments, activities and influence, and can no longer be regarded as at the periphery.[22] Interaction between headquarters and each subsidiary is likely to be dyadic, taking place between various actors at many different organizational levels and covering different exchanges, the outcome of which will be important for effective global performance.

- Such MNEs are loosely coupled political systems rather than tightly bonded, homogeneous, hierarchically controlled systems.[23] This runs counter to the traditional structure where linkages are described formally via the organization's structure and standardized procedures, and informally through interpersonal contact and socialization.[24]

Figure 2-8 attempts to depict such an intricate criss-crossing of relationships. One subsidiary may act as a nodal unit linked a cluster of satellite organizations. Thus, one center can assume responsibility for other units in its country or region. In line with this view, Ghoshal and Bartlett[25] have expanded their concept of the transnational to define the MNE as an inter-organizational system. This is comprised of a network of exchange relationships among different organizational units, including headquarters and national subsidiaries, as well as external organizations, such as host governments, customers, suppliers and competitors, with which the different units of the multinational must interact. These authors argue a new way of structuring is not the issue – it is more the emerging management philosophy, with its focus on management processes: 'The actual configuration of the processes themselves, and the structural shell within which they are embedded, can be very different depending on the businesses and the heritage of each company.'[26] Ghoshal and Bartlett cite GE, ABB and Toyota as prime examples of companies involved in developing such processes, with Intel and Corning, Philips and Alcatel, Matsushita and Toshiba regarded as companies embarking upon a network-type configuration.

The management of a multi-centered networked organization is complex. Apart from the intra-organizational network (comprising headquarters and the numerous subsidiaries), each subsidiary also has a range of external relationships (involving local suppliers, customers, competitors, host governments and alliance partners). The management of both the intra-organizational and inter-organizational spheres, and of the total integrated network, is crucial to global corporate performance. It involves what has been termed a less-hierarchical structure, featuring five dimensions:

- Delegation of decision-making authority to appropriate units and levels.
- Geographical dispersal of key functions across units in different countries.
- Delayering of organizational levels.
- De-bureaucratization of formal procedures.
- Differentiation of work, responsibility and authority across the networked subsidiaries.[27]

Research cited by Nohria and Ghoshal focuses on the capability of networking subsidiaries to package 'slack resources' (pools in capital, production or human resources beyond those required for local purposes) to stimulate 'local-for local', 'local-for-global' and 'global-for-global innovation processes'.[28] Integrated networks of these 'slack resource' pools are combined by way of interpersonal contacts, mentoring relationships and sophisticated communications networks in order to identify and distribute new products processes and technologies.

Beyond networks.   Doz, Santos and Williamson[29] have coined the term 'metanational' to describe firms comprised of three types of units. First, locally imbedded 'sensing units' are responsible for uncovering widely dispersed sources of engineering and market insights. Developing new technologies and processes can no longer be assumed to be the sole task of a conveniently located home-country headquarters research and development unit, or even a MNE-based center of excellence. Second, 'magnet' units are described as attracting these unpredictably dispersed innovative processes, creating a business plan to convert these innovations into viable services or products. Finally, a third set of units are responsible for marketing and producing adaptations of these products and services for a range of customers around the world. The metanational system is described as:

> a global tournament played at three levels. It is a race to identify and access new technologies and market trends ahead of the competition, a race to turn this dispersed knowledge into innovative products and services, and a race to scale and exploit these innovations in markets around the world.[30]

The place of the HR function in structural forms

As we point out in our treatment of the various forms, there has been little direct investigation into how the HR function develops in response to structural changes as a consequence of international growth. An exception is a study of the changing role of the corporate HR function in 30 UK firms.[31] The authors, Scullion and Starkey, found three distinct groups that they describe as follows:

- Centralized HR companies, characterized by large, well-resourced HR departments responsible for a wide range of functions. The key role for corporate HR was to establish and maintain control over world-wide top level management positions, such as divisional and subsidiary managers, so that strategic staffing was under central control. Companies in this group operated within product-based or matrix structures.

- Decentralized HR companies, characterized by devolving the HR responsibilities to a small group who confined their role to senior management at corporate HQ. This was consistent with the decentralized approach of other functions. Companies within this group operated within product or regional-based structures, with only one reporting using a matrix.

- Transition companies, characterized by medium-sized corporate HR departments staffed by a relatively small group at corporate HQ. They operated in a decentralized, product-based structure, though again one company reported using a matrix structure.

Scullion and Starkey note that the varied roles of corporate HR within these three groups impacted upon the way in which activities such as training and performance appraisal were handled, and the ability of corporate HR to plan for staff movements throughout the worldwide operations.

Different countries take different paths

The above discussion takes a generalist view of the growth of the internationalizing firm through the various stages to multinational status, and the correspondent organizational structures. However, it is important to note a cultural element. If, as Stopford and Wells, state, MNEs may develop global capabilities by an emphasis on product diversity, leading to worldwide product division structures, or alternately, by an emphasis on cultural responsiveness, leading to regional or area division structures, the question arises as to what role does the cultural origin of the multinational play in the path to globalization? See Figure 2-9 for a presentation of this issue.

As can be seen from Figure 2-9, European firms have tended to take a different structural path than their US counterparts. Franko's study of 70 European multinationals revealed that European firms moved directly from a functional 'mother–daughter' structure to a global structure with worldwide product or area

Cultural of origin

Figure 2-9

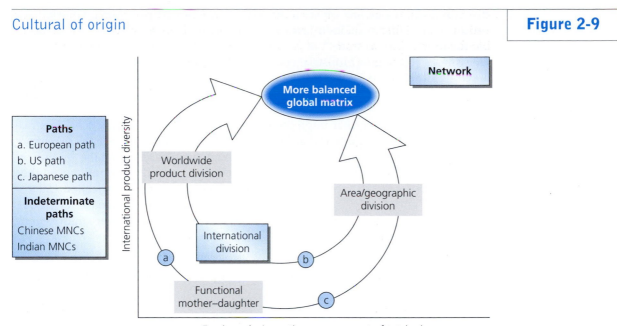

Foreign sales/operations as a per cent of total sales

Source: Adapted from J. Stopford and L. Wells, *Strategy and Structure of the Multinational Enterprise* (New York: Basic Books, 1972).

divisions, or to a matrix organization without the transitional stage of an international division.[32] Human resource management practices, changing to serve the needs of the new structure, adjusted accordingly. Swedish firms have traditionally adopted the mother–daughter structure, but Hedlund's work noted that this had changed. The Swedish multinationals in his study tended to adopt a mixture of elements of the mother–daughter structure and elements of the product division, at this stage of their internationalization process.[33] It may be that there is a preference for matrix-type structures within European firms, particularly Nordic MNEs. One could suggest that this structural form has better suited the more collaborative, group-oriented work organization found within these firms.

US firms that have experimented with the matrix form appear to have met with limited success. For example, as part of a reorganization process termed 'Ford 2000', the Ford Motor Company abandoned its regional structure in 1993 and adopted a form of global matrix organization characterized by a multidisciplinary product team approach with networked plants across regions. In the process, the European regional headquarters was moved to the USA in an attempt to develop global decision making. In November 2001, Ford announced a restructuring and plant rationalization that effectively took the company back to a regional structure.[34] Further restructuring, particularly of its North American operations in 2006, is underway as Ford seeks to retrieve its competitive position.

Japanese multinationals are evolving along similar lines to their US counterparts. Export divisions have become international divisions but, according to Ronen,[35] the rate of change was slower. The characteristics of Japanese organizational culture (such as the control and reporting mechanisms and decision-making systems), the role of trading companies and the systems of management appear to contribute to the slower evolution of the international division. In some cases, despite their high degree of internationalization, Japanese firms may not adapt their structure as they become more dispersed. As mentioned previously, Ghoshal and Bartlett were able to include Japanese firms in their description of the network multinational. A 1996 study[36] of 54 companies, taken from the *Fortune* 1991 list of the world's 500 largest industrial corporations revealed that the degree of internationalization differed between firms from the USA, Europe and Japan. The study also reports that the US multinationals in the sample gave more autonomy to their international operations than did their Japanese counterparts.

We should mention that internationalizing firms from other Asian nations may also vary in structural form and growth patterns. Korean conglomerates (*chaebols*) have had a stronger preference for growth-through-acquisitions than the 'greenfield' (building) approach taken by Japanese multinationals, and this has influenced their structural responses in terms of control and coordination. The so-called Chinese bamboo network/family firms may face significant challenges as their international activities expand and it becomes more difficult to maintain the tight family control that characterizes overseas-Chinese firms.

In 1995, only three mainland Chinese firms were listed in *Fortune*'s top 500 global companies. This number is expanding but relatively few Chinese firms have international operations.[37] Newly emerging Chinese multinationals, such as the white-goods manufacturer Haier, and PetroChina, an oil and gas producer, appear to be following an acquisition path, though there is little data on how these firms are integrating foreign operations. Some research has begun into the internationalization of Chinese MNEs. For example, Shen's[38] 2001 study of ten Chinese firms, mostly state owned enterprises of various sizes and from different industries, reports an incremental approach: moving into neighboring East and South East Asia before expanding into North America. These firms were at different stages of internationalization: four had foreign sales offices, three had sales offices and subsidiaries, and three were considered global in terms of number of foreign subsidiaries (either wholly owned or international joint ventures). Global area divisional or global functional structures were utilized. As with China, there is a similar relative paucity of information regarding Indian MNEs and their internationalization.

Some researchers have gone so far as to question the existence of a truly global firm. Doremus *et al.,*[39] find empirical support for their contention that institutional infrastructures (the cultural heritage codified into legislation and values related to banking and financial markets, research and development capabilities and patterns of technological change, as well as governmental and managerial preferences and strategic propensities) combine to limit the ability of firms to move too far beyond their regional homes. Three regional blocks are presented for multinational firms: North America, Europe (largely German-based multinationals) and Asia (largely Japanese-based multinationals). The authors report economic data to support their contention that while each of these regional powers have some impact outside of their own regions, practically no firms operate significantly in a balanced manner across all three regions of the world. Deep-seated differences in financial institutions, how technology is acquired and developed, and how products and services are consumed are all too divergent from each firm's region of origin for complete global cross-seeding to occur. According to Rugman, centers of regional competitive advantage may be created with some limited interventions outside of the regional core.[40]

Fashion or fit?

The above discussion has traced the evolution of the firm from domestic-oriented into a global-oriented firm. A note of caution should be added. Growth in the firm's international business activity does require structural responses, but the evolutionary process will differ across multinationals. Apart from the country of origin aspect, other variables – size of organization, pattern of internationalization, management policies and so on – also play a part. As Figure 2-9 illustrates, firms undergo stages of restructuring as they attempt to grapple with environment changes than require strategic responses.

Control mechanisms

As indicated in Figure 2-1 at the beginning of this chapter, international operations place additional stresses on control mechanisms. There is also additional stress on the firm's ability to coordinate resources and activities. As the chairman and chief executive officer of the French hotel and travel company, Accor, explained in a newspaper interview:[41]

> Accor has to be a global company, in view of the revolution in the service sector which is taking place . . . National [hotel chains] cannot optimise their operations. They cannot invest enough money . . . Globalisation brings considerable challenges which are often under-estimated. The principal difficulty is getting our local management to adhere to the values of the group . . . Every morning when I wake I think about the challenges of coordinating our operations in many different countries.

Figure 2-10 below presents two strategies for global control. It is important to note these two strategies are not independent or divorced from each other. Rather they present a difference in emphasis.

Traditionally multinational firms have emphasized more formal, structural forms of control. As presented earlier in the chapter, strategy is implemented via the factoring of work flows, the articulation of control by some combination of specialization characterized by functional, global product division, national, regional (area) divisions, or matrix structures. Structure results in hierarchies, functional authority and increasingly prescribed job descriptions, selection criteria, training standards and compensable factors. Human resource activities act to implement existing structural systems of control. Communication and relationships are formalized and prescribed and budgetary targets and 'rational', explicit, quantitative criteria dominate performance management systems.[42] Complementary, yet definitely secondary control is developed and maintained via more informal personal and social networks – the informal organization.

An alternative perspective has developed in response to perceived shortcomings in an over-reliance on bureaucratic structural controls in dealing with the significant variations in distance and people experienced in the far-flung activities and operations of multinational firms and presented in Chapter 1. The unique cultural interactions and the contextual and physical distances that characterized multinational operations may have outstripped the capabilities of solely structural and formal forms of control.[43] As long ago as 1981, William Ouchi termed the phrase 'clan control' to describe social control as a legitimate control system to supplement or replace traditional structural, bureaucratic control.[44] A more cultural focus emphasizes the group level potential of corporate culture, informal social processes, personal work networks and the investment in social capital to act as sources of more complete and nimble control in a complex multi-product, multicultural environment. On the individual level, an emphasis on persons (as opposed to jobs), their competencies and skills, and the investment in human capital become the

| **Figure 2-10** | Control strategies for multinational firms |

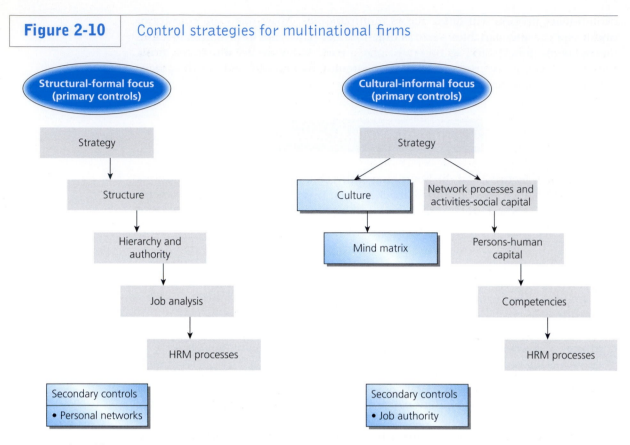

Source: Adapted from A. Engle and Y. Stedham, 'Von Nebenrolle zu Hautptrolle, von Statist ins Rampenlicht: Multinational and Transnational Strategies – Implications for Human Resource Practices', *Conference Proceedings of the Sixth Conference on International Human Resource Management,* Paderborn, Germany: University of Paderborn, 1998; and A. Engle, M. Mendenhall, R. Powers and Y. Stedham, 'Conceptualizing the Global Competency Cube: A Transnational Model of Human Resource', *Journal of European Industrial Training,* Vol. 25, No. 7, pp. 15–23.

focus of more customized human resource practices and processes.[45] Formal, structural controls still exist, but they are not the primary source of control.

Results from a survey of 390 Mexican subsidiaries of US MNEs by Gomez and Sanchez[46] led them to conclude that predicting the preferred combination of formal and informal controls a multinational might choose is problematic. The complexities related to subsidiary mandate, reliance on local or corporate technologies and skills, as well as the cultural distance between the corporate and host cultures need to be considered in determining the mix of formal and informal control. Clearly more research is called for in this topic area.[47] Returning to several of the elements in Figure 2-10, we will review informal control processes.

Control though personal relationships

A consistent theme in the descriptions of transnational and networked organization forms is the need to foster vital knowledge generation and diffusion through lateral communication via a network of working relationships. Networks are considered as part of an individual's or organization's *social capital:* contacts and ties, combined with norms and trust, that facilitate knowledge sharing and information exchanges between individuals, groups and business units.[48] As network relationships are built and maintained through personal contact, organizations need processes and forums where staff from various units can develop types of personal relationships that can be used for organizational purposes. For example, working in cross-functional and/or cross-border teams can assist in developing personal contacts. Training and development programs, held in regional centers or at headquarters, become an important forum for the development of personal networks that foster informal communication channels.

Control through corporate culture

Some advocates of more complex structural forms regard the use of cultural control as an effective informal control mechanism. Corporate culture is variously defined, but essentially it refers to a process of socializing people so that they come to share a common set of values and beliefs that then shape their behavior and perspectives. It is often expressed as 'our way of doing things'. Cultural control may be a contentious issue for some – evidence of multinational imperialism where corporate culture is superimposed upon national cultures in subsidiary operations. However, its proponents offer persuasive arguments as to its value as a management tool.[49] The emphasis is on developing voluntary adherence to corporate behavioral norms and expectations through a process of internalization of corporate values and beliefs.

The literature on corporate culture recognizes the role played by HR activities in fostering corporate culture. For example, Alvesson and Berg[50] regard HRM activities as important means of establishing corporate culture identity. HR activities that build corporate culture include recruitment and selection practices, as firms hire or 'buy' people who appear to hold similar values. Training and development programs, reward systems and promotion are also activities that reinforce company value systems.[51] Such reinforcement is considered to lead to more committed and productive employees who evince appropriate behavior and therefore reduce the need for formal control mechanisms. Placement of staff is another method. Some global firms have become even more systematic in their efforts to achieve control by way of shared corporate culture. As IHRM in Action Case 2-1 shows, these efforts can become a central element in IHRM strategy.

IHRM in Action Case 2-1

Globalizing Corporate Culture
'True Believers' in 'The Toyota Way'

Mikkabi, Japan is not the home to any renowned Buddhist temple or Shinto shrine, but it does act as a global repository for corporate philosophy and the missionary headquarters of Toyota. It is the location of the Toyota Institute. According to the Institute's general manager, Koki Konishi, 'We must prevent the Toyota way from getting more and more diluted as Toyota grows overseas.'

With 200 000 workers in 27 plants outside of the 18 plants in Japan, this global expansion has led to concerns about maintaining and yet adapting the MNE's core values around the world. This closed to the public institute, designed to socialize executives into Toyota's philosophies of collective problem solving, empowering production workers to so value quality that they will stop production lines in order to correct defect in real time, has been so successful that similar institutes are planned in Kentucky and Thailand. 'Toyota is growing more quickly than the company's ability to transplant its culture to foreign markets', according to Takaki Nakanishi, Tokyo-based auto analyst for J.P. Morgan Securities. 'This is a huge issue for Toyota, one of the biggest it will face in the coming years.'

Latonda Newton, a general manager responsible for North American training and development, experienced the Institute first hand. One of a 'class' of 40 managers from Japan, the USA, New Zealand and Singapore, Newton described a week of 12- to 14-hour days at the Institute. A series of opening lectures on the 'Toyota Way' from president Katsuaki Wantanabe, past president Fujio Cho and other top level executives are combined with a daily focus on more specific concepts and practices. These practices include *genchi genbutsu* – stressing that production problems can only be analyzed and solved at the source and not behind a desk, and the continuous improvement philosophy of *kaizen*. More interpersonal values are also communicated in the intense, week-long program. Topics include problem solving by factoring complex problems into smaller components, mutual respect in the workplace, consensus building and an understanding of Toyota's richly informative, yet complex production charts, factory screens and color-coded graphics that make up the cross-cultural vocabulary of the 'Toyota Way'.

Summary

The purpose of this chapter has been to identify the HR implications of the various options and responses that international growth places on the firm. This chapter focused on:

- The organizational context in which IHRM activities take place. Different structural arrangements have been identified as the firm moves along the path to multinational status – from export department through to more complex varieties such as the matrix, heterarchy, transnational and networked.

- Control and coordination aspects. Formal and informal mechanisms were outlined, with emphasis on control through personal networks and relationships, and control through corporate culture, drawing out HRM implications.

- How international growth affects the firm's approach to HRM. Firms vary from one another as they go through the stages of international development, and react in different ways to the circumstances they encounter in the various foreign markets. There is a wide variety of matches between IHRM approaches, organizational structure and stage of internationalization. For example, almost half the US firms surveyed by Dowling[52] reported that the operations of the HR function were unrelated to the nature of the firm's international operations. A study of nine subsidiaries of multinationals operating in Ireland by Monks[53] found that the majority adopted a local approach to the HR function, with headquarter's involvement often limited to monitoring the financial implications of HR decisions.

● Stages of development and organizational forms should not to be taken as normative. Research does suggest a pattern and a process of internationalization but firms do vary in how they adapt to international operations – we use nationality of the parent firm to demonstrate this.

Through the approach taken in this chapter, we have been able to demonstrate that there is an interconnection between IHRM approaches and activities and the organizational context, and that HR managers have a crucial role to play. In order to better perform this role, it would seem important that HR managers understand the various international structural options – along with the control and coordination demands imposed by international growth.

Discussion Questions

1   What are the stages a firm typically goes through as it grows internationally and how does each stage affect the HR function?

2   What are the specific HRM challenges in a networked firm?

3   Country of origin influences the firm's approach to organization structure. As MNEs from China and India internationalize, to what extent are they likely to differ from that observed for Japanese, European and US MNEs?

Further Reading

Bartlett, C., Ghoshal, S. and Beamish, P. (2008). *Transnational Management: Text, Cases and Readings in Cross-border Management,* 5th edn, Boston, MA: McGraw-Hill/Irwin.

Brewster, C., Sparrow, P. and Harris, H. (2005). 'Towards a New Model of Globalizing HRM', *International Journal of Human Resource Management,* 16(5): 949–70.

Enright, M. (2005). 'Regional Management Centers in the Asia-Pacific', *Management International Review,* 45, Special Issue (1): 59–82.

Kang, S.-C., Morris, S. and Snell, S. (2007). 'Relational Archetypes, Organizational Learning, and Value Creation: Extending Human Resource Architecture', *Academy of Management Review,* 32(1): 236–56.

Stiles, P. and Trevor, J. (2006). 'The Human Resource Department: Roles, Coordination and Influence', in G. Stahl and I. Björkman (eds), *Handbook of Research in International Human Resource Management,* Cheltenham: Edward Elgar, pp. 49–67.

Notes and References

1   For more on the potential of strategic and structural activities to impact international human resource processes and systems, see P. Evans, V. Pucik and J.-L. Barsoux, *The Global Challenge: Frameworks for International Human Resource Management* (Boston, MA: McGraw-Hill, 2002), particularly chapter 2.

2   A discussion of the 'administrative heritage' that may link MNE country of origin to a predisposition for certain strategies and structural options is presented by C. Bartlett, S. Ghoshal and P. Beamish, in *Transnational Management: Text, Cases and Readings in Cross-Border Management,* 5th edn (Boston, MA: McGraw-Hill/Irwin, 2008), pp. 333–40; T. Jackson, *International HRM: A Cross-Cultural Approach* (London: Sage Publications, 2002); and P. Buckley and P. Ghauri, 'Globalization, Economic Geography and the Strategy of Multinational Enterprises', *Journal of International Business Studies,* Vol. 35 (2004), pp. 81–98.

3   M. Svard and R. Luostarinen, *Personnel Needs in the Internationalising Firm,* FIBO Publication No. 19 (Helsinki: Helsinki School of Economics, 1982).

4 The organization's structure defines the tasks of individuals and business units within the firm and the processes that result from the intertwined tasks: identifying how the organization is divided up (differentiated) and how it is united (integrated).

5 B.M. Oviatt and P.P. McDougall, 'Towards a Theory of International New Ventures', *Journal of International Business Studies,* Vol. 25, No. 1 (1994), pp. 45–64.

6 J. Johanson and J.E. Vahlne, 'The Mechanism of Internationalisation', *International Marketing Review,* Vol. 7, No. 4 (1990), pp. 11–24; L. Welch and R. Luostarinen, 'Internationalisation: Evolution of a Concept', *Journal of General Management*, Vol. 14, No. 2 (1988), pp. 34–55.

7 A study of US service firms involved in international operations showed that a wholly owned subsidiary/branch office was the most common method, though engineering and architecture firms used direct exports and consumer services used licensing/franchising (K. Erramilli, 'The Experience Factor in Foreign Market Entry Behaviour of Service Firms', *Journal of International Business Studies,* Vol. 22, No. 3 (1991), pp. 479–501). Similar results were found in a study of Australian service firms (LEK Partnership, *Intelligent Exports and the Silent Revolution in Services,* Canberra: Australian Government Publishing Service, 1994).

8 J. Ricart, M. Enright, P. Ghemawat, S. Hart and T. Khanna, 'New Frontiers in International Strategy', *Journal of International Business Studies,* Vol. 35 (2004), pp. 175–200; D. Welch and L. Welch, 'Pre-expatriation: The Role of HR Factors in the Early Stages of Internationalization', *International Journal of Human Resource Management,* Vol. 8, No. 4 (1997), pp. 402–13.

9 See V. Pucik, 'Strategic Human Resource Management in a Multinational Firm', in H.V. Wortzel and L.H. Wortzel (eds), *Strategic Management of Multinational Corporations: The Essentials,* (New York: John Wiley, 1985), pp. 425.

10 N. Adler, *International Dimensions of Organizational Behavior,* 4th edn (Cincinnati, OH: South-Western, 2002), chap. 8; M. Bloom, G. Milkovich and A. Mitra, 'International Compensation: Learning How Managers Respond to Variations in Local Host Contexts', *International Journal of Human Resource Management,* Vol. 14, No. 8 (2003), pp. 1350–67.

11 Pucik, 'Strategic Human Resource Management in a Multinational Firm'.

12 C. Bartlett and S. Ghoshal, 'Organizing for Worldwide Effectiveness: The Transnational Solution', in R. Buzzell, J. Quelch and C. Barrett (eds), *Global Marketing Management: Cases and Readings,* 3rd edn (Reading, MA: Addison Wesley, 1992).

13 J.R. Galbraith and R.K. Kazanjian, 'Organizing to Implement Strategies of Diversity and Globalisation: The Role of Matrix Designs', *Human Resource Management,* Vol. 25, No. 1 (1986), p. 50. See also T.T. Naylor, 'The International Strategy Mix', *Columbia Journal of World Business,* Vol. 20, No. 2 (1985); and R.A. Pitts and J.D. Daniels, 'Aftermath of the Matrix Mania', *Columbia Journal of World Business,* Vol. 19, No. 2 (1984), for a discussion on the matrix structure.

14 W. Taylor, 'The Logic of Global Business: An Interview with ABB's Percy Barnevik', *Harvard Business Review,* March–April 1991, pp. 91–105. For a more complete presentation of ABB's strategic intent and structural and process qualities, see K. Barham and C. Heimer, *ABB: The Dancing Giant* (London: Financial Times/Pitman Publishing, 1998).

15 C.A. Bartlett and S. Ghoshal, 'Matrix Management: Not a Structure, a Frame of Mind', *Harvard Business Review,* July–August 1990, pp. 138–45.

16 S. Ronen, *Comparative and Multinational Management* (New York: John Wiley, 1986), p. 330.

17 P.J. Dowling, 'International HRM', in L. Dyer (ed.), *Human Resource Management: Evolving Roles and Responsibilities,* Vol. 1, ASPA/BNA Handbook of Human Resource Management Series (Washington, DC: BNA, 1988), pp. 228–257.

18 Galbraith and Kazanjian, 'Organizing to Implement Strategies', p. 50.

19 G. Hedlund, 'The Hypermodern MNC – A Heterarchy?', *Human Resource Management,* Vol. 25, No. 1 (1986), pp. 9–35.

20 G. Hedlund, 'A Model of Knowledge Management and the N-form Corporation', *Strategic Management Journal,* Vol. 15 (1994), pp. 73–90.

21 Bartlett and Ghoshal, 'Organizing for Worldwide Effectiveness', p. 66.

22 J. Birknishaw and N. Hood, *Multinational Corporate Evolution and Subsidiary Development* (London: Macmillan Press, 1998).

23 M. Forsgren, 'Managing the International Multi-centre Firm: Case Studies from Sweden', *European Management Journal,* Vol. 8, No. 2 (1990), pp. 261–7. Much of this work has been based on the concepts of social exchange theory and interaction between actors in a network.

24 J.I. Martinez and J.C. Jarillo, 'The Evolution of Research on Coordination Mechanisms in Multinational Corporations', *Journal of International Business Studies* (Fall 1989), pp. 489–514.

25 S. Ghoshal and C.A. Bartlett, 'The Multinational Corporation as an Interorganizational Network', *Academy of Management Review,* Vol. 8, No. 2 (1990), pp. 603–25.

26 S. Ghoshal and C. Bartlett, 'Building the Entrepreneurial Corporation: New Organizational Processes, New Managerial Tasks', *European Management Journal,* Vol. 13, No. 2 (1995), p. 145.

27 R. Marschan, 'Dimensions of Less-hierarchical Structures in Multinationals', in I. Björkman and M. Forsgren (eds), *The Nature of the International Firm* (Copenhagen: Copenhagen Business School Press, 1997).

28 N. Nohria and S. Ghoshal, *The Differentiated Network: Organizing Multinational Corporations for Value Creation* (San Francisco, CA: Jossey-Bass, 1997), pp. 28–32.

29 Y. Doz, J. Santos and P. Williamson, *From Global to Metanational: How Companies Win in the Knowledge Economy* (Boston, MA: Harvard Business School Press, 2001).

30 Y. Doz, J. Santos and P. Williamson, *From Global to Metanational,* p. 247.

31 H. Scullion and K. Starkey, 'In Search of the Changing Role of the Corporate Human Resource Function in the International Firm', *International Journal of Human Resource Management,* Vol. 11, No. 6 (2000), pp. 1061–81.

32 L. Leksell, 'Headquarter–Subsidiary Relationships in Multinational Corporations', unpublished doctoral thesis, Institute for International Economic Studies, University of Stockholm, Stockholm (1981).

33 G. Hedlund, 'Organization In-between: The Evolution of the Mother–Daughter Structure of Managing Foreign Subsidiaries in Swedish MNCs', *Journal of International Business Studies,* Fall (1984), pp. 109–23.

34 *Financial Times* series on The Global Company, October 15, 1997, p. 14; and *The Economist,* November 13, 2001.

35 S. Ronen, *Comparative and Multinational Management* (New York: John Wiley, 1986).

36 R.B. Peterson, J. Sargent, N.K. Napier and W.S. Shim, 'Corporate Expatriate HRM Policies, Internationalisation and Performance', *Management International Review,* Vol. 36, No. 3 (1996), pp. 215–30.

37 Yin, E. and Choi, C.J., 'The Globalization Myth: The Case of China', *Management International Review,* Vol. 45, Special Issue No. 1 (2005), pp. 103–20.

38 Shen, J., 'Factors Affecting International Staffing in Chinese Multinationals (MNEs)', *International Journal of Human Resource Management,* Vol. 17, No. 2 (2006), pp. 295–315.

39 P. Doremus, W. Keller, L. Pauley and S. Reich, *The Myth of the Global Corporation* (Princeton, NJ: Princeton University Press, 1998).

40 For additional empirical support for the idea of the regional multinational and the difficulties inherent in being a balanced global firm, see A. Rugman and R. Hodgetts, 'The End of Global Strategy', *European Management Journal,* Vol. 19, No. 4 (2001), pp. 333–43; and E. Schlie and G. Yip, 'Regional Follows Global: Strategy Mixes in the World Automotive Industry', *European Management Journal,* Vol. 18, No. 4 (2000), pp. 343–54.

41 Interview by Andrew Jack, *Financial Times,* October 13 (1997), p. 14.

42 A. Engle and P. Dowling, 'State of Origin: Research in Global Performance Management – Progress or a Lost Horizon?', *Conference Proceedings of the VII World Congress of the International Federation of Scholarly Associations of Management,* Berlin, 2006; G. Jones, *Organization Theory, Design and Change,* 5th edn (Upper Saddle River, NJ: Pearson/Prentice-Hall, 2007, chaps 4 and 5); R. Marchan, D. Welch and L. Welch, 'Control in Less-hierarchical Multinationals: the Role of Personal Networks and Informal Communication', *International Business Review,* Vol. 5, No. 2 (1996), pp. 137–50.

43 See C. Bartlett, S. Ghoshal and P. Beamish in *Transnational Management* for their discussion of a more complete form of control, more appropriate to advanced multinational firms, via a more balanced combination of structural 'anatomy', process 'physiology' and cultural 'psychology', pp. 343–7.

44 W. Ouchi, *Theory Z* (New York: Avon Books, 1981).

45 A. Engle, M. Mendenhall, R. Powers and Y. Stedham, 'Conceptualizing the Global Competence Cube: A Transnational Model of Human Resource Management', *European Journal of Industrial Training,* Vol. 25, No. 7 (2001), pp. 346–53.

46 C. Gomez and J. Sanchez, 'Human Resource Control in MNCs: A Study of the Factors Influencing the Use of Formal and Informal Control Mechanisms', *International Journal of Human Resource Management,* Vol. 6, No. 10 (2005), pp. 1847–61.

47 A prescriptive approach to developing a hybrid, more balanced formal and informal strategy of control is provided by F. Nilsson and N.-G. Olve, 'Control Systems in Multibusiness Companies: From Performance Management to Strategic Management', *European Management Journal,* Vol. 19, No. 4 (2001), pp. 344–58. An empirical assessment of 24 international manufacturing firms in the UK provided evidence of wide variance in the degree to which multinational firms

provide forums for informal control processes, some respondents appeared to rely on more formal control systems. P. Kidger, 'Management Structures in Multinational Enterprises: Responding to Globalization', *Employee Relations,* Vol. 24, No. 1 (2002), pp. 69–85; for a theoretical discussion of the potential relationships between social capital, HRM and corporate strategy, see S.-C. Kang, S. Morris and S. Snell, 'Relational Archetypes, Organizational Learning, and Value Creation: Extending Human Resource Architecture', *Academy of Management Review*, Vol. 32, No. 1 (2007), pp. 236–56.

48 J. Nahapiet and S. Ghoshal, 'Social Capital, Intellectual Capital, and the Organizational Advantage', *Academy of Management Review,* Vol. 23, No. 2 (1998), pp. 242–66; M. Hitt, L. Bierman, K. Uhlenbruck and K. Shimizu, 'The Importance of Resources in the Internationalization of Professional Service Firms: the Good, the Bad and the Ugly', *Academy of Management Journal,* Vol. 49, No. 6 (2006), pp. 1137–57.

49 D. Ravasi and M. Schultz, 'Responding to Organizational Identity Threats: Exploring the Role of Organizational Culture', *Academy of Management Journal,* Vol. 49, No. 3 (2006), pp. 433–58.

50 M. Alvesson and P. Berg, *Corporate Culture and Organizational Symbolism* (Berlin: Walter de Gruyter, 1992).

51 A. Engle and M. Mendenhall, 'Transnational Roles, Transnational Rewards: Global Integration in Compensation', *Employee Relations,* Vol. 26, No. 6 (2004), pp. 613–25; D. Welch and L. Welch, 'Commitment for Hire? The Viability of Corporate Culture as a MNC Control Mechanism', *International Business Review*, Vol. 15, No. 1 (2006), pp. 14–28.

52 P.J. Dowling, 'Hot Issues Overseas', *Personnel Administrator,* Vol. 34, No. 1 (1989), pp. 66–72.

53 K. Monks, 'Global or Local? HRM in the Multinational Company: The Irish Experience', *International Journal of Human Resource Management,* Vol. 7, No. 3 (1996), pp. 721–35.

The context of cross-border alliances and SMEs

Chapter Objectives

In the last chapter, we outlined how the international growth of MNEs places demands on management. In this chapter, the IHRM implications of other modes of international operations become our center of interest. Consequently, we move from an internal perspective on structure, control mechanisms and managerial responses to a global perspective which includes external partners.

In this chapter we will first concentrate on *cross-border alliances* with a special emphasis on *equity-based alliances*. These alliances are given priority here due to their association with complex IHRM processes and practices,[1] which is the main interest of study within this volume. Equity cross-border alliances include:

- Mergers and acquisitions (M&As).
- International joint ventures (IJVs).

At the end of the chapter we will address the *special case of globalizing small and medium-sized enterprises (SMEs)* while looking for respective IHRM responses. SMEs represent important elements in the world economy. However, in IHRM research they are often neglected. There is evidence that their approaches to international human resource management differ to a large extent from those of large MNEs and this is why we cover this topic in the present chapter. Chapters 2 and 3 complement each other and are designed to deliver insights in the most important organizational contexts for international human resource management.

Introduction to cross-border alliances

The strategic importance of alliances has increased in the course of globalization.[2] Cross-border alliances are cooperative agreements between two or more firms from different national backgrounds, which are intended to benefit all partners. As depicted in Figure 3-1 these comprise equity as well as non-equity arrangements.[3]

- A *non-equity cross-border alliance* 'is an investment vehicle in which profits and other responsibilities are assigned to each party according to a contract. Each party cooperates as a separate legal entity and bears its own liabilities.'[4] Examples include international technology alliances or strategic R&D alliances[5] as well as cooperative agreements in different functional areas such as marketing or production.[6]

- *Equity modes* involve a 'foreign direct investor's purchase of shares of an enterprise in a country other than its own'.[7] These include the establishment of subsidiaries as mentioned in Chapter 2, either through greenfield investments or acquisitions, as well as through joint ventures or mergers. The latter typically involve long-term collaborative strategies, which require the support of appropriate HR practices.[8] They represent typical cross-border equity-based alliances.

Equity as well as non-equity cross-border alliances pose specific challenges to international human resource management. Often, these are crucial to the success of the international operation. As Schuler and Tarique note, 'Some of the HR issues that are critical to the success of equity-based international or cross-border alliances may also rise in non-equity cross-border alliances, but they are often less central to the success of the alliance.'[9] Hence, the difference in HRM in equity and non-equity cross-border alliances is supposed to lie in the differing extent to which specific HR problems occur.[10] However, it has to be stated that there is a research deficit with respect to HRM in non-equity cross-border alliances[11] and it is beyond the scope of this chapter to discuss implications of all foreign entry modes in detail.[12]

Figure 3-1	Equity and non-equity modes of foreign operation

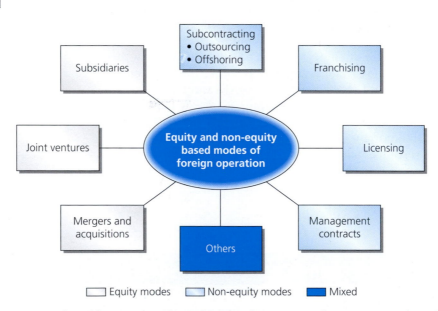

Source: Adapted from M. Kutschker and S. Schmid, *Internationales Management* (Munich and Vienna: R. Oldenbourg, 2004), p. 821.

Cross-border mergers and acquisitions

A *merger* is the result of an agreement between two companies to join their operations together. Partners are often equals. For example, the DaimlerChrysler merger was supposed to be a merger between equals in its first stage.[13] More information about this merger can be found in IHRM in Action Case 3-1.

An *acquisition,* on the other hand, occurs when one company buys another company with the interest of controlling the activities of the combined operations.[14] This was the case when the Dutch steel company Mittal, ranked second by volume in crude steel production in 2005, initiated a hostile takeover of the Luxembourg-based Arcelor group, ranked first in the same statistic.[15]

Figure 3-2 shows that a merger usually results in the formation of a new company while an acquisition involves the acquiring firm keeping its legal identity and integrating a new company into its own activities. The HR challenge in both cases consists of creating new HR practices and strategies that meet the requirements of the M&A.

Within the context of this international volume, our focus will be on cross-border mergers and acquisitions (M&As). This means that firms with headquarters located in two different countries are concerned. Many of the HRM challenges faced in mergers and in acquisitions are similar, and for this reason we will not further differentiate between these two entities, but summarize them and use the abbreviation M&A. UNCTAD defines cross-border M&As as follows:[16] 'Cross-border M&As involve partial or full takeover or the merging of capital, assets and liabilities of existing enterprises in a country by TNCs [transnational corporations] from other countries. M&As generally involve the purchase of existing assets and companies.'

Cross-border M&As have seen tremendous growth over the last two decades in part because of the phenomenon of globalization. 'Both the value and number of cross-border M&As rose in 2005, to US $716 billion (an 88% increase) and to 6,134 (a 20% increase) respectively.'[17] This is depicted in Figure 3-3.

One major reason to engage in mergers or acquisitions is often to facilitate the rapid entry into new markets.[18] Thus, 'mergers and acquisitions are a predominant feature of the international business system as companies attempt to strengthen their

The formation processes of M&As and HR challenges   **Figure 3-2**

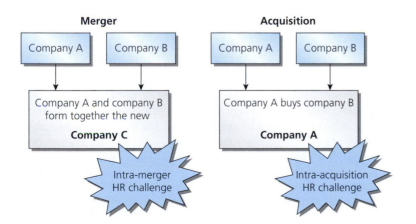

| **Figure 3-3** | Mergers and acquisitions in US billions |

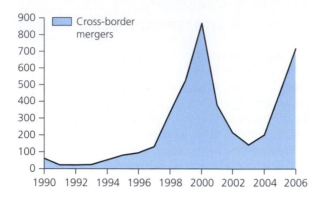

Source: UNCTAD (ed.), *World Investment Report, 2006* (New York and Geneva: United Nations, 2006).

market positions and exploit new market opportunities'.[19] Some of the factors that a firm takes into consideration when deciding on a target country include: the growth aspiration of the acquiring company, risk diversification, technological advantages, a response to government policies in a particular country, exchange rate advantages, favorable political and economic conditions, or an effort to follow clients.[20]

Despite the high yearly growth rates in the area of M&As there seems to be a gap between the expected added value and the benefits realized from a M&A.[21] However, there is growing appreciation that the way the M&A is managed during the different phases (especially in the post-merger integration phase) has an impact on its performance, and in turn on the added value created.[22] M&A management has been investigated from many different perspectives. The work of Larsson and Finkelstein[23] provides an excellent overview of M&As from different research fields including strategic management, economics, finance, organizational theory and human resource management.[24] Of course, all sources of research are important when explaining the phenomenon of M&A success.

For the purposes of this chapter, we are going to focus solely on HR and its role in employee relations. The quality of employee relations, ranging from employee support to employee resistance, is influenced by variables such as the similarity between the management styles of the two organizations,[25] the type of cross-border combinations, the combination potential in terms of efficiency gains, or the extent of organizational integration. There is evidence that employee resistance endangers M&A performance as it may hinder synergy realization.[26] For this reason, it is important that all M&As effectively manage issues where employee resistance in encountered, in order that employee support can evolve. This is a process in which the HRM function can play a major role.

A study by Birkinshaw *et al.*[27] found that the integration of tasks[28] between two companies is interdependent with human integration. The dimensions of human integration in this study included visibility and continuity of leadership, communication processes during integration, integrating mechanisms used, acquired personnel retained and voluntary personnel loss. Task and human integration interact in different phases to foster value creation in acquisitions:

In phase one, task integration led to a satisfying solution that limited the interaction between acquired and acquiring units, while human integration proceeded smoothly and led to cultural convergence and mutual respect. In phase two, there was renewed task integration built on the success of the human integration that has been achieved, which led to much greater interdependencies between acquired and acquiring units.[29]

Figure 3-4 summarizes the impact of the human integration and task acquisition on acquisition outcome.

Birkinshaw *et al.* conclude that the human integration process is especially difficult to manage and takes time. Complexity and the length of the integration process increase even more in the case of cross-border alliances.[30] One reason for this is that both of the firms undergoing acquisition processes are embedded in their own national, institutional and cultural settings.[31] Typical problems that arise in cross-border M&As involve the following:

- Within the first year of a merger, it is not uncommon for a company's top management level to lose up to 20 per cent of its executives. Over a longer time frame, this percentage tends to increase even further.[32]
- Personnel issues are often neglected.[33]
- Finally, a high number of M&As fail or do not produce the intended results.[34]

When a firm is acquired by another firm, so is its existing workforce. Considering this fact, we will describe the typical phases characterizing cross-border M&A processes and outline which HR practices are important at each of the different stages. At this point, it must be admitted that the extent to which these HR practices are carried out very much depends on the extent to which integration of the two companies is actually aspired. In the case of low integration (e.g. if the M&A is carried out mainly for portfolio reasons) both companies remain separate cultures. However, in the case of high integration, it is crucial for the M&A to meet the HR requirements of the different phases, which will be outlined in the next section.[35]

Impact of the human integration and task acquisition on acquisition outcome
Figure 3-4

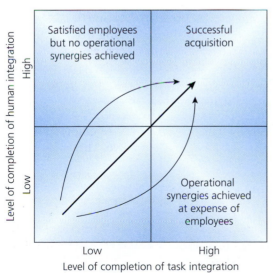

Source: J. Berkinshaw, H. Bresman and L. Hakanson, 'Managing the Post-acquisition Integration Process: How the Human Interaction and Task Integration Processes Interact to Foster Value Creation', *Journal of Management Studies,* Vol. 37, No. 3 (2000), pp. 395–425.

M&A phases and HR implications

Typically, mergers and acquisitions are characterized by different phases. Depending on the publication, these phases will have different names. However, the M&A process usually consists of the following steps:

- A *pre-M&A phase* including a screening of alternative partners based on an analysis of their strengths and weaknesses.

- A *due diligence phase*[36] which focuses more in-depth on analyzing the potential benefits of the merger. Here, product–market combinations, tax regulations and also compatibility with respect to HR and cultural issues are of interest.[37]

- In the *integration planning phase,* which is based on the results of the due diligence phase, planning for the new company is carried out.

- In the *implementation phase* plans are put into action.

Various studies have shown that the HR department becomes increasingly involved in the phases of M&A integration as the process evolves. For example, a study conducted in Germany of 68 M&As revealed that HR issues are only seriously considered once the integration strategy has actually been defined.[38] Schmidt refers to a study of 447 senior HR executives who represent mainly large companies with more than 1000 employees. Most participants were from North America, supplemented by companies from Europe, Latin America and Asia. He found that those companies which involved the HR department early in the process were more successful than others with a low HR involvement.[39] Both studies showed that the strongest involvement of the HR department took place in the last two phases of the M&A process. From this study Schmidt has derived best practices, which should be considered in the different M&A process phases (see Figure 3-5). They are complemented by culture-specific aspects, which are of special importance in cross-border M&As.

| **Figure 3-5** | HR activities in the phases of a cross-border M&A |

Pre-M&A phase
- Identification of people-related issues
- Planning for due diligence
- Assessing people
- Working out the organizational/cultural fit
- Forming the M&A steering team
- Educating the team on the HR implications

Due diligence phase
Estimating people-related
- Transactional costs
- Ongoing costs
- Savings
- Identifying and assessing cultural issues

Integration planning phase
- Developing employee culture-sensitive communication strategies
- Designing key talent retention programs
- Planning and leading integration efforts
- Developing a new strategy for the new entity
- Helping the organization cope with change
- Defining an organizational blueprint and staffing plan

Implementation and assessment phase
- Managing ongoing change, especially cultural change
- Managing employee communications
- Advising management on dealing with people issues
- Aligning HR policies, especially total rewards
- Monitoring the process of organizational and people-related integration activities
- Ensuring the capture of synergies via incentives
- Initiating learning processes for future M&As

Source: Adapted from J.A. Schmidt, 'The Correct Spelling of M&A Begins with HR', *HR Magazine,* Vol. 46, No. 6 (2001), pp. 102–8.

HR in the DaimlerChrysler merger

The merger

The merger between Chrysler and Daimler Benz was one of the largest in history. Both companies had started to screen the automobile industry for partners in 1997. In early 1998 Jürgen E. Schrempp, CEO of the German-based Daimler Benz company took the initiative and suggested a merger to Robert J. Eaton, CEO of the American-based Chrysler corporation. The merger contract was signed in May 1998.

HR in the different phases of the M&A

At *the beginning of the merger* 'soft' people skills were not an important issue to consider. Even in the second phase when the merger was negotiated HR issues continued to play a minor role. Negotiations were dominated by legal and financial aspects. Due to the strict secrecy at this stage, the corporate HR directors from both companies were not informed nor involved.

In the *integration planning phase* in August 1998, management teams from both firms developed strategies for the merged company. These teams identified a number of issues that had to be dealt with during the post-merger integration. With respect to HR one important challenge was to solve the remuneration problem: the German top managers earned much less than their American counterparts. The contrary was the case for the lower management levels. It was decided that the salaries for those German top managers who had international responsibility would be raised to US level. For a broader group of German managers a component of their salary would be linked to the company's profit and its share price. At this stage all employees were informed using various media such as letters, the intranet or films. Furthermore, there was a first awareness about cultural issues in the merger. The new board was composed of 18 members, including both Schrempp and Eaton as chairmen, eight board members from Chrysler and the same number from Daimler-Benz plus two from the Daimler subsidiaries Dasa and Debis.

During the *post-merger integration phase* mixed teams worked on more than 1000 projects identified by the post-merger integration coordination team. Only 43 projects were in the area of HR. They addressed topics such as corporate culture, employee profit-sharing, leadership styles, labor relations, global job evaluation, exchange programs and management development. The board member responsible for human resources was not included in the 'Chairman's Integration Council', the core of DaimlerChrysler's management structure during the post-merger integration phase. Within the first two years of the merger DaimlerChrysler lost about 20 top executives, especially from the Chrysler side. There is little evidence about a systematic retention program for this level. During the information campaign for the other levels the focus was on job security. Only two years after the merger DaimlerChrysler executives had admitted cultural problems. Examples included inappropriate humor, political correctness, perceived excessive formality, sexual harassment, private relationships and documentation of meetings. The company offered intercultural training for executives and management exchange programs.

Long-term effects

In 2000, profitability at Chrysler had sharply dropped and there was a 20 per cent decline in the DaimlerChrysler share price. At that time, the market capitalization of DaimlerChrysler was little more than that of Daimler Benz before the merger. Some years later, at the beginning of 2007 and after important financial losses mainly on the Chrysler side, media are discussing the possibility of a separation of Daimler and Chrysler. Although Chrysler had to close several production plants and had cut around 40 000 jobs during the first years following the merger, it had to admit important economic problems for the third time after the merger, endangering the overall success of the combined company.[40]

Source: This mini-case is adapted from T. Kühlmann and P.J. Dowling, 'DaimlerChrysler: A Case Study of a Cross Border Merger', in G.K. Stahl and M.E. Mendenhall, *Mergers and Acquisitions: Managing Cultures and Human Resources* (Stanford, CA: Stanford Business Books, 2005), pp. 351–63.

IHRM in Action Case 3-1 analyzes the case of the DaimlerChrysler merger with respect to the M&A phases and briefly outlines which HR measures were taken. If you compare the information given about the DaimlerChrysler merger with the list of HR activities outlined in Figure 3-4 you can analyze the strengths and the weaknesses from an HR perspective. What lessons could be learned from this process?

Strategic HRM and the role of the HR function in M&As

Aguilera and Dencker[41] suggest a strategic approach to HR management in M&A processes. Based on strategic HRM literature suggesting a fit between business strategy and HR strategy they argue that firms should match their M&A strategy with their HR strategy while relying on three conceptual tools:

> *Resources* are defined as tangible assets such as money and people, and intangible assets, such as brands and relationships. In the context of HRM in M&As decisions about resources involve staffing and retention issues, with termination decisions being particularly important. *Processes* refer to activities that firms use to convert the resources into valuable goods and services. For example, in our case, these would be training and development programs as well as appraisal and reward systems. Finally, *values* are the way in which employees think about what they do and why they do it. Values shape employee's priorities and decision making.[42]

These ideas deliver starting points for developing HR strategies for the newly created entity. Hence, they give hints on how to meet the intra-merger or intra-acquisition HR challenges outlined in Figure 3-2. Taking such a strategic approach and aligning the HRM activities with the M&A strategy with respect to resources, processes and values is also a challenging task for the HR manager to perform. The HR manager must develop a set of integrated HR activities which are not only in line with the business strategy but with the M&A strategy as well.[43] Based on the well-known work of Ulrich (1997),[44] the HR function can take the role of strategic partner (i.e. management of strategic human resources), an administrative expert (i.e. management of the firm's infrastructure), an employee champion (i.e. management of the employee contribution), or a change agent (i.e. management of transformation and change). In each phase of the M&A process each role involves different activities.

The role of expatriates in M&As

The role of expatriates has been discussed with respect to knowledge transfer between the acquiring and the acquired company. However, the transfer of embedded knowledge is not guaranteed by each international assignment. While some studies have revealed the importance of prior working experience with a specific host country or with a particular entry mode as a success factor for expatriates involved in the integration of mergers,[45] this has not been confirmed for acquisitions. In a study by Hébert *et al.*, prior experience did not have an impact on the performance of the acquired firm.[46]

In contrast to these findings, the above-mentioned study on M&As in Germany revealed that successful integration is dependent upon managers' industry experience, experience with similar projects and, particularly in the case of cross-border alliances, level of intercultural competence.[47] An emphasis on industry experience is in line with the suggestion by Hébert *et al.* who state that industry experience is an important asset when staffing an acquired subsidiary with an expatriate because it can lead to a transfer of best practices.[48]

These arguments have implications for the staffing of the post-merger integration team. Hébert *et al.*[49] suggest that acquiring companies should not completely rely on the placement of expatriates within the top management team of an acquired subsidiary. They suggest creating a strong team including a mix of both – expatriates and local members of top management – and that the acquisition integration be viewed as a learning process.

A study by Villinger (1996) of 35 acquisitions by Western MNEs in Hungary, the Czech Republic, Slovakia and Poland on post-acquisition managerial learning[50] highlights the importance of appropriate cross-border management skills. The author emphasizes that local language skills as well as sensitivity towards cultural differences are crucial for M&A success. It is especially important to note this when companies from developing countries represent the acquired firm in the M&A process. As Villinger[51] notes:

> Interestingly, although language and communication problems are clearly pointed out as the key barrier to successful learning from both sides, there seems to be a consensus that the command of the partner's language is mainly a requirement for eastern managers, and significantly less so for western partners. This may be surprising, as it can lead to a situation in which a hundred eastern European managers have to learn German, instead of a small number of German expatriates learning the local language. However, it may be argued that the language chosen for (future) communications will depend on the expected direction of 'the flow of learning' between the two partners.

A comparative approach to HRM in M&A processes

While it seems possible to identify the typical phases of M&A processes across nationalities and industries, the content of the HR measures appears to depend very much on the nationality and culture of the companies involved in the M&A. Child *et al.*[52] highlight the following HRM policy characteristics for the different countries of their investigation (USA, Japan, Germany, France, and UK):

- Performance-related pay is more popular in the USA than in Japan or Germany.
- Recruitment in the USA tends to be rather short-term as compared to Germany, France and the UK. While in Japan the lifetime orientation is less than before there is still a longer term focus than in the other countries.
- Training and career planning is most extensive in the USA.

Despite the fact that there are signs of convergence in HR practices across countries due to the increasing globalization of markets, companies' cultural and institutional differences and the resulting impact on HR still seems to be important.[53] This seems to also hold true when M&A processes are concerned and especially in the post-integration phase. Child *et al.*[54] summarize the results of their case study research as follows:

- Convergence across nationalities in HRM policies was evident in post-acquisition moves towards performance-related pay, training and team-based product development.
- Most acquirers also made adjustments to suit the local culture.

	Table 3-1				

Table 3-1 Post-acquisition trends in HRM practices

	USA	Japan	Germany	France	UK
Pay	Performance related	PRP growing	PRP growing	PRP growing	PRP growing
Recruitment	Short term	Lifetime	Long term	French long; local less so	Less short term than USA
Training	High; on course	On the job	Technical bias	To a ceiling	Increased; courses
Career planning	Little	Steady and slow	Ad hoc	Highly structured	Very variable
Product development	Team based	Team based	Team based		Not very team based
Culture	Top down	Bottom up; consensual	Top down	Top down	Top down
Appraisal	Regular and formal	Subtle, not transparent	Growing	Growing	Regular annual
Promotion	Fast and performance based	Slow and seniority based	Based on technical expertise	Emphasis on formal qualification; fast	Variable
Communications	Formal, need to know	Open when asked	Open and informal	Open and formal	Need-to-know approach

Source: J. Child, D. Faulkner and R. Pitkethly, *The Management of International Acquisitions* (Oxford: Oxford University Press, 2001), p. 172 (PRP = performance-related pay).

- US HRM reflected a short-term, individualistic, national business culture.
- Japanese HRM, although adopting some US methods, generally reflected long-term, consensual, team-based, collectivist national philosophies.
- French companies have also been influenced by IHRM best practice but still tend to display an ethnocentric approach that gives precedence to managers of French origin.
- German companies were the most anxious to adopt international practices in their acquisitions, even when these conflicted with their national tendencies. For example, they force themselves to be more informal.

Table 3-1 summarizes more details on the post-acquisition trends in HRM practices identified in the USA, Japan, France, Germany and the UK.

International equity joint ventures

International joint ventures (IJVs), the second type of equity-based cross-border alliance to be discussed in this chapter, have experienced tremendous growth during the last two decades as well. They will continue to represent a major means of global expansion for MNEs.[55] In emerging economies such as China they represent the dominating operation mode for MNEs' market entry.[56] According to a well-known definition by Shenkar and Zeira[57] an IJV is:

> A separate legal organizational entity representing the partial holdings of two or more parent firms, in which the headquarters of at least one is located outside the country of operation of the joint venture. This entity is subject to the joint control of its parent firms, each of which is economically and legally independent of the other.

An IJV can have two or more parent companies. Many IJVs, however, involve two parent companies. This is why we concentrate on this constellation in the following discussion. As will be outlined later, problems will get even more complex with more than two partners. The equity division between the parent companies of the joint venture may differ. In some cases the ratio is 50:50, in others the dominance of one partner becomes more obvious with a ratios of 51:49 or through various other combinations. This, of course, has implications for the control of the IJV; an issue which will be discussed later in this chapter. Figure 3-6 depicts the formation of an IJV. In contrast to M&As, the parent companies of an IJV keep their legal identity and an additional new legal entity representing the IJV is established. Figure 3-6 also indicates the level of complexity that an IJV represents for the human resource management function. For this reason IJVs clearly represent an important field of research for IHRM scholars.[58] The topics of research on IHRM in IJVs are very similar to those in M&As. In both cases, partners with different institutional, cultural and national backgrounds come together and must balance their interests. However, in IJVs, this challenge includes the following factors:

● On the one hand, HR must manage *relations at the interfaces between IJV and the parent companies.* The different partners that make up the IJV may possibly follow different sets of rules and this can lead to critical dualities[59] within the HR function.

● On the other side, the HR department must develop *appropriate HRM practices and strategies for the IJV entity itself.* HR has to recruit, develop, motivate and retain human resources at the IJV level.

Formation of an international equity joint venture   **Figure 3-6**

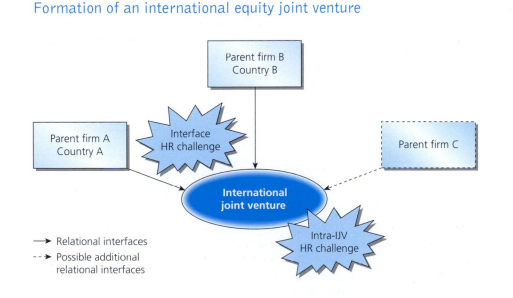

For the sake of the IJV's performance these two challenges have to be taken into consideration during the different phases of establishing and managing the joint venture.[60] These will be described later in this chapter (see Figure 3-7).

According to a literature analysis by Schuler, the main reasons for engaging in an IJV are as follows:[61]

- To gain knowledge and to transfer that knowledge.
- Host government insistence.
- Increased economies of scale.
- To gain local knowledge.
- To obtain vital raw materials.
- To spread the risks (e.g. share financial risks).
- To improve competitive advantage in the face of increasing global competition.
- Provide a cost effective and efficient response forced by the globalization of markets.

Special emphasis should be given to the knowledge transfer or learning objective.[62] IJVs provide an excellent opportunity to learn from another company in two ways.

| **Figure 3-7** | IJV development stages and HR implications |

IJV development stages	HR implications
Stage 1: Formation • Identifying reasons • Planning for utilization • Selecting dedicated manager • Finding potential partners • Selecting likely partners • Resolving critical issues • Negotiating the arrangement	• The more important learning is, the greater the role for HRM • Knowledge needs to be managed • Systematic partner selection is essential • Be thorough for compatibility • Ensure extensive communications and use skilled negotiators • Develop integrative strategies for learning
Stage 2: Development • Locating the IJV • Establishing the right structure • Getting the right senior managers	• Concerns of multiple sets of stakeholders need to be considered for long-term viability and acceptance • The structure will impact on the learning and knowledge management processes • Recruiting, selecting and managing senior staff are critical
Stage 3: Implementation • Establishing the vision, mission, values, strategy and structure • The people sharing this and learning from each other will provide direction to the IJV	• Need to design policies and practices with local–global considerations • Developing HR policies and practices • Staffing and managing the employees
Stage 4: Advancement and beyond • Learning from the partner • Transferring new knowledge to the parents • Transferring new knowledge to other locations	• Partners need learning capacity • HR systems need to be established to support knowledge flow to the parent

Source: Adapted from R.S. Schuler, 'Human Resource Issue and Activities in International Joint Ventures', *International Journal of Human Resource Management,* Vol. 12, No. 1 (2001), pp. 1–52.

First, each company has the chance to 'learn the other partner's skills'. This can include gaining know-how and process knowledge in specific functional areas such as R&D or acquiring local knowledge about a specific market or culture. Second, companies acquire working experience in cooperating with other firms. Thus, the IJV can be used as a medium for organizational learning processes as well.[63]

Unfortunately, there is evidence that many IJVs fail[64] or do not produce the expected results.[65] Major reasons for these failures can be traced back to the lack of interest in the human resource management and cross-cultural management aspects of international joint ventures.[66] These two issues will be addressed in the following sections.

IJV development stages and HRM implications

Similar to the M&A processes discussed earlier, the development of IJVs can also be described in development stages. Schuler distinguishes four stages: the formation, in which the partnership between the parent companies is the center of interest, the development and implementation of the joint venture itself, and the advancement of the activities.[67] Figure 3-7 summarizes the characteristic features of the different IJV stages and respective HR implications. It is important to remember that the different stages of development are not independent of each other. Activities in the first stage have an impact on activities in the second stage and so on. Furthermore, complexity can increase depending upon the number of parent companies [68] and countries involved in the joint venture.[69]

The stages model shows that compatibility between the IJV partners is most important when it comes to mutual learning opportunities between the parent companies and the joint venture. This aspect should be focused on from the beginning of a joint venture formation process. As all learning processes include communication processes and are carried out by people, the management of the human resources function at this point is critical. This encompasses all activities of the HR function including recruitment, selection, training and development, performance management and compensation. A strategic approach requires not only a strong compatibility of the various HR activities and practices, but also with the IJV-strategy.[70]

Within the different stages of IJV formation, the HR manager may take on many roles in order to meet the challenges of interaction between the parent company and the IJV:

- In the *partnership role*, HR managers should take all stakeholders' needs into account (including those of the counterparts in the other parent firm(s) and in the IJV) and demonstrate a thorough understanding of the business and the market.

- As a *change facilitator* and *strategy implementer*, HR managers should be able to conceptualize and implement new strategies involving trust-based communication and cooperation with relevant partners. This also requires the creation of a stable learning environment.

- As an *innovator*, the HR manager should be able to identify talent for executing IJV strategies and adapting to changes in the IJV stages.

- As a *collaborator*, the HR manager's strengths should lie in creating win-win situations characterized by sharing rather than competing between the different entities engaged in the joint venture.[71]

Of course, the HR roles are not exclusive. For the success of the IJV it is most important that the HR manager be able to combine aspects of all roles.

The importance of cross-cultural management in international joint ventures

As outlined in the previous section on 'A comparative approach to HRM in M&A processes', the national, institutional and cultural environments of a firm do indeed matter. Here, we will focus on cultural issues which play an important role in IJVs.[72] This information on comparative HRM as well as on cross-cultural HRM is relevant to both M&As and IJVs. In many studies, the implications of different cultural employee backgrounds coming together in an IJV have been in the center of interest. In the most recent studies, there is an especially strong focus on China.[73] Such a case is described in the following IHRM in Action Case 3-2, which

IHRM in Action Case 3-2

Collaboration, decision-making and loyalty in a German–Chinese joint venture: Beijing Lufthansa Center Co. Ltd

The joint venture

When in 1978 the People's Republic of China opened its frontiers for foreign investors, the need for modern hotels, apartments and office space that could meet Western requirements became obvious. Deutsche Lufthansa AG together with the government of the city of Beijing decided to cooperate in the establishment of a multifunctional service center. This was supposed to provide a logistical basis for international business travelers for whom China was an unknown territory at that time. The joint venture contract was signed in 1986, and in May 1992 the Beijing Lufthansa Center Co. Ltd was opened as one of the largest Chinese–German ventures.

Requirements for the selection of the management team

According to the legal requirements of joint ventures in China, the management team of a joint venture is composed with *equal representation* of both parties. For the selection of the German members their *technical abilities* and *industry as well as management know-how* were of major importance to ensure acceptance by their Chinese counterparts. Furthermore, an *understanding of Chinese culture*, combined with the ability to accept and cope with decision-making structures and the lifestyle of the foreign country were

important in creating an environment of cooperation and learning. Learning opportunities were a major motive in the Chinese decision to work in a joint venture.

Another important aspect was *language*. As many of the older Chinese were not able to speak English at that time, there was often a need for a translator. All documents had to be translated either into English or Chinese. For all important meetings there were translators. German managers took into account that this was time consuming and that not all information might have been transferred. Consequently, it would be useful for the cooperation and the atmosphere within the joint venture if the Germans also had Chinese language capabilities.

The German management team members were told that if they were able to influence the selection of their Chinese counterparts they needed to understand that *status and important contacts, as well as informal relationships within the administration and government,* played an important role in ensuring an important contribution to the joint venture's success.

Collaboration

Although all parties should have a common interest in the success of the joint venture *different perspectives* on specific topics can lead to conflict. This can have an impact on the choice of suppliers (foreign versus Chinese instead of quality considerations) or on the use of company cars representing important status symbols. The use of foreign consultants was favored by the Germans for quality reasons, while the Chinese voted for local consultants for cost reasons. The same was true in discussions concerning the need of expatriates. Chinese managers tried to avoid expensive expatriates while the German counterparts were convinced that they needed people with specific qualifications, which, according to them, could only be provided by expatriates. Again, the negotiations about these issues were very time consuming.

With respect to *decision making*, the joint venture contract stated that the general manager is responsible for daily business and that this person be supported by a Chinese deputy. These regulations ensured that the Chinese legal and cultural environment was sufficiently respected in the decision-making processes. However, in practice, this meant that the general manager could not decide anything without the Chinese deputy and decision processes became slow and complicated. This led to a change in the decision-making relationship between the general manager and the deputy, which gave more power to the deputy

and ensured that the general manager could take only a limited number of decisions without the deputy.

Loyalty

In many situations, strong loyalty to the parent company presented a problem because the managers did not put the common project at the center of interest. For example, it was reported that the Chinese managers didn't want to take decisions without consulting their parent firm, which again led to very slow decision processes. Here, the high degrees of power distance and uncertainty avoidance of the Chinese partners may have influenced this behavior. However, this approach endangers loyalty to the joint venture and such delays also discourage local employees and management from both sides. Another issue which led to difficulties involved the way in which expatriate managers viewed their jobs in the joint venture. For them, their positions were often just another step in their careers which could possibly lead to a higher position after the assignment. In this case, loyalty to the parent company was higher than loyalty to the joint venture.

Source: H.J. Probst, Human resources in a German-Chinese joint venture – experiences from the Beijing Lufthansa Center Co. Ltd.[74]

---

addresses the HR-related challenges of two different institutional and cultural environments working together in a common venture. This example illustrates how cultural differences matter in collaboration, decision making and loyalty in the German–Chinese joint venture of Beijing Lufthansa Center Co. Ltd. For further discussion and interpretation of the cultural differences refer to Chapter 9 where the host-country context is discussed more intensively.

The top management team and the role of expatriates in IJVs

As shown in IHRM in Action Case 3-2, the IJV's top management team has a high impact on the performance of the joint venture. The team's main task is to control the daily business operations of the IJV. The above-described case is typical when the two parent firms of an IJV share equal equity division. Usually, both have the right to be equally represented in the management team, and control of the key management positions is a critical issue when negotiating an IJV contract. Each firm tries to protect its own interests and to keep as much control as possible by staffing key positions with its own people.[75] Kabst[76] calls these IJV positions 'functional gatekeepers' – they try to protect their firm's assets in specific functional areas such as R&D, production or marketing.

Due to the fact that the parent companies compete for these few management positions, the top management team is usually composed of individuals from different cultural contexts. As in all multicultural teams, diversity may provide opportunities, but the individuals may also have problems working together. The critical challenge for a multicultural team heading an IJV is not only that it has to deal with different cultural expectations, but that it also has to balance various management styles and strategic objectives of the different parent firms. Li *et al.*[77] point out that identification with both the IJV and the parent firm can lead to significant role conflicts and divided loyalty for IJV managers: top management team 'members serving as control agents for the parent company often face the crisis of loyalty, commitment and organizational identity'.[78] As in the Beijing-Lufthansa case study, an exaggerated identification with the parent firm can affect communication and decision-making processes in the multicultural team and lead to lower commitment, and consequently, to problems in decision-making and unsatisfactory results. The relative status and power positions of the parent companies gain importance at the expense of the management of the IJV.[79]

To avoid intercultural conflicts, companies have started to recruit country experts from outside the company rather than repositioning internal technical experts, as the following example of a Western beverage company shows:

> The company has been investing heavily in China's growing beverage market and has set up six joint ventures with different local partners over the last five years. It has been rapidly building its China organizations by assessing managers from the headquarters to its joint ventures in China. However, due to their lack of knowledge about the local culture and market conditions, many of these managers had problems working in the local environment and left their positions in the joint ventures much earlier than at full term. In response to the high turnover rate, the company changed its recruiting strategy and began hiring expatriates who know the country well (e.g. degree holders in Chinese studies) for joint venture assignments in China. This, however, led to an unexpected problem. The 'country-expert' expatriates often took the side of the local partner whenever there were conflicts between the partners, rather than taking the side of the parent as was expected. The trust and loyalty of these country-expert expatriates was now doubted by their own parent firm.[80]

To address these problems and to increase IJV performance, Li *et al.* suggest taking explicit measures for improving organizational identity and identification at the IJV level.[81] Starting points for this process are discussed in the analysis of the HR implications of the IJV stages in Figure 3-7.

International SMEs

SMEs:[82] strategic importance and barriers to internationalization

The discussion about globalization and international management is very much dominated by the well-known names of MNEs from all over the world, while the role of small and medium-sized companies (SMEs) is infrequently discussed. SMEs can be defined using headcount, annual turnover or annual balance sheet total. Table 3-2 gives the latest definition developed by the European Commission. It is

SME definition			Table 3-2

Enterprise category	Headcount	Annual turnover	Annual balance sheet total
Medium-sized	<250	<€ 50 million	<€ 43 million
Small	<50	<€ 10 million	<€ 10 million

Source: European Commission (ed.), *The New SME Definition*, user guide and model declaration (Brussels: European Commission, 2005), p. 14.

important to note that there is no common worldwide accepted definition of SMEs and criteria as well as limits differ. The European Commission definition is very strict while other definitions include companies with up to 1000 employees as SMEs.[83] 'Depending on the issue, in addition qualitative criteria such as the identity of enterprise ownership and personal responsibility for the enterprise's activities should be taken into account as well.'[84]

It is often forgotten that small and medium-sized companies (SMEs) play an important role in the world economy as shown by the following figures:

● In the European Economic Area (EEA) and Switzerland there are more than 16 million enterprises. Less than 1 per cent are large enterprises, the rest are SMEs. Two-thirds of all jobs in this region are in SMEs, while one-third of all jobs are provided by large enterprises.[85] In many countries the percentage of employees working for enterprises with less than 20 employees amounts to more than 80 per cent.[86]

● SMEs constitute the backbone of the Asia-Pacific region, accounting for 90 per cent of enterprises, between 32 and 48 per cent of employment and between 80 and 60 per cent of gross domestic product in individual Asia-Pacific economies.[87]

● In the USA more than 80 per cent of total employment is with organizations with less than 20 employees.[88]

The strong position of SMEs in their national economies is not reflected to the same extent in the international business environment.[89] When internationalizing their operations, SMEs experience different challenges than large organizations. They have less experience with environmental contexts in different countries, less power to withstand the demand of host governments, less reputation and financial resources as well as fewer resources for managing international operations.[90] The top ten barriers to access to international markets as identified by a recent OECD survey on 978 SMEs worldwide include the following:

1 Shortage of working capital to finance exports.
2 Identifying foreign business opportunities.
3 Limited information to locate/analyze markets.
4 Inability to contact potential overseas customers.
5 Obtaining reliable foreign representation.
6 Lack of managerial time to deal with internationalization.

7 Inadequate quantity of and/or untrained personnel for internationalization.

8 Difficulty in managing competitor's prices.

9 Lack of home government assistance/incentives.

10 Excessive transportation/insurance costs.[91]

In many countries such as Singapore, Korea, South Africa and in the European Union, SME internationalization is promoted by policies of their home countries. As the *World Investment Report*[92] suggests:

> Policymakers need to support entrepreneurship and foster the creation of start-up MNEs, especially in knowledge-based industries. In terms of enterprise development countries make up for the lack of entrepreneurial talents and start-up candidates through the promotion of new industries and the creation of 'seed companies'. Spin-offs from public research institutes or from leading universities may also be encouraged, backed by relevant financial institutions.

IHRM features in SMEs

Much of our knowledge generated in the area of IHRM applies to large organizations.[93] While there is evidence that some recruitment or compensation practices are applicable to small organizations as well, the management of people in small organizations often differs from practices and strategies of established large organizations.[94] Although our understanding of IHRM in SMEs is still limited, there are some key points which we outline in this section of the chapter.

The importance of the founder/owner.

Internationalization process theory, which is derived from the behavioral model of uncertainty avoidance,[95] suggests that specific features of the owner or founder of an SME have an impact on the internationalization process of this particular enterprise.[96] The 'experiential market knowledge' of the managers is assumed to have a direct impact on the choice of foreign markets and thus, the internationalization process of the SME. This theoretical approach predicts that managers start the internationalization process in geographically and culturally close markets and that with increasing experience they move towards more distant markets. Consequently, in a globalizing SME the top managers responsible for internationalization decisions should have an international background to be prepared to take those decisions. Research on global start-ups or *born globals*,[97] which are characterized by an important international orientation and growth from inception have confirmed this:[98] 'the founders of international new ventures are more "alert" to the possibilities of combining resources from different national markets because of the competencies they developed from their earlier activities'.[99] Manolova *et al.* report that person-related factors such as international experiences/skills, international orientation, environmental perceptions and demographic factors such as age, education and tenure had systematic effects on the internationalization of small firms. Summarizing the results of their own study they state:[100]

> We expected that owners/founders who had international work experience, or established personal networks and relationships abroad would possess the skills necessary to conduct international business arrangements. Consistent with this, owners/founders or managers who have more positive perceptions of the international environment will also be more likely to internationalize their own small businesses.

Recruitment, selection and retention.   The above-mentioned barriers to SME internationalization included a scarcity of qualified international managers. Small firms may have more difficulties than large firms in recruiting adequate international managers.[101] It has been argued that many less-qualified employees are employed by SMEs because they do not meet the recruitment requirements of large organizations and were forced to work for SMEs as their second choice. As one interviewee in the study by MacMahon and Murphy[102] stated: 'You get these big multinationals who cream off the top graduates and production operatives which leaves a small business very vulnerable in terms of the quality and availability of labor.' Indeed, recruitment, selection and staffing have been shown to be problematic for SMEs because these firms are perceived to lack legitimacy as employers with a strong international orientation.[103]

Kühlmann[104] has analyzed the image of SMEs as employers on the external labor market in Germany. He found that perceived potential advantages of employment in SMEs as compared to large organizations included a good working atmosphere, less anonymity, a high degree of information and low requirements for mobility. Participants of the study perceived the following factors as disadvantages: career opportunities, employee benefits, progressiveness of the company, training programs, pay and international working opportunities. Figure 3-8 outlines the consequences of SME employer image for internationalization. The results indicate a self-fulfilling prophecy: potential job candidates think that SMEs do not have strong international operations and do not apply. Because the SMEs cannot recruit qualified international managers they are not as successful in international markets as they could be. In order to attract more applicants interested in international operations, Kühlmann suggests HR marketing activities for SMEs, which clearly communicate that the firm has a strong position in international markets and offers international career opportunities. If the small size of the firm makes it difficult to attract sufficient interest, he recommends cooperation with other SMEs in a similar situation.

SME employer image and internationalization

Figure 3-8

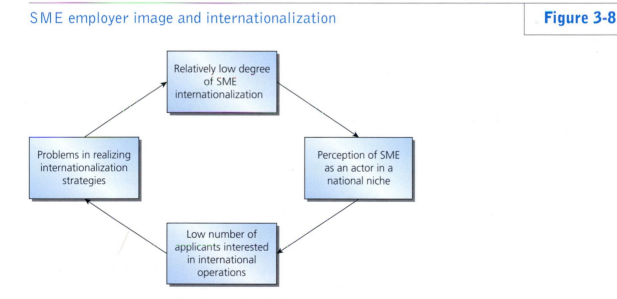

Source: Adapted from T.M. Kühlmann, Internationalization of medium-sized enterprises as a challenge for recruitment and development, p. 362.[104]

Furthermore, research[105] has shown that selection criteria of SMEs often include a general fit with the small organization or technical capabilities rather than requirements that refer to a future position with international responsibility. Small firms look for generalist knowledge rather than for specialists. However, it has to be stressed that the requirements for international managers in SMEs are similar to those identified in large organizations.[106] Consequently, internationalizing SMEs should rethink their selection criteria and define a set of international competencies.[107]

With respect to retaining key employees, the perceived advantages and disadvantages of working for a SME outlined in the image study cited above are useful indicators. The advantages need to be emphasized and SMEs should also consider improving, for example, the training opportunities or career paths of their key employees. Furthermore, the importance of financial benefits should be noted. In an empirical study of 449 German SMEs with up to 1000 employees, Weber and Kabst[108] found that financial participation programs were offered in more than 20 per cent of the companies – presumably to increase the manager's identification with the firm with the aim to create long-term retention of key personnel.

Human resource development: the challenge of learning.

Learning processes are of critical importance in the volatile global environment of modern business. This is especially true in cross-border alliances, which are ranked third as preferred foreign market entry strategies of SMEs, after export activities and subsidiaries.[109] Although organizational learning is a neglected area in SME research[110] early evidence indicates that it may differ between small and large organizations. Training and development activities tend to be rather short-term oriented in SMEs and are not supposed to meet long-term strategic needs.[111] The distinctive cultural features of a small organization indicate an informal learning approach using local networks and socialization[112] rather than formalized training.[113] Often, the focus is on acquiring tacit knowledge related to the specific context of the firm rather than on gaining explicit knowledge. Based on case study research, Anderson and Boocock have developed a model describing learning in the specific context of small organizations which is shown in Figure 3-9.

With respect to the specific case of the international environment, Brussig *et al.*[114] suggest that HRM should encourage staff in boundary spanning positions[115] (i.e. at the external interface of the SME) to pay attention to aspects relevant to internationalization decisions. On the one hand, this involves improving the capacity for perceiving relevant environmental developments – suggested training programs could include strategy and communication seminars. On the other hand, employees must be motivated to report and share their observations regularly and systematically which requires good communication within the company. Anderson and Boocock[116] conclude that:

> Those involved in HRD [human resource development] in smaller organizations . . . should resist the temptation to impose 'large firm thinking' into a small organizational context. In small firms there is a complex interaction between scarce resources, reliance on the motivations and abilities of a few key individuals and a necessary focus on short-term priorities. The study suggests that 'smallness' does not preclude generative learning, but the achievement of this is not universally relevant.

However, there is still a lack of knowledge about the 'optimal' balance between formal and informal training in SMEs[117] and the relationship between training and firm performance is still unresolved.[118] Another problem is that training is often perceived as an 'unaffordable luxury' in SMEs, particularly with regard to the training of expatriates.[119]

Learning in small organizations

Figure 3-9

Individual learning processes
- Formal learning may be undertaken to meet operational, technical learning needs
- Informal learning, based on experience, develops specialized and market knowledge
- Tacit knowledge is prevalent
- Learning is not explicitly planned or evaluated

Internal organizational context
- Prior experience of key decision makers is an important influence on learning culture
- Organizational culture 'filters' the knowledge that is acquired by individuals
- Structures of communication determine how/if knowledge will be disseminated within the organization

Learning in small organizations

External organizational environment
- Formal and informal business networks provide the main source of knowledge, ideas, advice and support for 'boundary spanners'
- Local and national agencies are perceived as less relevant and are used less frequently

Source: Adapted from V. Anderson and G. Boocock, 'Small Firms and Internationalization: Learning to Manage and Managing to Learn', *Human Resource Management Journal*, Vol. 12 (2002), p. 18.

Expatriate management.   As the previous sections have shown, an informal approach to human resource management still dominates in SMEs[120] – especially for expatriate employees.[121] Research on this topic is relatively scarce, but an empirical study by Weber and Kabst of 449 German SMEs with up to 1000 employees shows that expatriate assignments predominantly occur in the cases of joint ventures and wholly owned foreign subsidiaries. Sometimes also licensing agreements involve expatriates. After the challenge of recruiting people in foreign markets the internal recruitment of employees for international jobs is perceived as the most important problem for the investigated firms. This finding is in line with the above discussion concerning problems with SME recruiting. However, a positive sign of a systematic approach to expatriate management in SMEs is that more than 16 per cent of firms indicated that they send employees abroad for management development reasons (for a discussion of reasons for international assignments see Chapter 4). In terms of training the most important activities were language courses while cross-cultural training only played a minor role.[122] When SMEs needed cross-cultural training for potential expatriates, these employees were sent to external training institutions. Given the small number of expatriates, in-house training is not a viable option for most SMEs. The cultural integration of foreign acquisitions remains a challenge for SMEs.[123]

Limited resources of the HR department and outsourcing.   The list of barriers to internationalization of SMEs at the beginning of this section indicated that resources such as financial capital, qualified human capital to initiate and control internationalization processes and time are scarce. This in part explains why sophisticated management strategies are lacking and the appointment of HR specialists does not occur on the grounds that the costs cannot be justified with respect to the size of SMEs.[124] The focus of the small HR group in an SME is usually on administrative tasks and most important HR decisions are taken by the founder/owner of the enterprise.[125] The fact that most of the important HR activities are left to line managers is problematic for two reasons:[126]

> First, the complexity of many HR activities is likely to result in them becoming a significant drain on managerial time and resources. As such, HR tasks may interfere with managerial responsibilities that are directly related to revenue production. . . . Second, many HR tasks involve substantial complexity and, thus, the quality of HR decisions may well be affected that the general managers often lack significant training and expertise in HR.

On the national level, professional employer organizations have been discussed as possible providers of HR-related services – based on a contractual agreement with the SME, the professional employer organization can become the outsourced HR department for the respective firm. This option can lead to improved managerial satisfaction in SMEs and higher quality HR decisions.[127] Thus, outsourcing of HR practices represents a potentially valuable strategy to cope with the size-related deficiencies of HRM in SMEs. However, risks of outsourcing strategically important activities should always be closely monitored.

As an alternative we also found co-operations with large MNEs in the German automobile industry. Suppliers followed the car producers in foreign locations and benefited from the HR experience of the MNE. The latter supports small suppliers with its know-how about expatriate management, the environment of the relevant markets and its relationships with relevant governmental institutions for gaining visa and working permits. Furthermore, information about human resource management issues in the local country is shared. Thus, a symbiosis can emerge between the interests of the MNE in facilitating the effective functioning of its suppliers abroad and the interests of SMEs which need relevant specialized information in order to prevent mistakes and reduce costs.

Summary

In this chapter we have extended the discussion about the organizational context of MNEs conducted in Chapter 2 to other organizational forms, which pose specific problems to IHRM, i.e. cross-border alliances and globalizing SMEs. Cross-border M&As have seen a tremendous growth in the course of globalization. We have described their formation process as well as four important development phases: pre-M&A phase, due diligence phase, integration planning phase and implementation phase. In each of the phases specific strategic HR requirements need to be taken into account in order to effectively manage the M&A process. The role of expatriates is mainly discussed with respect to learning effects. A comparative approach to HR in M&As indicates the complexity that emerges from the institutional and cultural environments in which the firms are embedded.

The number of IJVs has increased significantly over the last few decades. In the chapter we have outlined the IJV formation process, which poses considerable challenges for the HR function. Four stages are identified for the development of IJVs (formation, development, implementation, advancement and beyond) which require specific HR measures and roles. We also addressed the importance of cross-cultural management in IJVs, which is an important factor for effective cooperation across all levels of the IJV, including the top management team. Both types of equity-based cross-border alliances are very similar involving both strategic, comparative and cross-cultural HRM issues as well as specified expatriate roles.

The third organization form we addressed was the case of the internationalized SME. In this case, different challenges have been identified. First we outlined the strategic importance of SMEs in international business and examined barriers to SME internationalization. We also addressed important IHRM features distinguishing SMEs from MNEs: the founder/owner of the SME; recruitment, selection and retention; human resource development with special emphasis on learning; expatriate management; and the limited resources of the HR department in SMEs and outsourcing opportunities.

Discussion Questions

1 Describe the formation process of cross-border mergers, acquisitions and international joint ventures. What are the major differences?

2 Describe the development phases of an M&A and the respective HR implications.

3 Outline the development phases of an IJV and the respective HR implications.

4 In which way do cultural and institutional differences impact the HR integration in M&As and in IJVs?

5 What are the barriers to internationalization for SMEs?

6 What are some of the typical challenges for HRM in internationalized SMEs?

Further Reading

Gong, Y., Shenkar, O., Luo, Y. and Nyaw, M.-K. (2005). 'Human Resources and International Joint Venture Performance: A System Perspective', *Journal of International Business Studies,* 36: 505–18.

Goulet, P.K. and Schweiger, D.M. (2006). 'Managing Culture and Human Resources in Mergers and Acquisitions', in G. Stahl and I. Björkman (eds), *Handbook of Research in International Human Resource Management,* Cheltenham *et al.*: Edward Elgar, pp. 385–404.

Schuler, R.S., Jackson, S.E. and Luo, Y. (2004). *Managing Human Resources in Cross-border Alliances,* London and New York: Routledge.

Stahl, G.K. and Mendenhall, M.E. (2005). *Mergers and Acquisitions: Managing Cultures and Human Resources,* Stanford, CA: Stanford Business Books.

Notes and References

1 R.S. Schuler and I. Tarique, 'Alliance Forms and Human Resource Issues: Implications, and Significance', in O. Shenkar and J.J. Reuer (eds), *Handbook of Strategic Alliances* (Thousand Oaks, CA: Sage Publications, Inc., 2006), pp. 219–39.

2 Ibid.

3 W.F. Cascio and M.G. Serapio, Jr, 'Human Resources Systems in an International Alliance: The Undoing of a Done Deal?', *Organizational Dynamics,* Vol. 19 (1991), pp. 63–74.

4 R.S. Schuler, S.E. Jackson and Y. Luo, *Managing Human Resources in Cross-border Alliances* (London and New York: Routledge, 2004), p. 2.

5 UNCTAD (ed.), *World Investment Report 2005* (New York and Geneva: United Nations, 2005), p. 126.

6 Schuler and Tarique, 'Alliance Forms and Human Resource Issues'.

7   UNCTAD (ed.), *World Investment Report 2005* (New York and Geneva: United Nations, 2005), p. 297.

8   J. Child and D. Faulkner, *Strategies of Cooperation* (Oxford and London: Oxford University Press, 1998).

9   Schuler and Tarique, 'Alliance Forms and Human Resource Issues', p. 220.

10   Schuler and Tarique, 'Alliance Forms and Human Resource Issues'.

11   For recent notable exceptions see for example the work by B.M. Lajara, 'The Role of Human Resource Management in the Cooperative Strategy Process', *Human Resource Planning,* Vol. 25 (2002), pp. 34–44; B.M. Lajara, F.G. Lillo and V.S. Sempere, 'Human Resources Management: A Success and Failure Factor in Strategic Alliances', *Employee Relations,* Vol. 25 (2003), pp. 61–80; P.S. Budhwar, H.K. Luthar and J. Bhatnagar, 'The Dynamics of HRM Systems in Indian BPO Firms', *Journal of Labor Research,* Vol. 27 (2006), pp. 339–60.

12   For an overview see D. Welch and L. Welch, 'Linking Operation Mode Diversity and IHRM', *International Journal of Human Resource Management,* Vol. 5 (1994), pp. 911–26.

13   T. Kühlmann and P.J. Dowling, 'DaimlerChrysler: A Case Study of a Cross-border Merger', in G.K. Stahl and M.E. Mendenhall, *Mergers and Acquisitions: Managing Cultures and Human Resources* (Stanford, CA: Stanford Business Books, 2005), pp. 351–64.

14   For other definitions see also R.S. Schuler, S.E. Jackson and Y. Luo, *Managing Human Resource in Cross-border Alliances,* p. 5.

15   UNCTAD (ed.), *World Investment Report, 2006* (New York and Geneva: United Nations, 2006), p. 123/225.

16   *Ibid.,* p. 15.

17   *Ibid.,* p. 13.

18   Greenfield FDI refers to investment projects that entail the establishment of new production facilities such as offices, buildings, plants and factories, as well as the movement of intangible capital (mainly services). See *ibid.,* p. 15.

19   J. Child, D. Faulkner and R. Pitkethly, *The Management of International Acquisitions* (Oxford: Oxford University Press, 2001), p. 1.

20   Schuler, Jackson and Luo, *Managing Human Resources in Cross-border Alliances;* Child, Faulkner and Pitkethly distinguish between market drivers, cost drivers, competitive drivers and government drivers for M&As. See Child, Faulkner and Pitkethly, *The Management of International Acquisitions*.

21   The same is true for international joint ventures. See K.W. Glaister, R. Husan and P.J. Buckley, 'Learning to Manage International Joint Ventures', *International Business Review,* Vol. 12 (2003), pp. 83–108.

22   Child, Faulkner and Pitkethly, *The Management of International Acquisitions*.

23   R. Larsson and S. Finkelstein, 'Integrating Strategic, Organizational, and Human Resource Perspectives on Mergers and Acquisitions: A Case Survey of Synergy Realization', *Organization Science,* Vol. 10 (1999), pp. 1–26. For the special case of acquisitions see a similar analysis by J. Birkinshaw, H. Bresman and L. Hakanson, 'Managing the Post-acquisition Integration Process: How the Human Integration and Task Integration Processes Interact to Foster Value Creation', *Journal of Management Studies,* Vol. 37 (2000), pp. 395–425.

24   Larsson and Finkelstein, 'Integrating Strategic, Organizational, and Human Resource Perspectives on Mergers and Acquisitions', state that the emphasis primarily was on the post-combination integration process investigating cultural and other conflicts. In the related HRM research, psychological aspects, communication and careers were important topics.

25   This is confirmed by the work of D.K. Datta, 'Organizational Fit and Acquisition Performance: Effects of Post-acquisition Integration', *Strategic Management Journal,* Vol. 12 (1991), pp. 281–97. In contrast, he didn't find an impact of differences in the evaluation and rewards systems on post-merger integration performance although 'reward systems are often employed to reinforce values, beliefs, and practices in an organization' (p. 292).

26   Larsson and Finkelstein, 'Integrating Strategic, Organizational, and Human Resource Perspectives on Mergers and Acquisitions'.

27   Birkinshaw, Bresman and Hakanson, 'Managing the Post-acquisition Integration Process'.

28   Task integration was measured by the initial plans for integration, integration mechanisms used, problems encountered during integration and task specialization during integration. See *ibid*.

29   *Ibid.,* p. 395.

30   J.A. Krug and D. Nigh, 'Executive Perceptions in Foreign and Domestic Acquisitions: An Analysis of Foreign Ownership and its Effect on Executive Fate', *Journal of World Business,* Vol. 36, No. 1 (2001), pp. 85–105.

31   R.V. Aguilera and J.C. Dencker, 'The Role of Human Resource Management in Cross-border Mergers and Acquisitions', *International Journal of Human Resource Management,* Vol. 15 (2004), pp. 1355–70.

32   See for example the IHRM in Action Case 4-1 and the study by Krug and Nigh, 'Executive Perceptions in Foreign and Domestic Acquisitions'.

33   Aguilera and Dencker, 'The Role of Human Resource Management in Cross-border Mergers and Acquisitions'.

34   A. Delios and P.W. Beamish, 'Survival and Profitability: The Roles of Experience and Intangible Assets in Foreign Subsidiary Performance', *Academy of Management Journal*, Vol. 44, No. 5 (2001), pp. 1028–38.

35   Schuler *et al*. differentiate between four types of integration: (1) The portfolio type, which has been mentioned in the text; (2) blending, i.e. the best elements from each culture are chosen; (3) a new company creation with a new culture that fits the new organization; (4) assimilation, where legitimacy is only assigned to one culture. See Schuler, Jackson and Luo, *Managing Human Resources in Cross-border Alliances*, p. 90.

36   Some experts argue that the due diligence phase is part of the first phase, which they call pre-combination. This is followed by a combination and integration stage and a solidification and assessment stage. See Schuler, Jackson and Luo, *Managing Human Resources in Cross-border Alliances*.

37   With respect to auditing human resource management see G.W. Florkowski and R.S. Schuler, 'Auditing Human Resource Management in the Global Environment', *International Journal of Human Resource Management*, Vol. 5, No. 4 (1994), pp. 827–51.

38   Successful M&As – The impact of human resource management, published in German language as: C. Geighardt, S. Armutat, H. Döring, M. Festing, C. Frühe, E. Nell and W. Werner (eds), *Erfolgreiche M&As – Was das Personalmanagement dazu beiträgt*, Praxispapiere 2-2007 (Düsseldorf: DGFP, 2007).

39   J.A. Schmidt, 'The Correct Spelling of M&A Begins with HR', *HR Magazine*, Vol. 46, No. 6 (2001), pp. 102–8.

40   See for example, www.welt.de/data/2007/02/12/1209254.html, 12 February 2007.

41   Aguilera and Dencker, 'The Role of Human Resource Management in Cross-border Mergers and Acquisitions'.

42   *Ibid.*, p. 1357.

43   E.M. Antila, 'The Role of HR Managers in International Mergers and Acquisitions: A Multiple Case Study', *International Journal of Human Resource Management*, Vol. 17 (2006), pp. 999–1020.

44   D. Ulrich, *Human Resource Champions: The Next Agenda for Adding Value and Delivering Results* (Boston, MA: Harvard Business School Press, 1997).

45   A. Delios and P.W. Beamish, 'Survival and Profitability: The Roles of Experience and Intangible Assets in Foreign Subsidiary Performance', *Academy of Management Journal*, Vol. 44 (2001), pp. 1028–38.

46   L. Hébert, P. Very and P.W. Beamish, 'Expatriation as a Bridge over Troubled Water: A Knowledge-based Perspective Applied to Cross-border Acquisitions', *Organization Studies*, Vol. 26 (2005), p. 1468.

47   Successful M&As – The impact of human resource management, published in German language as: Geighardt, Armutat, Döring, Festing, Frühe, Nell, and Werner, *Erfolgreiche M&As – Was das Personalmanagement dazu beiträgt*.

48   Hébert, Very and Beamish, 'Expatriation as a Bridge over Troubled Water', p. 1469.

49   *Ibid.*, pp. 1455–76.

50   R. Villinger, 'Post-acquisition Managerial Learning in Central East Europe', *Organization Studies*, Vol. 17 (1996), pp. 181–206.

51   *Ibid.*, p. 203.

52   Child, Faulkner and Pitkethly, *The Management of International Acquisitions*.

53   Katz and Darbishire (2001), Streeck (2001) and Pudelko (2006) discuss converging divergences in employment systems. With respect to employment systems they see an increasing divergence. However, in terms of workplace patterns at least Katz and Darbishire (2001) have identified a growing convergence. This is confirmed by research from the Cranet network mainly focusing on Europe (Brewster, 2006). Brewster, Mayrhofer and Morley (2004) give a more differentiated perspective. They distinguish between directional convergence and final convergence. The first is concerned with the question of whether the same trends can be observed in different countries, the latter addresses the results. Their conclusion, based on the Cranet data, is as follows: 'From a directional point of view, there seems to be a positive indication of convergence. However, when one looks at the question from a final convergence point of view, the answer is no longer a clear positive. None of the HR practices converged at the end of the decade. Rather, the maximum point of convergence is reached in the middle of the decade with signs of divergence after that' (Brewster, Mayrhofer and Morley 2004:434). Thus the results concerning the convergence or divergence of HRM systems including performance management systems are mixed. There is no

clear tendency although in an empirical study concerning the convergence-divergence debate in HRM Pudelko (2005) concludes that the majority of the HR managers investigated (originated from Germany, the USA and Japan) expect a convergence of HRM systems. See H. Katz and O. Darbishire, Review Symposium, Converging divergences: worldwide changes in employment system, *Industrial and Labor Relations Review,* Vol. 54, No. 3 (2001), pp. 681–716; W. Streeck, 'High Equality, Low Activity: The Contribution of the Social Welfare System to the Stability of the German Collective Bargaining Regime', Review Symposium, Converging Divergences, *Industrial and Labor Relations Review,* Vol. 54, No. 3 (2001), pp. 698–706; M. Pudelko, 'A Comparison of HRM Systems in the USA, Japan and Germany in their Socio-economic Context', *Human Resource Management Journal,* Vol. 16, No. 2 (2006), pp. 123–53; C. Brewster, *International Human Resource Management: If There is No 'Best Way', How Do We Manage?,* Inaugural Lecture (Greenlands, Henley-on-Thames: Henley Management College UK, 2006); C. Brewster, W. Mayrhofer and M. Morley (eds), *Human Resources: Evidence of Convergence?* (London: Elsevier, 2004).

54   Child, Faulkner and Pitkethly, *The Management of International Acquisitions,* p. 180.

55   Y. Gong, O. Shenkar, Y. Luo and M.-K. Nyaw, 'Human Resources and International Joint Venture Performance: A System Perspective', *Journal of International Business Studies,* Vol. 36 (2005), pp. 505–18.

56   K.-B. Chan, V. Luk and G.X. Wang, 'Conflict and Innovation in International Joint Ventures: Toward a New Sinified Corporate Culture or "Alternative Globalization" in China', *Asia Pacific Business Review,* Vol. 11, No. 4 (2005), pp. 461–82.

57   O. Shenkar and Y. Zeira, 'Human Resources Management in International Joint Ventures: Directions for Research', *Academy of Management Review,* Vol. 12 (1987), p. 547.

58   The following sources represent milestones in HRM-related IJV research: P. Lorange, 'Human Resource Management in Multinational Cooperative Ventures', *Human Resource Management,* Vol. 25 (1986), pp. 133–48; Shenkar and Zeira, 'Human Resources Management in International Joint Ventures' D.J. Cyr, *The Human Resource Challenge of International Joint Ventures* (Westport, CT and London: Quorum Books, 1995); R.S. Schuler, 'Human Resource Issues and Activities in International Joint Ventures', *International Journal of Human Resource Management,* Vol. 12, No. 3 (2001), pp. 1–52; Schuler, Jackson and Luo, *Managing Human Resource in Cross-border Alliances*; Gong, Shenkar, Luo and Nyaw, 'Human Resources and International Joint Venture Performance'.

59   P. Evans, V. Pucik and J.-L. Barsoux, *The Global Challenge: Frameworks for International Human Resource Management* (Boston, MA: McGraw-Hill, 2002).

60   For these challenges see Gong, Shenkar, Luo and Nyaw, 'Human Resources and International Joint Venture Performance'. Similar ideas can be found in K.W. Glaister, R. Husan and P.J. Buckley, 'Learning to Manage International Joint Ventures', *International Business Review,* Vol. 12 (2003), pp. 83–108.

61   Schuler, 'Human Resource Issues and Activities in International Joint Ventures', p. 4.

62   See for example D.J. Cyr, *The Human Resource Challenge of International Joint Ventures,* (Westport, CT and London: Quorum Books, 1995); P. Iles and M. Yolles, 'International Joint Ventures, HRM and Viable Knowledge Migration', *International Journal of Human Resource Management,* Vol. 13 (2002), pp. 624–41; H. Barkema, O. Shenkar, F. Vermeulen and J. Bell, 'Working Abroad, Working with Others: How Firms Learn to Operate International Joint Ventures', *Academy of Management Journal,* Vol. 40 (1997), pp. 426–43.

63   Glaister, Husan and Buckley, 'Learning to Manage International Joint Ventures'.

64   However, changes in the ownership structure do not necessarily reflect a failure but can also meet the necessities of a volatile global environment.

65   See, for example, S.H. Park and M.V. Russo, 'When Competition Eclipses Cooperation: An Event History Analysis of Joint Venture Failure', *Management Science,* Vol. 42, No. 6 (1996), pp. 875–91; A.B. Sim and M.Y. Ali, 'Determinants of Stability in International Joint Ventures: Evidence from a Developing Country Context', *Asia Pacific Journal of Management,* Vol. 17 (2000), pp. 373–97.

66   For an encompassing list of reasons for failures of international joint ventures see Schuler *et al., Managing Human Resources in Cross-border Alliances*.

67   Schuler, 'Human Resource Issues and Activities in International Joint Ventures', pp. 1–5.

68   See, for example P. Beamish and A. Kachra, 'Number of Partners and JV Performance', *Journal of World Business,* Vol. 39 (2004), pp. 107–20; D. Cyr, *The Human Resource Challenge of International Joint Ventures;* Schuler and Tarique, 'Alliance Forms and Human Resource Issues: Implications and Significance', in O. Shenkar and J. Reuer (eds), *Handbook of Strategic Alliances* (Thousand Oaks, CA: Sage Publications, Inc., 2006), pp. 219–39. D.R. Briscoe and

R.S. Schuler, *International Human Resource Management: Policies and Practices for the Global Enterprise,* 2nd edn (New York: Routledge, 2004).

69 Schuler and Tarique, 'Alliance Forms and Human Resource Issues: Implications and Significance'.

70 For fit-concepts in IHRM see for example J. Milliman, M.A. Glinow and N. Nathan, 'Organizational Life Cycles and Strategic International Human Resource Management in Multinational Companies: Implications for Congruence Theory', *Academy of Management Review,* Vol. 16, No. 2 (1999), pp. 318–39.

71 Schuler, 'Human Resource Issues and Activities in International Joint Ventures', p. 44.

72 For conceptual work see, for example, L. McFarlane Shore, B.W. Eagle and M.J. Jedel, 'China–United States Joint Ventures: A Typological Model of a Goal Congruence and Cultural Understanding and their Importance for Effective Human Resource Management', *International Journal of Human Resource Management,* Vol. 4 (1993), pp. 67–83, or P-X. Meschi and A. Roger, 'Cultural Context and Social Effectiveness in International Joint Ventures', *Management International Review,* Vol. 34 (1994), pp. 197–215.

73 S.H. Nam, 'Culture, Control and Commitment in International Joint Ventures', *International Journal of Human Resource Management,* Vol. 6 (1995), pp. 553–67, looks at US- and Japanese-affiliated banks in Korea. Y. Lu and I. Björkman, 'HRM Practices in China–Western Joint Ventures: MNC Standardization versus Localization', *International Journal of Human Resource Management,* Vol. 8 (1997), pp. 614–28; Lu and Björkman, 'The Management of Human Resources in Chinese–Western Joint Ventures', *Journal of World Business,* Vol. 34 (1999), pp. 306–24; Björkman and Lu, 'Institutionalization and Bargaining Power Explanations of HRM Practices in International Joint Ventures: The Case of Chinese–Western Joint Ventures', *Organization Studies,* Vol. 22 (2001), pp. 491–512; K.S. Chen and M. Wilson, 'Standardization and Localization of Human Resource Management in Sino-Foreign Joint Ventures', *Asia Pacific Journal of Management,* Vol. 20 (2003), pp. 397–408; K. Leung and J.Y.Y. Kwong, 'Human Resource Management Practices in International Joint Ventures in Mainland China: A Justice Analysis', *Human Resource Management Review,* Vol. 13 (2003), pp. 85–105; E.W.K. Tsang, 'Human Resource Management Problems in Sino-Foreign Joint Ventures', *International Journal of Manpower,* Vol. 15 (1994), pp. 4–21; L.M. Shore, B.W. Eagle and M.J. Jedel, 'China–United States Joint Ventures: A Typological Model of a Goal Congruence and Cultural Understanding and their Importance for Effective Human Resource Management', *International Journal of Human Resource Management,* Vol. 4 (1993), pp. 67–83, analyze China–Western joint ventures.

74 Based on H.J. Probst, Human resources in a German–Chinese joint venture – experiences from the Beijing Lufthansa Center Co. Ltd, published in German language as 'Human Resources in cinem deutsch chinesischen Joint Venture', Praxiserfahrungen am Beispiel der Beijing Lufthansa Center Co. Ltd, (Duisburg Working papers on East Asian Economic Studies No. 22, 1995).

75 Gong, Shenkar, Luo and Nyaw, 'Human Resources and International Joint Venture Performance'; J. Li, K. Xin, and M. Pillutla, 'Multi-cultural Leadership Teams and Organizational Identification in International Joint Ventures', *International Journal of Human Resource Management,* Vol. 13 (2002), pp. 320–37.

76 R. Kabst, 'Human Resource Management for International Joint Ventures: Expatriation and Selective Control', *International Journal of Human Resource Management,* Vol. 15, No. 1 (2004), pp. 1–16.

77 Li, Xin and Pillutla, 'Multi-cultural Leadership Teams and Organizational Identification in International Joint Ventures'. See also J.M. Frayne and M. Geringer, 'A Social Cognitive Approach to Examine Joint Venture General Manager Performance', *Group and Organizational Management,* Vol. 19 (1995), pp. 240–62. For the role of HRM policies as providers of control mechanisms see also Child, Faulkner and Pitkethly, *The Management of International Acquisitions.*

78 Li, Xin and Pillutla, 'Multi-cultural Leadership Teams and Organizational Identification in International Joint Ventures', p. 321.

79 *Ibid.,* pp. 320–37.

80 *Ibid.,* p. 322.

81 *Ibid.,* pp. 320–37.

82 This section is partly based on M. Festing, 'Globalization of SMEs and Implications for International Human Resource Management', *International Journal of Globalization and Small Business,* Vol. 2, No 1 (2007), pp. 5–18.

83 Internationalization of medium-sized enterprises, published in German language as: R. Kabst, *Internationalisierung mittelständischer Unternehmen* (München and Mering: Hampp, 2004).

84 http://www.ifm-bonn.org.

85 'UN-ECE Operational Activities: SME – Their Role in Foreign Trade', http://www.unece.org/indust/sme/foreignt.html, 17 February 2007.

86 http://stats.oecd.org/WBOS/default.aspx?DatasetCode=CSP6, 20 February 2007.

87 'UN-ECE Operational Activities: SME – Their Role in Foreign Trade', http://www.unece.org/indust/sme/foreignt.html, 17 February 2007.

88 http://stats.oecd.org/WBOS/default.aspx?DatasetCode=CSP6, 20 February 2007.

89 OECD (ed.), *Keynote Paper on Removing Barriers to SME Access to International Markets* (Geneva: OECD, 2006), http://www.oecd.org/dataoecd/4/16/37818320.pdf, 17 February 2007. For empirical evidence on the UK see H. Matlay and D. Fletcher, 'Globalization and Strategic Change: Some Lessons from the UK Small Business Sector', *Strategic Change,* Vol. 9 (2000), pp. 437–49.

90 For a discussion of SME barriers to internationalization in various contexts see S. Vachani, 'Problems of Foreign Subsidiaries of SMEs Compared with Large Companies', *International Business Review,* Vol. 14 (2005), pp. 415–39; M. Fujita, 'Small and Medium-sized Transnational Corporations: Salient Features', *Small Business Economics,* Vol. 7 (1995), pp. 251–71; D.A. Kirby and S. Kaiser, 'Joint Ventures as an Internationalization Strategy for SMEs', *Small Business Economics,* Vol. 21 (2003), pp. 229–42; Z.J. Acs, R. Morck, J.M. Shaver and B. Yeung, 'The Internationalization of Small and Medium-sized Enterprises: A Policy Perspective', *Small Business Economics,* Vol. 9 (1997), pp. 7–20; P.J. Buckley, 'International Technology Transfer by Small and Medium-sized Enterprises', *Small Business Economics,* Vol. 9 (1997), pp. 67–78; 'UN-ECE Operational Activities: SMEs – Their Role in Foreign Trade', http://www.unece.org/indust/sme/foreignt.html, 17 February 2007.

91 OECD (ed.), *Keynote Paper on Removing Barriers to SME Access to International Markets* (Geneva: OECD, 2006), http://www.oecd.org/dataoecd/4/16/37818320.pdf, 17 February 2007.

92 UNCTAD (ed.), *World Investment Report, 2006* (New York and Geneva: United Nations, 2006), p. 80.

93 V. Anderson and G. Boocock, 'Small Firms and Internationalization: Learning to Manage and Managing to Learn', *Human Resource Management Journal,* Vol. 12 (2002), pp. 5–24; A. Wilkinson, 'Employment Relations in SMEs', *Employee Relations,* Vol. 21 (1999), pp. 206–17.

94 For an excellent overview see M.S. Cardon and C.E. Stevens, 'Managing Human Resources in Small Organizations: What Do We Know?', *Human Resource Management Review,* Vol. 14 (2004), pp. 295–323; A.E. Barber, M.J. Wesson, Q.M. Roberson and M.S. Taylor, 'A Tale of Two Job Markets: Organizational Size and Its Effect on Hiring Practices and Job Search Behavior', *Personnel Psychology,* Vol. 52 (1999), pp. 841–67; Anderson and Boocock, 'Small Firms and Internationalization'.

95 J. Johanson and J.-E. Vahlne, 'The Internationalization Process of the Firm: A Model of Knowledge Development and Increasing Foreign Market Commitment', *Journal of International Business Studies,* Vol. 8, No. 1 (1977), pp. 23–32; J. Johanson and J.-E. Vahlne, 'The Mechanism of Internationalization', *International Marketing Review,* Vol. 7, No. 4 (1990), pp. 11–24; L. Melin, 'Internationalization as a Strategy Process', *Strategic Management Journal,* Vol. 13 (1992), pp. 99–118.

96 This finding is comparable to board internationalization of large companies. Knowledge and experiences gained in foreign markets are supposed to positively influence the extent and quality of firm internationalization. See, for example N. Athanassiou and D. Nigh, 'The Impact of the Top Management Team's International Business Experience on the Firm's Internationalization: Social Networks at Work', *Management International Review,* Vol. 42 (2002), pp. 157–81. For measurement issues of board internationalization see S. Schmid and A. Daniel, *Measuring Board Internationalization: Towards a More Holistic Approach,* ESCP-EAP Working Paper No. 21 (Berlin: ESCP-EAP European School of Management, 2006). For empirical evidence from the UK small business sector see H. Matlay and D. Fletcher, 'Globalization and Strategic Change: Some Lessons from the UK Small Business Sector', *Strategic Change,* Vol. 9 (2000), pp. 437–49.

97 M. Rennie, 'Global Competitiveness: Born Global', *McKinsey Quarterly,* Vol. 4 (1993), pp. 45–52; G.A. Knight, S.T. Cavusgil, 'The Born Global: A Challenge to Traditional Internationalization Theory', *Advances in International Marketing,* Vol. 8 (1996), pp. 11–26.

98 T.K. Madsen and P. Servais, 'The Internationalization of Born Globals: An Evolutionary Process', *International Business Review,* Vol. 6, No. 6 (1997), pp. 561–83.

99 P.P. McDougall, S. Shane and B.M. Oviatt, 'Explaining the Formation of International New Ventures: The Limits of Theories from International Business Research', *Journal of Business Venturing,* Vol. 9 (1994), p. 475.

100 T.S. Manolova, C.G. Brush, L.F. Edelman and P.G. Greene, 'Internationalization of Small Firms', *International Small Business Journal*, Vol. 20 (2002), p. 22.

101 I.O. Williamson, 'Employer Legitimacy and Recruitment Success in Small Businesses', *Entrepreneurship Theory and Practice*, Vol. 25, Issue 1 (2000), pp. 27–42.

102 J. MacMahon and E. Murphy, 'Managerial Effectiveness in Small Enterprises: Implications for HRD', *Journal of European Industrial Training*, Vol. 23 (1999), p. 32.

103 M.S. Cardon and C.E. Stevens, 'Managing Human Resources in Small Organizations: What Do We Know?', *Human Resource Management Review*, Vol. 14 (2004), pp. 295–323.

104 Internationalization of medium-sized enterprises as a challenge for recruitment and development, published in German language as T.M. Kühlmann, 'Internationalisierung des Mittelstandes als Herausforderung für die Personalauswahl und – entwicklung, in Gerhard und Lore Kienbaum Stiftung', in J. Gutmann and R. Kabst (eds), *Internationalisierung im Mittelstand. Chancen – Risken – Erfolgsfaktoren* (Wiesbaden: Gabler, 2000), pp. 357–71.

105 This has been confirmed in literature analysis by Cardon and Stevens, Managing human resources in small organizations: What do we know?. *Human Resource Management Review*, Vol. 14 (2004), pp. 295–323. However, this study does not focus explicitly on *international* SMEs.

106 Globalization of SMEs – experiences and recommendations for human resource management, published in German language as DGFP (ed.), *Globalisierung in kleinen und mittleren Unternehmen. Erfahrungen und Ansatzpunkte für das Personalmanagement*, Praxispapiere (Düsseldorf: DGFP, forthcoming).

107 *Ibid.*

108 Internationalization of medium-sized enterprises – organization form and human resource management, published in German language as W. Weber and R. Kabst, 'Internationalisierung mittelständischer Unternehmen: Organisationsform und Personalmanagement, in Gerhard und Lore Kienbaum Stiftung', in J. Gutmann and R. Kabst (eds), *Internationalisierung im Mittelstand. Chancen – Risken – Erfolgsfaktoren* (Wiesbaden: Gabler, 2000), pp. 3–92.

109 *Ibid.*

110 Anderson and Boocock, 'Small Firms and Internationalization'.

111 R. Hill and J. Stewart, 'Human Resource Development in Small Organizations', *Journal of European Industrial Training*, Vol. 24 (2000), pp. 105–17.

112 M.S. Cardon and C.E. Stevens, 'Managing Human Resources in Small Organizations: What Do We Know?', *Human Resource Management Review*, Vol. 14 (2004), pp. 295–323.

113 Globalization of SMEs – experiences and recommendations for human resource management, published in German language as DGFP (ed.), *Globalisierung in kleinen und mittleren Unternehmen. Erfahrungen und Ansatzpunkte für das Personalmanagement*.

114 M. Brussig, L. Gerlach and U. Wilkens, 'The Development of Globalization Strategies in SMEs and the Role of Human Resource Management', Paper presented at the Global Human Resource Management Conference, Barcelona 2001.

115 J.D. Thompson, *Organizations in Action* (New York: McGraw-Hill, 1967); A.H. Aldrich, *Organizations & Environments* (Englewood Cliffs, NJ: Prentice Hall, 1979).

116 Anderson and Boocock, 'Small Firms and Internationalization', p. 20.

117 Cardon and Stevens, 'Managing Human Resources in Small Organizations'.

118 D.J. Storey, 'Exploring the Link Among Small Firms, Between Management Training and Firm Performance: A Comparison Between the UK and Other OECD Countries', *International Journal of Human Resource Management*, Vol. 15 (2004), pp. 112–133.

119 MacMahon and Murphy, 'Managerial Effectiveness in Small Enterprises', p. 29.

120 B. Kotey and P. Slade, 'Formal Human Resource Management Practices in Small Growing Firms', *Journal of Small Business Management*, Vol. 43 (2005), pp. 16–40; Storey, 'Exploring the Link Among Small Firms Between Management Training and Firm Performance': J.S. Hornsby and D.F. Kuratko, 'Human Resource Management in U.S. Small Businesses: A Replication and Extension', *Journal of Developmental Entrepreneurship*, Vol. 8 (2003), pp. 73–92.

121 For an exception see H. Harris and L. Holden, 'Between Autonomy and Control: Expatriate Managers and Strategic HRM in SMEs', *Thunderbird International Business Review*, Vol. 43, No. 1 (2001), pp. 77–100.

122 Internationalization of medium-sized enterprises – organization form and human resource management, published in German language as W. Weber and R. Kabst, 'Internationalisierung mittelständischer Unternehmen: Organisationsform und Personalmanagement, in Gerhard und Lore Kienbaum Stiftung', in J. Gutmann and R. Kabst (eds), *Internationalisierung im Mittelstand. Chancen – Risken – Erfolgsfaktoren* (Wiesbaden: Gabler, 2000), pp. 3–92.

123 Globalization of SMEs – experiences and recommendations for human resource management, published in German language as DGFP (ed.), *Globalisierung in kleinen und mittleren Unternehmen. Erfahrungen und Ansatzpunkte für das Personalmanagement*.

124 N. Kinnie, J. Purcell, S. Hutchinson, M. Terry, M. Collinson and H. Scarbrough, 'Employment Relations in SMEs: Market-driven or Customer-shaped?, *Employee Relations*, Vol. 21 (1999), pp. 218–35; B.S. Klaas, J. McClendon and T.W. Gainey, 'Managing HR in the Small and Medium Enterprise: The Impact of Professional Employer Organizations', *Entrepreneurship Theory and Practice*, Vol. 25, Issue 1 (2000), pp. 107–24.

125 Internationalization of medium-sized enterprises as a challenge for recruitment and development, published in German language as Kühlmann, 'Internationalisierung des Mittelstandes als Herausforderung für die Personalauswahl und – entwicklung, in Gerhard und Lore Kienbaum Stiftung'.

126 Klaas, McClendon and Gainey, 'Managing HR in the Small and Medium Enterprise', p. 107.

127 *Ibid.,* pp. 107–24.

Staffing international operations for sustained global growth

Chapter Objectives

The previous chapters have concentrated on the global environment and organization contexts. We now focus on the 'managing people' aspect. The aim is to establish the role of HRM in sustaining international business operations and growth. We cover the following:

- Issues relating to the various approaches to staffing foreign operations.
- The reasons for using international assignments: position filling, management development and organizational development.
- The various types of international assignments: short term, extended and longer term; and non-standard arrangements: commuter, rotator, contractual and virtual.
- The role of expatriates and non-expatriates in supporting international business activities.
- Return on investment of international assignments.
- The role of the corporate HR function in MNEs.

Introduction

The purpose of this chapter is to expand on the role of IHRM in sustaining global growth. We examine the various approaches taken to staffing international operations and the allocation of human resources to the firm's various international operations to ensure effective strategic outcomes. The pivotal role of international assignments is outlined. We conclude with a discussion on the role of the HR function within this context, particularly examining the issue of centralization and decentralization of the HR function and its activities.

Approaches to staffing

There are staffing issues that internationalizing firms confront that are either not present in a domestic environment, or are complicated by the international context in which these activities take place. Take, for example, the following scenario. A US MNE wishes to appoint a new finance director for its Irish subsidiary. It may decide to fill the position by selecting from finance staff available in its parent operations (that is, a PCN); or to recruit locally (a HCN); or seek a suitable candidate from one of its other foreign subsidiaries (a TCN).

The IHRM literature uses four terms to describe MNE approaches to managing and staffing their subsidiaries. These terms are taken from the seminal work of Perlmutter,[1] who claimed that it was possible to identify among international executives three primary attitudes – *ethnocentric, polycentric* and *geocentric* – toward building a multinational enterprise, based on top management assumptions upon which key product, functional and geographical decisions were made. To demonstrate these three attitudes, Perlmutter used aspects of organizational design; such as decision making, evaluation and control, information flows and complexity of organization. He also included 'perpetuation', which he defined as 'recruiting, staffing, development'. A fourth attitude – *regiocentric* – was added later.[2] We shall consider the connection between these four categories and staffing practices, and examine the advantages and disadvantages of each approach.

Ethnocentric

Few foreign subsidiaries have any autonomy and strategic decisions are made at headquarters. Key positions in domestic and foreign operations are held by headquarters' personnel. Subsidiaries are managed by staff from the home country (PCNs).

There are often sound business reasons for pursuing an ethnocentric staffing policy:

- A perceived lack of qualified host-country nationals (HCNs).
- The need to maintain good communication, coordination and control links with corporate headquarters. For firms at the early stages of internationalization, an ethnocentric approach can reduce the perceived high risk. When a multinational acquires a firm in another country, it may wish to initially replace local managers with PCNs to ensure that the new subsidiary complies with overall corporate objectives and policies, or because local staff may not have the required level of competence. Thus, an ethnocentric approach to a particular foreign market situation could be perfectly valid for a very experienced multinational. Having your own person, in whom you can place a degree of trust to 'do the right thing', can moderate the perceived high risk involved in foreign activities. This has been referred to by Bonache, Brewster and Suutari as 'assignments as control'.[3]

An ethnocentric policy, however, has a number of disadvantages:[4]

- It limits the promotion opportunities of HCNs, which may lead to reduced productivity and increased turnover among that group.
- The adaptation of expatriate managers to host countries often takes a long time, during which PCNs often make mistakes and poor decisions.

● When PCN and HCN compensation packages are compared, the often-considerable income gap in favor of PCNs is often viewed by HCNs as unjustified.

● For many expatriates a key overseas position means new status, authority and an increase in standard of living. These changes may affect expatriates' sensitivity to the needs and expectations of their host country subordinates. They can be very different and international managers have to understand this as the case in IHRM in Action Case 4-1 illustrates.

Expatriates are also very expensive to maintain in overseas locations. A recent study by PriceWaterhouseCoopers[5] reports that the average expatriate assignment cost per annum is US$ 311000 with a range of between US$ 103000 and US$ 396000. It is interesting to note that the average expatriate management costs amount to US$ 22378 as compared to the management of an average employee of US$ 3000.

IHRM in Action Case 4-1

What works at home does not necessarily work abroad: Impressions from working in Poland

Rainer van Daak was born in Frankfurt/Germany. Currently, he is working as an international sales manager for a German international electronics company in Warsaw/Poland. Below he summarizes some aspects of his working experience in Poland.

All my colleagues here are Polish. In my company, I'm the only foreigner in Poland, and also the only one in the whole of Eastern Europe! A lot of people want to work for the parent company in the US and I know people who have gone to Australia or Singapore. I think people are afraid to come to Eastern Europe because salaries are lower. But I can recommend working in Poland. It's a good experience. There are jobs here and a lot more people can speak English these days.

The working culture is different though. People are not so punctual and projects tend to start at the last minute. I think Germans like to be ready in advance. You can be a German-style manager and push everyone or you can be a friend.

People don't take things from your experience. They have their own way of doing things. You can try to suggest doing things a different way and switching back if it doesn't work. But they don't even want to try. It's really hard for a manager.

Polish people are really smart and Polish universities are really good. You see this in the field of electronics. International companies come here to hire Polish developers. Poles are very inventive. They haven't always had access to parts so they improvise and look at things differently.

Please discuss the challenges of taking an ethnocentric staffing approach.

Source: European Commission, *Europeans on the Move – Portraits of 31 Mobile Workers* (Luxemburg: Office for Official Publications of the European Communities, 2006).

Polycentric

The MNE treats each subsidiary as a distinct national entity with some decision-making autonomy. Subsidiaries are usually managed by local nationals (HCNs), who are seldom promoted to positions at headquarters, and PCNs are rarely transferred to foreign subsidiary operations. The main advantages of a polycentric policy, some of which address shortcomings of the ethnocentric policy identified above, are:

- Employing HCNs eliminates language barriers, avoids the adjustment problems of expatriate managers and their families and removes the need for expensive cultural awareness training programs.
- Employment of HCNs allows a multinational company to take a lower profile in sensitive political situations.
- Employment of HCNs is less expensive, even if a premium is paid to attract high-quality applicants.
- It gives continuity to the management of foreign subsidiaries. This approach avoids the turnover of key managers that, by its very nature, results from an ethnocentric approach.

A polycentric policy, however, has its own disadvantages:

- Bridging the gap between HCN subsidiary managers and PCN managers at corporate headquarters. Language barriers, conflicting national loyalties and a range of cultural differences (for example, personal value differences and differences in attitudes to business) may isolate the corporate headquarter's staff from the various foreign subsidiaries. The result may be that a multinational firm could become a 'federation' of independent national units with nominal links to corporate headquarters.
- Career paths of HCN and PCN managers. Host-country managers have limited opportunities to gain experience outside their own country and cannot progress beyond the senior positions in their own subsidiary. Parent-country managers also have limited opportunities to gain overseas experience. As headquarter's positions are held only by PCNs, the senior corporate management group will have limited exposure to international operations and, over time, this will constrain strategic decision making and resource allocation.

Of course, in some cases the host government may dictate that key managerial positions are filled by its nationals. Alternatively, the multinational may wish to be perceived as a local company as part of a strategy of local responsiveness. Having HCNs in key, visible positions assists this.

Geocentric

Here, the MNE is taking a global approach to its operations, recognizing that each part (subsidiaries and headquarters) makes a unique contribution with its unique competence. It is accompanied by a worldwide integrated business, and nationality is ignored in favor of ability. This is a major goal the European telecommunications company Vodafone would like to achieve. As a company speaker said:

> We want to create an international class of managers. In our view, the right way to do it is to have people close to one another, sharing their different approaches and understanding how each different part of the company now faces specific business challenges in the same overall scenario. We want to

develop a group of people who understand the challenges of being global on the one hand and are still deeply rooted in the local countries on the other. Our target is to develop an international management capability that can leverage our global scale and scope to maintain our leadership in the industry.[6]

There are three main advantages to this approach:

- It enables a multinational firm to develop an international executive team which assists in developing a global perspective and an internal pool of labor for deployment throughout the global organization.
- It overcomes the 'federation' drawback of the polycentric approach.
- It supports cooperation and resource sharing across units.

As with the other staffing approaches, there are disadvantages associated with a geocentric policy:

- Host governments want a high number of their citizens employed and may utilize immigration controls in order to force HCN employment if enough people and adequate skills are available, or require training of a HCN over a specified time period to replace a foreign national.
- Many Western countries require companies to provide extensive documentation if they wish to hire a foreign national instead of a local national. Providing this documentation can be time-consuming, expensive and at times futile. Of course, the same drawback applies to an ethnocentric policy. A related issue, that will be discussed later, is the difficulty of obtaining a work permit for the accompanying spouse or partner.
- A geocentric policy can be expensive to implement because of increased training and relocation costs. A related factor is the need to have a compensation structure with standardized international base pay, which may be higher than national levels in many countries.
- Large numbers of PCNs, TCNs and HCNs need to be sent abroad in order to build and maintain the international team required to support a geocentric staffing policy. To successfully implement a geocentric staffing policy, therefore, requires a longer lead time and a more centralized control of the staffing process. This necessarily reduces the independence of subsidiary management in these issues, and this loss of autonomy may be resisted by the subsidiary.

Welch[7] has identified IHRM barriers that may impede a multinational from building the staffing resources required to sustain the geocentric policy that is implicit in globalization literature. The barriers – staff availability, time and cost constraints, host government requirements and ineffective HRM policies – reflect the issues surrounding the geocentric approach listed in the literature reviewed above. While there may be a genuine predisposition among top managers at headquarters regarding the staffing of its global operations, leveraging critical resources in order to build the necessary international team of managers may prove to be a major challenge.

Regiocentric

This approach reflects the geographic strategy and structure of the MNE. Like the geocentric approach, it utilizes a wider pool of managers but in a limited way. Staff may move outside their countries but only within the particular geographic region. Regional managers may not be promoted to HQ positions but enjoy a degree of regional autonomy in decision making.[8] For example, a US-based firm could create three regions: Europe, the Americas and Asia-Pacific. European staff would be transferred throughout the European region (say a Briton to Germany, a French national to Belgium and a German to Spain). Staff transfers to the Asian-Pacific region from Europe would be rare, as would transfers from the regions to headquarters in the USA.

The advantages of using a regiocentric approach are:

● It allows interaction between executives transferred to regional headquarters from subsidiaries in the region and PCNs posted to the regional headquarters.

● It reflects some sensitivity to local conditions, since local subsidiaries are staffed almost totally by HCNs.

● It can be a way for a multinational to gradually move from a purely ethnocentric or polycentric approach to a geocentric approach.[9]

There are some disadvantages in a regiocentric policy:

● It can produce federalism at a regional rather than a country basis and constrain the organization from taking a global stance.

● While this approach does improve career prospects at the national level, it only moves the barrier to the regional level. Staff may advance to regional headquarters but seldom to positions at the parent headquarters.

A philosophy toward staffing

In summary, based on top management attitudes, a multinational can pursue one of several approaches to international staffing. It may even proceed on an ad hoc basis,[10] rather than systematically selecting one of the four approaches discussed above. A danger with this approach, according to Robinson[11] is that: 'The firm will opt for a policy of using parent-country-nationals in foreign management positions by default, that is, simply as an automatic extension of domestic policy, rather than deliberately seeking optimum utilization of management skills.'

This option is really a policy by default; there is no conscious decision or evaluation of appropriate policy. The 'policy' is a result of corporate inertia, inexperience, or both. The major disadvantage here (apart from the obvious one of inefficient use of resources) is that the firm's responses are reactive rather than proactive, and a consistent human resources strategy that fits its overall business strategy is difficult to achieve.

Table 4-1 summarizes the advantages and disadvantages of using the three categories of staff – PCNs, HCNs and TCNs.

While the various attitudes have been a useful way of demonstrating the various approaches to staffing foreign operations, it should be stressed that:

● The above categories refer to managerial attitudes that reflect the socio-cultural environment in which the internationalizing firm is embedded and are based on Perlmutter's study of US firms.

● These attitudes may reflect a general top management attitude, but the nature of international business often forces adaptation upon implementation. That is, a firm may adopt an ethnocentric approach to all its foreign operations, but a particular host government may require the appointment of its own people

| The advantages and disadvantages of using PCNs, TCNs and HCNs | Table 4-1 |

Parent-country nationals

Advantages
- Organizational control and coordination is maintained and facilitated.
- Promising managers are given international experience.
- PCNs may be the best people for the job because of special skills and experiences.
- There is assurance that subsidiary will comply with company objectives, policies, etc.

Disadvantages
- The promotional opportunities of HCNs are limited.
- Adaptation to host country may take a long time.
- PCNs may impose an inappropriate HQ style.
- Compensation for PCNs and HCNs may differ.

Third-country nationals

Advantages
- Salary and benefit requirements may be lower than for PCNS.
- TCNs may be better informed than PCNs about the host-country environment.

Disadvantages
- Transfers must consider possible national animosities (e.g. India and Pakistan).
- The host government may resent hiring of TCNs.
- TCNs may not want to return to their own countries after assignment.

Host-country nationals

Advantages
- Language and other barriers are eliminated.
- Hiring costs are reduced and no work permit is required.
- Continuity of management improves, since HCNs stay longer in positions.
- Government policy may dictate hiring of HCNs.
- Morale among HCNs may improve as they see career potential.

Disadvantages
- Control and coordination of HQ may be impeded.
- HCNs have limited career opportunity outside the subsidiary.
- Hiring HCNs limits opportunities for PCNs to gain foreign experience.
- Hiring HCNs could encourage a federation of national rather than global units.

in the key subsidiary positions; so, for that market, a polycentric approach is mandatory. In such instances a uniform approach is not achievable.

● As will be outlined in further detail later, the strategic importance of the foreign market, the maturity of the operation and the degree of cultural distance between the parent and host country, influence the way in which the firm approaches a particular staffing decision.[12] In some cases a MNE may use a combination of approaches. For example, it may operate its European interests in a regiocentric manner and its Southeast Asian interests in an ethnocentric way, until there is greater confidence in operating in that region of the world.

● The approach to policy on executive nationality tends to reflect organizational needs. For instance, if the multinational places a high priority on organizational control, then an ethnocentric policy will be adopted. However, there are difficulties in maintaining a uniform approach to international staffing. Therefore, strategies in different countries may require different staffing approaches.

Because of these operating realities, it is sometimes difficult to precisely equate managerial attitudes towards international operations with the structural forms we presented in Chapter 2. The external and internal contingencies facing the particular internationalizing firm influence its staffing choices. These include the following:

● *Context specificities.* The local context of the headquarters as well as of the subsidiary can be described by cultural and institutional variables (for a detailed description of cultural and institutional variables in the host-country context see Chapter 9). Cultural values may differ to a high extent between the headquarters and the host-country context. For example, Tarique, Schuler and Gong see the cultural similarity between parent country and subsidiary country as a moderator in the relationship between MNE strategy and subsidiary staffing.[13] Gong has found that MNEs tend to staff cultural distant subsidiaries with PCNs and that this has a positive effect on labor productivity.[14] The institutional environment includes, for example, the legal environment or the education system.[15] The latter may be directly linked to staff availability on the local labor market. Another effect is the host-country-effect, which implies that subsidiaries are influenced by their local environment.[16] In addition, the type of industry the firm is active in may have an impact as well.

● *Company specific variables.* These are mainly depicted from the framework on strategic HRM in multinational enterprises introduced in Chapter 1. The most relevant variables are MNE structure and strategy, international experience, corporate governance and organizational culture, which describe the MNE as a whole.[17]

● *Local unit specificities.* As the staffing approach may vary with the cultural and institutional environment it may also be dependent on the specificities of the local unit. An important factor here is the establishment method of the subsidiary, i.e., whether it is a greenfield investment, a merger, an acquisition or a shared partnership.[18] Furthermore, the strategic role of a subsidiary, its strategic importance for the MNE as a whole and the related questions of the need of control and the locus of decision may play important roles for staffing decisions.[19]

Determinants of staffing choices[20]

Figure 4-1

- **IHRM practices.** Selection, training and development, compensation and career management including expatriation as well as repatriation in a broader firm context – covered later in this book – play an important role in the development of effective policies required to sustain a preferred staffing choice.

These four groups of factors are supposed to systematically affect staffing practices. Due to situational factors individual staffing decisions might be taken in a non-expected way. Further, it has to be acknowledged that there are interdependencies between the determining variables outlined in Figure 4-1. However, for analytical reasons only the impact on the staffing choices, which is in the center of interest in this chapter, is discussed. Figure 4-1 illustrates the suggested linkages.

The above model may be helpful in drawing together the various contextual, organizational and HR-related issues in determining staffing choices. For example, a firm that is maturing into a networked organization (company specificity) will require IHRM approaches and activities that will assist its ability to develop a flexible global organization that is centrally integrated and coordinated yet locally responsive – a geocentric approach. However, a key assumption underlying the geocentric staffing philosophy is that the multinational has sufficient numbers of high-caliber staff (PCNs, TCNs and HCNs) constantly available for transfer anywhere, whenever global management needs dictate.[21]

As we discussed earlier, it is not easy to find or nurture the required numbers of high-quality staff (firm-specific and situation variables), nor assign them to certain operations due to host-country requirements (context specificities). For example, a study by Richards[22] of staffing practices and subsidiary performance of US multinationals in the UK and Thailand, found a link between perceptions of subsidiary performance, subsidiary location and staffing. Subsidiaries in Thailand appeared to perform better with a HCN in charge than a PCN.

Many studies investigating the determinants of staffing policies have been conducted in MNEs originating from developed countries. Recently, a study of Chinese MNEs has confirmed that Western models are generally applicable to Chinese MNEs as well.[23] However, the author points out that the same categories sometimes have different meanings. It is interesting to note that in this study culturally determined factors such as trust and personal morality have proved to be of special importance for staffing decisions. Overall, it seems that the different determinants of staffing choices outlined above all have an important impact, although the model as a whole is yet to be empirically tested.

Transferring staff for international business activities

The above discussion demonstrates the options for staffing key positions in foreign operations. We will now look at the HR consequences of these approaches and the broader implications in terms of:

● The reasons for using international assignments.
● Types of international assignments.
● The role of expatriates and non-expatriates.
● The role of inpatriates

Reasons for international assignments

Given the difficulties surrounding international assignments, it is reasonable to question why multinationals persist in using expatriates. Certainly, there are ebbs and flows associated with the number of staff moved internationally. Frequently, predictions are made that expatriates will become like dinosaurs as firms implement localization strategies, replacing expatriates with HCNs as a way of containing employment costs. For example, in a 2005 survey of 203 companies by the consulting firm PriceWaterhouseCoopers,[24] participants expected their use of expatriates would continue to grow in response to pressures for internationally mobile staff. This trend was despite the global environment volatility and may be regarded as evidence of a continuing commitment to international business operations.[25] A 2005 survey of global trends in international assignments, by the consulting firm GMAC Global Relocation Services, LLC (GMAC GRS),[26] confirmed this trend. It indicated that 47 per cent of participating firms expected an increase in the number of expatriates, compared to 39 per cent in its 2004 survey.[27] The increase is expected for short-term as well as for long-term assignments.[28] Why? As a practitioner involved in expatriate management explains:[29]

> As I talk to people, they say they wish they could shrink the expatriate population because of the expense in terms of benefits, services and support. And as long as I've been in this business, people say they are going to scale down on expats but it never happens. Until we have people all over the world with the skills they need, employers are going to have to continue to send expatriates.

The international management and IHRM literature has consistently identified three key organizational reasons for the use of various forms of international assignments:

● *Position filling*. The organization has a need and depending on the type of position and the level involved will either employ someone locally or transfer a suitable candidate. The 2002 global survey, by the consulting firm GMAC GRS,[30] asked respondents to indicate their primary objectives for international assignments. The most common reason was to fill a skills gap, followed by the launch of a new endeavor and technology transfer. In the 2004 survey, firms ranked to fill a skills gap as the primary reason, followed by launch of a new endeavor and building management expertise. Likewise, Wong's study[31] of two Japanese department stores in Hong Kong found that short-term job filling was the main reason for using expatriate staff rather than for long-term development and socialization of individuals. However, this seems to have changed. Interestingly, a recent study by PriceWaterhouseCoopers[32] has revealed that the problem of staff availability has decreased in the last five years. Instead, the costs of staff are an important driver, at least for European organizations.

● *Management development*. Staff can be moved into other parts of the organization for training and development purposes and to assist in the development of common corporate values. For this reason, we see headquarters' staff transferred to subsidiary operations, or subsidiary staff transferring into the parent operations, or to other subsidiary operations. Assignments may be for varying lengths of time and may involve project work as well as a trainee position. The perceived link between international experience and career development can be a motivation for staff to agree to such transfers.

● *Organization development*. Here strategic objectives of the operation come into play: the need for control; the transfer of knowledge, competence, procedures and practices into various locations; and to exploit global market opportunities, as we outlined in Chapter 1. As a result organizational capabilities enabling a firm to compete in global markets might be developed.[33] Indeed, the 2002 PriceWaterhouseCoopers Report mentioned above found that greater staff mobility assisted in supporting a global corporate culture and assisted the cross-fertilization of ideas and practices. One participant from an insurance firm is quoted as saying: 'To create a truly global organization, we will have to embed a culture of cross-border mobility into the organization's genetic code, which will take 10 years.' International assignments allow staff to gain a broader perspective, as they become familiar with more than one operation.

A study of 64 organizations by the CIPD (2001)[34] indicates that sending people on international assignments for management development reasons is as important as the need for filling positions due to a lack of local expertise. 57.8 per cent of the assignments were supposed to serve the career development goal and 56.3 per cent were initiated because of a lack of qualified HCNs. However, also organization and control played an important role (transfer of expertise: 53.1 per cent; control of local operations: 20.3 per cent; coordination of global policy: 7.8 per cent). As this study confirms, these reasons are not mutually exclusive and international assignments often achieve multiple objectives.

Types of international assignments

Employees are transferred internationally for varying lengths of time depending on the purpose of the transfer and the nature of the task to be performed. Companies tend to classify types according to the length or duration of the assignment:

- *Short term:* up to three months. These are usually for troubleshooting, project supervision, or a stopgap measure until a more permanent arrangement can be found.
- *Extended:* up to one year. These may involve similar activities as that for short-term assignments.
- *Long term:* varies from one to five years, involving a clearly defined role in the receiving operation (such as managing director of a subsidiary). The long-term assignment has also been referred to as a *traditional expatriate assignment*.

Table 4-2 illustrates some of the differences between short-term and traditional expatriate assignments. It should be noted that definitions of short-term and long-term assignments vary and depend upon organizational choices.

Within these three broad categories, it is possible to find what are termed non-standard assignments:

- *Commuter assignments.* Special arrangements where the person concerned commutes from the home country on a weekly or bi-weekly basis to the place of work in another country. Cross-border workers or daily commuters are not included. Usually the family of the assignee stays in the home country. For

Table 4-2	Differences between traditional and short-term assignments

	Traditional assignments	Short-term assignments
Purpose	• Filling positions or skills gaps • Management development • Organizational development	• Skills transfer/problem solving • Management development • Managerial control
Duration	Typically 12–36 months	Typically up to 6 months or 12 months.
Family's position	Family joins the assignee abroad	Assignee is unaccompanied by the family
Selection	Formal procedures	Mostly informal, little bureaucracy
Advantages	• Good relationships with colleagues • Constant monitoring	• Flexibility • Simplicity • Cost-effectiveness
Disadvantages	• Dual-career considerations • Expensive • Less flexibility	• Taxation • Side-effects (alcoholism, high divorce rate) • Poor relationships with local colleagues • Work permit issues

Source: Adapted from M. Tahvanainen, D. Welch and V. Worm, 'Implications of Short-term International Assignments', *European Management Journal,* Vol. 23, No. 6 (2005), p. 669.

example, the person lives in London but works in Moscow. In 2001, more than half of the 82 companies from 13 nationalities investigated in a study by PriceWaterhouseCoopers expected a further increase in the use of commuter assignments.[35]

● *Rotational assignments.* Employees commute from the home country to a place of work in another country for a short, set period followed by a break in the home country – used on oil rigs or in other hardship locations, for example. Again, the family usually remains in the home country. Out of all non-standard assignments companies expected the lowest growth rates for this type of assignment.[36]

● *Contractual assignments.* Used in situations where employees with specific skills vital to an international project are assigned for a limited duration of six to twelve months. Research and development (R&D) is one area that is using multinational project teams and lends itself to short-term contractual assignments in conjunction with longer-term assignments and virtual teams.[37] According to the above-mentioned study by PriceWaterhouseCoopers contractual assignments only play a slightly more important role than rotational assignments.

● *Virtual assignment.* Where the employee does not relocate to a host location but manages, from home-base, international responsibilities for a part of the organization in another country. In this case the manager heavily relies on communications technologies such as telephone, email or video conferences. Furthermore, frequent visits to the host country are necessary. The PriceWaterhouseCoopers[38] survey found that 28 per cent of the surveyed firms anticipated an increasing use of virtual assignments, compared with 17 per cent in a similar survey two years previous. A total of 65 per cent of respondents who use virtual assignments reported having seen an increase in the number of virtual assignments used by their company and the same proportion indicated an expected increase in the next two years. The main reasons given by responding firms for experimenting with the virtual assignment were similar to those given for other non-standard forms of international assignments: the shortage of mobile staff prepared to accept longer term postings, and for cost containment reasons.

Some of these arrangements assist in overcoming the high costs of international assignments. However, non-standard assignments are not always effective substitutes for the traditional expatriate assignment. As the PriceWaterhouseCoopers 2000 report's authors point out: 'There are real concerns about the viability of commuter arrangements over an extended period of time due to the build up of stress resulting from intensive travel commitments and the impact on personal relationships.'[39]

Most of the research into assignment issues has been around the long-term assignment type, mainly because it forms the bulk of international assignments. In contrast, short-term and extended assignments have received limited research attention.[40] It is similar in terms of the non-standard assignments. For example, Welch, Worm and Fenwick[41] comment: 'while non-standard assignments have long been used in conjunction with, or instead of, traditional expatriate assignments, this has yet to translate into a comparable body of academic inquiry'. Their study into the use of virtual assignments in Australian and Danish firms has suggested that while there are certain advantages of operating virtually (such as not having to relocate a family unit), there are disadvantages that may affect successful work outcomes. These are:

● *Role conflict, dual allegiance and identification issues*. Between the person in the home location and the virtual work group in the foreign location. For example, to whom does the virtual assignee 'belong' – the home location where the person physically resides for most of the time, or to the foreign unit? How much time should be devoted to the 'virtual' work responsibilities versus the 'real' work?

● *Interpersonal relations and work relationships*. Given that much of the work is done through electronic media, the potential for cultural misunderstandings increases, and the geographical distance means normal group interaction is not possible. Communication is mainly through conference calls, videoconferencing and emails, and depends on good skills in using these media. Frequent visits between the two locations are required to support the working of this arrangement as not everything can be settled virtually. Face-to-face meetings are still required.

Virtual assignments tend to be used for regional positions – such as European Marketing Manager, where the person is mainly coordinating a number of countries' marketing activities but is based at a regional center. The 2000 PriceWaterhouseCoopers' study found that virtual assignments were more common in Europe with no companies indicating the use of such arrangements in the Asia-Pacific region. Geographical distance in terms of flight hours and time zones were the main difficulties encountered in operating virtually between operations in Europe and Asia Pacific.

The roles of an expatriate

As mentioned above, the reasons for using expatriates are not mutually exclusive. They do however underpin expectations about the roles staff play as a consequence of being transferred from one location to another country. These roles are delineated in Figure 4-2.

| Figure 4-2 | The roles of an expatriate |

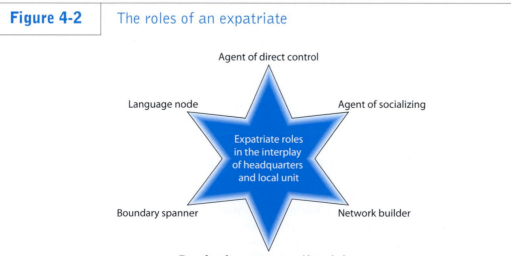

The expatriate as an agent of direct control

The use of staff transfers can be regarded as a bureaucratic control mechanism,[42] where the primary role is that of ensuring compliance through direct supervision. Harzing[43] found that German companies tend towards this form of control. She labels expatriates who are such agents as 'bears', arguing that the analogy reflects the level of dominance of this type of expatriate control. To a certain extent, using expatriates for control reflects an ethnocentric predisposition, but this can be important in ensuring subsidiary compliance, enabling strategic objectives for local operations to be achieved.

The expatriate as an agent of socialization

This role is related to the use of corporate culture as an informal control mechanism we examined in Chapter 2. There is an implicit expectation that expatriates assist in the transfer of shared values and beliefs. Harzing describes expatriates who transfer corporate values as 'bumble-bees'. However, as Fenwick et al.[44] point out there has been little empirical investigation as to how effective expatriates have been as agents of socialization. In fact, attempts to instil corporate values and norms ritualized in the form of certain expected behaviors often have negative results at the subsidiary level.

International assignments do assist in knowledge sharing and competence transfer, and encourage adoption of common work practices, aspects of which may comprise elements of corporate culture. Staff in the various organizational units may be exposed to different viewpoints and perspectives that will shape their behavior and may reinforce their feeling of belonging. In their study, Goodall and Roberts[45] relate a reaction by a Chinese employee in the Chinese operation of a European oil company. Her time in the parent's operation in Europe enabled her to appreciate how the company valued its name and reputation, and was able to better understand the company's code of conduct and attitude towards occupational health and safety.

Expatriates as network builders

As we discussed in Chapter 2, international assignments are viewed as a way of developing social capital:[46] fostering interpersonal linkages that can be used for informal control and communication purposes. Naturally, as employees move between various organizational units, their network of personal relationships changes, leading to Harzing's analogy of expatriates as 'spiders' to describe this role. How these employees are utilized is person-dependent. People tend to nurture and protect their networks, to be very selective about the way they use their connections, and to evaluate the potential damage to key individuals in their networks if the connection was to be used inappropriately. In their study of project teams and networks, Schweiger et al.[47] provide the following example of how international assignments assisted network development:

> I depended heavily on the contacts I had developed over the years. The time spent in international assignments was invaluable. I knew important people in several key operations. I knew how they operated and what was important to them. They also knew that I was credible and would help them when the opportunity arose.

Further, as Marschan *et al.*[48] explain: 'People may be introduced to each other but not form the type of relationship on which productive networks are built.' Take the case of Laura, an American expatriate, who has worked in India for several years, and built up a strong network comprising subsidiary staff, key host-government officials, clients, suppliers and the like. She is now being transferred to the Canadian operations, and, Angelo, from the Italian subsidiary is taking her place. Laura may take Angelo around and introduce him to key individuals in this personal network, but it will not guarantee that Angelo will be readily accepted into that network of critical contacts.

While short-term assignments may not allow the expatriate to develop as wide a range of contacts in one location as a traditional assignment allows, over time, they can increase the number and variety of networks, giving opportunity for the transfer of ideas and competence.[49] Duration of the assignment, therefore, will have an impact on the person's ability to develop networks.

Expatriates as boundary spanners

Boundary spanning refers to activities, such as gathering information, that bridge internal and external organizational contexts. Expatriates are considered boundary spanners because they can collect host-country information, act as representatives of their firms in the host country and can influence agents. For example, attending a social function at a foreign embassy can provide the expatriate with an opportunity to network, gather market intelligence and promote the firm's profile at a high level. Networking activity emerged as a way in which expatriates from various nationalities operating in Hong Kong were able to engage in boundary spanning activities.[50]

Expatriates as language nodes

Marschan-Piekkari *et al.*[51] found that Finnish expatriates working for the elevator company Kone, sometimes became what they termed language nodes. They give as an example, a Finn (whom they refer to as Mr X) who learned to speak Spanish while working as an expatriate in the firm's South American operations. Upon repatriation back to the Finnish headquarters, Mr X finds that he becomes 'the man in Finland who speaks Spanish'. Kone employees from the firm's Spanish-speaking operations, including Mexico, would call Mr X, preferring to conduct queries and gain information from him in Spanish, and check information sent to them in English.

Transfer of competence and knowledge

Overall, international assignments are seen as an effective way of accomplishing multiple objectives. In fact, one could argue that there are elements of competence and knowledge transfer in all the roles we have identified. However, evidence as to the effectiveness of expatriates in conducting their numerous roles is sparse. Factors that may affect effectiveness include:

● The creation of an environment of openness and support for cross-fertilization of ideas and implementation of 'best practice'.

- The need for knowledge and information to travel dyadically, that is, between the expatriate and the host location, and back to the expatriate's home location, if the multinational is to benefit from international assignments as a mechanism for competence and knowledge transfer.

- Despite the recognition of the importance of personal networks in knowledge and information transfer, staffing decisions often are made without regard to their effect on network relationships. In many cases there is not a strategic approach controlling these effects.

- There is a link between the duration of the assignment and the effective transfer of knowledge and competences. Some knowledge and competence may be transferred quickly while other skills and knowledge (particularly where a high level of tacitness is present) may take longer.

- Naturally, much of what is transferred depends on the expatriate concerned in terms of ability to teach others, and motivation to act as an agent of knowledge and competence transfer. For example, Goodall and Roberts[52] quote the experience of a Colombian HCN working for a European oil company:

> It is important that there is really a transfer of technology between expat [expatriate] and Colombian. And during the last two years nothing is learned. The expat goes and then they bring another expat. . . . There should be more of a formal commitment to training, a follow-up. They [expatriates] should be evaluated on coaching with Columbians.

A final point: Bolino and Feldman[53] make an interesting observation that when expatriates are assigned for position filling due to a lack of appropriate local staff, such expatriates are often forced to take over some of the responsibilities of their colleagues due to differences in knowledge and competence levels. Consequently, they argue, that expatriates often spend significant time on less challenging tasks to help out co-workers and train them. In such cases, while the expatriates may assist in skills transfer, over time their own level of competence may decrease as they are not developing their own expertise. Thus, when expatriates return to their home operation, they may find that their knowledge is obsolescing.

The roles of non-expatriates

The above discussion has centered on the international assignment. What has tended to be overlooked is that a considerable amount of international business involves what can be called non-expatriates: people who travel internationally yet are not considered expatriates, as they do not relocate to another country. That is, non-expatriates are international business travelers[54] – persons for whom a large proportion of their role involves constant international visits to foreign markets, subsidiary units, international projects and the like. Where this group is referred to, they are popularly termed 'road warriors', 'globetrotters', 'frequent fliers' or even 'flexpatriates'.[55]

International travel is an essential component of their work, such as international sales staff whose job is almost totally comprised of international travel and managers whose job entails numerous, periodic visits to international operations.

International sales representatives attend trade fairs, visit foreign agents and distributors, demonstrate new products to potential clients and negotiate sales contracts. Various staff will visit foreign locations to deal with host-country government officials, alliance partners, subcontracting firms and foreign suppliers.

In spite of emails and videoconferencing, international business travel is increasing.[56] People still prefer to conduct certain business activities, hold meetings and interact face-to-face. As Mintzberg *et al.*[57] note:

> Why do so many effective international managers get into airplanes rather than pick up telephones when they need to communicate seriously? As we move from written communication (letters, e-mail) to strictly oral (telephones) to face-to-face forms, communication appears to become richer and more nuanced.

However, international business travel can make heavy demands on staff. For example, the Norwegian firm, Moelven, a global player in the timber industry, when developing its operations in the Russian market in the early 1990s, initially through importing, had to become highly involved in building personal relationships with key individuals in Russia:

> One manager from the purchasing department responsible for imports commented: 'Personal contacts were so important that during the first three years [of] dealing with the Russians, I had between 50 and 100 trips to Russia, talking to suppliers and maintaining the personal networks'.[58]

Apart from the resource implications, there are issues relating to the management of international business travelers that do not seem to be addressed in the IHRM literature. This may be due to the fact that this category of staff does not include expatriates on traditional or non-standard assignments. The international component of their work is performed within the context of their 'normal' duties. Regardless, there are several important issues that should be considered. There is a high level of stress involved for those whose job responsibilities contain a large proportion of international business travel. In one of the few articles on this issue, DeFrank *et al.*[59] identify the following factors as stressors:

- *Home and family issues.* Such as missing important anniversaries and school events. The more frequent the travel, the greater the potential for family and marital relationships to be strained.

- *Work arrangements.* The 'domestic' side of the job still has to be attended to even though the person is traveling internationally. Modern communications allow work to accompany them, so the business traveller is expected to deal with home-base issues while remote from the office via modem. When the traveler returns to the home office, they may face crises, backlogs of paperwork and so forth.

- *Travel logistics.* Airline connections, hotel accommodation and meeting schedules.

- *Health concerns.* Poor diet, lack of physical exercise, lack of sleep, coping with jetlag, and exposure to disease and other illnesses (such as SARS and deep vein thrombosis).

- *Host-culture issues.* As international business is conducted in other cultural settings, the person is still expected to be able to operate in unfamiliar environments and handle cultural differences effectively. However, the limited empirical and anecdotal evidence suggests that non-expatriates do not receive the same level of cross-cultural training as expatriates – if any.

The above list contains the negatives associated with international business travel. However, there are positives. People involved in this side of international business will relate the excitement and thrills of conducting business deals in foreign locations, the lifestyle (top hotels, business-class travel, duty-free shopping), and its general exotic nature as the reasons why they enjoy international business travel, despite its very real negatives.

Non-expatriate business travelers also perform many of the roles of expatriates – in terms of being agents for socialization, network-builders, boundary spanners and language nodes. From the limited evidence available, however, it would seem that the management of staff using these forms of arrangements falls to the functional or line managers involved rather than the HR department as such.

The role of inpatriates

If organizations work on a global scale they need sufficient qualified staff to meet the requirements of globalization. As we have discussed above a shortage of multicultural managers possessing global leadership competencies may limit the opportunities of an MNE to gain competitive advantage. To support this process, a new term for the management development of a specific type of HCN called inpatriation has recently occurred.

As we have outlined in Chapter 1 inpatriates are mainly distinguished from expatriates by definition. They include international assignments of HCNs or TCNs from a foreign location to the headquarters of the MNE. Inpatriates are supposed to serve as 'linking pins' between the different organizational units of an MNE. They are:

> expected to share their local contextual knowledge with HQ staff in order to facilitate effective corporate activities in these local markets. At the same time they are socialized in the HQ corporate culture and learn firm-specific routines and behaviors that enable them to master future management tasks within the organization. As a result, inpatriates seem to act both as knowledge senders and receivers.[60]

Collings and Scullion[61] have identified the following key drivers for recruiting inpatriate managers:

- The desire to create a global core competency and a cultural diversity of strategic perspectives in the top management team,[62] thus, increasing the capability of organizations to 'think global and act local'.

- The desire to provide career opportunities for high-potential employees in host countries, i.e. HCNs and TCNs.

- The emergence of developing markets which often represent difficult locations for expatriates in terms of quality of life and cultural adjustment.

Inpatriates represent a phenomenon, which can be observed to an increasing extent in addition to the traditional expatriation.[63] For example, the German MNE Bosch had employed 519 inpatriates in January 2006. While this number is still small compared to the current number of expatriates (1059) it is nevertheless significant given that 15 years ago Bosch had assigned only 300 expatriates to foreign locations.[64] It indicates the tremendous process of internationalization that has taken place within this company and that is associated with a need of international managers in all parts of the organization, being able to realize bilateral knowledge transfer between the foreign unit represented by the inpatriate and the headquarters.

However, the strategy of inpatriation also underlines that the strategic importance of the headquarters is still prevailing, indicating that the knowledge of the culture, the structure and the processes specific to the headquarters are still important requirements for vertical career advancement. Despite inpatriation, career opportunities for HCNs and TCNs are often limited. Usually, the assignment to the headquarters aims at training the manager for a top management position back home in the foreign subsidiary. Especially if firms aim at open sky policies,[65] i.e. offering career opportunities independently from the nationality, inpatriation can only be a first step, reflecting a rather ethnocentric approach. Harvey and Buckley[66] conclude that in this case 'inpatriation may be a dangerous process'. While it might be more difficult for inpatriates than for PCNs to realize a vertical career in the headquarters, they experience the same integration and repatriation problems as expatriates during and after their international assignment. Consequently, they may not reach the same return on investment for their international assignment as expatriates. This can only be guaranteed if career opportunities for inpatriated HCNs or TCNs exist as well in the headquarters. In this case inpatriation can be an important step in realizing a geocentric orientation within the MNE and thus an open sky for HCN and TCN managers.

Return on investment of international assignments

From an organizational perspective international assignments are a very risky and costly way of developing employees.[67] Consequently, the question arises whether they are worth it. This question gains even more importance as companies are becoming more cost sensitive when managing expatriates.[68]

Traditionally the success of an international assignment has been measured using expatriates' failure rates (including premature return from the assignment or unexpected quit during, as well as after, the assignment),[69] the financial costs associated with the assignment as well as the performance of the expatriate.[70] The PriceWaterhouseCoopers survey on *International Assignments* (2005) reveals that companies have an increasing interest in measuring the value of international assignments in a more differentiated way.[71] They suggest to use a return on investment (ROI) approach. This concept has only recently been applied to international assignments and expatriate management activities.[72] According to McNulty and Tharenou: 'expatriate ROI should be defined as a calculation in which the financial and non-financial benefits to the MNC are compared to the financial and non-financial costs of the international assignment, as appropriate to the assignments purpose'.[73]

While the expenses associated directly with the assignment such as the salary or the relocation costs may be relatively easy to quantify, it is more complex to estimate the administrative costs of running an international assignment.[74] McNulty and Tharenou suggest to analyze all IHRM support activities including assignment planning, expatriate selection, administering the relocation program, expatriate compensation, training and development, family support practices, performance management, repatriation and retention in the context of the assignment purpose with respect to costs and benefits in order to calculate expatriate ROI. Even more complexity is expected when management development outcomes shall be assessed. Here, the focus should be on the extent to which the assignee has developed a global mindset and/or on the quality of the acquired global leadership skills.[75] Figure 4-3

Indicators for calculating return-on-investment on international assignments   **Figure 4-3**

INVESTMENT
Direct costs of the assignment
- Employees salary
- Taxes
- Housing
- Shipment of household goods
- Education assistance for dependents
- Spouse support
- Cross-cultural training
- Goods and service allowance
- Repatriation logistics
- Reassignment costs

Administrative costs of running an international assignment program
- Home-based HR support (assignment planning, selection and compensation management)
- Assignment location or host-based HR support
- Post-assignment placement costs
- Post-assignment career tracking costs

Adjustment costs
- Settling in services
- Spouse and family support
- Cross-cultural and language adjustments
- Destination familiarization and house-hunting trips

RETURN
Quantifiable assignment objectives, e.g.
- Open a new office (finding a location, establishing an office, hiring and training local employees)
- Increase a company's sales by a specified amount over a certain period of time

Non-quantifiable assignment objectives with respect to organization development, e.g.
- Strengthening the corporate culture in the local entity
- Improving the relationship with a joint-venture partner
- Providing knowledge transfer between headquarters and foreign location

Non-quantifiable assignment objectives with respect to management development, e.g.
- Understanding an international market critical to the business
- Networking in another country to build a new client base
- Integrating into the local work environment
- Providing effective feedback to subordinates in a manner appropriate to the local culture
- Making presentations to an international audience in a foreign language
- Working well across multiple time zones and cultures

Source: Adapted from Y. M. McNulty, and P. Tharenou, "Expatriate return on investment", *International Studies of Management and Organization,* Vol. 34, No. 3 (2004), pp. 68–95; L. Johnson, "Measuring International Assignment Return on Investment", *Compensation Benefits Review,* Vol. 37, No. 2 (2005), pp. 50–54.

gives an impression about the indicators that may be used to calculate a ROI on a single international assignment. It has to be noted here that a 'one-best' ROI formula for international assignments does not exist because the objectives pursued with each assignment are likely to be different.[76]

For determining expatriate ROI McNulty and Tharenou recommend an approach comprising four steps:[77]

1 Identifying financial and non-financial costs and benefits.

2 Linking the costs and benefits to the purpose of the long-term assignment.

3 Identifying the appropriate antecedents from a system's perspective.

4 Conducting the calculation at an appropriate time within the context of the assignment's purpose.

In a recent study Johnson[78] as well as the GMAC Global Relocation Trends Survey[79] found that only 14 per cent of the investigated companies have measured expatriate ROI. If ROI was measured half of the investigated companies in the GMAC GRS survey indicated that they defined it as 'accomplished assignment objectives at expected cost'.[80] It is interesting to note that according to the PriceWaterhouseCoopers study the costs of managing an international assignment program represent 7 per cent of the total costs including compensation, long-term benefits and allowances.[81]

As we have outlined above international management development has become a major goal associated with international assignments. In this case all investment is focused on retaining the internationally experienced manager in the company with a long-term career perspective. But as expatriation represents an important transition point within the career of an employee it includes several career risks. 'Expatriation, as a specific time period in one's career, might be conducive to a change of organization, particularly when the individual does not feel that an international assignment is beneficial to his or her career within the expatriation organization.'[82] Therefore it is important to focus research on how companies can retain expatriated employees. Stahl and Cerdin[83] outlined that organizations not providing effective IHRM support practices tend to end up with dissatisfied managers, likely to leave the company. Surveys have shown that the turnover of repatriated assignees amounts up to percentages between 14 and 23.[84] Considering that the PriceWaterhouseCoopers study (2006) has revealed important performance increases during and after an international assignment these turnover rates mean important losses for the firms not able to amortize their investments in the human capital of their international managers. This indicates the importance of post-assignment career tracking as an issue for MNEs.

The role of the corporate HR function in MNEs

Having considered the approaches to staffing, and examined international assignments and the role of expatriates and non-expatriates, we now turn our attention to the role played by the corporate HR function in managing people in a multinational context.

Much of the IHRM literature is focused on whom to place in control of foreign operations and activities. However, like other functional areas, HR professionals in multinationals face strategic choices. First, can we manage our people like a global product? The concept of a global internal labor market does imply some belief that it is possible to deploy human resources in much the same way as other resources. However, comparative HRM and cross-cultural management literature suggest that standardizing work practices and HRM activities is not the same as product standardization. In contrast globalization occurs at the level of the particular function.[85]

Second, what HR matters require central control and what can be delegated to subsidiary HR managers? The answer partly depends on organizational and administrative imperatives and the economic and political imperatives of the host location. For example, the desire for control and coordination may stress a geocentric approach to staffing that requires standardized policies to encourage equal treatment to all staff on international assignments (that is, an administrative imperative). Legal constraints, cost considerations and host-government directives may require compromises in terms of staffing (economic and political imperatives).

Scullion and Starkey[86] remark that there has been little empirical research into the corporate HR function's role and how it may change over time.[87] As we discussed in Chapter 2, as the firm internationalizes it is required to make structural and processual changes and we indicated ways in which the HR department may need to respond. We outlined Scullion and Starkey's finding from a study of 30 British-owned international companies where they identified centralized, decentralized and transition HR companies. The roles of the various HR departments in these three organizational categories reflect the structural differences. These are summarized in Table 4-3 below. As you would expect, there is a direct link between the structure of the company and the roles of the HR function. However, there was a common approach to the management of key executive staff across the three organizational types, suggesting the need for coordination and integration of international activities that, in turn, requires greater central control over key managerial staff.

A related aspect in terms of centralization and decentralization is the nature of the activities performed by the HR function. The above table indicates a primary concern of corporate HR departments to be able to deploy staff throughout the worldwide operations of the multinational and this is a major driver of centralization, whether supported by formal mechanisms or not. Multinationals may also centralize training and development programs. For example, Motorola, a US multinational, has its own 'university'; Lufthansa, the German airline and Ikea, the Swedish furniture retailer have their own 'business schools'. Hiring of HCNs tends to be devolved to the local level given the need for adherence to local hiring practices.

Another driver is the level of sophistication within the firm regarding its international business operations. The more mature the firm, the more likely it has centralized those HR activities it considers strategic. The position of the corporate HR function is also dependent on its profile within the top executive team. For many firms, despite the impact that international growth has on a firm's HR activities, the

Various roles of corporate HR		Table 4-3
Centralized HR companies	*Decentralized HR companies*	*Transition HR companies*
• Large well-resourced HR departments • Key role: management of all high-grade management positions worldwide • Key activities: planning international assignments and performance management globally, identifying high-potential staff	• Small HR departments • Key role: managing elite corporate managers • Key activities: influencing operating units to support international assignments, supporting decentralized HR	• Medium-sized HR departments • Key role: management and career development of senior managers and expatriates • Key activities: persuading divisional managers to release key staff using informal and subtle methods, strategic staffing

Source: Adapted from H. Scullion and K. Starkey, 'In Search of the Changing Role of the Corporate Human Resource Function in the International Firm', *International Journal of Human Resource Management,* Vol. 11, No. 6 (2000), pp. 1061–81.

precise nature and extent of that impact on corporate performance is not well understood by many senior managers. Possible explanations are:

● HR managers only become involved in strategic decisions when there is a critical mass of expatriates to be managed.

● Senior management is more likely to recognize HR issues when international assignments become of significant strategic value, and therefore are more likely to leverage the required resources.

● There is often a considerable time lag before HR constraints on international expansion come to the attention of senior corporate management.

● As we discussed in Chapter 1, a global perspective, through a broader view of issues, enables the development of more effective corporate policies. The need for a global perspective applies to staff in the corporate HR department, at the regional HR level and divisional and business units HR managers. HR managers could undertake international assignments themselves to gain appreciation of both global corporate and local unit concerns. The use of international assignments can be supplemented with frequent meetings of corporate and subsidiary HR managers. Smaller firms with limited resources may find it impossible to finance international assignments, but they may be able to identify other ways to globally orientate HR staff such as an annual visit to key overseas subsidiaries.

In line with the above issues, Novicevic and Harvey[88] argue that corporate HR staff need to redefine their traditional role as bureaucratic administrators and become 'influencers' over areas of subsidiary practices, such as encouraging career ladders to assist in global staffing decisions, and designing performance appraisal and compensation systems and policies that support lateral integration and informal communication. These types of activities, it is suggested, will enhance what these authors call homogenization of best practices while endeavoring to maintain specific capabilities and responsiveness at the local subsidiary level, thus ensuring the relevance of the corporate HR function. This describes what is meant if a company moves from international human resource management, which essentially means managing an international workforce to global human resource management including all HR activities worldwide.[89]

Summary

This chapter has expanded on the role of staffing international operations for sustaining international business operations. The following issues were discussed:

● We have outlined the various approaches to staffing international operations – ethnocentric, polycentric, geocentric and regiocentric and discussed their advantages and disadvantages. In addition we presented a model delineating factors that may determine the choice of these options: context specificities, company characteristics, features of the local unit as well as IHRM practices.

● Primary reasons for using international assignments include position filling, management development and organization development. There are indicators that the importance of management development increases.

- Various types of international assignments can be distinguished: short, extended and long term (traditional); and non-standard forms such as commuter, rotational, contractual and virtual assignments. All are presented including implications for the firm as well as for the individual.

- Roles of the expatriates are complex. They can act as an agent for direct control, as an agent for socialization, as a network builder, as a boundary spanner and as a language node. These various roles of the expatriate help to explain why expatriates are utilized and illustrate why international assignments continue to be an important aspect of international business from the organization's perspective.

- We placed emphasis of the issue that non-expatriates are also critical to international business operations. International business travelers present their own challenges, such as the effect of frequent absences on family and home life, the possible negative health effects and other stress factors. The management of such individuals though does not appear to fall within the domain of the HR department.

- Another important development in IHRM is the discussion about inpatriates. This is a group of employees who only differ by definition from expatriates because it includes only those employees who are sent to the headquarters by foreign locations and not those who are assigned by the headquarters.

- In line with the increasing need of companies to control costs and develop metrics we pointed out the importance and the possibilities to measure expatriate return on investment (ROI).

- Finally, the importance of the role of the corporate HR function as the firm grows internationally is acknowledged, building on sections from Chapters 1 and 2.

Discussion Questions

1 Outline the main characteristics of the four approaches to international staffing.

2 Which factors determine the choice of a staffing approach? Would a MNE choose the same staffing approach worldwide? Place your arguments in the context of the model outlining determinants of staffing choices.

3 What are the reasons for using international assignments?

4 What is the role of inpatriates? Do inpatriates guarantee a geocentric staffing policy?

5 Why is it important to measure return on investment of international assignments? Which indicators can be used?

6 As a newly appointed Project Manager of a research team, you consider that you will be able to manage the project virtually from your office in London, even though the other six members are located in Munich. This will solve your personal dilemma as your family does not want to be relocated. The project has a six-month deadline. What factors should you need to consider in order to make this virtual assignment effective?

Further Reading

Benito, G.R.G., Tomassen, S., Bonache-Perez, J. and Pla-Barber, J. (2005). 'A Transaction Cost Analysis of Staffing Decisions in International Operations', *Scandinavian Journal of Management,* 21: 101–26.

Collings, D. and Scullion, H. (2006). 'Global Staffing', in G. Stahl and I. Björkman (eds), *Handbook of Research in International Human Resource Management,* Cheltenham: Edward Elgar, pp. 141–57.

Scullion, H. and Collings, D.G. (eds) (2006). *Global Staffing,* London and New York: Routledge.

Tarique, I., Schuler, R. and Gong, Y. (2006). 'A Model of Multinational Staffing Composition', *The International Journal of Human Resource Management,* 17(2): 207–24.

Torbiörn, I. (2005). 'Staffing Policies and Practices in European MNCs: Strategic Sophistication, Culture-bound Policies or Ad-hoc Reactivity', in H. Scullion and M. Linehan (eds), *International human resource management: A critical text,* Basingstoke: Palgrave Macmillan, pp. 47–68.

Notes and References

1 H.V. Perlmutter, 'The Tortuous Evolution of the Multinational Corporation', *Columbia Journal of World Business,* Vol. 4, No. 1 (1969), pp. 9–18.

2 D.A. Heenan and H.V. Perlmutter, *Multinational Organization Development* (Reading, MA: Addison-Wesley, 1979).

3 J. Bonache, C. Brewster and V. Suutari, 'Expatriation: A Developing Research Agenda', *Thunderbird International Business Review,* Vol. 43, No. 1 (2001), pp. 3–20.

4 Y. Zeira, 'Management Development in Ethnocentric Multinational Corporations', *California Management Review,* Vol. 18, No. 4 (1976), pp. 34–42.

5 PriceWaterhouseCoopers (eds), *Measuring the Value of International Assignments* (London: PriceWaterhouseCoopers, 2006).

6 PriceWaterhouseCoopers (eds), *Managing Mobility Matters 2006* (London: PriceWaterhouseCoopers, 2006), p. 28.

7 D. Welch, 'HRM Implications of Globalization', *Journal of General Management,* Vol. 19, No. 4 (1994), pp. 52–68.

8 Heenan and Perlmutter, *Multinational Organization Development.*

9 A.J. Morrison, D.A. Ricks and K. Roth, 'Globalization versus Regionalisation: Which Way for the Multinational?', *Organizational Dynamics,* Winter (1991), pp. 17–29.

10 I. Torbiörn, 'Staffing Policies and Practices in European MNCs: Strategic Sophistication, Culture-bound Policies or Ad-hoc Reactivity', in H. Scullion and M. Linehan (eds), *International Human Resource Management: A Critical Text* (Basingstoke: Palgrave Macmillan, 2005), pp. 47–68.

11 R.D. Robinson, *International Business Management: A Guide to Decision Making,* 2nd edn (Hinsdale, IL: Dryden, 1978), p. 297.

12 N. Boyacigiller, 'The Role of Expatriates in the Management of Interdependence, Complexity and Risk in Multinational Corporations', *Journal of International Business Studies,* Vol. 21, No. 3 (1990), pp. 357–81, and D.E. Welch, 'Determinants of International Human Resource Management Approaches and Activities: A Suggested Framework', *Journal of Management Studies,* Vol. 31, No. 2 (1994), pp. 139–64.

13 I. Tarique, R. Schuler and Y. Gong, 'A Model of Multinational Staffing Composition', *International Journal of Human Resource Management,* Vol. 17, No. 2 (2006), pp. 207–24.

14 See the results of a study among Japanese subsidiaries by Y. Gong, 'Subsidiary Staffing in Multinational Enterprises: Agency, Resources, and Performance', *Academy of Management Journal,* Vol. 45, No. 6, (2003), pp. 728–39. A similar analysis has been carried out by Y. Thompson and M. Keating, 'An Empirical Study of Executive Nationality Staffing Practices in Foreign-owned MNC Subsidiaries in Ireland', *Thunderbird International Business Review,* Vol. 46, No. 6 (2004), pp. 771–97.

15 For an institutional perspective see the national business systems approach by R.D. Whitley, *European Business Systems: Firms and Markets in Their National Contexts* (London: Sage Publications, 1992).

16 For a discussion of European staffing approaches see I. Torbiörn, 'Staffing Policies and Practices in European MNCs'.

17 For a similar discussion see C.M. Vance and Y. Paik, *Managing a Global Workforce: Challenges and Opportunities in International Human Resource Management* (Armonk, NY and London: M.E. Sharpe, 2006).

18 For a discussion of these factors on subsidiary HRM see Y. Kim and S.J. Gray, 'Strategic Factors Influencing International Human Resource Management Practices: An Empirical Study of

Australian Multinational Corporations', *International Journal of Human Resource Management,* Vol. 16, No. 5 (2005), pp. 809–30.

19   For the issue of subsidiary consideration see M.M. Novicevic and M. Harvey, 'Staffing Architecture for Expatriate Assignments to Support Subsidiary Cooperation', *Thunderbird International Business Review,* Vol. 46, No. 6, (2004), pp. 709–24. For a discussion of the impact of different subsidiary strategies see J. Bonache and Z. Fernandez, 'Strategic Staffing in Multinational Companies: A Resource-based Approach', in C. Brewster and H. Harris, *International HRM: Contemporary Issue in Europe* (London and New York: Routledge, 2004), pp. 163–82. For a resource dependence perspective on the emergence of IHRM strategies see M. Festing, J. Eidems and S. Royer, 'Strategic Issues and Local Constraints in Transnational Compensation Strategies: An Analysis of Cultural, Institutional and Political Influences', *European Management Journal,* Vol. 25, No. 2 (2007), pp. 118–31.

20   This figure is informed by the work of D. Welch, 'Determinants of International Human Resource Management Approaches and Activities: A Suggested Framework', *Journal of Management Studies,* Vol. 31, No. 2 (1994), p. 150; and H. De Cieri and P.J. Dowling, 'Strategic International Human Resource Management in Multinational Enterprises: Developments and Directions, in G.K. Stahl and I. Björkman (eds), *Handbook of Research in International Human Resource Management* (Cheltenham: Edward Elgar, 2006), pp. 15–35; Y. Thompson and M. Keating, 'An Empirical Study of Executive Nationality Staffing Practices in Foreign-owned MNC Subsidiaries in Ireland', *Thunderbird International Business Review,* Vol. 46, No. 6 (2004), pp. 771–797; Festing, Eidems and Royer, 'Strategic Issues and Local Constraints in Transnational Compensation Strategies'.

21   Welch, 'HRM Implications of Globalization'.

22   M. Richards, 'US Multinational Staffing Practices and Implications for Subsidiary Performance in the UK and Thailand', *Thunderbird International Business Review,* Vol. 34, No. 2 (2001), pp. 225–42.

23   J. Shen, 'Factors Affecting International Staffing in Chinese Multinationals (MNEs)', *International Journal of Human Resource Management,* Vol. 17, No. 2 (2006), pp. 295–315.

24   PriceWaterhouseCoopers (eds), *International Assignments: Global Policy and Practice Key Trends 2005* (London: PriceWaterhouseCoopers, 2005).

25   Important destinations include China in the first place, however, closely followed by Central and Eastern Europe, especially from the perspective of European companies, and the Indian subcontinent. See PriceWaterhouseCoopers, *International Assignments.*

26   GMAC Global Relocation Services in conjunction with US National Foreign Trade Council Inc. and SHRM Global Forum, *Global Relocation Trends: 2005 Survey Report* (Woodbridge, IL: GMAC, 2005).

27   GMAC Global Relocation Services in conjunction with US National Foreign Trade Council Inc. and SHRM Global Forum, *Global Relocation Trends: 2003/2004 Survey Report* (Woodbridge, IL: GMAC, 2004).

28   PriceWaterhouseCoopers, *International Assignments.*

29   K. Blassingame, '"C" Change Recommended for Expat. Management', *Employee Benefit News,* Vol. 15, No. 10 (2001), p. 12.

30   GMAC Global Relocation Services in conjunction with US National Foreign Trade Council Inc. and SHRM Global Forum, *Global Relocation Trends: 2002 Survey Report* (Woodbridge, IL: GMAC, 2002).

31   May M.L. Wong, 'Internationalising Japanese Expatriate Managers', *Management Learning,* Vol. 32, No. 2 (2001), pp. 237–51.

32   PriceWaterhouseCoopers (eds), *Managing Mobility Matters 2006* (London: PriceWaterhouse-Coopers, 2006).

33   Based on a literature review on German IHRM studies Harzing concludes that all key reasons for international assignments can lead to organization development 'defined as the increase of the company's potential to succeed and to compete in the international market' (Harzing 2001: 368). See A.-W. Harzing, 'Of Bears, Bumble-bees, and Spiders: The Role of Expatriates in Controlling Foreign Subsidiaries', *Journal of World Business,* Vol. 36, No. 4 (2001), pp. 366–79. With respect to IHRM, Morris *et al.* distinguish between integrative and creative capabilities to meet the challenges of the global market. See S.S. Morris, A.A. Snell and P.M. Wright, A Resource-based View of International Human Resources: Toward a Framework of Integrative and Creative Capabilities', in Stahl and Björkman (eds), *Handbook of Research in International Human Resource Management,* pp. 433–48.

34   Cited in P. Sparrow, C. Brewster and H. Harris, *Globalizing Human Resource Management* (London and New York: Routledge, 2004), p. 138.

35   PriceWaterhouseCoopers (eds), *Managing a Virtual World: Key Trends 2000/2001* (London: PriceWaterhouseCoopers, 2001).

36   While the increase of this type of assignment during the last two years amounted to 11 per cent a further increase within the next two years was expected by 18 per cent of the investigated companies. See PriceWaterhouseCoopers, *Managing a Virtual World: Key Trends 2000/2001.*

37   A. Mendez, 'The Coordination of Globalised R&D Activities through Project Teams Organization: An Exploratory Empirical Study', *Journal of World Business,* Vol. 38, No. 2 (2003), pp. 96–109.

38   PriceWaterhouseCoopers (eds), *Managing a Virtual World: International Non-standard Assignments, Policy and Practice* (London: PriceWaterhouseCoopers, 2000).

39   *Ibid.,* p. 11.

40   D.E. Welch and L.S. Welch, 'Linking Operation Mode Diversity and IHRM', *International Journal of Human Resource Management,* Vol. 5, No. 4 (1994), pp. 911–26; and M. Tahvanainen, D. Welch and V. Worm, 'Implications of Short-term International Assignments', *European Management Journal,* Vol. 23, No. 6 (2005), pp. 663–73.

41   D.E. Welch, V. Worm and M. Fenwick, 'Are Virtual Assignments Feasible?', *Management International Review,* Vol. 43, Special Issue No. 1 (2003), p. 98.

42   For a literature review and discussion on the use of staff transfers as a control mechanism, see D. Welch, M. Fenwick and H. De Cieri, 'Staff Transfers as a Control Strategy: An Exploratory Study of Two Australian Organizations', *International Journal of Human Resource Management,* Vol. 5, No. 2 (1994), pp. 473–89.

43   A.-W. Harzing, 'Of Bears, Bumble-bees, and Spiders'.

44   M.S. Fenwick, H.L. De Cieri and D.E. Welch, 'Cultural and Bureaucratic Control in MNEs: The Role of Expatriate Performance Management', *Management International Review,* Vol. 39 (1999), pp. 107–24.

45   K. Goodall and J. Roberts, 'Only Connect: Teamwork in the Multinational', *Journal of World Business,* Vol. 38, No. 2 (2003), pp. 150–64.

46   S.S. Morris, A.A. Snell and P.M. Wright, 'A Resource-based View of International Human Resources: Toward a Framework of Integrative and Creative Capabilities', in Stahl and Björkman (eds), *Handbook of Research in International Human Resource Management,* pp. 433–48.

47   D.M. Schweiger, T. Atamer and R. Calori, 'Transnational Project Teams and Networks: Making the Multinational more Effective', *Journal of World Business,* Vol. 38 (2003), pp. 127–40.

48   R. Marschan, D. Welch and L. Welch, 'Control in Less-hierarchical Multinationals: The Role of Personal Networks and Information Communication', *International Business Review,* Vol. 5, No. 2 (1996), pp. 137–150.

49   J. Birkinshaw and N. Hood, 'Unleash Innovation in Foreign Subsidiaries', *Harvard Business Review,* March (2001), pp. 131–7.

50   K.Y. Au and J. Fukuda, 'Boundary Spanning Behaviors of Expatriates', *Journal of World Business,* Vol. 37 (2002), pp. 285–96.

51   R. Marschan-Piekkari, D. Welch and L. Welch, 'Adopting a Common Corporate Language: IHRM Implications', *International Journal of Human Resource Management,* Vol. 10, No. 3 (1999), pp. 377–90.

52   Goodall and Roberts, 'Only Connect', p. 159.

53   M.C. Bolino and D.C. Feldman, 'Increasing the Skill Utilization of Expatriates', *Human Resource Management,* Vol. 39, No. 4 (2000), pp. 367–79.

54   D.E. Welch, L.S. Welch and V. Worm, 'The International Business Traveller: A Neglected but Strategic Human Resource', *International Journal of Human Resource Management,* Vol. 18, No. 2 (2007), pp. 173–83.

55   H. Mayerhofer, L.C. Hartmann, G. Michelitsch-Riedl and I. Kollinger, 'Flexpatriate Assignments: A Neglected Issue in Global Staffing', *International Journal of Human Resource Management,* Vol. 15, No. 8 (2004), pp. 1371–89.

56   American Express, 'International Travellers Optimistic About Travel for 2003', 9 October 2002 press release. Website accessed 19 May 2003.

57   H. Mintzberg, D. Dougherty, J. Jorgensen and F. Westley, 'Some Surprising Things About Collaboration: Knowing How People Connect Makes it Work Better', *Organizational Dynamics,* Vol. 25, No. 1 (1996), p. 62.

58   L.S. Welch, G.R.G. Benito, P.R. Silseth and T. Karlsen, 'Exploring Inward-outward Linkages in Firms' Internationalization: A Knowledge and Network Perspective', in S. Lundan (ed.), *Network Knowledge in International Business* (Cheltenham: Edward Elgar, 2002), pp. 216–31.

59   R.S. DeFrank, R. Konopaske and J.M. Ivancevich, 'Executive Travel Stress: Perils of the Road Warrior', *Academy of Management Executive,* Vol. 14, No. 2 (2000), pp. 58–71.

60   B.S. Reiche, 'The Inpatriate Experience in Multinational Corporations: An Exploratory Case Study in Germany', *International Journal of Human Resource Management,* Vol. 19, No. 9 (2006), p. 1580.

61 D. Collings and H. Scullion, 'Global Staffing', in Stahl and Björkman (eds), *Handbook of Research in International Human Resource Management*, pp. 141–57.

62 Similar ideas can be found in M.G. Harvey, C. Speier and M.M. Novicevic, 'The Role of Inpatriation in Global Staffing', *International Journal of Human Resource Management*, Vol. 10, No. 3 (2001), pp. 459–76.

63 M.G. Harvey, M.M. Novicevic and C. Speier, 'Strategic Global Human Resource Management: The Role of Inpatriate Managers', *Human Resource Management Review*, Vol. 10, No. 2 (2000), pp. 153–75.

64 Careers and repatriation, published in German language as: G. Heismann, 'Einmal Karriere und zurück', Lufthansa Exclusive, 7 (2006), pp. 80–5.

65 Open sky – essentials and limits of management development in a global corporate culture, published in German language as: M. Festing and B. Müller, 'Open Sky – Möglichkeiten und Grenzen der Personalentwicklung in einer globalen Unternehmenskultur', in W. Auer-Rizzi, S. Blazejewski, W. Dorow and G. Reber (eds), *Unternehmenskulturen in globaler Interaktion.* Analysen, Erfahrungen, Lösungsansätze (Wiesbaden: Gabler, 2007), pp. 327–43.

66 M.G. Harvey and M.R. Buckley, 'Managing Inpatriates: Building a Global Core Competency', *Journal of World Business*, Vol. 32, No. 1 (1997), pp. 35–52.

67 S. Perkins, *International Reward and Recognition*, Research Report (London: CIPD, 2006).

68 For example, the GMAC 2005 report has revealed that 65 per cent of the investigated companies make efforts to reduce international assignment expenses. See GMAC Global Relocation Services in conjunction with US National Foreign Trade Council Inc. and SHRM Global Forum, *Global Relocation Trends: 2005 Survey Report*.

69 For a critical discussion on expatriate failure rates see A.-W. Harzing and C. Christensen, 'Expatriate Failure: Time to Abandon the Concept?', *Career Development International*, Vol. 9, No. 7 (2004), pp. 616–26.

70 D.G. Collings and H. Scullion, 'Strategic Motivations for International Transfers: Why Do MNCs Use Expatriates?', in H. Scullion and D.G. Collings (eds), *Global Staffing* (London and New York: Routledge, 2006), pp. 39–56.

71 This discussion can be placed in the broader context of 'HR affordability', which is reflected in an increased interest in metrics. See C. Brewster, P. Sparrow and H. Harris, 'Towards a New Model of Globalizing HRM', *International Journal of Human Resource Management*, Vol. 16 (2005), pp. 949–70.

72 Scullion and Collings (eds), *Global Staffing*.

73 Y.M. McNulty and P. Tharenou, 'Expatriate Return on Investment', *International Studies of Management and Organization*, Vol. 34, No. 3 (2004), pp. 68–95 (quoting from p. 88). A similar definition can be found in L. Johnson, 'Measuring International Assignment Return on Investment', *Compensation Benefits Review*, Vol. 37, No. 2 (2005), p. 53.

74 For a transaction cost theoretical analysis of staffing decisions see G.R.G Benito, S. Tomassen, J. Bonache-Perez and J. Pla-Barber, 'A Transaction Cost Analysis of Staffing Decisions in International Operations', *Scandinavian Journal of Management*, Vol. 21 (2005), pp. 101–26. For an agency theory-based analysis see Y. Gong, 'Subsidiary Staffing in Multinational Enterprises: Agency, Resources, and Performance', *Academy of Management Journal*, Vol. 45, No. 6 (2003), pp. 728–39. For the use of economic theories in international human resource management see M. Festing, 'International Human Resource Management and Economic Theories of the Firm', in Stahl and Björkman (eds), *Handbook of Research in International Human Resource Management*, pp. 449–62.

75 See, for example J.S. Osland, A. Bird, M. Mendenhall and A. Osland, 'Developing Global Leadership Capabilities and Global Mindset: A Review', in Stahl and Björkman (eds), *Handbook of Research in International Human Resource Management*, pp. 197–222; P. Caligiuri, 'Developing Global Leaders', *Human Resource Management Review*, Vol. 16, No. 2 (2006), pp. 219–28; M. Mendenhall, T.M. Kühlmann and G.K. Stahl (eds), *Developing Global Business Leaders* (Westport, CT: Greenwood Publishing Group, 2000).

76 McNulty and Tharenou, 'Expatriate Return on Investment'.

77 *Ibid.*, p. 89.

78 L. Johnson, 'Measuring International Assignment Return on Investment', *Compensation Benefits Review*, Vol. 37, No. 2 (2005), pp. 50–4. A similar result is reported in the Mercer International Assignments Survey 2005/2006.

79 GMAC Global Relocation Services in conjunction with US National Foreign Trade Council Inc. and SHRM Global Forum, *GMAC Global Relocation Trends: 2005 Survey Report*.

80 *Ibid.*, p. 16.

81 PriceWaterhouseCoopers (eds), *Measuring the Value of International Assignments*.

82 G.K. Stahl and J.-L. Cerdin, Global Careers in French and German Multinational Corporations',
    Journal of Management Development, Vol. 23, No. 9 (2004), p. 887.

83 Stahl and Cerdin, Global Careers in French and German Multinational Corporations',
    pp. 885–902.

84 M. Festing and B. Mueller, 'Expatriate Careers and the Psychological Contract – An Empirical
    Study on the Impact of International Human Resource Management', paper presented at the 9th
    Conference on International Human Resource Management, Tallin, Estonia 2007;
    PriceWaterhouseCoopers (eds), *Measuring the Value of International Assignments;* GMAC Global
    Relocation Services in conjunction with US National Foreign Trade Council Inc. and SHRM
    Global Forum, *GMAC Global Relocation Trends: 2005 Survey Report.*

85 For similar arguments see P.R. Sparrow, 'Globalization of HR at Functional Level: Exploring the
    Issues through International Recruitment, Selection and Assessment Processes', International
    Programs Visiting Working papers, Cornell University (2006).

86 H. Scullion and K. Starkey, 'In Search of the Changing Role of the Corporate Human Resource
    Function in the International Firm', *International Journal of Human Resource Management,*
    Vol. 11, No. 6 (2000), pp. 1061–81.

87 For a recent review see as well H. Scullion and J. Paauwe, 'Strategic HRM in Multinational
    Companies', in H. Scullion and M. Linehan (eds), *International Human Resource Management:
    A Critical Text* (Basingstoke: Palgrave Macmillan, 2005), pp. 22–46.

88 M. Novicevic and M. Harvey, 'The Changing Role of the Corporate HR Function in Global
    Organizations of the Twenty-first Century', *International Journal of Human Resource
    Management,* Vol. 12, No. 8 (2001), pp. 1251–68.

89 C. Brewster, P. Sparrow and H. Harris, 'Towards a New Model of Globalizing HRM', *International
    Journal of Human Resource Management,* Vol. 16 (2005), pp. 949–70; P.R. Sparrow,
    'Globalization of HR at Functional Level: Exploring the Issues through International Recruitment,
    Selection and Assessment Processes', International Programs Visiting Working Papers, Cornell
    University 2006.

Recruiting and selecting staff for international assignments

Chapter Objectives

The focus of this chapter is on recruitment and selection activities in an international context. We will address the following issues:

- The myth of the global manager.
- The debate surrounding expatriate failure.
- Factors moderating intent to stay or leave the international assignment.
- Selection criteria for international assignments.
- Dual career couples.
- Are female expatriates different?

Introduction

Hiring and then deploying people to positions where they can perform effectively is a goal of most organizations, whether domestic or international. *Recruitment* is defined as searching for and obtaining potential job candidates in sufficient numbers and quality so that the organization can select the most appropriate people to fill its job needs. *Selection* is the process of gathering information for the purposes of evaluating and deciding who should be employed in particular jobs. It is important to note that recruitment and selection are discrete processes and both processes need to operate effectively if the firm is effectively to manage its staffing process. For example, a firm may have an excellent selection system for evaluating candidates but if there are insufficient candidates to evaluate then this selection system is less than effective. Both processes must operate effectively for optimal staffing decisions to be made. We shall return to this point later in the chapter.

Some of the major differences between domestic and international staffing are first that many firms have predispositions with regard to who should hold key positions in headquarters and subsidiaries (i.e. ethnocentric, polycentric, regiocentric and geocentric staffing orientations) and second, the constraints imposed by host governments (e.g. immigration rules with regard to work visas and the common requirement in most countries to require evidence as to why local nationals should not be employed rather than hiring foreigners) which can severely limit the firm's ability to hire the right candidate. In addition, as Scullion and Collings[1] note, most expatriates are recruited *internally* rather than externally, so the task of persuading managers (particularly if they are primarily working in a domestic environment) to recommend and/or agree to release their best employees for international assignments remains a key issue for international HR managers.

In this chapter, we will explore the key issues surrounding international recruitment and selection, with a focus on selection criteria. Implicit in much of the discussion and research about selecting staff for international assignments is that there are common attributes shared by persons who have succeeded in operating in other cultural work environments – that is, the so-called global manager. Our discussion on this topic centers around four myths: that there is a universal approach to management; that all people can acquire appropriate behaviors; there are common characteristics shared by global managers; and there are no impediments to global staff mobility. We then consider various factors – such as expatriate failure, selection criteria, dual career couples and gender – that impact on the multinational's ability to recruit and select high calibre staff for deployment internationally. For convenience, we will use the term 'multinational' throughout this chapter, but it is important to remember that the issues pertain variously to all internationalizing companies – regardless of size, industry, stage in internationalization, nationality of origin and geographical diversity. We continue to use the term expatriate to include all three categories: PCNs (parent-country nationals), TCNs (third country nationals) and HCNs (host-country nationals) transferred into headquarters' operations, although much of the literature on expatriate selection is focused only on PCNs.

Issues in staff selection

The myth of the global manager

Multinationals depend on being able to develop a pool of international operators from which they can draw as required. Such individuals have been variously labeled 'international managers' or 'global managers'. The concept of a global manager appears to be based on the following myths or assumptions.

Myth 1: there is a universal approach to management.
The view that there is a universal approach to management persists, despite evidence from research to the contrary, and many multinationals continue to transfer home-based work practices into their foreign operations without adequate consideration as to whether this is an appropriate action. The persistence of a belief in universal management may be evidence of a lingering ethnocentric attitude or perhaps an indicator of inexperience in international operations. However, as we discussed in Chapter 1 in relation to the convergence–divergence debate, work practices have, to a certain extent, converged through the transfer of technology and 'best practice' and this process is supported by the global spread of management education programs that reflect the dominant Western approach to management. Linked to this process is the belief in the power of organizational culture as a moderator of cultural differences in the work setting.

Myth 2: people can acquire multicultural adaptability and behaviors. Some people can adopt culturally appropriate behaviors but that does not apply all the time in all cultural settings.[2] It depends, as we will examine later, on the individual's reaction to a particular cultural environment, as it is not always easy to put into practice what you know is the right way to behave and some individuals have much better effectiveness and coping skills than others.[3] Effectiveness skills are defined as the ability to successfully translate the managerial or technical skills into the foreign environment, whereas coping skills enable the person to become reasonably comfortable, or at least survive, in a foreign environment. Those who are able to function adequately in other cultural settings may be regarded as having good effectiveness and coping skills. As we examine later in this chapter, cultural adjustment has been linked to expatriate performance and influences how international assignments are perceived.

Myth 3: there are common characteristics shared by successful international managers. The body of literature on expatriate selection tends to reflect this approach, as we will explore in the next section of this chapter. It is possible to identify predictors of success, in that a person who has certain characteristics, traits and experience is more likely to perform effectively in foreign environments than a person who does not share this profile. However, this has to be countered by other factors involved – not just in the selection process, but also in the way the person responds to the foreign location. It is also unclear how the identified predictors of success should be measured.

Myth 4: there are no impediments to mobility. We have mentioned that particularly large multinationals are endeavoring to develop and exploit an internal labor market from which expatriates – international managers – can be drawn. As Forster[4] points out, firms may have become more global in their operations but their people have not. The barriers to furthering a geocentric staffing policy – staff availability, time and cost constraints and host-government requirements – reveal how the multinational's ability to deploy what may be the best person into a particular position can be curtailed. That some multinationals are experimenting with alternatives such as the virtual assignment is indicative of this constraint.

Compounding the above myths is the way in which the term 'global manager' is sometimes used to describe a person who has a global 'mindset', though often international experience is a prerequisite for building the global perspective required. Baruch[5] argues that there is no consistent way to characterize a global manager. He suggests that the basic qualities commonly listed – intelligence, motivation, adaptability and entrepreneurship – are the same requirements for any successful manager today.

Profile of an expatriate

Table 5-1 shows the current profile of an expatriate, drawn from results of a 2005 GMAC GRS worldwide survey of 125 multinationals representing both small and large organizations. For 46 per cent of respondents, the company headquarters was located outside of the USA (a record high response from non-US firms). As the results show, while the largest group of expatriates are PCNs, this group is not the majority and the HCN and TCN groups are significant. Most expatriates are male (77 per cent), aged 30–49 (66 per cent), married (61 per cent) and accompanied by

Table 5-1	Current expatriate profile

Expatriate category	PCN	(44%)	HCN TCN	(29%) (27%)
Gender	Male	(77%)	Female	(23%)
Age	30–49	(66%)	20–29	(16%)
Marital status	Married	(61%)	Single	(28%)
			Partner	(11%)
Accompanied by	Spouse	(81%)	Children	(52%)
Duration	1–3 years	(53%)	Short term	(27%)
			Permanent	(20%)
Primary reason	Fill a position			
Prior international experience	12%			

Source: Adapted from 'Global Relocation Trends: 2005 Survey Report', GMAC Global Relocation Services, National Foreign Trade Council and SHRM Global Forum (2006), GMAC GRS.

a spouse (81 per cent) and children (52 per cent). While the majority of assignments are 1–3 years (53 per cent), a total of 27 per cent of assignments are classified as short term (i.e. less than one year). The primary reason for the assignment is to fill a position and, interestingly, only 12 per cent of assignees had prior international experience.

Given the important roles commonly assigned to expatriates, it is logical to assume that MNEs take great care in their selection process. What is evident from the now considerable literature on the topic is that the selection of expatriates is complex. Indeed, predicting future performance potential when hiring or promoting staff is challenging at the best of times, but operating in foreign environments certainly adds another level of uncertainty. For this reason, before we take a critical look at criteria for expatriate selection, we should consider the current debate surrounding expatriate non-performance.

Expatriate failure

There are three questions related to failure: its definition, the magnitude of the phenomenon and the costs associated with failure. We shall treat these separately before examining the reasons attributed to expatriate failure and the link to selection criteria.

What do we mean by expatriate failure?

The term expatriate failure has been defined as the premature return of an expatriate (that is, a return home before the period of assignment is completed). In such a case, an expatriate failure represents a selection error, often compounded by ineffective expatriate management policies. There has been some discussion in the literature about the usefulness of defining expatriate failure so narrowly. An expatriate may be ineffective and poorly adjusted yet, if not recalled, the person will not be considered a failure. Because of an inability either to effectively handle the new responsibilities or to adjust to the country of assignment, performance levels may be diminished. These results will not be immediately apparent but can have long-term negative consequences in terms of subsidiary performance. However, if the expatriate remains for the duration of the assignment, to all intents and purposes, the assignment will have been considered a success.

Thus, the premature return rate is not a perfect measure of success or failure, and may underestimate the problem. For example, in his study of 36 British-based firms, Forster[6] used the broadest definition of failure (that is, including under-performance and retention upon completion of the assignment). Forster found that a high proportion of staff do struggle to cope with their overseas assignments, concluding:

> If we accept that a broader definition of EFRs [expatriate failure rates] is warranted, then it can be argued that the actual figure of those who are 'failing' on IAs [international assignments] could be somewhere between 8 per cent and 28 per cent of UK expatriates and their partners.

Support for broadening the definition of expatriate failure comes from a 1997/98 Price Waterhouse[7] study of international assignment policy and practice among European multinationals (including US subsidiaries). Unlike previous surveys of this kind, the study added 'under-performance' to its definition of assignment failure, and found:

> The rates for employees currently under-performing on assignment as a result of difficulties in adapting to their cultural surroundings are even higher. 29% of companies report a rate in excess of one in twenty, with 7% reporting a rate over one in ten.

What is the magnitude of the phenomenon we call expatriate failure?

Tung's[8] highly cited 1981 article could be said to have started the discussion about expatriate failure and, more particularly, the inability of US nationals to handle an international assignment. Her results suggested that expatriate failure was of more concern to US firms: 24 per cent of the US firms in her sample (n = 80) had recall rates below 10 per cent; compared to 59 per cent of the West European (n = 29) and 76 per cent of the Japanese firms (n = 35) reporting recall rates of less than 5 per cent. Later studies appear to confirm Tung's European results[9] in terms of expatriate failure. However, many studies that explore expatriate failure and expatriate adjustment persist in quoting high US rates of failure, variously reporting it as falling between 30 to 50 per cent and even higher.

Harzing[10] has questioned the reported failure rates in the US literature, claiming there is 'almost no empirical foundation for the existence of high failure rates when measured as premature re-entry'. More recently, Christensen and Harzing have questioned the value of the whole concept of expatriate failure, arguing that 'it might well be time to abandon the concept of expatriate failure altogether and instead draw on the general HR literature to analyze problems related to turnover and performance management in an expatriate context'.[11]

When we delve further into this issue to establish how large the problem actually is, one finds a suggestion of a declining rate. Evidence can be gained from two global surveys, conducted in 2002 and 2005. The first was a survey of 300 multinationals (46 per cent North American, 28 per cent European, and 9 per cent UK) from a wide range of industries by US-based consulting firm, ORC Worldwide.[12] They report that almost 56 per cent of respondents did not know the return rate of their expatriates. Those who keep records indicated, on average, that less than

10 per cent of their international assignments ended in early recall. The second survey by GMAC Global Relocation Services, LLC (GMAC GRS) mentioned earlier asked responding firms to indicate their attrition rate – that is, expatriate turnover, including early recall from an international assignment, and upon completion of the assignment. Again, we find that some firms (36 per cent) could not answer, as they did not have the figures. Those that did have the information indicated that 21 per cent left the firm during an assignment and 23 per cent within one year of returning from an assignment. It would have been useful to find out why so many of the responding firms in these two surveys did not keep records on assignment failures. Perhaps this is because it is not seen as an important issue?

Respondents in the ORC Worldwide survey were also asked to define a failed assignment. Seventy-two per cent defined it as 'early return of the expatriate'. The other definitions were: 'unmet business objectives' (71 per cent); 'problems at assignment location' (49 per cent); and 'unmet career development objectives' (32 per cent). It would appear multinationals are recognizing that there are many aspects to a failed assignment, though it is not clear from the report if responding firms were separating out under-performance from early recall. Unmet business objectives, problems at assignment location and unmet career development may be reasons for early recall rather than a definition.

From the above discussion, though, we can draw a number of conclusions:

1 Broadening the definition of expatriate failure beyond that of premature return is warranted. Following up broad surveys with interviews with responding firms may assist in this.

2 Regardless of the definition or precise amount of 'failure', its very exposure as a problem has broadened the issue to demonstrate the complexity of international assignments. In fact, one could argue that the so-called persistent myth of high US expatriate failure rates has been a positive element in terms of the attention that has subsequently been directed towards expatriation practices. It has certainly provoked considerable research attention into the causes of expatriate failure.

3 The evidence about expatriate failure rates is somewhat inconclusive. Recent studies suggest that high failure rates reported in the 1980s have not persisted for US nationals. Though recent reports do not break results down into nationality groups, US firms form the largest group in these surveys. The European studies reported above were conducted at various intervals since Tung's original study, and do not include the same countries. Further, non-US researchers have been reporting from regional or single country perspectives (see for example, Björkman and Gertsen[13] who found expatriate failure rates of less than 5 per cent for Nordic firms; Dowling and Welch[14] reported similar results for Australian firms).

4 The above studies tend not to differentiate between types of expatriate assignments, the level of 'international' maturity,[15] or firm size – factors that may influence failure in its broadest sense.

5 It may be that companies operating internationally have since become more aware of the problems associated with expatriate failure and have learned how to avoid them. That is, multinationals have become more sophisticated in their approach to IHRM activities. Benchmarking against other firms may have assisted in the development of an awareness of international assignment issues.

What are the costs of failure?   These can be both *direct* and *indirect*. Direct costs include airfares and associated relocation expenses, and salary and training. The precise amount varies according to the level of the position concerned, country of destination, exchange rates and whether the 'failed' manager is replaced by another expatriate.

The 'invisible' or indirect costs are harder to quantify in money terms but can prove to be more expensive for the company. Many expatriate positions involve contact with host-government officials and key clients. Failure at this level may result in loss of market share, difficulties with host-government officials and demands that expatriates be replaced with HCNs (thus affecting the multinational's general staffing approach). The possible effect on local staff is also an indirect cost factor, since morale and productivity could suffer.[16]

Failure also, of course, has an effect on the expatriate concerned, who may lose self-esteem, self-confidence and prestige among peers.[17] Future performance may be marked by decreased motivation, lack of promotional opportunities, or even increased productivity to compensate for the failure. Finally, the expatriate's family relationships may be threatened. These are additional costs to organizations that are often overlooked.

Factors moderating performance

Naturally, the debate about the degree to which expatriate failure occurs has been accompanied by investigation and speculation about why failure occurs. Expatriates tend to have a higher profile, so reducing the rate of incidence is of some strategic importance as multinationals continue to rely on expatriates and therefore wish to encourage mobility. Consequently, there has been considerable research that has attempted to identify factors that may moderate performance and affect the decision to stay or leave the international assignment. The primary intention has been to link reasons for early recall to predictors of success and thereby generate selection criteria that may assist multinationals in their staffing decisions. While the focus has predominately been on cross-cultural adjustment, other factors have been identified, as shown in Figure 5-1. We will base our examination of the issue around this figure.

Inability to adjust to the foreign culture

This factor has been a consistent reason given for expatriate failure – and has been the subject of considerable interest to researchers. Again, we must acknowledge the pioneering contribution of Tung's[18] study in providing the impetus for this interest. She found national differences in the responses between the US and Japanese firms. Asked to rank reasons for failure in descending order of importance, US firms ranked 'inability of the spouse to adjust' as the most important, whereas this was ranked fifth for the Japanese firms. For the European firms, 'inability of the spouse to adjust' was the only consistent response provided.

Tung[19] noted that the relatively lower ranking of 'inability of spouse to adjust' by Japanese respondents is not surprising, given the role and status to which Japanese society relegates the spouse. However, other social factors may contribute to this finding. Because of the extremely competitive nature of the

Figure 5-1	International assignments: factors moderating performance

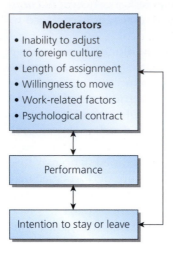

Japanese education system, the spouse commonly opts to remain in Japan with the children, particularly where male offspring are concerned. The Japanese word for these unaccompanied male expatriates is *tanshin funin* or bachelors-in-exile.[20] Thus, in many cases, the spouse is not a factor in expatriate failure. Unlike the debate around the magnitude of the problem, research over the past 20 years has shown a consistent ranking of 'inability of the spouse/partner/family' as a primary cause of early recall. The GMAC GRS 2005 global survey mentioned above reported the following reasons for early return (in rank order):

1 family concerns
2 accepted new position in the company
3 completed assignment early
4 cultural adjustment challenges
5 security concerns
6 career concerns.

The persistence of family concerns as a reason for early return over several decades since Tung's findings were published, despite company programs to try to alleviate the problem, indicate how difficult an international assignment can be for some. It certainly explains why so much attention has been given to expatriate adjustment and confirms the importance of the selection process.

While there is limited evidence (at least readily accessible and in English) regarding expatriate experiences from other Asian countries, accounts indicate that expatriates from these countries may face similar adjustment problems. For example, Selmer *et al.*[21] report that spouses and children of Chinese expatriates in Hong Kong were normally not permitted to accompany the expatriates. While adjustment was not the focus of this study, the authors found that most of the respondents would have liked to have had their family with them, and conclude that the precarious situation of the families was not conducive to the pursuit of an international career.

The process of adjustment

The dilemma is that adjustment to a foreign culture is multifaceted, and individuals vary in terms of their reaction and coping behaviors. The concept of an adjustment cycle or curve, depicted in Figure 5-2, is helpful in demonstrating the typical phases that may be encountered during cultural adjustment. The curve (sometimes referred to as the U-Curve,) is based on psychological reactions to the assignment and comprises certain phases.[22]

Phase 1 commences with reactions prior to the assignment – the expatriate may experience a range of positive and negative emotions such as excitement, anxiety, fear of the unknown, or a sense of adventure. There can be an upswing of mood upon arrival in the assignment country that produces what has been referred to as the 'honeymoon' or 'tourist' phase. Then, as the novelty wears off, realities of everyday life in the foreign location begin to intrude, homesickness sets in, and a downswing may commence – a feeling that 'the party is over'[23] – which can create negative appraisals of the situation and the location leading to a period of crisis – *Phase 2*. This can be a critical time, and how the individual copes with the psychological adjustment at this phase has an important outcome in terms of success or failure. There is a suggestion that 'failure as an early recall' may be triggered at this point (indicated by the dotted arrow in Figure 5-2). Once past this crisis point, as the expatriate comes to terms with the demands of the new environment, there is a pulling up – *Phase 3* – as the person begins to adjust to the new environment. This levels off over time to what has been described as healthy recovery – *Phase 4*.

However, when considering the above U-Curve, one should remember the following points:

● The U-Curve is not normative. Some people do not experience this U-Curve. Individuals will differ in their reactions to the foreign location.

● The time period involved varies, and there is no conclusive statistical support for the various phases. Black and Mendenhall[24] point out that the U-Curve describes these phases but does not explain how and why people move through the various phases.

● There may be other critical points during the assignment – beyond Phase 4 – that may produce downturns, negative reactions and upswings (that is, a cyclical wave rather than a U-Curve).

The phases of cultural adjustment   **Figure 5-2**

Source: Adapted from H. De Cieri, P.J. Dowling and K.F. Taylor, 'The Psychological Impact of Expatriate Relocation on Partners', *International Journal of Human Resource Management,* Vol. 2, No. 3 (1991) p. 380.

Despite these limitations, however, expatriates often relate experiencing these phases, and awareness of the psychological adjustment process can assist the expatriate adopt positive coping behaviors. We should also note that family members experience the phases differently, and not necessarily move through the various phases at the same time as each other. How accompanying family members handle cultural adjustment is important, as there can be a spill-over effect – an unhappy spouse may affect the expatriate's ability to adjust, and thus impact on performance. For example, in their study of US managers in Japan, Korea, Taiwan and Hong Kong, Black and Stephens[25] found a high correlation between spouse and expatriate adjustment. Companies can assist in the cultural adjustment of the expatriate and employee by using volunteer employees who have worked abroad as expatriates to 'adopt' a visiting family and assist in their adjustment.

Length of assignment

There is some evidence that length of assignment does contribute to adjustment and performance. For example, the average assignment for Japanese firms tends to be four to five years, compared with the figure shown in Table 5.1 of 1–3 years for 53 per cent of the sample of the GMAC GRS 2005 survey. A longer assignment allows the expatriate more time to adjust to the foreign situation and become productive.[26] Japanese firms often do not expect the expatriate to perform up to full capacity until the third year; the first year of the foreign assignment is seen mainly as a period of adjustment to the foreign environment.

Willingness to move

In a situation where an employee is a reluctant expatriate or accompanied by reluctant family members, it is more likely that they may interpret negatively events and situations encountered in the new environment. In their survey of 405 US managers and their spouse/partners, Brett and Stroh[27] found a significant causal relationship between the manager and the spouse's willingness to move. They conclude that managers who are most ready for international relocations are those whose spouses are also supportive of that move – a not surprising finding. Other studies support the importance of a positive outlook. For example, Hamill[28] reported that the reasons for lower British expatriate failure rates were that British managers were more internationally mobile than US managers, and that perhaps British companies had developed more effective expatriate policies. Dowling and Welch[29] note that the respondents in their research perceived an expatriate posting as a desirable appointment – an opportunity to travel and live overseas – leading to a positive outlook on the foreign assignment. Willingness to relocate as a predictor of success should include the views of family members and is also associated with the perceived desirability of the location of the international assignment.

Work environment-related factors

Gregersen and Black[30] studied 220 American expatriates in four Pacific Rim countries. They found a positive correlation between what they term 'intent to stay in the overseas assignment' and the PCN's commitment to the local company, adjustment to interaction with HCNs, and adjustment to general living conditions. Adjustment to the work role itself however, was negatively associated with 'intent to stay'. Support for these factors as moderators has come from a study by Shaffer *et al.*[31] of expatriates working in ten US multinationals. However, Bolino and Feldman[32] extended this to include skills utilization and commitment to the organization. Their study of 268 expatriates from six Fortune 500 companies found that effective skill utilization was significantly related to job satisfaction, organization commitment and intent to finish the international assignment.

Job autonomy is also a powerful factor influencing expatriate turnover.[33] Another moderator is the perceived level of organizational support – from home as well as from the host unit.[34] Further, once the expatriate has mastered, or nearly completed, the assigned work, other factors may surface and assume relative importance. For instance, if the work becomes less demanding and no longer so time-consuming, the expatriate may have time to pay more attention to negative cross-cultural experiences that the family is encountering. These negative experiences can become distorted when combined with lack of challenge at work and thus sow seeds for early recall, or under-performance.

Selection criteria

We now have a fuller understanding of the phenomenon called expatriate failure, and the multifaceted nature of international assignments, and why developing appropriate selection criteria has become a critical IHRM issue. It should be noted that selection is a two-way process between the individual and the organization. A prospective candidate may reject the expatriate assignment, either for individual reasons, such as family considerations, or for situational factors, such as the perceived toughness of a particular culture.

It is a challenge for those responsible for selecting staff for international assignments to determine appropriate selection criteria. Figure 5-3 illustrates the factors involved in expatriate selection, both in terms of the individual and the specifics of the situation concerned. It should be noted that these factors are inter-related. We base the following discussion around this Figure.

Factors in expatriate selection   Figure 5-3

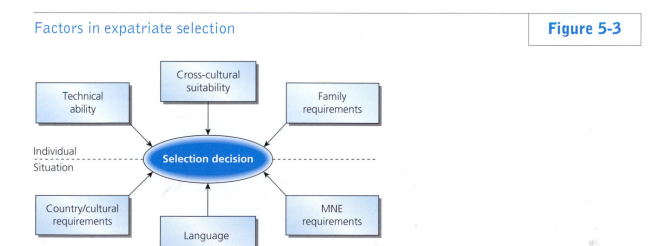

Technical ability

Naturally, the person's ability to perform the required tasks is an important consideration. Technical and managerial skills are therefore an essential criterion. Indeed, research findings consistently indicate that multinationals place heavy reliance on relevant technical skills during the expatriate selection process.[35] For example, the ORC Worldwide 2002 survey mentioned earlier found that 72 per cent of responding firms selected assignees on the basis of skills or competencies for the job. This is not surprising given that 'position filling' is the most common reason for an international assignment. Reinforcing the emphasis on technical skills is the relative ease with which the multinational may assess the candidate's potential, as technical and managerial competence can be determined on the basis of past performance. Since expatriates are predominantly internal recruits, personnel evaluation records can be examined and checked with the candidate's past and present superiors. The dilemma though is that past performance may have little or no bearing on one's ability to achieve a task in a foreign cultural environment.

Cross-cultural suitability

As we have already discussed, the cultural environment in which expatriates operate is an important factor in determining successful performance. Apart from the obvious technical ability and managerial skills, expatriates require cross-cultural abilities that enable the person to operate in a new environment. There appears to be a consensus that desirable attributes should include cultural empathy, adaptability, diplomacy, language ability, positive attitude, emotional stability and maturity.[36]

In practice, while inter-cultural competence is recognized as important, it is difficult to precisely define what this comprises, let alone assess a candidate's suitability in this regard. One has to take into consideration aspects such as the individual's personality, attitude to foreigners, ability to relate to people from another cultural group and so on. Multinationals may indicate that, for example, relational abilities are an important expatriate selection criterion, but few will assess a candidate's relational ability through a formal procedure such as judgement by senior managers or psychological tests. As we will discuss shortly, testing procedures are not necessarily the answer.

Family requirements

The contribution that the family, particularly the spouse, makes to the success of the overseas assignment is now well documented, as we mentioned above in relation to the impact of the accompanying spouse/partner on early return. Despite the importance of the accompanying spouse/partner, as Shaffer and Harrison[37] point out, the focus has been on the expatriate. From the multinational's perspective, expatriate performance in the host location is the important factor. However, the interaction between expatriate, spouse/partner and family members' various adjustment experiences is now well documented.

It should be pointed out the spouse (or accompanying partner) often carries a heavy burden. Upon arrival in the country of assignment, the responsibility for settling the family into its new home falls on the spouse, who may have left behind a career, along with friends and social support networks (particularly relatives). In developing countries the employment of house servants is quite common but this is an aspect of international living that many Westerners from developed countries have some difficulty adjusting to. It is often not possible for the spouse/partner to work in the country of assignment and the well-being and education of the children may be an ongoing concern for the spouse. Though the majority of spouses are female, accompanying male spouses/partners face similar problems of adjustment.[38] In fact, when one adds cultural adjustment problems to such a situation, it is perhaps not so surprising to find that some couples seek to return home prematurely.

Despite studies that emphasize the link between the favorable opinion of the spouse to the international assignment and expatriate adjustment, companies appear reluctant to include the spouse/partner in the selection process, treating it in a peripheral way.[39] As a survey by Price Waterhouse[40] found:

> Compared to our 1995 survey, the number of companies which routinely interview an employee's spouse or partner as part of the selection process has increased slightly, from 9% to 11%. However, overall, fewer companies involve the spouse or partner in the selection process under any circumstances, rising from half in 1995 to two-thirds currently. Of the companies which do interview the spouse or partner, 12% interview them on their own. Given that more than a third of the companies believe the assignments that either failed, or had been ended prematurely, due to a spouse or partner's difficulties with adapting to life in the host location, it is perhaps a little surprising that companies are not attributing more importance to assessing their suitability.

The 2002 ORC Worldwide survey did not address the involvement of the spouse/partner in the selection process, though reports that assistance was provided to help the accompanying person cope with the international assignment.

Apart from the accompanying partner's career, there are family considerations that can cause a potential expatriate to decline the international assignment. Disruption to children's education is an important consideration, and the selected candidate may reject the offered assignment on the grounds that a move at this particular stage in his or her child's life is inappropriate. The care of aging or invalid parents is another consideration. While these two reasons have been noted in various studies, what has been somewhat overlooked is the issue of single parents. Given increasing divorce rates, this may become a critical factor in assignment selection and acceptance where the custody of children is involved. The associated legal constraints, such as obtaining the consent of the other parent to take the child (or children) out of the home country, and visiting/access rights, may prove to be a major barrier to the international mobility of both single mothers and single fathers.

Country/cultural requirements

As discussed in Chapter 1, international firms are usually required to demonstrate that a HCN is not available before the host government will issue the necessary work permit and entry visa for the desired PCN or TCN. In some cases, the multinational may wish to use an expatriate and has selected a candidate for the international assignment, only to find the transfer blocked by the host government. Many developed countries are changing their legislation to facilitate employment-related immigration which will make international transfers somewhat easier – for example the European Union Social Charter allows for free movement of citizens of member countries within the EU. It is important that HR staff keep up-to-date with relevant legislative changes in the countries in which the MNE is involved.

Our IHRM in Action Case below shows how one US MNE's careful planning allowed it to obtain the required number of PCN visas to successfully launch its business in Australia.

An important, related point is that generally a work permit is granted to the expatriate only. The accompanying spouse or partner may not be permitted to work in the host country. Increasingly, multinationals are finding that the inability of the spouse to work in the host country may cause the selected candidate to reject the offer of an international assignment. If the international assignment is accepted, the lack of a work permit for the accompanying spouse or partner may cause difficulties in adjustment and even contribute to failure. For these reasons, as reported above, some multinationals provide assistance in this regard.

Further, the host country may be an important determinant. Some regions and countries are considered 'hardship postings': remote areas away from major cities or modern facilities; or war-torn regions with high physical risk. Accompanying family members may be an additional responsibility that the multinational does not want to bear. There may be a reluctance to select females for certain Middle East or South East Asian regions and in some countries a work permit for a female expatriate will not be issued. These aspects may result in the selection of HCNs rather than expatriates.

To overcome this problem, a group of more than 20 large multinationals (including Shell, British Airways, Unilever, PricewaterhouseCoopers and Siemens) has established an organization called 'Permits Foundation',[41] in an attempt to promote the improvement of work permit regulations for spouses of expatriates. It also aims to raise government awareness of the connection between work permits and employee mobility.

IHRM in Action Case 5-1

Citibank Plans for Changing Staffing Needs

Banks, along with oil and construction companies, remain heavy users of PCN employees, because these industries require very specific (sometimes firm-specific) skills frequently not found in foreign locations. In the mid-1980s Australia offered a once-only opportunity for foreign banks to enter the local market. Citibank already held a limited banking license that allowed it to operate in Australia as a merchant bank and finance company. A year before the licenses were to be awarded, Citibank sent one of its senior HR managers on a year-long assignment to Sydney to assess the staffing implications of an application to the Australian government for a banking license. First, an assessment was made as to how many PCN visas would be required. Then, a detailed summary was prepared for the Australian immigration department that demonstrated the history of Citibank's investment in training Australian nationals, with career examples of HCNs who were now employed by Citibank in Australia, in other foreign locations, and in the USA. This proved to be a successful strategy: Citibank received one of the 16 licenses on offer and all of the PCN work permits it requested.

MNE requirements

Situational factors often have an influence on selection decisions. For example, the MNE may consider the proportion of expatriates to local staff when making selection decisions, mainly as an outcome of its staffing philosophy. However, operations in particular countries may require the use of more PCNs and TCNs than would normally be the case, as multinationals operating in parts of Eastern Europe and China are discovering. This will affect the selection ratio – that is, PCN:TCN: HCN. Other situational factors include the following:

- *The mode of operation involved.* Selecting staff to work in an international joint venture may involve major input from the local partner, and could be heavily constrained by the negotiated agreement on selection processes.[42]

- *The duration and type of the assignment.*[43] Family members tend not to accompany an expatriate when the assignment is only for three to six months, so family requirements would not normally be a relevant factor in the selection decision in such cases.

- *The amount of knowledge transfer* inherent in the expatriate's job in the foreign operation. If the nature of the job is to train local staff, then the MNE may include training skills as a selection criterion.

Language

The ability to speak the local language is an aspect often linked with cross-cultural ability. However, we have chosen to stress language as situation-determined in terms of its importance as a factor in the selection decision. Language skills may be regarded as of critical importance for some expatriate positions, but lesser in others, though some would argue that knowledge of the host country's language is an important aspect of expatriate performance, regardless of the level of position.

Differences in language are recognized as a major barrier to effective cross-cultural communication.[44] Yet, in terms of the other selection criteria we have examined above, from the multinational's perspective, language is placed lower down the list of desirable attributes. For example, the ORC Worldwide survey results rank language ability as the fifth most important selection criteria. In the past, US multinationals have tended to place a relatively low importance on foreign language skills. For example, in a 1990 study of US multinationals, Fixman[45] found that foreign language skills were rarely considered an important part of international business success. She comments: 'Language problems were largely viewed as mechanical and manageable problems that could be solved individually'. This view is also confirmed by the consistent and relatively poor performance of young Americans on polls of geographic literacy sponsored by the National Geographic Education Foundation. In the most recent 2006 poll[46] of young American adults between the ages of 18 and 24 the following results were reported:

- 50 per cent of the sample thought it was 'important but not absolutely necessary' to know where countries in the news are located.

- 75 per cent did not know that a majority of Indonesia's population of 245 million is Muslim (making it the largest Muslim country in the world).

- 74 per cent of the sample thought that English was the most commonly spoken language in the world, rather than Mandarin Chinese.

There are signs that in a post 9/11 world, the USA is beginning to refocus on some of these issues. Recently, the Committee on Education and the Workforce of the US Congress[47] has examined the issue of international and foreign language studies and the Chair of the Committee noted that:

> Congress created Title VI in the National Defense Education Act of 1958 to address a sense of crisis caused by U.S. citizens' lack of knowledge of other countries and cultures. This program remains the federal government's leading mechanism for supporting programs that produce Americans with expertise in foreign languages and international studies, including international business . . . Continued federal support for these programs reflects the significance and growing relevance of language and area studies, diplomacy, national security, and business competitiveness.

This level of commitment is encouraging, but as we noted in Chapter 1, the task of internationalizing business education in the USA is a large one and will require considerable resources and persistence for significant progress to be made.

Another component to language as a situation factor in the selection decision is the role of the *common corporate language*. As previously discussed, many multinationals adopt a common corporate language as a way of standardizing reporting systems and procedures. This is not, perhaps, an issue for PCN selection within multinationals from the Anglo-Saxon world (Britain, the USA, Canada, Australia and New Zealand) where the chosen corporate language remains the same as that of the home country. However, it becomes an expatriate selection issue for multinationals from non-English-speaking countries that adopt English as the corporate language, unless the posting is to a country with a shared language. For instance, a Spanish multinational, using Spanish as the corporate language, selecting a PCN to head its new subsidiary in Mexico, does not face the same language issue as a Spanish multinational, with English as its corporate language, selecting a PCN to its US facility. For the latter, fluency in English would be required. Lack of fluency in the corporate language, therefore, can be a selection barrier. Prospective candidates may be eliminated from the potential pool due to a lack of at least competency in the common language.[48] Language ability therefore may limit the MNE's ability to select the most appropriate candidate.

The use of selection tests

Although there is a consensus among scholars and practitioners that personal characteristics (or traits) are important, there is considerable debate about how such personal characteristics can be reliably and accurately measured. Personality and psychological tests have been used in the selection process, but the effectiveness of such tests as predictors of cultural adjustment is questioned. For example, Torbiörn[49] comments that though desirable personality traits are specified and recommended, the tests or criteria to assess these traits are seldom convincingly validated. Likewise, Willis[50] states that if tests are used they should be selected with care and regard for reliability and validity because, while some tests may be useful in suggesting potential problems, there appears to be little correlation between test scores and performance. He further adds that most of the relevant tests have been devised in the USA and, therefore, may be culture-bound. Use of such tests without careful modification on non-American nationals adds another question mark to their reliability and validity as predictors of expatriate success. It is important that HRM staff in all locations are aware of the debate surrounding the use of selection tests, particularly the culture-bound nature of psychometric tests designed for PCNs.

Another constraint is that in some countries (the UK and Australia for instance) there is controversy about the use of psychological tests.[51] There is also a different pattern of usage across countries – the use of such tests is very low in Germany.[52] The 1997/98 Price Waterhouse survey reported only 12 per cent used formal assessment centers, and some companies 'indicated through their comments that they also use psychometric tests'. The majority of respondents (85 per cent) mainly assessed expatriate suitability through the traditional interview process. More recent surveys have not addressed this aspect of selection. The difficulty of predicting success, then, seems to be related to the lack of valid and reliable screening devices to identify, with certainty, managers who will succeed in a foreign assignment. The crucial variables affecting the adjustment of the individual and family are not only difficult to identify or measure, but the complex relationship between personality factors and ability to adjust to another culture is not well understood.[53]

Another drawback of expatriate selection based on traits or characteristics is the subjective nature of the scoring of abilities, especially those classified as personal and environmental characteristics. Nevertheless, models derived from this approach have value in that they provide some guidelines that can be applied during the selection process, rather than mere reliance on the potential manager's domestic record as a predictor.[54] One such model is that offered by Mendenhall and Oddou.[55] They propose a four-dimensional approach that attempts to link specific behavioral tendencies to probable overseas performance:

- The self-oriented dimension – the degree to which the expatriate expresses an adaptive concern for self-preservation, self-enjoyment and mental hygiene.

- The perceptual dimension – the expertise the expatriate possesses in accurately understanding why host nationals behave the way they do.

- The others-oriented dimension – the degree to which the expatriate is concerned about host-national co-workers and desire to affiliate with them.

- The cultural-toughness dimension – a mediating variable that recognizes that acculturation is affected by the degree to which the culture of the host country is incongruent with that of the home country.

The evaluation of the candidate's strengths and weaknesses on these four dimensions, Mendenhall and Oddou suggested, will focus appropriate attention on cross-cultural ability and behavior, thus complementing technical ability assessment.

Equal employment opportunity issues

In the recruitment and selection process, multinationals must address the issue of equal employment opportunity (EEO) for employees in all employment locations. This involves taking into consideration the increasingly conflicting national laws on employment. As Jain, Sloane and Horwitz[56] mention, mandatory retirement and hiring ages are illegal in some countries such as the USA and some other countries but remain a legal requirement in other countries.

Determining which law applies where, and which has precedence, is a problem without a specific solution. The USA has a comprehensive statute (Title VII of the Civil Rights Act of 1964) to cover many EEO situations. In 1991 the US Supreme Court[57] held that this Act does not apply outside the territorial borders of the USA. The case involved an American citizen who claimed that he had been illegally discriminated against while working overseas for a US corporation. A naturalized citizen born in Lebanon, the plaintiff began working for Aramco Corporation in Texas in 1979 and was transferred by the company to work in Saudi Arabia in 1980, where he worked until 1984, when he was discharged. The Court rejected the person's claim that he had been harassed and ultimately discharged by Aramco Corporation on account of his race, religion and national origin. This decision had important implications for the status and protection of Americans working abroad for US firms and the Civil Rights Act was subsequently amended by the US Congress in 1991 to extend protection to all US citizens working overseas.

Equal employment opportunity laws are expressions of social values with regard to employment and reflect the values of a society or country.[58] In parts of the Middle East, Africa, Asia and Latin America, women are perceived to have a lower social status and are not universally employed. On the other hand, with the increasing rate of female entry into the workforce, many Western countries have introduced legislation to cover sex discrimination. Multinationals must be aware of legislation and ensure subsidiary compliance where appropriate in selecting expatriates.

Expatriate selection in practice: the role of the coffee machine

As we indicated at the beginning of the section on selection criteria, most multinationals admit that technical and/or managerial skills are the dominant, sometimes only, criteria used. We have suggested that reliance on technical skills is mainly due to the fact that most international assignments are 'position filling'. Of the factors outlined in Figure 5-3 above, technical skills is perhaps the easiest to measure. It could be argued that Figure 5-3 represents a best practice or ideal selection model which many MNEs do not in fact use. Harris and Brewster[59] have argued that expatriate selection, in reality, often tends to be an ad hoc process which they describe as the 'coffee-machine' system.

Harris and Brewster suggest that executives chatting around the coffee-machine (or water cooler) can start the selection process through a casual conversation about an assignment need confronting one of them. Another executive can volunteer the name of a potential expatriate thus starting an informal short list of candidates. What happens next, according to Harris and Brewster, is that the multinational's processes are then activated to legitimize the decision that has, in effect, already been taken around the coffee machine. Harris and Brewster relate that this process was the most common form of selection process they encountered in their study of UK firms. They then derived a typology of selection systems to explain variations found in the way expatriate selection is conducted, detailed in Table 5-2.

Harris and Brewster regard the coffee-machine scenario as an example of the informal/closed cell in their typology. It is of course possible to find examples of formal, open selection processes in firms as well as informal or closed systems. Harris and Brewster note that the process can be influenced by the maturity of the multinational, its stage in the internationalization process and its size or industry. The type of position involved, the role of the HR function in the process and whether the multinational is reactive rather than proactive where international assignment selection is involved remain key factors in how selection processes work in multinationals.

| Harris and Brewster's selection typology | Table 5-2 |

	Formal	*Informal*
OPEN	• Clearly defined criteria • Clearly defined measures • Training for selectors • Open advertising of vacancy (internal/external) • Panel discussions	• Less defined criteria • Less defined measures • Limited training for selectors • No panel discussions • Open advertising of vacancy • Recommendations
CLOSED	• Clearly defined criteria • Clearly defined measures • Training for selectors • Panel discussions • Nominations only (networking/reputation)	• Selectors' individual preferences determine selection criteria and measures • No panel discussions • Nominations only (networking/reputation)

Source: H. Harris and C. Brewster, 'The Coffee-Machine System: How International Selection Really Works', *International Journal of Human Resource Management,* Vol. 10, No. 3 (1999), p. 493. Reproduced with permission.

Dual career couples

So far, we have focused on selecting suitable candidates for international assignments. We will now consider an emerging constraint – the dual career couple – on the available pool of candidates, thus hindering the recruitment and selection process. The rise in dual career couples, along with the aging population and other family-related situations, combine to make more people immobile. Employees are prepared to state the grounds for refusal as 'family concerns'. That this has become more acceptable as a reason reflects a significant shift in thinking about the role of non-work aspects impinging on work-related matters.

The increase in the number of dual-career couples is a worldwide trend, one that is posing a dilemma for both companies and employees alike. This is not surprising given that accepting a traditional international assignment will impact upon the career of the potential candidate's spouse or partner. The ORC Worldwide 2002 survey focused on the issue of dual careers and international assignments. A major finding was that spousal or dual career issues were the most common reasons for rejecting international assignments reported by North American and European firms, but were rarely cited by Asian firms. Rather, concern for children and ageing parents were barriers to assignment acceptance for this group. Likewise, the GMAC GRS 2005 survey cites spouse career concerns as the third most frequent reason for assignment refusal.

Multinationals are being forced to select from a diminishing pool of candidates who may be less qualified. This has strategic implications for staffing policies, and may be a reason why more TCNs are being utilized. As we noted when discussing the expatriate profile in Table 5-1, 27 per cent of expatriates were TCNs in the 2005 GMAC GRS survey. While cost containment remains a major driver of localization (that is, replacing expatriates with HCNs), staff availability is also a factor.[60] Reflecting this global trend, the impact of the accompanying spouse/partner's career orientation upon the international assignment is an emerging area of research. It seems that career orientation not only affects the couple's willingness to move, but also may negatively affect performance and retention in the foreign location.[61] Some multinationals are endeavoring to come up with solutions to the dual-career challenge. These can be divided into two categories: finding alternative arrangements and making the assignments more 'family-friendly'.

Alternative assignment arrangements

There are a number of alternative assignment arrangements that can be identified in international staffing:

Short-term assignments.   In the ORC Worldwide 2002 survey, 72 per cent of responding firms used short-term assignments (compared with 26 per cent in a 1996 ORC survey) as an alternative means of satisfying the international assignment need.

Commuter assignments (sometimes referred to as 'commuter marriages').   The spouse may decide to remain in the home country, and the couple works out ways to maintain the relationship with the help of the firm. Alternatively, couples may move to jobs in adjoining countries, or within the same geographical region to make commuting (relationship-maintenance) easier. Multinationals often adjust compensation benefits to fit with agreed arrangements. The ORC survey found that 46 per cent of responding firms had such arrangements (compared with 19 per cent in 1996).

Other arrangements.   Other arrangements included in the ORC 2002 report findings were:

- Unaccompanied assignments   50 %
- Replacing assignments with business travel   57 %
- Virtual assignments   16 %.

Only 23 per cent of respondents in a similar study by ORC Worldwide in 1995 reported the use of unaccompanied assignments.

There has been little attention given to the advantages and disadvantages of these non-standard assignments in terms of the individual employees, their spouses and the strategic objectives that prompt the use of international rather than local staff. While these arrangements may have short-term benefits in overcoming reluctance to move, how effective they will be in encouraging dual career couples to accept international assignments over time is yet to be determined.

Family-friendly policies

Inter-company networking.   Here the multinational attempts to place the accompanying spouse or partner in a suitable job with another multinational – sometimes in a reciprocal arrangement. To illustrate: a US multinational may enter into an agreement with a German multinational also operating in, say, China, that they find a position within their respective Chinese facilities for each other's accompanying partner (that is, 'you find my expatriate's spouse a job and work visa, and I will do likewise for you'). Alternatively, a local supplier, distributor, or joint venture partner may agree to employ the accompanying spouse/partner.

Job-hunting assistance.   Here the multinational provides spouse/partner assistance with the employment search in the host country. This may be through employment agency fees, career counselling, or simply work permit assistance. Some may provide a fact-finding trip to the host location before the actual assignment. The 2005 GMAC GRS survey reports that 31 per cent of responding firms assisted in finding the accompanying spouse/partner employment by funding job-finding and executive search fees.

Intra-company employment.   This is perhaps a logical but often a somewhat difficult solution. It means sending the couple to the same foreign facility, perhaps the same department. Not all multinationals (or all couples) are comfortable with the idea of having a husband and wife team in the same work location and there can often be difficulties obtaining work visas for such arrangements.

On-assignment career support.   Motorola[62] is an example of how a multinational may assist spouses to maintain and even improve career skills through what Motorola calls its Dual-Career Policy. This consists of a lump-sum payment for education expenses, professional association fees, seminar attendance, language training to upgrade work-related skills and employment agency fees. There are conditions attached, such as the spouse must have been employed before the assignment. Thus, if the spouse is unable to find suitable employment, the time can be spent on career development activities.

Other examples of on-assignment assistance are providing help in establishing contacts and paying for lost spouse income. The idea is to maintain skills so that the spouse may find work upon re-entry into the home country. These attempts demonstrate that creative thinking can assist multinationals to overcome this potential barrier. It is not possible to comment with authority on how effective the above assistance schemes are in terms of overcoming the dual career barrier. However, it is clear that multinationals are attempting to address the issue and create solutions for this barrier to mobility.

Are female expatriates different?

Our final issue in terms of selection for international assignments is related to gender. The typical expatriate tends to be male: 23 per cent in the GMAC GRS 2005 survey were females, 14 per cent in the ORC 2002 survey. The authors of both these surveys make the point that the proportion of females is increasing. For example, the ORC report compares the 2002 situation to that of their 1992 survey where only 5 per cent of expatriates were female. One can go further back to a 1984 article, in which Adler[63] reported a survey of international HR practices in over 600 US and Canadian companies that found only 3 per cent of the 13 338 expatriates identified were female. She found that female expatriates tended to be employed by companies with over 1 000 employees in the banking, electronics, petroleum and publishing industries. It has been argued that as the proportion of women in the domestic workforce continues to increase, and as international experience becomes an essential criterion for career progression within multinationals, we will see more international managers who are female.

Over the past decade or so, researchers have attempted to discover why so few expatriates are female. Is it because they were unwilling to relocate? Is it attitudinal? Does it reflect a somewhat externalized belief that men in some cultures, such as certain Asian countries, do not like reporting to female managers, particularly foreign women, and therefore women should not be posted overseas, creating what has been referred to as 'the glass border that supports the glass ceiling'.

A number of studies challenge some of the attitudes regarding the suitability of females for international assignments. For example, Stroh, Varma and Valy-Durbin[64] found that US and Canadian women are interested in and likely to accept international assignments, though there are variations between those with children and those without. However the women in this study tended to believe that their firms were hesitant to ask them to accept an international assignment, though supervisors (whether male or female) did not necessarily share that belief. Further, performance of female expatriates was found initially to be affected by host-country prejudice regarding the role of women in certain countries – considered as culturally tough assignment locations. However, the longer the women were on such assignments, the less they perceived that prejudice was a barrier to effectiveness. Caligiuri and Tung,[65] in their study of female and male expatriates in a US-based multinational found that females can perform equally as well as their male counterparts regardless of a country's attitude toward women in managerial positions.

Taking a different approach in her study of Austrian female expatriates, Fischlmayr[66] used the concepts of external and self-established barriers to explore why women are under-represented in international assignments. These are listed in Table 5-3.

Through 21 interviews with HR managers and female expatriates in Austrian multinationals from various industries and positions, Fischlmayr found that attitudes of HR directors were a major barrier to the selection of female expatriates, though self-established barriers were also very strong. Females in Austrian companies often had to specifically request an international assignment whereas their male colleagues were required to take international assignments. Further, some women regarded that their age was decisive in terms of others' perceptions and expectations about their behavior. The older the woman, the easier it is. Fischlmayr concludes that women are partly to blame for their under-representation.

Mayrhofer and Scullion[67] report on the experiences of male and female expatriates in the German clothing industry. They found that women were sent into a diverse number of countries, including those with an Islamic influence. Overall, there were few differences in the experiences of both gender groups, though female expatriates placed more value on integration of spouse/family issues prior to and during the assignment than did the males in the sample.

Barriers to females taking international assignments	Table 5-3

External barriers	Self-established barriers
• HR managers reluctant to select female candidates • Culturally tough locations or regions preclude female expatriates • Those selecting expatriates have stereotypes in their minds that influence decisions	• Some women have limited willingness to relocate • The dual career couple • Women are often a barrier to their own careers by behaving according to gender-based role models

Source: Based on the literature reviewed in I.C. Fischlmayr, 'Female Self-Perception as Barrier to International Careers?', *International Journal of Human Resource Management,* Vol. 13, No. 5 (2002), pp. 773–83.

Assignment lengths in this industry tended to be shorter and involved various forms of non-standard assignments, and there were generally more female managers than perhaps found in other industries. More women than men were assigned for longer assignment terms, and these authors conclude that the higher proportion of women in the industry appeared to make gender less of an issue. However, this did not apply at the top senior management positions where women were less represented. Mayrhofer and Scullion conclude that there are still barriers to female expatriates in terms of senior expatriate positions.

A further contribution comes from a study by Napier and Taylor[68] of female expatriates from various countries working in Japan, China and Turkey. The women fell into three categories: traditional expatriates, 'trailers' who were spouses/partners of male expatriates, and 'independents' – professional women who could be called self-selected expatriates. Napier and Taylor found that gaining credibility with local clients was a major issue. Accommodating cultural differences, maintaining a social life and a need for appropriate interpersonal skills were important factors in coping with work demands. Networks became important for both business and social contexts. Being a minority (foreign females) meant higher visibility than they were used to and could be a positive in terms of getting access to key clients and customers.

What emerges as common across the various studies on female expatriates is that assignment location, level of organization support, spouse/partner satisfaction and inter-cultural experiences are important in terms of performance. The list of moderators is similar to those we discussed in general terms earlier in this chapter. What does appear to differentiate female and male expatriates is the degree to which these moderators affect individual performance and the value placed on cultural awareness training prior to the international assignment. The dual career issue may prove to be a greater barrier for female mobility as males are more reluctant to accompany their spouse/partner.

Summary

This chapter has addressed key issues affecting recruitment and selection for international assignments. We have covered:

- Four myths related to the concept of a global manager: that there is a universal approach to management; that people can acquire multicultural adaptability and behaviors; that there are common characteristics successful international managers share; and that there are no impediments to mobility.

- The debate surrounding the definition and magnitude of expatriate failure.

- Cultural adjustment and other moderating factors affecting expatriate intent to stay and performance. These included duration of the assignment, willingness to move and work-related factors.

- Individual and situational factors to be considered in the selection decision. Evaluation of the common criteria used revealed the difficulty of selecting the right candidate for an international assignment and the importance of including family considerations in the selection process.

- Dual career couples as a barrier to staff mobility, and the techniques multinationals are utilizing to overcome this constraint.

- Female expatriates and whether they face different issues to their male counterparts.

It is also clear that, while our appreciation of the issues surrounding expatriate recruitment and selection has deepened in the past 30 years, much remains to be explored. The field is dominated by US research into predominantly US samples of expatriates, though there has been an upsurge in interest from European academics and practitioners. Will the factors affecting the selection decision be similar for multinationals emerging from countries such as China and India? If more multinationals are to encourage subsidiary staff to consider international assignments as part of an intra-organizational network approach to management, we will need further understanding of how valid the issues discussed in this chapter are for all categories of staff from different country locations. It is apparent, though, that staff selection remains critical. Finding the right people to fill positions, particularly key managers – whether PCN, TCN or HCN – can determine international expansion. However, effective recruitment and selection is only the first step.

Discussion Questions

1 What is the difference between a global manager and a global mindset?
2 Should multinationals be concerned about expatriate failure? If so, why?
3 What are the most important factors involved in the selection decision?
4 Are female expatriates different?
5 Discuss the proposition that most expatriate selection decisions are made informally, as suggested by the 'coffee-machine' solution.

Further Reading

Boudreau, J., Ramstad, P. and Dowling, P.J. (2003). 'Global Talentship: Toward a Decision Science Connecting Talent to Global Strategic Success', in W.H. Mobley and P.W. Dorfman (eds), *Advances in Global Leadership,* Vol. 3, Oxford: Elsevier Science, pp. 63–99.

International Studies of Management & Organization (2004). Special issue on Expatriation in the New Millenium, guest ed. Moshe Banai, 34(3).

Scullion, H. and Collings, D. (eds) (2006). *Global Staffing,* London: Routledge.

Tarique, I., Schuler, R. and Gong, Y. (2006). 'A Model of Multinational Enterprise Subsidiary Staffing Composition', *International Journal of Human Resource Management,* 17(2): 207–24.

Notes and References

1 H. Scullion and D. Collings, 'International Recruitment and Selection', in H. Scullion and D. Collings (eds), *Global Staffing* (London, Routledge, 2006), pp. 59–86.

2 For a recent review of the culture literature, see K. Leung, R. Bhagat, N. Buchan, M. Erez and C. Gibson, 'Culture and International Business: Recent Advances and Their Implications for Future Research', *Journal of International Business Studies,* Vol. 36, No. 4 (2005), pp. 357–78.

3 F.T. Murray and A.H. Murray, 'Global Managers for Global Businesses', *Sloan Management Review,* Vol. 27, No. 2 (1986), pp. 75–80.

4 N. Forster, 'The Myth of the "International Manager"', *International Journal of Human Resource Management,* Vol. 11, No. 1 (2000), pp. 126–42. See also C.A. Bartlett and S. Ghoshal, 'The Myth of the Generic Manager: New Personal Competencies for New Management Roles', *California Management, Review,* Vol. 40, No. 1 (1997), pp. 92–116.

5 Y. Baruch, 'No Such Thing as a Global Manager', *Business Horizons,* January–February (2002), pp. 36–42.

6 N. Forster, 'The Persistent Myth of High Expatriate Failure Rates', *International Journal of Human Resource Management,* Vol. 8, No. 4 (1997), p. 430.

7 Price Waterhouse (eds), *International Assignments: European Policy and Practice* (London: Price Waterhouse, 1997).

8 R.L. Tung, 'Selection and Training of Personnel for Overseas Assignments', *Columbia Journal of World Business,* Vol. 16, No. 1 (1981), pp. 68–78; R.L. Tung, 'Selection and Training Procedures of US, European and Japanese Multinationals', *California Management Review,* Vol. 25, No. 1 (1982), pp. 57–71; and R.L. Tung, 'Human Resource Planning in Japanese Multinationals: A Model for US Firms?', *Journal of International Business Studies* (Fall 1984), pp. 139–49.

9 C. Brewster, *The Management of Expatriates,* Human Resource Research Centre Monograph Series, No. 2 (Bedford: Cranfield School of Management, 1988). In a pilot study, Hamill investigated the IHRM practices and policies of seven British multinationals. He found that the failure rate among British expatriates was significantly lower (less than 5 per cent) than that reported for US multinationals (J. Hamill, 'Expatriate Policies in British Multinationals', *Journal of General Management,* Vol. 14, No. 4 (1989), pp. 19–33; E. Marx, *International Human Resource Practices in Britain and Germany* (London: Anglo-German Foundation, 1996).

10 A.-W. Harzing, 'The Persistent Myth of High Expatriate Failure Rates', *International Journal of Human Resource Management,* Vol. 6, No. 2 (1995), p. 458.

11 C. Christensen and A.-W. Harzing, 'Expatriate Failure: Time to Abandon the Concept?', *Career Development International,* Vol. 9, No. 7 (2004), pp. 616–26.

12 Organizational Resource Councelors Inc, 'Dual Careers and International Assignments Survey' (2002). The organization changed its name to ORC Worldwide in 2003.

13 I. Björkman and M. Gertsen, 'Corporate Expatriation: An Empirical Study of Scandinavian Firms', in 'Proceedings of the Third Symposium on Cross-Cultural Consumer and Business Studies', Honolulu (December 1990). Danish firms did not respond to Tung's survey, but the Swedish and Norwegian firms did.

14 P.J. Dowling and D. Welch, 'International Human Resource Management: An Australian Perspective', *Asia-Pacific Journal of Management,* Vol. 6, No. 1 (1988), pp. 39–65. Although precise records were not kept, the four companies estimated failure rates of less than 5 per cent.

15 For example, Enderwick and Hodgson explain the absence of 'expatriate failure' in their study of New Zealand firms may be due to their early stages in internationalization. See P. Enderwick and D. Hodgson, 'Expatriate Management Practices of New Zealand Business', *International Journal of Human Resource Management,* Vol. 4, No. 2 (1993), pp. 407–23.

16 M.E. Mendenhall and G. Oddou, 'The Overseas Assignment: A Practical Look', *Business Horizons* (September–October, 1988), pp. 78–84.

17 M. Mendenhall and G. Oddou, 'The Dimensions of Expatriate Acculturation: A Review', *Academy of Management Review,* Vol. 10 (1985) pp. 39–47.

18 Tung, 'Selection and Training Procedures'.

19 *Ibid*.

20 *Focus Japan,* 'Tanshin Funin: Bachelors in Exile', December 1990, p. 4.

21 J. Selmer, B.P. Ebrahimi and L. Mingtao, 'Career Management of Business Expatriates from China', *International Business Review,* Vol. 11, No. 1 (2002), pp. 17–33.

22 For a review and assessment of the U-Curve, see J.S. Black and M. Mendenhall, 'The U-Curve Adjustment Hypothesis Revisited: A Review and Theoretical Framework', *Journal of International Business Studies,* Vol. 22, No. 2 (1991), pp. 225–47.

23 H. De Cieri, P.J. Dowling and K.F. Taylor, 'The Psychological Impact of Expatriate Relocation on Partners', *International Journal of Human Resource Management,* Vol. 2, No. 3 (1991), pp. 377–414; M. Kauppinen, *Antecedents of Expatriate Adjustment: A Study of Finnish Managers in the United States* (Helsinki: Helsinki School of Economics Press, 1994).

24 Black and Mendenhall, 'The U-Curve Adjustment Hypothesis Revisited'.

25 J.S. Black and G.K. Stephens, 'The Influence of the Spouse on American Expatriate Adjustment and Intent to Stay in Pacific Rim Overseas Assignments', *Journal of Management,* Vol. 15, No. 4 (1989), pp. 529–44. See also, M. Kauppinen, *Antecedents of Expatriate Adjustment,* for support of this finding.

26 Tung, 'Selection and Training Procedures'.

27 J.M. Brett and L.K. Stroh, 'Willingness to Relocate Internationally', *Human Resource Management,* Vol. 34, No. 3 (1995), pp. 405–24.

28 Hamill, 'Expatriate Policies in British Multinationals'.

29 P.J. Dowling and D. Welch, 'International Human Resource Management'. One US personnel director interviewed by the authors pointed out that attributing expatriate recall to 'failure of spouse to adjust' was at times a simplistic explanation. He postulated that, apart from the probability of the expatriate blaming his wife for his own failure to adjust, some astute spouses may see the expatriate's poor performance and trigger the early recall to limit damage to the expatriate's career.

30 H.B. Gregersen and J.S. Black, 'A Multifaceted Approach to Expatriate Retention in International Assignments', *Group & Organization Studies,* Vol. 15, No. 4 (1990), pp. 461–85.

31 M.S. Shaffer, D.A. Harrison and K.M. Gilley, 'Dimensions, Determinants, and Differences in the Expatriate Adjustment Process', *Journal of International Business Studies,* Vol. 30, No. 3 (1999), pp. 557–81.

32 M.C. Bolino and D.C. Feldman, 'Increasing the Skill Utilization of Expatriates', *Human Resource Management,* Vol. 39, No. 4 (2000), pp. 367–79.

33 See for example M. Birdseye and J. Hill, 'Individual, Organizational/Work and Environmental Influences on Expatriate Turnover Tendencies: An Empirical Study', *Journal of International Business Studies,* Vol. 26, No. 4 (1995), pp. 787–813; and E. Naumann, "Organizational Predictors of Expatriate Job Satisfaction", *Journal of International Business Studies,* Vol. 24, No. 1 (1993), pp. 61–79.

34 M. Kraimer, S.J. Wayne and R.A. Jaworski, 'Sources of Support and Expatriate Performance: The Mediating Role of Expatriate Adjustment', *Personnel Psychology,* Vol. 54 (2001), pp. 71–92.

35 A.L. Hixon, 'Why Corporations Make Haphazard Overseas Staffing Decisions', *Personnel Administrator,* Vol. 31, No. 3 (1986), pp. 91–4; M.E. Mendenhall, E. Dunbar and G. Oddou, 'Expatriate Selection, Training and Career-Pathing: A Review and a Critique', *Human Resource Planning,* Vol. 26, No. 3 (1987), pp. 331–45; J. McEnery and G. DesHarnais, 'Culture Shock', *Training and Development Journal,* Vol. 44, No. 4 (1990), pp. 43–7; I. Björkman and M. Gertsen, 'Selecting and Training Scandinavian Expatriates: Determinants of Corporate Practice', *Scandinavian Journal of Management,* Vol. 9, No. 2 (1993), pp. 145–64. E. Marx, *International Human Resource Practices in Britain and Germany;* Price Waterhouse (eds), *International Assignments: European Policy and Practice* (1997).

36 P. Caligiuri, 'The Big Five Personality Characteristics as Predictors of Expatriate's Desire to Terminate the Assignment and Supervisor-rated Performance', *Personnel Psychology,* Vol. 53 (2000), pp. 67–88.

37 M.A. Shaffer and D.A. Harrison, 'Forgotten Partners of International Assignments: Development and Test of a Model of Spouse Adjustment', *Journal of Applied Psychology,* Vol. 86, No. 2 (2001), pp. 238–54.

38 M. Harvey, 'The Executive Family: An Overlooked Variable in International Assignments', *Columbia Journal of World Business,* Spring (1985), pp. 84–93. See also, A. Thompson, 'Australian Expatriate Wives and Business Success in South East Asia', *Euro-Asian Business Review,* Vol. 5, No. 2 (1986), pp. 14–18; and J.E. Harris, 'Moving Managers Internationally: The Care and Feeding of Expatriates', *Human Resource Planning,* Vol. 12, No. 1 (1989), pp. 49–53.

39 J.S. Black and G.K. Stephens, 'The Influence of the Spouse on American Expatriate Adjustment and Intent to Stay in Pacific Rim Overseas Assignments', *Journal of Management,* Vol. 15, No. 4 (1989), p. 541; see also H. De Cieri, P.J. Dowling and K.F. Taylor, 'The Psychological Impact of Expatriate Relocation on Partners', *International Journal of Human Resource Management,* Vol. 2, No. 3 (1991), pp. 377–414; and Brewster, *The Management of Expatriates.*

40 Price Waterhouse (eds), *International Assignments: European Policy and Practice.*

41 See www.permitsfoundation.com/home.htm for the home page of the Permits Foundation.

42 S.N. As-Saber, P.J. Dowling and P.W. Liesch, 'The Role of Human Resource Management in International Joint Ventures: A Study of Australian-Indian Joint Ventures', *International Journal of Human Resource Management,* Vol. 9, No. 5 (1998), pp. 751–66.

43 D. Welch and L. Welch, 'Linking Operation Mode Diversity and IHRM', *International Journal of Human Resource Management,* Vol. 5, No. 4 (1994), pp. 911–26.

44 D. Victor, *International Business Communication* (New York: HarperCollins, 1992).

45 C. Fixman, 'The Foreign Language Needs of US-based Corporations', *ANNALS,* AAPSS, Vol. 51 (September 1990), p. 25.

46 'National Geographic-Roper Public Affairs 2006 Geographic Literacy Study'. A copy of this report is available on the National Geographic website: www.nationalgeographic.com/.

47 News update provided by the US Congress Education and the Workforce Committee. Accessed on 4 May 2006 at www.house.gov/ed_workforce/press109/first/04apr/t6042205.htm. See also the report *International Education and Foreign Language Studies in Higher Education* (ISBN 0160749123) published by this Congress Committee in 2005.

48 R. Marschan-Piekkari, D. Welch and L. Welch, 'Adopting a Common Corporate Language', *International Journal of Human Resource Management,* Vol. 10, No. 3 (1999), pp. 377–90.

49 I. Torbiörn, *Living Abroad: Personal Adjustment and Personnel Policy in the Overseas Setting* (New York: John Wiley, 1982).

50 H.L. Willis, 'Selection for Employment in Developing Countries', *Personnel Administrator,* Vol. 29, No. 7 (1984), p. 55.

51 See, for example, P. Sparrow and J.-M. Hiltrop, *European Human Resource Management in Transition* (Hemel Hempstead: Prentice Hall, 1994); P.J. Dowling, 'Psychological Testing in Australia: An Overview and an Assessment', in G. Palmer, (ed.) *Australian Personnel Management: A Reader* (Sydney: Macmillan, 1988).

52 Marx found that only 4.4 per cent of the German companies in her survey used such tests, compared with 15.2 per cent in the UK firms. See Marx, *International Human Resource Practices in Britain and Germany.*

53 Hixon, 'Why Corporations Make Haphazard Overseas Staffing Decisions'.

54 G.M. Baliga and J.C. Baker, 'Multinational Corporate Policies for Expatriate Managers: Selection, Training, Evaluation', *Advanced Management Journal,* Vol. 50, No. 4 (1985), pp. 31–8. See also J.S. Black, 'The Relationship of Personal Characteristics with the Adjustment of Japanese Expatriate Managers', *Management International Review,* Vol. 30, No. 2 (1990), pp. 119–34, for a review and discussion of cross-cultural adjustment.

55 Mendenhall and Oddou, 'The Dimensions of Expatriate Acculturation'. For a review of the Type A literature, see V.A. Price, *Type A Behaviour Pattern: A Model for Research and Practice* (New York: Academic Press, 1982).

56 H.C. Jain, P.J. Sloane and F.M. Horwitz, *Employment Equity and Affirmative Action: An International Comparison* (Armonk, NY: M.E. Sharpe, 2003).

57 EEOC vs Arabian American Oil Co., 111 S. Ct. 1227 (1991). For an excellent commentary on this case, see G.L. Clark, 'The Geography of Civil Rights', *Environment and Planning D: Society and Space,* Vol. 10 (1992), pp. 119–21. For details on the amendment see Civil Rights Act of 1991, § 109(a), 105 Stat. 1077, codified at 42 U.S.C. § 2000e(f).

58 For a review of this area see Jain, Sloane and Horwitz, *Employment Equity and Affirmative Action.*

59 H. Harris and C. Brewster, 'The Coffee-Machine System: How International Selection Really Works', *International Journal of Human Resource Management,* Vol. 10, No. 3 (1999), pp. 488–500.

60 M.G. Harvey, 'The Impact of Dual-Career Families on International Relocations', *Human Resource Management Review,* Vol. 5, No. 3 (1995), pp. 223–44.

61 G.K. Stephens and S. Black, 'The Impact of Spouse's Career-Orientation on Managers during International Transfers', *Journal of Management Studies,* Vol. 28, No. 4 (1991), p. 425.

62 The Conference Board, *Managing Expatriates' Return,* Report Number 1148-98-RR (New York: The Conference Board, 1996).

63 N.J. Adler, 'Women in International Management: Where Are They?', *California Management Review,* Vol. 26, No. 4 (1984), pp. 78–89.

64 L.K. Stroh, A. Varma and S.J. Valy-Durbin, 'Why are Women Left at Home: Are They Unwilling to Go on International Assignments?', *Journal of World Business,* Vol. 35, No. 3 (2000), pp. 241–55.

65 P.A. Caligiuri and R.L. Tung, 'Comparing the Success of Male and Female Expatriates from a US-based Multinational Company', *International Journal of Human Resource Management,* Vol. 10, No. 5 (1999), pp. 763–82.

66 I.C. Fischlmayr, 'Female Self-Perception as Barrier to International Careers?', *International Journal of Human Resource Management,* Vol. 13, No. 5 (2002), pp. 773–83.

67 W. Mayrhofer and H. Scullion, 'Female Expatriates in International Business: Empirical Evidence from the German Clothing Industry', *International Journal of Human Resource Management,* Vol. 13, No. 5 (2002), pp. 815–36.

68 N.K. Napier and S. Taylor, 'Experiences of Women Professionals Abroad: Comparisons Across Japan, China and Turkey', *International Journal of Human Resource Management,* Vol. 13, No. 5 (2002), pp. 837–51.

International training and development

Chapter Objectives

Training aims to improve employees' current work skills and behavior, whereas development aims to increase abilities in relation to some future position or job. In this chapter, we examine how the international assignment is a vehicle for both training and development, as reflected in the reasons why international assignments continue to play a strategic role in international business operations. The role of training in preparing and supporting personnel on international assignments is also considered. We examine the following issues:

- The role of training in supporting expatriate adjustment and on-assignment performance.
- Components of effective pre-departure training programs such as cultural awareness, preliminary visits and language skills. Relocation assistance and training for trainers are also addressed.
- The effectiveness of pre-departure training.
- The developmental aspect of international assignments.
- Training and developing international management teams.
- Trends in international training and development.

Reflecting the general literature on this topic, the focus of the chapter is on the traditional, expatriate assignment. However, where possible we will draw out training and development aspects relating to short-term assignments, non-standard assignments and international business travelers.

Introduction

In order to compete successfully in a global market, more firms are focusing on the role of human resources as a critical part of their core competence and source of competitive advantage. As Kamoche[1] comments: 'the human resource refers to the accumulated stock of knowledge, skills, and abilities that the individuals possess, which the firm has built up over time into an identifiable expertise'. Training and development activities are part of the way in which the multinational builds its stock of human resources – its human capital. An indication of the importance of this is the increasing number of multinationals that have established their own 'universities' or 'schools'. Motorola, McDonald's and Disney universities are good examples of these in-house training centers. Several European, Japanese and Korean firms have similar arrangements, such as the Lufthansa Business School and the Ericsson Management Institute.

The international assignment in itself is an important training and development tool:

- Expatriates are trainers, as part of the transfer of knowledge and competence between the various units – a major rationale for the use of international assignments. Whether implicitly or explicitly stated, they are expected to assist the multinational train and develop HCNs – that is, train their replacements.

- Expatriates are also expected to ensure that systems and processes are adopted, and inevitably they will be engaged in showing how these systems and processes work, as well as monitoring the effective performance of HCNs.

- One of the reasons for international assignments is management development. A move into another area – job rotation – is a useful way for employees to gain a broader perspective. It assists in developing capable people who form the required pool of global operators, as discussed in earlier chapters.

Therefore, the way in which a MNE anticipates and provides suitable training for international assignments is an important first step. This is reflected in the growth of interest in, and provision of, pre-departure training to prepare expatriates and accompanying family members for the international assignment.

Figure 6-1 is a schematic representation of the structure of this chapter. It shows the link between international recruitment and selection, which we covered in Chapter 5, and training and development activities. Most expatriates are internal hires, selected from within the multinational's existing operations though, as indicated by the dotted arrow in Figure 6-1, some expatriates may be hired externally for an international assignment. We will now consider the various elements related to expatriate training and development in the context of managing and supporting international assignments.

Figure 6-1 International training and development

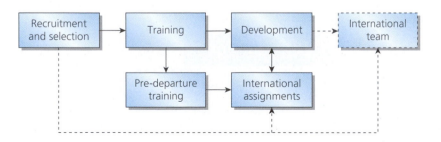

The role of expatriate training

Given that the primary selection criterion for most MNEs is technical ability, it is not surprising to find that most of the literature is devoted to expatriate pre-departure training activities that are mainly concerned with developing cultural awareness. Attention to this aspect has been fuelled by the reported link between expatriate failure rates and cultural adjustment discussed in Chapter 5. Therefore, once an employee has been selected for an expatriate position, pre-departure training is considered to be the next critical step in attempting to ensure the expatriate's effectiveness and success abroad, particularly where the destination country is considered culturally tough. In Figure 6-1 on the facing page, pre-departure training is indicated as a subset of general training. Effective cultural training, it is advocated, assists individuals to adjust more rapidly to the new culture. As Earley[2] points out, 'A major objective of intercultural training is to help people cope with unexpected events in a new culture.'

The limited, predominately US-based, research into this area reveals that a large number of US multinationals have been reluctant to provide even a basic level of pre-departure training, though this is slowly changing. Particular interest in the area began with Tung's[3] study on expatriation practices, including the use of pre-departure training programs. Her results showed that US multinationals tended to use training programs for expatriates less frequently than European and Japanese firms (32 per cent compared with 69 per cent and 57 per cent, respectively). The US attitude to the provision of pre-departure training appeared to persist through the 1980s. For example, a 1984 study of one thousand US multinationals found that only 25 per cent offered extensive pre-departure training programs;[4] while a 1989 study of US firms found that only 13 per cent of respondents indicated that they would offer expatriates a pre-departure program.[5] Among the various reasons cited by firms in these studies was that top management did not believe pre-departure training was necessary or effective.[6] So, while the potential benefits of cultural awareness training are widely acknowledged, such training was down-graded or not offered by a large number of US multinationals.[7] A 1997 survey of European firms (including subsidiaries of non-European multinationals) found only 13 per cent of responding firms always provided expatriates with access to cultural awareness courses, though a further 47 per cent provided briefings for culturally 'challenging' postings (compared with 21 per cent in a 1995 survey).[8]

MNEs appear to be more positive about the provision of training over the last few years, possibly in part due to the growth in numbers of providers of pre-departure training that multinationals can access. For example, the Global Relocation Trends Survey reports by the consulting firm GMAC Global Relocation Services, LLC (GMAC GRS) (in conjunction with the US National Foreign Trade Council and the SHRM Global Forum) also covered pre-departure training. The majority of firms in these surveys are US based (79 per cent in the 2004 survey). The data on provision of cross-cultural training (CCT) is somewhat consistent between the 2002 and 2004 GMAC GRS surveys, as shown in Table 6.1.

Previously, multinational firms placed less priority on providing pre-departure training for the spouse and family.[9] However, perhaps due to increasing recognition of the interaction between expatriate performance and family adjustment, more multinationals are now extending their pre-departure training programs to include the spouse/partner and children. This is reflected in the GMAC GRS figures above, and in another survey – the 2002 survey of dual careers and international

Table 6-1	Availability of cross-cultural training in MNEs

	GMAC 2002	*GMAC 2004*
CCT available:	64 per cent	62 per cent
CCT attendance optional	76	74
Provided to:		
• Employee only	2 per cent	5 per cent
• Employee and spouse	29	27
• Whole family	33	28
• None	36	40

Source: Global Relocation Trends Survey reports provided by GMAC Global Relocation Services, LLC. All Rights Reserved.

assignments by ORC Worldwide. The latter report's authors commented that provision of pre-departure training for accompanying spouses and partners continued to increase. However, as Table 6.1 shows, the percentage of firms which make CCT *optional* remains very high (74 per cent in 2004) so it is possible that many expatriates still receive very little training. In a recent review of CCT Littrell and Salas suggest that a lack of synthesis in the area of CCT research has made it difficult for managers to implement CCT. Their review provides a number of research-based guidelines as to how MNEs can enhance the success of their CCT programs.[10]

Components of effective pre-departure training programs

Studies indicate that the essential components of pre-departure training programs that contribute to a smooth transition to a foreign location include: cultural awareness training, preliminary visits, language instruction and assistance with practical, day-to-day matters.[11] We will look at each of these in turn.

Cultural awareness programs

It is generally accepted that, to be effective, the expatriate employee must adapt to and not feel isolated from the host country. A well-designed, cultural awareness training program can be extremely beneficial, as it seeks to foster an appreciation of the host country's culture so that expatriates can behave accordingly, or at least develop appropriate coping patterns. Without an understanding (or at least an acceptance) of the host-country culture in such a situation, the expatriate is likely to face some difficulty during the international assignment. Therefore, cultural awareness training remains the most common form of pre-departure training.

The components of cultural awareness programs vary according to country of assignment, duration, purpose of the transfer, and the provider of such programs. As part of her study of expatriate management, Tung[12] identified five categories of pre-departure training, based on different learning processes, type of job, country of assignment and the time available. These were: area studies programs that include environmental briefing and cultural orientation; culture assimilators; language train-ing; sensitivity training; and field experiences. To understand possible variations in expatriate training, Tung proposed a contingency framework for deciding the nature and level of rigor of training. The two determining factors were the degree of inter-action required in the host culture and the similarity between the individual's na-tive culture and the new culture. The related training elements in her framework involved the content of the training and the rigor of the training. Essentially, Tung argued that:

- If the expected interaction between the individual and members of the host culture was low, and the degree of dissimilarity between the individual's native culture and the host culture was low, then training should focus on task- and job-related issues rather than culture-related issues. The level of rigor necessary for effective training should be relatively low.

- If there was a high level of expected interaction with host nationals and a large dissimilarity between the cultures, then training should focus on cross-cultural skill development as well as on the new task. The level of rigor for such training should be moderate to high.

Tung's model specifies criteria for making training method decisions – such as degree of expected interaction and cultural similarity. One limitation of the model is that it does not assist the user to determine which specific training methods to use or what might constitute more or less rigorous training.

More than a decade later, Tung[13] revisited her earlier work and reported that her original recommendations held, though with some changes:

- Training should be more orientated to life-long learning than 'one-shot' programs with an area-specific focus.
- There should be more emphasis on provision of foreign language training.
- There should be emphasis on the levels of communication competence, not just verbal communication, so the person becomes bicultural and bilingual, which enables an easier transition between one culture and another.
- Cross-cultural training assists in managing diversity.
- The preview of the expatriate position should be realistic, as this facilitates effective performance.

Mendenhall and Oddou extended Tung's model and this was refined subsequently by Mendenhall, Dunbar and Oddou[14] who proposed three dimensions: training methods; levels of training rigor; and duration of the training relative to degree of interaction and culture novelty (see Figure 6-2). This model provides useful guide-lines for determining an appropriate program. For example, if the expected level of interaction is low and the degree of similarity between the individual's home culture and the host culture is high, the length of the training should probably be less than a week. Methods such as area or cultural briefings via lectures, movies, or books would provide the appropriate level of training rigor.[15]

On the other hand, if the individual is going overseas for a period of two to twelve months and is expected to have some interaction with members of the host culture, the level of training rigor should be higher and its length longer (one to four weeks). In addition to the information-giving approaches, training methods such as culture assimilators and role-plays may be appropriate.[16] If the individual is going to a fairly novel and different host culture and the expected degree of inter-action is high, the level of cross-cultural training rigor should be high and training

| **Figure 6-2** | The Mendenhall, Dunbar and Oddou cross-cultural training model |

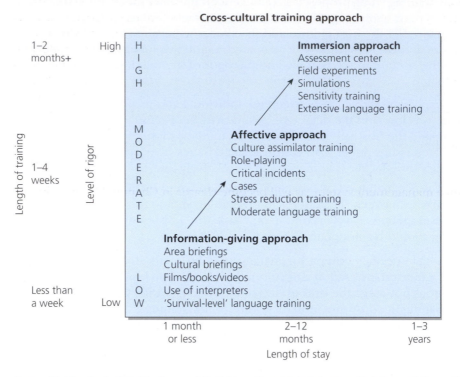

Source: M. Mendenhall, E. Dunbar, and G. Oddou, 'Expatriate Selection, Training and Career-Pathing: A Review and Critique', *Human Resource Management,* Vol. 26 (1987), pp. 338. Reprinted with permission.

should last as long as two months. In addition to the less rigorous methods already discussed, sensitivity training, field experiences and intercultural experiential workshops may be appropriate training methods in this situation.

Later, Black and Mendenhall[17] concluded that the earlier model, like that of Tung's, was primarily 'cultural' in nature, with little integration of the individual's new tasks and the new host culture. Black and Mendenhall therefore proposed what they described as an extensive theoretically based model using Bandura's social learning theory and prior cultural awareness training models. They take three aspects of social learning theory – attention, retention and reproduction – and show how these are influenced by individual differences in expectations and motivation, and the incentives to apply learned behaviors in the foreign location. This approach recognizes that effective training is only the first step and that the expatriate's willingness and ability to act upon that training in the new environment is crucial to effective performance.

An obvious practical limitation of Black and Mendenhall's model is that insufficient time is often given as a reason why multinationals do not provide pre-departure training. It would therefore be difficult to develop appropriate pre-departure training programs in such cases. Other contextual and situational factors – such as, cultural toughness, length of assignment and the nature/type of the job – may have a bearing on the content, method and processes involved in the cultural awareness training program. More importantly, monitoring and feedback should be recognized as important components of individual skill development, particularly as adjustment and performance are the desired outcomes of cultural awareness training.

Figure 6-3 draws together the components of the three models reviewed above. It stresses the importance of attention paid by the potential expatriate to the behaviors and probable outcomes of a cultural awareness training program; the individual's ability and willingness to retain learned behaviors; and their reproduction as appropriate in the host location. Poor performance could be addressed by clarifying incentives for more effective reproduction of the required level of behavior, or by providing additional cultural awareness training during the international assignment. Therefore, we combine adjustment and performance and link it to the performance management system; whereas Black and Mendenhall have adjustment and performance as separate outcomes, with adjustment leading to performance. We argue that performance affects adjustment in many instances. Further, it seems important that adjustment and performance be linked to the MNE's performance management system, as will become clearer in Chapter 11 where we address performance management systems and issues.

Preliminary visits

One technique useful in orienting international employees is to send them on a preliminary trip to the host country. A well-planned trip overseas for the candidate and spouse provides a preview that allows them to assess their suitability for and interest in the assignment. Such a trip also serves to introduce expatriate candidates to the business context in the host location and helps encourage more informed

Cultural awareness training and assignment performance   **Figure 6-3**

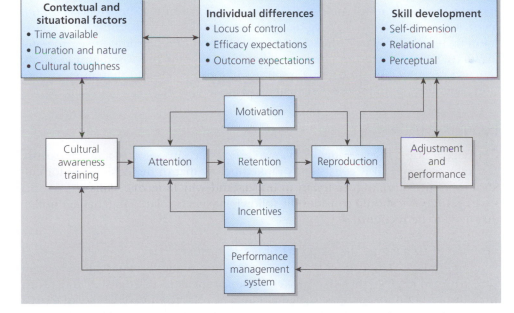

Source: Adapted from Tung (1981),[12] Mendenhall, Dunbar and Oddou (1987),[14] Black and Mendenhall (1990),[7] and J.S. Black and M.E. Mendenhall, 'A Practical but Theory-based Framework for Selecting Cross-cultural Training Methods', in M. Mendenhall and G. Oddou (eds), *Readings and Cases in International Human Resource Management* (Boston, MA: PWS-Kent, 1991).

pre-departure preparation. When used as part of a pre-departure training program, visits to the host location can assist in the initial adjustment process.

The 1997 European survey mentioned above reported that 53 per cent of firms always provided preliminary visits and a further 38 per cent indicated such use in certain circumstances. The average length of visit was about a week. The country of assignment was a determining factor. Visits were not provided if the country concerned was already known to the expatriate (perhaps from a previous visit either on firm-related business or as a tourist), or was perceived as culturally close (e.g. Zurich to Frankfurt, or New York to Toronto). Unfortunately, the 2002 and 2004 surveys by GMAC GRS, and the 2002 ORC Worldwide survey, do not deal with preliminary visits. However, a study of expatriates from Germany, the US, Korea and Japan working in Singapore, and Singaporean repatriates and expatriates did include preliminary visits as part of pre-departure training. Osman-Gani[18] reports that of these five groups, only the US expatriates rated preliminary visits as important, ranking it second behind cross-cultural training.

Obviously, the prospective assignee may reject the assignment on the basis of the preliminary visit. As one firm in the 1997 European study[19] is reported to have admitted: 'We do not provide pre-assignment visits where conditions are so poor that nobody would want to go.' Most firms that utilize preliminary visits, though, weigh the cost of a preliminary visit against premature recall and under-performance risks. A potential problem is that the aim of the preliminary visit is often twofold – part of the selection decision and part of pre-departure training. The multinational could send mixed signals if it offers the preliminary visit as part of the selection process but the prospective assignee finds upon arrival in the proposed country of assignment that they are expected to make decisions regarding suitable housing and schools. Such treatment could be interpreted as 'accepting the preliminary visit equals accepting the assignment', thus negating its role in the decision-making process. Where multinationals use the preliminary visit to allow the assignee (and spouse) to make a more informed decision about accepting the overseas assignment, it should be used solely for that purpose. Combined with cultural awareness training, the preliminary visit is a useful component of a pre-departure program. Exposure to the expatriate community, if one exists in the proposed host location, can also be a positive outcome. Brewster and Pickard[20] found that an expatriate community has an influence on expatriate adjustment.

Language training

Language training is a seemingly obvious, desirable component of a pre-departure program. However, it is consistently ranked below that of the desirability for cultural awareness training. In trying to understand why language skills are given a lower priority we should consider the following aspects related to language ability that need to be recognized.

The role of English as the language of world business. It is generally accepted that English is the language of world business, though the form of English is more 'international English' than that spoken by native speakers of English.[21] India is an attractive location for foreign call centers due, in part, to the availability of a large English-speaking population from which to recruit employees. The willingness of Chinese nationals to acquire English fluency is confirming the dominance of English. Multinationals from the Anglo-Saxon or English-speaking countries such as the United Kingdom, the USA, Canada, Australia and New Zealand often use the

dominant role of English as a reason for not considering language ability in the selection process, and for not stressing language training as part of pre-departure programs. Tung[22] reports that a 12 country study of almost 3 000 executives found that respondents from the USA the UK, Canada and Australia – all English-speaking countries – deemed language skills as unimportant. This is in contrast to executives from Europe, Asia and South America, however, who considered knowledge of a foreign language as critical to success.

A similar attitude emerged from a study of US multinationals' foreign language needs. Fixman[23] found that foreign language skills were seldom included as part of cross-cultural understanding, and that language problems were largely viewed as mechanical and manageable problems that could easily be solved. As Pucik[24] comments, an exclusive reliance on English diminishes the MNE's linguistic capacity. The resultant lack of language competence has strategic and operational implications as it limits the multinational's ability to monitor competitors and process important information. For example, translation services, particularly those external to the firm, cannot make strategic inferences and firm-specific interpretations of language specific data. Fixman[25] raises the question of protecting important technology in international joint venture activities: 'It would seem that the less one understands of a partner's language, the less likely one is to detect theft of technology.' Perhaps more importantly, as Wright and Wright[26] in their study of British firms point out, to accept English as the de facto language of international business gives the advantage to the other person:

> The other speaker controls what is communicated and what is understood. The monolingual English speaker has less room to maneuver, no possibility of finding out more than he is given. His position forces him to be reactive rather than proactive in the relationship. What he says and understands is filtered through the other speaker's competence, over which he has no control.

Disregarding the importance of foreign language skills may reflect a degree of ethnocentrism. A study by Hall and Gudykunst[27] has shown that the lower the level of perceived ethnocentrism in an MNE, the more training it provides in cultural awareness and language training. It also reflects a degree of perhaps unconscious arrogance on the part of expatriates from English-speaking countries. However, more firms are including language training as evidenced by recent surveys. For example, the ORC Worldwide 2002 survey revealed that provision of language training to spouses and partners, as part of pre-departure training programs, had markedly increased. A total of 59 per cent of the responding firms provided language training prior to departure, and 74 per cent provided language training while the person was on assignment. In fact, it was the most common form of spousal assistance while on assignment – and is reflected in the 2004 survey where 60 per cent of responding firms indicated provision of language training as part of their spousal assistance package, though when this was provided was not outlined, though one respondent volunteered: 'language training is a top challenge'.[28] (See also the discussion on language ability as a selection criterion in Chapter 5.)

Host-country language skills and adjustment. Clearly, the ability to speak a foreign language can improve the expatriate's effectiveness and negotiating ability. As Baliga and Baker[29] point out, it can improve managers' access to information regarding the host country's economy, government and market. Of course, the degree of fluency required may depend on the level and nature of the position that the expatriate holds in the foreign operation, the amount of interaction with external stakeholders such as government officials, clients, trade officials, as well as with host-country nationals.

In a survey of 400 expatriates by Tung,[30] the importance of language skills was identified as a critical component in assignment performance. Respondents indicated that ability to speak the local language, regardless of how different the culture was to their home country, was as important as cultural awareness in their ability to adapt and perform on assignment. Knowledge of the host-country language can assist expatriates and family members gain access to new social support structures outside of work and the expatriate community.

Language skills are therefore important in terms of task performance and cultural adjustment. Its continued omission from pre-departure training can be partly explained by the length of time it takes to acquire even a rudimentary level of language competence. Hiring language competent staff to enlarge the 'language pool' from which potential expatriates may be drawn is one answer, but its success depends on up-to-date information being kept on all employees, and frequent language auditing to see whether language skills are maintained.[31]

Knowledge of the corporate language. As previously mentioned, multinationals tend to adopt (either deliberately or by default) a common company language to facilitate reporting and other control mechanisms. Given its place in international business, quite often English becomes the common language within these multinationals. Expatriates can become language nodes, performing as communication conduits between subsidiary and headquarters, due to their ability to speak the corporate language. It also can give added power to their position in the subsidiary, as expatriates – particularly PCNs – often have access to information that those not fluent in the corporate language are denied. An expatriate fluent in the parent-company language and the language of the host subsidiary can perform a gate-keeping role, whatever the formal position the expatriate may hold.

Most MNEs use staff transfers as part of its corporate training program, with HCN recruits spending time at corporate headquarters. These training programs will normally be conducted in the corporate language. Fluency in the corporate language is, therefore, usually a prerequisite for international training assignments and may constrain the ability of subsidiary employees to attend and benefit from such training. An exception to this pattern would be an example where key new line managers from important emerging markets may be trained in their own language at the corporate headquarters – a practice which the McDonald's Corporation follows at its corporate training facility in Chicago.[32] Pre-departure training programs often may need to include both the language of the host country and the corporate language.

Practical assistance

Another component of a pre-departure training program is that of providing information that assists in relocation. Practical assistance makes an important contribution toward the adaptation of the expatriate and his or her family to their new environment. Being left to fend for oneself may result in a negative response toward the host country's culture, and/or contribute to a perceived violation of the psychological contract. Many multinationals now take advantage of relocation specialists to provide this practical assistance, for example, in finding suitable accommodation and schools. Further language training for the expatriate and family could be provided, particularly if such training was not possible before departure. Usually, during the assignment, host-country HR staff will organize any further orientation programs and language training. However, it is important that corporate HRM staff act as a liaison to the sending line manager as well as the HR department in the foreign location to ensure that practical assistance is provided.

Training for the training role

Expatriates are often used for training because of a lack of suitably trained staff in the host location. Consequently, expatriates often find themselves training HCNs as their replacements. The obvious question is how are expatriates prepared for this training role? There is little research on this question. We do know from the cross-cultural management literature that there are differences in the way people approach tasks and problems, and that this can have an impact on the learning process.[33] The ability to transfer knowledge and skills in a culturally sensitive manner perhaps should be an integral part of pre-departure training programs – particularly if training is part of the expatriate's role in the host country.

One way that MNEs could improve the quality and content of the training offered to expatriates in their role of training HCNs as their replacements would be to better utilize the knowledge transfer process when expatriates are repatriated. A paper by Lazarova and Tarique[34] has examined this issue and argues that effective knowledge transfer occurs when there is a fit between individual readiness to transfer knowledge and organizational receptivity to knowledge. Specifically they propose that:

> Organizations should try to match the level of intensity of their knowledge transfer mechanisms to the type of knowledge gained abroad. Thus, highly intense extraction tools (e.g. assigning repatriates to strategic teams) should be used to acquire international knowledge with high tacitness and high specificity. . . . Such knowledge would be transferred most effectively through rich mechanisms involving frequent communication between the repatriate and other organizational members. Organizations can use low intensity extraction tools (e.g. presentations, intranet) to acquire explicit international knowledge (e.g. information on banking laws and regulations in a particular foreign market).

Training and the company code of conduct

As a result of high-profile cases related to ethical behavior and corporate governance, the 2004 GMAC GRS survey asked responding firms if they were instituting programs to train expatriates regarding the company's code of conduct. A total of 37 per cent indicated that they had. However, since the form this training took and when it was delivered was not specified it is difficult to evaluate the significance of this response.

TCN and HCN expatriate training

Anecdotal evidence suggests that in some firms pre-departure training may not be provided to TCNs being transferred to another subsidiary, and for HCNs transferred into the parent country operations. Where it is provided, it may not be to the extent of that available to PCNs. This omission could create perceptions of inequitable treatment in situations where PCNs and TCNs work in the same foreign location, and affect adjustment to the international assignment. Not considering the need for HCNs transferred to the parent organization reflects an ethnocentric attitude.[35]

There may be a link between the amount of training, particularly cross-cultural, and assignment length. HCNs transferred to either headquarters or to another subsidiary are often short-term, project-based assignments or for management development purposes. As such, they may not be regarded as 'genuine' expatriate postings, thus falling outside the ambit of the HR function. In order to design and implement TCN and HCN pre-departure training, local management, particularly those in the HR department, need to be conscious of the demands of an international assignment – just as we have discussed in terms of corporate/headquarters HR staff. There perhaps needs also to be recognition and encouragement of this from headquarters, and monitoring to ensure that sufficient subsidiary resources are allocated for such training.

Provision of training for non-traditional expatriate assignments

In theory, all staff should be provided with the necessary level of pre-departure training given the demands of the international assignment. Cultural adjustment is inherent in international staff transfers. Pre-departure training should also be provided for employees on short-term assignments, on non-standard assignments such as commuting, and to international business travelers. However, there is a paucity of information regarding pre-departure training for non-standard assignments.

Short-term and non-standard assignments.
Given the generally low level of provision of pre-departure training to traditional expatriates, it is not surprising to find that those on short-term and non-standard assignments receive little or no preparation before departure. The oversight may be due to lack of time, which is a standard reason for non-provision of pre-departure training.

This may be why multinationals are beginning to use modern technology to overcome time and resource constraints. For example, the GMAC GRS 2004 survey referred to earlier asked respondents if they used CD-based and Web-based cross-cultural programs. Only 16 per cent (compared to 21 per cent in 2002) of responding firms used such facilities, of which:

- 65 per cent used CD and Web-based programs as additional forms of support for in-person programs (compared to 60 per cent in 2002).

- 30 per cent used CD and Web-based programs as stand-alone alternatives (compared to 41 per cent in 2002).

- 5 per cent indicated that CD and Web-based programs were the only form of pre-departure training offered (compared to 16 per cent in 2002).

The 2004 survey does not report on the specifics of this training. However, in the 2002 survey, more detail was made available. For example, one firm explained that employees on short-term assignments were provided with access to Web-based information, while longer-term expatriates were provided with both in-person and Web-based programs. The 2002 GMAC GRS data revealed that firms with smaller expatriate populations (1–25 and 51–100) were more likely to use CD or Web-based cross-cultural training, than did firms with 101 or more expatriates.

International business travelers.   Non-expatriates tend to be a forgotten group, yet for many firms they may comprise the largest contingent of employees involved in international business. International business travelers are flying into and out of foreign operations performing a myriad of tasks, including training. For example, explaining new product development, or service, or process, to HCN employees that will involve demonstrations, seminar presentations and other methods of information dissemination. Such internal company interaction usually will involve the use of the corporate language. Therefore, non-expatriates need to be aware that HCNs will differ in their level of competence. It is easy to equate intelligence with language fluency: perceiving lack of fluency as a sign of stupidity. Company briefings and training sessions will need to take into account local variances in how people conduct themselves in formal situations and approach the 'classroom' situation.

International business travelers may be providing new product information to foreign agents or distributors. These activities naturally involve cross-cultural interaction. Competence in the local language or at least an ability to work with and through interpreters may be required. The same applies to those conducting negotiations with host government officials, prospective clients, suppliers and subcontractors. All these activities are strategically important yet there is little in the literature regarding the provision of training for these roles. From the limited, mainly anecdotal, information available, it would seem that non-expatriates learn on the job, and gradually acquire the knowledge and skills to function effectively in various countries and situations.[36] For a recent review of the international business traveler literature see Welch and Worm.[37]

The effectiveness of pre-departure training

The objective of pre-departure training is to assist the expatriate to adjust to the demands of living and working in a foreign location. The question is how effective is such training and what components have been considered to be essential by those who have been provided pre-departure training?

The GMAC GRS surveys asked firms to indicate the value of cross-cultural preparation for expatriate success as shown in Table 6.2. For the 2004 survey, over two-thirds of the respondents indicated that cross-cultural training was 'of great value' or 'of high value'. However, it should be noted that information on how the responding firms

Perceived value of cross-cultural preparation of expatriates		Table 6-2

Value rating	GMAC 2002	GMAC 2004
Of great value	35%	36%
Of high value	45%	37%
Of medium value	17%	21%
Of little value	Not available	6%

Source: Global Relocation Trends Survey reports provided by GMAC Global Relocation Services, LLC. All rights reserved.

evaluated their training was not provided in either survey – a common problem with many surveys of training utilization.

Several academic studies have attempted to assess the effectiveness of pre-departure training. Eschbach, Parker and Stoeberl[38] report the results of a study of 79 US repatriates. They measured cognitive, affective and experiential cross-cultural training, and language training, provided by the company or self-initiated. The amount and type of training, based on the models of Tung and Black *et al.* described earlier in this chapter, was included. Expatriates with integrated cross-cultural training exhibited cultural proficiency earlier, and appeared to have greater job satisfaction, than those with lesser training. Repatriates commented that there was a need for accurate, up-to-date cultural and language training for expatriates and spouses and many considered that preliminary visits should be used.

The second study was a meta-analysis of the cross-cultural training literature.[39] The conclusion reached was that the effectiveness of cross-cultural training was somewhat weaker than expected due to:

- Limited data as few organizations systematically evaluate or validate the effectiveness of their training programs or make them available to the public.
- The use of a mixture of different training methods, making evaluation of which method is most effective difficult to isolate.
- The large diversity in cultures that expatriates face.
- The interaction between individual differences between expatriates and the work environment they face. What works for one person may not work for another. Thus, the effects of cross-cultural training can be as diverse as the countries to which expatriates are assigned.

The authors add that traditional training methods may underestimate the complexity of international business life, where expatriate managers are required to perform complex jobs across multiple cultural contexts, sometimes on the same day or even within the hour. Training programs that capture this reality are difficult to find and many existing cross-cultural training programs have yet to prove their utility.[40]

Developing staff through international assignments

International assignments have long been recognized as an important mechanism for developing international expertise. The expected outcomes are:

- *Management development.* Individuals gain international experience, which assists in career progression, while the multinational gains through having a pool of experienced international operators on which to draw for future international assignments.
- *Organizational development.* International assignments also provide a multinational with a way of accumulating a stock of knowledge, skills and abilities upon which it can base its future growth. A global mindset is an important side benefit, as key personnel take a broader view. Further, as discussed previously, expatriates are agents of direct control and socialization and assist in the transfer of knowledge and competence.

We shall now consider these outcomes, first from the perspective of the individual, and then from the multinational's viewpoint.

Individual development

An international assignment can be compared to job rotation, a management development tool that seeks to provide certain employees with opportunities to enhance their abilities by exposing them to a range of jobs, tasks and challenges. It is therefore not surprising to find an implicit assumption that an international assignment has *per se* management development potential. Along with expected financial gain, perceived career advancement is often a primary motive for accepting international assignments. This is particularly the case in smaller population advanced economies (e.g. The Netherlands, Australia, Sweden and New Zealand) where the relatively small local economy is not big enough to generate growth and international activities provide the opportunity for ongoing revenue growth. In such a situation, employees understand that international experience is frequently a requirement for further career advancement. However, there is a paucity of research that demonstrates the link between an international assignment and career advancement. Two exceptions are studies by Feldman and Thomas, and Naumann.[41] While these studies confirm career expectations as motives, the expatriates involved were taken from those currently on assignment. Overall, there remains a need for research that establishes career paths as a direct consequence of international assignments.

There are two possible explanations for this lack of interest in the career outcomes of international assignments:

- Companies and academics have been somewhat preoccupied with the process of expatriation from the organization's perspective. It is important to understand the roles played by the various IHRM activities so that proper management and support for expatriates can be provided to reduce under-performance and improve cost-effectiveness.

- Surveys consistently report that expatriates consider career progression as a primary motive for accepting international assignments. Such a consistency of response – that is, career advancement as a reason for accepting an overseas assignment – has masked the issue of whether these career expectations are, indeed, met. In other words, we know why people accept international assignments, but we do not have a clear picture of when and how these expectations are met, and the consequences to both the individual and the multinational if the expected career outcomes are not met.

Developing international teams

Expatriates may gain individual management development from the international assignment, as we have previously discussed. The international assignment often is the 'training ground' for the international 'cadre' in Figure 6-4. International teams can be formed from those who have had international experience, though the international assignment itself may be an assignment to an international team, or to form an international team.

It is frequently argued that multinationals, especially in networked organizations, would benefit from using international teams as:

- A mechanism for fostering innovation, organizational learning and the transfer of knowledge.

- A means of breaking down functional and national boundaries, enhancing horizontal communication and information flows.

Figure 6-4 Developing international teams through international assignments

- A way of encouraging diverse inputs into decisions, problem solving and strategic assessments.
- A way of developing a global perspective.
- A way of developing shared values, thus assisting in the use of informal, normative control through socialization.

Research and development and international projects are common situations where teamwork is utilized and forms the basis of much of the literature on multinational teams, a sub-set of which is the virtual team, where members are geographically dispersed (see Figure 6-4).

To a certain extent, international assignments achieve teambuilding by exposing employees to various parts of the global organization. Consequently, expatriates develop local networks that often persist after completion of the assignment. These predominantly informal networks can later be activated for work situations, such as providing membership of project teams. Not everyone will wish to become part of an international 'cadre', but to create an effective global pool of international operators, many multinationals are conscious that they need to provide international experience to many levels of managers, regardless of nationality. A small cadre comprised only of PCNs may defeat the purpose of having a team of experienced employees who are capable of operating in multiple environments on various types of tasks and jobs. For example, Peterson[42] found that Western-based multinationals operating in Central and Eastern Europe were increasing the use of TCN and HCN expatriate transfers as a way of widening the 'corporate talent pool'.

While the international assignment plays an important role in both management and organizational development, its effectiveness depends on the individuals concerned, the type of multinational and contextual factors. For example, Caligiuri and Di Santo[43] argue that certain personality characteristics that have been identified as expatriate predictors of success cannot be developed through international assignments. In other words, individual characteristics such as dogmatic or authoritarian tendencies are not likely to be altered through an expatriate experience. However, Caligiuri and Di Santo do suggest that individuals can learn to be more sensitive to the challenges of working in another country – that is, become culturally aware. This knowledge and experience would prove valuable when working in an international team comprised of colleagues from other nationalities.

The MNE needs to be able to provide the resources and support for those working in international teams such as R&D projects. Managers supervising international teams, for example, will need to understand processes such as group dynamics, especially how national cultures affect group functioning. Those who have previous experience of international assignments and teams will be better placed than those who have not. Perhaps this is why some MNEs are placing greater stress on the need for international experience and are prepared to use expatriates despite the cost and difficulties often associated with international assignments. For recent reviews of the literature on developing international teams see Gibbs,[44] Maznevski et al.[45] and Caligiuri and Tarique.[46]

Trends in international training and development

There are a number of emerging and continuing trends in international training and development that we can briefly comment on. First, although the pressure from globalization continues to push MNEs towards a convergent approach to training and development, there is a continuing pressure from many countries (particularly developing countries) for localization of training and development initiatives of which MNEs must be mindful. Al-Dosary and Rahman[47] have reviewed the benefits and problems associated with localization of training and development. Second, there is a growing realization that although globalization is having a major impact on business processes and associated training and development efforts in MNEs, there is evidence that for competence development and learning, it is still necessary to consider the impact and importance of the national context and institutions on such efforts (see Geppert).[48] Third, there is increasing awareness of the important role of non-governmental organizations (NGOs) in international training and development (see Chang, and Brewster and Lee for recent reviews).[49] Fourth, with the rise of China as an economic superpower, there is increasing interest in all aspects of training and development with a focus on China (see Wang et al., Zhao, Zhang et al., Zhu, and Wang and Wang for recent reviews).[50] Finally, there is a realization in the training and development literature that the field must address global, comparative and national level contexts for training and development, just as the international HRM field is beginning to do so (see Metcalfe and Rees[51] for a recent review).

Summary

This chapter has concentrated on the issues relating to training and developing expatriates for international assignments. In the process, we have discussed:

- The role of expatriate training in supporting adjustment and on-assignment performance.
- The components of effective pre-departure training programs such as cultural awareness, preliminary visits, language skills, relocation assistance and training for trainers.
- How cultural awareness training appears to assist in adjustment and performance and therefore should be made available to all categories of staff selected for overseas postings, regardless of duration and location.

- The need for language training for the host country and in the relevant corporate language.
- The impact that an international assignment may have on an individual's career.
- The international assignment as an important way of training international operators and developing the international 'cadre'. In this sense, an international assignment is both training (gaining international experience and competence) and managerial and organizational development.
- How international assignments are connected to the creation of international teams.
- Trends in international training and development.

Discussion Questions

1 What are some of the challenges faced in training expatriate managers?

2 Assume you are the HR director for a small company that has begun to use international assignments. You are considering using an external consulting firm to provide pre-departure training for employees, as you do not have the resources to provide this 'in-house'. What components will you need covered? How will you measure the effectiveness of the pre-departure training program provided by this external consultant?

3 How does an international assignment assist in developing a 'cadre' of international operators? Why is it necessary to have such a 'cadre'?

4 Why do some MNEs appear reluctant to provide basic pre-departure training?

Further Reading

Caligiuri, P. and Tarique, I. (2006). 'International Assignee Selection and Cross-cultural Training and Development', in G. Stahl and I. Björkman (eds), *Handbook of Research in International Human Resource Management,* Cheltenham: Edward Elgar, pp. 302–22.

Festing, M. (2001). 'The Effects of International Human Resource Management Strategies on Global Leadership Development', in M. Mendenhall, T. Kuehlmann and G. Stahl (eds), *Developing Global Business Leaders: Policies, Processes, and Innovation*, Westport, CT: Quorum Books, pp. 37–57.

Littrell, L.N. and Salas, E. (2005). 'A Review of Cross-cultural Training: Best Practices, Guidelines, and Research Needs', *Human Resource Development Review*, 4(3): 305–34.

Osman-Gani, A. and Jacobs, R. (2005). 'Technological Change and Human Resource Development Practices in Asia: A Study of Singapore-based Companies', *International Journal of Training and Development,* 9(4): 271–80.

Notes and References

1 K. Kamoche, 'Strategic Human Resource Management with a Resource-Capability View of the Firm', *Journal of Management Studies,* Vol. 33, No. 2 (1996), p. 216.

2 P.C. Earley, 'Intercultural Training for Managers: A Comparison', *Academy of Management Journal*, Vol. 30, No. 4 (1987), p. 686.

3 R. Tung, 'Selection and Training Procedures of US, European, and Japanese Multinationals', *California Management Review,* Vol. 25, No. 1 (1982), pp. 57–71. Tung also asked those respondents who reported no formal training programs to give reasons for omitting these programs. Again, differences were found between the three regions. The US companies cited

a trend toward employment of local nationals (45 per cent); the temporary nature of such assignments (28 per cent); the doubtful effectiveness of such training programs (20 per cent); and lack of time (4 per cent). The reasons given by European multinationals were the temporary nature of such assignments (30 per cent); lack of time (30 per cent); a trend toward employment of local nationals (20 per cent); and the doubtful effectiveness of such programs. Responses from the Japanese companies were lack of time (63 per cent) and doubtful effectiveness of such programs (37 per cent).

4   J.C. Baker, 'Foreign Language and Departure Training in US Multinational Firms', *Personnel Administrator,* July (1984), pp. 68–70.

5   D. Feldman, 'Relocation Practices', *Personnel,* Vol. 66, No. 11 (1989), pp. 22–5. See also J. McEnery and G. DesHarnais, 'Culture Shock', *Training and Development Journal,* April (1990), pp. 43–7.

6   M. Mendenhall and G. Oddou, 'The Dimensions of Expatriate Acculturation', *Academy of Management Review,* Vol. 10, No. 1 (1985), pp. 39–47; and Y. Zeira, 'Overlooked Personnel Problems in Multinational Corporations', *Columbia Journal of World Business,* Vol. 10, No. 2 (1975), pp. 96–103.

7   J.S. Black and M. Mendenhall, 'Cross-Cultural Training Effectiveness: A Review and a Theoretical Framework for Future Research', *Academy of Management Review,* Vol. 15, No. 1 (1990), pp. 113–36.

8   Price Waterhouse, *International Assignments: European Policy and Practice* (London: Price Waterhouse, 1997/1998).

9   K. Barham and M. Devine, *The Quest for the International Manager: A Survey of Global Human Resource Strategies,* Ashridge Management Research Group, Special Report No. 2098 (London: The Economist Intelligence Unit 1990). See also, D. Welch, 'Determinants of International Human Resource Management Approaches and Activities: A Suggested Framework', *Journal of Management Studies,* Vol. 31, No. 2 (1994), pp. 139–64.

10 L.N. Littrell and E. Salas, 'A Review of Cross-Cultural Training: Best Practices, Guidelines, and Research Needs', *Human Resource Development Review,* Vol. 4, No. 3 (2005), pp. 305–34.

11 See, for example, M. Mendenhall and G. Oddou, 'Acculturation Profiles of Expatriate Managers: Implications for Cross-Cultural Training Programs', *Columbia Journal of World Business,* Winter (1986), pp. 73–9.

12 R. Tung, 'Selecting and Training of Personnel for Overseas Assignments', *Columbia Journal of World Business,* Vol. 16 (1981), pp. 68–78.

13 R.L. Tung, 'A Contingency Framework of Selection and Training of Expatriates Revisited', *Human Resource Management Review,* Vol. 8, No. 1 (1998), pp. 23–37.

14 M. Mendenhall and G. Oddou, 'Acculturation Profiles of Expatriate Managers'; M. Mendenhall, E. Dunbar and G. Oddou, 'Expatriate Selection, Training and Career-Pathing: A Review and Critique', *Human Resource Management,* Vol. 26 (1987), pp. 331–45.

15 Earley advocates the use of both documentary and interpersonal methods to prepare managers for intercultural assignments (see P. Earley, 'International Training for Managers: A Comparison of Documentary and Interpersonal Methods', *Academy of Management Journal,* Vol. 30, No. 4 (1987), pp. 685–98. Baliga and Baker suggest that the expatriates receive training that concentrates on the assigned region's culture, history, politics, economy, religion and social and business practices. They argue that only with precise knowledge of the varied components of their host culture can the expatriate and family grasp how and why people behave and react as they do (see G. Baliga and J.C. Baker, 'Multinational Corporate Policies for Expatriate Managers: Selection, Training, and Evaluation', *Advanced Management Journal,* Autumn (1985), pp. 31–8).

16 For further information on the use of cultural assimilators, see R.W. Brislin, 'A Culture General Assimilator: Preparation for Various Types of Sojourns', *International Journal of Intercultural Relations,* Vol. 10 (1986), pp. 215–34; and K. Cushner, 'Assessing the Impact of a Culture General Assimilator', *International Journal of Intercultural Relations,* Vol. 13 (1989), pp. 125–46.

17 J.S. Black and M. Mendenhall, 'A Practical but Theory-Based Framework for Selecting Cross-Cultural Training Methods', *Human Resource Management,* Vol. 28, No. 4 (1989), pp. 511–39.

18 A.M. Osman-Gani, 'Developing Expatriates for the Asia-Pacific Region: A Comparative Analysis of Multinational Enterprise Managers from Five Countries Across Three Continents', *Human Resource Development Quarterly,* Vol. 11, No. 3 (2000), pp. 213–35.

19 Price Waterhouse, *International Assignments: European Policy and Practice,* p. 35.

20 C. Brewster and J. Pickard, 'Evaluating Expatriate Training', *International Studies of Management and Organization,* Vol. 24, No. 3 (1994), pp. 18–35.

21 C. Wright and S. Wright, 'Do Languages Really Matter? The Relationship between International Business Success and a Commitment to Foreign Language Use', *Journal of Industrial Affairs,*

Vol. 3, No. 1 (1994) pp. 3–14. These authors suggest that international English is perhaps a better term than 'poor' or 'broken' English.

22 Tung, 'A Contingency Framework of Selection and Training of Expatriates Revisited'.

23 C. Fixman, 'The Foreign Language Needs of US-Based Corporations', *Annals, AAPSS*, 511 (September 1990).

24 V. Pucik, 'Strategic Human Resource Management in a Multinational Firm', in H.V. Wortzel and L.H. Wortzel (eds), *Strategic Management of Multinational Corporations: The Essentials* (New York: John Wiley, 1985).

25 C. Fixman, 'The Foreign Language Needs of US-Based Corporations', p. 36.

26 Wright and Wright, 'Do Languages Really Matter?', p. 5.

27 P. Hepner Hall and W.B. Gudykunst, 'The Relationship of Perceived Ethnocentrism in Corporate Cultures to the Selection, Training, and Success of International Employees', *International Journal of Intercultural Relations,* Vol. 13 (1989), pp. 183–201.

28 GMAC 2004 *Global Survey* (Oak Brook, IL: GMAC Global Relocation Services), p. 44.

29 Baliga and Baker, 'Multinational Corporate Policies'.

30 R.L. Tung and Arthur Andersen, *Exploring International Assignees' Viewpoints: A Study of the Expatriation/Repatriation Process* (Chicago, IL: Arthur Andersen, International Executive Services, 1997).

31 R. Marschan, D. Welch and L. Welch, 'Language: The Forgotten Factor in Multinational Management', *European Management Journal,* Vol. 15, No. 5 (1997), pp. 591–7; see also Fixman, 'The Foreign Language Needs of US-Based Corporations'.

32 The first author had the opportunity a number of years ago to visit McDonald's Hamburger University in Chicago and observe training for new store managers from a number of developing markets such as countries from Eastern Europe and Russia. The training facility was able to conduct a number of simultaneous training programs with full simultaneous translation into the native language of the participants.

33 See for example, H. Park, S.D. Hwang and J.K. Harrison, 'Sources and Consequences of Communication Problems in Foreign Subsidiaries: The Case of United States Firms in South Korea', *International Business Review,* Vol. 5, No. 1 (1996), pp. 79–98; and A. Rao and K. Hashimoto, 'Intercultural Influence: A Study of Japanese Expatriate Managers in Canada', *Journal of International Business Studies,* Vol. 27, No. 3 (1996), pp. 443–66.

34 M. Lazarova and I. Tarique, 'Knowledge Transfer Upon Repatriation', *Journal of World Business,* Vol. 40 (2005), pp. 361–73, quotation from p. 370.

35 M. Harvey, '"Inpatriation" Training: The Next Challenge for International Human Resource Management', *International Journal of Intercultural Relations,* Vol. 21, No. 3 (1997), pp. 393–428.

36 An exception is an article by R.S. DeFrank, R. Konopaske and J.M. Ivancevich, 'Executive Travel Stress: Perils of the Road Warrior', *Academy of Management Executive,* Vol. 14, No. 2 (2000), pp. 58–71. However, the authors only devote one paragraph to host culture issues.

37 D. Welch and V. Worm, 'International Business Travelers: A Challenge for IHRM', in G. Stahl and I. Björkman (eds), *Handbook of Research in International Human Resource Management* (Cheltenham: Edward Elgar, 2006), pp. 283–301.

38 D.M. Eschbach, G.E. Parker and P.A. Stoeberl, 'American Repatriate Employees' Retrospective Assessments of the Effects of Cross-Cultural Training on their Adaptation to International Assignments', *International Journal of Human Resource Management,* Vol. 12, No. 2 (2001), pp. 270–87.

39 M.A. Morris and C. Robie, 'A Meta-Analysis of the Effects of Cross-Cultural Training on Expatriate Performance and Adjustment', *International Journal of Training and Development,* Vol. 5, No. 2 (2001), pp. 112–25. The authors define meta-analysis as 'a method developed in the late 1970s to summarize and integrate research findings from multiple articles . . . to resolve conflicting findings of multiple studies on the same topic by combining their results in a systematic fashion', pp. 113–14.

40 J. Selmer, I. Torbiön and C.T. de Leon, 'Sequential Cross-Cultural Training for Expatriate Business Managers: Pre-departure and Post-arrival', *International Journal of Human Resource Management,* Vol. 9, No. 5 (1998), pp. 831–40.

41 D.C. Feldman and D.C. Thomas, 'Career Issues Facing Expatriate Managers', *Journal of International Business Studies,* Vol. 23, No. 2 (1992), pp. 271–94; E. Naumann, 'A Conceptual Model of Expatriate Turnover', *Journal of International Business Studies,* Vol. 23, No. 3 (1992), pp. 449–531.

42 R.B. Peterson, 'The Use of Expatriates and Inpatriates in Central and Eastern Europe Since the Wall Came Down', *Journal of World Business,* Vol. 38 (2003), pp. 55–69.

43 P. Caligiuri and V. Di Santo, 'Global Competence: What is It, and Can It be Developed Through Global Assignments?', *Human Resource Planning,* Vol. 24, No. 3 (2001), pp. 27–35.

44 J. Gibbs, 'Decoupling and Coupling in Global Teams: Implications for Human Resource Management', in G. Stahl and I. Björkman (eds), *Handbook of Research in International Human Resource Management* (Cheltenham: Edward Elgar, 2006), pp. 347–63.

45 M. Maznevski, S. Davison and K. Jonsen, 'Global Virtual Team Dynamics and Effectiveness', in G. Stahl and I. Björkman (eds), *Handbook of Research in International Human Resource Management* (Cheltenham: Edward Elgar, 2006), pp. 364–84.

46 P. Caligiuri and I. Tarique, 'International Assignee Selection and Cross-cultural Training and Development', in G. Stahl and I. Björkman (eds), *Handbook of Research in International Human Resource Management* (Cheltenham: Edward Elgar, 2006), pp. 302–22.

47 A. Al-Dosary and S. Rahman, 'Saudization (Localization) – A Critical Review', *Human Resource Development International,* Vol. 8, No. 4 (2005), pp. 495–502.

48 M. Geppert, 'Competence Development and Learning in British and German Subsidiaries of MNCs: Why and How National Institutions Still Matter', *Personnel Review,* Vol. 34, No. 2 (2005), pp. 155–77.

49 W. Chang, 'Expatriate Training in International Nongovernmental Organizations: A Model for Research', *Human Resource Development Review,* Vol. 4, No. 4 (2005), pp. 440–61; C. Brewster and S. Lee, 'HRM in Not-for-profit International Organizations: Different, But Also Alike', in H. Larsen and W. Mayrhofer (eds), *European Human Resource Management* (London: Routledge, 2006).

50 J. Wang, G. Wang, W. Ruona and J. Rojewski, 'Confucian Values and the Implications for International HRD', *Human Resource Development International,* Vol. 8, No. 3 (2005), pp. 311–26; C. Zhao, 'Management of Corporate Culture through Local Managers' Training in Foreign Companies in China: A Qualitative Analysis', *International Journal of Training and Development,* Vol. 9, No. 4 (2005), pp. 232–55; D. Zhang, Z. Zhang and B. Yang, 'Learning Organization in Mainland China: Empirical Research on its Application to Chinese State-owned Enterprises', *International Journal of Training and Development,* Vol. 8, No. 4 (2004), pp. 258–73; C. Zhu, *Human Resource Management in China: Past, Current and Future HR Practices in the Industrial Sector* (London: Routledge, 2004); J. Wang and G. Wang, 'Exploring National Human Resource Development: A Case of China Management Development in a Transitioning Context', *Human Resource Development Review,* Vol. 5, No. 2 (2006), pp. 176–201.

51 B. Metcalfe and C. Rees, 'Theorizing Advances in International Human Resource Development', *Human Resource Development International,* Vol. 8, No. 4. (2005), pp. 449–65.

International compensation

Chapter Objectives

In the introductory chapter we described international HR managers as grappling with complex issues. International managers must: (1) manage more activities from a broader perspective, (2) be more involved in the lives of their far-flung employees, (3) balance the needs of PCNs, HCNs and TCNs, (4) control exposure to financial and political risks, and (5) be increasingly aware of and responsive to host country and regional influences. All of these issues and concerns are brought out in a discussion of compensation issues. In this chapter we:

- Examine the complexities that arise when firms move from compensation at the domestic level to compensation in an international context.

- Detail the key components of an international compensation program.

- Outline the two main approaches to international compensation and the advantages and disadvantages of each approach.

- Examine the special problem areas of taxation, valid international living cost data and the problem of managing TCN compensation.

- Examine recent developments and global compensation issues.

Introduction

Global compensation practices have recently moved far beyond the original domain of expatriate pay. Compensation is increasingly seen as: a mechanism to develop and reinforce a global corporate culture,[1] a primary source of corporate control, explicitly linking performance outcomes with associated costs,[2] and the nexus of increasingly strident, sophisticated and public discourses on central issues of corporate governance in an international context.[3]

Increased *complexities* in global pay include the growing use of outsourced activities and subsequent labor pricing needs,[4] balancing centralization and decentralization of incentives, benefits and pensions, given the technical capabilities of Web-based human resource information systems (HRIS),[5] and balancing the need for more accurate and detailed performance metrics on international assignees with the realities of a cost-sensitive environment resulting from maturing global competitiveness.[6]

Increasingly domestic pay practices of long standing have been questioned as firms move into the global arena. These overt *challenges* to deeply held national and corporate values and pay systems include challenges to the universal applicability of incentive pay programs[7] and what some critics view as out of control executive compensation programs, often driven by US-based multinational pay systems.[8] Critiques of US-based MNE pay for executives have recently expanded to include challenges to the effectiveness of legal and institutional forms of corporate governance and the roles, responsibilities and pay practices of corporate boards, compensation committees and the use of executive pay consultants.[9]

Greater *choice*, the growing ability to systematically identify and implement heretofore novel or unrecognized pay practices, may be seen to result from increases in the transparency of pay practices around the world due to increased global media attention and reach, changes in corporate reporting regulations, the sheer number of assignments across borders, as well as the impact of the World Wide Web.[10] It remains to be seen if this increased choice will translate into a predictable set of global pay practices.

These complexities, challenges and choices facing managers involved in global compensation decisions do not change two primary areas of focus. These individuals must manage highly complex and turbulent local details while concurrently building and maintaining a unified, strategic pattern of compensation policies, practices and values.

For multinationals to successfully manage compensation and benefits requires knowledge of employment and taxation law, customs, environment and employment practices of many foreign countries; familiarity with currency fluctuations and the effect of inflation on compensation; and an understanding of why and when special allowances must be supplied and which allowances are necessary in what countries – all within the context of shifting political, economic and social conditions. The level of local knowledge needed in many of these areas requires specialist advice and many multinationals retain the services of consulting firms that may offer a broad range of services or provide highly specialized services relevant to HRM in a multinational context.[11]

Because of its complexity and expense, much of the discussion in this chapter addresses PCN compensation. However, issues relevant to TCNs and HCNs are also described because they are becoming more important to the success of many multinationals.[12] For example, in most Western countries a driver may be considered a luxury, only available to very senior managers. In developing economies a driver is economical in terms of cost, effectiveness and safety. Apart from the expectation that managers use drivers, parking is frequently chaotic in developing countries (especially in large cities) and the driver also performs the function of a parking attendant. In some developing countries it is quite common for the police to arrest drivers involved in traffic accidents and leave them in detention while responsibility and damages are assessed. Such a risk is unacceptable to most firms. Many multinationals do not allow their expatriate employees to drive at all in some developing countries and provide local drivers for both the expatriate and spouse.

Indeed, expatriate compensation – long the preoccupation of global HR executives – is increasingly seen more as a component of a more balanced, albeit complex, system of worldwide pay.[13] National and regional differences in the meaning, practice and tradition of pay remain significant sources of variation in the international firm. Yet these contextual sources of complexity must be balanced with strategic intent and administrative economy.[14] Rather than seeing pay as an ethnocentric extension of an essentially domestic strategy, pay systems are increasingly becoming truly global – with truly global objectives.[15]

Objectives of international compensation

When developing international compensation policies, a firm seeks to satisfy several objectives. First, the policy should be consistent with the overall strategy, structure and business needs of the multinational. Second, the policy must work to attract and retain staff in the areas where the multinational has the greatest needs and opportunities. Thus, the policy must be competitive and recognize factors such as incentive for foreign service, tax equalization and reimbursement for reasonable costs. Third, the policy should facilitate the transfer of international employees in the most cost-effective manner for the firm. Fourth, the policy must give due consideration to equity and ease of administration.

The international employee will also have a number of objectives that need to be achieved from the firm's compensation policy. First, the employee will expect the policy to offer financial protection in terms of benefits, social security and living costs in the foreign location. Second, the employee will expect a foreign assignment to offer opportunities for financial advancement through income and/or savings. Third, the employee will expect issues such as housing, education of children and recreation to be addressed in the policy. (The employee will also have expectations in terms of career advancement and repatriation, as discussed in Chapter 8.)

If we contrast the objectives of the multinational and the employee, we of course see the potential for many complexities and possible problems, as some of these objectives cannot be maximized on both sides. The 'war stories' about problems in international compensation that we see in HR practitioner magazines is testimony to these complexities and problems. However, if we take away the specialist jargon and allow for the international context, are the competing objectives of the firm and the employee *fundamentally* different from that which exists in a domestic environment? We think not. We agree with the broad thrust of an article by Milkovich and Bloom[16] which argues that firms must rethink the traditional view that local conditions dominate international compensation strategy. We will return to these issues at the end of the chapter after we have covered some of the technical aspects and complexities of compensation in an international context.

Key components of an international compensation program

The area of international compensation is complex primarily because multinationals must cater to three categories of employees: PCNs, TCNs and HCNs. In this section, we discuss key components of international compensation as follows.

Base salary

The term base salary acquires a somewhat different meaning when employees go abroad. In a domestic context, base salary denotes the amount of cash compensation serving as a benchmark for other compensation elements (such as bonuses and benefits). For expatriates, it is the primary component of a package of allowances, many of which are directly related to base salary (e.g. foreign service premium, cost-of-living allowance, housing allowance) as well as the basis for in-service benefits and pension contributions. It may be paid in home or local country currency. The base salary is the foundation block for international compensation whether the employee is a PCN or TCN. Major differences can occur in the employee's package depending on whether the base salary is linked to the home country of the PCN or TCN, or whether an international rate is paid. (We will return to this issue later in the chapter.)

Foreign service inducement/hardship premium

Parent-country nationals often receive a salary premium as an inducement to accept a foreign assignment or as compensation for any hardship caused by the transfer. Under such circumstances, the definition of hardship, eligibility for the premium, and amount and timing of payment must be addressed. In cases in which hardship is determined, US firms often refer to the US Department of State's *Hardship Post Differentials Guidelines* to determine an appropriate level of payment. As Ruff and Jackson[17] have noted, however, making international comparisons of the cost of living is problematic. It is important to note, though, that these payments are more commonly paid to PCNs than TCNs. Foreign service inducements, if used, are usually made in the form of a percentage of salary, usually 5 to 40 per cent of base pay. Such payments vary, depending upon the assignment, actual hardship, tax consequences and length of assignment. In addition, differentials may be considered; for example, a host country's work week may be longer than that of the home country, and a differential payment may be made in lieu of overtime, which is not normally paid to PCNs or TCNs.

Allowances

Issues concerning allowances can be very challenging to a firm establishing an overall compensation policy, partly because of the various forms of allowances that exist. The *cost-of-living allowance* (COLA), which typically receives the most attention, involves a payment to compensate for differences in expenditures between the home country and the foreign country (to account for inflation differentials, for example). Often this allowance is difficult to determine, so companies may use the services of organizations such as ORC Worldwide (a US-based firm)[18] or ECA International (based in Britain).[19] These firms specialize in providing COLA information on a global basis, regularly updated, to their clients. The COLA may also include payments for housing and utilities, personal income tax, or discretionary items.[20]

The provision of a *housing allowance* implies that employees should be entitled to maintain their home-country living standards (or, in some cases, receive accommodation that is equivalent to that provided for similar foreign employees and peers). Such allowances are often paid on either an assessed or an actual basis. Other alternatives include company-provided housing, either mandatory or optional; a fixed housing allowance; or assessment of a portion of income, out of which actual housing costs are paid. Housing issues are often addressed on a case-by-case basis, but as a firm internationalizes, formal policies become more necessary and efficient. Financial assistance and/or protection in connection with the sale or leasing of an expatriate's former residence is offered by many multinationals. Those in the banking and finance industry tend to be the most generous, offering assistance in sale or leasing, payment of closing costs, payment of leasing management fees, rent protection and equity protection. Again, TCNs receive these benefits less frequently than PCNs.

There is also a provision for *home leave allowances.* Many employers cover the expense of one or more trips back to the home country each year. The purpose of paying for such trips is to give expatriates the opportunity to renew family and business ties, thereby helping them to avoid adjustment problems when they are repatriated. Although firms traditionally have restricted the use of leave allowances to travel home, some firms give expatriates the option of applying the allowances to foreign travel rather than returning home. Firms allowing use of home leave allowances for foreign travel need to be aware that expatriate employees with limited international experience who opt for foreign travel rather than returning home may become more homesick than other expatriates who return home for a 'reality check' with fellow employees and friends.[21]

Education allowances for expatriates' children are also an integral part of any international compensation policy. Allowances for education can cover items such as tuition, language class tuition, enrolment fees, books and supplies, transportation, room and board and uniforms. (While not common in the USA, it is quite common in many countries for high-school students to wear uniforms.) The level of education provided for, the adequacy of local schools and transportation of dependents who are being educated in other locations may present problems for multinationals. PCNs and TCNs usually receive the same treatment concerning educational expenses. The cost of local or boarding school for dependent children is typically covered by the employer, although there may be restrictions, depending on the availability of good local schools and on their fees. Attendance at a university may also be provided for, when deemed necessary.

Relocation allowances usually cover moving, shipping and storage charges; temporary living expenses; subsidies regarding appliance or car purchases (or sales); and down payments or lease-related charges. Allowances regarding perquisites (cars, club memberships, servants,[22] and so on) may also need to be considered (usually for more senior positions, but this varies according to location). These allowances are often contingent upon tax-equalization policies and practices in both the home and the host countries.

Increasingly, many MNEs are also offering *spouse assistance* to help guard against or offset income lost by an expatriate's spouse as a result of relocating abroad. Although some firms may pay an allowance to make up for a spouse's lost income, US firms are beginning to focus on providing spouses with employment opportunities abroad, either by offering job-search assistance or employment in the firm's foreign office (subject to a work visa being available).

To summarize, MNEs generally pay allowances in order to encourage employees to take international assignments and to keep employees 'whole' relative to home standards. We will present more about this concept later in the chapter. In terms of housing, companies usually pay a tax-equalized housing allowance in order to discourage the purchase of housing and/or to compensate for higher housing costs. This allowance is adjusted periodically based on estimates of both local and foreign housing costs.

Benefits

The complexity inherent in international benefits often brings more difficulties than when dealing with compensation. Pension plans are very difficult to deal with country-to-country, as national practices vary considerably. Transportability of pension plans, medical coverage and social security benefits are very difficult to normalize. Therefore, firms need to address many issues when considering benefits, including:

● Whether or not to maintain expatriates in home-country programs, particularly if the firm does not receive a tax deduction for it.
● Whether firms have the option of enrolling expatriates in host-country benefit programs and/or making up any difference in coverage.
● Whether expatriates should receive home-country or host-country social security benefits.

Most US PCNs typically remain under their home countries' benefit plan. In some countries, expatriates cannot opt out of local social security programs. In such circumstances, the firm normally pays for these additional costs. European PCNs and TCNs enjoy portable social security benefits within the European Union. Laws governing private benefit practices differ from country to country, and firm practices also vary. Not surprisingly, multinationals have generally done a good job of planning for the retirement needs of their PCN employees, but this is generally less the case for TCNs.[23] There are many reasons for this: TCNs may have little or no home-country social security coverage; they may have spent many years in countries that do not permit currency transfers of accrued benefit payments; or they may spend their final year or two of employment in a country where final average salary is in a currency that relates unfavorably to their home-country currency. How their benefits are calculated and what type of retirement plan applies to them may make the difference between a comfortable retirement in a country of their choice and a forced penurious retirement elsewhere.

In addition to the already discussed benefits, multinationals also provide vacations and special leave. Included as part of the employee's regular vacation, annual home leave usually provides airfares for families to return to their home countries. Rest and rehabilitation leave, based on the conditions of the host country, also provides the employee's family with free airfares to a more comfortable location near the host country. In addition to rest and rehabilitation leave, emergency provisions are available in case of a death or illness in the family. Employees in hardship locations often receive additional leave expense payments and rest and rehabilitation periods.

Approaches to international compensation

There are two main options in the area of international compensation – the *Going Rate Approach* (also referred to as the Market Rate Approach) and the *Balance Sheet Approach* (sometimes known as the Build-up Approach). In this section we describe each approach and discuss the advantages and disadvantage inherent in each approach.[24]

The Going Rate Approach

The key characteristics of this approach are summarized in Table 7-1. With this approach, the base salary for the international transfer is linked to the salary structure in the host country. The multinational usually obtains information from local compensation surveys and must decide whether local nationals (HCNs), expatriates of the same nationality or expatriates of all nationalities will be the reference point in terms of benchmarking. For example, a Japanese bank operating in New York would need to decide whether its reference point would be local US salaries, other Japanese competitors in New York, or all foreign banks operating in New York. With the Going Rate Approach, if the location is in a low-pay county, the multinational usually supplements base pay with additional benefits and payments.

There are advantages and disadvantages of the Going Rate Approach, summarized in Table 7-2. The advantages are: there is equality with local nationals (very

Going Rate Approach	Table 7-1

- Based on local market rates
- Relies on survey comparisons among:
  - Local nationals (HCNs)
  - Expatriates of same nationality
  - Expatriates of all nationalities
- Compensation based on the selected survey comparison
- Base pay and benefits may be supplemented by additional payments for low-pay countries

Advantages and disadvantages of the Going Rate Approach	Table 7-2

Advantages	Disadvantages
- Equality with local nationals - Simplicity - Identification with host country - Equity amongst different nationalities	- Variation between assignments for same employee - Variation between expatriates of same nationality in different countries - Potential re-entry problems

effective in attracting PCNs or TCNs to a location that pays higher salaries than those received in the home country); the approach is simple and easy for expatriates to understand; expatriates are able to identify with the host country; and there is often equity amongst expatriates of different nationalities.

There are also disadvantages with the Going Rate Approach. First, there can be variation between assignments for the same employee. This is most obvious when we compare an assignment in an advanced economy with one in a developing country, but also between assignments in various advanced economies where differences in managerial salaries and the effect of local taxation can significantly influence an employee's compensation level using the Going Rate Approach. Not surprisingly, individual employees are very sensitive to this issue. Second, there can be variation between expatriates of the same nationality in different locations. A strict interpretation of the Going Rate Approach can lead to rivalry for assignments to locations which are financially attractive and little interest in locations considered to be financially unattractive.

Finally, the Going Rate Approach can pose problems upon repatriation when the employee's salary reverts to a home-country level that is below that of the host-country. This is not only a problem for firms in developing countries, but also for firms from many countries where local managerial salaries are well below that of the USA, which is the world market leader in managerial salaries.[25] For example, a survey by Towers Perrin[26] of total compensation for CEOs around the world reported the following results for various countries (all figures in US dollars):

- USA: $2 164 952
- United Kingdom: $1 184 936
- Italy: $1 137 326
- Canada: $1 068 964
- Singapore: $1 033 274
- Mexico: $1 002 357
- Belgium: $987 387
- The Netherlands: $862 711
- Australia: $707 747
- China (Hong Kong): $651 339
- Venezuela: $467 868
- Argentina: $431 300

As this list shows, a manager from Argentina or The Netherlands would be very positive about a Going Rate approach to compensation if they were offered senior expatriate assignments in the USA, but would have some difficulties adjusting back to local salaries on their repatriation to their home country.

The Balance Sheet Approach

The key characteristics of this approach (which is the most widely used approach for international compensation) are summarized in Table 7-3. The basic objective is to '*keep the expatriate whole*'[27] (that is, maintaining relativity to PCN colleagues and compensating for the costs of an international assignment) through maintenance of home-country living standard plus a financial inducement to make the

The Balance Sheet Approach	**Table 7-3**

- Basic objective is maintenance of home-country living standard plus financial inducement
- Home-country pay and benefits are the foundations of this approach
- Adjustments to home package to balance additional expenditure in host country
- Financial incentives (expatriate/hardship premium) added to make the package attractive
- Most common system in usage by multinational firms

package attractive. This approach links the base salary for PCNs and TCNs to the salary structure of the relevant home country. For example, a US executive taking up an international position would have his or her compensation package built upon the US base-salary level rather than that applicable to the host country. The key assumption of this approach is that foreign assignees should not suffer a material loss due to their transfer, and this is accomplished through the utilization of what is generally referred to as the *Balance Sheet Approach*. According to Reynolds:

> The balance sheet approach to international compensation is a system designed to equalize the purchasing power of employees at comparable position levels living overseas and in the home-country, and to provide incentives to offset qualitative differences between assignment locations.[28]

There are four major categories of outlays incurred by expatriates that are incorporated in the Balance Sheet Approach:

1 *Goods and services* – home-country outlays for items such as food, personal care, clothing, household furnishings, recreation, transportation and medical care.

2 *Housing* – the major costs associated with housing in the host country.

3 *Income taxes* – parent-country and host-country income taxes.

4 *Reserve* – contributions to savings, payments for benefits, pension contributions, investments, education expenses, social security taxes, etc.

Where costs associated with the host-country assignment exceed equivalent costs in the parent country, these costs are met by both the firm and the expatriate to ensure that parent-country equivalent purchasing power is achieved.

Table 7-4 shows a typical spreadsheet for an expatriate assignment using the Balance Sheet Approach. In this example, an Australian expatriate is assigned to a country called New Euphoria which has a Cost-of-Living-Index of 150 relative to Australia and an exchange rate of 1.5 relative to the Australian dollar. In addition to a foreign service premium, a hardship allowance is also payable for this location. Housing is provided by the firm, and a notional cost for this is recognized by a 7 per cent deduction from the package, along with a notional tax deduction (we discuss taxation later in the chapter). The expatriate can see from this spreadsheet what components are offered in the package and how the package will be split between Australian currency and New Euphoria currency.

There are advantages and disadvantages of the Balance Sheet Approach, summarized in Table 7-5. There are three main advantages. First, the Balance Sheet Approach provides equity between foreign assignments and between expatriates of

Table 7-4	Expatriate compensation worksheet

Employee: Brian Smith
Position: Marketing Manager
Country: New Euphoria
Reason for change: New Assignment
Effective date of change   1 February 2008

Item	Amount A$ PA	Paid in Australian dollars A$ PA	Paid in local currency NE$ PA
Base salary	200000	100000	150000
Cost of living allowance	50000		75000
Overseas service premium (20%)	40000	40000	
Hardship allowance (20%)	40000	40000	
Housing deduction (7%)	−14000	−14000	
Tax deduction	−97000	−97000	
TOTAL	219000	69000	225000

COLA Index = 150

Table 7-5	Advantages and disadvantages of the Balance Sheet Approach

Advantages	Disadvantages
• Equity ○ Between assignments ○ Between expatriates of the same nationality • Facilitates expatriate re-entry • Easy to communicate to employees	• Can result in great disparities ○ Between expatriates of different nationalities ○ Between expatriates and local nationals • Can be quite complex to administer

the same nationality. Second, repatriation of expatriates is facilitated by this emphasis on equity with the parent country as expatriate compensation remains anchored to the compensation system in the parent country. Third, this approach is easy to communicate, as Table 7-4 illustrates.

There are two main disadvantages of the Balance Sheet Approach. First, this approach can result in considerable disparities – both between expatriates of different nationalities and between PCNs and HCNs. Problems arise when international staff are paid different amounts for performing the same (or very similar) job in the host location, according to their different home base salary. For example, in the Singapore regional headquarters of a US bank, a US PCN and a New Zealand TCN may perform the same banking duties but the American will receive a higher salary than the New Zealander because of the differences in US and New Zealand base-salary levels. As noted above, differences in base-salary levels can also cause difficulties between expatriates and HCNs. Traditionally, this has referred to the problem of highly paid PCNs being resented by local HCN employees because these 'foreigners' are perceived as being excessively compensated (and because they are blocking career opportunities for locals).

However, feelings of resentment and inequity can also run in the other direction. For instance, as indicated above, the USA has the highest level of managerial compensation in the world. Thus, a firm which establishes a subsidiary in the USA (or acquires a US business) may find that if it uses a Balance Sheet Approach, its expatriates may be substantially underpaid compared to local American employees. While the logic of the balance sheet states that being tied to the home country assists in repatriation because the expatriate identifies with the home country, research in equity theory[29] suggests that employees do not always assess compensation issues in a detached and rational way.

The issue of base salary differences is also a concern for US employees working for foreign firms operating in the USA. Many non-US multinationals are reluctant to pay high US salaries to US employees who are offered international assignments (as HCNs into the firm's home-country operations, or as TCNs). US employees are equally reluctant to accept the lower salaries paid in the firm's home country. Thus, the Balance Sheet Approach not only can produce disparities, but also may act as a barrier to staff acceptance of international assignments.

A second problem with the Balance Sheet Approach is that while this approach is both elegant and simple as a concept, it can become quite complex to administer. Complexities particularly arise in the areas of tightly integrated private and government fund transfers; or, put more plainly, taxes and pensions.

Taxation

This aspect of international compensation is probably the one that causes the most concern to HR practitioners and expatriates (both PCNs and TCNs), as taxation generally evokes emotional responses.[30] No one enjoys paying taxes, and this issue can be very time consuming for both the firm and the expatriate. To illustrate the potential problems, an assignment abroad can mean being a US expatriate is taxed both in the country of assignment and in the USA. This dual tax cost, combined with all of the other expatriate costs, makes some US multinationals think twice about making use of expatriates. It is important to note that Section 911 of the US Internal Revenue Service Code contains provisions permitting a substantial deduction on foreign-earned income, but US expatriates must file with the IRS and usually also with the host-country tax office during their period of foreign service. This requirement is more onerous than for some other nationalities who may not be required to declare their total global income to their home-country taxation authority.

Multinationals generally select one of the following approaches to handling international taxation:

- *Tax equalization.* Firms withhold an amount equal to the home-country tax obligation of the PCN, and pay all taxes in the host country.

- *Tax protection.* The employee pays up to the amount of taxes he or she would pay on compensation in the home country. In such a situation, the employee is entitled to any windfall received if total taxes are less in the foreign country than in the home country. In her review of global compensation, Stuart[31] adds two other approaches: (1) ad hoc (each expatriate is handled differently, depending upon the individual package agreed to with the firm); and (2) laissez-faire (employees are 'on their own' in conforming to host-country and home-country taxation laws and practices). However, neither of these approaches are recommended and we shall focus on tax equalization and tax protection, as these are the most common approaches.

Tax equalization is by far the more common taxation policy used by multinationals.[32] Thus, for a PCN, tax payments equal to the liability of a home-country taxpayer with the same income and family status are imposed on the employee's salary and bonus. Any additional premiums or allowances are typically paid by the firm, tax-free to the employee. As multinationals operate in more and more countries, they are subject to widely discrepant income tax rates. It is also important to note that just focusing on income tax can be misleading, as the shares of both personal and corporate taxes are rising in the OECD countries.[33] For example, if we look at selected maximum federal marginal tax rates (see Table 7-6) the 'top five' highest taxation countries are The Netherlands, Belgium, France, Australia and China. The USA is significantly below the rates for these five countries.[34]

Table 7-6	Maximum marginal federal tax rates

Country	Maximum marginal rate (%)
Argentina	35.00
Australia	47.00
Belgium	50.00
Brazil	27.50
Canada	29.00
China (Hong Kong)	20.00
China	45.00
France	48.09
Germany	42.00
India	33.66
Italy	43.00
Japan	37.00
Malaysia	28.00
Mexico	33.00
Netherlands	52.00
Poland	40.00
Singapore	22.00
South Africa	40.00
South Korea	35.00
Spain	29.16
Sweden	26.00
Switzerland	11.50
Taiwan	40.00
United Kingdom	40.00
United States	35.00
Venezuela	34.00

Source: Adapted from Towers Perrin, *Worldwide Total Remuneration 2005–2006*[35]

Many multinationals have responded to this complexity and diversity across countries by retaining the services of international accounting firms to provide advice and prepare host-country and home-country tax returns for their expatriates. Increasingly, firms are also outsourcing the provisions of further aspects of the total expatriate compensation packages including a variety of destination services in lieu of providing payment in a package.[36] When multinationals plan compensation packages, they need to consider to what extent specific practices can be modified in each country to provide the most tax-effective, appropriate rewards for PCNs, HCNs and TCNs within the framework of the overall compensation policy of the firm.

As one international HRM manager noted, the difficulties in international compensation 'are not compensation so much as benefits'. Pension plans are very difficult to compare or equalize across nations, as cultural practices vary considerably. Transportability of pension plans, medical coverage and social security benefits are very difficult to normalize.[37] Therefore, companies need to address many issues when considering benefits, including:

- Whether or not to maintain expatriates in home-country programs, particularly if the company does not receive a tax deduction for it.
- Whether companies have the option of enrolling expatriates in host-country benefit programs and/or making up any difference in coverage.
- Whether host-country legislation regarding termination affects benefit entitlement.
- Whether expatriates should receive home-country or host-country social security benefits.
- Whether benefits should be maintained on a home-country or host-country basis, who is responsible for the cost, whether other benefits should be used to offset any shortfall in coverage, and whether home-country benefit programs should be exported to local nationals in foreign countries.

Differences in national sovereignty are also at work in the area of mandated public and private pension schemes, what many nations refer to as 'social security' programs. Table 7-7 highlights the differences in mandated degree of contribution (ranging from a low of 0 per cent to a high of over 60 per cent) as well as the mix of employer–employee contribution.

For many international firms, expatriate assignments are likely to increase in distance, number and duration over an employee's career, and more and more firms may create cadres of permanent international assignees – called 'globals' by some firms. The inherent complexity and dynamism of culturally embedded and politically volatile national tax and pension processes promise to tax the resources, time and attention of international human resource managers for the foreseeable future. Seamless networks of global firms, their specialist consultants and local and regional public and private interests are a goal, not yet a reality.

International living costs data

Obtaining up-to-date information on international living costs is a constant issue for multinationals. As we noted at the beginning of this chapter, the level of local knowledge required in many areas of IHRM requires specialist advice. Consequently, many multinationals retain the services of consulting firms that may offer a broad range of services or provide highly specialized services relevant to HRM in a multinational context. With regard to international living costs, a number of consulting firms offer

Table 7-7	Social security contributions by employers and employees

Country	Employer contribution rate (%)	Employee contribution rate (%)	Total contribution rate (%)
Argentina	17.00	17.00	34.67
Australia	0.00*	0.00*	0.00*
Belgium	34.69	13.07	47.76
Brazil	20.00	11.00	31.00
Canada	4.95	4.95	9.90
China (Hong Kong)	0.00	0.00	0.00
China	43.50	18.00	61.50
France	**	**	**
Germany	16.90	16.90	33.80
India	13.59	1.75	0.00
Italy	**	**	**
Japan	11.07	11.07	22.13
Malaysia	1.80	0.50	2.30
Mexico	29.00	4.00	33.00
Netherlands	0.00*	32.60	32.60
Poland	16.26	26.96	43.22
Singapore	0.00*	0.00*	0.00*
South Africa	1.00	1.00	2.00
South Korea	6.66	6.66	13.32
Spain	23.60	4.70	28.30
Sweden	24.26	7.00	31.26
Switzerland	5.05	5.05	10.10
Taiwan	4.55	1.30	5.85
United Kingdom	12.80	11.00	23.00
United States	6.20	6.20	12.40
Venezuela	9.00	4.00	13.00

*When the contributions are at zero, they are funded out of the General Tax Revenue and range from zero to very high values
**Varies
Source: Adapted from Towers Perrin, *Worldwide Total Remuneration 2005–2006.*[38]

regular surveys calculating a cost-of-living index that can be updated in terms of currency exchange rates. A recent survey of living costs[39] in selected cities ranked the ten most expensive cities as Tokyo, Osaka, London, Moscow, Seoul, Geneva, Zurich, Copenhagen, Hong Kong and Oslo. The first US city in the index was New York, ranked as the 13th most expensive city. The least expensive city was Asuncion (Paraguay).

MNEs using the balance sheet approach must constantly update compensation packages with new data on living costs which is an ongoing administrative requirement. This is an important issue to expatriate employees and forms the basis of many complaints if updating substantially lags behind any rise in living costs. Multinationals must also be able to respond to unexpected events such as the currency and stock market crash that suddenly unfolded in a number of Asian countries in late 1997. Some countries such as Indonesia faced a devaluation of their currency (the Ruphiah) by over 50 per cent against the US dollar in a matter of weeks. This event had a dramatic impact on prices, the cost of living and the cost of servicing debt for Indonesian firms with loans denominated in a foreign currency such as the US dollar. There is also much debate about what should be in the 'basket of goods' which consulting firms use as the basis for calculating living costs around the world. For example, the Swiss Bank UBS uses the 'Big Mac Index' to measure living costs around the world.[40]

According to Table 7-8, it takes just over three hours for the average worker in Nairobi to earn enough for a Big Mac. In Los Angeles, Miami and Tokyo, the global burger can be bought for a mere 10 minutes' effort.[41]

Range of working times required to buy one Big Mac	**Table 7-8**

City	Minutes
Chicago	9
Los Angeles, Miami, Tokyo	10
New York	12
Hong Kong	12
Toronto	13
Zurich, Montreal, Dublin, Luxembourg,	14
Basel, Frankfurt, Vienna	15
Geneva, Copenhagen, Amsterdam, Berlin, London, Nicosia	16
Lugano, Taipei	17
Oslo, Brussels, Sydney	18
Auckland, Helsinki, Stockholm, Paris	19
Dubai, Singapore	20
Madrid, Milan, Athens	21
Vilnius, Lagos	57
Manila	59
Jakarta	64
Mexico City	72
Caracas,	74
Kiev, Lima	75
Bucarest	76
Bogota	90
Mumbai	104
Karachi	132
Nairobi	181

Notes: Price of one Big Mac divided by weighted average hourly pay across 13 occupations
Source: UBS, Prices and Earning 2005.[42]

It is also possible to take a wider view and focus on *business costs* rather than living costs for expatriates, because the multinational firm is interested in the overall cost of doing business in a particular country as well as the more micro issue of expatriate living costs. *The Economist* Intelligence Unit[43] calculates such indices, which measure the relative costs of doing business in different economies by compiling statistics relating to wages, costs for expatriate staff, air travel and subsistence, corporation taxes, perceived corruption levels, office and industrial rents and road transport. Generally the developed countries tend to rank as more expensive than developing countries because their wage costs are higher.

Differentiating between PCNs and TCNs

As we have indicated, one of the outcomes of the balance sheet approach is to produce differentiation between expatriate employees of different nationalities because of the use of nationality to determine the relevant home-country base salary. In effect, this is a differentiation between PCNs and TCNs. Many TCNs have a great deal of international experience because they often move from country to country in the employ of one multinational (or several) headquartered in a country other than their own (for example, an Indian banker may work in the Singapore branch of a US bank). As Reynolds[44] has observed, there is no doubt that paying TCNs according to their home-country base salary can be less expensive than paying all expatriates on a PCN scale (particularly if the multinational is headquartered in a country such as the USA or Germany which has both high managerial salaries and a strong currency), but justifying these differences can be very difficult. Nonetheless, it is common practice for MNEs to use a home-country balance sheet approach for TCNs. Evidently, the reduction in expenses outweighs the difficulty of justifying any pay differentials. However, as firms expand internationally, it is likely that TCN employees will become more valuable and firms may need to rethink their approach to compensating TCNs.

As a starting point, multinational firms need to match their compensation policies with their staffing policies and general HR philosophy. If, for example, a firm has an ethnocentric staffing policy, its compensation policy should be one of keeping the expatriate *whole* (that is, maintaining relativity to PCN colleagues plus compensating for the costs of international service). If, however, the staffing policy follows a geocentric approach (that is, staffing a position with the 'best person', regardless of nationality), there may be no clear 'home' for the TCN, and the firm will need to consider establishing a system of *international base pay* for key managers, regardless of nationality, that is paid in a major reserve currency such as the US dollar or the Euro. This system allows firms to deal with considerable variations in base salaries for managers.

Tentative conclusions: patterns in complexity, challenges and choices

As outlined at the opening of the chapter, international compensation administration may be more complex than its domestic counterpart, but is only slowly and fitfully evolving from a dominant domestic state of origin.[45] Domestic pay patterns – that is norms and assumptions, pay strategies and practices, as well as pay forms and administration – are increasingly challenged as executives in MNEs are exposed to alternative pay forms, varying legal and institutional contexts and the rapidly changing realities of global competitiveness.

Recent developments in the study of global pay issues may be seen to operate at three distinct vertical levels: the basic level of cultural values and assumptions; the intermediate level of pay strategy, practices and systems design; and the surface (artefact) level of pay administration and form[46] – see Figure 7-1. On a second, horizontal level, firms must individually determine how to strike a balance between traditional, internally based models and explanations of pay and those more externally focused models and explanations of pay that comprise a global challenge to the status quo.[47] Globalizing firms must individually choose between internally and externally focused assumptions, strategies and practices. This combined choice is the complex 'context' of pay for any given global firm. Pay context is the pivotal center column in Figure 7-1.

On the level of basic explanations, firms can choose to emphasize firm-specific theories of job worth (such as resource-based views of the firm,[48] behavioral theory,[49] or new institutional economics models)[50] or they may emphasize firm

Complexity, challenges and choices in global pay   **Figure 7-1**

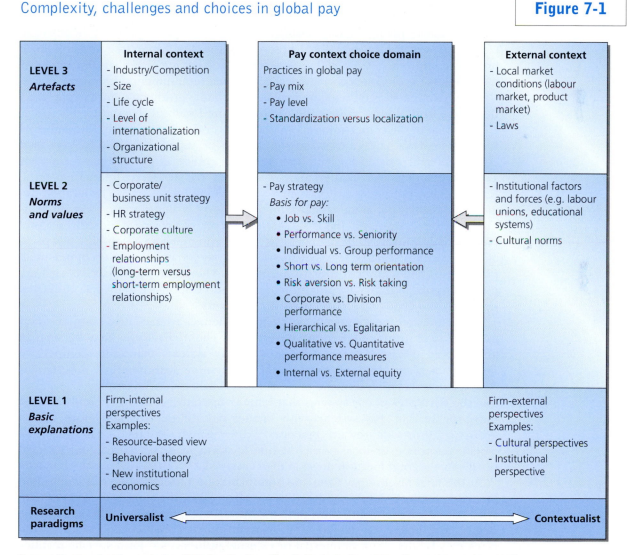

Source: Reprinted with permission. © Marion Festing, Allen D. Engle, Sr, Peter J. Dowling and Bernadette Müller.

external theories of job worth (such as cultural and institutional perspectives).[51] These theories may be implicit and not articulated by pay practitioners, and yet these assumptions may indirectly drive all other pay processes. On the more explicit, and more widely investigated, level of norms and values, pay strategy may be seen as some combination of internal, corporate norms (derived from and consistent with pay strategy, IHRM strategy, and traditional employment relationships – practised 'psychological contracts') and external, environmental norms (derived from labor unions, educational systems, and local or regional institutional sources) that may vary significantly by geographic region.

Pay strategy may be defined in terms of a series of interlocking strategic choices on: basis of pay (job versus skill, performance versus seniority),[52] unit of aggregation (paying individuals, groups, organizations, short- versus long-term orientation to pay),[53] patterns of variation in pay (variability or risk in pay, hierarchical versus egalitarian pay orientation),[54] and an overall focus on internal equity – as captured by job evaluation systems – as opposed to external equity – as captured by market surveys.[55] 'Universal' pay systems may be preferred by corporate pay planners rather than having to deal with myriad 'local' systems. Ease of administration and the standardization of practices are attractive and can contribute to simplicity in global assignments, resolving disputes related to perceived inequities or policy inconsistencies, etc. However, local or regional 'host contexts' and/or firm strategy may influence firms to compromise these global preferences and strategically align pay practices more or less in conformance with local or regional requirements.[56] Strategic necessity and contextual requirements may incrementally grudgingly 'move' pay practices away from a universalized and toward a more localized character.[57]

Note that in the center column of Figure 7-1, under 'basis for pay', a number of levels of analysis have emerged to supplement or augment traditional job-based pay. Firms may provide a *person* with personal 'choice' in pay and pay for his/her skills or competencies.[58] Alternately, a firm may pay at the traditional *job* level, realizing that even standard jobs may vary tremendously across geographic regions. Firms may pay at the task *group* or plant level of aggregation.[59] Finally, firms may provide 'customized' pay at the *national* level, or provide standardized 'core' pay for all employees in the global *firm*.[60] Increasingly, we may combine pay packages across these vertical levels of analysis and pay for a combination of personal, job, group, national, or corporate purposes.[61] These composite pay systems are more complex, but they are also more flexible and responsive to diverse employee demands and changing global business conditions.

Recall our earlier comments on global challenges to executive compensation practices and forms of corporate governance. These challenges may be seen as an ongoing debate between advocates of pay systems that value competitive individualism and result in 'hierarchical' pay systems with large pay differentials for executives, market sensitive professions and other 'critical' employee groups[62] and the advocates of pay systems that value cooperative collectivism and result in more 'egalitarian' pay systems with smaller pay differentials and more shared group or firm-wide reward practices.[63] Increasingly, multinational firms that violate corporate or local norms in one location in order to respond to local norms in a second location do so at their own risk.[64]

At the final level of pay form and administration (artefacts) we may determine that pay practices such as pay mix (between base pay, the nature and extent of benefits, use of long-term and short-term incentives, etc.), overall level of pay, and the degree to which pay is standardized across all units or customized to local conditions may be the result of internal or external influences.[65] Firm specific realities (such as operating in a monopolistic industry, a low degree of internationalization, and simple organizational design) may mitigate for standardized pay practices. Conversely, strongly held local values, institutions and regulations, an advanced level of internationalization and decentralized organizational designs may mitigate for more flexible, localized pay practices.[66]

Summary

In this chapter, we have examined the complexities that arise when firms move from compensation at the domestic level to compensation in an international context. It is evident from our review that compensation policy becomes a much less precise process than is the case in the domestic HR context. To demonstrate this complexity, we have:

- Detailed the key components of an international compensation program.

- Outlined the two main approaches to international compensation (the Going Rate and the Balance Sheet) and the advantages and disadvantages of each approach.

- Outlined special problem areas such as taxation, obtaining valid international living costs data and the problems of managing TCN compensation.

- Presented a model of global pay that highlights the complexity and yet familiarity of pay practices in the global context. It is this combination of pay decisions based on strategic global standardization and sensitivity to changing local and regional conditions that characterizes the state of international pay practices.

- Posited that a strategic yet sensitive balance can only be achieved by creating and maintaining professional networks, comprised of home office and local affiliate HR practitioners, outsourcing selected activities through specialist consultants, and a close cooperation with local and regional governments and other key local institutions.

Discussion Questions

1 What should be the main objectives for a multinational firm with regard to its compensation policies?

2 Describe the main differences in the Going Rate and Balance Sheet Approaches to international compensation.

3 What are the key differences in salary compensation for PCNs and TCNs? Do these differences matter?

4 What are the main points that MNEs must consider when deciding how to provide benefits?

5 Why is it important for MNEs to understand the compensation practices of other countries?

6 Explain how balancing the interests of global and local, occupational and functional perspectives might play out in a compensation decision scenario.

Further Reading

Bonache, J. (2006). 'The Compensation of Expatriates: A Review and a Future Research Agenda', in G. Stahl and I. Björkman (eds), *Handbook of Research in International Human Resource Management,* Cheltenham: Edward Elgar, pp. 158–75.

Festing, M. (2006). 'International Human Resource Management and Economic Theories of the Firm', in G. Stahl and I. Björkman (eds), *Handbook of Research in International Human Resource Management,* Cheltenham: Edward Elgar, pp. 449–63.

Festing, M., Eidems, J. and Royer, S. (2007). 'Strategic Issues and Local Constraints in Transnational Compensation Strategies: An Analysis of Cultural, Institutional and Political Influences', *European Management journal,* April, Vol. 25, Issue 2: 118–31.

Lowe, K., Milliman, J., De Cieri, H. and Dowling, P. (2002). 'International Compensation Practices: A Ten-country Comparative Analysis', *Human Resource Management,* 41(1): 45–66.

Notes and References

1 See J. Kerr and J. Slocum, 'Managing Corporate Culture Through Reward Systems', *Academy of Management Executive,* Vol. 19, No. 4 (2005), pp. 130–8; and P. Evans, V. Pucik and J. Barsoux, *The Global Challenge: A Framework for International Human Resource Management* (Boston, MA: McGraw-Hill, 2002), particularly pp. 327–41.

2 E. Locke, 'Linking Goals to Monetary Incentives', *Academy of Management Executive,* Vol. 18, No. 4 (2004), pp. 130–3; F. Luthans and A. Stajkovic, 'Reinforce for Performance: The Need to Go Beyond Pay and Even Rewards', *Academy of Management Executive,* Vol. 13, No. 2 (1999), pp. 49–57; and A. Pomeroy, 'Executive Briefing: Global Pay for Performance', *HR Magazine,* Vol. 51, No. 4, April (2006), p. 18.

3 Martin Hilb presents a well-written and thorough introduction to this interesting topic area in *New Corporate Governance: Successful Board Management Tools,* 2nd edn (Berlin: Springer Publishing, 2006); a fascinating critique of contemporary executive pay and governance is provided by L. Bebchuck and J. Fried in *Pay Without Performance: The Unfulfilled Promise of Executive Compensation* (Cambridge, MA: Harvard University Press, 2004).

4 D. Kirby, 'Strategies for Assessing Global Markets', *Workspan,* Vol. 47, No. 12, December (2004), pp. 44–5.

5 A. Wright, 'Don't Settle for Less – Global Compensation Programs Need Global Compensation Tools', *Employee Benefit Plan Review,* March (2004), pp. 14–18; D. Robb, 'Unifying Your Enterprise With a Global HR Portal', *HR Magazine,* Vol. 51, No. 3, March (2006), pp. 109–15.

6 K. Chou and H. Risher, 'Point/Counterpoint: Pay for Performance', *Workspan,* Vol. 48, No. 9, September (2005), pp. 28–37; S. Troutman and S. Ross, 'Rationalizing Global Incentive Pay Plans: Look At the Big Picture, Part One', *Workspan,* Vol. 48, No. 8, August (2005), pp. 18–22, 'Part Two', *Workspan,* Vol. 48, No. 9, September (2005), pp. 52–6, 'Part Three', *Workspan,* Vol. 48, No. 10, October (2005), pp. 30–3. Also see E. Krell, 'Evaluating Returns on Expatriates', *HR Magazine,* Vol. 50, No. 3, March (2005), pp. 60–5, and S. Nurney, 'The Long and The Short of It: When Transitioning From Short-term to Long-term Expatriate Assignments, Consider the Financial Implications', *HR Magazine,* Vol. 50, No. 3, March (2005), pp. 91–4.

7 Chou and Risher, 'Point/Counterpoint'; D. Green, 'In the Global Reward Environment One Size Doesn't Fit All', *Workspan,* Vol. 48, No. 10, October (2005), pp. 34–8; and P. Gooderham, M. Morley, C. Brewster and W. Mayrhofer, 'Human Resource Management: A Universal Concept?', in C. Brewster, W. Mayrhofer and M. Morley (eds) *Human Resource Management in Europe: Evidence of Convergence?* (Oxford: Elsevier Butterworth-Heinemann, 2004), pp. 1–26.

8 See Hilb, *New Corporate Governance;* Bebchuck and Fried, *Pay Without Performance;* as well as A. Pomeroy, 'Executive Briefing: With Executive Comp Go Your Own Way', *HR Magazine,* Vol. 50, No. 1, November (2005), p. 14; E. Poutsma, P. Ligthart and R. Schouteten, 'Employee Share Schemes in Europe – The Influence of US Multinational', *Management Revue,* Vol. 16, No. 1 (2005), pp. 99–122; 'New Ideas-Compensation: Institutional Investors Say Executives Are Overpaid: Need Stronger Pay-For-Performance Strategies', www.watsonwyatt.com contribution, *Workspan,* Vol. 49, No. 2, February, 2006, p. 14; M. Hovy, 'Future Global Remuneration Strategies: Compliance, Defiance or Alignment?', *Workspan,* Vol. 48, No. 2, February (2005), pp. 34–8. M. Hope's 'An Interview with Geert Hofstede', *Academy of Management Executive,* Vol. 18, No. 1 (2004), pp. 75–9 includes the provocative quote from Hofstede: 'A present fad is the myth of the magical powers of top executives. The importance of management in general, and top management in particular, is overrated and top managers are overpaid. In many cases

top managers have been brought in who turn out to be parasites on their corporation rather than assets to its real success. The importance of the people who do the work is underrated, although this trend differs between countries and parts of the world' (p. 78). Challenges indeed.

9   See Hilb, *New Corporate Governance,* as well as S. Tyson and F. Bournois (eds), *Top Pay and Performance: International and Strategic Approach* (Oxford: Elsevier Butterworth-Heinemann, 2005); 'New Ideas-Compensation: US CEO and Director Pay On the Rise', www.conference-board.org, in *Workspan,* Vol. 49, No. 1, January (2006), p. 14; M. Thompson, 'Investors Call For Better Disclosure of Executive Compensation in Canada', *Workspan Focus: Canada,* supplement to *Workspan,* February (2006), pp. 4–6; G. Morgenstern, 'Advice on Boss's Pay May Not Be So Independent', *New York Times,* April 10, 2006. (www.newyorktimes.com/2006/04/10/business/10pay.html).

10   For a recent example and discussion of transparency in pay see D. McHugh, 'Nine German Firms Reveal Executive Pay', *Lexington Herald Leader,* Thursday, August 26 (2004), B8; and A. Engle and P. Dowling, 'Global Rewards: Strategic Patterns in Complexity', Conference Proceedings of the International Conference of Human Resource Management in a Knowledge Based Economy, Ljubljana, Slovenia, June, 2004.

11   For example, specialized firms such as P-E International in Britain provide a survey of Worldwide Living Costs while Price Waterhouse offers a worldwide consulting service called 'Global Human Resource Solutions', which covers a broad range of international HR issues.

12   C. Reynolds, *2000 Guide to Global Compensation and Benefits* (San Diego, CA: Harcourt Professional Publishing, 2000), pp. 3, 15–16.

13   Reynolds, *2000,* Chapters 5 and 28; Y.-S. Hsu, 'Expatriate Compensation: Alternative Approaches and Challenges', *WorldatWork Journal,* Vol. 16, No. 1 (2007), pp. 15–19.

14   See K. Lowe, J. Milliman, H. DeCeiri and P. Dowling, 'International Compensation Practices: A Ten-Country Comparative Analysis', *Human Resource Management,* Vol. 41, No. 1, Spring (2002), pp. 45–66; S. Overman, 'In Sync: Harmonizing Your Global Compensation Plans May Be Done More "In Spirit" Than to the Letter', *HR Magazine,* Vol. 45, No. 3, March (2000), pp. 86–92; K. Bensky, 'Developing a Workable Global Rewards System', *Workspan,* Vol. 45, No. 10, October (2002), pp. 44–8; and E. Scott and R. Burke, 'Taming the Beast: Aligning Global Sales Incentives', *Workspan,* Vol. 50, No. 3, March (2007), pp. 44–9.

15   M. Bloom and G.T. Milkovich, 'A SHRM Perspective on International Compensation and Rewards Systems', *Research in Personnel and Human Resource Management,* Supplement 4, (Greenwich, CT: JAI Press, 1999), pp. 283–303; V. Pucik, 'Human Resources in the Future: An Obstacle or A Champion of Globalization?', *Human Resource Management,* Vol. 36, No. 1, Spring (1997), pp. 163–7.

16   G.T. Milkovich and M. Bloom, 'Rethinking International Compensation', *Compensation and Benefits Review,* Vol. 30, No. 1 (1998), pp. 15–23.

17   H.J. Ruff and G.I. Jackson, 'Methodological Problems in International Comparisons of the Cost of Living', *Journal of International Business Studies,* Vol. 5, No. 2 (1974), pp. 57–67.

18   To view the Web page of ORC Worldwide, see www.orcinc.com/.

19   To view the Web page of ECA International, see www.eca-international.com/.

20   *Ibid*.

21   The experience of the first author in his research on expatriates and their families is that for some expatriates (particularly expatriates with little international experience), using home leave allowances for foreign travel can intensify feelings of homesickness. Without the benefit of returning home to mix with employees and friends it is possible to idealize what they remember of their experience at work and home and fail to come to a measured judgement of what is good and bad in both their host and home environments. Overall, it would seem prudent for MNEs to take the view that home leave allowances should normally be used for the purpose they are provided – to give employees and their families the opportunity to renew family and business ties, thereby increasing the probability of reduced adjustment problems when they are repatriated.

22   It is common in Asia and many developing countries in other regions for expatriates and local business people to employ maids and cooks in their houses. As stated in an earlier note when discussing employment of drivers, it may be expected that an expatriate would employ servants and to not do so would be judged negatively as this would be depriving local people of employment. Not surprisingly, this is one benefit which expatriate spouses miss when they return to their home country.

23   Trends in Expatriate Compensation, *Bulletin to Management,* 18 October (1990), p. 336.

24   The material in the tables describing the two main approaches to international compensation is based on various sources – the research and consulting experience of the first author and

various discussions on this topic with a range of HR managers and consultants in Australia and the USA.

25 In interviews conducted by the first author with senior management of Australian firms operating internationally, repatriation difficulties was one of the major reasons cited for not following a Going Rate Approach with Australian expatriates.

26 *Worldwide Total Remuneration 2005–2006,* New York: Towers Perrin, p. 20. Total compensation included basic salary, variable bonus, compulsory company contributions, voluntary company contributions, perquisites and long-term incentives. See also the Towers Perrin website (www.towers.com) for further information.

27 See B.W. Teague, *Compensating Key Personnel Overseas* (New York: The Conference Board, 1972), and J.J. Martoccho, *Strategic Compensation,* 3rd edn (Upper Saddle River, NJ: Pearson/Prentice-Hall, 2004) for more detailed discussions of the concept of keeping the expatriate 'whole'.

28 This discussion of the Balance Sheet Approach follows the presentation in Chapter 5 of the *2000 Guide to Global Compensation and Benefits,* ed. C. Reynolds (San Diego, CA: Harcourt Professional Publishing, 2000).

29 See Chapter 3 of T.J. Bergmann, V.G. Scarpello and F.S. Hills, *Compensation Decision Making,* 3rd edn (Fort Worth, TX: Dryden Press, 1998) for a review of equity theory applied to compensation.

30 R. Cui, 'International Compensation: The Importance of Acting Globally', *WorldatWork Journal,* Vol. 15, No. 4 (2006), pp. 18–23.

31 P. Stuart, 'Global Payroll – A Taxing Problem', *Personnel Journal,* October (1991), pp. 80–90.

32 *Ibid.;* tax equalization can become a potential area of familial contention and more complex when dual career families seek tandem international assignments, as presented by G. Aldred in 'Dual Career Support: Strategies for Designing and Providing Career Support for International Assignee Partners', *GMAC Strategic Advisor, 2, 6,* February 2006, pp. 1–4 (www.gmacglobalrelocation.com).

33 'Tax Burdens', *The Economist,* 2 November, 2000 (accessed online on 18 July 2003: www.economist.com).

34 *Worldwide Total Remuneration 2005–2006,* p. 32, Towers Perrin, see also the Towers Perrin website (www.towers.com) for further information.

35 *Ibid.*

36 'Global Relocation Trends 2002 Survey Report' (2002), GMAC Global Relocation Services, accessed through Society for Human Resource Management Global Website (www.shrmglobal.org).

37 R. Schuler and P. Dowling, *Survey of SHRM/I Members* (New York: Stern School of Business, New York University, 1988).

38 Worldwide Total Remuneration 2005–2006 (New York: Towers Perrin), p. 34. See also the Towers Perrin website (www.towers.com) for further information.

39 '*Finfacts Global/Worldwide 2005/2006 Cost of Living Ranking*', by Mercer Human Resource. (Accessed on 1 May 2006.) For further reading go to http://www.finfacts.com.

40 Price and Earnings: A Comparison of Purchasing Power Around the Globe (Zurich: UBS AG, Wealth Management Research, 2005).

41 More details at http://www.ubs.com/1/g/ubs_ch/wealth_mgmt_ch/research.html.

42 Accessed from http:www.ubs.com/e/ubs_ch/bb_ch/market_information.Referen3.0002.file.dat/ 3.9_PL_e.pdf.

43 See www.eiu.com/index.asp for *The Economist* Intelligence Unit website.

44 C. Reynolds, 'Cost-Effective Compensation', *Topics in Total Compensation,* Vol. 2, No. 1 (1988), p. 320.

45 G. Milkovich and J. Newman, *Compensation,* 8th edn (Boston, MA: McGraw-Hill/Irwin Pub., 2005), Chapter 16.

46 See E. Schein, *Organizational Culture and Leadership* (San Francisco, CA: Jossey-Bass Pub., 1985).

47 P. Dowling, A. Engle, M. Festing and B. Mueller, 'Complexity in Global Pay: A Meta-Framework', *Conference Proceedings of the 8th Conference on International Human Resource Management,* Cairns, Australia, June, 2005, CD-ROM indexed by title and first author's name; C. Brewster, 'Strategic Human Resource Management: The Value of Different Paradigms', *Management International Review,* Vol. 39, No. 3 (1999), pp. 45–64.

48 J. Barney, 'Firm Performance and Sustained Competitive Advantage', *Journal of Management,* Vol. 17, No. 1 (1991), pp. 99–120.

49 See J.G. March and H.A. Simon, *Organizations* (New York: Wiley and Sons, Inc., 1958).

50 O. Williamson, 'Efficient Labor Organization', in F. Stephens (ed.), *Firms, Organization and Labour* (London: MacMillan, 1984), pp. 87–118.

51 As in M. Armstrong and H. Murlis, *Reward Management: A Handbook of Remuneration Strategy and Practice* (London: Kogan Page Limited, 1991). Also see G.T. Milkovich and M. Bloom, 'Rethinking International Compensation', *Compensation and Benefits Review,* Vol. 30, No. 1 (1998), pp. 15–23.

52 A. Engle and M. Mendenhall, 'Transnational Roles, Transnational Rewards: Global Integration In Compensation', *Employee Relations,* Vol. 26, No. 6 (2004), pp. 613–25.

53 L. Gomez-Mejia and T. Welbourne, 'Compensation Strategies In a Global Context', *Human Resource Planning,* Vol. 14, No. 1 (1991), pp. 29–41; R. Heneman, C. von Hippel, D. Eskew and D. Greenberger, 'Alternative Rewards in Unionized Environments', in R. Heneman (ed.), *Strategic Reward Management* (Greenwich, CT: Information Age Pub., 2002), pp. 131–52.

54 Gomez-Mejia and Welbourne, 'Compensation Strategies In a Global Context'; M. Bloom and G.T. Milkovich, 'A SHRM Perspective on International Compensation and Reward Systems', *Research in Personnel and Human Resource Management, Supplement 4* (Greenwich, CT: JAI Press, 1991), pp. 283–303.

55 Milkovich and Newman, 'A SHRM Perspective on International Compensation and Reward Systems'.

56 M. Festing, J. Eidems and S. Royer, 'Strategic Issues and Local Constraints in Transnational Compensation Strategies: An Analysis of Cultural, Institutional and Political Influences', *European Management Journal,* April, Vol. 25, Issue 2 (2007), pp. 118–31.

57 M. Bloom, G.T. Milkovich and A. Mitra, 'International Compensation: Learning From How Managers Respond to Variations in Local Host Contexts', *International Journal of Human Resource Management,* Vol. 14 (2003), pp. 1350–67. Also see A. Mitra, M. Bloom and G.T. Milkovich, 'Crossing a Raging River: Seeking Far-Reaching Solutions to Global Pay Challenges', *World at Work Journal,* Vol. 11, No. 2 (2002), pp. 6–17.

58 J. Boudreau, P. Ramstad and P. Dowling, 'Global Talentship: Toward a Decision Science Connecting Talent to Global Strategic Success', in W.H. Mobley and P.W. Dorfman (eds), *Advances in Global Leadership,* Vol. 3 (Oxford: Elsevier Science, 2003), pp. 63–99. Also see A. Engle, M. Mendenhall, R. Powers and Y. Stedham, 'Conceptualizing the Global Competency Cube: A Transnational Model of Human Resource', *Journal of European Industrial Training,* Vol. 25, No. 7 (2001), pp. 346–53.

59 E.E. Lawler III, *Rewarding Excellence* (San Francisco, CA: Jossey-Bass Pub., 2000); C. Garvey, 'Steer Teams With the Right Pay', *HR Magazine,* Vol. 47, No. 5, May (2002), pp. 71–8.

60 G.T. Milkovich and M. Bloom, 'Rethinking International Compensation', *Compensation and Benefits Review,* Vol. 30, No. 1 (1998), pp. 15–23.

61 G.T. Milkovich and M. Bloom, 'Rethinking International Compensation'. Also see A. Engle and M. Mendenhall, 'Transnational Roles and Transnational Rewards: Global Integration in Compensation', *Employee Relattons,* Vol. 26, No. 6 (2004), pp. 613–25.

62 Milkovich and Newman, *Compensation,* pp. 75–7, 80–1.

63 *Ibid.*

64 H. Timmons, 'Pay Debated at British Bank's Meeting', *The New York Times,* May 31, 2003.

65 A. Katsoudas, S. Olsen and P. Weems, 'New Trends in Global Equity Rewards', *Workspan,* Vol. 50, No. 3 (2007), pp. 28–33.

66 See Dowling, Engle, Festing and Mueller, 'Complexity in Global Pay'; Bloom, Milkovich and Mitra, 'International Compensation'.

Re-entry and career issues

Chapter Objectives

While the preceding chapters have concentrated on the management and support of international assignments, this chapter deals with what could be called the post-assignment stage. Re-entry, though, raises issues for both the expatriate and the multinational, some of which may be connected to events that occurred during the international assignment. We treat this stage as part of the international assignment. We examine:

● The process of re-entry or repatriation.

● Job-related issues.

● Social factors, including family factors that affect re-entry and work adjustment.

● Multinational responses to repatriate concerns.

● Staff availability and career issues.

● Return on investment (ROI) and knowledge transfer.

● Designing a repatriation program.

Introduction

It is evident from the preceding chapters that there have been considerable advances in our understanding and knowledge of the issues surrounding the management and support of expatriates in terms of recruitment and selection, pre-departure training and compensation. As Figure 8-1 indicates, the expatriation process also includes repatriation: the activity of bringing the expatriate back to the home country.

While it is now more widely recognized by managers and academics that repatriation needs careful managing, attention to this aspect of international assignments has been somewhat belated. In the past, the unpredictable and incremental nature of globalization led to reactive assignments, and re-entry to the firm was left unspoken or dealt with informally on an ad hoc basis. As more expatriates completed their assignments, firms were faced with organizing these returns in a more

| Figure 8-1 | Expatriation includes repatriation |

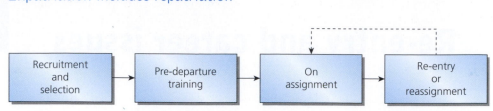

planned pattern that allowed for a more strategic and complete use of the returning employee's newfound experiences and insights, while at the same time easing the repatriates return to their 'home' country and firm.[1]

Re-entry into the home country presents new challenges. The repatriate (returning person) is coping with what has been termed *re-entry shock,* or reverse culture shock. While people frequently expect life in a new country to be different, they may be less prepared for homecoming to present problems of adjustment. As a consequence, it can be a traumatic experience for some,[2] even more than what was encountered in the foreign location. From the multinational's perspective, repatriation is frequently considered as the final stage in the expatriation process (as indicated in Figure 8-1), but the multinational's ability to attract future expatriates is affected by the manner in which it handles repatriation.[3]

In this chapter, we focus on the key factors associated with re-entry: including how the repatriation process is handled by the individual and the receiving work unit; as well as family adjustment. We will also explore how repatriation affects the successful 'closure' of the foreign assignment, its impact on future career paths within the multinational, and the effect on staff mobility. The reasons for the international assignment and its outcomes are assessed – that is, how the multinational recoups its investment in human capital, and the process of knowledge and competence transfer upon re-entry. It should be noted that what is written about the re-entry process centers on the traditional expatriate assignment, based predominantly on experiences of repatriated PCNs.

The repatriation process

Typically, on completion of the international assignment, the multinational brings the expatriate back to the home country, though not all international assignments end with a transfer home. Some expatriates may agree to become part of the multinational's international team of managers – as indicated by the dotted arrow in Figure 8-1 – and thus have consecutive overseas assignments. In the event that one of these consecutive assignments involves the expatriate returning to the home-country operations, it will be treated as 'just another posting' rather than re-entry or repatriation. For example, John Jones is moved from his home base in the US parent operations to Japan for two years. He then spends four years in China, followed by one year in headquarters in the USA before moving on to another position in the English operations. That one-year period spent at headquarters is not treated as re-entry back into the home-country operations. In contrast, Mary Smith has spent three years working in China and is repatriated back to the USA into a defined position at headquarters.

As outlined in Figure 8-2, repatriation may be seen to encompass three phases. First, before the global assignment, MNEs may act to assign home sponsors or mentors and hold them responsible for keeping the expatriate in touch with changing conditions in the home country. Ideally, such sponsors might have relevant expatriate assignments as part of their own work history. Web-based indices of relevant national, regional, industrial or firm websites may be provided. These ongoing communication protocols may be formal or informal.[4] By initially creating this network of personal and media links the expatriate may be able to keep up with the changes in the home country, work unit, the larger firm as well as changes in the local or regional community while on assignment. This more systematic updating may contribute to more realistic expectations on the part of the expatriate, reducing culture shock upon return.

Second, during the assignment, 'home leave', work-related information exchanges, sponsor communications and a systematic pre-return orientation process can all facilitate realistic expectations and ease the return. Allowing for periodic returns to the home country will help the expatriate and her/his family to reconnect with firm employees, family and friends and catch up with changing business conditions. Some MNEs allow their expatriates to use their holidays to visit more exotic, once-in-a-lifetime locations closer to the host country.[5] In some cases, this is not a wise policy for the employer as by doing this, some expatriates lose their perspective of how things may be changing in their home country and may develop a somewhat 'rose-colored' view of life back at home.[6] Work-related information exchanges are part of any expatriate assignment. Through these regular and ongoing task-related communications, rich information about changes in home personnel, power politics, strategic developments and less work-related updates can be passed on to the expatriate. Ongoing and regular communications with the sponsor during the assignment and a systematic pre-return orientation will be discussed in detail later in the chapter. These two activities may become more intense in the months or weeks immediately prior to the return.

Repatriation activities and practices   Figure 8-2

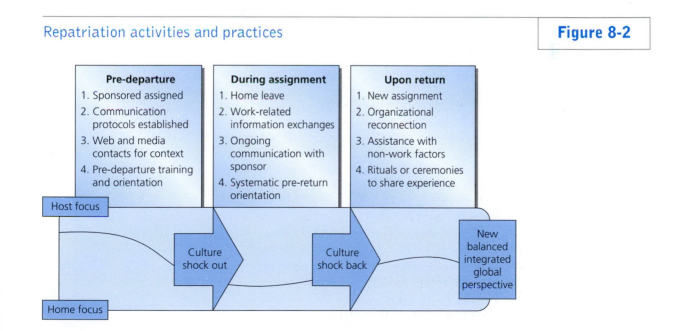

Finally, upon return a series of immediately practical and more long-term activities combine during what is normally a very restricted time frame. Multinational firms can be less effective in their use of expatriates by either being too vague and unfocused about repatriates, or they can try to be too efficient by expecting the returning expatriate to jump back into the home assignment before the issues and processes related to return are resolved – literally before their 'bags are unpacked'.[7] Practical issues upon return relate to housing – for longer-term assignments homes are sometimes sold and new house searches and short-term accommodation must be found. Schools for children, new shopping patterns and family survival activities in new locations are required. Expatriates must be assigned a new work space, and given a whole new orientation to the MNE. The new job assignment and local work group must be encountered and understood. On a broader scale, the repatriated must reconnect with the local social network of the MNE, and personal and career dynamics may have to be adjusted in new and potentially unpredictable ways.[8] Changes and adjustments for societal, firm and job dynamics on the personal, family, job, organizational and career levels are involved in this final stage.

Note the two stages of culture shock represented at the bottom in Figure 8-2. The overemphasis on a home focus, at the expense of a focus on the host assignment can lead to problems with performance on assignment and premature return as outlined in Chapters 4 and 5. At the same time, an overemphasis on host activities, at the expense of some awareness of changes at home can lead to a second culture shock upon return. The goal of any set of expatriation/repatriation practices should result in the successful integration of home and host experiences. Achieving this more balanced set of transitions is not always easy. For example, in 1996, Harzing[9] conducted a comprehensive survey of 287 subsidiaries of nearly 100 different multinationals. She reported that 52 per cent of sampled firms experienced repatriate re-entry problems. A fictionalized IHRM in Action, Case 8-1 provides a sense of this concern.

IHRM in Action Case 8-1

Repatriation and loss prevention at ISCAM

On his last day of work at ISCAM, Wayne Bullova wrote up his letter of resignation, took the five weeks of vacation he was due and walked through the February snow across the downtown Denver street to open his own safety and security consulting firm. Only three years earlier, Wayne had jumped at the chance to take the assignment as Loss Prevention and Safety Director at ISCAM's new regional center in Peru. As a global mining engineering firm with decades of international activities,

ISCAM had done a very good job of preparing Wayne and his family for the differences between Lima and Denver. The children had quickly adjusted to the American school, surprisingly his Mexican-born wife had enjoyed being involved in both the expatriate community and the local Peruvian church group associated with the Cathedral, and Wayne had immediately enjoyed the increased responsibilities and centrality of his new role. As an ex-US Army Ranger Captain, his security role did provide occasional adrenalin rushes as he responded to Sendero Luminoso activities in mine sites around Huaneayo, but the evident success of the counter-terrorism and security protocols he developed were gratifying.

His return to Denver, some six months ago, was a different matter. He knew that things would be different at home after the corporate restructuring that occurred a year into his expatriate assignment. His long-time mentor and friend, Herman Balkin, had taken a reportedly very generous early retirement package after a long-simmering executive power struggle unpredictably came to a head. Several restructuring 'aftershocks' relocated many of his colleagues outside of Colorado. During his assignment in Peru Wayne was more and more frustrated as his informal corporate intelligence network dissolved and the role of his liaison was passed around among a series of increasingly junior, and to his mind clueless, executives.

The assignment he was promised by the company president was 'rethought' and when he returned six months ago he spent the better part of a month trying to get an office and understand his new job. Everyone he talked to had a different perspective on what he was being asked to do. He felt claustrophobic, and to make matters worse, the new counter-terrorism and security

protocols he had developed and used, with great success, in Peru were either systematically ignored or so modified by his supervisors that they were unrecognizable.

At a Bronco's football game he shared his growing frustrations with Balkin. On the home front, the new house they had purchased upon return – having sold their home at the advice of the HR director at the time of the international assignment – was expensive, hard to heat, and placed them in a city school district that the children were having problems with. He had looked at private schools, but the tuitions were astronomical and his salary was not much more than it had been three years ago. His wife had started to complain about Denver winters again. At work, Wayne felt as if he had returned to a totally different world. Balkin asked if ISCAM had asked Wayne to renew his executive non-competition agreement. Wayne replied that ISCAM had not. 'Well, there you go', said Balkin, 'Let's do what we have talked about for years. With your technical expertise and my industry contacts, we can work for ourselves – at least we will know who our bosses are and what the job is.'

Source: Fictionalized synthesis from several interviews.

The problems outlined above may provoke staff turnover, in that repatriates may leave the organization. The GMAC Global Relocation Services, LLC (GMAC GRS)[10] global surveys (referred to in previous chapters) provide data on repatriate turnover. Firms in the 2006 survey indicated that 23 per cent of repatriates left the company within the first year. The 2004 survey reported 13 per cent of repatriates left with the first year, and 10 per cent within two years. This compares with the 2002 survey where responding firms admitted a 44 per cent expatriate turnover rate, half of whom left their firms within the first year of re-entry. The 2006 survey notes that, for surveyed firms, retaining expatriate talent remains a considerable challenge. Explanations for repatriate turnover ranged as follows:

- 'Employees with international experience are more likely to leave the company' (2002 survey).
- 'Most expatriates leave to pursue other expatriate assignments that they view as beneficial to their careers' (2004 survey).
- 'Expatriates anticipate a lack of attractive positions to return to in the home country and seek out better opportunities outside their company' (2006 survey).

It should be remembered that 39 per cent of the multinationals in the 2002 GMAC GRS survey did not know their expatriate attrition rate, and this figure almost doubled in the 2004 survey, with 69 per cent of responding firms indicating that they did not know when expatriates left. Given this, the percentage of exiting employees could be higher. Why are an increasing number of firms seemingly ignoring the fate of repatriates? The answer may lie in the following comment by the GMAC GRS 2004 report's authors:

> To a great extent, this [increase] can be explained by the nature of the expatriate-tracking process itself. In general, expatriates are tracked in order to apply and record specially developed payroll and benefits packages and to comply with tax-reporting requirements. Once expatriates complete their assignments, these considerations expire. Consequently the key motivation for tracking them also disappears. The concept of tracking the employment status of expatriates after they complete their assignments is nonetheless a valuable one in its own right.[11]

Given the reasons why international assignments are used, the direct and indirect costs involved, and the various roles that are assigned to expatriates – as discussed in Chapter 4 – it seems important to understand why re-entry is problematic yet of seemingly lesser importance to researchers and practitioners than other stages of the international assignment. To this end, we now examine factors that may contribute to re-entry problems, considering the process first from the individual's perspective, and then the multinational's viewpoint.

Individual reactions to re-entry

As with cross-cultural adjustment, the re-entry process is a complex interaction of several factors. It is possible to group the major factors that have been identified as moderators of re-entry readjustment into two categories – job-related factors and social factors – as depicted in Figure 8-3, which we now discuss.

Job-related factors

These factors center around future employment prospects as a consequence of the international assignment, value being placed on the person's international experience, coping with new role demands and the loss of status and financial benefits upon re-entry. We shall examine these factors in turn.

Career anxiety.   When surveyed, expatriates consistently list two motivators for accepting an international assignment: career advancement and financial gain.[12] It is not surprising then that a prime factor in re-entry is career anxiety. This can emerge prior to the physical relocation, even before Phase 1 in Figure 8-3, and can affect productivity during the last couple of months of the international assignment as the person contemplates the re-entry process. So, what prompts career anxiety? The causes range across the following and are often interrelated:

● *No post-assignment guarantee of employment*. This is becoming the reality for the majority of those on international assignments. For example, 68 per cent of respondents in the 2004 GMAC GRS survey did not provide post-assignment employment guarantees. This figure is similar to that of the 2002 survey,

Factors influencing repatriate adjustment

Figure 8-3

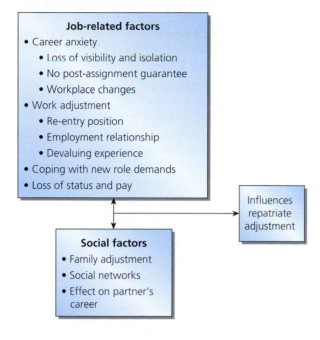

Job-related factors
- Career anxiety
  - Loss of visibility and isolation
  - No post-assignment guarantee
  - Workplace changes
- Work adjustment
  - Re-entry position
  - Employment relationship
  - Devaluing experience
- Coping with new role demands
- Loss of status and pay

Social factors
- Family adjustment
- Social networks
- Effect on partner's career

Influences repatriate adjustment

where 70 per cent of respondents did not give a guarantee. One respondent in the 2002 survey explained: 'We provide no guarantee for employment. We do guarantee to bring the person home, and if a suitable position is not readily available, they have three months.'[13] In other words, repatriation more often leads to redundancy, as the 1990s trend away from re-entry job guarantees continues. A 1998 survey by Price Waterhouse (now PriceWaterhouseCoopers) survey[14] reported a decrease in post-assignment job guarantees from 69 per cent in their 1995 survey to 46 per cent in 1998.

Studies that break down general trends into regions and countries reveal some differences. The Tung-Arthur Andersen 1997 survey of 49 North American firms reported that the majority (almost 60 per cent) did not guarantee a position at home upon successful completion of the overseas assignment.[15] In her study of international HR practices in German and UK firms, Marx[16] found that the majority of German firms offered a guaranteed job upon return from the foreign assignment, whereas the majority of UK firms admitted that they were not able to offer jobs upon repatriation. Marx suggests that Continental European firms may have to provide such guarantees in order to attract expatriates. However, a respondent in the 2002 GMAC GRS survey explained that: 'Our approach depends on the base [sending] country. Europeans have a labor contract, and the U.S. does not.'[17] Given the lack of job security, it is not surprising that career anxiety commences prior to homecoming, and acts as a readjustment moderator upon re-entry if career outcomes are not realized.

- *A fear that the period overseas has caused a loss of visibility* and isolation – as captured in the phrase: 'out of sight, out of mind'.[18] Again, this fear can commence towards the end of the international assignment as the person begins to consider the re-entry process, and depends on various elements: the amount of contact that the person has had with the home organization; the position level concerned; whether the person is aware well in advance of the type of re-entry job awaiting in the home country. Lack of information may increase the level of anxiety leaving the person with a decided impression that the company has not planned adequately, or that a mediocre or makeshift job awaits.[19] If there is no post-assignment job guarantee, the anxiety level will be understandably high.

● *Changes in the home workplace.* Anxiety can be exacerbated by informal communication from home-based colleagues about organizational changes. It may be that the multinational is in the process of a major restructuring, the aftermath of a merger or acquisition, or sale of divisions or business units. These changes are usually accompanied by job shedding. Knowledge of such changes and potential or real job loss naturally will add to the level of anxiety, particularly if the expatriate does not have a guaranteed job upon repatriation.

Another issue here is that restructuring can affect the host-country operations – such as closure of a plant, dissolving of a joint venture or merging of operations post acquisition. This may leave the expatriate stranded, or force an early repatriation which has not been planned.[20] If similar changes are also occurring in the home country, then availability of suitable positions will have been reduced. One repatriate who was placed in such a position explains:

> The division I worked for was reorganized, and the subsidiary I worked for was placed under stringent cost-cutting guidelines, which forced me to return earlier than anticipated. My re-entry was very cold, with little support in finding a job since previous management had been fired.[21]

Work adjustment.   Black, Gregersen and Mendenhall[22] argue that work adjustment has an important impact on a person's intent to stay with the organization. Career anxiety is one moderating factor, but others may also lead to readjustment problems:

● *The employment relationship.* An individual's career expectations may be based on clear messages sent by top management to the effect that an international assignment is a condition for career progression. That is, verbal or written statements such as: 'We are an international company and we need internationally oriented people who have worked in our overseas facilities.' These pronouncements can be made in the context of the need for a global orientation or mindset where a definite link is made between international experience and global managers.

Perceptions regarding expected career outcomes also are influenced by comments made by HR or line managers during the recruitment and selection stage. For example, the line manager may suggest to a younger employee: 'You should volunteer for that international assignment. It would be a smart career move at this stage in your life.' If others have been promoted upon repatriation, it may be perceived to be the 'norm', thus reinforcing the perception that international assignments lead to promotion upon re-entry.

For these reasons, the person believes promotion should follow based on successful performance while abroad and if the re-entry position does not eventuate within a reasonable time frame, then career anxiety is justified. A study by Lazarova and Caligiuri[23] of 58 repatriates from four North American-based companies found that repatriation support practices are positively related to perceptions of organizational support, and these affect repatriates' intention to stay or leave the organization. The psychological contract is a moderator of re-entry readjustment as well as on-assignment adjustment and performance. The repatriate may believe that the performance overseas warrants promotion: that signals were given by the organization that effective performance in the international assignment would result in career advancement. When the expected promotion does not eventuate, the repatriate may feel there is no option but to exit the organization. It is important to note that the psychological contract concerns perceptions and expectations, complicated by the fact that the MNE representative making statements about career outcomes prior to the international assignment is not necessarily the person who is responsible for re-entry decisions about job placement and promotion.

● *Re-entry position.* It would seem for some that promotion is a primary issue as the following comment from a repatriate reveals.[24] 'Get a promotion before the return! You are forgotten while overseas, and you start all over on the return. The promotions go to people who have been in a position for extended periods; nothing done overseas counts in this company.'

Fears surrounding future employment and career development can materialize. Peers are promoted ahead of the repatriated manager, and the repatriate sometimes is placed in a position that is, in effect, a demotion. The situation may be exacerbated if the repatriate had held a senior position in the foreign location and now finds himself (or herself) at a less senior level. As a consequence, the re-entry position is frequently judged by whether it matches the repatriate's career expectation, particularly when the international assignment has caused considerable family disruption; such as a forced break in the career of the accompanying partner, or difficulties experienced with the education of the children involved. Put simply, the repatriate wants the 'end to justify the means', so that the family unit is fully compensated for the sacrifices it has made in expectation of career advancement. Suutari and Brewster, in their study of Finnish expatriates, report that most repatriates left only after they felt that they had given the company sufficient time to find more suitable positions. These authors identified an 'external pull factor': external recruiters were actively 'head-hunting' repatriates either during the assignment or upon return.[25]

A question put to responding firms in the GMAC GRS surveys concerned the career impact of international experience. Firms were asked to compare the careers of expatriates with those of employees without international experience. Table 8.1 provides the following results:

Career impacts of international assignments			Table 8-1
	2005 survey	*2004 survey*	*2002 survey*
Expatriates were promoted faster	37 per cent	34 per cent	36 per cent
Expatriates obtained new positions in the company more easily	36 per cent	35 per cent	33 per cent
Expatriates changed employers more often	24 per cent	23 per cent	23 per cent
Not sure about the career link to international experience	40 per cent	40 per cent	35 per cent

The GMAC GRS 2002 report's authors made the following comment:

> We find it disturbing that each year, a high percentage of respondents are not sure about the impact that an international assignment has on an expatriate's career. How can one make a convincing case for accepting an assignment if one cannot determine the impact that the assignment will have on an expatriate's career?

A similar comment was made regarding the 2004 survey results: 'It was disturbing that so many respondents lack the information needed to make a convincing case for accepting these assignments.'[26] This sentiment was echoed in the 2005 PricewaterhouseCoopers report on global trends in policies and practices related to international assignments: 'further research into why [repatriate] assignees seek alternative employment should be high on an organization's agenda'.[27]

Stroh[28] found that the best predictors of repatriate turnover were whether the company had a career development plan; and whether the company was undergoing turbulence, such as downsizing. She argues that lower rates of repatriate turnover are more likely in organizations that planned for the repatriation of their employees and provided career development planning for them. We will return to the career aspects later in this chapter.

● *Devaluing the overseas experience.* Career progression is important but to be promoted upon re-entry signifies that international experience is important and valued by the organization. Consider the following comments made by a number of expatriates:

> I think that our corporation can benefit from the experience I gained abroad, but no one asked me for any information. It is as if I never went.[29]

> When I came home, I was assigned to a newly created, undefined staff job, where I had no friends, no contacts, and no access to management.[30]

> The problem is when one comes back from an international assignment it may happen that there is no position for the person to return to. Sometimes it is necessary to be a supplementary person in a department and one has to wait for a job. That is not very nice to come back to.[31]

> They didn't bother to say 'thank you for the job you did in [country X]'. And quite frankly, it was such a tremendous job, it was a huge, huge, *huge* project, and it went quite well.[32]

As these comments reveal, the re-entry position may be a less challenging job with reduced responsibility and status than that held either during the international assignment, or prior to the period overseas, in 'holding' positions such as a task force or project team, or in temporary positions engaged in duties that do not appear to exploit their newly gained international expertise.[33] For some, the return position is frequently a lateral move rather than a promotion.[34] The positions do not seem to be related, nor draw upon, experiences and skills the person may have acquired during the international assignment – that is, giving the impression that such experience is devalued.

Furthering the sense of the devaluing of international experience is the reactions of work colleagues. Suggestions can be met with xenophobic responses[35] – along the lines of 'you are at home now', or 'it won't work here'. Some repatriates report a general lack of interest. For example, Stroh, Gregersen and Black[36] quote an interviewee: 'Returning repatriates should be warned about the extreme lack of interest Americans usually show in anything outside their own world.'

Coping with new role demands.

Along with career issues, a mismatch of expectations affects the repatriate's perception of the role associated with network position. A role is the organized set of behaviors that are assigned to a particular position. Although an individual may affect how a role is interpreted and performed, the role itself is predetermined, usually defined in the job description.[37] Effective role behavior is an interaction between the concept of the role, the interpretation of expectations, the person's ambitions and the norms inherent in the role. Figure 8-4 illustrates the elements of the repatriate's role as a focus for a discussion of the readjustment issues related to role behavior.

Readjustment problems may occur because, although the repatriate is attempting to function back in the home country, his or her role conception remains influenced by that of the foreign assignment. The message being sent (denoted by the direction of the arrow in Figure 8-4) by the home company (the role sender) has crossed the cultural boundary. The person has been operating for some time in the foreign location and consequently may have made significant changes to his or her role behavior.[38] For example, an American working in Indonesia may have altered his managerial style and be more authoritarian based on messages sent by the foreign subsidiary; or it could be that the time in the Indonesian subsidiary has reinforced an authoritarian tendency. Conflict is likely to occur if the repatriate does not resume the managerial behavior appropriate to the US context upon return.

Torbiörn[39] contends that as long as the repatriate's 'identity and basic values are still bound up in the culture of the home country, the strain of adjusting to conditions at home will be slight'. However, while the repatriate may retain the role conception, and the cultural norms regarding behavior appropriate to that role, the

---

The repatriate role	**Figure 8-4**

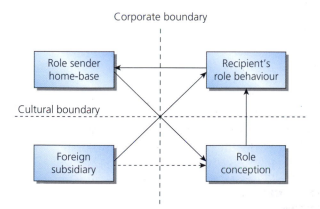

Source: Adapted from I. Torbiörn, 'The Structure of Managerial Roles in Cross-cultural Settings', *International Studies of Management & Organization,* Vol. 15, No. 1 (1985).

foreign subsidiary's influence may linger, indicated by the dotted arrow in Figure 8-4, and what is communicated to the home company, in the form of role behavior, will not conform to the home company's expectations. As shown by the broken line between the role sender and role recipient boxes at the top of Figure 8-4, there is a 'corporate boundary' to be crossed in the communication of the role conception between the role recipient (the repatriate) and the role sender (the home company). The role sender, however, may not recognize the cultural and corporate boundaries that affect the repatriate's role conception and role behavior, thus unwittingly contributing to readjustment problems.

While research in this area is limited, in their study of 125 repatriate managers from four large US multinationals, Black and Gregersen[40] found that role clarity, rather than role conflict, was significantly related to work adjustment. Discussing these findings, the authors explain that role conflict may be an important factor in expatriate assignments due to conflicting role signals between home office and the foreign subsidiary; whereas role conflict upon return most likely stems from conflicting job signals from different individuals within the home operation. They add: 'While there are advantages in providing jobs that are clear and free from role conflicts, it is perhaps more important for firms to provide clear jobs upon repatriation.' In other words, role clarity emerges as an aspect of healthy repatriation.

A further contribution to our understanding of repatriate readjustment comes from Black and Gregersen's finding regarding role discretion. Role discretion refers to the freedom to adjust the work role to fit the individual, making it easier for the person to utilize past, familiar behavior, thus reducing the level of uncertainty in the new job that assists adjustment. They found that, for their sample, role discretion had a positive impact upon adjustment; a finding that appears to confirm earlier studies on the relationship between role discretion, role clarity and work adjustment.[41] In a later survey of Finnish repatriates, Gregersen found fairly consistent results in terms of role clarity and role discretion with those of American repatriates. He comments:

> The consistent results between American and Finnish managers suggest that greater role discretion upon repatriation seems to facilitate repatriation adjustment. In addition, the importance of role clarity to work adjustment suggests that Finnish and American firms may want to provide clearer jobs upon repatriation.[42]

However, it would appear that, for North American companies at least, role clarity and role discretion remains a repatriation issue. It emerged as important in Baughn's[43] survey of US repatriates. The category 'reduced responsibility and autonomy on the job' was ranked second, after 'career advancement', as a major concern upon repatriation for respondents in the Tung-Arthur Andersen survey mentioned earlier. These findings lend added support to the importance of role clarity, role conflict and role discretion in work adjustment after re-entry.[44]

Further, the above studies suggest that the corporate boundary in Figure 8-4 may be stronger than the 'cultural boundary', in terms of the repatriate role. Limited support for this conclusion comes from the results of a study by Forster,[45] who surveyed 124 employees recently repatriated back to the United Kingdom. Analysis of the responses indicated five predictors for repatriation maladjustment (in ranked order):

- Length of time abroad.
- Unrealistic expectations of job opportunities in the home company.

- Downward job mobility.
- Reduced work status.
- Negative perceptions of the help and support provided by employers during and after repatriation.

Job-related factors were found to be more important than non-work and family factors.

A point that is not directly addressed, but may help to explain the inter-relationships between the variables found significant in the above studies, is that the period overseas does alter the person. The experiences of living and working in another country can affect the person's self-efficacy (the degree to which an individual believes that he or she can execute a set of behaviors). As well, the expatriate position commonly involves a more demanding job position. Learning how to successfully cope with the various challenges encountered during the foreign assignment may give the person more self-confidence, along with a broader perspective.[46] These changes may be subtle for some people, for others they can be profound, and may be influenced by factors such as length of time spent abroad, country of assignment and individual differences such as age and personality. As a result, the reverse culture shock experienced by the repatriate may be as much a function of the degree to which the person has altered, as to the changes that have occurred in the home country, as indicated in Figure 8-5.

Likewise identity has been recognized as an aspect linking international assignments, career development and repatriation,[47] though there has been limited research on how a repatriate's identity construction is positively or negatively related to the international experience. What is evident from anecdotal evidence, however, is that repatriates note a change in perspective post assignment. The process of redefining oneself is not restricted to professional competence but may include self-development aspects such as self-confidence, flexibility and tolerance. The challenge is to align this 'new self' to expectations organization and family members have that are based on what the repatriate considers as 'what I was before, not whom I have become'.

The period of time spent overseas is an important aspect. The longer the person is away from the home country, the more likely there will be readjustment

---

The readjustment challenge   **Figure 8-5**

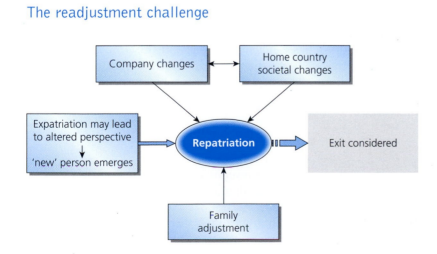

problems upon return.[48] Another contributing factor to re-entry adjustment may be the length of time that the repatriate is kept in a so-called 'holding pattern'. This may be acceptable as an interim measure, but the longer repatriates are treated as temporary, the more likely they are to become anxious about the future, and have less commitment to the home work unit and the parent organization.[49] Other workplace changes may affect readjustment. The repatriate often encounters changes in the formal and informal information channels in the home organization, particularly if there has been widespread restructuring and downsizing. Technological advances in the multinational may render the repatriate's functional skills and knowledge outdated. Unless there was sufficient contact with the expatriate during the international assignment, the person will be unprepared for these changes. When coupled with other job-related problems, these changes make work adjustment a difficult process.

Loss of status and pay.   Usually, at least for PCNs, the international assignment is a form of promotion. It carries greater autonomy, a broader area of responsibility (because of the smaller size of the overseas subsidiary), and, at the top management level, a prominent role in the local community. The result is higher status. Some expatriates use the term *kingpin* to describe their positions overseas. Upon return, the repatriate is expected to resume his or her position within the home company, with the loss of status and autonomy. In effect, the repatriate is treated as just another company executive. This shift may cause readjustment problems. For example, a repatriate can find that, whereas in the foreign operation he/she was the key decision-maker, now he/she has to seek permission from a superior.

Compounding the problem is the loss of expatriate premiums. As Conway states, 'More commonly, employees are brought home to resume life on a scale that may be significantly less comfortable than what they had grown used to abroad. Pay is usually lower in absolute terms.'[50] A similar finding is reported by the Tung-Arthur Andersen survey referred to earlier. However, in their study of 21 US firms, Napier and Petersen[51] found that most of the repatriates in their sample felt that their personal finances were better *after* the assignment than *before,* even though they were not as favorable as before the overseas assignment. Napier and Petersen explain that the total compensation package received while on assignment was greater than before, thus allowing the person to return to the USA with increased savings.

Another contributing factor is that the returning manager may no longer be able to afford to buy a home similar to the one sold a few years before. A US study suggests that the current practice of providing expatriates with better housing than they had at home may contribute to repatriation problems. That is, a drop in the standard of housing conditions has a negative impact on the adjustment of US repatriates.[52] This creates somewhat of a dilemma for US HR managers. As we discussed in Chapter 5, the amount of support provided for the expatriate and family is critical to adjustment and intent to stay in the foreign location, but may have a negative effect on re-entry.

Social factors

The familiar surrounds of the home environment may ease the transition, or at least the cultural adjustment will not be as demanding as that confronted in the foreign country. However, the international experience can distance the repatriate, and his or her family, socially and psychologically. If the expatriate position gave the person a high profile, involving interaction with the social and economic elite, the return home may bring with it some measure of social disappointment, thus reinforcing the *kingpin* syndrome. The financial loss of the compensation premium, housing subsidy and related benefits can exacerbate these feelings.

Family adjustment.

It must be stressed here that, where spouses, partners and children are involved, each family member is experiencing his or her own readjustment problems. For some returnees, re-entry is a shock. It is as if they had pressed the 'pause' button as they flew out of the country, and expected life at home to remain in the 'freeze frame'. Re-entry reminds them that life is not static. Others may have, as a coping behavior in the foreign location, glamorized life back home, and now have to come to terms with reality; to accept the negative as well as the positive aspects of home. For example, the foreign country may have appeared more expensive in relative terms, but upon repatriation, the family is confronted with a higher level of inflation in the home country than was previously the case. Conversely, life at home may now seem dull and unexciting in contrast, and the family unit may begin to glamorize the life they left behind in the foreign location. These reactions can be compounded if the family income has been reduced upon repatriation. Of course, the income level depends on whether spouses/partners worked while in the foreign location, and how quickly they find suitable jobs upon repatriation.

Social networks.

Naturally, impressions generated about changes in the home country may depend on how effectively the family has been able to keep up to date with events back home. One could expect that the coverage by satellite television news channels such as CNN and BBC World, and global-oriented newspapers, make it easier for US and UK expatriates to follow their home events, than those coming from smaller countries such as Australia or The Netherlands. However, with the rapid advances in the Internet, wireless and mobile phone technology, digital cameras and email, it is now significantly easier to stay in touch, though this depends on the availability of, and access to, television cable networks, computer facilities and Internet connections in the foreign location.

Re-establishing social networks can also be difficult, especially if the family has been repatriated to a different state or town in the home country. Families who return to their previous domestic locations often find that friends have moved away. Repatriated spouses may find their friends have re-entered the workforce and are no longer available for social activities. There can be a sense of loss as the level of attention and support from the multinational is withdrawn: 'The 'phone does not ring. We went from a very close [expatriate] community to here where everyone is very busy with their own lives.'[53] Many repatriates report that people show little interest in hearing about their expatriate experiences, which can make conversation uncomfortable.[54] As one US repatriate relates: 'It was very difficult discussing my experiences with my co-workers and friends because Americans refuse to accept that life somewhere else could be as good or better than in the USA.'[55]

Children may also find re-entry difficult. Coming back to school, attempting to regain acceptance into peer groups, and being out-of-touch with current slang, sport and fashion can cause problems. However, there are few reported studies in the literature that focus on children's repatriation. An exception is a study of 40 Japanese children that found the children faced difficulties reintegrating into both their peer groups and the Japanese educational system.[56] One can speculate though that the more difficult the re-entry process for the children, the greater the 'spill-over' effect for the repatriate.

Effect on partner's career.   Partners encounter difficulties in re-entering the workforce, particularly if the partner has not been able to work outside the home prior to, or during, the foreign assignment, but now desires to find outside employment; either as part of a re-entry coping strategy, or due to altered family circumstances. Negative experiences during the job search may affect the partner's self-worth, compounding the readjustment process, and even causing tension in the relationship. For those who held positions prior to the overseas assignment, difficulties in re-entering the workforce may depend on: occupation,[57] length of time abroad, unemployment levels in the home country, and personal characteristics such as age and gender.[58]

There is a dearth of research into the effects of the foreign assignment and repatriation upon the partner's career, and many questions surrounding this issue remain unexplored:

- Do new employers consider the value of the time overseas to 'compensate' for the forced career disruption? One study reported: 'being a trailing spouse during the expatriate's international assignment constitutes a damaging gap in their employment history'.[59]

- Have those partners who were able to work during the foreign assignment found employment in career-related jobs, and been able to progress upon repatriation?

- Do male 'trailing' partners face different challenges upon repatriation than do females? In one of the few reported studies into dual-career expatriates, Harvey[60] found a difference between female expatriate managers' expectations prior to and after expatriation, exposing the need for support for the male trailing partner. The overseas assignment was the focus of Harvey's study, but one could assume that the same results would hold true upon repatriation. More recently, Linehan and Scullion[61] looked at the repatriation process of female expatriates working in various European companies but did not consider the career aspect of the accompanying spouse/partner.

Readjustment of the expatriate, whether male-led or female-led, may be linked with concerns about the effect that the foreign assignment might have on the partner's career. Given that dual-career couples are on the increase, and that more females expect overseas assignments, the issue of the partner's career is likely to become a major factor determining staff availability for future overseas assignments. A 2002 global survey by ORC Worldwide[62] found that job-search assistance (20 per cent), c.v./résumé preparation (20 per cent) and career counselling (18 per cent) were the most common forms of spousal assistance upon re-entry. The report's authors comment:

> Surprisingly, the provision of these three important support mechanisms has decreased since the previous increase in the 1996 survey. Taking into account the increased recognition of the dual career issues and their significance for successful assignments leading to the growth in pre-assignment and on-assignment spousal assistance, this decrease in the support on repatriation was unexpected.

Our analysis has revealed how various factors influence re-entry and readjustment at the individual level. These moderating factors can combine in hard to predict ways, creating a volatile situation that may lead to the repatriate's unforeseen and debilitating exit from the multinational.

Multinational responses

The above sections have considered the re-entry and career issues from the perspective of the individual repatriate. We shall now examine the issues from the viewpoint of the multinational. Early studies into the issue of repatriation indicated that it was somewhat neglected by multinationals. For example, Mendenhall, Dunbar, and Oddou[63] concluded that US human resource professionals may be unaware of the challenges facing repatriated managers. Commenting on the results of his 1989 study Harvey[64] noted that: 'Even though many executives have experienced difficulties upon repatriation, [US] multinational companies have seemingly not addressed the issues related to repatriation with the same level of interest as preparing executives for expatriation.'

A 1997 survey found that only 27 per cent of responding firms indicated they held re-entry sessions to discuss issues, such as career objectives, performance and plan for re-entry. The majority of these firms indicated that they waited up to 90 days before initiating such sessions.[65] There would seem to have been some progress lately. For example, the GMAC GRS data shows that in 2002, 73 per cent of responding firms held re-entry discussions, compared with 86 per cent in 2004. The timing and formality of these re-entry discussions varies. For example, in 2004, 44 per cent of respondents held repatriation discussions before departure, mostly on an informal basis.

The GMAC GRS surveys do not report on spousal or family involvement in re-entry discussions, but these aspects were raised in the ORC Worldwide 2002 Report. As mentioned earlier in this chapter, job search assistance, résumé preparation and career counselling were the most common forms of assistance. However, the report does not indicate if this was negotiated before or during the international assignment or upon re-entry, and if it was part of a re-entry discussion.

Managing the process of repatriation should be of concern to multinationals that desire to maximize the benefits of international assignments and create a large internal labor market. A well-designed repatriation process is important in achieving these objectives, for three main reasons: staff availability, return on investment and knowledge transfer. These are now discussed.

Staff availability and career expectations

The way the multinational handles repatriation has an impact on staff availability for current and future needs, as indicated in Figure 8-6. Re-entry positions signal the importance given to international experience. If the repatriate is promoted or given a position that obviously capitalizes on international experience, other members of the multinational interpret international assignments as a positive career move. On the other hand, if the multinational does not reward expatriate performance, tolerates a high turnover among repatriates, or is seen to terminate a repatriate's employment upon re-entry, then the workforce may interpret the acceptance of an international assignment as a high-risk decision in terms of future career progression within the organization. The multinational's ability to attract high-calibre staff for international assignments is thereby lessened, and this can have a negative effect on the multinational's activities in the long term.

Lately, there has been some discussion about international assignments and *boundaryless careers*. The term 'boundaryless career' appears to have been coined in recognition of shifts occurring in the employment relationship, particularly in

| **Figure 8-6** | Linking repatriation process to outcomes |

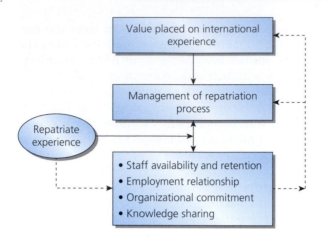

Western countries. The traditional hierarchical career path, with definable stages (such as junior, middle and senior manager), assumed long-term employment within one organization – the so-called job-for-life where one climbed the corporate ladder. Today, employees are tending to switch jobs more frequently, either voluntarily or involuntarily as economic circumstances change, such as unemployment as a result of organizational restructuring, or reskilling as jobs disappear. 'The boundaryless careerist . . . is the highly qualified mobile professional who builds his or her career competencies and labor market value through transfers across boundaries.'[66] Careers then are becoming discontinuous in the sense that the person moves between organizations, and may have periods of unemployment, or self-employment, or contract work interspersed with more traditional employment arrangements. International assignments, particularly for career expatriates or global managers, are sometimes regarded as boundaryless in that the assignment places the person in another organization, most commonly a subsidiary or an international joint venture. Accompanying this view is the notion that the individual rather than the organization is responsible for career management: the term 'protean' (after the Greek god Proteus who could change into any form)[67] is sometimes used to reflect the idea of a self-directed, continuous learning, career.

Multinationals are reinforcing the notion of protean and boundaryless careers when they do not guarantee repatriates positions upon re-entry. As Stahl *et al*.[68] found in their large study of 494 German managers posted to 59 countries: 'the vast majority of expatriates viewed their international assignment as an opportunity for skill development and future career advancement, even though it may not be with their current company, [which] supports the notion of boundaryless careers'. In such cases, commitment to the organization (an outcome in Figure 8-6) is replaced by commitment to one's career. Such a change may restrict the ability of the organization to attract high-calibre individuals to undertake international assignments – that is, staff availability – thus affecting the quality as well as the quantity of suitable candidates and the development of a cadre of global operators.

Similar results were found in a study of German and Singaporean expatriates. Both of these groups reported concerns with their firms' ability to facilitate their careers upon return from international assignments, provide in-company opportunities to use the new knowledge and skills they had gained during their international assignments, or provide them with new positions having the responsibility, autonomy and compensation at levels that met their expectations. They did feel as if these international assignments enhanced their opportunities among other possible employers and facilitated the development of their own intercultural and professional or managerial skills.[69]

In some instances firms may choose to select 'international itinerants', that is 'professional managers who over their careers are employed for their ability, by at least two business organizations that are not related to each other, in at least two different countries',[70] instead of selecting in-house candidates that will have to be repatriated to the MNE. By selecting these individuals in lieu of internal candidates, overall costs may be reduced, ongoing support costs can be managed, and – germane to our discussion – repatriation activities can be eliminated. The two main disadvantages of using of these types of assignees relate to a lack of in-depth firm knowledge by the itinerants and problems the MNE may have in selecting and controlling itinerants.[71]

However, in the literature, contradicting evidence also exists on the issue of boundaryless careers. Other researchers suggest that expatriate careers still correspond very much to the traditional model of the organizational career, especially in the case of a global corporate philosophy including the development of global leaders.[72] Festing and Müller[73] found in a study of 168 alumni of a European business school that in cases where international assignments had an important strategic value for the MNE and were accompanied by a high level of IHRM activity, expatriates had rather traditional career expectations aiming at a long-term employment relationship with their employer. In these cases the retention rates of international managers after the international assignment were high. This indicates that the organizational context may at least partly influence the emergence of expatriate career patterns and confirm the relationships outlined in Figure 8-6, i.e. that IHRM measures such as repatriation programs influence the outcomes in terms of the employment relationship in general and specifically employee retention rates and commitment.

How actively the MNE manages – as a matter of strategy or circumstances – an international assignee's career may vary substantially. Career management is conceptualized in an analysis of 194 UK-based firms by Baruch and Peiper as being more or less sophisticated and with more or less involvement by the firm in an employee's career. 'Basic' and 'formal' practices, comprised of less sophisticated career practices and low levels of involvement, are characterized by practices such as common career paths, written personal career planning, job posting and lateral moves. More sophisticated practices with higher levels of firm involvement in an employee's career are described as 'multidirectional' and 'active planning' forms of career. These models are characterized by practices related to in-depth career counselling, succession planning, a strong link between performance management systems and career planning, peer appraisals and upward appraisal processes.[74] Little is known at this time about the factors that determine how much time, energy and effort returning expatriates and executives in MNEs will put into career practices designed to maintain existing work relationships, as opposed to readily looking for external job opportunities upon return or seeing repatriation turnover as an inevitable cost of doing business globally.

Return on investment (ROI)

Expatriates are expensive, especially expatriates from first-world advanced economies. Where possible, multinationals try to localize positions through the employment of HCNs, but not all positions can or should be localized. As we discussed in Chapter 4, the alternative, which more companies are utilizing or experimenting with, is a short-term or non-standard assignment to replace the traditional expatriate form. Cost containment is the driver here along with staff immobility. For example, 79 per cent of firms in a 2005 global survey by Price-WaterhouseCoopers[75] identified cost reduction as important or very important in the evolution of international assignment practices, and the GMAC GRS surveys continue to indicate that cost containment continues to drive assignment trends.

However, faced with the business reality that expatriates will always be with us, the question is how to ensure the organization reaps the benefits of international assignments regardless of duration and form. Black and Gregersen[76] calculate that a US multinational spends around one million dollars on each expatriate over the duration of a foreign assignment. They argue that, if approximately one in four repatriates exits the firm within a year of repatriation: 'It represents a substantial financial and human capital loss to the firm, especially if the skills, knowledge, and experience that the individual gains are important to the firm and scarce in the internal or external labor markets.'

Getting a return on this investment would appear to be an important objective, but not easy to achieve. First, there is a matter of definition. Respondents in the GMAC GRS 2002 survey were asked if ROI could be defined as 'accomplishing the assignment objectives at the expected cost'. A total of 96 per cent of respondents agreed with this definition – a figure that dropped to 10 per cent in the 2004 survey, increasing slightly to 14 per cent in 2005. It is not clear whether the 2004 respondents misunderstood the question, or disagreed with the GMAC GRS offered definition. In one of the few articles that considered ROI on international assignments, McNulty and Tharenou[77] recognize that a meaningful definition should include a cost-benefit analysis of financial and non-financial data, measured against the purpose of the assignment. Identifying direct costs is relatively easy as relocation expenses, an itemized compensation package and other international assignee entitlements are accessible. The indirect, intangible, non-financial costs are more problematical. These include the non-direct costs of expatriate failure or under-performance (as identified in Chapter 5) and the opportunity cost of not using a HCN.

Placing monetary value on the benefits of the international assignment is also a challenge as the intangibles – such as knowledge and skills transfer, management development and relationship/network building – are somewhat invisible, often tacit and person-bound. It is difficult to measure intellectual, social and human capital gains – improvements in the stock of knowledge and competence that result from a successful repatriation process. ROI analysis also focuses on the international assignment period, and can be an exercise to justify cost reduction measures (such as replacing expatriates with HCNs) rather than considering gains that accrue to the organization through repatriated staff.

Although firms participating in the GMAC GRS surveys tracked assignment costs, only 46 per cent of respondents in the 2004 survey compared estimated with actual costs, and only 37 per cent in the 2005 survey. Difficulties encountered in attempts to measure ROI were:

- Receiving feedback from the business unit concerned.
- Tracking international assignments in a systematic way.
- No formal planning.
- A lack of objective measures.

● Too many decisions being made without realizing the costs relating to the international assignment.

● Globalization is a 'must' for us (so the ROI almost doesn't matter).

More importantly, there is a link between value placed on the international experience and strategic outcomes (see Figure 8-6). As the authors of the GMAC GRS 2004 Survey Report[78] argue:

> If management is not aware of the return on investment (or lack of return) for international assignments, how can expatriates be recognized and rewarded for making signal contributions to their firm's success? Until companies sharpen their pencils and learn to measure the impact of international assignments on the corporate bottom line, they will be unable to convince international-assignment candidates that acceptance of such assignments will have a positive impact on their careers.

Further, employees will perform their own ROI calculations, based on perceived and actual costs and benefits, and these calculations will influence their willingness to accept an international assignment – or repeat the experience. Aligning corporate objectives with individual expectations is not an easy task, and compounds attempts to balance costs and benefits for both parties.

Knowledge transfer

A common theme in current international business that is stressed by company managers is the need for cross-fertilization of ideas and practices that assist in developing and maintaining competitive advantage. International assignments are a primary method of achieving this objective. As the PriceWaterhouseCoopers 2002[79] report concludes: 'Organizations need to make sure that their business strategies are supported by sound mobility strategies . . . The need to move key employees around the business, regardless of national boundaries, will be increasingly vital to the success of a global organization.'

Given the roles played by expatriates, along with their cost, it is reasonable to expect that multinationals would endeavor to retain key staff and to extract and build upon their international experience. However, as we have seen in our examination of re-entry and career issues, a relatively high turnover of repatriate staff seems acceptable. That 69 per cent of responding firms in the 2004 GMAC GRS survey do not know their expatriate attrition rate is evidence of this (a jump from 39 per cent in 2002). One GMAC GRS respondent commented: 'There is a high level of investment with a low value on the experience.'[80] More telling is the continuing trend not to guarantee post-assignment positions so that the organization has greater flexibility over employment levels.

We can draw several conclusions regarding repatriate attrition rates. First, despite the rhetoric, knowledge transfer is treated as a one-way activity. Expatriates are sent on international assignments and effectiveness is determined on the performance of their ascribed roles and work responsibilities. Any transfer of knowledge and competence occurs in the host location and remains there. Expatriates return to their home base and are reassigned or resign. Consider the following comments about international assignment objectives volunteered by responding firms in the 2002 GMAC GRS survey.[81]

● The primary reason for an expatriate assignment is to go into a country and train someone who is local to do a specific job function and then return home.

● Work is project oriented. We send expatriates to complete projects and leave.
● Expatriates develop local management talent.
● Our main reason for sending expatriates is to supplement national staff capacity, provide training and coaching, and provide professional expertise.
● We view these as developmental assignments to broaden employee experience.

More recent surveys reinforce these findings. There is no mention about an international assignment being part of transferring knowledge and competence around the organization, or even as a two-way process. The point here is that while performing their tasks in the host location, expatriates develop skills and gain experience, knowledge and network relationships that can then be used upon repatriation in some way or another. For example, a project manager working in Russia can report, on re-entry to his UK home base, technical problems encountered and solutions that were developed to overcome these problems, thus sharing the experience. However, not all of the knowledge about that project is explicit. Much will remain tacit and person-bound. What is codified and made explicit often is retained within the project team, even though some of the information and knowledge could be applicable to other projects or types of business concerning Russia, such as important contacts, management styles and some technical solutions. In addition, international assignments vary in terms of purpose, duration, location and nature and these differences affect the acquisition and transfer of knowledge and skills.

HCNs transferred to headquarters for developmental reasons, for example, may benefit through such exposure but the experience will remain person-bound if the home unit does not allow the repatriated HCN opportunities to share knowledge and information. Contacts at headquarters can be used for personal advantage. A similar case can be made for TCNs transferred back from another subsidiary. The aims of cross-fertilization of ideas and best practices given to justify cross-border movement of staff require the right environment to facilitate sharing of information and knowledge. The 'not-invented-here' mindset (or xenophobia) can operate to devalue repatriate contributions.

What knowledge and skills are acquired through a typical international assignment? A study of 19 Austrian repatriates provides some answers. Based on in-depth interviews, Fink *et al.*[82] classified repatriate knowledge into five categories:

● *Market specific knowledge.* Local system (political, social, economic), local language and local customs.
● *Personal skills.* Inter-cultural knowledge, self-confidence (that is, ability to make quick decisions), flexibility, tolerance.
● *Job-related management skills.* Communication, project management, problem solving.
● *Network knowledge.* Meeting diverse people – clients, suppliers, subsidiary personnel, other expatriates.
● *General management capacity.* An enlarged job description, broader job responsibilities, exposure to other parts of the organization.

The range of knowledge and skills listed comprise both tacit and explicit knowledge. The authors consider that the first four categories are useful for the sending organization, while the last (general management capacity) is most beneficial to the individual. Fink *et al.* conclude that repatriate knowledge may be useful in enhancing a firm's competitiveness, but acknowledge the difficulties in capitalizing on this, particularly if repatriates exit before such knowledge has been transferred. They also point out that the size of the firm, and its stage in the internationalization process, is a critical factor. The Austrian firms in their sample were SMEs who did not have need for a large number of 'general managers' and thus were unable to meet repatriate expectations based on their newly acquired skills and knowledge.

The trend towards not providing post-assignment position guarantees suggests that multinationals accept loss of experience, knowledge and competence; that repatriates effectively forced to leave the organization will take with them what could be vital and valuable, allowing competing firms to reap the benefits of a substantial investment in human capital. Those who remain in the organization may not be motivated to share.[83] Perhaps this seemingly downgrading of the repatriate experience is partly due to the fact that many firms are unaware of the benefits of the international assignment to both the firm and the individual as ROI calculations, clearly linked to the nature and purpose of the assignment, are not performed. As Downes and Thomas[84] found, multinationals that valued international experience were rewarded by loyal employees who contributed to the intellectual capital base of their companies. Unfortunately, that repatriates become an under-utilized resource has been a consistent finding in studies and surveys examining repatriation.[85]

Blakeney, Oddou and Osland recommend that HR practitioners in multinational firms take a wider, more systematic view of the expatriate-repatriate cycle, and focus on: (1) identifying the critical, implicitly held knowledge assets inherent in expatriation/repatriation, and (2) reduce the sources of resistance to knowledge transfer inherent in the motivation and capabilities of the repatriate as well as the structural and cultural impediments inherent in the receiving unit at home. This can be done by building trust and enhancing the shared sense of social identity between the repatriate and the receiving unit.[86] Practically speaking, HR practices that combine a unified expatriation/repatriation cycle that explicitly emphasizes knowledge transference in each stage of the process (namely, in selection, pre-departure and in country training, mentoring or coaching, designing the international assignment, re-entry training, returnee job assignment and selection as well as the training of the returnees own managers) will assist in the successful transfer of knowledge. More formal activities, including seminars by repatriates as post-assignment 'action learning' exercises and the development of knowledge disseminating teams and databases made up to index the expertise of repatriates, can facilitate progress.[87]

Recent empirical research by Tung points out the potential for patterns of international careers, in this case careers in MNEs moving back and forth between China and North America, to contribute to outward foreign direct investment strategies for MNEs.[88] These humans capital flows are only now being documented and a rudimentary understanding of the complex relationships between government policies, cultural solidarity in the face of diasporas, and personal career ambitions is beginning to emerge.

Designing a repatriation program

While there is no simple, quick solution, preparing the repatriate and family for re-entry appears to have some value. The potential for mismatch of expectations regarding the future may be addressed as part of pre-re-entry training before the return, and discussed during re-entry counseling sessions (sometimes referred to as debriefing) between the receiving organization in the home country

Table 8-2	Topics covered by a repatriation program

- Preparation, physical relocation and transition information (what the company will help with)
- Financial and tax assistance (including benefit and tax changes; loss of overseas allowance)
- Re-entry position and career path assistance
- Reverse culture shock (including family disorientation)
- School systems and children's education, and adaptation
- Workplace changes (such as corporate culture, structure, decentralization)
- Stress management, communication-related training
- Establishing networking opportunities
- Help in forming new social contacts

and the repatriate. In today's parlance, such sessions would enable both parties to 'take a reality check'.

What should be covered in formal repatriation programs? Table 8-2 is an amalgam of the lists suggested by respondents in the various surveys referred to above.

Some MNEs assign the expatriate a *mentor* (also referred to as a company contact, sponsor, or 'godfather'). The mentor is usually in a more senior position than the expatriate, from the sending work unit, and knows the expatriate personally. The rationale behind the use of a mentor is to alleviate the 'out-of-sight, out-of-mind' feeling discussed earlier through the provision of information (such as, workplace changes) on a regular basis, so that the expatriate is more prepared for conditions faced upon re-entry. A mentor should also ensure that the expatriate is not forgotten when important decisions are made regarding positions and promotions.

A survey of re-entry practices in 152 multinational companies from the USA, Europe and Asia[89] found that 26 per cent of respondents provided mentors for their expatriates; though this was related to various organizational factors:

- Size of expatriate workforce. Firms with more than 250 expatriates were more likely to assign mentors (43 per cent) than those with 55–100 expatriates (15 per cent).

- Which work unit was responsible for the expatriate. Mentors are more likely if corporate HR formulates expatriate policy (in 35 per cent of cases); and when the expatriate is managed by a separate international assignments unit (in 41 per cent of cases) rather than at the divisional level (18 per cent).

- Nationality of responding company. 35 per cent of Continental European firms reported the use of mentors compared to 20 per cent in US firms. This result compares with findings from a study of European-based multinationals: over a quarter used a career mentor/sponsor system, with a further 19 per cent indicating that such a scheme would be introduced in the future.

Linehan and Scullion[90] found that 40 of the 50 females in their study had experienced mentoring relationships, and believed that their management positions were partially due to that relationship. The mentors provided contact and support from the home organization which also facilitated re-entry and reduced the 'out-of-sight, out-of-mind' syndrome. Their experiences led them to adopt mentoring roles in their new domestic positions.

It is reasonable to suggest the practice of mentoring, to be effective, has to be managed. For example, what happens when the mentor retires or leaves the firm – two likely events in a multinational undergoing radical restructuring? Who monitors the mentor's performance? Recent surveys have not specifically covered the practice of mentoring, though 12 per cent of responding firms in the 2002 GMAC GRS survey indicated they used mentors. Firms in a 1997/98 Price Waterhouse survey[91] defined mentoring duties to include:

- Maintaining contact with the expatriate throughout the assignment.
- Ensuring expatriates are kept up to date with developments in the home country.
- Ensuring expatriates are retained in existing management development programs.
- Mentors are responsible for assisting expatriates with the repatriation process, including helping them with a repatriation position.

It may be that having a mentor assists the expatriate to adjust during the foreign assignment but, by itself, does not necessarily help re-entry. Stroh[92] concludes that her study: 'did not show that having a mentoring program would make an independent contribution to repatriate retention rate', though there was a suggested link between assignment of a mentor, career development and repatriate retention. In other words, an effective mentor is likely to alert the firm of the imminent return of the repatriate and thus affects the re-entry position; or the practice is part of a managed repatriation program.

Caligiuri and Lazarova[93] recommend no less than 12 proactive strategies to maximize the likelihood that the professional, financial and emotional issues faced by repatriates and their families will be dealt with and repatriates will be able to return with an integrated and balanced set of experiences which will be available to the MNE (see the lowest segment of the right column of Figure 8-2). These proactive strategies include:

- Managing expectations via pre-departure briefings on what can be expected during the assignment and upon return.
- Multiple career planning sessions focusing on career objectives and performance indicators, carried out by HR managers or a purpose-built team of past repatriates and relevant executives.
- Written repatriate agreements when feasible to clarify the types of assignments available upon return.
- Previously mentioned mentoring programs that continue on into the repatriate's post-assignment career. This practice may act to notify the firm of any post-assignment dissonance and reduce turnover.
- Again, as mentioned above, extended home visits to keep up with social, family and organizational changes.
- Reorientation programs to provide the repatriate with a briefing on changes in strategy, policies and organization.
- Personalized reorientation by the MNE so the repatriate and her/his family may deal with the emotionally charged issues of social readjustment, schools, family dynamics and lifestyle changes inherent in return.
- Personalized financial and tax advice as well as access to interim financial benefits such as short-term loans – similar to the professional advice available to executives.

- Providing some kind of an adjustment period upon return that may or may not include a vacation or reduced work load.

- Improved employee satisfaction and commitment upon return will potentially translate into a more globally capable firm.[94] Visible and concrete expressions of the repatriate's value to the firm (in the form of promotion, public ceremonies or a completion bonus) may be required to seal and reinforce this new, more globally encompassing relationship between the multinational firm and the repatriate.

In terms of empirical evidence of practices, GMAC GRS's 2005 survey of trends in global relocation reports 81 per cent of responding firms discussed repatriation upon return, while 59 per cent discussed repatriation before the employee left for the assignment. At the same time, 57 per cent of responding firms did not offer post-assignment guarantees but 83 per cent reported they identified a new job (via transfers) within the firm. Responding firms stated they felt the practice of highlighting opportunities for the repatriate to use their international experience was useful to reduce turnover upon return (64 per cent), followed by the practices of providing a variety of assignments for the repatriate to select from (50 per cent) and repatriation assistance (43 per cent).[95]

Even with all of these practices, employee attrition remains a concern; 21 per cent of repatriates leave during the assignment, 23 per cent leave within one year of return and 20 per cent exit by the second year. These rates are twice those reported for all employees.[96]

While recognition of the importance of repatriation programs is increasing, and companies are experimenting with other measures such as mentors, other avenues could be explored, such as using repatriates as an important information source. Inviting repatriates to assist in developing repatriation programs may contribute to relevant and effective policies. It may also have a desirable side-effect upon readjustment, simply by giving participating repatriates a sense that they are not an under-utilized resource, and that the firm recognizes they can make a valuable contribution to the expatriation process. It is, naturally, important that wherever possible the multinational ensures equity of treatment between PCN, TCN and HCN expatriates.

Summary

This chapter has been concerned with the repatriation process. We have covered:

- The repatriation process. One may conclude that in re-entry, the broader socio-cultural context of the home country takes a backstage position – unlike in the expatriation adjustment phase, where the foreign culture can be overwhelming.[97] Cultural novelty has been found to affect adjustment and, for the majority of repatriates, coming home to the familiar culture may assist in readjustment. Indeed, given the more profound effect that job-related factors appear to have, *re-entry shock* is perhaps a more accurate term to describe the readjustment process experienced upon repatriation.

● Job-related issues centered on career issues upon re-entry. Factors that affected career anxiety were: no post-assignment guarantee of employment; fear that the period overseas had caused a loss of visibility; changes in the home workplace that affect re-entry positions; and the employment relationship. The re-entry position was an important indicator of future career progression and the value placed on international experience. Coping with new role demands was another factor in readjustment, along with loss of status and pay.

● Social factors explored were loss of social standing – the kingpin syndrome – and the accompanying loss of the expatriate lifestyle. Family readjustment was also important. A specific aspect was the effect of the international assignment upon the spouse/partner's career, such as being re-employed and having international experience recognized.

● Multinational responses to repatriates' concerns focused on re-entry procedures. We looked at how repatriation affected staff availability, whether companies were measuring and obtaining a return on investment through international assignments, and the contribution of repatriates to knowledge transfer. The concepts of protean and boundaryless careers were introduced in terms of the international assignment and career outcomes.

● Designing effective repatriation programs, including the use of mentors and available forms of technology.

While the focus of this chapter has been repatriation in the general sense, the issue of career expatriates should be raised. The repatriation literature reviewed in preparation for this chapter makes little mention of the process of managing the return of those who have been part of the international team of managers (or cadre) – those who have worked outside their home countries for lengthy periods of time. For this strategically important group of employees, at some point repatriation may coincide with retirement. One is left with the impression that those who return to retire in their home country are no longer of concern to their firms. However, one could expect that these individuals would require special counselling to assist not only the transition back to the home country, but from work to retirement as well.

Viewing repatriation as part of the expatriation process, as suggested in Figure 8-2, should remind those responsible for expatriation management of the need to prepare repatriates for re-entry and to recognize the value of the international experience to both parties.

Discussion Questions

1 What factors contribute to re-entry shock?

2 How can multinationals assist dual career couples' repatriation?

3 Placing value on the international assignment assists repatriate retention. Discuss this statement.

4 What are the elements of a good mentoring system for international assignees?

5 What aspects would you include in a pre-repatriation program?

Further Reading

Bossard, A. and Peterson, R. (2005). 'The Repatriate Experience as Seen by American Expatriates', *Journal of World Business,* 40(4): 9–28.

Harvey, M. and Novicevic, M. (2006). 'The Evolution from Repatriation of Managers in MNEs to "Patriation" in Global Organizations', in G. Stahl and I. Björkman (eds), *Handbook of Research in International Human Resource Management,* Cheltenham: Edward Elgar, pp. 323–46.

Mayerhofer, H., Hartmann, L.C. and Herbert, A. (2004). 'Career Management Issues for Flexpatriate International Staff', *Thunderbird International Business Review,* 46(6): 647–66.

Tung, R. (2007). 'The Human Resource Challenge to Outward Foreign Direct Investment Aspirations from Emerging Economies: The case of China', *International Journal of Human Resource Management,* 18(5): 868–89.

Notes and References

1   See L. Stroh, J.S. Black, M. Mendenhall and H. Gregersen, *International Assignments: An Integration of Strategy, Research and Practice* (Mahiwah, NJ: Lawrence Erlbaum, 2005); M. Harvey and M. Novicevic, 'The Evolution from Repatriation of Managers in MNEs to "Patriation" in Global Organizations', in G. Stahl and I. Björkman (eds), *Handbook of Research in International Human Resource Management* (Cheltenham: Edward Elgar, 2006), pp. 323–343.

2   R. Moran, 'Coping with Re-entry Shock', *International Management* (December 1989), p. 67; M.G. Harvey, 'Repatriation of Corporate Executives: An Empirical Study', *Journal of International Business Studies,* Vol. 20, No. 1 (Spring 1989), pp. 131–44.

3   Stroh, *et al., International Assignments;* Harvey, 'Repatriation of Corporate Executives'.

4   Y. Paik, B. Segand and C. Malinowski, 'How to Improve Repatriation Management: Are Motivations and Expectations Congruent Between the Company and Expatriates?', *International Journal of Management,* Vol. 23 (2002), pp. 635–48; Stroh, *et al., International Assignments.*

5   J.S. Black, H. Gregersen and M. Mendenhall, 'Towards a Theoretical Framework for Repatriation Adjustment', *Journal of International Business Studies,* Vol. 23 (1992), pp. 737–60.

6   The first author has seen a number of examples over the years where expatriate families have taken their holidays in other locations rather than returning to their home country and have subsequently developed a rather unrealistic picture which led to difficulties when the reality of subsequent repatriation resulted in adjustment difficulties.

7   Stroh, *et al., International Assignments,* pp. 215–16.

8   W. Mayrhofer, M. Meyer, A. Iellatchitch and M. Schiffinger, 'Careers and Human Resource Management: A European Perspective', *Human Resource Management Review,* Vol. 14 (2004), pp. 473–98; Stroh, *et al., International Assignments,* pp. 199–217.

9   A-W. Harzing, *Environment, Strategy, Structure, Control Mechanisms, and Human Resource Management in Multinational Companies,* Company Report (Limburg, The Netherlands: University of Limburg, 1996).

10 GMAC-Global Relocation Services, US National Foreign Trade Council and SHRM Global Forum, *Global Relocation Trends 2002 Survey Report* (2002); *2004 Survey Report;* and *2006 Survey Report.* These reports are available from the GMAC Global Relocation Services website: www.gmacglobalrelocation.com/survey.html.

11 GMAC, *2004 Survey Report,* p. 54.

12 R.L. Tung and Arthur Andersen, *Exploring International Assignees' Viewpoints: A Study of the Expatriation/Repatriation Process* (Chicago, IL: Arthur Andersen, International Executive Services, 1997); D.C. Feldman and D.C. Thomas, 'Career Issues Facing Expatriate Managers', *Journal of International Business Studies,* Vol. 23, No. 2 (1992), pp. 271–94.

13 GMAC-GRS survey, *2002 Survey Report,* p. 51.

14 Price Waterhouse Europe, 'International Assignments: European Policy and Practice', Price Waterhouse International Assignment Services Europe (1997).

15 Tung and Arthur Andersen, *Exploring International Assignees' Viewpoints.*

16 E. Marx, *International Human Resource Practices in Britain and Germany* (London: Anglo-German Foundation for the Study of Industrial Society, 1996).

17 GMAC-GRS survey, *2002 Survey Report,* p. 51.

18 Harzing, *Environment, Strategy, Structure, Control Mechanisms;* D. Osborn, 'The International Mobility of French Managers', *European Management Journal,* Vol. 15, No. 5 (1997), pp. 584–90.

19 S. Black and H.B. Gregersen, 'When Yankee Comes Home: Factors Related to Expatriate and Spouse Repatriation Adjustment', *Journal of International Business Studies*, Vol. 22, No. 4 (1991), pp. 671–94.

20 M. Bolino and D.C. Feldman, 'Increasing the Skill Utilization of Expatriates', *Human Resource Management*, Vol. 39, No. 4 (2000), pp. 367–79.

21 L.K. Stroh, H.B. Gregersen and J.S. Black, 'Closing the Gap: Expectations Versus Reality Among Repatriates', *Journal of World Business*, Vol. 33, No. 2 (1998), p. 119.

22 J.S. Black, H.B. Gregersen and M.E. Mendenhall, 'Toward a Theoretical Framework of Repatriation Adjustment', *Journal of International Business Studies*, Vol. 23, No. 4 (1992), pp. 737–60.

23 M. Lazarova and P. Caligiuri, 'Retaining Repatriates: The Role of Organizational Support Practices', *Journal of World Business*, Vol. 36, No. 4 (2001), pp. 389–401.

24 Stroh, Gregersen and Black, 'Closing the Gap', p. 119.

25 V. Suutari and C. Brewster, 'Repatriation: Empirical Evidence from a Longitudinal Study of Careers and Expectations among Finnish Expatriates', *International Journal of Human Resource Management*, Vol. 14, No. 7 (2003), pp. 1132–51.

26 GMAC, *2004 Survey Report*, p. 49.

27 PricewaterhouseCoopers, 'International Assignments: Global Policy and Practice Key Trends 2005', Human Resource Services. Downloaded from company website.

28 L.K. Stroh, 'Predicting Turnover among Repatriates: Can Organizations Affect Retention Rates?', *International Journal of Human Resource Management*, Vol. 6, No. 2 (1995), p. 450.

29 Lazarova and Caligiuri, 'Retaining Repatriates', p. 395.

30 Stroh, Gregersen and Black, 'Closing the Gap', p. 120.

31 M. Linehan and H. Scullion, 'Repatriation of European Female Corporate Executives: An Empirical Study', *International Journal of Human Resource Management*, Vol. 13, No. 2 (2002), pp. 259–60.

32 A.B. Bossard and R.B. Peterson, 'The Repatriate Experience as Seen by American Expatriates', *Journal of World Business*, Vol. 40 (2005), p. 17.

33 Stroh, Gregersen and Black, 'Closing the Gap'. See also R.L. Tung, 'Career Issues in International Assignments', *Academy of Management Executive*, Vol. 2, No. 3 (1988), pp. 241–4; and H.B. Gregersen, 'Commitments to a Parent Company and a Local Work Unit during Repatriation', *Personnel Psychology*, Vol. 45, No. 1 (Spring 1992), pp. 29–54; R.L. Tung, 'A Contingency Framework Revisited', *Human Resource Management Review*, Vol. 8, No. 1 (1998), pp. 23–37.

34 R.L. Tung and E.L. Miller, 'Managing in the Twenty-first Century: The Need for Global Orientation', *Management International Review*, Vol. 30, No. 1 (1990), pp. 5–18; D. Allen and S. Alvarez, 'Empowering Expatriates and Organizations to Improve Repatriation Effectiveness', *Human Resource Planning*, Vol. 21, No. 4 (1998), pp. 29–39.

35 M.R. Hammer, W. Hart and R. Rogan, 'Can You Go Home Again? An Analysis of the Repatriation of Corporate Managers and Spouses', *Management International Review*, Vol. 38, No. 1 (1998), pp. 67–86.

36 Stroh, Gregersen and Black, 'Closing the Gap', p. 120.

37 H. Mintzberg, *The Nature of Managerial Work* (Englewood Cliffs, NJ: Prentice-Hall, 1973), p. 54.

38 L. Gomez-Mejia and D.B. Balkin, 'The Determinants of Managerial Satisfaction with the Expatriation and Repatriation Process', *Journal of Management Development*, Vol. 6, No. 1 (1987), pp. 7–17.

39 I. Torbiörn, 'The Structure of Managerial Roles in Cross-cultural Settings', *International Studies of Management & Organization*, Vol. 15, No. 1 (1985), p. 69.

40 Black and Gregersen, 'When Yankee Comes Home', p. 688.

41 H.B. Gregersen and J.S. Black, 'A Multifaceted Approach to Expatriate Retention in International Assignments', *Group and Organization Studies*, Vol. 15, No. 4 (1990), pp. 461–85; also Torbiörn, 'The Structure of Managerial Roles in Cross-cultural Settings'.

42 H.B. Gregersen, 'Coming Home to the Arctic Cold: Finnish Expatriate and Spouse Repatriation Adjustment and Work-Related Outcomes', Paper presented at the Academy of International Business Meeting, Brussels (November 1992), p. 23.

43 C. Baughn, 'Personal and Organizational Factors Associated with Effective Repatriation', in J. Selmar (ed.), *Expatriate Management: New Ideas for International Business* (Westport CT: Quorum Books, 1995).

44 Black, Gregersen and Mendenhall, 'Toward a Theoretical Framework of Repatriation Adjustment'.

45 N. Forster, 'The Forgotten Employees? The Experience of Expatriate Staff Returning to the UK', *International Journal of Human Resource Management*, Vol. 5, No. 2 (1994), pp. 405–25.

46 N.K. Napier and R.B. Peterson, 'Expatriate Re-entry: What Do Expatriates Have to Say?', *Human Resource Planning,* Vol. 14, No. 1 (1991), pp. 19–28.

47 For a review of this literature, see E. Kohonen, 'Developing Global Leaders through International Assignments: An Identity Construction Perspective', *Personnel Review,* Vol. 34, No. 1 (2005), pp. 22–36.

48 Black and Gregersen, 'When Yankee Comes Home', p. 686; Baughn, 'Personal and Organizational Factors Associated with Effective Repatriation'.

49 Harvey, 'Repatriation of Corporate Executives'; and Stroh, 'Predicting Turnover among Repatriates'.

50 M. Conway, 'Reducing Expatriate Failure Rates', *Personnel Administrator,* Vol. 29, No. 7 (1984), pp. 31–8.

51 Napier and Petersen, 'Expatriate Re-entry', p. 24.

52 Black and Gregersen, 'When Yankee Comes Home'.

53 H. De Cieri, P.J. Dowling and K.F. Taylor, 'The Psychological Impact of Expatriate Relocation on Partners', *International Journal of Human Resource Management,* Vol. 2, No. 3 (1991), p. 403.

54 M.G. Harvey, 'The Other Side of Foreign Assignments: Dealing with the Repatriation Dilemma', *Columbia Journal of World Business,* Vol. 17, No. 1 (1982), pp. 52–9; R. Savich and W. Rodgers, 'Assignment Overseas: Easing the Transition Before and After', *Personnel,* August (1988), pp. 44–8.

55 Baughn, 'Personal and Organizational Factors Associated with Effective Repatriation', p. 224.

56 W. Enloe and P. Lewin, 'Issues of Integration Abroad and Readjustment to Japan of Japanese Returnees', *International Journal of Intercultural Relations,* Vol. 11 (1987), pp. 223–48.

57 G.K. Stevens and S. Black, 'The Impact of Spouse's Career-Orientation on Managers During International Transfers', *Journal of Management Studies,* Vol. 28, No. 4 (1991), pp. 417–28.

58 Black and Gregersen, 'When Yankee Comes Home'.

59 The Conference Board, *Managing Expatriates' Return: A Research Report* (New York: The Conference Board, Report No. 1148–96RR, 1997), p. 16.

60 M.G. Harvey, 'Dual-Career Expatriates: Expectations, Adjustment and Satisfaction with International Relocation', *Journal of International Business Studies,* Vol. 28, No. 3 (1997), pp. 627–58.

61 Linehan and Scullion, 'Repatriation of European Female Corporate Executives'.

62 Organization Resources Counselors Inc. (now ORC Worldwide), *Dual Careers and International Assignments Survey* (New York: ORC Worldwide, 2002), p. 7.

63 M. Mendenhall, E. Dunbar and G. Oddou, 'Expatriate Selection, Training and Career-pathing: A Review and a Critique', *Human Resource Planning,* Vol. 26, No. 3 (1987), pp. 331–45.

64 Harvey, 'The Other Side of Foreign Assignments'.

65 The Conference Board, *Managing Expatriates' Return,* p. 28.

66 D.C. Thomas, M.B. Lazarova, and K. Inkson, 'Global Careers: New Phenomenon or New Perspectives?', *Journal of World Business,* Vol. 40, No. 4 (2005), p. 341.

67 See for example, J.M. Mezias and T.A. Scandura, 'A Needs Driven Approach to Expatriate Adjustment and Career Development: A Multiple Mentoring Perspective', *Journal of International Business Studies,* Vol. 36, No. 5 (2005), pp. 519–39.

68 G.K. Stahl, E.L. Miller and R.L. Tung, 'Toward the Boundaryless Career: A Closer Look at the Expatriate Career Concept and the Perceived Implications of an International Assignment', *Journal of World Business,* Vol. 37 (2002), p. 222.

69 See G. Stahl and C. Chua, 'Global Assignments and Boundaryless Careers: What Drives and Frustrates International Assignees?', in M. Morley, N. Heraty and D. Collins (eds), *International Human Resource Management and International Assignments* (Basingstoke: Palgrave Macmillan, 2006), pp. 133–52.

70 M. Banai and W. Harry, 'Boundaryless Global Careers: The International Itinerants', in M. Morley, N. Heraty and D. Collins (eds), *International Human Resource Management and International Assignments* (Basingstoke: Palgrave Macmillan, 2006), pp. 153–80, especially p. 157.

71 *Ibid.*

72 Y. Baruch and Y. Altman, 'Expatriation and Repatriation in MNCs: A Taxonomy', *Human Resource Management',* Vol. 41, No. 2 (2002), pp. 239–59.

73 M. Festing and B. Müller, 'Antecedents and Outcomes of Expatriate's Psychological Contracts: Framework and Empirical Results', Paper presented at the Academy of Management Annual Meeting, Philadelphia/USA, August 2007.

74 For more on the sophistication and commitment to career management, see Y. Baruch and M. Peiper, 'Career Management Practices: An Empirical Survey and Implications', *Human Resource Management,* Vol. 39, No. 4 (2000), pp. 347–66; J. Richardson and M. Mallon, 'Career

Interrupted: The Case of the Self-Directed Expatriate', *Journal of World Business,* Vol. 40, No. 4 (2005), pp. 409–20; and D. Thomas, M. Lazarova and K. Inkson, 'Global Careers: New Phenomenon or New Perspectives?', *Journal of World Business,* Vol. 40 (2005), pp. 340–7.

75   PriceWaterhouseCoopers, 'International Assignments: Global Policy and Practice Key Trends', 2005.

76   Black and Gregersen, 'When Yankee Comes Home'.

77   Y.M. McNulty and P. Tharenou, 'Expatriate Return on Investment', *International Studies of Management & Organization,* Vol. 34, No. 3 (2004), pp. 68–95.

78   GMAC Survey 2004, p. 8.

79   PriceWaterhouseCoopers, *International Assignments* (2002), p. 28.

80   GMAC Survey 2002, p. 56.

81   *Ibid.,* p. 40.

82   G. Fink, S. Meierewert and U. Rohr, 'The Use of Repatriate Knowledge in Organizations', *Human Resource Planning,* Vol. 28, No. 4 (2005), pp. 30–6.

83   M. Lazarova and I. Tarique, 'Knowledge Transfer upon Repatriation', *Journal of World Business,* Vol. 40, No. 4 (2005), pp. 361–73.

84   M. Downes and A.S. Thomas, 'Managing Overseas Assignments to Build Organizational Knowledge', *Human Resource Planning,* Vol. 22, No. 4 (1999), pp. 31–48.

85   See for example, R.L. Tung and Arthur Andersen, *Exploring International Assignees' Viewpoints;* Price Waterhouse Europe, 'International Assignments: European Policy and Practice'; Lazarova and Caligiuri, 'Retaining Repatriates'.

86   R. Blakeney, G. Oddou and J. Osland, 'Repatriate Assets: Factors Impacting Knowledge Transfer', in M. Morley, N. Heraty and D. Collins (eds), *International Human Resource Management and International Assignments* (Basingstoke: Palgrave Macmillan, 2006), pp. 181–99.

87   As reported by Blakeney *et al.,* 'Repatriate Assets'. Colgate-Palmolive developed a database of repatriate skills, as 'the company saw the value of having information on each manager's knowledge/experience with particular cultures and disseminating knowledge about local markets throughout its global operations', p. 194. For a more in-depth discussion of potential relationships between knowledge mapping processes, career development and strategic activities in transnational firms, see A. Engle, P. Dowling and M. Mendenhall, 'Transnational Trajectories: Emergent Strategies of Globalization and a New Context for Strategic HRM in MNEs' (working paper, 2007).

88   R. Tung, 'The Human Resource Challenge to Outward Foreign Direct Investment Aspirations from Emerging Economies: The Case of China', *International Journal of Human Resource Management,* May, Vol. 18, Issue 5 (2007), pp. 868–89.

89   The Conference Board, *Managing Expatriates' Return.*

90   Linehan and Scullion, 'Repatriation of European Female Corporate Executives'.

91   Price Waterhouse Europe, 'International Assignments', p. 32.

92   Stroh, 'Predicting Turnover among Repatriates', p. 454.

93   P. Caligiuri and M. Lazarova, 'Strategic Repatriation Policies to Enhance Global Leadership Development', in M. Mendenhall, T. Kuhlmann and G. Stahl (eds), *Developing Global Leaders: Policies, Processes and Innovations* (Westport, CT: Quorum Books, 2001), pp. 243–56.

94   Stroh, *et al., International Assignments.*

95   GMAC, *Global Relocation Trends: 2005 Survey Report,* p. 15.

96   *Ibid.*

97   Black and Gregersen, 'When Yankee Comes Home'.

IHRM in the host-country context

Chapter Objectives

For a long time the discussion of IHRM has concentrated on managing an international workforce. As has been outlined in detail, the focus was mainly on expatriate management, particularly on assigning parent-country nationals to foreign locations and the related management implications.

As a result of increasing globalization, the scope of IHRM has broadened and now includes a spectrum of questions – these concern a larger group of the MNE workforce including employees from the headquarters as well as from foreign locations. The following chapter addresses these aspects by outlining the importance of the various facets of the host-country context.

First, we will discuss the most important drivers shaping the interplay between global standardization and the localization of human resource practices in a multinational context. These include the following drivers:

- Standardization drivers are MNE strategy and structure, maturity and age, and corporate culture.
- Localization drivers are the host country's cultural and institutional environment, the mode of operation and subsidiary role.

We will then outline measures which support the development of a balance of globalization and the localization of HRM. Afterwards, we address the global code of conduct as a device for controlling employee behavior worldwide.

The last part of this chapter focuses on the strategic importance of offshoring. While looking at India and China as important offshoring locations, we will discuss the HR-related issues of this strategy and the corresponding HRM implications.

Introduction

In Chapter 2, we covered the internationalization process of the MNE and its structural implications. In Chapter 3, the focus was on cross-border alliances and the distinct situation of international SMEs. Up until this point, we have discussed a wide range of responses to the managerial challenges encountered in international business operations. Yet, increasing global competition involves the need for many multinationals to realize both global integration and local responsiveness.[1] In this chapter we discuss what this means for human resource activities in MNEs in particular. The balance between these two pressures will vary depending on the extent to which a multinational adopts a more global or local approach.[2] Morris *et al*.[3] describe the challenge of this balance as follows:

> Multinationals develop integrative HR practices by sharing best practices from all parts of the firm to create a worldwide system that strives for consistency and to gain efficiencies of scale and scope across several different countries. At the same time each overseas affiliate has to recognize and to develop HR practices that are appropriate for their local markets, employment laws, cultural traditions and the like in order to offer local advantages.

In order to gain a better understanding of how MNEs might balance these global and local pressures in HRM systems, the host-country environment becomes relevant. As we will outline in the following sections, here, the cultural and institutional embedding of an organization plays an important role. Parent organizations, as well as subsidiaries, are each rooted in their particular country-specific environment characterized by distinct systems of norms, values and assumptions, which all impact organizational behavior. Due to similar country-specific socializations, employees of the same unit usually react similarly to management practices. The parent organization must recognize that its particular way of managing human resources reflects the assumptions and values of a specific context and that these may not be appropriate abroad. Foreign affiliates may have other preferred ways of management which are more effective on a local level.

Effective multinational management requires sensitivity and adaptation to the various host-country requirements and customs regarding employment, such as hiring, reward and promotion practices, and respect for local cultural and institutional traditions. Mismatches between cultural, social and/or political attributes of HRM practices in the parent country and in the foreign locations may result in dysfunctional effects such as problems in attracting and retaining employees, labor relations conflicts or ineffective employee behavior.

The need for consistency of, and conformity to, corporate goals and objectives is driven from the strategic business orientation of the MNE, accompanied by an underlying presumption that it is possible to achieve unity of purpose through all employees worldwide adopting corporate values and codes of conduct. It is reflected in headquarters' predispositions, as we reviewed in Chapter 4, when looking at staff placement in subsidiary operations: whom to place in key positions and what positions can and should be localized. Even in mature multinationals, what has been termed 'lingering ethnocentrism' is evident in the way in which the parent company approaches subsidiary management, particularly in the use of control and coordination mechanisms.[4] How to accomplish the interplay between headquarters and foreign affiliates, however, is complicated.

These challenges of the 'think global, act local' mantra are incorporated in the idea of the 'transnational firm',[5] which has driven much of multinational management thinking over the past decades.[6] The idea of the global mindset is compelling. The message is to encourage all employees to appreciate 'a bigger picture' – to recognize interdependencies and interrelationships between units, and between units and headquarters, so that resource sharing and knowledge transfer succeed and are for the benefit of the corporate 'whole'. This is reflected in the recent intense discussion about developing global leaders and global leadership competencies.[7]

In this chapter, we will explore how a MNE's HRM practices in host-country contexts are shaped by the interaction between the various parties involved. We will also look at the trade-offs that occur while managing people in a multinational context. Again, we recognize that the current thinking on these issues has been shaped mostly by the investigation of larger multinationals and their relationships with a network of diverse subsidiaries, but much of this research is relevant to all firms operating internationally.

Standardization and localization of HRM practices

Controlling cross-border operations of a MNE centers around what processes, routines, procedures and practices can be and should be transferred abroad and to what degree these require country-specific adaptation, if any, to be effectively implemented at the local level. In the processes of transferring systems and know-how the role of people is critical. The management of people – probably the most culture-bound resource in an international context – is faced by a high level of complexity because of the diverse cultural environment of a MNE.[8]

As discussed in previous chapters, expatriates are frequently used to oversee the successful implementation of appropriate work practices. At some point, however, multinational management replaces expatriates with local staff with the expectation that these work practices will continue as planned. This approach is based on assumptions that appropriate behavior will have been instilled in the local workforce through training programs and hiring practices, and that the multinational's way of operating has been accepted by the local staff in the manner intended. In this way, the multinational's corporate culture will operate as a subtle, informal control mechanism – a substitution of direct supervision.

However, this depends on the receptivity of the local workforce to adhere to corporate norms of behavior, the effectiveness of expatriates as agents of socialization and whether cost considerations have led the multinational to localize management prematurely. Here, the role of appropriate human resource management activities becomes crucial. The *aim of global standardization* of HRM practices is to reach the above-mentioned consistency, transparency and an alignment of a geographically fragmented workforce around common principles and objectives.[9] The use of common management practices is intended to foster a feeling of equal treatment among managers involved in cross-border activities and, at the same time, aims at a common understanding of what is expected from the employees. Furthermore, consistent systems facilitate the administration processes by increasing operational efficiencies.[10]

The aim *of realizing local responsiveness* is to respect local cultural values, traditions, legislation or other institutional constraints such as government policy and/or education systems regarding HRM and work practices. As mentioned above, attempting to implement methods and techniques that have been successful in one environment can be inappropriate in another.[11]

The challenge of many multinationals is to create a *system that operates effectively in multiple countries* by exploiting local differences and interdependencies and at the same time sustaining global consistency. Unilever, for example, uses the same recruitment criteria and appraisal system on a worldwide basis to ensure a particular type of managerial behavior in each subsidiary. However, features of the national education systems and skill levels must be considered.[12]

This discussion has shown that the standardization–localization choice that confronts the multinational in an area of operation such as marketing, applies to the management of the global workforce as well. This is due to the fact that HRM carries out a strategic support function within the firm. However, as has been indicated above, the extent to which HRM systems are standardized or localized depends on various interdependent factors. We call this the 'HRM balance between standardization and localization'. Figure 9-1 illustrates important drivers that either foster standardization or localization. To sum up, the exact balance of a firm's HRM standardization–localization choice is based on factors of influence such as strategy,

| **Figure 9-1** | Balancing the standardization and localization of human resource management in MNEs |

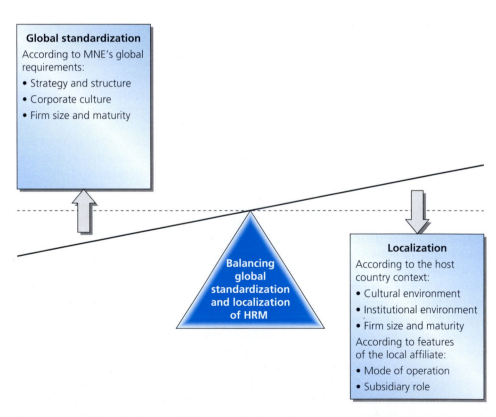

Source: Adapted from M. Festing, J. Eidems and S. Royer, 'Strategic Issues and Local Constraints in Transnational Compensation Strategies: An Analysis of Cultural, Institutional and Political Influences', *European Management Journal,* Vol. 25, No. 2 (2007), pp. 118–31.

structure, firm size and maturity. The strength of corporate culture plays an important role on the standardization side, while the cultural and institutional environment, including features of the local entity such as operation mode and subsidiary role, play an important role on the localization side. As Harzing[13] confirms, there exists a continuum of advantages for both standardization and localization.

Factors driving standardization

The factors driving the standardization of human resource management practices in MNEs have been discussed in the first three chapters of this volume. *Strategic issues* are included in the model on strategic international HRM in multinational enterprises (Figure 1-5). The organizational context including various organizational *structures* and their impact on HRM, as well as considerations about *organizational culture* are all subjects of the second chapter. The impact of *firm size* has been discussed in the context of SMEs outlining important differences between HRM in SMEs and MNEs in Chapter 3. Closely linked to the firm size and the *stage of maturity* is the degree of international experience.[14] For example, Motorola's or IBM's experiences in China reflect their large size and the fact that they already had a wealth of international experience upon which their management could draw when considering entry into a transitional economy like China. As these firms are familiar with the complexity of international operations, they are better prepared to cope with an additional new environment and better practised in finding appropriate HRM solutions than other firms with less international experience. A smaller multinational or a relative newcomer to international business may not have the same level of experience, the competencies or the needed resources with respect to HRM.

All of these factors are dependent upon each other. The relationship suggested in the literature explains that a large MNE with a long international history and extensive cross-border operations:

● pursues a multinational or transnational corporate strategy[15]

● supported by a corresponding organizational structure[16] that is

● reinforced by a shared worldwide corporate culture.[17]

However, in practice, we do not always observe perfect adherence to these factors in all MNEs. For example, a worldwide corporate culture may not be shared by all employees in all subsidiaries.[18] This factor should, nonetheless, at least be the target of many firms hoping to cope with the challenges of globalization.

In such highly internationalized organizations we often find attempts to standardize HRM practices on a worldwide basis. Of course, this approach is not appropriate for the whole workforce but aims at a group of managers who are working at the cross-border boundaries of the firm in the headquarters or in foreign locations, i.e., international boundary spanners.[19] A good example of a company which has attempted to globally standardize compensation practices is Schering AG, a German pharmaceutical company, which introduced a global performance system for top managers worldwide.[20] Within the context of a new strategic orientation, Schering implemented a standardized bonus system for top executives that aimed at strengthening the performance culture in the company and facilitating a common orientation for all managers. The corporate element of the bonus system consisted of a standardized bonus structure. As the cultural acceptance for variable bonuses varied across Schering's subsidiaries, the proportion between the fix and variable part of the total compensation package of managers was adapted to the country-specific conditions. The Schering example not only shows us that the implementation of global standards is possible, but at the same time, it also makes it clear that local adaptations and exceptions to the standards are often needed. The factors driving the localization of HRM practices are outlined in the next section.

Factors driving localization

As has been depicted in Figure 9-1, factors driving localization include the cultural and institutional environment and features of the local entity itself. We will discuss these factors in the following paragraphs.

The cultural environment

In Chapter 1, we identified national culture as a moderating variable in IHRM. We explained how members of a group or society share a distinct way of life with common values, attitudes and behaviors that are transmitted over time in a gradual, yet dynamic, process. The significance of national culture is underlined by the statement that most inhabitants of a country share the same mental program.[21] There is evidence that culture has an important impact on work and HRM practices. Sparrow, for example, has identified cultural influences on reward behavior such as 'different expectations of the manager–subordinate relationship and their influence on performance management and motivational processes'.[22] Triandis[23] found that cultures wherein work is based on more integrated personal social 'relationships' may value a more complete balance of intrinsic and extrinsic rewards, while cultures characterized by personal independence and isolation ('individualism') as well as rapidly changing personal and social contexts may emphasize extrinsic rewards – given the absence of a strong and enduring social matrix that attributes meaning and power to intrinsic rewards. The examples indicate that the effectiveness of standardized practices might differ in various cultural contexts.

A first orientation to the features that characterize a culture is delivered by cross-cultural management studies. In Chapter 1 we pointed to the importance of the seminal work by the Dutch researcher Hofstede.[24] In addition to Hofstede's work, other intercultural studies have also been conducted that have made important contributions to our knowledge about cultural differences in an organizational context.[25] Here, we introduce central concepts of the most recent encompassing survey conducted by House *et al.*[26] This is the Global Leadership and Organizational Behavior Effectiveness Research Program (GLOBE), a cooperation of 170 researchers from 62 cultures representing all major regions of the world. The study aims at explaining the impact of culture on leadership behavior and organizational processes. The GLOBE-activities started in 1991 with a long-term orientation and have developed a worldwide spread using a multiphase, multi-method cross-cultural research design. Three out of four research phases have been completed. At this stage, the GLOBE-group has delivered data from questionnaires filled out by 17 000 middle managers active in three industries and representing 62 societies. The cultural dimensions are partly based on the dimensions identified by Hofstede and partly based on further theoretical considerations. A summary of the culture construct definitions and respective sample items is given in Table 9-1. While these dimensions are simplified and can only be applied at a societal level and not used for predicting individual behavior, they may nevertheless give indications as to where important cultural differences can be expected. These may have an impact on the standardization–localization balance.

Culture construct definitions and sample questionnaire items	Table 9-1

Cultural construct definitions	Specific questionnaire item
Power distance: The degree to which members of a collective expect power to be distributed equally.	Followers are (should be) expected to obey their leaders without question.
Uncertainty avoidance: The extent to which a society, organization, or group relies on social norms, rules and procedures to alleviate unpredictability of future events.	Most people lead (should lead) highly structured lives with few unexpected events.
Humane orientation: The degree to which a collective encourages and rewards individuals for being fair, altruistic, generous, caring and kind to others.	People are generally (should be generally) very tolerant of mistakes.
Collectivism I (institutional collectivism): The degree to which organizational and societal institutional practices encourage and reward collective distribution of resources and collective action.	Leaders encourage (should encourage) group loyalty even if individual goals suffer.
Collectivism II (in-group collectivism): The degree to which individuals express pride, loyalty and cohesiveness in their organizations and families.	Employees feel (should feel) great loyalty toward this organization.
Assertiveness: The degree to which individuals are assertive, confrontational and aggressive in their relationship with others.	People are (should be) generally dominant in their relationships with each other.
Gender egalitarianism: The degree to which a collective minimizes gender inequality.	Boys are encouraged (should be encouraged) more than girls to attain a higher education.
Future orientation: The extent to which individuals engage in future-oriented behaviors such as delaying gratification, planning and investing in the future.	More people live (should live) for the present rather than for the future.
Performance orientation: The degree to which a collective encourages and rewards group members for performance improvement and excellence.	Students are encouraged (should be encouraged) to strive for continuously improved performance.

Source: R.J. House, P.J. Hanges, M. Javidan, P.W. Dorfman and V. Gupta (eds) *Culture, Leadership and Organizations: The GLOBE Study of 62 Societies,* (Thousand Oaks, CA: Sage Publications Inc., 2004), p. 30.

It is beyond the scope of this chapter to discuss the implications of all cultural dimensions identified in the GLOBE study and how conflicts between extreme culture-specific differences in values can be solved with respect to the standardization–localization balance of HRM in MNEs. However, the following example can illustrate this with respect to the decision about variable and/or fixed pay in the context of the dimension 'uncertainty avoidance'. Results of a study by Lowe *et al.*[27] indicate that employees in the USA, Taiwan, Mexico and Latin America prefer variable pay incentives while their counterparts in Australia and Japan only moderately emphasize this kind of pay. Research shows that seniority-based pay in terms of a fixed salary is more likely to be found in countries with higher levels of uncertainty avoidance such as Greece and Portugal.[28] This cultural dimension points out the extent to which people are risk averse. Risk-taking managers are often advocates of large incentive payments while risk-adverse managers are less accepting of high income variability, which may be involved in performance-based pay. These culture-based arguments illustrate that while a MNE may aim at a strong corporate performance orientation, local forces that do not share the same culture, may alter the extent to which this is possible.[29]

It can be concluded that appropriate corporate HRM practices can help support the cohesion between different units of the MNE. Subsidiary staff may have a strong identification with the local unit, but the challenge is to foster employee identification at the global level through globally accepted HRM practices.[30] If the HRM practices do not match local norms and values, they must be adapted to the distinct features of the host-country culture. Multinationals might solve such culture-based divergences in the perception of the appropriateness of human resource management measures by allowing for certain well-defined exceptions which provide opportunities for local adaptation while assuring consistency with corporate guidelines. There are indications that the extent of cultural distance between headquarters and subsidiaries will also have a bearing on the degree to which human resource and work practices require adaptation.[31] The larger the cultural distance the more important are forces for local adaptation. This is an aspect which MNEs must keep in mind when deciding on the standardization–localization balance.

The institutional environment

In addition to national or regional culture, institutional settings shape the behavior and expectations in subsidiaries.[32] The institutionalism perspective[33] indicates that institutional pressures may be powerful influences on human resource practices.[34] According to Whitley,[35] institutional norms and values may be based on the features of a *national business system*. Elements which are relevant to HRM are, for example, the characteristics of the education system or the industrial relations system.

For example, in Germany, the dual vocational training system, which provides theoretical learning opportunities in part-time schools and practical experience in companies, is widespread. More than 60 per cent of an age group is involved in dual vocational training for more than 350 professions.[36] This kind of training represents a well-accepted qualification in Germany, whereas in other countries such as France, this system is non-existent or restricted to lower qualifications. The pervasiveness and reputation of such a training system has an impact on IHRM. More specifically, for example, the recruitment process and the selection criteria reflect the importance of these qualifications. Another example of institutional factors which can have HRM-related effects are the 'scope of labor legislation and its regency of codification, [it] creates new codes of conduct through issues such as sex discrimination, equal pay for equal work, and minimum wages.'[37] Thus, for legitimacy reasons, it can make sense for some organizations to offer specific benefits or advantages, for example, even if they are very expensive and normally would not be offered due to efficiency considerations.

The impact of the institutional environment on IHRM is shown in the following example, which addresses staffing decisions. A study by As-Saber *et al.*[38] found that there was a clear preference for using HCNs in key positions by multinationals operating in India. The authors suggest that a major reason for HCN preference was the belief that an Indian would know more than an expatriate manager could learn in years on the job. As you will recall from Chapter 4, localization of HR staff positions is more likely to ensure that local customs and host-government employment regulations are followed. Khilji[39] found that, although foreign multinationals in Pakistan had formulated policies, implementation was low 'because managers brought up and trained in a hierarchical and centralized set-up resist sharing power and involving employees in decision making'. This occurred despite the host country's expectation that multinationals would transfer their best practices and act as a positive force in the introduction of what was regarded as desirable Western management styles. However, the multinationals in Khilji's study had taken a polycentric approach, with HCNs in key positions, including that of the HR manager.

Liberman and Torbiörn,[40] in their study of eight European subsidiaries of a global firm, found variation in the degree to which employees adopted corporate norms. They suggest that at the start of a global venture, differences in management practices are attributable to cultural and institutional factors whereas commonalities might be explained by a common corporate culture. Empirical results confirmed this. In some countries, employees were agreeable towards wearing of company clothing emblazoned with its logo, as such action did not challenge their national culture. In another focus of the study, there was great resistance to the implementation of performance assessment for non-managerial positions as it went against existing practice in one of the subsidiaries. Taylor[41] found that Chinese employees working in Japanese plants in their home country perceived team briefings and other such forums as a new form of rhetoric, replacing nationalist and Communist Party propaganda of the past, and this information was consequently considered of little value by workers and managers. These examples underline the importance of finding adequate solutions for the standardization–localization balance.

These above-described effects illustrate phenomena identified by the theoretical lens of institutionalism. The *country-of-origin effect* implies that multinationals are shaped by institutions existing in their country of origin and that they attempt to introduce these parent-country-based HRM practices in their foreign subsidiaries.[42] This is especially the case in an ethnocentric firm. The country-of-origin effects are stronger in non-restrictive local environments than in very restrictive countries. For example, US American multinationals are more flexible in importing their HRM practices in British affiliates than in German units because the British employment law is not as strict as that in Germany and it leaves more choices to the enterprises.[43] However, there is also evidence that MNEs tend to limit the export of practices typical for the country-of-origin to those that are considered to be their core competences.[44]

The *host-country effect* refers to the extent to which HRM practices in subsidiaries are impacted by the host-country context. For example, foreign MNEs in Germany are not free in their choice of pay levels or pay mixes. This is regulated by collective wage agreements, which are typical for the German environment and must be accepted. A similar effect exists in the headquarters. Here, HRM activities are influenced by the home-country environment. We call these effects *home-country effects.* This differentiation reflects the discussion on home and host-country environment, which is typical for MNEs. The home-country effect is the basis for the above-described country-of-origin effect, describing MNEs that try to transfer HRM activities shaped by their home-country environment to foreign locations.

This discussion has shown that the institutional context has an impact on HRM in several different ways. We have seen that not only the host country's institutional context can foster localization, but that forces exist from the country-of-origin as well. Sometimes *reverse diffusion,* i.e. the transfer of practices from foreign locations to the headquarters, can be observed.[45] For example, there is evidence that American MNEs learn from their subsidiaries in the United Kingdom.[46] Edwards *et al.*[47] have reported that a 'shared service' approach to organizing the HR function was developed in the UK and then introduced in the American headquarters. Relationships of the different effects between the institutional environment and the MNE units are delineated in Figure 9-2.

Conclusions on the host-country environment

In the preceding two sections we outlined how the cultural and institutional environment may influence HRM and, in particular, attempts at global

---

Figure 9-2 | Institutional effects on MNEs

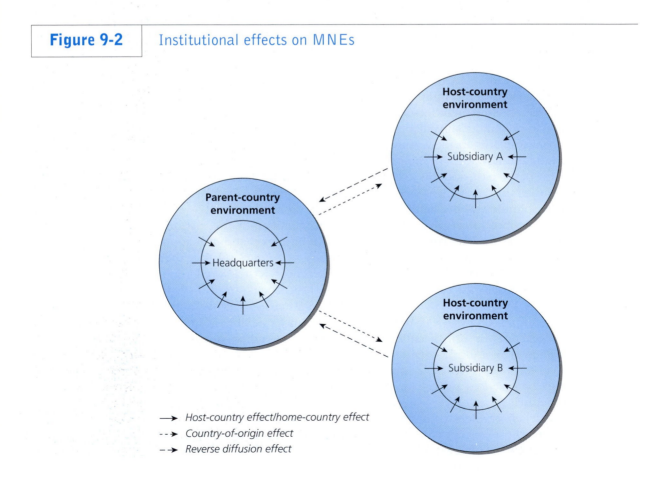

→ Host-country effect/home-country effect
--→ Country-of-origin effect
--→ Reverse diffusion effect

standardization and local responsiveness. Table 9-2 summarizes these ideas and gives examples of environmental differences, which could lead to problems when MNEs attempt to introduce worldwide standardized HRM practices. Within this context, it is important to recall the discussion on the convergence and divergence of HRM and work practices, as mentioned in the first chapter.

Examples of the impact of the cultural and institutional context on HRM practices		**Table 9-2**

HRM practices	Impact of the cultural context	Impact of the institutional context
Recruitment and selection	• In *societies low on 'in-group collectivism'* individual achievements represent important selection criteria. • In *societies high on 'in-group collectivism'* the emphasis in the recruiting process is more on team-related skills than on individual competencies.	*Education system* The reputation of educational institutions such as public and private universities varies in different countries. This is reflected in the recruiting processes (i.e., HR marketing) and selection criteria of the firms in those countries.
Training and development	• In societies *high on gender egalitarianism* women have the same chances for vertical career advancement as men. • In societies *low on gender egalitarianism* female managers are rare.	*Education system* Education systems differ between different countries (existence of a dual vocational training system, quality and reputation of higher education institutions). This has an effect on the training needs perceived and fulfilled by MNEs.
Compensation	• In societies *high on uncertainty avoidance* employees tend to be rather risk averse and prefer fixed compensation packages or seniority-based pay. • In societies *low on uncertainty avoidance* employees tend to be rather risk-taking and accept high income variability through performance-based pay.	*Legislation and industrial relations* Legislation such as the regulation of minimum wages or respective union agreements with respect to compensation have an impact on the firm's compensation choices with respect to pay mix and pay level.
Task distribution	• Societies *high on collectivism* tend to emphasize group work. • Societies *high on individualism* rather attribute individual responsibilities in the work system.	*Legislation and norms* Legislations and respective norms support gender-based division of labor to a differing extent in different countries. While in some countries the percentage of female managers is relatively high, in other countries it is not common that women work at all.

Mode of operation abroad

When addressing the mode of operation, it is helpful to examine this from the level of the local affiliate. Thus, we turn to firm-endogenous factors to determine the balance between global standardization and localization. Chapters 2 and 3 discussed the various modes of foreign operations and their associated HRM practices. A study by Buckley et al.[48] provides two examples of how the mode of operation either inhibits or facilitates work standardization. In late 1978, the Chinese government announced an open-door policy and commenced economic reforms aimed at moving the country from a centrally planned to a market economy. Western firms that entered China early were more or less forced to enter into joint ventures with state-owned enterprises (SOEs), whereas those entering later have been able to establish wholly owned subsidiaries (WOSs).

One case in the Buckley et al. study is Shanghai Bell – a joint venture formed in 1983 between a Belgian telecommunications firm (now Alcatel Bell), the Belgian government and the Chinese Postal and Telecommunications Industries Corporation (PTIC). There was a gradual transfer of relevant technology by the Belgian firm, with a long-term reliance on Belgian expatriates. The Belgian firm had limited control over the Chinese employees in the joint venture and was constrained by its partner's expectations and differing goals.

The second case researched was much different. The US telecommunications firm, Motorola, established a wholly owned operation in Tianjin, China, in 1992. Changing conditions in China meant that Motorola could effectively build a 'transplant factory': importing production equipment, organizational processes and practices from either the parent or other subsidiaries in its global network. This enabled Motorola to integrate the Chinese operation into the broader corporate network and to localize management. These have been supported by HRM initiatives such as a special management training program (CAMP – China Accelerated Management Program),[49] English language training and transfer of Chinese employees into the US operations. Motorola has been able to transfer its processes and systems, such as Six Sigma quality control, bringing its technology, knowledge and work practices, supported by HRM activities, into the new facilities in China relatively quickly.

Ownership and control are therefore important factors that need to be taken into consideration when multinationals attempt to standardize work and HRM practices. A firm's ability to independently implement processes and procedures is naturally higher in wholly owned subsidiaries while the question of control in international joint ventures (IJV) remains a concern for multinational firms. Complementarities between IJV partners and the degree of interdependence between the IJV and other parts of the multinational have proven to be important influences on effective IJV operation and the transfer of work practices. For example, Yan's[50] study of 87 IJVs operating in China revealed the importance of defining a strategic objective for the IJV when determining work practices. Yan concluded that task-related influence in an IJV plays an important role in directly shaping HRM practices.

This discussion here and in Chapter 3 indicates that the achievement of an acceptable balance in the standardization and localization of HRM practices is less problematic in wholly owned subsidiaries than in cross-boarder alliances. However, in the latter, the balance also depends on many features of a particular alliance including ownership and control issues. As we will discuss in the next section, it is important to further differentiate wholly owned subsidiaries. We will therefore now introduce the concept of a subsidiary role.

Subsidiary role

The subsidiary role specifies the position of a particular unit in relation to the rest of the organization and defines what is expected of it in terms of contribution to the efficiency of the whole MNE. Subsidiaries can take different roles.[51] Studies have examined how subsidiary roles can differ related to subsidiary function, power and resource relationships, initiative-taking, host-country environment, the predisposition of top management and the active championing of subsidiary managers.[52] Subsidiaries may be initiators as well as producers of critical competences and capabilities that contribute as specific profit centers to the competitive advantage of the whole multinational. Centers of excellence at the subsidiary level can be viewed as an indication of how some network-multinationals are recognizing that levels of expertise differ across the organization and that not all innovation and 'best practice' originates from the center – that is from headquarters. The Japanese electronics firm Hitachi's establishment of an R&D center in China is an example of building up the existing R&D facility to the status of a global center for the development of air conditioners.[53]

We will now discuss the well-known typology of subsidiary roles by Gupta and Govindarajan.[54] Based on their interpretation of a MNE as a network of capital, product and knowledge flows, they attribute the highest importance to knowledge flows. They differentiate between (1) the magnitude of knowledge flows, i.e., the intensity of the subsidiary's engagement in knowledge transfer, and (2) the directionality of transactions, which means whether subsidiaries are knowledge providers or recipients. The differentiation between knowledge in- and outflows leads to the following typology (see Table 9-3).

Subsidiaries characterized as *global innovators* provide significant knowledge for other units and have gained importance as MNEs move towards the transnational model. This role is reflected in an IHRM[55] orientation in which the parent firm develops HRM policies and practices which are then transferred to its overseas affiliates.[56]

The *integrated player* also creates knowledge but at the same time is recipient of knowledge flows. Thus, a subsidiary characterized by this role can represent an important knowledge node in the MNE network.[57] This should be supported by a highly integrated HRM orientation. Thus, the HRM practices and policies between headquarters and subsidiaries are very similar, probably characterized by a high extent of global standardization and localized elements when this is needed.

Gupta and Govindarajan's four generic subsidiary roles		**Table 9-3**

	Low outflow	High outflow
Low inflow	Local innovator	Global innovator
High inflow	Implementer	Integrated player

Source: Adapted from A. Gupta and V. Govindarajan, 'Knowledge Flows and the Structure of Control within Multinational Corporations', *Academy of Management Review*, Vol. 16, No. 4 (1991), pp. 768–92.

Implementers rely heavily on knowledge from the parent or peer subsidiaries and create a relatively small amount of knowledge themselves. If the IHRM system is export-oriented, i.e., global HRM decisions are mainly made in the parent company, then the local subsidiaries are responsible for the implementation process at the local level.

In the *local innovator* role, subsidiaries engage in the creation of relevant country/region-specific knowledge in all key functional areas because they have complete local responsibility. The HRM systems in such polycentric firms only have weak ties with the headquarters. As every subsidiary operates independently from the parent company and from other subsidiaries this independence results in a number of localized HRM policies and practices.

Harzing and Noorderhaven[58] have recently tested this typology and found empirical support in a sample of 169 subsidiaries of MNEs headquartered in The Netherlands, France, Germany, the UK, Japan and the USA:

> In comparison to earlier studies, our results show an increasing differentiation between subsidiaries, as well as an increase in the relative importance of both knowledge and product flows between subsidiaries suggesting that MNCs are getting closer to the ideal type of the transnational company.[59]

A development towards the ideal type of the transnational corporation involves more subsidiaries engaging in high-knowledge outflows, and thus, taking on the role of *global innovator* or *integrative players*. The difficulties in transferring knowledge and competence with respect to management practices from the subsidiary level – whether from a designated 'center of excellence'[60] or not – to the rest of the network are similar to the difficulties that we discussed in the context of headquarters to subsidiary transfer. The 'sticky' nature of knowledge, for example, applies regardless of its origins, but the designated role of the subsidiary and the standing of its management are critical in determining the spread and adoption of subsidiary initiated practices.

Stickiness represents one reason why some firms move towards an export-oriented approach to IHRM rather than an integrative management orientation.[61] Another major barrier to an integrative approach can be what Birkinshaw and Ridderstråle[62] describe as 'the corporate immune system'. Subsidiary initiatives are often met with significant resistance. Individuals within the organization resist change, or support low-risk projects, and are wary of ideas that challenge their own power base. Michailova and Husted use the terms 'knowledge-sharing hostility' and 'knowledge hoarding' to explain non-sharing behaviors identified in their study of firms operating in Russia.[63]

Increasing the mobility of managers is one way to break down these barriers and produce corporate rather than subsidiary champions who are prepared to disseminate information about subsidiary initiatives and capabilities, and recommend adoption in other parts of the organization where appropriate. Tregaskis,[64] in her study of R&D centers, reports how one firm found that personal relationships formed through visits of key staff to other units facilitated information sharing and the eventual adoption of new products by other subsidiaries. Face-to-face interactions were important in building trust and exchanges of tacit knowledge which might be possible in the context of corporate or regional meetings. Hence, frequent personal exchanges between the MNE units via individual encounters or regional or global meetings are essential in the processes of successful identification and transfer of knowledge.[65]

This discussion has indicated how the subsidiary role and related processes of knowledge transfer may impact the balance of standardization and localization in HRM. Recalling the power and resource relationships outlined at the beginning of this section, it must be stressed that powerful subsidiaries may have a stronger position in influencing the standardization–localization balance than those affiliates active in less significant markets or with rather unspecific skills.[66] Birkinshaw and Ridderstråle[67] define the structural power and resource-based power of subsidiaries *vis-à-vis* the corporate headquarters as two basic sources of influence within networks and distinguish between 'core' subsidiaries and 'peripheral' subsidiaries. There is evidence that those subsidiaries controlling large market volumes and possessing strategically important function-specific skills within the MNE network have a strong impact on the standardization–localization balance.[68]

Measures creating the HRM balance between standardization and localization

Various studies[69] have investigated coordination, communication and control processes between parent organizations and subsidiaries. The analysis of these mechanisms contributes to our understanding about how the balance between globalization and localization is achieved.

Here, we will follow the distinction between structural/formal and informal/subtle coordination mechanisms used by Martinez and Jarillo.[70] These authors define coordination as 'the process of integrating activities that remain dispersed across subsidiaries'.[71] The essential difference between these two groups of coordination mechanisms is that the latter is person oriented whereas the former is not. Martinez and Jarillo attribute the non-person-oriented coordination mechanisms to simple strategies of internationalization. More complex strategies, however, require a higher coordination effort. A high degree of coordination is usually realized by using both the non-person-oriented coordination mechanisms and person-oriented coordination mechanisms.[72]

In the context of corporate IHRM practices and policies, non-person-oriented coordination devices include, for example, written material on HRM practices such as handbooks or information leaflets, either provided in print or via the intranet. However, as this is a one-way communication device, it can only supplement the complex process of balancing global and local needs. It does not meet the requirements of a complex transnational approach to IHRM. Here, person-oriented coordination is indispensable.

As has already been indicated in the context of knowledge transfer between subsidiaries, HR managers from the headquarters as well as from the foreign affiliates must exchange their knowledge, expectancies and experiences on the different local contexts. Therefore, meetings and common project work using a respective supporting infrastructure such as intranet platforms[73] are essential throughout the process of developing and implementing the standardization–localization balance in IHRM. Furthermore, powerful line managers acting as opinion leaders should be involved in the process as well in order to achieve broad support for the transnational HRM measures. Finally, a high importance placed on the respective HRM solution by the corporate top management is essential for the success of the initiative.[74]

Code of conduct – monitoring HRM practices in the host country

An issue that has been somewhat overlooked in the IHRM literature is the need to monitor the HRM practices used in the host country. This is even more important in cases of cross-border alliances: Many multinationals, particularly in the textile, clothing and footwear (TCF) industries, and other consumer goods industries such as electrical goods, do not establish their own manufacturing operations.

A critical issue in the management of the international supply chain is ensuring that quality standards are met. However, particularly for multinationals with well-known brands, such as Nike, Levi Strauss, Benetton, Reebok and Adidas, the major management challenge has been the reaction of its Western consumers to alleged employment practices used by its subcontractors in countries such as India, China, Turkey, Indonesia, El Salvador, Honduras, the Dominican Republic and the Philippines. Various multinationals have been accused of condoning work practices such as the use of child labor, long working hours for minimal pay and unsafe working environments – conditions that would not be permitted in their home countries. Public uproar in the 1990s resulted in various actions by governments, the United Nations and non-government organizations (NGOs) to try to enforce codes of conduct also for subcontractors through their multinational partners.[75] Some multinationals, with corporate reputations and valuable brands at stake, quickly introduced their own codes of conduct.[76] These codes of conduct included, for example, acceptable working conditions, no child labor and minimum wages. There is now a universal standard, similar to the ISO 9000 quality standard, called the Social Accountability 8000, whose principles are drawn from the UN human rights conventions.[77]

While the code of conduct approach initially appeared to handle the public relations issue, ongoing enforcement has proven difficult. The role of HRM related to a global code of conduct may include the following:

- Drawing up and reviewing codes of conduct.
- Conducting a cost–benefit analysis to oversee compliance of employees and relevant alliance partners.
- Championing the need to train employees and alliance partners in elements of the code of conduct.
- Checking that performance and rewards systems take into consideration compliance to codes of conduct.

IHRM in Action Case 9-1 illustrates one example of a firm which has established a global code of conduct. On the basis of this case, you can discuss what internal and external effects such a code of conduct may have for the MNE.

Managing human resources in 'offshoring countries'

The concept of offshoring and its strategic importance

Offshoring is an important trend for reaching competitive advantage in the globalized economy.[78] In this section we will give special emphasis to the context of host countries, which are typical recipients for offshoring activities of MNEs. For these

Degussa's global code of conduct

The firm

Degussa group is a multinational corporation with a market leadership position in the sector of specialty chemistry. The group is represented worldwide on all five continents and based in more than 300 locations. The cornerstone for Degussa was placed in 1843 in Frankfurt, Germany; after several acquisitions, today 44 000 employees work for this company worldwide. Since June 2004, the Degussa group has been a 100 per cent subsidiary of Rag AG. Due to its important size and long history as well as its broad international experience, Degussa operates relatively independently from the parent company. Key production facilities, sales and marketing offices of Degussa can be found in around 60 countries, whereas the business activity focuses on Europe, North America and Asia. In 2005, Degussa generated sales of EUR 11.8 billion; almost three-quarters of this sales volume were generated outside of Germany.

The organization

Degussa has a decentralized organization within a global business framework. This is achieved through business units, which have full accountability for local operations. However, to maintain strategic control of its international business, strategic management decisions are mainly made in the headquarters – this philosophy is also reflected in the structure of the management board which consists solely of German managers.

To foster a corporate strategy and a new corporate culture known as 'Blue Spirit', a set of supporting principles including Degussa's Global Social Policy, guiding missions which are incorporated in management practices (e.g., a bonus system for executives linked to corporate goals) as well as a Global Code of Conduct were developed. The aim is to bring together several different corporate cultures and to create one company in which every employee at every site feels as though he or she is part of a common whole.

The Global Code of Conduct

The Global Code of Conduct aims at supporting the employees in their daily work and providing them with reference points. In the course of growing globalization, the variety of relevant markets and cultures has increased. The expectations of employees as well as customers are becoming more complex and different national and cultural backgrounds gain importance in the day-to-day work in this multinational company. The Code of Conduct is binding for every Degussa staff member and is applied in all subsidiaries as well as in the parent company. In addition, the code includes guidelines which control interactions with the corporate environment as well as with the public and governmental agencies or institutions. Even in countries (like for example India) where local rules and laws have other standards, the Global Code of Conduct is enforced. In case regional requirements go beyond the Degussa Code, the firm is forced to adapt to these conditions and has to include respective deviations within the Code.

Every employee worldwide is expected to comply with the Global Code of Conduct. Degussa has appointed various compliance officers in different units to ensure that the rules are respected. In addition, these officers might answer any related questions to assist employees in complying with these rules. Beyond this, local HR departments offer training sessions, information and publications to ensure that all employees are familiar with the Code. All employees are encouraged to name strengths and weaknesses and to actively participate in the continuing further development of this Global Code of Conduct.

Content of the Global Code of Conduct: compliance rules for the Degussa group

1.   Scope and objectives
2.   Business conduct
2.1 Managing business transactions
2.2 Business relations
2.3 Conflicts of interest
2.4 Insider trading
2.5 Maintaining the confidentiality of internal information
2.6 Political involvement and contributions
2.7 Ethics

3.   Technical issues
3.1 Competition and antitrust law
3.2 Foreign trade, export and terrorism controls
3.3 Tax law
3.4 Environmental protection, safety, occupational health and quality
3.5 Data protection
3.6 IT security
4.   Practical implementation of compliance rules

Source: Based on information obtained from Degussa's website, and 'Consult' – Kienbaum Kundenmagazin, Kienbaum Human Resources Management Consulting, 1/2007, pp. 1–7.

offshoring countries we will discuss HRM implications[79] because this trend leads to a revolution in the global division of labor. New interfaces emerge that need to be managed.[80]

Unfortunately, there is no common and worldwide accepted definition for the term 'offshoring'. Frequently, it is used as a subcategory of outsourcing, which can be defined as 'the act of transferring some of a company's recurring interval activities and decision rights to outside providers, as set in a contract'.[81] Depending on whether these offshoring activities are equity based or not we can differentiate between captive offshoring, i.e., involving an affiliated firm, and outsourcing with a non-affiliated firm. While offshoring has a long tradition, for example, in the automobile industry, it has recently gained importance in the service industry and especially in the information technology (IT) sector.[82]

The main locations for service offshoring activities of European companies are the United Kingdom, Ireland, Spain and Portugal in Western Europe and Poland, Hungary and Romania in Eastern Europe. Nearly half of the projects go to Asia.[83] On a global scale, current leading beneficiaries, for example, of IT offshoring include Ireland and India. A recent PriceWaterhouseCoopers survey gives an overview of foreign locations in which companies plan to begin business operations in the near future. The results show that India and China are expected to be the most important locations for future foreign business operations (see Figure 9-3). These two countries together represent 40 per cent of the world's supply of labor.[84]

For example, in India the development of offshoring was a result of strong support by the government to help the country meet those requirements that have an impact on the choice of the location for offshored activities. This choice depends on costs (labor and trade costs), the quality of institutions (particularly legislation) and infrastructure (particularly telecommunications), the tax and investment regime and the skills of the employees (particularly language and computer skills).[85] A prominent example for offshoring activities are international call-centers. 'But, in fact, offshoring of services also includes more sophisticated, high value-added activities, such as accounting, billing, financial analysis, software development, architectural design, testing, and research and development.'[86]

As mentioned previously, in this chapter we will concentrate on the two most important countries for future foreign operations, India and China. Although it is beyond the scope of this chapter to deliver an encompassing description and analysis

Target countries for future foreign business operations

Figure 9-3

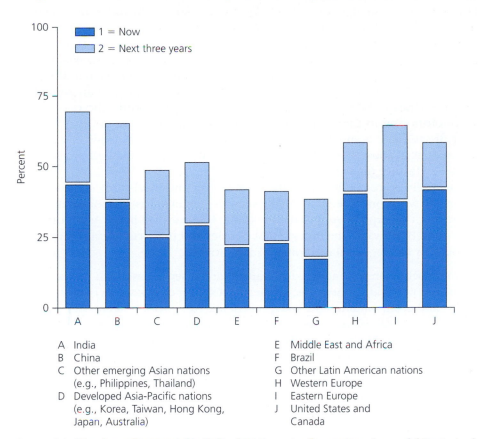

A   India
B   China
C   Other emerging Asian nations
     (e.g., Philippines, Thailand)
D   Developed Asia-Pacific nations
     (e.g., Korea, Taiwan, Hong Kong,
     Japan, Australia)

E   Middle East and Africa
F   Brazil
G   Other Latin American nations
H   Western Europe
I   Eastern Europe
J   United States and
     Canada

Source: PriceWaterhouseCoopers (ed.), *Technology Executive Connections: Successful Strategies for Talent Management* (USA: PriceWaterhouseCoopers, 2006), p. 43.

of the employment relations systems and approaches to HRM, we will analyze the situation with respect to offshoring and draw implications for HRM in each country. Finally, emerging issues for HRM in offshoring countries will be discussed.

Offshoring and HRM in India

As mentioned above, India has developed a flourishing business process outsourcing (BPO) industry[87] and respective competencies. The technological infrastructure and the qualification as well as the motivation of the employees are perceived as benefits by Western investors and partners.

Furthermore, each year 3.1 million graduates enter the workforce and 20 per cent of the population speaks English.[88] Indian graduates are prepared to work for salaries, which used to be 80 per cent lower than those of their Western counterparts. To capitalize on this cost advantage, US firms such as IBM, Hewlett-Packard and Electronic Data Systems have outsourced software development to Indian suppliers.[89] Other multinationals, such as General Electric, have used the availability of a highly educated yet relatively cheap labor force to establish their call centers in various parts of India. Local staff employed in these call centers are trained to speak English complete with particular accent and use of appropriate idiom, so that

US, UK and Australian customers are often unaware that their 'local' call has been diverted to a call center in India.

However, problems have also been reported from Indian BPOs and many of them are associated with HRM issues. For example, annual personnel turnover rates range from 20 to 80 per cent and a shortage exists considering the high demand for a skilled workforce, especially in middle management. As some HR managers have reported, only half of the candidates even show up for a job interview.[90] This shortage and the high demand for skilled workers have led to an annual increase in salaries of between 10 and 20 per cent. Consequently, the cost advantages of offshoring to India are in danger. Additional issues are the problems of worker dissatisfaction and conflicts caused by stress as well as cases of reported sexual and racial abuse.[91] All of these factors can lead to a decrease in productivity and thus, to further financial losses.[92]

These findings are confirmed by the results of an empirical study conducted by Mehta *et al.*, who concluded that HRM issues are perceived as a major weakness in BPO firms.[93] This represents a challenge to the HRM of BPO firms. As reported by Sparrow and Budhwar,[94] the Indian HRM policies and practices are still very much influenced by castes, social relationships and politics.

> At times, selection, promotion and transfer are based on ascribed status and social and political connections, so there is a strong emphasis on collectivism – family and group attainments take precedence over work outcomes. . . . Motivational tools are more likely to be social, interpersonal, and even spiritual. In such conditions, the employee's orientation emphasizes personalized relationships rather than performance.[95]

These issues lead to a HRM system, which is characterized by informalities and less rationality.[96] This might contradict the previously discussed attempts for a global standardization of HRM policies and practices by MNEs.[97] However, a study conducted in 51 BPO companies situated close to New Delhi revealed that the work settings were designed to guarantee maximum customer satisfaction. Furthermore, the authors discovered a more formal, structural and rational approach to HRM – similar to those in developed countries. Nevertheless, with respect to HRM practices and their effects on the employees, weaknesses have also been identified. The emphasis on career development and training was lower than in Western firms. Further HRM issues to be addressed in the future included: increasing attrition rates, the prevention of psychological and stress-related problems, more flexibility in the workplace (part-time jobs do not currently exist), and the creation of a more interesting work environment to help build long-term relationships with well-qualified employees.[98] Only if the employees' needs are met by HRM measures is retention possible.[99]

Offshoring and HRM in China

China is one of the fastest growing economies in the world. It is a country well-known for inexpensive manufacturing, although costs in this sector are rising.[100] Currently, salaries in China are even lower than in India. However, the total number of graduates is only half that which India produces, and the percentage of English-speaking graduates is also much lower.[101] While Chinese universities produce a high number of science and technology graduates, students come from an educational system in which they were rarely encouraged to take initiative and deliver creative solutions although these are major requirements by MNEs.[102] Consequently, the Chinese economy suffers from a skills shortage similar to that in India, especially for those jobs which require both technical as well as management know-how.[103] Similar turnover rates and the same tendency of increasing salaries for highly skilled employees can also be observed in China.[104] Reported problems or barriers to working with local entities not only include difficulties of staff recruitment and retention, but also problems in cross-cultural communication, poor working practices in supplier firms and corrupt staff behavior.[105]

For Western MNEs who are planning to offshore activities to China, it is important to understand the role played by network connections called *guanxi:* dyadic personal relationships between people. Tung and Worm[106] explain that while these relationships bear similarities to the Western practice of networking, there are differences: *guanxi* are contingent upon conditions such as asymmetry, reciprocity and necessity. The authors stress the importance of *guanxi* for successful business operations in China but recognize the difficulties this poses for Western executives. They suggest that *hiring practices* for key positions should take into account prospective Chinese employees' *guanxi*. The difficulty is being able to assess whether prospective employees have the right *guanxi*.

Multinationals find that they need to invest in *training* so that employees learn how to properly use equipment, operate systems and the like. What actions can these firms take to gain the benefits of this investment in human capital? Obviously, it is not easy to prevent employees from leaving the operation. The poaching of skilled employees is a business reality. Shanghai Bell was an early entrant into the Chinese market and became the 'academy for the industry', experiencing high staff turnover to both Chinese and foreign-owned competitors.[107] In post-reform China, employees tend to change jobs frequently in pursuit of higher wages, and not in an effort to develop their skills.[108] To a certain extent, this may be traced back to the employment system that existed prior to reforms associated with the transition to a market economy. Guaranteed continuation of employment, along with various welfare and benefits offered to employees, such as accommodation, medical treatment, childcare and pensions, has been referred to as the 'iron rice bowl'.[109] In exchange for job security, employees had little freedom to move to another work unit – that is, they were unable to quit or transfer jobs and were locked into a dependency relationship with their enterprises. Respectively, managers were deprived of their right to fire or lay off unqualified or non-productive employees.[110]

While companies operating in China are endeavoring to *reduce their attrition rates,* through the provision of additional benefits and staff development programs, Chinese employees are beginning to recognize compensation differentials and that is having an impact upon job attitudes. A fair environment and good management practices are emerging as the essential tools for retaining Chinese employees, rather than above-market compensation alone. Goodall and Roberts,[111] in their study of a European oil company operating in China, cite the example of one employee who found that being part of a wider organizational network was incentive enough to stay with the multinational.

The above-mentioned recruitment, qualification and retention problems require HRM practices which meet the needs of highly skilled human resources socialized in the Chinese context. However, HRM in China has only recently evolved and is challenging the former administrative system.[112] The transition is difficult because of the previous strong influence of the state and a current highly competitive situation:[113]

Until quite recently, the personnel function in SOEs [state-owned enterprises] was confined to job allocation, personnel record filing, and the provision of welfare benefits. The primary task for personnel management was to keep the employees politically and ideologically sound. Many of the HR functions which are familiar to their western counterparts were beyond the experience of personnel staff in China.[114]

From this analysis Cooke derives key features that describe the current state of HRM in China:[115]

● There is no systematic approach for linking HRM with the business strategy.

● Despite a surplus of labor, many companies face recruiting and retention problems.

● There is no systematic link between performance management, reward and long-term motivation.

● There is a lack in coherence and continuity of enterprise training.

However, research also shows differences between different types of enterprises.[116] Venter[117] points out that resource-rich companies, often characterized by foreign ownership, have a more encompassing approach to HRM, which includes formal education as a selection mechanism selecting the educational elite and continuing to develop them through extensive training programs. To cope with the problem of high turnover rates it is suggested that procedural justice as well as measures for increasing commitment within the organization may be helpful.[118] To sum up, employee needs must be met by respective HRM practices and the creation of a satisfying work environment.

Summarizing emerging issues

From this brief analysis of the situation in offshore countries, important issues emerge with respect to the role of HRM as well as skill shortages and the resulting consequences. Eventually, in this context, the role of ex-host-country nationals (EHCNs) is discussed.

A possible role for HRM.   As we have seen from the discussion above, offshoring activities can fail. Common reasons for this include the unsatisfactory quality of products or services, problems of management control, the rapid turnover of local staff and language problems. A recent CIPD survey on 'Offshoring and the Role of HR' conducted in more than 600 companies in the UK has revealed that the involvement of the HR department in offshoring decisions and processes was limited. Based on the survey results CIPD identified the following roles for HRM:[119]

● Consultation with unions/employee representatives.

● Manpower planning, considering the scope for employee redeployment.[120]

● Contributing to the internal communication strategy.

● Identifying training needs.

● Designing new jobs which stem from offshoring operations.

● Highlighting potential risks, such as the implications of employment regulation both in the home country and in foreign locations.

This discussion clearly shows that there are still starting points for strengthening the local HRM systems in Indian and Chinese firms. This measure would be further supported if HRM played a more important role in offshoring decisions and processes.

Skill shortages and the resulting consequences in a broader regional context.

Skill shortage represents a major problem in the offshoring countries of India and China. According to a recent PriceWaterhouseCoopers survey,[121] 41 per cent of 153 respondents from all over the world have reported problems in recruiting technical talent in emerging countries. Even more companies (47 per cent) find it difficult to retain well-qualified staff. However, this is not a phenomenon that only exists in these countries. For a long time, skill shortage has also been the focus of discussion in the context of developed Western countries. Examples include Ireland[122] or Canada.[123] Table 9.4 below shows the areas in which companies perceive talent to be scarce today and within the next three years.

Where talent is scarce				**Table 9-4**

	Overall	North America	Europe	Asia-Pacific
Today	45%	33%	51%	40%
Next 3 years	66%	66%	63%	73%

Source: PriceWaterhouseCoopers (ed.), *Technology Executive Connections: Successful Strategies for Talent Management* (USA: PriceWaterhouseCoopers, 2006), p. 19.

Considering the high unemployment rates, for example, in several EU countries, these figures might seem astonishing. But as a senior HR executive of a large technology division of Siemens Corporation, Germany states: 'For technical degrees, things are becoming more competitive. We are having greater difficulty – experiencing a longer time to hire for qualified graduates and especially for more senior positions.'[124] As this example shows, the skill shortage problem prevails in other parts of the world as well. The problem threatens to increase with changing workforce demographics as well as changes in attitudes and values.[125]

However, the consequences for the offshoring countries of India and China are striking. The scarcity of labor supply and the resulting competition between employers lead to tremendous turnover rates[126] and resulting salary increases. These factors endanger the cost advantages Western MNEs are looking for in offshoring countries. As one respondent of the above-mentioned PriceWaterhouseCoopers survey stated:

Compensation levels in many of the emerging markets are increasing to the point where we no longer view India and now even China as necessarily low-cost countries. . . . Our operations in India and China are already looking at offshoring to Indonesia and, believe it or not, Vietnam.[127]

It is interesting to note, however, that this development is also shared by companies originating from offshoring countries such as India and China. Due to the skill shortage, Chinese companies already look for offshore opportunities themselves.[128] This seems to reflect another step in the course of globalization.

Coping with skill shortages: the role of returning HCNs.

Another important issue that might be addressed when discussing skill shortages in emerging countries points to a group of people who originate from these countries, have studied abroad and return back to their home countries. These individuals have been described as 'ex-host-country nationals' (EHCNs) by Tung and Lazarova[129] in an empirical study of EHCNs in Central and Eastern Europe. They state that especially in these transitional economies 'where there is a significant shortage of local talent . . . EHCNs appear to be a good source of supply for much needed competencies and skills to enable these countries to survive and thrive in the global economy'.[130] This is confirmed by Saxenian: She states that if those highly skilled employees decide to return home they are accelerating the technological developments in their home countries.[131] In her research, she discusses the cases of China and India. In an empirical investigation of Chinese university students in Canada, Tung found that the majority was receptive to the idea of returning to China.[132] However, in their study of Eastern European EHCNs Tung and Lazarova report re-adaptation problems when EHCNs return to their home countries. This indicates that there is a risk whether the EHCNs will stay in their countries of origin and whether they will be as effective and successful as they are supposed to be. If they decide not to return to their home country after their studies there is a danger of 'brain drain'.[133] This is critical in a situation of skill shortage in an emerging country.[134] The findings by Tung and Lazarova of reintegration problems of EHCNs have important implications for HRM practitioners because they indicate that EHCNs might expect to be treated in a similar way to expatriates with careful reintegration into their countries of origin. According to Tung and Lazarova, returning HCNs can be regarded as a 'brain gain' and represent a valuable measure to cope with the challenge of skill shortages in host-country locations.

Summary

This chapter has focused on issues relating to HRM and work practices in the host-country context. We examined the following areas:

- In the first part of this chapter we explained the importance of a balance of HRM standardization and localization in MNEs. As major drivers for standardization we referred to MNE strategy and structure, firm maturity and age, as well as corporate culture, issues which were discussed in previous chapters. Localization drivers included the host country's cultural and institutional environment, the mode of operation and the subsidiary role. We also pointed out the importance of personal contacts and meetings for realizing an adequate integrative HRM approach.

- We went on to discuss another measure which can have an important effect on controlling the behavior of human resources in host countries and with this we introduced the concept of a code of conduct. In IHRM in Action Case 9-1, we outlined the example of the Global Code of Conduct at the German MNE Degussa.

- In the last part of the chapter we addressed the special situations of both India and China – countries currently subject to massive offshoring activities, especially in the service sector. In this discussion, we stressed the implications of skill shortages and other challenges for HRM.

Discussion Questions

1 What are the determinants of the balance of standardization and localization in human resource management in MNEs?

2 How does a subsidiary's role affect its ability to transfer ideas and work practices to other parts of the global network? What is the impact of the resources controlled by the respective affiliate?

3 What contributes to the poaching of subsidiary employees? What steps can be taken to recruit and retain key employees?

4 What are typical HRM problems in offshoring organizations? How can companies, for example in India and in China, design their human resource management systems to avoid these problems?

Further Reading

Carr, S., Inkson, K. and Thorn, K. (2005). 'From Global Careers to Talent Flow: Reinterpreting "brain drain"', *Journal of World Business,* 40: 386–98.

Engle, A.D. and Mendenhall, M. (2004). 'Transnational Roles, Transnational Rewards: Global Integration in Compensation', *Employee Relations,* 26(6): 613–25.

Geppert, M. and Williams, K. (2006). 'Global, National and Local Practices in Multinational Corporations: Towards a Sociopolitical Framework', *International Journal of Human Resource Management,* 17(1): 49–69.

House, R.J., Hanges, P.J., Javidan, M., Dorfman, P.W. and Gupta, V. (eds) (2004). *Culture, Leadership and Organizations: The GLOBE Study of 62 Societies,* Thousand Oaks, CA: Sage.

Notes and References

1 C.A. Bartlett, S. Ghoshal and P.W. Beamish, *Transnational Management: Text, Cases and Readings in Cross-border Management* (Boston, MA: McGraw-Hill, 2008). A.W.K. Harzing and N. Noorderhaven, 'Knowledge Flows in MNCs: An Empirical Test and Extension of Gupta and Govindarajan's Typology of Subsidiary Roles', *International Business Review,* Vol. 15 (2006), pp. 195–214; J.B. Hocking, M. Brown, A.-W. Harzing, 'Balancing Global and Local Strategic Contexts: Expatriate Knowledge Transfer, Applications and Learning within a Transnational Organization', *Human Resource Management,* forthcoming.

2 P. Evans, V. Pucik and J.-L. Barsoux, *The Global Challenge: Frameworks for International Human Resource Management* (Boston, MA: McGraw-Hill, 2002).

3 S.S. Morris, S.A. Snell and P.M. Wright, 'A Resource-based View of International Human Resources: Toward a Framework of Integrative and Creative Capabilities', in G. Stahl and I. Björkman (eds), *Handbook of Research in International Human Resource Management* (Cheltenham: Edward Elgar, 2006), pp. 433–48.

4 S. Blazejewski and W. Dorow, *Corporate Cultures in Global Interaction: A Management Guide* (Gütersloh: Bertelsmann Foundation, 2007).

5 Bartlett, Ghoshal, and Beamish, *Transnational Management.*

6 A. Engle, M. Mendenhall, R. Powers and Y. Stedham, 'Conceptualizing the Global Competency Cube: A Transnational Model of Human Resource', *Journal of European Industrial Training,* Vol. 25, No. 7 (2001), pp. 346–53.

7 See, for example, A.J. Morrison, 'Developing a Global Leadership Model', *Human Resource Management,* Vol. 39, No. 2/3 (2000), pp. 117–31; N.J. Adler, 'Shaping History: Global Leadership in the Twenty-first Century', in H. Scullion and M. Linehan, *International Human Resource Management: A Critical Text* (Basingstoke and New York: Palgrave MacMillan, 2005), pp. 281–97; J.S. Osland, A. Bird, M. Mendenhall and A. Osland, 'Developing Global Leadership Capabilities and Global Mindset: A Review', in G.K. Stahl and I. Björkman (eds), *Handbook of Research in International Human Resource Management* (Cheltenham: Edward Elgar, 2006), pp. 197–222; P. Caligiuri, 'Developing Global Leaders', *Human Resource Management Review,* Vol. 16, No. 2 (2006), pp. 219–28; M.E. Mendenhall, T.M. Kühlmann and G.K. Stahl, *Developing Global Business Leaders* (Westport, CT: Greenwood Publishing Group, 2000). See also Chapter 8 in this volume.

8   P.M. Rosenzweig and N. Nohria, 'Influences on Human Resource Management Practices in Multinational Corporations', *Journal of International Business Studies,* Vol. 25, No. 2 (1994), pp. 229–51.

9   P. Evans, V. Pucik and J.-L. Barsoux, *The Global Challenge: Frameworks for International Human Resource Management* (Boston, MA: Irwin/McGraw-Hill, 2002); R. White, 'A Strategic Approach to Building a Consistent Global Rewards Program', *Compensation and Benefits Review,* Vol. 37, No. 4 (2005), pp. 23–40.

10 M. Bloom, G.T. Milkovich and A. Mitra, 'International Compensation: Learning from How Managers Respond to Variations in Local Host Contexts', *International Journal of Human Resource Management,* Vol. 14, No. 8 (2002), pp. 1350–67.

11 P. Lawrence and J. Lorsch, 'Differentiation and Integration in Complex Organizations', *Administrative Science Quarterly,* Vol. 12 (1967), pp. 1–30; N. Forster and R. Whipp, 'Future of European Human Resource Management: A Contingent Approach', *European Management Journal,* Vol. 13, No. 4 (1995), pp. 434–42. P. Gunnigle, K.R. Murphy, J.N. Cleveland, N. Heraty and M. Morley, 'Localization in Human Resource Management: Comparing American and European Multinational Corporations', *Advances in International Management,* Vol. 14 (2002), pp. 259–84.

12 K. Kamoche, 'Strategic Human Resource Management within a Resource-capability View of the Firm', *Journal of Management Studies,* Vol. 33 (1996), pp. 213–33.

13 A.W.K. Harzing, *Managing the Multinationals: An International Study of Control Mechanisms* (Cheltenham: Edward Elgar, 1999).

14 For an analysis of the impact of organizational factors on global standardization with special emphasis on international experience see B. Myloni, A.-W. Harzing and H. Mirza, 'The Effect of Corporate-level Organizational Factors on the Transfer of Human Resource Management Practices: European and US MNCs and their Greek subsidiaries', *International Journal of Human Resource Management,* forthcoming.

15 N.J. Adler and F. Ghadar, 'Strategic Human Resource Management: A Global Perspective', in R. Pieper (ed.), *Human Resource Management: An International Comparison* (Berlin and New York: De Gruyter, 1991), pp. 235–60.

16 Bartlett, Ghoshal and Beamish, *Transnational management.*

17 See Chapter 2.

18 Blazejewski and Dorow, *Corporate Cultures in Global Interaction.*

19 J.D. Thompson, *Organizations in Actions* (New York: McGraw-Hill, 1967); A.H. Aldrich, *Organizations & Environments* (Englewood Cliffs, NJ: Prentice Hall, 1979).

20 Further details can be found in M. Festing, J. Eidems, S. Royer and F. Kullak, *When in Rome Pay as the Romans Pay? Considerations about Transnational Compensation Strategies and the Case of a German MNE,* ESCP-EAP Working Paper No. 22 (Berlin: ESCP-EAP European School of Management, 2006). Schering AG was acquired by Bayer AG in 2006 and is now Bayer Schering Pharma AG.

21 G. Hofstede, *Culture and Organizations: Software of the Mind* (London: McGraw-Hill, 1991).

22 P. Sparrow, 'International Rewards Systems: To Converge or Not to Converge?', in C. Brewster and H. Harris (eds), *International HRM: Contemporary Issues in Europe* (London: Routledge, 2004), pp. 102–19. See also G.T. Milkovich and M. Bloom, 'Rethinking International Compensation', *Compensation and Benefits Review,* Vol. 30, No. 1 (1998), pp. 15–23.

23 H. Triandis, 'Generic Individualism and Collectivism', in M. Gannon and K. Newman (eds), *The Blackwell Handbook of Cross-cultural Management* (Oxford: Blackwell Business Pub., 2002), pp. 16–45.

24 G. Hofstede, *Culture's Consequences: International Differences in Work-related Values* (Beverly Hills, CA: Sage, 1980).

25 E.T. Hall and M. Hall, *Understanding Cultural Differences* (Yarmouth: Intercultural Press, 1990); C. Hampden-Turner and F. Trompenaars, *The Seven Cultures of Capitalism: Value Systems for Creating Wealth in the United States, Britain, Japan, Germany, France, Sweden, and The Netherlands* (New York: Doubleday, 1993); H.W. Lane and J.J. DiStefano, *International Management Behavior: From Policy to Practice,* 4th edn (Cambridge: Blackwell Pub., 2000).

26 R.J. House, P.J. Hanges, M. Javidan, P.W. Dorfman and V. Gupta (eds), *Culture, Leadership and Organizations: The GLOBE Study of 62 Societies* (Thousand Oaks, CA: Sage, 2004).

27 K. Lowe, J. Milliman, H. DeCieri and P.J. Dowling, 'International Compensation Practices: A Ten-country Comparative Analysis', *Human Resource Management,* Vol. 41, No. 1 (2002), pp. 45–66.

28 R. Schuler and N. Rogovsky, 'Understanding Compensation Practice Variations Across Firms: The Impact of Culture', *Journal of International Business Studies,* Vol. 29, No. 1 (1998), pp. 159–77.

29 This example is adapted from M. Festing, J. Eidems and S. Royer, 'Strategic Issues and Local Constraints in Transnational Compensation Strategies: An Analysis of Cultural, Institutional and Political Influences', *European Management Journal,* Vol. 25, No. 2 (2001), pp. 118–31.

30 C. Reade, 'Dual Identification in Multinational Corporations: Local Managers and their Psychological Attachment to the Subsidiary versus the Global Organization', *International Journal of Human Resource Management,* Vol. 12, No. 3 (2001), pp. 405–24.

31 W. Liu, 'The Cross-national Transfer of HRM Practices in MNCs: An Integrative Research Model', *International Journal of Manpower,* Vol. 25, No. 6 (2004), pp. 500–17. For a general discussion on cultural distance see, for example, O. Shenkar, 'Cultural Distance Revisited: Towards a More Rigorous Conceptualization and Measurement of Cultural Differences', *Journal of International Business Studies,* Vol. 32, No. 3 (2001), pp. 519–36.

32 A well-known definition for institutions is the following: institutions consist of cognitive, normative and regulative structures and activities that provide stability and meaning to social behaviour. See W.R. Scott, *Institutions and Organizations* (Thousand Oaks, CA: Sage, 1995), p. 33.

33 P.J. DiMaggio and W.W. Powell, 'The Iron Cage Revisited: Institutional Isomorphism and Collective Rationality in Organizational Fields', *American Sociological Review,* Vol. 48 (1983), pp. 47–160; R.D. Whitley, *European Business Systems: Firms and Markets in Their National Contexts* (London: Sage, 1992); R.D. Whitley, *Business Systems in East Asia: Firms, Markets and Societies* (London: Sage, 1992).

34 A. Ferner, 'Country of Origin Effects and HRM in Multinational Companies', *Human Resource Management Journal,* Vol. 7, No. 1 (1997), pp. 19–37.

35 Whitley, *Business Systems in East Asia;* Whitley, *European Business Systems.*

36 Federal Ministry of Education and Research (ed.), *Education in Germany* (Bonn/Berlin: Federal Ministry of Education and Research, 2004).

37 P. Sparrow, 'International Rewards Systems: To Converge or Not to Converge?', in C. Brewster and H. Harris (eds), *International HRM: Contemporary Issues in Europe* (London: Routledge, 2004), p. 103.

38 S.N. As-Saber, P.J. Dowling and P.W. Liesch, 'The Role of Human Resource Management in International Joint Ventures: A Study of Australian-Indian Joint Ventures', *International Journal of Human Resource Management,* Vol. 9, No. 5 (1998), pp. 751–66.

39 S.E. Khilji, 'Modes of Convergence and Divergence: An Integrative View of Multinational Practices in Pakistan', *International Journal of Human Resource Management,* Vol. 13, No. 2 (2002), pp. 232–53.

40 L. Liberman and I. Torbiörn, 'Variances in Staff-related Management Practices at Eight European Country Subsidiaries of a Global Firm', *International Journal of Human Resource Management,* Vol. 11, No. 1 (2000), pp. 37–59.

41 B. Taylor, 'Patterns of Control Within Japanese Manufacturing Plants in China: Doubts about Japanization in Asia', *Journal of Management Studies,* Vol. 36, No. 6 (1999), pp. 853–73.

42 Ferner, 'Country of Origin Effects and HRM in Multinational Companies'.

43 Human resource management of US American enterprises in the United Kingdom, published in German language as: A. Ferner, P. Almond, P. Butler, I. Cark, T. Colling, T. Edwards and L. Holden, 'Das Human Resource Management amerikanischer Unternehmen in Großbritannien', in H. Wächter and R. Peters (eds), *Personalpolitik amerikanischer Unternehmen in Europa* (München and Mering: Hampp, 2004); A. Ferner, P. Almond and T. Colling, 'Institutional Theory and the Cross-national Transfer of Employment Policy: The Case of "Workforce Diversity" in US Multinationals', *Journal of International Business Studies,* Vol. 36 (2005), pp. 304–21.

44 M. Pudelko and A.-W. Harzing, 'HRM Practices in Subsidiaries of US, Japanese and German MNCs: Country-of-origin, Localization or Dominance Effect', *Human Resource Management,* forthcoming.

45 T. Edwards, P. Almond, I. Clark, T. Colling and A. Ferner, 'Reverse Diffusion in US Multinationals: Barriers from the American Business System', *Journal of Management Studies,* Vol. 42 (2005), pp. 1261–86.

46 A. Ferner, J. Quintanilla and M. Varul, 'Country-of-origin Effects, Host-country Effects, and the Management of HR in Multinationals', *Journal of World Business,* Vol. 36, No. 2 (2001), pp. 107–27.

47 T. Edwards, P. Almond, I. Clark, T. Colling and A. Ferner, 'Reverse Diffusion in US Multinationals: Barriers from the American Business System', *Journal of Management Studies,* Vol. 42 (2005), pp. 1261–86.

48 P.J. Buckley, J. Clegg and H. Tan, 'The Art of Knowledge Transfer: Secondary and Reverse Transfer in China's Telecommunications Manufacturing Industry', *Management International Review,* Vol. 43, Special Issue 2 (2003), pp. 67–93.

49 Motorola, Company website information, December 2002.

50 Y. Yan, 'A Comparative Study of Human Resource Management Practices in International Joint Ventures: The Impact of National Origin', *International Journal of Human Resource Management,* Vol. 14, No. 4 (2003), pp. 487–510.

51 For example, A. Gupta and V. Govindarajan, 'Knowledge Flows and the Structure of Control within Multinational Corporations', *Academy of Management Review,* Vol. 16, No. 4 (1991), pp. 768–92; A. Gupta and V. Govindarajan, 'Organizing for Knowledge Flows within MNCs', *International Business Review,* Vol. 3, No. 4 (1991), pp. 443–58; J. Birkinshaw and. A.J. Morrison, 'Configurations of Strategy and Structure in Subsidiaries of Multinational Corporations', *Journal of International Business Studies,* Vol. 26, No. 4 (1995), pp. 729–54; J. Birkinshaw and N. Hood, 'Multinational Subsidiary Evolution: Capability and Charter Change in Foreign Owned Subsidiary Companies', *Academy of Management Review,* Vol. 23, No. 4 (1998), pp. 773–95; B. Ambos and W.D. Reitsberger, 'Offshore Centers of Excellence: Social Control and Success', *Management International Review,* Vol. 44 (2004) pp. 51–66; K. Ferdows, 'Mapping International Factory Networks', in K. Ferdows (eds), *Managing International Manufacturing* (Amsterdam: North-Holland, 1989), pp. 3–21; K. Ferdows, 'Making the Most of Foreign Factories', *Harvard Business Review,* Vol. 75 (1997), pp. 73–88.

52 See, for example, Birkinshaw and Hood, 'Multinational Subsidiary Evolution'.

53 T. Ying, 'Electronics Giant to Open R&D Company', *China Daily,* 26–27 March (2005), p. 4.

54 Gupta and Govindarajan, 'Knowledge Flows and the Structure of Control within Multinational Corporations'.

55 Human resource management implications are mainly based on S. Taylor, S. Beechler and N. Napier, 'Toward an Integrative Model of Strategic International Human Resource Management', *Academy of Management Review,* Vol. 21, No. 4 (1996), pp. 959–85.

56 Harzing and Noorderhaven, 'Knowledge Flows in MNCs'.

57 *Ibid.*

58 *Ibid.*

59 *Ibid.,* p. 195.

60 For a recent study on centers of excellence see B. Ambos and W.D. Reitsperger, 'Offshore Centers of Excellence: Social Control and Success', *Management International Review,* Vol. 44, Special Issue No. 2 (2004), pp. 51–65.

61 Morris, Snell and Wright, 'A Resource-based View of International Human Resources'.

62 J. Birkinshaw and J Ridderstråle, 'Fighting the Corporate Immune System: A Process Study of Subsidiary Initiatives in Multinational Corporations', *International Business Review,* Vol. 8, No. 2 (1999), p. 154.

63 S. Michailova and K. Husted, 'Knowledge-sharing Hostility in Russian Firms', *California Management Review,* Vol. 45, No. 3 (2003), pp. 59–77.

64 O. Tregaskis, 'Learning Networks, Power and Legitimacy in Multinational Subsidiaries', *International Journal of Human Resource Management,* Vol. 14, No. 3 (2003), pp. 431–47.

65 Taylor, Beechler and Napier, 'Toward an Integrative Model of Strategic International Human Resource Management'.

66 Festing, Eidems and Royer, 'Strategic Issues and Local Constraints in Transnational Compensation Strategies'.

67 J. Birkinshaw and J Ridderstråle, 'Fighting the Corporate Immune System', pp. 149–80.

68 Festing, Eidems and Royer, 'Strategic Issues and Local Constraints in Transnational Compensation Strategies'. For other resource-dependent oriented analyses see Y. Kim, 'Different Subsidiary Roles and International Human Resource Management: An Exploratory Study of Australian Subsidiaries in Asia', *Journal of Asia-Pacific Business,* Vol. 4 (2002), pp. 39–60; B. Myloni, A.-W. Harzing and H. Mirza, 'The Effect of Corporate-level Organizational Factors on the Transfer of Human Resource Management Practices: European and US MNCs and their Greek Subsidiaries', *International Journal of Human Resource Management,* forthcoming.

69 Gupta and Govindarajan, 'Knowledge Flows and the Structure of Control within Multinational Corporations'; Harzing, *Managing the Multinationals.*

70 J.I. Martinez and J.C. Jarillo, 'The Evolution of Research on Coordination Mechanisms in Multinational Corporations', *Journal of International Business Studies,* Vol. 19 (1989), pp. 489–514.

71 J.I. Martinez and J.C. Jarillo, 'Coordination Demands of International Strategies', *Journal of International Business Studies,* Vol. 21 (1991), p. 431.

72 For a further discussion in the context of IHRM strategies see M. Festing, 'International HRM in German MNCs', *Management International Review,* Vol. 37, Special Issue No. 1 (1997), pp. 43–64.

73 A PriceWaterhouseCoopers report points out that global workforce management includes the management of a respective database. For example, 70 000 employees of IBM have their profile online. PriceWaterhouseCoopers (eds), *Technology Executive Connections: Successful Strategies for Talent Management* (USA: PriceWaterhouseCoopers, 2006), p. 40.

74 These insights are based on an interview by one of the authors with the Head of HR of a transnational organization.

75 J.P. Doh and T.R. Gay, 'Globalization and Corporate Social Responsibility: How Non-Governmental Organizations Influence Labor and Environmental Codes of Conduct', *Management International Review,* Vol. 44, Special Issue No. 2 (2004), pp. 7–29.

76 J.P. Sajhau, *Business Ethics in the Textile, Clothing and Footwear (TCF) Industries: Codes of Conduct,* Working Paper (Geneva: International Labour Office, Sectoral Activities Programme, 1997).

77 For standards for codes of conduct refer also to L. Paine, R. Deshpande, J.D. Margolis and K.E. Bettcher, 'Up to Code: Does Your Company's Conduct Meet World-class Standards?', *Harvard Business Review,* December (2005), pp. 122–33.

78 UNCTAD (ed.), *World Investment Report 2004* (New York and Geneva: United Nations, 2004).

79 For a general discussion on entry mode choice including offshoring refer to WTO (ed.), *World Trade Report 2005,* III – Thematic Essays, C – Offshoring Services: Recent Developments and Prospects (Geneva: World Trade Organization, 2005).

80 UNCTAD, *World Investment Report 2004.* See as well S. Schmid and M. Daub, *Service Offshoring Subsidiaries – Towards a Typology,* Working Paper No. 12 (Berlin: ESCP-EAP European School of Management, 2005).

81 WTO (ed.), *World Trade Report 2005,* III – Thematic Essays, C – Offshoring Services: Recent Developments and Prospects (Geneva: World Trade Organization, 2005), p. 266.

82 *Ibid.,* p. 267. See as well S. Schmid and M. Daub, *Service Offshoring Subsidiaries – Towards a Typology.*

83 UNCTAD (ed.), *Service Offshoring Takes Off in Europe,* issued jointly by UNCTAD and Roland Berger Strategy Consultants (Geneva and New York: UNCTAD, 2004).

84 *Financial Times* (London, England), July 20, 2006.

85 UNCTAD, *Service Offshoring Takes Off in Europe.*

86 UNCTAD (ed.), *Offshoring – At the Tipping Point?* (Geneva and New York: UNCTAD, 2004).

87 For different types of outsourcing in India see S. Bhowmik, 'Work in a Globalizing Economy: Reflections on Outsourcing in India', *Labour, Capital and Society,* Vol. 37 (2004), pp. 76–96.

88 I. Hunter, *The Indian Offshore Advantage: How Offshoring is Changing the Face of HR* (Aldershot: Gower Publishing, 2006).

89 J. Shankar, 'Growth Surge Drives Subcontinent Boom', *The Australian,* June 17 (2003), p. 34.

90 *Financial Times* (London, England), July 20 (2006).

91 With these examples, the importance of the global codes of conduct mentioned earlier in this chapter is supported.

92 P.S. Budhwar, H.K. Luthar and J. Bhatnagar, 'The Dynamics of HRM Systems in Indian BPO Firms', *Journal of Labor Research,* Vol. 27, No. 3 (2006), pp. 339–60.

93 A. Mehta, A. Armenakis, N. Mehta and F. Irani, 'Challenges and Opportunities of Business Process Outsourcing in India', *Journal of Labor Research,* Vol. 27, No. 3 (2006), pp. 323–38.

94 P. Sparrow and P.S. Budhwar, 'Competition and Change: Mapping the Indian HRM Recipe Against World Wide Patterns', *Journal of World Business,* Vol. 32 (1997), pp. 224–42. See also: D.S. Sainni and P.S. Budhwar, 'HRM in India', in P.S. Budhwar, *Managing Human Resources in Asia-Pacific* (London and New York: Routledge, 2004), pp. 113–39.

95 Budhwar, Luthar and Bhatnagar, 'The Dynamics of HRM Systems in Indian BPO Firms', p. 345.

96 For further information about the Indian HRM system refer to Sainni and Budhwar, 'HRM in India'.

97 I. Björkman, 'Transfer of HRM to MNC Affiliates in Asia-Pacific', in P. Budhwar (ed.), *Managing Human Resources in Asia-Pacific* (London: Routledge, 2004), pp. 253–67. For differences

between Indian and foreign firms with respect to performance appraisal practices and management values see S.C. Amba-Rao, J.A. Petrick, J.N.D. Gupta and T.J. Von der Embse, 'Comparative Performance Appraisal and Management Values Among Foreign and Domestic Firms in India', *International Journal of Human Resource Management,* Vol. 11, No. 1 (2000), pp. 60–89; As-Saber, Dowling and Liesch, 'The Role of Human Resource Management in International Joint Ventures'.

98   Budhwar, Luthar and Bhatnagar, 'The Dynamics of HRM Systems in Indian BPO firms'.

99   PriceWaterhouseCoopers, *Technology Executive Connections: Successful Strategies for Talent Management,* p. 42.

100   *International Herald Tribune,* April 20 (2005).

101   Budhwar, Luthar and Bhatnagar, 'The Dynamics of HRM Systems in Indian BPO firms'.

102   B. Einhorn, 'A Dragon in R&D: China's Labs May Soon Rival its Powerhouse Factories – and Multinationals are Flocking in for Tech Innovation', *Business Week,* October 26 (2006).

103   PriceWaterhouseCoopers, *Technology Executive Connections: Successful Strategies for Talent Management; Financial Times,* London, England, July 20 (2006).

104   *International Herald Tribune,* April 20 (2005).

105   B. Wilkinson, M. Eberhardt, J. McLaren and A. Millington, 'Human Resource Barriers to Partnership Sourcing in China', *International Journal of Human Resource Management,* Vol. 16, No. 10 (2005), pp. 1886–900.

106   R.L. Tung and V. Worm, 'Network Capitalism: The Role of Human Resources in Penetrating the China Market', *International Journal of Human Resource Management,* Vol. 12, No. 4 (2001), pp. 517–34.

107   P.J. Buckley, J. Clegg and H. Tan, 'The Art of Knowledge Transfer: Secondary and Reverse Transfer in China's Telecommunications Manufacturing Industry', *Management International Review,* Vol. 43 (2003), pp. 67–93.

108   C.J. Zhu, 'Human Resource Development in China During the Transition to a New Economic System', *Asia Pacific Journal of Human Resources,* Vol. 35, No. 3 (1997), pp. 19–44. The same is true in other Asian countries. Evidence is reported by N. Kathri, C.T. Fern and P. Budhwar, 'Explaining Employee Turnover in an Asian Context', *Human Resource Management Journal,* Vol. 11, No. 1 (2001), pp. 54–74.

109   D.Z. Ding, K. Goodall and M. Warner, 'The End of the 'Iron Rice-bowl': Whither Chinese Human Resource Management?', *International Journal of Human Resource Management,* Vol. 11, No. 2 (2000), pp. 217–37; M. Warner, 'Human Resource Management in China Revisited: Introduction', *International Journal of Human Resource Management,* Vol. 15, No. 4 (2004), pp. 617–34.

110   C.J. Zhu and P.J. Dowling, 'Staffing Practices in Transition: Some Empirical Evidence from China', *International Journal of Human Resource Management,* Vol. 13, No. 4 (2002), pp. 569–97.

111   K. Goodall and J. Roberts, 'Only Connect: Teamwork in the Multinational', *Journal of World Business,* Vol. 38, No. 2 (2003), pp. 150–64.

112   F.L. Cooke, 'HRM in China', in P.S. Budhwar, *Managing Human Resources in Asia-Pacific* (London and New York: Routledge, 2004), pp. 17–34.

113   Zhu and Dowling, 'Staffing practices in transition'.

114   Cooke, 'HRM in China', p. 26.

115   Cooke, 'HRM in China'. This is confirmed by an empirical study by Glover and Siu. These authors have discussed the need for a better quality management initiative in China. In their study they found poor standards of training, dissatisfaction with the pay level and inadequate communication structures. L. Glover and N. Siu, 'The Human Resource Barriers to Managing Quality in China', *International Journal of Human Resource Management,* Vol. 11, No. 5 (2000), pp. 867–82.

116   See, for example, F.L. Cooke, 'Foreign Firms in China: Modelling HRM in a Toy Manufacturing Corporation', *Human Resource Management Journal,* Vol. 14, No. 3 (2004), pp. 31–52. D.Z. Ding, K. Goodall and M. Warner, 'The End of the 'Iron Rice-bowl'.

117   K. Venter, 'Building on Formal Education: Employers' Approaches to the Training and Development of New Recruits in the People's Republic of China', *International Journal of Training and Development,* Vol. 7, No. 3 (2003), pp. 186–202.

118   N. Khatri, C.T. Fern and P. Budhwar, 'Explaining Employee Turnover in an Asian Context', *Human Resource Management Journal,* Vol. 11, No. 1 (2001), pp. 54–74.

119   www.peoplemanagement.co.uk, 26 January (2007).

120   Strategic decisions taken at corporate headquarters such as plant rationalization can result in the closure of host-country operations, as multinationals divest and withdraw, or de-internationalize.

For example, in 2003, the US automobile manufacturer, Ford Motor Corporation, closed five of its 11 plants in Europe, resulting in job losses. The English car-assembly plant had been in operation for almost 71 years. Some staff were retained in the R&D (engine design) center in England, but job losses are an inevitable outcome of such actions; see 'Ford in Europe: Historical Time Line', Cologne, 3 March 2003, company website: news release section.

121 PriceWaterhouseCoopers, *Technology Executive Connections: Successful Strategies for Talent Management*. The survey generated responses from senior executives based in five principal regions: 30 per cent Asia, 41 per cent Europe, 23 per cent North America, 5 per cent Middle East and Africa and 1 per cent Latin America.

122 S. McGuiness and J. Bennett, 'Examining the Link between Skill Shortages, Training Composition and Productivity Levels in the Construction Industry: Evidence from Northern Ireland', *International Journal of Human Resource Management,* Vol. 17, No. 2 (2006), pp. 265–79.

123 R.J. Burke and E. Ng, 'The Changing Nature of Work and Organizations: Implications for Human Resource Management', *Human Resource Management Review,* Vol. 16, No. 1 (2006), pp. 86–94.

124 PriceWaterhouseCoopers, *Technology Executive Connections: Successful Strategies for Talent Management,* p. 21.

125 Burke and Ng, 'The Changing Nature of Work and Organizations'.

126 It is not just China and India where there is a high turnover of subsidiary staff. Firms operating in Russia have faced similar issues, as a study by Camiah and Hollinshead highlights. Demand for Russians with foreign language skills and experience working in Western companies is high and such individuals can generally move freely between jobs. Khatri, Chong Tze and Budhwar report similar job-hopping behaviours in Singapore and other Asian countries. N. Camiah and G. Hollinshead, 'Assessing the Potential for Effective Cross-cultural Working between "New" Russian Managers and Western Expatriates', *Journal of World Business,* Vol. 38, No. 3 (2003), pp. 245–61; N. Khatri, F. Chong Tze and P. Budhwar, 'Explaining Employee Turnover in an Asian Context', *Human Resource Management Journal,* Vol. 11, No. 1 (2001), pp. 54–74.

127 PriceWaterhouseCoopers, *Technology Executive Connections: Successful Strategies for Talent Management,* p. 40. Chinese wages and salaries are still lower than in Europe or in the USA. However, a worker in a sneaker factory earns 30 per cent more than a colleague in Vietnam and 15 per cent more than a colleague in Indonesia. See *International Herald Tribune,* April 20 (2005).

128 *Financial Times* (London, England), July 20 (2006).

129 R.L. Tung and M. Lazarova, 'Brain Drain versus Brain Gain: An Exploratory Study of Ex-host Country Nationals in Central and Eastern Europe', *International Journal of Human Resource Management,* Vol. 17, No. 11 (2006), pp. 1853–72.

130 *Ibid.,* p. 1871.

131 A. Saxenian, 'From Brain Drain to Brain Circulation: Transnational Communities and Regional Upgrading in India and China', *Studies in Comparative International Development,* Vol. 40, No. 2 (2005), pp. 35–61.

132 R. Tung, 'The Human Resource Challenge to Outward Foreign Direct Investment Aspirations from Emerging Economies: The Case of China', *International Journal of Human Resource Management,* Vol. 18, Issue 5 (2007), pp. 868–89.

133. Y. Baruch, P.W. Budhwar and N. Kathri, 'Brain Drain: Inclination to Stay Abroad After Studies', *Journal of World Business,* Vol. 42 (2007), p. 99. For a critical view on brain drain see S.C. Carr, K. Inkson and K. Thorn, 'From Global Careers to Talent Flow: Reinterpreting "brain drain"', *Journal of World Business,* Vol. 40 (2005), pp. 386–98.

134 However, as skill shortages exist in many countries, Carr *et al.* replace the term 'brain drain' by describing talent flows across borders and Tung and Lazarova at least see a positive notion of brain gain. Carr, Inkson and Thorn, 'From Global Careers to Talent Flow; Tung and Lazarova, 'Brain Drain versus Brain Gain'.

International industrial relations

Chapter Objectives

In this chapter we:

- Discuss the key issues in international industrial relations and the policies and practices of multinationals.
- Examine the potential constraints that trade unions may have on multinationals.
- Outline key concerns for trade unions.
- Discuss recent trends and issues in the global workforce context.
- Discuss the formation of regional economic zones such as the European Union and the impact of opponents to globalization.

Introduction

In this chapter we will use the more traditional term 'industrial relations' to describe the broad field of study that looks at wider issues of work and employment. We recognize that newer terms such as 'employee relations' and 'employment relations' are also used in the literature but prefer to use the traditional term in the global context as do organizations such as the International Organization of Employers and the International Labor Office.[1]

Before we examine the key issues in industrial relations as they relate to multinational firms, we need to consider some general points about the field of international industrial relations.[2] First, it is important to realize that it is difficult to compare industrial relations systems and behavior across national boundaries; an industrial relations concept may change considerably when translated from one industrial relations context to another.[3] The concept of collective bargaining, for example, in the USA is understood to mean negotiations between a local trade union and management; in Sweden and Germany the term refers to negotiations between an employers' organization and a trade union at the industry level. Cross-national differences also emerge as to the objectives of the collective bargaining process and the enforceability of collective agreements. Many European unions continue to view the collective bargaining process as an ongoing class struggle between labor and capital, whereas in the USA union leaders tend toward a pragmatic economic view of collective bargaining rather than an ideological view. Second, it is very important to recognize in the international industrial relations field that no industrial relations system can be understood without an appreciation of its historical origin.[4] As Schregle[5] has observed,

> A comparative study of industrial relations shows that industrial relations phenomena are a very faithful expression of the society in which they operate, of its characteristic features and of the power relationships between different interest groups. Industrial relations cannot be understood without an understanding of the way in which rules are established and implemented and decisions are made in the society concerned.

An interesting example of the effect of historical differences may be seen in the structure of trade unions in various countries. Poole[6] has identified several factors that may underlie these historical differences:

● The mode of technology and industrial organization at critical stages of union development.

● Methods of union regulation by government.

● Ideological divisions within the trade union movement.

● The influence of religious organizations on trade union development.

● Managerial strategies for labor relations in large corporations.

As Table 10-1 shows, union structures differ considerably among Western countries. These include industrial unions, which represent all grades of employees in

---

Table 10-1	Trade union structure in leading Western industrial societies

Australia	general, craft, industrial, white-collar
Belgium	industrial, professional, religious, public sector
Canada	industrial, craft, conglomerate
Denmark	general, craft, white-collar
Finland	industrial, white-collar, professional and technical
Great Britain	general, craft, industrial, white-collar, public sector
Japan	enterprise
The Netherlands	religious, conglomerate, white-collar
Norway	industrial, craft
Sweden	industrial, craft, white-collar and professional
Switzerland	industrial, craft, religious, white-collar
USA	industrial, craft, conglomerate, white-collar
West Germany	industrial, white-collar

Source: M. Poole, *Industrial Relations: Origins and Patterns of National Diversity* (London: Routledge & Kegan Paul, 1986), p. 79.

an industry; craft unions, which are based on skilled occupational groupings across industries; conglomerate unions, which represent members in more than one industry; and general unions, which are open to almost all employees in a given country. These differences in union structures have had a major influence on the collective bargaining process in Western countries. Some changes in union structure are evident over time; for example, enterprise unions are increasingly evident in industrialized nations. Enterprise unions are common in Asia-Pacific nations, although there are national variations in their functions, and in the proportion of enterprise unions to total unions.

The less one knows about how a structure came to develop in a distinctive way, the less likely one is to understand it. As Prahalad and Doz[7] note, the lack of familiarity of multinational managers with local industrial and political conditions has sometimes needlessly worsened a conflict that a local firm would have been likely to resolve. Increasingly, MNEs are recognizing this shortcoming and admitting that industrial relations policies must be flexible enough to adapt to local requirements. This is evidently an enduring approach, even in firms that follow a non-union labor relations strategy where possible, as IHRM in Action Case 10-1 points out. Although the case is some years old, the key points made remain relevant to current international industrial relations.

IHRM in Action Case 10-1

Advice for companies going global

The key to successfully expanding overseas is to become one with the culture of the location, even if it means unionization of employees, Michael R. Quinlan, chairman and chief executive officer of McDonald's Corp., tells conferees at a meeting of the Human Resources Management Association of Chicago.

After opening fast-food restaurants in 53 nations, McDonald's has learned that it must follow the established practices of a foreign country to succeed there, Quinlan says. For example, a number of European countries and Australia have very strict unionization standards, and operations there are unionized as a condition of doing business. Acknowledging that McDonald's has had some 'horrible union fights around the world', Quinlan advises employers considering expansion into other nations to 'do it their way, not your way'.

The main implication of dealing with unions is the increased cost of wages and benefits, according to Quinlan. Still, he adds that he does not feel unionization has interfered with employees' loyalty to McDonald's, or to the company's philosophy of service and employee motivation. Declaring that unions do not 'bring much to the equation' of the employee/employer relationship, Quinlan says McDonald's is 'basically a non-union company' and intends to stay that way.

Another source of difficulty for McDonald's in its expansion overseas lies in the fact that fast-food restaurants are unfamiliar in most nations. Opening the first McDonald's inside the Communist-bloc, in Yugoslavia, took 12 years, Quinlan notes. He also points out that the company's policy is to staff its restaurants, from crew through management, only with nationals – for the 3300 foreign outlets, the corporation employs only 35 expatriate US citizens, and its goal is to have 100 per cent local employees within five years.

Source: Reproduced with permission from Bulletin to Management, a weekly report of news and trends for HR Managers, Vol. 42, No. 9 (March 7, 1991) pp. 66, 71. Copyright 1991 by the Bureau of National Affairs, Inc. http://www.bna.com/products/hr

Key issues in international industrial relations

The focus of this chapter is on the industrial relations strategies adopted by multinationals rather than the more general topic of comparative industrial relations.[8] We have already covered the emerging topic of 'offshoring of labor' in Chapter 9, in this chapter, we examine the central question for industrial relations in an international context, which concerns the orientation of MNEs to organized labor.

Industrial relations policies and practices of multinational firms

Because national differences in economic, political and legal systems produce markedly different industrial relations systems across countries, multinationals generally delegate the management of industrial relations to their foreign subsidiaries. However, a policy of decentralization does not keep corporate headquarters from exercising some coordination over industrial relations strategy. Generally, corporate headquarters will become involved in or oversee labor agreements made by foreign subsidiaries because these agreements may affect the international plans of the firm and/or create precedents for negotiations in other countries. Further, Marginson *et al.*[9] found that the majority of the firms in their study monitored labor performance across units in different countries. Comparison of performance data across national units of the firm creates the potential for decisions on issues such as unit location, capital investment and rationalization of production capacity. The use of comparisons would be expected to be greatest where units in different countries undertake similar operations. For recent reviews of the literature in this area, see the work of Gunnigle and his colleagues.[10]

Much of the literature on the industrial relations practices of multinationals tends to be at a more cross-national or comparative level. There is, however, some research on industrial relations practices at the firm level. Empirical research has identified a number of differences in multinational approaches to industrial relations. Indeed, a number of studies have examined differences in the propensity of multinational headquarters to intervene in, or to centralize control over, matters such as industrial relations in host locations. Multinational headquarters involvement in industrial relations is influenced by several factors, as detailed below.

The degree of inter-subsidiary production integration.   According to Hamill,[11] a high degree of integration was found to be the most important factor leading to the centralization of the industrial relations function within the firms studied. Industrial relations throughout a system become of direct importance to corporate headquarters when transnational sourcing patterns have been developed, that is, when a subsidiary in one country relies on another foreign subsidiary as a source of components or as a user of its output.[12] In this context, a coordinated industrial relations policy is one of the key factors in a successful global production strategy.[13] One early example of the development of an international policy for industrial relations can be seen in the introduction of employee involvement across Ford's operations.[14]

Nationality of ownership of the subsidiary.   There is evidence of differences between European and US firms in terms of headquarters' involvement in industrial relations.[15] A number of studies have revealed that US firms tend to exercise greater centralized control over labor relations than do British or other European firms.[16] US firms tend to place greater emphasis on formal management controls and a close reporting system (particularly within the area of financial control) to ensure that planning targets are met. In his review of empirical research of this area, Bean[17] showed that foreign-owned multinationals in Britain prefer single-employer bargaining (rather than involving an employer association), and are more likely than British firms to assert managerial prerogative on matters of labor utilization. Further, Hamill[18] found US-owned subsidiaries to be much more centralized in labor relations decision making than British-owned. Hamill attributed this difference in management procedures to the more integrated nature of US firms, the greater divergence between British and US labor relations systems than between British and other European systems, and the more ethnocentric managerial style of US firms.

International human resource management approach.

In earlier chapters, we discussed the various international human resource management approaches utilized by multinationals; these have implications for international industrial relations. Interestingly, an ethnocentric predisposition is more likely to be associated with various forms of industrial relations conflict.[19] Conversely, it has been shown that more geocentric firms will bear more influence on host-country industrial relations systems, due to their greater propensity to participate in local events.[20]

MNE prior experience in industrial relations.

European firms have tended to deal with industrial unions at industry level (frequently via employer associations) rather than at firm level. The opposite is more typical for US firms. In the USA, employer associations have not played a key role in the industrial relations system, and firm-based industrial relations policies are the norm.[21]

Subsidiary characteristics.

Research has identified a number of subsidiary characteristics to be relevant to centralization of industrial relations. First, subsidiaries that are formed through acquisition of well-established indigenous firms tend to be given much more autonomy over industrial relations than are greenfield sites set up by a multinational firm.[22] Second, according to Enderwick, greater intervention would be expected when the subsidiary is of key strategic importance to the firm and the subsidiary is young.[23] Third, where the parent firm is a significant source of operating or investment funds for the subsidiary, that is, where the subsidiary is more dependent on headquarters for resources, there will tend to be increased corporate involvement in industrial relations and human resource management.[24] Finally, poor subsidiary performance tends to be accompanied by increased corporate involvement in industrial relations. Where poor performance is due to industrial relations problems, multinationals tend to attempt to introduce parent-country industrial relations practices aimed at reducing industrial unrest or increasing productivity.[25]

Characteristics of the home product market.

An important factor is the extent of the home product market[26] – an issue which was discussed in detail in Chapter 1. If domestic sales are large relative to overseas operations (as is the case with many US firms), it is more likely that overseas operations will be regarded by the parent firm as an extension of domestic operations. This is not the case for many European firms, whose international operations represent the major part of their business. Lack of a large home market is a strong incentive to adapt to host-country institutions and norms. There is evidence of change in the European context: since the implementation of the single European market in 1993, there has been growth in large European-scale companies (formed via acquisition or joint ventures) that centralize management organization and strategic decision making. However, processes of operational decentralization with regard to industrial relations are also evident.[27]

Management attitudes towards unions.
An additional important factor is that of management attitudes or ideology concerning unions.[28] Knowledge of management attitudes concerning unions may provide a more complete explanation of multinational industrial relations behavior than could be obtained by relying solely on a rational economic model. Thus, management attitudes should also be considered in any explanation of managerial behavior along with such factors as market forces and strategic choices. This is of particular relevance to US firms, since union avoidance appears to be deeply rooted in the value systems of American managers.[29]

As Table 10-2 shows, of the ten developed economies listed, Sweden has the highest level of union membership while the USA, France and Korea have low levels of union density. Hence, managers from these countries may be less likely to have extensive experience with unions than managers in many other countries. Overall, Table 10-2 shows that union density growth has declined. This decline in union density in many countries may been explained by economic factors such as reduced public-sector employment, reduced employment in manufacturing

Table 10-2	Union membership for selected countries

	Union density (%)		Union density growth (%)
	1995	2000	1990–2000
Australia	35	25	−39
Canada	34	31	−11
France	10	10	stable
Germany	29	24	−25
Italy	38	36	−8
Japan	24	21	−16
Korea	14	12	−29
Sweden	83	79	−1
UK	32	29	−24
USA	15	13	−19

Source: Adapted from G. Bamber, S. Ryan and N. Wailes, 'Globalization, Employment Relations and Human Resources Indicators in Ten Developed Market Economies: International Data Sets', *International Journal of Human Resource Management,* Vol. 15, No. 8 (2004), Table 18.

industries as a share in total employment, and increased competition; it is also suggested to be associated with decentralization of industrial relations to business unit level, changes in governance and legislative changes. Union membership decline is also linked to the introduction of new forms of work organization, globalization of production and changes in workforce structure.[30]

Although there are several problems inherent in data collection for a cross-national comparison of union density rates, several theories have been suggested to explain the variations among countries. Such theories consider economic factors such as wages, prices and unemployment levels; social factors such as public support for unions; and political factors. In addition, studies indicate that the strategies utilized by labor, management and governments are particularly important.[31]

Another key issue in international industrial relations is industrial disputes. Hamill[32] examined strike-proneness of multinational subsidiaries and indigenous firms in Britain across three industries. Strike-proneness was measured via three variables – strike frequency, strike size and strike duration. There was no difference across the two groups of firms with regard to strike frequency, but multinational subsidiaries did experience larger and longer strikes than local firms. Hamill suggests that this difference indicates that foreign-owned firms may be under less financial pressure to settle a strike quickly than local firms – possibly because they can switch production out of the country.

Overall, it is evident that international industrial relations are influenced by a broad range of factors. Commenting on the overall results of his research, Hamill[33] concluded that:

> general statements cannot be applied to the organization of the labor relations function within MNEs. Rather, different MNEs adopt different labor relations strategies in relation to the environmental factors peculiar to each firm. In other words, it is the type of multinational under consideration which is important rather than multinationality itself.

Trade unions and international industrial relations

Trade unions may limit the strategic choices of multinationals in three ways: (1) by influencing wage levels to the extent that cost structures may become uncompetitive; (2) by constraining the ability of multinationals to vary employment levels at will; and (3) by hindering or preventing global integration of the operations of multinationals.[34] We shall briefly examine each of these potential constraints.

Influencing wage levels

Although the importance of labor costs relative to other costs is decreasing, labor costs still play an important part in determining cost competitiveness in most industries. The influence of unions on wage levels is therefore, important. Multinationals that fail to successfully manage their wage levels will suffer labor cost disadvantages that may narrow their strategic options.

Constraining the ability of multinationals to vary employment levels at will

For many multinationals operating in Western Europe, Japan and Australia, the inability to vary employment levels at will may be a more serious problem than wage levels. Many countries now have legislation that limits considerably the ability of firms to carry out plant closure, redundancy or layoff programs unless it can be shown that structural conditions make these employment losses unavoidable. Frequently, the process of showing the need for these programs is long and drawn-out. Plant closure or redundancy legislation in many countries also frequently specifies that firms must compensate redundant employees through specified formulae such as two week's pay for each year of service. In many countries, payments for involuntary terminations are quite substantial, especially in comparison to those in the USA.

Trade unions may influence this process in two ways: by lobbying their own national governments to introduce redundancy legislation; and by encouraging regulation of multinationals by international organizations such as the Organization for Economic Cooperation and Development (OECD). (Later in this chapter we describe the *Badger* case, which forced Raytheon to finally accept responsibility for severance payments to employees made redundant by the closing down of its Belgian subsidiary.) Multinational managers who do not take these restrictions into account in their strategic planning may well find their options severely limited. In fact, recent evidence shows that multinationals are beginning to consider the ability to dismiss employees to be one of the priorities when making investment location decisions.[35]

Hindering or preventing global integration of the operations of multinationals

In recognition of these constraints, many multinationals make a conscious decision not to integrate and rationalize their operations to the most efficient degree, because to do so could cause industrial and political problems. Prahalad and Doz[36] cite General Motors as an example of this 'sub-optimization of integration'. GM was alleged in the early 1980s to have undertaken substantial investments in Germany (matching its new investments in Austria and Spain) at the demand of the German metalworkers' union (one of the largest industrial unions in the Western world) in order to foster good industrial relations in Germany. One observer of the world auto industry suggested that car manufacturers were sub-optimizing their manufacturing networks partly to placate trade unions and partly to provide redundancy in sources to prevent localized social strife from paralyzing their network. This sub-optimization led to unit manufacturing costs in Europe that were 15 per cent higher, on average, than an economically optimal network would have achieved. Prahalad and Doz drew the following conclusion from this example:[37]

> Union influence thus not only delays the rationalization and integration of MNEs' manufacturing networks and increases the cost of such adjustments (not so much in the visible severance payments and 'golden handshake' provisions as through the economic losses incurred in the meantime), but also, at least in such industries as automobiles, permanently reduces the efficiency of the integrated MNC network. Therefore, treating Labor relations

as incidental and relegating them to the specialists in the various countries is inappropriate. In the same way as government policies need to be integrated into strategic choices, so do labor relations.

The response of trade unions to multinationals

Trade union leaders have long seen the growth of multinationals as a threat to the bargaining power of labor because of the considerable power and influence of large multinational firms. While it is recognized that multinationals are 'neither uniformly anti-union nor omnipotent and monolithic bureaucracies',[38] their potential for lobbying power and flexibility across national borders creates difficulties for employees and trade unions endeavoring to develop countervailing power. There are several ways in which multinationals have an impact upon trade union and employee interests. Kennedy[39] has identified the following seven characteristics of MNEs as the source of trade union concern about multinationals:

● *Formidable financial resources.* This includes the ability to absorb losses in a particular foreign subsidiary that is in dispute with a national union and still show an overall profit on worldwide operations. Union bargaining power may be threatened or weakened by the broader financial resources of a multinational. This is particularly evident where a multinational has adopted a practice of transnational sourcing and cross-subsidization of products or components across different countries. 'The economic pressure which a nationally based union can exert upon a multinational is certainly less than would be the case if the company's operations were confined to one country.'[40]

● *Alternative sources of supply.* This may take the form of an explicit 'dual sourcing' policy to reduce the vulnerability of the multinational to a strike by any national union. Also, temporary switching of production in order to defeat industrial action has been utilized to some extent, for example, in the automotive industry.[41]

● *The ability to move production facilities to other countries.* A reported concern of employees and trade unions is that job security may be threatened if a multinational seeks to produce abroad what could have, or previously has, been manufactured domestically. National relative advantages provide MNEs with choice as to location of units. Within the EU, for example, evidence suggests that multinational management are locating skill-intensive activities in countries with national policies promoting training and with relatively high labor costs. Conversely, semi-skilled, routinized activities are being located in countries with lower labor costs.[42] Threats by multinationals, whether real or perceived, to reorganize production factors internationally, with the accompanying risk of plant closure or rationalization, will have an impact on management–labor negotiations at a national level. However, technical and economic investments would reduce a multinational's propensity to relocate facilities.

● *A remote locus of authority* (i.e. the corporate head office management of a multinational firm). While many multinationals report decentralization and local responsiveness of HRM and industrial relations, trade unions and works councils have reported that the multinational decision-making structure is opaque and the division of authority obscured. Further, employee representatives may not be adequately aware of the overall MNE organizational strategy and activities.[43]

- *Production facilities in many industries.* As Vernon[44] has noted, most multinationals operate in many product lines.
- *Superior knowledge and expertise in industrial relations.*
- *The capacity to stage an 'investment strike',* whereby the multinational refuses to invest any additional funds in a plant, thus ensuring that the plant will become obsolete and economically non-competitive.

Many of the points made by Kennedy would now be recognized as characteristics of the process now described as *offshoring* (also discussed in Chapter 9). This topic will remain a key issue within the broader debate concerning globalization and the employment consequences of globalization. For recent reviews of offshoring, see Auer *et al.*,[45] Cooke,[46] and Pyndt and Pedersen.[47]

Another issue reported by trade unions is their claim that they have difficulty accessing decision makers located outside the host country and obtaining financial information. For example, according to Martinez Lucio and Weston:

> Misinformation has been central to the management strategy of using potential investment or disinvestment in seeking changes in certain organizations . . . For example, in companies such as Heinz, Ford, Gillette and General Motors, workers have established that they had on occasions been misinformed by management as to the nature of working practices in other plants.[48]

The response of labor unions to multinationals has been threefold: to form international trade secretariats (ITSs); to lobby for restrictive national legislation; and finally, to try and achieve regulation of multinationals by international organizations.

International trade secretariats (ITSs)

ITSs function as loose confederations to provide worldwide links for the national unions in a particular trade or industry (e.g., metals, transport and chemicals). The secretariats have mainly operated to facilitate the exchange of information.[49] The long-term goal of each ITS is to achieve transnational bargaining with each of the multinationals in its industry. Each ITS has followed a similar program to achieve the goal of transnational bargaining.[50] The elements of this program are: (1) research and information, (2) calling company conferences, (3) establishing company councils, (4) companywide union–management discussions, and (5) coordinated bargaining. Overall, the ITSs have met with limited success, the reasons for which Northrup[51] attributes to: (1) the generally good wages and working conditions offered by multinationals, (2) strong resistance from multinational firm management, (3) conflicts within the labor movement, and (4) differing laws and customs in the industrial relations field.

Lobbying for restrictive national legislation

On a political level, trade unions have for many years lobbied for restrictive national legislation in the USA and Europe. The motivation for trade unions to pursue restrictive national legislation is based on a desire to prevent the export of jobs via multinational investment policies. For example, in the USA, the AFL-CIO has lobbied strongly in this area.[52] A major difficulty for unions when pursuing this strategy is the reality of conflicting national economic interests. In times of economic downturn, this factor may become an insurmountable barrier for trade union officials. To date, these attempts have been largely unsuccessful, and, with the increasing internationalization of business, it is difficult to see how governments will be persuaded to legislate in this area.

Regulation of multinationals by international organizations

Attempts by trade unions to exert influence over multinationals via international organizations have met with some success. Through trade union federations such as the European Trade Union Confederation (ETUC) and the International Confederation of Free Trade Unions (ICFTU), the labor movement has been able to lobby the International Labor Organization (ILO), the United Nations Conference on Trade and Development (UNCTAD),[53] the Organization for Economic Cooperation and Development (OECD) and the European Union (EU). The ILO has identified a number of workplace-related principles that should be respected by all nations: freedom of association; the right to organize and collectively bargain, abolition of forced labor and non-discrimination in employment. In 1977 the ILO adopted a code of conduct for multinationals (Tripartite Declaration of Principles Concerning MNEs and Social Policy).[54] The ILO code of conduct, which was originally proposed in 1975, was influential in the drafting of the OECD guidelines for multinationals, which were approved in 1976. These voluntary guidelines cover disclosure of information, competition, financing, taxation, employment and industrial relations, and science and technology.[55]

A key section of these guidelines is the *umbrella* or *chapeau clause* (the latter is the more common term in the literature) that precedes the guidelines themselves. This clause states that multinationals should adhere to the guidelines 'within the framework of law, regulations and prevailing Labor relations and employment practices, in each of the countries in which they operate'. Campbell and Rowan[56] state that employers have understood the chapeau clause to mean compliance with local law supersedes the guidelines while labor unions have interpreted this clause to mean that the guidelines are a 'supplement' to national law. The implication of this latter interpretation is significant: a firm could still be in violation of the OECD guidelines even though its activities have complied with national law and practice. Given the ambiguity of the chapeau clause and the fact that the OECD guidelines are voluntary, it is likely that this issue will remain controversial.

There is also some controversy in the literature as to the effectiveness of the OECD guidelines in regulating multinational behavior.[57] This lack of agreement centers on assessments of the various challenges to the guidelines. The best known of these challenges is the *Badger* case. The Badger Company was a subsidiary of Raytheon, a US-based multinational. In 1976 the Badger Company decided to close its Belgian subsidiary, and a dispute arose concerning termination payments.[58] Since Badger (Belgium) NV had filed for bankruptcy, the Belgian labor unions argued that Raytheon should assume the subsidiary's financial obligations. Raytheon refused, and the case was brought before the OECD by the Belgian government and the International Federation of Commercial, Clerical, Professional and Technical Employees (FIET), an international trade secretariat. The Committee on International Investments and MNEs (CIIME) of the OECD indicated that paragraph six of the guidelines (concerned with plant closures) implied a 'shared responsibility' by the subsidiary and the parent in the event of a plant closing. Following this clarification by the CIIME and a scaling down of initial demands, Badger executives and Belgian government officials negotiated a settlement of this case.

Blanpain[59] concludes that the *Badger* case made clear the responsibility of the parent company for the financial liability of its subsidiary, but that this responsibility is not unqualified. As to whether the *Badger* case proved the 'effectiveness' of the OECD guidelines, Jain[60] and Campbell and Rowan[61] point out that the Belgian unions devoted considerable resources to make this a test case and had assistance from both American unions (which, through the AFL-CIO, lobbied the US Department of State) and the Belgian government in their negotiations with the OECD and Badger executives. Liebhaberg[62] is more specific in his assessment:

> Despite an outcome which those in favour of supervision consider to be positive, the Badger Case is a clear demonstration of one of the weaknesses in the OECD's instrument, namely that it does not represent any sort of formal undertaking on the part of the twenty-four member states which are signatories to it. The social forces of each separate country must apply pressure on their respective governments if they want the guidelines applied.

A recent development with the OECD guidelines (which are addressed by 36 OECD and non-OECD governments) has been the follow-up procedures. The system of National Contact Points promotes observance of the guidelines by MNEs operating in or from the governments' territories. It appears that this system is now having some influence on MNE behavior in the industrial relations area. As the Chair of the 2005 Annual Meeting of the National Contact Points (NCPs) noted:

> The NCPs' reports suggest that many adhering governments have deepened their use of the Guidelines in the context of a 'whole of government' approach to corporate responsibility. They have expanded their promotion with and through embassy networks, export credit and investment guarantee programs and other specialized agencies and Ministries. Taken together, the NCP reports on promotion attest to the ongoing vigour of adhering countries' commitment to the Guidelines.[63]

Recognizing the limitations of voluntary codes of conduct, European trade unions have also lobbied the Commission of the European Union to regulate the activities of multinationals.[64] Unlike the OECD, the Commission of the EU can translate guidelines into law, and has developed a number of proposals concerning disclosure of information to make multinationals more 'transparent'.[65] These are discussed in more detail in the next section.

Regional integration: the European Union (EU)

Regional integration such as the development of the European Union (EU) has brought significant implications for industrial relations.[66] In the Treaty of Rome (1957), some consideration was given to social policy issues related to the creation of the European Community. In the EU, the terms 'social policy' or 'social dimension' are used to cover a number of issues including in particular labor law and working conditions, aspects of employment and vocational training, social security and pensions. There have been a number of significant developments in EU social policy over the past four decades. The Social Charter of the Council of Europe came into effect in 1965. In 1987, the major objective of the implementation of the Single European Act was to establish the Single European Market (SEM) on 31 December 1992, in order to enhance the free movement of goods, money and people within the SEM. The social dimension aims to achieve a large labor market by eliminating the barriers that restrict the freedom of movement and the right of domicile within the SEM. The European Community Charter of the Fundamental Social Rights of Workers (often referred to simply as the Social Charter) was introduced in 1989, and has guided the development of social policy in the 1990s.[67] Naturally, the social dimension has been the subject of much debate: proponents defend the social dimension as a means of achieving social justice and equal treatment for EU citizens, while critics see it as a kind of 'social engineering'.[68]

At the signing of the Treaty on European Union in Maastricht in February 1992, Britain was allowed to opt out of the social policy agreements. The other 11 member states were party to a protocol (The Social Policy Protocol), which allows them to agree their own directives without Britain's participation.[69] With the election of the Blair Labor government in Britain in 1997, this anomaly was resolved when all members of the EU signed the Treaty of Amsterdam on 17 June 1997. This means that there now exists a single coherent legal basis for action by the EU member states with regard to social policy.

The Social Chapter in the Treaty of Amsterdam opens with a general statement of objectives.[70] Its first Article (Article 117 of the EC Treaty), drawn largely from Article 1 of the Maastricht Social Agreement, begins with a reference to fundamental social rights such as those in the European Social Charter of 1961 and the Social Charter of 1989. It then sets out the objectives for the EU: to support and complement the activities of the member states in a number of listed areas. These include improvement of working conditions and of the working environment in the interest of workers' health and safety, information and consultation of workers, integration of persons excluded from the labor market and equality of opportunity, and at work, between men and women. However, the Treaty excludes matters of pay, the right of association and the right to strike or to lock out. The European Commission department responsible for social policy is known as Directorate-General for Employment, Social Affairs and Equal Opportunities.[71]

Disclosure of information and European Works Councils

The EU has introduced a range of directives related to the social dimension. Of the directives concerned with multinationals, the most contentious has been the Vredeling Directive (associated with Henk Vredeling, a former Dutch member of the EU Commission).[72] The Seventh (Vredeling) Directive's requirement of disclosure of company information to unions faced strong opposition led by the then conservative British government and employer representatives. They argued that employee involvement in consultation and decision making should be voluntary. The European Works Councils (EWC) Directive was approved on 22 September 1994 and implemented two years later. Under the terms of the Treaty of Amsterdam, this directive applies to all EU member states. This was the first pan-European legislation that regulated collective relationships between multinationals and employees. The directive requires EWCs to be established in multinationals with at least 1000 employees, having 100 or more employees in each of two member states. According to Chesters, more than 1000 multinationals, including around 200 US-based firms, are affected by the EWC directive.[73] The directive is designed to provide coverage to all employees, whether unionized or not. The EWC directive aims to enhance employees' rights to information and consultation in general, and provide rights to information regarding international corporate decisions that would significantly affect workers' interests.[74] Partly in response to the EWC directive, firms such as General Motors and Heinz have subsidized visits of worker representatives to other plants and provided information and forums for discussion at the European level.[75]

Obviously, all firms operating in the EU will need to become familiar with EU directives and keep abreast of changes. While harmonization of labor laws can be seen as the ultimate objective, Michon[76] argues that the notion of a European social community does not mean a unification of all social conditions and benefits, or, for that matter, of all social systems. However, the EU does aim to establish minimal standards for social conditions that will safeguard the fundamental rights of workers. A recent study on European Works Councils by Gilman and Marginson[77] summarized these somewhat conflicting trends in the following way:

> The salience of both country and sector influences on the provisions of EWC agreements places a question mark against the perspective that sees EWCs as primarily international extensions of national structures of information and consultation. The influence of national systems of industrial relations on the provisions of EWC agreements is important, but the similarities within particular sectors, which cross national borders, reflects a more general process of 'converging divergences' (Katz and Darbishire, 2000) under which growing divergence in industrial relations arrangements and practice within national systems is occurring alongside increased cross-border convergence of practices within given sectors.

The issue of social 'dumping'

One of the concerns related to the formation of the SEM was its impact on jobs. There was alarm that those member states that have relatively low social security costs would have a competitive edge and that firms would locate in those member states that have lower labor costs. The counter-alarm was that states with low-cost labor would have to increase their labor costs, to the detriment of their competitiveness.[78] There are two industrial relations issues here: the movement of work from one region to another and its effect on employment levels; and the need for trade union solidarity to prevent workers in one region from accepting pay cuts to attract investment, at the expense of workers in another region. There is some, although not as much as was expected, evidence of 'social dumping' in the EU.[79] It is likely that this issue will be a contentious one in Europe for some time and multinationals need to be aware of this debate when doing business in Europe.[80]

One of the key reasons it is likely that the question of social dumping will remain a live issue is the recent further expansion of the EU with ten new members accepted, most relatively low-income states, some of whom have not fully completed their transition from a communist system. The EU through the 'Lisbon Strategy' has recently recommitted itself to the European Employment Strategy with ambitious targets to be achieved by 2010. As Ingham et al.[81] have recently concluded, the likelihood of the EU being able to meet the targets set out in the European Employment Strategy is remote.

Summary

The literature reviewed in this chapter and the discussion surrounding the formation of regional economic zones such as the European Union and the Asia Pacific Economic Cooperation (APEC)[82] supports the conclusion that transnational collective bargaining has yet to be attained by trade unions.[83] As Enderwick[84] has noted:

> The international operations of MNEs do create considerable impediments in effectively segmenting labor groups by national boundaries and stratifying groups within and between nations. Combining recognition of the overt segmentation effects of international business with an understanding of the dynamics of direct investment yields the conclusion that general multinational collective bargaining is likely to remain a remote possibility.

Enderwick argues that trade unions should opt for less ambitious strategies in dealing with multinationals, such as: (1) strengthening national union involvement in plant-based and company-based bargaining; (2) supporting research on the vulnerability of selective multinationals; and (3) consolidating the activities of company-based ITSs. Despite setbacks, especially with the regional economic integration issues discussed in this chapter, it is likely that trade unions and the ILO will pursue these strategies and continue to lobby where possible for the regulation of multinationals via the European Commission and the United Nations.

It is also likely that opponents of globalization will continue to attempt to influence public opinion in the developed economies with campaigns against selected MNEs with industrial relations policies and practices being a particular target. The recent campaign against Wal-Mart, utilizing the documentary film *Wal-Mart: The High Cost of Low Price*,[85] is an example of such a campaign. One of the key points made in the film is that Wal-Mart employees have either poor medical coverage or none at all. However, as the business magazine *Fortune*[86] astutely points out, in a globalized economy: 'American companies can't continue paying the world's highest health-care costs. Don't blame Wal-Mart; blame America's inability to devise a national health care plan that takes the burden off employers.'

With globalization, what was once a domestic issue has now become in part an international issue and in turn raises public policy questions as to what health-care costs can US firms be expected to fund in a globalized economy. It is likely that the impact of globalization on international industrial relations will be an ongoing issue in the foreseeable future.

Discussion Questions

1 Why is it important to understand the historical origins of national industrial relations systems?

2 In what ways can trade unions constrain the strategic choices of multinationals?

3 Identify four characteristics of MNEs that give trade unions cause for concern.

4 How have trade unions responded to MNEs? Have these responses been successful?

5 What is 'social dumping' and why should unions be concerned about it?

6 Can you give other examples of documentary films which are critical of large multinational firms?

Further Reading

Bamber, G., Lansbury, R. and Wailes, N. (eds) (2004). *International and Comparative Employment Relations,* 4th edn, London: Sage.

Cooke, W.N. (2006). 'Multinational Companies and Global Human Resource Strategy', in P. Boxall, J. Purcell and P. Wright (eds), *Oxford Handbook of Human Resource Management,* Oxford: Oxford University Press, pp. 489–509.

Jacoby, S.M. (2004). *The Embedded Corporation: Corporate Governance and Employment Relations in Japan and the United States,* Princeton, NJ: Princeton University Press.

Katz, H. and Darbishire, O. (2000). *Converging Divergences,* Ithaca, NY: ILR Press.

Shen, J. (2007). *Labour Disputes and Their Resolution in China,* Oxford: Chandos Publishing.

Notes and References

1 See www.ioe-emp.org/en/policy-areas/international-industrial-relations/index.html for the International Organisation of Employers and www.ilo.org/ for the International Labour Organization.

2 These introductory comments are drawn from J. Schregle, 'Comparative Industrial Relations: Pitfalls and Potential', *International Labour Review,* Vol. 120, No. 1 (1981), pp. 15–30.

3 This point is also referred to as the *emic-etic* problem. See Chapter 1 for a detailed discussion of this point.

4 O. Kahn-Freund, *Labour Relations: Heritage and Adjustment* (Oxford: Oxford University Press, 1979). Also see R.B. Peterson and J. Sargent, 'Union and Employer Confederation Views on Current Labour Relations in 21 Industrialized Nations', *Relations Industrielles,* Vol. 52, No.1 (1997), pp. 39–59.

5 J. Schregle, 'Comparative Industrial Relations', p. 28.

6 M. Poole, *Industrial Relations: Origins and Patterns of National Diversity* (London: Routledge, 1986).

7 C.K. Prahalad and Y.L. Doz, *The Multinational Mission: Balancing Local Demands and Global Vision* (New York: The Free Press, 1987).

8 For general reviews of the comparative industrial relations literature, see T. Kennedy, *European Labour Relations* (Lexington, MA: Lexington Books, 1980); R. Bean, *Comparative Industrial Relations: An Introduction to Cross-National Perspectives* (New York: St. Martin's Press, 1985); Poole, *Industrial Relations*; G. Bamber, R. Lansbury and N. Wailes (eds), *International and Comparative Employment Relations,* 4th edn (London: Sage, 2004).

9 P. Marginson, P. Armstrong, P.K. Edwards and J. Purcell, 'Extending Beyond Borders: Multinational Companies and the International Management of Labour', *International Journal of Human Resource Management,* Vol. 6, No. 3 (1995), pp. 702–19; also see M. Martinez Lucio and S. Weston, 'New Management Practices in a Multinational Corporation: The Restructuring of Worker Representation and Rights', *Industrial Relations Journal,* Vol. 25, (1994), pp. 110–21.

10 See the following publications by Gunnigle and his colleagues: P. Gunnigle, D.G. Collings and M.J. Morley, 'Accommodating Global Capitalism: Industrial Relations in American MNCs in Ireland', in A. Ferner, J. Quintanilla and C. Sanchez-Runde (eds), *Multinationals and the Construction of Transnational Practices: Convergence and Diversity in the Global Economy* (London: Palgrave Macmillan, 2006); P. Gunnigle, D. Collings and M. Morley, 'Exploring the Dynamics of Industrial Relations in US Multinational: Evidence from the Republic of Ireland', *Industrial Relations Journal,* Vol. 36, No. 3 (2005), pp. 241–56; P. Almond, T. Edwards, T. Colling, A. Ferner, P. Gunnigle, M. Muller-Camen, J. Quintanilla and H. Waechter, 'Unraveling Home and Host Country Effects: An Investigation of the HR Policies of an American Multinational in Four European Countries', *Industrial Relations,* Vol. 44, No. 2 (2005), pp. 276–306; I. Clark, P. Almond, P. Gunnigle and H. Waechter, 'The Americanisation of the European business system?', *Industrial Relations Journal,* Vol. 36, No. 6 (2005), pp. 494–517.

11 J. Hamill, 'Labour Relations Decision-making within Multinational Corporations', *Industrial Relations Journal,* Vol. 15, No. 2 (1984), pp. 30–4.

12 S.H. Robock and K. Simmonds, *International Business and Multinational Enterprises,* 4th edn (Homewood, IL: Irwin, 1989); Marginson, Armstrong, Edwards and Purcell, 'Extending Beyond Borders'.

13 D.F. Hefler, 'Global Sourcing: Offshore Investment Strategy for the 1980's', *Journal of Business Strategy,* Vol. 2, No. 1 (1981), pp. 7–12.

14 K. Starkey and A. McKinlay, *Strategy and the Human Resource: Ford and the Search for Competitive Advantage* (Oxford: Blackwell, 1993).

15 B.C. Roberts and J. May, 'The Response of Multinational Enterprises to International Trade Union Pressures', *British Journal of Industrial Relations,* Vol. 12 (1974), pp. 403–16.

16 See J. La Palombara and S. Blank, *Multinational Corporations and National Elites: A Study of Tensions* (New York: The Conference Board, 1976); A.B. Sim, 'Decentralized Management of Subsidiaries and Their Performance: A Comparative Study of American, British and Japanese Subsidiaries in Malaysia', *Management International Review,* Vol. 17, No. 2 (1977), pp. 45–51; and Y.K. Shetty, 'Managing the Multinational Corporation: European and American Styles', *Management International Review,* Vol. 19, No. 3 (1979), pp. 39–48.

17 Bean, *Comparative Industrial Relations.*

18 Hamill, 'Labour Relations Decision-making'.

19 See P. Marginson, 'European Integration and Transnational Management–Union Relations in the Enterprise', *British Journal of Industrial Relations,* Vol. 30, No. 4 (1992), pp. 529–45.

20 Martinez Lucio and Weston, 'New Management Practices in a Multinational Corporation'.

21 See Bean, *Comparative Industrial Relations*; D. Bok, 'Reflections on the Distinctive Character of American Labour Law', *Harvard Law Review,* Vol. 84 (1971), pp. 1394–1463; and J.P. Windmuller and A. Gladstone (eds), *Employers Associations and Industrial Relations: A Comparative Study* (Oxford: Clarendon Press, 1984).

22 Hamill, 'Labour Relations Decision-making'.

23 P. Enderwick, 'The Labour Utilization Practices of Multinationals and Obstacles to Multinational Collective Bargaining', *Journal of Industrial Relations,* Vol. 26, No. 3 (1984), pp. 354–64.

24 P.M. Rosenzweig and N. Nohria, 'Influences on Human Resource Management Practices in Multinational Corporations', *Journal of International Business Studies,* Vol. 25, No. 2 (1994), pp. 229–51.

25 Hamill, 'Labour Relations Decision-making'.

26 Also see Bean, *Comparative Industrial Relations.*

27 P. Marginson and K. Sisson, 'The Structure of Transnational Capital in Europe: The Emerging Euro-Company and its Implications for Industrial Relations', in R. Hyman and A. Ferner (eds), *New Frontiers in European Industrial Relations* (Oxford: Blackwell, 1994); K. Williams and M. Geppert, 'The German Model of Employee Relations on Trial: Negotiated and Unilaterally Imposed Change in Multi-national Companies', *Industrial Relations Journal,* Vol. 37, No. 1 (2006), pp. 48–63.

28 For an interesting discussion of the importance of understanding ideology, see G.C. Lodge, 'Ideological Implications of Changes in Human Resource Management', in D.R.E. Walton and P.R. Lawrence, *HRM Trends and Challenges* (Boston, MA: Harvard Business School Press, 1985).

29 T.A. Kochan, R.B. McKersie and P. Cappelli, 'Strategic Choice and Industrial Relations Theory', *Industrial Relations,* Vol. 23, No. 1 (1984), pp. 16–39.

30 See V. Frazee, 'Trade Union Membership is Declining Globally', *Workforce,* Vol. 3, No. 2 (1998), p. 8; *World Labour Report 1997–98: Industrial Relations, Democracy and Social Stability* (Geneva: ILO, 1997); W. Groot and A. van den Berg, 'Why Union Density has Declined', *European Journal of Political Economy,* Vol. 10, No. 4 (1994), pp. 749–763.

31 See Bean, *Comparative Industrial Relations;* Poole, *Industrial Relations;* and J. Visser, 'Trade Unionism in Western Europe: Present Situation and Prospects', *Labour and Society,* Vol. 13, No. 2 (1988), pp. 125–82.

32 J. Hamill, 'Multinational Corporations and Industrial Relations in the UK', *Employee Relations,* Vol. 6, No. 5 (1984), pp. 12–16.

33 Hamill, 'Labour Relations Decision-making', p. 34.

34 This section is based in part on Chapter 5, 'The Impact of Organized Labour', in Prahalad and Doz, *The Multinational Mission.*

35 For example, the decision by Hoover to shift some of its production from France to Scotland in the early 1990s appeared to be influenced by the ease with which the employer could implement layoffs. See D. Goodhart, 'Ground Rules for the Firing Squad', *Financial Times,* Feb. 15 (1993) p. 8.

36   Prahalad and Doz, *The Multinational Mission.*

37   *Ibid.*, p. 102.

38   M. Allen, 'Worldly Wisdom', *New Statesman and Society,* Vol. 6 (1993), pp. xii.

39   Kennedy, *European Labour Relations.*

40   Bean, *Comparative Industrial Relations,* p. 191.

41   *Ibid.*

42   Marginson, Armstrong, Edwards and Purcell, 'Extending Beyond Borders'.

43   B. Mahnkopf and E. Altvater, 'Transmission Belts of Transnational Competition? Trade Unions and Collective Bargaining in the Context of European Integration', *European Journal of Industrial Relations,* Vol. 1, No. 1 (1995), pp. 101–17.

44   R. Vernon, *Storm over the Multinationals: The Real Issues* (Cambridge, MA: Harvard University Press, 1977).

45   P. Auer, G. Besse and D. Meda (eds), *Offshoring and the Internationalization of Employment: A Challenge for a Fair Globalization?* (Geneva: International Labour Organization, 2006).

46   W. Cooke, 'Exercising Power in a Prisoner's Dilemma: Transnational Collective Bargaining in an Era of Corporate Globalization?', *Industrial Relations Journal,* Vol. 36, No. 4 (2005), pp. 283–302.

47   J. Pyndt and T. Pedersen, *Managing Global Offshoring Strategies* (Copenhagen: Copenhagen Business School Press, 2006).

48   M. Martinez Lucio and S. Weston, 'Trade Unions and Networking in the Context of Change: Evaluating the Outcomes of Decentralization in Industrial Relations', *Economic and Industrial Democracy,* Vol. 16 (1995), p. 244.

49   For a detailed analysis of ITSs, see R. Neuhaus, *International Trade Secretariats: Objectives, Organization, Activities,* 2nd edn (Bonn: Friedrich-EbertStiftung, 1982). For an overview of international Labour politics and organizations, see T. Boswell and D. Stevis, 'Globalisation and International Labour Organizing: A World-System Perspective', *Work and Occupations,* Vol. 24, No. 3 (1997), pp. 288–308.

50   N. Willatt, *Multinational Unions* (London: Financial Times, 1974).

51   H.R. Northrup, 'Why Multinational Bargaining Neither Exists Nor Is Desirable', *Labour Law Journal,* Vol. 29, No. 6 (1978), pp. 330–42. Also see J. Gallagher, 'Solidarity Forever', *New Statesman & Society* (1997), p. 10.

52   See Kennedy, *European Labour Relations*; and R.B. Helfgott, 'American Unions and Multinational Enterprises: A Case of Misplaced Emphasis', *Columbia Journal of World Business,* Vol. 18, No. 2 (1983), pp. 81–6.

53   Up to 1993 there was a specialized UN agency known as the United Nations Centre on Transnational Corporations (UNCTC), which had published a number of reports on MNEs (see for example, *Transborder Data Flows: Transnational Corporations and Remote-sensing Data* (New York: UNCTC, 1984); and *Transnational Corporations and International Trade: Selected Issues* (New York: UNCTC, 1985). Since 1993, the responsibilities of the UNCTC have been assigned to UNCTAD. For further information, see the UNCTAD website at www.unicc.org/unctad/en/aboutorg/inbrief.htm. See Boswell and Stevis, 'Globalisation and International Labour Organizing', for more information on these international organizations.

54   See B. Leonard, 'An Interview with Anthony Freeman of the ILO', *HRMagazine,* Vol. 42, No. 8 (August 1997), pp. 104–9. For coverage of the ongoing debate on international Labour standards and globalization, see E. Lee, 'Globalisation and Labour Standards: A Review of Issues', *Management International Review,* Vol. 136, No. 2 (1997), pp. 173–89; and R.N. Block, K. Roberts, C. Ozeki and M.J. Roomkin, 'Models of International Labour Standards', *Industrial Relations,* Vol. 40, No. 2 (April 2001), pp. 258–86.

55   For a detailed description and analysis of the OECD Guidelines for Multinational Enterprises, see D.C. Campbell and R.L. Rowan, *Multinational Enterprises and the OECD Industrial Relations Guidelines,* Industrial Research Unit (Philadelphia, PA: The Wharton School, University of Pennsylvania, 1983); and R. Blanpain, *The OECD Guidelines for Multinational Enterprises and Labour Relations, 1982–1984: Experiences and Review* (Deventer, The Netherlands: Kluwer, 1985).

56   Campbell and Rowan, *Multinational Enterprises and OECD.*

57   J. Rojot, 'The 1984 Revision of the OECD Guidelines for Multinational Enterprises', *British Journal of Industrial Relations,* Vol. 23, No. 3 (1985), pp. 379–97.

58   For a detailed account of this case see R. Blanpain, *The Badger Case and the OECD Guidelines for Multinational Enterprises* (Deventer, The Netherlands: Kluwer, 1977).

59   R. Blanpain, *The OECD Guidelines for Multinational Enterprises and Labour Relations, 1976–1979: Experience and Review* (Deventer, The Netherlands: Kluwer, 1979).

60 H.C. Jain, 'Disinvestment and the Multinational Employer: A Case History from Belgium', *Personnel Journal,* Vol. 59, No. 3 (1980), pp. 201–5.

61 Campbell and Rowan, *Multinational Enterprises and OECD.*

62 B. Liebhaberg, *Industrial Relations and Multinational Corporations in Europe* (London: Cower, 1980), p. 85.

63 'OECD Guidelines to Multinational Enterprises: 2005 Annual Meeting of the National Contact Points', Report by the Chair, Meeting Held in June 2005, p. 3, www.oecd.org/investment. See also the special issue of *Transnational Corporations Journal,* Vol. 14, No. 3 (2005) on Voluntary Codes of Conduct for Multinational Corporations: Promises and Challenges.

64 C.S. Jensen, J.S. Madsen and J. Due, 'A Role for a Pan-European Trade Union Movement? Possibilities in European IR-regulation', *Industrial Relations Journal,* Vol. 26, No. 1 (1995), pp. 4–18; Mahnkopf and Altvater, 'Transmission Belts of Transnational Competition?'.

65 G.W. Latta and J.R. Bellace, 'Making the Corporation Transparent: Prelude to Multinational Bargaining', *Columbia Journal of World Business,* Vol. 18, No. 2 (1983), pp. 73–80; J.T. Addison and W.S. Siebert, 'Recent Developments in Social Policy in the New European Union', *Industrial and Labour Relations Review,* Vol. 48, No. 1 (1994), pp. 5–27; and N. Donnelly and C. Rees, *Industrial Relations and Multinational Companies in the European Community: The Work of the International Companies Network,* Warwick Papers in Industrial Relations no. 54 (Warwick: Warwick Business School, 1995).

66 See, for example, P. Teague, 'EC Social Policy and European Human Resource Management', in C. Brewster and A. Hegewisch (eds), *Policy and Practice in European Human Resource Management* (London: Routledge, 1994); and L. Ulman, B. Eichengreen and W.T. Dickens (eds), *Labour and an Integrated Europe* (Washington, DC: The Brookings Institution, 1993).

67 Commission of the European Communities, *Community Charter of the Fundamental Social Rights of Workers* (Luxembourg: Office for Official Publications of the European Communities, 1990).

68 See, for example, J. Lodge, 'Social Europe: Fostering a People's Europe?', in ed. J. Lodge (ed.), *European Community and the Challenge of the Future* (London: Pinter, 1989); J. Addison and S. Siebert, 'The Social Charter of the European Community: Evolution and Controversies', *Industrial and Labour Relations Review,* Vol. 44, No. 4 (1991), pp. 597–625; and M. Hall, 'Industrial Relations and the Social Dimension of European Integration: Before and After Maastricht', in R. Hyman and A. Ferner (eds), *New Frontiers in European Industrial Relations* (Oxford: Blackwell, 1994).

69 J. Pickard, 'Maastricht Deal Worries the Multinationals', *PM Plus,* January (1992), p. 4; B. Fitzpatrick, 'Community Social Law after Maastricht', *Industrial Law Journal,* Vol. 21, No. 3 (1992), pp. 199–213; and B. Bercusson and J.J. Van Dijk, 'The Implementation of the Protocol and Agreement on Social Policy of the Treaty on European Union', *The International Journal of Comparative Labour Law and Industrial Relations,* Vol. 11, No.1 (1995), pp. 3–30.

70 The Treaty of Amsterdam revised the Treaties on which the European Union was founded. For further information see http://europa.eu.int/abc/obj/amst/en/index.htm and http://www.europarl.eu.int/basicdoc/en/default.htm.

71 See http://europa.eu.int/comm/dgs/employment_social/index_en.htm.

72 For a detailed analysis of the Vredeling Directive, see D. Van Den Bulcke, 'Decision Making in Multinational Enterprises and the Information and Consultation of Employees: The Proposed Vredeling Directive of the EC Commission', *International Studies of Management and Organization,* Vol. 14, No. 1 (1984), pp. 36–60.

73 See M. Gold and M. Hall, 'Statutory European Works Councils: The Final Countdown?', *Industrial Relations Journal,* Vol. 25, No. 3 (1994), pp. 177–86; and Marginson, 'European Integration and Transnational Management–Union Relations in the Enterprise'.

74 Addison and Siebert, 'Recent Developments in Social Policy'; P. Knutsen, 'Corporatist Tendencies in the Euro-Polity: the EU Directive of 22 September 1994, on European Works Councils', *Economic and Industrial Democracy,* Vol. 18, No. 2 (1997), pp. 289–323.

75 Martinez Lucio and Weston, 'Trade Unions and Networking in the Context of Change'.

76 F. Michon, 'The "European Social Community": A Common Model and Its National Variations? Segmentation Effects, Societal Effects', *Labour and Society,* Vol. 15, No. 2 (1990) pp. 215–36. Also see E. Szyszczak, 'Future Directions in European Union Social Policy Law', *Industrial Law Journal,* Vol. 24, No. 1 (1995), pp. 19–32.

77 M. Gilman and P. Marginson, 'Negotiating European Works Councils: Contours of Constrained Choice', *Industrial Relations Journal,* Vol. 33, No. 1 (2002), pp. 36–51.

78 W. Nicoll and T.C. Salmon, *Understanding the European Community* (Hertfordshire: Philip Allan, 1990) p. 191.

79 C.L. Erickson and S. Kuruvilla, 'Labour Costs and the Social Dumping Debate in the European Union', *Industrial and Labour Relations Review,* Vol. 48, No. 1 (1994), pp. 28–47.

80 For further reading see M. Muller-Camen, P. Almond, P. Gunnigle, J. Quintanilla and A. Tempel, 'Between Home and Host Country: Multinationals and Employment Relations in Europe', *Industrial Relations Journal,* Vol. 32, No. 5 (2001), pp. 435–48.

81 M. Ingham, H. Ingham, H. Bicak and M. Altinay, 'The Impact of (More) Enlargement on the European Employment Strategy', *Industrial Relations Journal,* Vol. 36, No. 6 (2005), pp. 456–77. See also P. Marginson and G. Meardi, 'European Union Enlargement and the Foreign Direct Investment Channel of Industrial Relations Transfer', *Industrial Relations Journal,* Vol. 37, No. 2 (2006), pp. 92–110.

82 M. Zanko, 'Change and Diversity: HRM Issues and Trends in the Asia-Pacific Region', *Asia Pacific Journal of Human Resources,* Vol. 41, No. 1 (2003), pp. 75–87.

83 See H. Ramsey, 'Solidarity At Last? International Trade Unionism Approaching The Millenium', *Economic and Industrial Democracy,* Vol. 18, No. 4 (1997), pp. 503–37; and Jensen, Madsen and Due, 'A Role for a Pan-European Trade Union Movement?'.

84 Enderwick, 'The Labour Utilization Practices of Multinationals', p. 357.

85 See www.walmartmovie.com/ and www.walmartmovie.com/teaser_qhi.php.

86 G. Colvin, 'Don't Blame Wal-Mart: The Giant Retailer Isn't Evil – Just Caught Up in the Global Economy', *Fortune,* November 28 (2005), p. 41.

Performance management

Chapter Objectives

The aim of this chapter is to draw together the relevant literature on performance management in the international context as it relates to IHRM. The concentration is on the subsidiary context, reflecting the bias towards subsidiary management in the international business and performance management literature. The focus is on identifying those aspects that require a substantial modification of traditional performance management (especially appraisal criteria, the roles of various actors in the processes and processes themselves) that are imposed by international operations. We specifically address the following aspects:

● Multinational performance management at the global and local level: considering aspects such as non-comparable data, the volatility of the global environment, the effect of distance and level of subsidiary maturity.

● Performance management as part of a MNE's control system.

● Factors associated with expatriate performance, including compensation package, task and role, headquarters' support, host environment factors and cultural adjustment.

● Performance management of expatriates and non-expatriates, and for those on non-standard tasks and assignments such commuter and virtual.

● Issues related to the performance appraisal of international employees.

Introduction

The complexities of managing performance in a firm's various globally distributed facilities have received a great deal of professional and academic attention in the last decade. As presented in Chapters 2 and 3, diversity in productions and operations, geographical dispersal and varieties in modes of operations all combine to make performance measurement and the creation of performance management processes that are simultaneously locally relevant and globally comparable a major challenge for HRM practitioners.[1] Monitoring performance and ensuring conformity to agreed-upon standards are significant elements in the managerial control system of a multinational firm; and yet, as Cascio has stated, 'the terrain of global performance management systems is largely uncharted'.[2]

In this chapter, we differentiate between 'performance management' and 'performance appraisal'. *Performance management* is a process that enables the multinational to evaluate and continuously improve individual, subsidiary unit and corporate performance, against clearly defined, pre-set goals and targets. Figure 11-1 illustrates the major issues, actors and decision processes related to performance management in the international context. This model will allow us to investigate the complex interaction between local and global contexts for performance and the tasks of the actors, performance criteria, purposes for, and timing of performance management as these elements relate to individual and firm outcomes. It provides a convenient starting point for our exploration of the link between the multinational's internationalization strategies, its goals for individual units in terms of contribution to global profitability and the performance management of individual employees, whether PCN, TCN or HCN. The aspects of these relationships are critical as an individual's performance is appraised (or evaluated) according to expectations of appropriate outcomes and behavior that contribute to organizational goal attainment.

| **Figure 11-1** | Perspectives, issues, actions and consequences in MNE performance management |

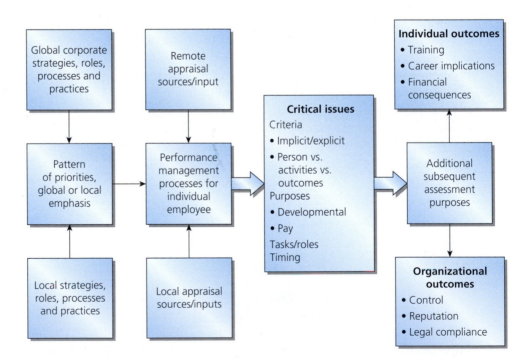

Source: Adapted from A. Engle and P. Dowling, 'State of Origin: Research in Global Performance Management: Progress or a Lost Horizon?', *Conference Proceeding of the VIIIth World Congress of the International Federation of Scholarly Associations of Management,* Berlin, September, 2006.

Multinational performance management

While its general strategic position may be international, multinational, global or transnational[3] (depending on, for instance, its size, industry and geographic dispersal), a multinational makes strategic choices based on economic and political imperatives. Within this context, as indicated in Figure 11-1, the MNE has specific expectations for each of its foreign subsidiaries, cooperative ventures and other forms of operation modes, in terms of market performance and contribution to total profits and competitiveness. When evaluating subsidiary performance against these expectations, however, it is important to recognize various constraints that may affect goal attainment. These include the following constraints outlined below.

Whole versus part

By its very nature, a multinational is a single entity that faces a global environment, which means that it simultaneously confronts differing national environments. Integration and control imperatives often place the multinational in the position where it decides that the good of the whole is more important than one subsidiary's short-term profitability. An example provided by Pucik,[4] is where a multinational establishes an operation in a particular market where its main global competitor has a dominant position. The objective of entering the market is to challenge the competitor's cash flow with aggressive pricing policies. Pucik explains that:

> The balance sheet of this particular subsidiary might be continually in the red, but this strategy, by tying up the competitor's resources, may allow substantially higher returns in another market. The difficulties in quantifying such a global strategy in terms of the usual return-on-investment objectives are obvious.

Another situation is where the multinational establishes a joint venture in a particular market in order to have a presence there, even though it has low expectations in the short term, and may provide minimum resources to the venture. Therefore, the consequences of such global decisions for subsidiary management must be taken into consideration for performance appraisal.

Non-comparable data

Frequently, the data obtained from subsidiaries may be neither interpretable nor reliable, as the following examples illustrate:[5]

> Sales in Brazil may be skyrocketing, but there are reports that the Brazilian government may impose tough new exchange controls within a year, thus making it impossible for the multinational to repatriate profits. Does this mean that the MNE is performing effectively? Is the subsidiary performing effectively?
>
> Sales in Peru may be booming, but headquarters management was unaware that under Peruvian accounting rules, sales on consignment are counted as firm sales. How should the headquarters accounting system handle these sales relative to sales from other subsidiaries, which do not consider sales on consignment as firm sales?

As Garland *et al.*[6] explain, physical measures of performance may be easier to interpret than in the above examples, but difficulties may still arise. For instance, notions of what constitutes adequate quality control checks can vary widely from one country to another, import tariffs can distort pricing schedules, or a dock strike in one country can unexpectedly delay supply of necessary components to a manufacturing plant in another country. Further, local labor laws may require full employment at plants that are producing at below capacity. These factors can make an objective appraisal of subsidiary performance problematic, and may complicate the appraisal of individual subsidiary managers.

Volatility of the global environment

The turbulence of the global environment requires that long-term goals be flexible in order to respond to potential market contingencies. According to Pucik,[7] an inflexible approach may mean that subsidiaries could be pursuing strategies that no longer fit the new environment. Consider, for example, the impact on international business of major events in the past two decades or so, such as: the collapse of communist rule in the late 1980s in Eastern Europe and the former Soviet Union; the adoption of the Euro (€) as the single currency by most of the European Union countries; Chinese market reforms; the Severe Acute Respiratory Syndrome (SARS) and bird flu epidemics; the spread of international terrorism; the Gulf Wars; rising oil prices; high-profile corporate collapses; and the adoption of international accounting standards (IAS).

Each of these events has had profound implications for the global and local strategies of multinationals. Because subsidiaries operate under such volatility and fluctuation, they must tailor long-term goals to the specific situation in a given market. Problems arise when subsidiary managers perceive that goals and deadlines set by a distant headquarters strategy team are unrealistic and inflexible, due to a failure to take into account local conditions that change as a result of a volatile environment. Obviously, involving regional and subsidiary managers in strategic planning assists in overcoming this perception.

Separation by time and distance

Judgements concerning the congruence between the multinational and local subsidiary activities are further complicated by the physical distances involved, time-zone differences, the frequency of contact between the corporate head-office staff and subsidiary management and the cost of the reporting system.[8] Developments in sophisticated worldwide communications systems, such as fax machines, video telephone conferences and email, do not fully substitute for 'face-to-face' contacts between subsidiary managers and corporate staff. In some areas, the telecommunications system may be so overloaded, or underdeveloped, that reliable telephone, fax services and Internet connections cannot be assumed. It is often necessary to meet personally with a manager to fully understand the problems that managers must deal with. For this reason, many multinational corporate managers spend a considerable amount of time traveling in order to meet expatriate and local managers in foreign locations. It is then possible for HR corporate staff, when designing performance management systems, to take account of country-specific factors.

Alternately, the growing use of Web-based platforms of human resource information systems that now include performance management modules may be seen as a response – by larger, more sophisticated and well-funded multinationals – to the separations of time, distance and culture experienced by multinational firms. These strategies may be driven by the complexity and inherent uncertainty of global performance and a sense that successfully competing in the global market-place will require increased efficiency of operations. And yet the potential of these technical systems to control and coordinate activities and actors within the firm may be limited by unspoken or ill-articulated roles, processes, practices, criteria and purposes.[9]

Variable levels of maturity

According to Pucik,[10] without the supporting infrastructure of the parent, market development in foreign subsidiaries is generally slower and more difficult to achieve than at home, where established brands can support new products and new business areas can be cross-subsidized by other divisions. As a result, more time may be needed to achieve results than is customary in a domestic market, and this fact ought to be recognized in the performance management process. Further, variations in customs and work practices between the parent country and the foreign subsidiary need to be considered. For example,

> One does not fire a Mexican manager because worker productivity is half the American average. In Mexico, that would mean that this manager is working at a level three or four times as high as the average Mexican industrial plant. Here we need relevant comparative data, not absolute numbers; our harassed Mexican manager has to live with Mexican constraints, not European or American ones, and these can be very different. The way we measure worker productivity is exactly the same, but the numbers come out differently because of that environmental difference.[11]

In summary, there are a number of significant constraints that must be taken into account when considering foreign subsidiary performance. Because performance measurement is primarily based on strategic factors, it affects the appraisal and success of the subsidiary's chief executive (or managing director) most directly.

Control and performance management

Although it is not often described as such, performance management is a part of a multinational's control system. You may recall from the discussion of control mechanisms in Chapter 2 that performance targets are a part of formal control. Through formal control mechanisms, and communication through the feedback and appraisal aspects, performance management also contributes to shaping corporate culture, both formally and informally,[12] thereby acting as an informal control mechanism as well as part of the bureaucratic control system. Employees are rewarded for adopting appropriate work behaviors and this in turn reinforces normative control. Figure 11-2 illustrates the performance–behavior–outcomes linkage. It is through formal and informal control mechanisms that the multinational achieves the consistency, coordination and compliance of desired behavior and outcomes to implement its global strategy. These behaviors and outcomes are expected at all levels and areas – at headquarters as well as in subsidiary operations.

In a sense, by adopting a performance management approach, MNEs are drawing on a number of human resource management activities to realize

Figure 11-2   MNE control and performance

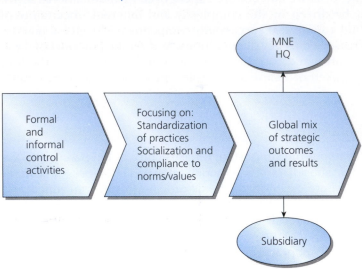

performance goals set during the performance appraisal process. Its proponents argue, somewhat convincingly, that effective performance management is beneficial to both the individual and the firm. As Tahvanianen [13] points out, strong goal setting and appraisal are key elements of an individual performance management system that also may include training and development, and performance-related pay.

Performance management of international employees

Having considered the broader context, we now turn our attention to individual performance management. Consistent with our general approach, we use the term 'expatriate' to cover PCNs, TCNs and those HCNs on assignment to headquarters. We also address performance management issues relating to those on non-standard and short-term assignments (such as commuter and virtual) and non-expatriates (international business travelers). Given the broad scope, and the fact that often issues are common to both expatriates and non-expatriates, we have decided to use the term 'international employees' when all these various groups are involved.

As discussed in Chapter 4, international assignments vary in terms of the duration and scope of physical relocation required. That is, from traditional expatriate assignments when expatriates and, usually, their family members relocate; to virtual assignments, where no physical relocation by employees or their families is required. When attempting to manage the performance of staff working across the multinational, it is essential to consider all these variables in relation to the nature of the international assignment. The following sections also identify some performance management issues associated with expatriate and non-expatriate international assignments.

Expatriate performance management

As noted in Chapters 4 and 5, expatriation remains a key dimension of multinational enterprise and performance. When attempting to determine expatriate performance, it is important to consider the impact of the following variables and their interrelationship:

● The compensation package.

● The task – the assignment task variables and role of the expatriate.

● Headquarters' support.

● The environment in which performance occurs – the subsidiary or foreign facility.

● Cultural adjustment – of the individual and the accompanying family members.

Figure 11-3 depicts these variables and forms the basis upon which we will explore both the nature of the international assignment, how performance is managed, the criteria for assessment and the other elements that comprise an effective performance management system.

Compensation package.   We examined the issues surrounding compensation in Chapter 7. However, it is essential that we recognize the importance of remuneration and reward in the performance equation. Perceived financial benefits, along with the career progression potential associated with an overseas assignment, are often important motives for accepting the posting. If these expectations are not realized during the assignment, the level of motivation and commitment is likely to decrease, thus affecting performance.

Task.   As outlined earlier, expatriates are assigned to foreign operations to fulfil specific tasks. Hays[14] identified four such tasks:

● The *chief executive officer,* or subsidiary manager, who oversees and directs the entire foreign operation.

● The *structure reproducer* carries the assignment of building or reproducing in a foreign subsidiary a structure similar to that which he or she knows from another part of the company. He or she could be building a marketing

---

Variables affecting expatriate performance   **Figure 11-3**

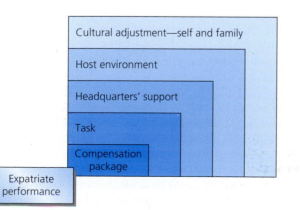

framework, implementing an accounting and financial reporting system, or establishing a production plant, for example.

- The *troubleshooter* is the individual who is sent to a foreign subsidiary to analyze and solve a particular operational problem.

- The *operative* is the individual whose assignment is to perform functional job tasks in an existing operational structure, in generally lower level, supervisory positions.

Interesting presentations on executive performance management have recently been provided as part of a wider discussion of 'corporate governance'. Issues of performance criteria (an over-reliance on 'shareholder value' models of executive performance) and the evolving roles, responsibilities and institutional safeguards to assure a complete, accurate and unbiased assessment of top level managers are widely cited for this critical task group.[15]

In a recent review of cross-cultural performance management systems, Caligiuri identifies four basic types of international assignments: 'technical assignments' – short-term knowledge transference activities, said to make up 5 to 10 per cent of expatriate assignments; 'developmental assignments' – focusing on in-country performance and the acquisition of local or regional understanding by the assignee, said to make up 5 to 10 per cent of assignments; 'strategic assignments' – high-profile activities that focus on developing a balanced global perspective, said to make up 10 to 15 per cent of assignments; and 'functional assignments' – described as more enduring assignments with local employees that involve the two-way transfer of existing processes and practices, said to make up between 55 and 80 per cent of assignments.[16] Accurately assessing performance in the tasks inherent in technical and functional assignments may well involve a limited number of sources and focus on more concrete output criteria (projects completed, contracts signed, etc.). Assessing progress in developmental and strategic assignments, given their more complex, subjective tasks, are likely to involve a wider variety of local and global participants and perspectives.[17]

Task variables are generally considered to be more under a multinational's control than environmental factors. Because of this relative control, task variables can be better assessed and more easily changed, depending, of course, on the level of position, and the nature of the task assignment. Along with the specifics of the task, the multinational, like any other organization, determines the role that accompanies each task position. A role is the organized set of behaviors that are assigned to a particular position. Although an individual may affect how a role is interpreted and performed, the role itself is predetermined.[18] For the expatriate (role recipient), the parent company (role sender) predetermines his or her role in the foreign assignment, and role expectations may be clearly communicated to the expatriate before departure. Black and Porter[19] found that American expatriates working in Hong Kong exhibited similar managerial behavior to those remaining in the US. In their discussion of this finding, these authors suggest that the US multinationals involved communicated role expectations by omitting to provide cross-cultural training before departure. In the absence of incentives to modify their role behavior when abroad, it is not surprising that the expatriates concerned performed as they did. This study reminds us that the transmission of expatriate role conception is culturally bound. As Torbiörn[20] explains:

> The content of the managerial role, as perceived by both the individual manager and the parent company, is affected by organizational norms, in terms of parent-company expectations of the manager, and by the set of

cultural norms that the manager holds in relation to other cultural and organizational norms that may be represented by other role senders. Organizational and cultural norms thus interactively determine the role content of the manager.

The difficulty this presents for the expatriate manager is that the role is defined in one country, but performed in another. That is, the cultural norms regarding the set of behaviors that define 'a manager in the US' may not be the same as those considered appropriate for a manager's role in Indonesia.

Communication of role conception from the multinational to the expatriate is indicated by the straight arrows in Figures 11-4 and 11-5. Role conception is also communicated to the role recipient by host-country stakeholders (e.g., subsidiary employees, host-government officials, customers, suppliers, etc.) as shown by the dashed arrows. This, however, crosses a cultural boundary. Role behavior provides the feedback loop, again at two levels: the parent and the host-country stakeholders. Trying to perform to differing expectations may cause role conflict. If the PCN

| PCN role conception | **Figure 11-4** |

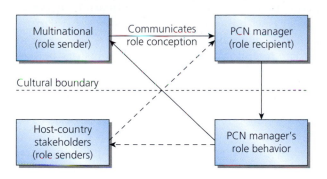

Source: Adapted from I. Torbiörn, 'The Structure of Managerial Roles in Cross-cultural Settings', *International Studies of Management & Organization,* Vol. 15, No. 1 (1985), p. 60.

| TCN role conception | **Figure 11-5** |

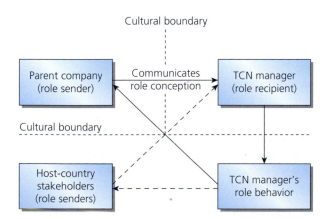

Source: Adapted from I. Torbiörn, 'The Structure of Managerial Roles in Cross-cultural Settings', *International Studies of Management & Organization,* Vol. 15, No. 1 (1985), p. 60.

manager adapts his role behavior according to the role conception communicated in the host environment, it may conflict with that predetermined at headquarters. Janssens'[21] study of expatriate performance indicated that role conflict is likely to result in situations where the international manager has an understanding of the host-country culture and realizes that the use of headquarters' procedures or actions may lead to ineffective management. She postulates that the higher the degree of intercultural interaction, the more problems the expatriate has with role conflict.

From the perspective of headquarters, commitment to the parent is perceived as important, given the part that the PCN plays in transferring know-how and 'the company way of doing things' into the subsidiary. This helps to explain the preference for using headquarters' standards in expatriate performance appraisal as a control mechanism.[22] If the PCN is perceived to identify too closely with host-subsidiary concerns, he or she may be recalled (the term 'going native' has, in the past, often been used to describe this perception). Some MNEs will restrict the length of stay to no more than three years to contain the possibility of PCN identification with local concerns. Because of the importance given to the parent as role sender in performance appraisal, a PCN may elect to ignore role communication sent from the host-country stakeholders if they consider that performance appraisal is determined by how role behavior conforms to headquarters' expectation. After all, the expatriate's career is with the parent, not the host subsidiary.

Some empirical support for such a view comes from work by Gregersen and Black[23] in their study of US expatriate retention and dual commitments (to the parent and the local organizations). They found, at the correlational level, commitment to the parent and to the local operation were both positively related to intent to stay. However, 'regression analysis indicated that when controlling for certain demographic and attitudinal variables, commitment to the parent company appears to be slightly more relevant to expatriates' intention to stay'. Role conflict was found to affect commitment to the parent company, but was unrelated to commitment to the host company. Another intervening variable may be that of role autonomy. For example, job discretion emerged as an important aspect from a survey of 115 US expatriates working in various countries by Birdseye and Hill.[24] They found that: 'Foreign work methods may be more structured than their American counterparts (perhaps more procedures and protocols) and that individuals have less discretion in how they approach tasks and problems.' These authors conclude that individuals are likely to blame this lack of discretion on the organization, the job and the location – in that order. A similar finding emerged from a study of US domestic and international relocation by Feldman and Tompson.[25] The degree of change in job duties was positively related to adjustment, while the degree of change in the organization was negatively related to adjustment. Thus, role conflict and role autonomy appear to be important elements in job satisfaction and task performance.

Role clarity emerged as an important variable in a meta-analysis of expatriate adjustment and performance. Integrating studies on expatriate adjustment, the authors[26] found that:

> role clarity and work adjustment was the second largest effect . . . suggesting that the uncertainty regarding objectives, goals, and role requirements is the strongest stressor in expatriates' overseas work environments. In addition, role clarity also has a moderate potential to spill over and minimize nonwork difficulties.

Role expectations are likely to be more complex for the TCN than the PCN, as the role is defined by and performed in two different countries. That is, role conception crosses two cultural boundaries, as shown in Figure 11-5. Parent and host-country role senders may have differing expectations of role behavior that, in turn, are different to the accepted managerial behavior defined by the prevailing norms in the TCN's own country. For example, a US manager working for a Dutch multinational posted as a TCN in Indonesia may face added difficulties. The American's role behavior may be deemed inappropriate by both the parent (Dutch multinational) and the host nationals (Indonesians). As Torbiörn[27] points out:

> The task of the PCN manager could be described as one of realizing the expectations of a psychologically close, but physically distant stakeholder [parent] in an environment containing other role senders [host-country stakeholders] who are psychologically distant, but physically close . . . The TCN manager must try to meet the expectations of role senders who are all psychologically distant in a context that is also psychologically distant.

However, as you may recall from our discussion of the rationale for using TCNs, often the country of assignment is perceived by headquarters as culturally close and this may be an important factor which influences the decision to use a TCN (e.g., a German multinational decides to transfer a Canadian into the USA rather than a German). As there are very few studies that specifically examine TCN performance management issues,[28] we can only assume that many of the aspects relating to PCNs discussed above will apply to the TCN situation. An American manager working in Indonesia, for instance, whether as a PCN or TCN, may encounter lack of job discretion – with perhaps the same effect in terms of performance – depending on the strength of other intervening variables. For example, differing role senders may exacerbate the situation through conflicting role expectations.

The preceding discussion demonstrates the importance of considering the role that accompanies each task position. Given that task performance is a core component of expatriate appraisal, it is also necessary to recognize that it does not occur in isolation. Many individuals and firms rank job ability as the primary ingredient relating to their expected probability of success in the international assignment, as discussed in Chapter 5. Certain types of tasks, however, require significantly more interaction with host-country stakeholders. Thus, the task variables should not be evaluated in isolation from the subsidiary environment context.

Another factor relating to task variables that warrants consideration is the similarity of the job the individual is assigned abroad to the job that they held domestically. Some types of tasks require an individual to operate within a given structure, while other tasks demand the creation of the structure. Individuals vary greatly in their ability to conceive and implement a system and their tolerance for lack of structure and ambiguity. Some multinationals have experienced failure abroad because they assumed that an individual could be effective in setting up a structure, such as a marketing system, based on evidence of good performance within the existing marketing structure in the domestic corporation.[29]

Headquarters' support.   The expatriate assignment differs from a domestic relocation as it involves the transfer of the individual and accompanying family members into a foreign environment, outside their normal cultural comfort zones. The individual's primary motivation for accepting the assignment may be career or financially orientated, but this is often mixed with a genuine feeling of loyalty and commitment to the sending organization. As mentioned previously, the process of adjustment to the foreign location typically produces, to varying degrees, a range of emotional and psychological reactions to unfamiliar situations encountered over the period of the stay in the host country. The level of headquarters' support provided to the individual and the family is an important performance variable.

Host environment.   The environment has an impact on any job, but it becomes of primary importance with regard to expatriate management. According to Gregersen *et al.*,[30] the international context – with its differing societal, legal, economic, technical and physical demands – can be a major determinant of expatriate performance. Consequently, expatriate performance should be placed within its international as well as its organizational context. Therefore, the five major constraints identified above in terms of multinational strategy and goal setting for the subsidiary are important considerations for expatriate performance management.

The type of operation to which the expatriate is assigned is important. For instance, it may be relatively easier to perform in a wholly owned subsidiary than in a joint venture with a state-owned enterprise in China. Conflicting goals between the parent companies are a common problem within international joint ventures and can make the expatriate's job more difficult. An expatriate IJV manager may have difficulty trying to serve two masters and experience a high level of uncertainty regarding the effect of differing goal expectations for the IJV upon their performance appraisal. Similarly, the stage of the international business will influence the success of the expatriate. An expatriate overseeing the establishment of a new facility in a foreign country, especially in a developing or emerging market, will face different challenges and constraints to one who is posted into a mature operation.

Cultural adjustment.   The process of cultural adjustment may be a critical determinant of expatriate job performance. Indeed, much of the literature reviewed in our discussion of the cause of expatriate 'failure' covers the process of adjustment. It is likely that expatriates and their families will have some difficulty adjusting to a new environment, and this will impact on the manager's work performance. The dilemma is that adjustment to a foreign culture is multifaceted, and individuals vary in terms of their reaction and coping behaviors. Determining the relevance of adjustment to the new environment when assessing expatriate work performance may be problematical.

The five variables – compensation package, task, headquarters' support, host environment and cultural adjustment – reviewed above, and shown in Figure 11-3, are not mutually exclusive, but interact in a way that has significant implications for the appraisal of international employees' performance. Designers and users of performance management systems need to be conscious of, and responsive to, the impact of these variables.

A cross-cultural context for performance management

As noted in Figure 11-1, corporate and local strategies and role expectations create much of the potential for complexity and conflict in the definitions underlying criteria, processes and standards that make up performance management. Regional and national institutional, regulatory and historical contexts can impact the character of the criteria selected, task definitions, the timing and even the purposes of performance management. We present three European examples of the relationship between national context and firm level practices. Nordic performance management (particularly Danish, Finnish and Swedish firms) have been described as decentralized, based on a broad range of hard and soft criteria (the 'balanced scorecard'), and strategically linked to identify and support changes in operational-level activities.[31]

In France, legal and cultural factors combine to create a performance management system characterized by administrators with a high level of legal expertise – even though France's labor laws allow some flexibility in assessing performance, within a merit-based, and non-discriminatory framework. It is seen as a system linked to motivation and developing intellectual capital via coaching and competency-based assessments, with tasks often facilitated by the acceptance of advanced forms of technology. Centralization in processes, implicit or non-transparent procedures, and a propensity to have more or less favorable impressions of individuals based on the prestige of their previous university-corporate-governmental experiences, and a strong link between assessment and hierarchical remuneration may be seen to result from widely held cultural norms and values within certain segments of French society.[32] As with any national assessment, care must be taken not to overgeneralize. Practices in France vary by size of the firm – with larger firms being more open to a wider variety of performance management practices and criteria than smaller firms – as well as by industry, level of internationalization and occupational level of employee.[33]

By contrast, and with the same caveats against overgeneralization, performance management in Germany must adjust to a much more precisely delineated set of legal and institutional factors. A strong tradition of collective bargaining – be it on the plant, firm or industry level – plant level codetermination and a centuries-old tradition of vocational training all contribute to performance management systems characterized by a high level of worker input via works councils, consensus building processes and activities, a long-term career focus, valuing flexibility in task capability to enhance long-term job security and a high value placed on specialized technical knowledge.[34]

Processes tend to be more consensual, explicit, ongoing and informal in a day-to-day setting, yet roles, standards, criteria, purposes, schedules and consequences are explicitly formalized and regulated via codetermination. Performance-based pay, as a consequence or outcome of the performance management system has been much slower to gain widespread acceptance amongst German firms. This may be to the use of short-term performance criteria to trigger British and US models of performance-based pay. German firms tend to focus on linking performance management results to drive long-term training and development activities.[35]

Performance management of non-expatriates

In Chapter 4, non-expatriates (i.e. the international business traveler, or 'frequent flyer') were described as employees whose work involved international travel but who are not considered international assignees because they do not relocate to another country. Performance management issues may also impact upon the performance of another group: commuters. This is a form of non-standard assignment outlined in Chapter 4 where the person does not completely relocate but commutes between their home country and their office in another country. For instance, an executive who considers 'home' to be a suburb of London, but who, from Monday morning to Friday night, lives and works in Germany while the family remains in London.[36] In Chapter 4, we also discussed the trend towards the use of virtual assignments to overcome staff immobility. Instead of moving into the host environment, the person manages the international position from the home country using a combination of regular communication link-ups and frequent trips to the foreign location.

As yet, little is really known about the implications of such international business travel, whether as part of a non-standard assignment, or as a component of a specific job, on individual performance. However, it is possible to suggest some performance management challenges:

● How to determine performance criteria and goals related to the effective conduct of non-standard assignments, especially virtual assignees. As indicated in Figure 11-1, agreement on performance criteria is an important component of the performance management process. This requires the link between each employee's performance and the achievement of the multinational's strategic goals and objectives to be clearly established and understood. However, as the role conceptions in Figures 11-4 and 11-5 above show, shared conceptions of roles and expectations are complicated by the numbers of cultures and organizational contexts involved. With virtual assignees, monitoring and evaluating a physically and geographically distant group of employees is problematical. It is 'management by remote control'. In addition, the virtual assignee may be faced with dual goals – that of the domestic-located job, and the virtual work group. Therefore, the perennial challenge of effectively communicating the strategic links between the assignee's performance and organizational strategy is likely to be magnified.[37]

● An understanding of the criteria for performance is generally advocated as a highly participative process between supervisor and employee.[38] As with the traditional expatriate assignment, work conducted through non-standard assignments and international travel still is conducted across cultural and national boundaries, and thereby subject to cultural differences in norms about acceptable or preferred levels of participation.

● Isolating the international dimensions of job performance might not be as straightforward as in traditional expatriate assignments. It may depend on the level of difficulty inherent in the performance criteria set and how individual performance levels are determined.

● Outstanding performance, under-performance or failure in non-expatriate and non-standard assignments will challenge the performance appraisal process.

● As we shall explore in a later section of this chapter, regular feedback on progress towards those performance goals is most usually provided through the performance appraisal activity. Performance feedback for assignees will only be relevant if it reflects the international contexts in which they are performed.[39] Those enduring concerns of who conducts performance appraisals, how and based on what performance data, may be intensified when it involves increasing numbers of others outside head office with whom the assignee is working.

● One key function of performance appraisal feedback is that it provides opportunities to improve performance by identifying performance gaps that might be eliminated with training and development. Cross-cultural awareness and competence training will still be relevant for non-expatriates. However, a detailed analysis of other pre-departure and ongoing training that might be required for non-expatriate assignments is yet to be conducted.

- Employee expectations about rewards for performance and as elements of their working conditions, together with motivation are important aspects of individual performance. In multinationals, the management of links between performance and rewards is already complex, due to the specialized local knowledge required across multiple employment and legal environments. The challenges for IHRM are to determine what to reward when dealing with non-expatriate assignments, and the way compensation for each type of international assignment fits with global compensation strategy.

- The impact of non-standard assignments on host-country national co-workers should also be considered – particularly in terms of the impact on these staff of international business travelers and commuters who 'drop in, drop out'.

Performance appraisal of international employees

Now that we have an understanding of the variables likely to influence performance, including the nature of the international assignment being performed, we can discuss the criteria by which performance is to be appraised (or evaluated – the terms are used interchangeably in the relevant literature). We note that the focus on expatriate management is also reflected in the literature about the performance appraisal of international staff, and much of the following discussion reflects that emphasis. However, aspects of expatriate performance appraisal are also relevant to the appraisal of non-expatriates and these, along with the aspects that distinguish between the two categories of international staff, will be highlighted.

As shown in Figure 11-1, individual performance management involves a set of decisions on the dimensions and level of performance criteria, task and role definitions, and the timing of the formal and informal aspects of the appraisal. Traditionally, it comprises a formal process of goal setting, performance appraisal and feedback. Data from this process is often used to determine pay and promotion, and training and development requirements. Company goals influence the individual's salient task set, against which job goals and standards are established and measured. There are differences in the way this process is handled within companies. For example, in Germany and Sweden it is common for employees to have input into job goal setting, whereas in other countries such as the USA, job goals tend to be assigned.[40] In addition, the type and length of assignment appears to influence how performance management is handled. For example, a study of Finnish firms revealed that those on short-term assignments were treated the same as any other employee in the company, and there was more flexibility in the timing of the performance review for those assigned to projects.[41]

Performance criteria

The global firm's ability to measure an employee's individual contribution to performance and to assess the aggregate contribution of human capital to strategic progress is a complex and timely topic in organizational studies.[42] Goals tend to be translated into performance appraisal criteria so specificity and measurability issues are important aspects, and we need to recognize that hard, soft and contextual goals are often used as the basis for performance criteria. *Hard goals* are objective, quantifiable and can be directly measured – such as return-on-investment (ROI), market share, etc.

Soft goals tend to be relationship or trait-based, such as leadership style or interpersonal skills. *Contextual goals* attempt to take into consideration factors that result from the situation in which performance occurs. For example, MNEs commonly use arbitrary transfer pricing and other financial tools for transactions between subsidiaries to minimize foreign-exchange risk exposure and tax expenditures. Another consideration is that all financial figures are generally subject to the problem of currency conversion, including sales and cash positions. Further complications arise because host governments can place restrictions on repatriation of profits and currency conversion. The nature of the international monetary system and local accounting differences may preclude an accurate measurement of results. The dilemma this poses is that the use of transfer pricing and other financial tools is necessary because of the complexity of the international environment. Multinationals cannot allow subsidiaries to become autonomous in financial management terms, and place controls on subsidiary managers. Thus, the financial results recorded for any particular subsidiary do not always reflect accurately its contribution to the achievements of the corporation as a whole. Therefore, such results should not be used as a primary input in performance appraisal.[43] For this reason, a performance management approach is now advocated, rather than traditional performance appraisal, as it allows clarification of goals and expectations of performance against those goals.

Janssens[44] suggests that performance appraisal of subsidiary managers against hard criteria is often supplemented by frequent visits by headquarter staff, and meetings with executives from the parent company. Soft criteria can be used to complement hard goals, and take into account areas that are difficult to quantify, such as leadership skills, but their appraisal is somewhat subjective and, in the context of both expatriate and non-expatriate assignments, more complicated due to cultural exchanges and clashes. However, relying on hard criteria such as financial data to evaluate how well a manager operates a foreign subsidiary does not consider the way results are obtained and the behaviors used to obtain these results.[45] Concern with questionable ethical practices led to the enactment of the US Foreign Corrupt Practices Act (FCPA), which may prompt an increased use of behavioral as well as results data to appraise the performance of managers in foreign subsidiaries.[46] (We discuss the FCPA in more detail in Chapter 12.) However, an appraisal system that uses hard, soft and contextual criteria builds upon the strengths of each while minimizing their disadvantages.[47] Using multiple criteria wherever possible is therefore recommended in the relevant literature. In addition, job analysis must, as Harvey[48] suggests, generate criteria that adequately capture the nature of international work as opposed to the domestic context, in order to provide valid appraisal information.

Who conducts the performance appraisal

Another issue is who conducts the performance appraisal. Typically, employees are appraised by their immediate superiors, and this can pose problems for subsidiary chief executive officers (or managers). They work in countries geographically distant, yet are evaluated by superiors back at headquarters who are not in a position to see on a day-to-day basis how the expatriate performs in the particular situation. Consequently, subsidiary managers tend to be assessed according to subsidiary performance, with a reliance on hard criteria similar to that applied to heads of domestic units or divisions. Of course, there is a danger that a subsidiary manager will take decisions and implement local strategies that favor short-term performance to the detriment of longer-term organizational goals.

Appraisal of other employees is likely to be conducted by the subsidiary's CEO, or the immediate host-country supervisor, depending upon the nature and level of the position concerned.[49] With regard to expatriate performance appraisal, host-country managers may have a clearer picture of expatriate performance and can take into consideration contextual criteria. However, they may have culturally bound biases (e.g. about role behavior) and lack an appreciation of the impact of the expatriate's performance in the broader organizational context. As the IHRM in Action Case 11-1 illustrates, some expatriates may prefer to have parent-company evaluators given that their future career progression may depend on how the appraisal data is utilized back at headquarters. This may be especially so in cases where foreign operations are relatively less important than, say, domestic US operations.[50] Others may prefer a host-country appraisal if they perceive it as a more accurate reflection of their performance.

Multiple raters are sometimes used in the domestic context – such as the technique referred to as 360-degree feedback. It has been argued that, given the cross-cultural complexity of the foreign assignment, a team of evaluators should be used for performance appraisal. For example, Gregersen *et al.*[51] found that most firms

---

IHRM in Action Case 11-1

A rainy expatriate performance appraisal

Richard Hoffman, a Quebecois Chemical Engineer working for a Canadian-based energy firm, was given a three-year expatriate assignment in Venezuela as a technical liaison and environmental protection project manager. His local project supervisor was Jean, a French engineer who had lived in French Guiana and then Venezuela for over 20 years. Richard thought that as a Francophone from Quebec, he and Jean would be able to build a quick working relationship. Rich sent Jean an early email (in French, and not the usual corporate English) containing what he thought of as the five most significant goals associated with his assignment – similar to the management by objectives section of the more or less standard performance appraisal forms he had filled out for years during earlier assignments in Edmonton, Toronto and at corporate headquarters in Montreal. After several months with no response from Jean, Richard caught Jean in the hallway between meetings and asked him about the email and his progress to date. 'Don't worry about that', Jean responded blandly, 'Just keep working to the deadlines and I will check with your co-workers and the other project managers on your work. Where did you go to engineering school by the way?'

Richard waited another six months and was becoming increasingly anxious as the firm's annual review week approached. He finally caught up with Jean on a rainy Friday in the lobby of the office building as they both waited for their drivers to arrive. When asked about the upcoming performance review, Jean snorted and said. 'C'est tout fini, it's all been taken care of. Make an appointment with my assistant Louisa next week and we can go over the report we have sent to Montreal.' As Jean stepped gingerly into the rainy Caracas parking lot, Richard thought back to the last few weeks with his team, the sometimes loud disagreements with his fellow project managers, and wondered if it was too late in the day to call his old supervisor in Toronto.

Source: Based on the synthesis of a series of expatriate experiences.

(81 per cent) in their survey of HR directors in 58 US multinationals used more than one rater when assessing expatriate performance. The immediate superior (in either the home or host country), the expatriate as self-rater, and the HR manager (either home or host-country based) were commonly used as multiple evaluators of US expatriate performance. Likewise, a survey of 99 Finnish internationally operating companies reported that, for 79 per cent of respondents, expatriate performance appraisal was conducted by the superior located in Finland.[52] Often though, this was simply because there was no suitable person in the host country to conduct such appraisals. The GMAC Global Relocation Services, LLC (GMAC GRS) surveys, mentioned in previous chapters, include questions regarding expatriate performance. Host-country performance reviews were used by 69 per cent of responding firms in the 2004 survey, compared to 65 per cent in 2002; home country-based reviews were used by 50 per cent and 43 per cent in 2004 and 2002 respectively (the numbers do not total as respondents were allowed multiple answers – some firms combine both home and host-country reviews). For the virtual assignment situation, the use of multiple appraisers would most likely be the most accurate way to determine performance. However, the availability of knowledgeable, trained raters may constrain the approach taken in the international context.

Standardized or customized performance appraisal forms

Domestic companies commonly design performance appraisal forms for each job category, particularly those using a traditional performance appraisal approach rather than performance management. Such standardization assists in the collection of accurate performance data on which personnel decisions can be made, and allows for cross-employee comparisons. The question often posed is should these standardized forms be adapted when used for appraising international managers? As Gregersen *et al.*[53] argue:

> In principle, performance appraisal systems are designed carefully and often presumed to be static. Valid reasons exist for maintaining standard, traditionally used appraisals (e.g., when the system has been tested, has identified baselines, and reduces future development costs). These reasons are valid as long as the context of the performance does not change. In the expatriate setting, however, the performance context does change, and sometimes it changes dramatically. Given a global context, previous testing and established baselines grounded in domestic situations can become meaningless.

Despite this, they found in their sample of US firms that 76 per cent in fact used the same standardized appraisal forms for expatriate appraisal.[54] Employees who relocate within the multinational and non-expatriate assignees who also cross cultural boundaries in their performance context do not always feel headquarters-based appraisal forms allow for consideration of the critical success factors of their performance like cross-cultural competence.[55]

Frequency of appraisal

In practice, formal appraisal is commonly on a yearly basis, and this appears to extend to international performance systems, even though the domestic-oriented literature on this topic recommends an ongoing combination of formal and informal performance appraisal and feedback. For example, the majority of the US companies in the Gregersen *et al.* study referred to above reported annual appraisal practices. It is interesting to note that the US companies using annual appraisal systems were more likely to use standard appraisal forms and hard criteria. In their discussion of this finding, Gregersen *et al.* comment that replicating domestic practices requires less effort in collecting and interpreting the data, and that the preference for following the domestic system might reflect lack of international experience within the companies in the sample. As only 28 per cent of the HR respondents in their study reported having been on international assignments themselves, they might not be aware of the need to take contextual criteria into consideration, or see a need for the customization of their expatriate performance systems.

Performance feedback.   An important aspect of an effective performance management system is the provision of timely feedback of the appraisal process. One of the problems with annual appraisal is that employees do not receive the consistent frequent feedback considered critical in order to maintain or improve their performance. The performance literature also suggests that regular feedback is an important aspect in terms of meeting targets and revising goals, as well as assisting in motivation of work effort. The difficulty for the expatriate who is being evaluated by a geographically distant manager is that timely, appropriate feedback is only viable against hard criteria.

For virtual assignees, this is further complicated when geographic dispersion dictates reliance on email communication. Interpersonal relations and an effective choice of communication medium are two factors influencing virtual workgroup relations.[56] Milliman *et al.*[57] reported two critical incidents involving miscommunication between managers working on a virtual assignment in the USA and Malaysia. Email feedback about his Malaysian counterpart's good performance provided to the Malaysian by the American head of the project generated a cycle of cross-cultural conflict. This threatened the virtual team's performance when the Malaysian sought to transfer out of the team. Adopting an organizational learning approach, the researchers analyzed the miscommunication and its consequences. They concluded that the two managers concerned had different views about what constituted 'the primary source of job performance, how performance feedback is provided, what role the subordinate will have in communicating with a superior, how conflict is handled, and what communication styles are expected'. The approach used to analyze these incidents provides a useful IHRM starting point for developing effective cross-cultural performance feedback communication skills.

Appraisal of HCN employees

The discussion so far has omitted the issue of appraising the performance of HCN employees. To a certain extent, this reflects the limited research on the topic in the context of IHRM, though there is a growing body of literature on comparative HRM practices. What is important to mention here is that the practice of performance appraisal itself confronts the issue of cultural applicability.[58] Performance appraisal in different nations can be interpreted as a signal of distrust or even an insult. In Japan, for instance, it is important to avoid direct confrontation to 'save face', and this custom affects the way in which performance appraisal is conducted. A Japanese manager cannot directly point out a work-related problem or error committed by a subordinate:

> Instead, he is likely to start discussing with the subordinate about the strong
> points of that person's work, continuing with a discussion about the work on
> a relatively general level. Then he might continue to explain the consequences

of the type of mistake committed by the subordinate, still without directly pointing out the actual mistake or the individual employee. From all this, the subordinate is supposed to understand his mistake and propose how to improve his work.[59]

One way to overcome the dilemma of cultural adaptation is to use host-country nationals to assist in devising a suitable system for appraising subsidiary employees and to advise on the conduct of the appraisal. The need for local responsiveness may affect the multinational's ability to effectively implement a standardized approach to performance management at all levels within the global operation.[60]

As we discussed in relation to PCNs and TCNs, the level of position involved is an important consideration. Should a multinational appoint a HCN as its subsidiary manager then much of what we covered in terms of goals (particularly hard goals) and performance measures could be expected to apply to the HCN. In terms of task performance and potential role conflict, as can be seen from Figure 11-6, Torbiörn[61] recognizes that HCN managers face particular role concerns that are different from those of the PCN and TCN manager. The HCN manager is expected to perform a role that is conceptualized by a psychologically and physically distant parent company, but enacted in an environment with other role senders who are both psychologically and physically close.

Parent-company role conception is communicated to the HCN, but it crosses the cultural boundary, as does feedback expressed as the HCN's role behavior (the straight arrows in Figure 11-6). Input from 'host-country' role senders, though, does not cross a cultural boundary. The HCN receives role expectations and enacts role behaviors in his or her own cultural environment. For subsidiary staff below the top management level, one would expect that the performance management system be localized to take into consideration local behavioral norms

---

| **Figure 11-6** | HCN role conception |

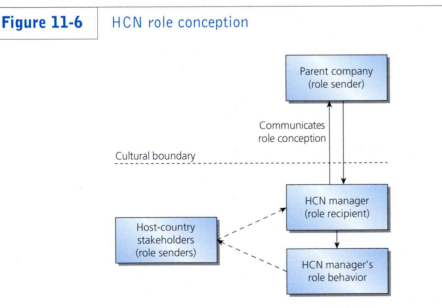

Source: Adapted from I. Torbiörn, 'The Structure of Managerial Roles in Cross-cultural Settings', *International Studies of Management & Organization,* Vol. 15, No. 1 (1985), p. 61.

of work behavior. Torbiörn's model depicts only HCN managerial role conception and communication.

Conflict may arise in cases where HCNs report to a PCN expatriate manager who also conducts their performance appraisal. In a way, this is the reverse of the discussion surrounding local managers appraising the performance of expatriates in terms of cultural bias. The difference, of course, is the impact that parent-company standards have on the performance management system and the degree to which localization is permitted in a standardized approach.[62] It may not be culturally sensitive to use appraisal techniques such as 360-degree feedback, for instance. In practice, US multinationals have often used the same appraisal form for HCNs as for their domestic employees. Sometimes the forms are translated from English; sometimes they are not. Both approaches have drawbacks. As discussed above, while some companies are developing information systems to assist in performance appraisal, the widespread use of computer-generated data is hampered by the legal constraints imposed by some host governments or by concerns about personal privacy.

An aspect that is overlooked in the limited literature is the potential for role conflict for those HCNs transferred into the parent's operations.[63] For that period, the HCN may be evaluated according to role behavior expectations communicated by role senders that are physically close but psychologically distant, in an environment that is also psychologically distant. The HCN is then transferred, usually back into his or her home country, and may experience difficulties in readjusting role behavior.

In relation to performance appraisal generally, it seems that the process remains problematic, irrespective of cultural impacts. For example, a study by Gerringer *et al*. reported a common finding across ten countries/regions, which was the failure of performance appraisal to fulfil its development purpose. The study formed part of the Best Practices in International HRM project – a multiple-year, multiple-researcher, multi-national project.[64] The ten countries/regions were Australia, Canada, China, Indonesia, Japan, Korea, Latin America, Mexico, Taiwan and the USA. The researchers noted: 'It appears that the potential of appraisal is not fully realized in current practice, not only (as widely believed) in the US, but also in most other countries.'[65]

Recent reviews on global performance management describe a more and more widespread use of performance management systems by multinational firms, formal reviews tend to be annual or biannual, online systems are still in the minority (20 per cent of responding firms), but one-third of the firms stated they had plans to move to online systems. Objective and subjective criteria are used, and training based on the results of the performance management process is growing. Systems capabilities related to consistency within the far-flung system in the firm, integrating performance management into other HR activities (such as succession planning and compensation) and linking performance management to strategic planning while incorporating the leadership of senior management are seen as critical if performance management is to contribute to the control of MNEs.[66]

The criticality of balancing global (parent) processes, practices, roles and norms with local or regional equivalents is of ongoing interest to students of global performance management. Investigating the impact of high context cultures on selecting and valuing implicit, explicit-subjective or explicit-objective forms of performance criteria is an ongoing activity. The effects of legal and regulatory contexts on the aforementioned processes, practices and norms, and the widening range of tasks and assignments required of employees in multinational firms all combine to make performance management a complex, yet critical area of human resource management.

Summary

Technical competence is a necessary but not sufficient condition for successful international performance. Cross-cultural interpersonal skills, sensitivity to foreign norms and values, and ease of adaptation to unfamiliar environments are just a few of the managerial characteristics most multinational firms seek when selecting international managers. The added challenge is the effective management and appraisal of performance across all of the multinational's operations. Therefore, we have explored in this chapter:

- The basic components of a performance management system that is conscious of and responds to the organizational, national and international elements.

- Multinational performance aspects: whole (global) versus part (subsidiary); non-comparable data; the volatility of the global environment; the effect of distance; and the level of maturity. Performance management as a control mechanism was briefly discussed.

- Factors associated with expatriate performance: the compensation package; task and role; headquarters' support; host-environment factors; and cultural adjustment.

- The performance management of non-expatriates and those on non-standard assignments. We used the virtual assignment as an illustration of some of the aspects that need to be considered in these non-traditional assignment types.

- The issues relating to the performance appraisal of international employees.

- Appraisal of HCN managers and employees in subsidiary operations.

Broadening out the discussion to the multinational level, and addressing performance management and appraisal concerns related to non-expatriates and those on non-standard assignments, has been useful to remind us that there are many dimensions to international business operations that need to be considered when designing an effective performance management system in the multinational context.

Discussion Questions

1 In the section on the volatility of the global environment, several world events were listed that have had profound implications for the global and local strategies of MNEs. Select a recent world event, identify the specific HR implications that may arise from this, and devise policies as to how these may be handled.

2 Discuss the major factors associated with appraisal of expatriate managerial performance.

3 'One of the dangers of performance appraisal is that, because the focus is so much on a particular individual, the teamwork aspect gets lost. In an international location, it is perhaps desirable to focus more on how the PCN has settled in and is operating as part of a team rather than as an individual at the possible detriment of the team.' Do you agree with this statement?

4 Why is it important to include hard, soft and contextual goals when assessing managerial performance?

5 In what ways would the role of a manager working in a non-standard international assignment arrangement differ from that of a typical expatriate manager?

Further Reading

Cascio, W. (2006). 'Global Performance Management Systems', in G. Stahl and I. Björkman (eds), *Handbook of Research in International Human Resource Management*, Cheltenham: Edward Elgar, pp. 176–96.

Milliman, J., Nason, S., Zhu, C. and De Cieri, H. (2002). 'An Exploratory Assessment of the Purposes of Performance Appraisals in North and Central America and the Pacific Rim', *Asia Pacific Journal of Human Resources,* 40(1): 105–22.

Shay, J.P. and Baack, S.A. (2004). 'Expatriate Assignment, Adjustment and Effectiveness: An Empirical Examination of the Big Picture', *Journal of International Business Studies,* 35: 216–32.

Shih, H., Chiang, Y. and Kim, I. (2005). 'Expatriate Performance Management from MNEs of Different National Origins', *International Journal of Manpower,* 26(2): 157–76.

Notes and References

1 Excellent overviews of research in this area are provided by P. Caligiuri, 'Performance Measurement in a Cross-cultural Context', in W. Bennett, C. Launce and J. Woehr (eds), *Performance Management: Current Perspectives and Future Challenges* (Mahwah, NJ: Lawrence Erlbaum Associates, 2006), pp. 227–44; and W. Cascio, 'Global Performance Management Systems', in G. Stahl and I. Björkman (eds), *Handbook of Research in International Human Resource Management* (Cheltenham: Edward Elgar, 2006), pp. 176–96.

2 Cascio, 'Global Performance Management Systems', p. 193.

3 C.A. Bartlett and S. Ghoshal, 'Managing Across Borders: New Strategic Requirements', *Sloan Management Review* (Summer, 1987), pp. 7–17.

4 V. Pucik, 'Strategic Human Resource Management in a Multinational Firm', in H.V. Wortzel and L.H. Wortzel (eds), *Strategic Management of Multinational Corporations: The Essentials* (New York: John Wiley, 1985), pp. 429, 430.

5 J. Garland, R.N. Farmer and M. Taylor, *International Dimensions of Business Policy and Strategy,* 2nd edn (Boston, MA: PWS-KENT, 1990), p. 193.

6 *Ibid.*

7 Pucik, 'Strategic Human Resource Management in a Multinational Firm', p. 430.

8 *Ibid.*

9 A. Engle and P. Dowling, 'State of Origin: Research in Global Performance Management: Progress or a Lost Horizon?', *Conference Proceedings of the VIIIth World Congress of the International Federation of Scholarly Associations of Management,* Berlin, September, 2006; J. Kochanski and A. Sorensen, 'Managing Performance Management', *Workspan,* Vol. 48, No. 9 (2006), pp. 20–7; and J. Ryder, 'The Future of HR Technology', *HR Magazine,* Vol. 50, No. 3 (2005), pp. 67–9.

10 Pucik, 'Strategic Human Resource Management in a Multinational Firm'.

11 Garland, Farmer and Taylor, *International Dimensions of Business Policy and Strategy,* p. 193.

12 M. Fenwick, H. De Cieri and D. Welch, 'Cultural and Bureaucratic Control in MNEs: The Role of Expatriate Performance Management', *Management International Review,* Vol. 39, Special Issue No. 3 (1999), pp. 107–24.

13 M. Tahvanainen, *Expatriate Performance Management* (Helsinki: Helsinki School of Economics Press, 1998).

14 Richard Hays, 'Expatriate Selection: Insuring Success and Avoiding Failure', *Journal of International Business Studies,* Vol. 5, No. 1 (1974), pp. 25–37. Tung appears to have based her initial studies on these categories (see R. Tung, 'Selection and Training of Personnel for Overseas Assignments', *Columbia Journal of Word Business,* Vol. 16, No. 1 (1981), pp. 68–78).

15 M. Hilb, *New Corporate Governance: Successful Board Management Tools,* 2nd edn (Berlin: Springer Publishing, 2006); and F. Malik, *Effective Top Management* (Frankfurt: Wiley-VCH, 2006).

16 Caligiuri, 'Performance Measurement in a Cross-cultural Context'.

17 For more on how the purposes and roles inherent in assignments may impact upon the characteristics of performance management systems see Engle and Dowling, 'State of Origin'.

18 H. Mintzberg, *The Nature of Managerial Work* (Englewood Cliffs, NJ: Prentice-Hall, 1973), p. 54.

19 J.S. Black and L.W. Porter, 'Managerial Behaviors and Job Performance: A Successful Manager in Los Angeles May Not Succeed in Hong Kong', *Journal of International Business Studies,* Vol. 22, No. 1 (1991), pp. 99–113.

20 I. Torbiörn, 'The Structure of Managerial Roles in Cross-Cultural Settings', *International Studies of Management & Organization,* Vol. 15, No. 1 (1985), pp. 52–74, quote from p. 59.

21 M. Janssens, 'Evaluating International Managers' Performance: Parent Company Standards as Control Mechanism', *International Journal of Human Resource Management,* Vol. 5, No. 4 (1994), pp. 853–73.

22 *Ibid*.

23 H.B. Gregersen and J.S. Black, 'A Multifaceted Approach to Expatriate Retention in International Assignments', *Group & Organization Studies,* Vol. 15, No. 4 (1990), p. 478.

24 M.G. Birdseye and J.S. Hill, 'Individual, Organization/Work and Environmental Influences on Expatriate Turnover Tendencies: An Empirical Study', *Journal of International Business Studies,* Vol. 26, No. 4 (1995), p. 800.

25 D.C. Feldman and H.B. Tompson, 'Expatriation, Repatriation, and Domestic Geographical Relocation: An Empirical Investigation of Adjustment to New Job Assignments', *Journal of International Business Studies,* Vol. 24, No. 3 (1993), pp. 507–29.

26 P. Bhaskar-Shrinivas, M.A. Shaffer and D.M. Luk, 'Input-Based and Time-Based Models of International Adjustment: Meta-Analytic Evidence and Theoretical Extensions', *Academy of Management Journal,* Vol. 48, No. 2 (2005), p. 272.

27 Torbiörn, 'The Structure of Managerial Roles in Cross-cultural Settings', p. 59.

28 For example, in one of the few articles on this topic, Chadwick looks at the TCN assignment in general and does not specifically address performance. Rather, the focus is on fair treatment and equity regarding compensation (W.F. Chadwick, 'TCN Expatriate Manager Policies', in Jan Selmer (ed.), *Expatriate Management: New Ideas for International Business* (Westport, CT: Quorum Books, 1995).

29 M. Conway, 'Reducing Expatriate Failure Rates', *Personnel Administrator,* July (1984), pp. 31–7.

30 H.B. Gregersen, J.M. Hite and J.S. Black, 'Expatriate Performance Appraisal in U.S. Multinational Firms', *Journal of International Business Studies,* Vol. 27, No. 4 (1996), pp. 711–38.

31 See F. Nilsson and M. Kald, 'Recent Advances in Performance Management: The Nordic Case', *European Management Journal,* Vol. 20, No. 3 (2002), pp. 235–45; V. Suutari and M. Tahvanainen, 'The Antecedents of Performance Management amongst Finnish Expatriates', *International Journal of Human Resource Management,* Vol. 13, No.1 (2002), pp. 55–75; and M. Tahvanainen, 'Expatriate Performance Management: The Case of Nokia Telecommunications', *Human Resource Management,* Vol. 39, No. 2 (2000), pp. 267–76.

32 M. Festing and C. Bartzantny, 'Performance Management in Germany and France', in A. Varma, P. Budhwar and A. DeNisi (eds), *Performance Management Across the Globe* (London: Routledge, in press); and P. Gooderham, O. Nordhaug and K. Ringdal, 'Institutional and Rational Determinants of Organizational Practices: Human Resource Management in European Firms', *Administrative Science Quarterly,* Vol. 44 (1999), pp. 507–31.

33 Festing and Bartzantny, 'Performance Management in Germany and France'; and M. Tahrvanainen and V. Suutari, 'Expatriate Performance Management in MNCs', in H. Scullion and M. Lineham (eds), *International HRM: A Critical Text* (Basingstoke: Macmillan, 2005), pp. 91–113.

34 M. Dickmann, 'Implementing German HRM Abroad: Desired, Feasible, Successful?', *International Journal of Human Resource Management,* Vol. 34, No. 2 (2003), pp. 265–83.

35 For more on Anglo-Saxon approaches to performance-based pay see H. Aguinis, *Performance Management* (Upper Saddle River, NJ: Pearson Education, 2007), particularly Chapter 10. For more information related to German performance management see M. Festing and C. Bartzantny, 'Performance Management in Germany and France'; and M. Pudelko, 'A Comparison of HRM Systems in the USA, Japan and Germany in Their Socioeconomic Context', *Human Resource Management Journal,* Vol. 16, No. 2 (2006), pp. 123–53.

36 M. Fenwick, 'On International Assignment: Is Expatriation the Only Way to Go?', *Asia Pacific Journal of Human Resources,* Vol. 42, No. 3 (2003), pp. 365–77.

37 D. Welch, V. Worm and M. Fenwick, 'Are Virtual Assignments Feasible?', *Management International Review,* Vol. 43, Special Issue No.1 (2003), pp. 95–114; P. Caligiuri, 'Performance Measurement in a Cross-cultural Context'.

38 See for example M. Armstrong, *Performance Management* (London: Kogan Page, 1994); and P. Stiles, L. Gratton, C. Truss, V. Hope-Hailey and P. McGovern, 'Performance Management and the Psychological Contract', *Human Resource Management Journal,* Vol. 7, No. 1 (1997), pp. 57–66.

39 M. Harvey, 'Focusing the International Personnel Performance Appraisal Process', *Human Resource Development Quarterly,* Vol. 8, No. 1 (1997) pp. 41–62.

40 Tahvanainen, *Expatriate Performance Management.*

41 M. Tahvanainen, D. Welch and V. Worm, 'Implications of Short-term International Assignments', *European Management Journal,* Vol. 23, No. 6 (2005), pp. 663–73.

42 For a well-presented and far-reaching discussion of the relationship between strategic purpose and talent management, see J. Boudreau and P. Ramstad, *Beyond HR: The New Science of Human Capital* (Boston, MA: Harvard Business School Press, 2007).

43 Pucik, 'Strategic Human Resource Management'.

44 Janssens, 'Evaluating International Managers' Performance'.

45 R.W. Beatty, 'Competitive Human Resource Advantages Through the Strategic Management of Performance', *Human Resource Planning,* Vol. 12, No. 3 (1989), pp. 179–94.

46 K.F. Brickley, *Corporate Criminal Liability: A Treatise on the Criminal Liability of Corporations, Their Officers and Agents,* Cumulative supplement (Deerfield, IL: Clark Boardman Callaghan, 1992). Enacted in 1977, the FCPA addresses the problem of questionable foreign payments by US multinationals and their managers. The act was amended by Congress in 1988 to include substantial increases in the authorized criminal fines for organizations and new civil sanctions for individuals violating the FCPA.

47 Tahvanainen, *Expatriate Performance Management;* and Gregersen, Hite and Black, 'Expatriate Performance Appraisal in U.S. Multinational Firms'.

48 Harvey, 'Focusing the International Personnel Performance Appraisal Process'.

49 Tahvanainen, *Expatriate Performance Management.*

50 E. Naumann, 'Organizational Predictors of Expatriate Job Satisfaction', *Journal of International Business Studies,* Vol. 24, No. 1 (1993), pp. 61–80.

51 Gregersen, Hite and Black, 'Expatriate Performance Appraisal in U.S. Multinational Firms'.

52 Tahvanainen, *Expatriate Performance Management.*

53 Gregersen, Hite and Black, 'Expatriate Performance Appraisal in U.S. Multinational Firms', p. 716.

54 It should be remembered that these authors take a traditional performance appraisal approach, rather than utilize the newer performance management literature that we discuss in this chapter. It may be that the goal setting stressed in the performance management literature will assist standardization.

55 Cascio, 'Global Performance Management Systems' and Engle and Dowling, 'State of Origin'.

56 See W. Cascio and S. Shurygailg, 'E-leadership in Virtual Firms', *Organizational Dynamics,* Vol. 31 (2003), pp. 362–75.

57 J. Milliman, S. Taylor and A. Czaplewski, 'Cross-Cultural Performance Feedback in Multinational Enterprises: Opportunity for Organizational Learning', *Human Resource Planning,* Vol. 25, No. 3 (2002), pp. 29–43.

58 See, for example, N.J. Adler, *International Dimensions of Organizational Behavior,* 4th edn. (Cincinnati, OH: South Western/Thomson, 2002); S. Schneider, 'National vs. Corporate Culture: Implications for Human Resource Management', *Human Resource Management,* Vol. 27 (1988), pp. 231–46; and G.P. Latham and N.K. Napier, 'Chinese Human Resource Management Practices in Hong Kong and Singapore: An Exploratory Study', in G. Ferris, K. Rowland and A. Nedd (eds), *Research in Personnel and Human Resource Management,* Vol. 6 (Greenwich, CT: JAI, 1989).

59 J.V. Koivisto, 'Duality and Japanese Management: A Cosmological View of Japanese Business Management', paper presented at the European Institute of Advanced Studies in Management Workshop, *Managing in Different Cultures,* Cergy, Group Essec, France, November 23–24, 1992.

60 Caligiuri, 'Performance Measurement in a Cross-cultural Context' and Engle and Dowling, 'State of Origin'.

61 Torbiörn, 'The Structure of Managerial Roles in Cross-Cultural Settings'.

62 Engle and Dowling, 'State of Origin'.

63 The performance appraisal of 'inpatriates' is briefly covered in M. Harvey and M. Buckley, 'Managing Inpatriates: Building a Global Core Competency', *Journal of World Business,* Vol. 32, No. 1 (1997), pp. 35–52. For a more general overview of the role of 'inpatriates' in control processes for multinational firms, see M. Harvey and M. Novicevic, 'The Evolution from Repartiation of Managers in MNEs to "Inpatriation" in Global Organizations', in G. Stahl and I. Björkman (eds), *Handbook of Research in International Human Resource Management* (Cheltenham: Edward Elgar, 2006), pp. 323–46.

64 J. Gerringer, C. Frayne and J. Milliman, 'In Search of "Best Practices" in International Human Resource Management: Research Design and Methodology', *Asia Pacific Journal of Human Resources,* Vol. 40, No. 1 (2002), pp. 9–37.

65   J. Milliman, S. Nason, C. Zhu and H. De Cieri, 'An Exploratory Assessment of the Purposes of Performance Appraisals in North and Central America and the Pacific Rim', *Asia Pacific Journal of Human Resources,* Vol. 40, No. 1 (2002), p. 117.

66   See Cascio's, 'Global Performance Management Systems', discussion as well as a survey of 278 firms from 15 countries reported in P. Bernthal, R. Rogers and A. Smith's, *Managing Performance: Building Accountability for Organizational Success* (Pittsburgh, PA: Development Dimensions International, 2003).

IHRM trends: complexity, challenges and choices in the future

Chapter Objectives

In this final chapter, we identify and comment on observed trends and future directions regarding:

- International business ethics and HRM.
- Mode of operation and IHRM.
- Ownership issues relating to IHRM requirements of organizations other than the large multinational, such as:
  - family-owned firms
  - non-government organizations (NGOs).
- Safety and security issues.

Introduction

In this book, we have explored the IHRM issues relating to managing people in a multinational context. To that end, we have focused on the implications that the process of internationalization has for the activities and policies of HRM. We now turn our attention to developments that have not previously been emphasized in the general IHRM literature and the challenges they present to IHRM: international business ethics, mode of operation, family-owned firms, non-government organizations (NGOs), and the developing role of IHRM in contributing to safety, security and dealing with global terrorism. In a sense, these topics reflect what some Japanese MNEs refer to as the 'general affairs' aspect of IHRM; the expectation that the human resource function will be the first line of defence in dealing with unpredictable and emergent issues from the many and varied environments and constituency groups that make up the complexity of MNEs.[1]

In the sections that follow we return to a discussion of some issues that distinguish HRM in MNEs. Revisiting the model of strategic HRM in MNEs presented in Chapter 1, Figure 12-1 contains highlights in **bold** of those issues and topics that are unique or distinct for MNEs. These topics include ethical issues associated with *external factors* such as country-regional characteristics, *internal factors* such as mode of operation, *external factors* related to safety, security and terrorism as industry or regional characteristics, and trends in research on the HR function and practices as these issues relate to *strategic HRM* and HR practices among MNEs.

External factors: international business ethics and HRM

Global organizations face a challenge: should they apply their own values everywhere they do business, irrespective of the cultural context and standard of local practices? To appreciate the dilemma, take the situation of a multinational that has assigned a PCN to manage its operations in a host country where bribery is commonly practiced, child labor is used and workplace safety is wanting. Whose standards should prevail? Those of the MNE's parent country or the host country?

There are three main responses to this question. The first involves ethical relativism, the second ethical absolutism and the third, ethical universalism. For the *ethical relativist,* there are no universal or international rights and wrongs, it all depends on a particular culture's values and beliefs. For the ethical relativist, when in Rome, one should do as the Romans do. Unlike the relativist, the *ethical*

| **Figure 12-1** | Returning to topics of strategic HRM in multinational enterprises |

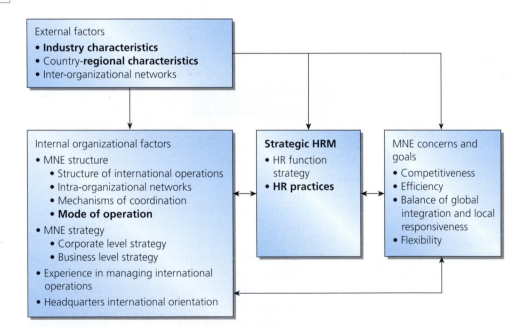

Source: Adapted from H. De Cieri and P.J. Dowling, 'Strategic Human Resource Management in Multinational Enterprises: Theoretical and Empirical Developments', in P.M. Wright *et al.* (eds), *Research in Personnel and Human Resource Management: Strategic Human Resources in the 21st Century,* Supplement 4 (Stamford, CT: JAI Press, 1999).

absolutist believes that when in Rome, one should do what one would do at home, regardless of what the Romans do. This view of ethics gives primacy to one's own cultural values. Opponents of this view argue that ethical absolutists are intolerant individuals who confuse respect for local traditions with ethical relativism. It must be noted that while some behaviors are wrong wherever they are practiced (e.g. bribery of government officials), other behaviors may be tolerated in their cultural context (e.g. the practice of routine gift giving between Japanese business people). In contrast to the ethical relativist, the *ethical universalist* believes there are fundamental principles of right and wrong which transcend cultural boundaries, and that MNEs must adhere to these fundamental principles or global values.

The existence of universal ethical principles can also be seen in the agreements that exist among nations that are signatories to the United Nations Declaration of Human Rights and a number of international accords such as the Guidelines for Multinational Enterprises adopted by the Organization of Economic Cooperation and Development (OECD). The need for international accords and corporate codes of conduct has grown commensurately with the spread of international business and the considerable growth of offshoring (as outlined in Chapter 9), but translating ethical principles and values into practice in the international business domain is an enormous task in the absence of a supranational legislative authority. Efforts to make progress in this area have centered on regulation, the development of international accords and the use of education and training programs.

New global developments on the criminalization of bribery

Bribery and corruption tends to top the list of the most frequent ethical problems encountered by international managers.[2] Bribery involves the payment of agents to do things that are inconsistent with the purpose of their position or office in order to gain an unfair advantage. Bribery can be distinguished from so-called gifts and 'facilitating' or 'grease' payments. The latter are payments to motivate agents to complete a task they would routinely do in the normal course of their duties. While most people do not openly condone bribery, many argue for a lenient approach based on the view that bribery is necessary to do business (the ethical relativist's argument). However, it is now generally agreed that bribery undermines equity, efficiency and integrity in the public service; undercuts public confidence in markets and aid programs; adds to the cost of products; and may affect the safety and economic well-being of the general public.

For these reasons, there has been an international movement to criminalize the practice of bribery. In 1977 the United States enacted the Foreign Corrupt Practices Act (FCPA) to prohibit US-based firms and US nationals from making bribery payments to foreign government officials. In addition, payments to agents violate the Act if it is known that the agent will use those payments to bribe a government official. The Act was amended in 1988 to permit 'facilitating' payments but mandates record-keeping provisions to help ensure that illegal payments are not disguised as entertainment or business expenses. The FCPA has in the past been criticized for placing US firms at a competitive disadvantage since European and Asian firms did not face criminal prosecution for paying bribes to foreign officials[3] but the evidence on the competitive disadvantage of the FCPA is mixed. The FCPA has also been criticized by some for being ethnocentric while others saw it as moral leadership on the part of the USA.[4]

In the absence of adequate international self-regulation to control bribery and corruption, the US lobbied other nation-states for almost two decades to enact uniform domestic government regulation to provide a level playing field. Finally, in December 1996 the United Nations adopted the Declaration Against Corruption and Bribery in International Commercial Transactions that committed UN members to criminalize bribery and deny tax deductibility for bribes. A year later the Declaration was endorsed by 30 member nations, and four non-member nations of the OECD adopted the Convention on Combating Bribery of Foreign Public Officials in International Business Transactions (OECD Convention). Under the OECD Convention members agreed to establish domestic legislation by the end of 1998 criminalizing the bribing of foreign public officials on an extraterritorial basis. The OECD Convention came into force in February 1999 and as of 2007 had been ratified by 36 countries. Each member state is required to undergo a peer review and to provide a report reviewing its implementation of the Convention. Country reports are available on the OECD website.[5] The OECD Convention requires sanctions to be commensurate with domestic penalties applicable to bribery of public officials.

Given the seriousness of offences and penalties in the OECD Convention, it is imperative that enterprises involved in global business take active steps to manage their potential exposure. Also, although the OECD Convention currently addresses the supply side of corruption in the public sector, it is likely that the ambit of the Convention will be expanded to include bribery in the private sector as well as the demand side of bribery. HR professionals have an important role to play in instituting a strategic plan for legal compliance and developing corporate codes for voluntary compliance. They can also provide training in understanding the difference between corrupt bribery payments, gifts, and allowable facilitation payments and the development of negotiation skills to handle problem situations that may arise in sensitive geographical regions and industries. The debate over payments to foreign officials is likely to continue for many years to come.

The Berlin-based non-government lobby group, Transparency International (TI) publishes an annual Corruption Perceptions Index. The index measures perceptions, not actual levels of corruption for over 50 countries and is based on international surveys of business people and financial journalists. The ranking is scored from zero (most corrupt) to ten (least corrupt). Table 12-1 shows the country rank of the top 22 least corrupt countries in descending order from the 2006 index. Finland, Iceland and New Zealand (all small population advanced economies) are the top equal-ranked three least corrupt countries. The countries perceived to be most corrupt are Guinea, Iraq, Myanmar and Haiti which are ranked at the bottom of the list of 163 countries.[6]

The public and financial consequences of a bribery scandal can be significant for an MNE. The IHRM in Action Case 12-1 below provides a sense of the actual and reputational costs of unethical conduct for a MNE.

Challenges for the HR function of the multinational firm

Managers involved in international business activities face many of the same ethical issues as those in domestic business, but the issues are made more complex because of the different social, economic, political, cultural and legal environments

| | Transparency International Corruption Perceptions Index 2006 | **Table 12-1** |

Country rank	Country/territory	2006 CPI score*
1	Finland	9.6
	Iceland	9.6
	New Zealand	9.6
4	Denmark	9.5
5	Singapore	9.4
6	Sweden	9.2
7	Switzerland	9.1
8	Norway	8.8
9	Australia	8.7
	Netherlands	8.7
11	Austria	8.6
	Luxembourg	8.6
	United Kingdom	8.6
14	Canada	8.5
15	Hong Kong	8.3
16	Germany	8.0
17	Japan	7.6
18	France	7.4
	Ireland	7.4
20	Belgium	7.3
	Chile	7.3
	USA	7.3

* CPI score relates to perceptions of the degree of corruption as seen by business people and risk analysts, and ranges between 10 (highly clean) and 0 (highly corrupt).

Source: Adapted from the Transparency International Corruption Perceptions Index 2006 (www.transparency.org).

in which MNEs operate. Firms which opt consciously or by default to leave ethical considerations up to individual employees not only contribute to the pressures of operating in a foreign environment (and perhaps contribute to poor performance or early recall of the expatriate), but also allow internal inconsistencies that affect total global performance.

When MNEs select international assignees, their ability to manage with integrity could be a job-relevant criterion and any pre-departure training or orientation program should include an ethics component that includes discussion of ethical dilemmas which expatriates may encounter. In designing training programs to meet the challenges of multinational business, the HR function should not only raise the issue of cultural relativities but also the extent to which moral imperatives transcend national and cultural boundaries. To avoid the temptation to cut 'ethical corners', expatriates should not be placed under unreasonable pressure to deliver good financial results and they must be given feedback and reinforcement. Performance appraisals, compensation programs and regular

'Too Little Too Late?' Siemens belatedly wakes up to reputation risk

Dateline: Frankfurt

It is a dense, dramatic account of police raids, arrests and the investigation into allegations that at least Euro200m ($265m) was siphoned out of secret bank accounts in Liechtenstein, Austria and Switzerland. A page-turning airport thriller? No, the 20-F filing submitted by Siemens, a German conglomerate, to the Securities and Exchange Commission in Washington, DC on 11 December. At the same time, the firm restated its earnings to take account of uncertainties over transactions being investigated by state prosecutors in at least three countries.

The purpose of these murky dealings remains unclear: was it a case of self-enrichment by crooked employees or something more sinister – carefully laundered bribes to win Siemens business in some of the 190 countries in which it operates? Siemens insists that it was a victim of crime not an accessory to it. It is investigating Euro420m of suspicious payments to consultants over the past seven years. Meanwhile, six present and former employees, including one former board member arrested on 12 December, are in custody.

In the flow of adverse publicity since police raided 30 of its offices a month ago, Siemens has tried to show that it is taking appropriate action. It announced the formation of a 'task force' to clarify and standardize its employees' business practices. It also appointed an ombudsman to encourage internal whistleblowing. But for Transparency International (TI), an anti-corruption campaign group, this was not enough. It had already suspended Siemens's membership of its German chapter in 2004 because of the company's reluctance to be transparent about an unresolved bribery case in Italy. (The case was settled last month without admission of guilt.) Siemens's sluggish reaction to investigations in Liechtenstein triggered a letter last month from TI warning that the firm's membership would be liable for termination after 15 December.

At an emergency board meeting this week Siemens announced new measures to show how determined it is to change its culture. It appointed a law firm to investigate the company's compliance and control systems. And it appointed Michael Hershman, an anti-corruption expert and one of the founders of TI (a nice touch), to review anti-corruption controls and training at Siemens. But will this be enough to save the company's reputation or its planned joint venture, Nokia Siemens Networks, which is due to start business on 1 January? The reputation risk could give Nokia grounds to pull out.

Some of Siemens' problems stem from the 1990s, before Germany and other nations signed the OECD's anti-bribery convention in 1999. Yet the Italian case post-dates the convention and another case in Greece concerns preparations for the 2004 Olympics. Siemens and the Munich prosecutors point to evidence that in the latest shenanigans the suspects 'banded together' to defraud the firm. There is only so much one can do, sighs a Siemens' spokesman, against 'criminal energy'.

But even poor supervision and control, rather than connivance with bribery, are bad enough. It cannot help appearances that Heinrich von Pierer, who was chief executive of Siemens in the 1990s before bribery was outlawed, still heads the supervisory board. He was supposed to steer the company through its transition to OECD anti-bribery rules and compliance with America's Sarbanes-Oxley Act, which requires greater disclosure and personal responsibility from executives. Worst of all for Germany's reputation as export champion of the world is the suspicion that it may owe some of its prowess to secret bank accounts and slush funds.

Klaus Kleinfeld, Siemens' chief executive since January 2005, may escape the full wrath of shareholders. But he still has plenty to do to reach self-imposed profit targets for some of the group's worse-performing divisions such as business systems, which is loss-making, and communications, where profits are sliding. The constant bad publicity cannot help.

Source: *Economist*, 16 December 2006, Vol. 381, Issue 8508, pp. 65–6.

trips home are important instruments in developing and maintaining ethical cultures.

The difficulties involved when massive, highly standardized firms attempt to be sensitive to local customs and values while becoming more international, is personified by Wal-Mart, the giant US retailer. The highly successful low-cost strategy (with its attendant standardization, scale and scope economies) that characterizes this would-be MNE has become a magnet for concerns, protests and social commentary all over the world. Issues related to offshoring procurement (especially from China), the consequences of a relentless low-cost strategy on direct employee and contractor wages, health-care benefits, working conditions and job security, and the competitive impact of Wal-Mart's 'super-stores' on traditional local retail establishments, city center infrastructure and small-population communities have initiated a worldwide discussion of the economic, social and political consequences of global business.[7]

Little is presently known about the evolving roles and responsibilities for HRM in balancing the economic imperatives of cost control and global standardization with the social and institutional realities of citizenship in a widening range of diverse contexts – particularly in terms of the development of labor sourcing, compensation and employee relations strategies.[8] However, it seems clear that these are likely to remain dominant issues in international business in the twenty-first century.

Internal factors: mode of operation and IHRM

We have stressed the need to broaden the scope of IHRM beyond that of subsidiary operations. While not downplaying its importance, for many MNEs, managing and staffing subsidiary units is only one aspect of international business operations, though the weighting given to subsidiary management will vary significantly according to the nature of international activities and the size of the internationalizing firm (see Chapter 1). The fact that external parties are involved in contractual modes, joint ventures and strategic alliances imposes management and HR constraints that are not usually present in wholly owned operations. While the HR implications of international joint ventures have received considerable attention in the literature,[9] there remains a need for studies that consider the HR implications of contractual modes where the firm is operating at arm's length. Training, for instance, is often an important part of contractual modes, playing a key role in the transfer of technology and systems, inculcation of company culture, and acting as a screening process (for example, in selecting suitable franchisees). As a result, staff may be primarily involved in short-term assignments to deliver training in foreign locations, rather than as traditional expatriates.

Family-owned firms

Often, family-owned firms are treated as a sub-set of SMEs (which we discussed in Chapter 3). However, large multinationals can be family-owned, though the definition of what constitutes family ownership varies across countries. An excellent example of a large MNE that remains family owned is the Bechtel Corporation which is a global engineering, construction and project management company which is headquartered in San Francisco.[10] Firms that later become publicly owned often retain members of the founding family as major stockholders. The long involvement of the Ford family in the management of the US automobile company, the Ford Motor Company, is an example of a situation in which family concerns have received wide media coverage in the context of international business decision making.

A factor that may contribute to the demise, or take-over, of a family firm is the way in which management succession is handled. Replacing top management is often seen as a challenge, but handing over control can be fraught with conflict and turmoil when family businesses are involved. HR planning takes on a different dimension in the context of family-owned firms and gives rise to much speculation in high-profile MNEs such as Aldi (German supermarket chain) and News Limited (Murdoch's media group, including the London *Times*, *New York Times*, Sky Channel and Fox). Another aspect is the way the internationalization process is handled within family-owned firms. There has been a suggestion that Asian family firms try to keep as much control as possible within the immediate or at least the extended family. A study by Yeung[11] of the internationalization of three Chinese family-owned Hong Kong firms found that these firms were able to meet the challenges of growth while still preserving their family management and structure, though control through socialization was used when non-family managers were placed in key positions. As Yeung points out, the globalization of family firms has been a remote topic in international business studies.

Non-government organizations (NGOs)

The globalization of trade and business has provoked a vigorous debate within national states, and often is expressed in anti-globalization rallies and protests. The activities of environmental groups such as Greenpeace highlight how these organizations have also become internationalized. They tend to have national 'managers' in various countries, and variations of structural forms for coordination and accountability. Aid agencies such as the Red Cross, the Red Crescent, World Vision and Médecins Sans Frontieres (Doctors without Borders) are prominent examples of NGOs. They may utilize different organizational structures and have members who may internalize to a greater degree the shared values and beliefs due to the nature of the organization's mission and activities, than may be found in a for-profit multinational. Nonetheless, in terms of global control and operations, there may be similar managerial concerns to those of, for instance, oil companies. Physical risk – such as the danger of staff being taken hostage, and of having property damaged – is common to firms operating in hostile contexts. As Fenwick[12] identifies, non-profit organizations have been largely ignored in IHRM research, possibly because IHRM 'reflects the traditional management ethos of effectiveness and efficiency rather than the non-profit ethos of values-driven, charitable and philanthropic ideals'.[13] It would seem that the need to broaden the focus of the IHRM field to include NGOs will be necessary, as the impact and influence of NGOs is more than likely to continue well into the twenty-first century.

External factors: challenges in an uncertain world: safety, security and counterterrorism[14]

Traditionally, many domestic and international human resource managers have been responsible for legal compliance and training issues related to safety in the workplace.[15] As national and international regulations related to workplace safety expanded, specific professional standards of practice, reporting mechanisms and roles were specified in the area of corporate risk management.[16] Risk categories associated with natural disaster protocols, emergency and disaster preparedness plans for MNE plant and facilities, workplace violence policies, industrial theft and sabotage protocols, and 'hardening' individual facilities to enhance in-house security have emerged and a growing body of professional and academic literature exists. Less clear are the particular roles, expectations and portfolios of responsibilities that IHRM managers and directors have been called upon to incorporate into their existing responsibilities. Intuitively, in smaller MNEs – operating in less sensitive industries and less turbulent markets – the IHRM generalists will be called on to incorporate these protocols by outsourcing technical security systems and personnel as required.[17] In larger organizations, particularly MNEs operating in more public and sensitive industries and/or more socially and politically turbulent regions of the world, significant investment in developing integrated, coordinated and specialized risk management practices within the HR function is warranted. Many MNEs have developed their own idiosyncratic systems and processes in response to a history of 'critical incidents' which the firm has experienced over years or even decades – e.g. the kidnapping of an executive, a natural disaster impacting a key facility, or an airline or private aircraft disaster that decimated the executive cadre of the MNE.

Not surprisingly, executives in most MNEs are unwilling to discuss the protocols processes, systems and structures in place in this sensitive area. More recently emerging risk categories relate to cyberterrorism, political terrorist groups targeting specific firms and industries and the risks inherent in pandemics, such as SARS, avian flu and airborne contaminants (as discussed in Chapter 1). As a working set of corporate risk assessment categories, a starting point for a MNE-specific audit, would include the following five areas:

- *In-facility emergency and disaster preparedness* – including being in compliance with local safety laws and standards (e.g. occupational safety and health administration rules in the USA), creating a command center and triage area, protocols for transport-evacuation and the systematic location of employees, liaison with public-sector emergency workers, and media relations.

- *In-facility security* – comprised of perimeter security, search protocols into and out of facilities (truck inspections, deliveries, etc.), internal search protocols (lockers, etc.), bomb threat procedures, risk control for violence in the facility and threats to management (including training on warning signs, protection of property and equipment and safeguarding executives), protection and lighting in parking areas and the use of cameras in the workplace.

- *Industrial espionage, theft and sabotage* – activities to secure internal communications (emails, telephones, etc.), open records protection, employee privacy regulations, clearly defined physical inspections and search processes.

- *Cyberterrorism* – hardware, software and human systems to deal with hacking, information theft, internal sabotage, the sabotage of software systems and the development and maintenance of an architecture of back-up systems and multiple independent operations for information systems.

● *Out-of-facility fire and travel risks* – providing traveling managers with portable five-minute air packs, travel policies prohibiting employees staying in hotel rooms above the seventh floor (most aerial ladder trucks only reach to the sixth floor), policies prohibiting top-level managers from traveling on the same airline flight/private aircraft, hotel evacuation training if traveling teams of employees are staying at the same hotel.[18]

According to Czinkota *et al.,* analytically, IHRM managers may be able to assess the potential risk from terrorist threats at three levels of analysis: *primary* – 'at the level of the individual person and firm'; at the *micro level* – 'specific regions, industries or levels in international value chains'; and at the *macro level* – 'the effect of a terrorist attack on the global environment . . . the world economy, consumer demand for goods and services, and reactions by supranational organizations such as the United Nations'.[19] As an example of micro-level risk analysis, the travel/hospitality industry is particularly sensitive to terrorist events or natural disasters that may inhibit travel in general, travel to a certain region or country, or to specific travel destinations.[20] On the primary and micro levels:

> It is useful to distinguish the most vulnerable links in firm's value chains . . . From the individual [firm's] perspective, it is more useful to view terrorism at the micro level wherein input sourcing, manufacturing, distribution, and shipping and logistics are likely to be the most vulnerable areas.[21]

Surveys of multinational chief executives in 2004 by PriceWaterhouseCoopers and the Rand Corporation-Europe report terrorism is perceived as one of the five greatest threats to business growth and a significant threat to their organization.[22] Other research and survey results report CEOs and CFOs have increased their investments in risk management and security systems in the range of 10 per cent per year since 2001 and expect those increases to continue.[23] By systematically analyzing people and processes, IHRM professionals may contribute to 'stabilizing risk'[24] through recommendations that 'harden' processes in the value chain, recruit people with capabilities and skills relevant for these kinds of processes and train employees in these processes and systems.

In a similar vein, Gillingham presents risk analysis in terms of partitioning security risk into an external environmental dimension (geographic region of operation) and an internal company dimension (industry, firm media profile, national affiliation associated with the company). Low-risk companies in low-risk environments do not need to invest as heavily in security systems and protocols. High-risk companies in low-risk environments should follow security strategies that focus on hardening individual sites. Low-risk companies in high-risk environments can follow security strategies that disperse activities across the region and build redundant infrastructure, so that value chain activities in the high-risk region can be provided by out of region units. High-risk companies in high-risk environments must invest much more in quite elaborate risk management strategies.[25] Much remains to be understood in this rapidly evolving area, and the expectations, standards and practices of IHRM executives and professionals as they relate to safety and security are in flux. According to Czinkota *et al.:* 'In depth case studies on firms directly affected by terrorism will also serve to provide grounded information as to the nature of the relationships between types of terrorism and their specific effects, and facilitate the development of models and theory.'[26] A similar conclusion can be reached in terms of the need for a better understanding of these challenges facing IHRM in MNEs.

Strategic HRM: research issues and theoretical developments

The field of IHRM has been slow to develop as a rigorous body of theory. There are a number of reasons for this:

- There are major methodological problems involved in the area of international management and IHRM. These problems greatly increase the complexity of doing international research and, as Adler[27] noted some years ago, it is often quite difficult to solve these problems with the rigor usually required of within-culture studies by journal editors and reviewers. The major methodological problems in this area are:

  — *Defining culture and the emic-etic distinction.* The problems of defining culture and the emic-etic distinction were discussed in Chapter 1.
  — *Static group comparisons.* An enduring issue in international research is that virtually all cross-cultural comparisons are based on 'static group designs'.[28] The difficulty with static group comparisons in international research is that subjects are not randomly assigned from a superordinate population to different levels of a treatment variable. In practice, it is impossible for cross-cultural researchers to avoid this methodological problem. This difficulty is further compounded by ill-defined notions of culture as an independent variable. As Malpass[29] has observed,

  > No matter what attribute of culture the investigator prefers to focus upon or to interpret as the causative variable, any other variable correlated with the alleged causative variable could potentially serve in an alternative explanation of a mean difference between two or more local populations.

  As a practical solution to this problem, Malpass recommends that investigators should attempt to obtain data on as many rival explanations as possible and then demonstrate that they are less plausible (by conducting post hoc statistical analyses, for example) than the investigator's favored interpretation.[30]
  — *Translation and stimulus equivalence.* Researchers need to be aware that problems may arise when translating concepts central to one culture into the language of another culture. Triandis and Brislin[31] argue that translation problems should be a starting point for research, rather than a data collection frustration. The decentering technique – translating from the original to the target language and back again through several iterations – is advocated. This technique allows the researcher to test if there is any emic coloring of the concepts under investigation. A related point is that non-native speakers need to translate research findings into English for publication in English-language journals.

- International studies are invariably more expensive than domestic studies. International research takes more time, involves more travel and frequently requires the cooperation of host-country organizations, government officials and researchers. Developing a stream of research is consequently much more difficult. An example, though, of how academics can overcome some of these difficulties is the 'best practice' country/regional study and analysis of ten countries' approaches to HRM, involving a diverse team of academics from various countries.[32]

Until relatively recently, many management and HR researchers have regarded the IHRM field as a marginal academic area. This attitude was reflected in the relatively small number of stand-alone business school courses in IHRM – a situation which is changing, particularly in Europe and the Asia-Pacific region, but less so in the USA. A strong positive development was the establishment of a dedicated journal in the field (*International Journal of Human Resource Management*) in 1990 by Professor Michael Poole at Cardiff University that has had a significant impact on the development of research in the field of IHRM. An increasing number of books which have focused on HRM in particular regions such as Latin America,[33] Central and Eastern Europe,[34] the Middle-East,[35] Europe,[36] Africa,[37] and the Asia Pacific[38] have also made a valuable contribution to the IHRM literature.

The human resource function in MNEs

As presented in Chapter 1, the sheer complexity of the IHRM function in MNEs has led to a fundamental re-examination of the purposes, actors, roles and relationships between line managers and staff HR specialists, between subsidiary HR staff and corporate HR specialists, between MNE employees and outsourced contractors, and between the various HR actors within the MNE hierarchy (e.g. HR members on the Board of Directors, at Vice President level or reporting directly to a board member).[39] An analysis of HR staffing practices in 17 European countries and Japan by Brewster *et al.*[40] led to the following conclusions:

- Larger MNEs have proportionately smaller HR departments (measured by ratio of HR staff to total head count), while smaller firms, perhaps more engaged in transactional administration and reacting to daily issues, have proportionately larger HR departments.

- HR ratio varies with industry sector, such that firms with lower levels of internal and external interdependence and standardized work outputs require less HR activity, while sectors characterized by more external networking, more organic, and unpredictable, non-routine work outputs are associated with more HR headcount.

- National regulatory heritage, in the form of regulatory complexity, creates a context for HR activities. Japan, characterized by mandatory transactions, has larger HR staffs, while the former communist nations of Central and Eastern Europe, reacting to the deregulation associated with changes from planned economies and the widespread acceptance of 'market forces', has smaller HR staffs. Beyond these patterns, how transactional or strategic HR becomes is not clearly related to the size of the HR staff.

- More resources spent on training and employee development, HR presence on the Board and the absence of unions are all associated with larger HR staffs.

- Institutionally, where roles and relationships are more formally established by bureaucratic systems, trade union contracts or government mandates, HR departments are smaller.[41]

Clearly, disentangling the complex relationships between those institutional, industrial and historical contingencies that may contribute to the pattern of IHRM philosophies, strategies, policies, practices and capabilities of an MNE, industry or nation remains a rich area for future research.[42]

Summary and concluding remarks

Throughout this book, we have endeavored to highlight the challenges faced by firms as they confront human resource management concerns related to international business operations. This chapter has been concerned with identified trends and future challenges – both managerial and academic – that are likely to have an impact on IHRM, as a function and as a scientific field of study. We specifically addressed:

- International business ethics and HRM.
- Modes of operation other than wholly owned subsidiaries, and the IHRM activities that are required, such as training for contractual and project operations.
- Ownership issues relating to family-owned firms, and non-government organizations (NGOs) and the IHRM challenges specific to these organizations as they grow internationally that have remained relatively under-identified, despite their continuing importance in international business and global activities.
- The complex assessment and planning activities related to safety, security and counterterrorist efforts.
- Research issues in IHRM, and developments that are endeavoring to assist in understanding the intricacies and interrelationships between the IHRM function and IHR activities, firm internationalization and strategic directions and goals.

A consistent theme throughout this book has been the way in which IHRM requires a broader perspective of what operating internationally involves, and a clear recognition of the range of issues pertaining to all categories of staff operating in different functional, task, and managerial capacities is essential. As Poole[43] stated in his editorial in the first issue of the *International Journal of Human Resource Management* in 1990, 'international human resource management archetypically involves the world-wide management of people in the multinational enterprise'.

Discussion Questions

1 What is your view of international initiatives to criminalize foreign bribery?

2 Identify a number of HRM problems that typically arise with expatriate assignments. In what ways might the core ethical values and guidelines identified in this chapter apply to them?

3 Why is management succession frequently an issue for family-owned firms?

4 Beyond checklists and systemic analysis, what actions can MNEs take to reduce risks related to terrorism? What roles can HRM take in these processes?

5 What IHRM activities would be pertinent to the sending, by Médecins Sans Frontieres, of a medical team into a country such as Bangladesh?

Further Reading

Cascio, W. (2006). 'Decency Means More Than "Always Low Prices": A Comparison of Costco to Wal-Mart's Sam's Club', *Academy of Management Perspective,* 20(3): 26–37.

Scullion, H. and Linehan, M. (eds) (2005). *International Human Resource Management: A Critical Text,* Basingstoke: Palgrave/Macmillan.

Shen, J. and Edwards, V. (2006). *International Human Resource Management in Chinese Multinationals,* London: Routledge.

Stahl, G. and Björkman, I. (eds) (2006). *Handbook of Research in International Human Resource Management,* Cheltenham: Edward Elgar.

Suder, G. (ed.) (2004). *Terrorism and the International Business Environment: The Security-Business Nexus,* Cheltenham: Edward Elgar.

Suder, G. (ed.) (2006). *Corporate Strategies Under International Terrorism and Adversity,* Cheltenham: Edward Elgar.

Notes and References

1 See T. Jackson, *International HRM: A Cross-cultural Approach,* Chapter 5, 'The Motivating Organization: The Japanese Model' (London: Sage Publications, 2002), pp. 107–26; E. Ikegami, *The Taming of the Samurai: Honorific Individualism and the Making of Modern Japan* (Cambridge, MA: Harvard University Press, 1995); and J. Abegglen and G. Stalk, *Kaisha: The Japanese Corporation* (New York: Basic Books, 1985).

2 See www.oecd.org/topic/0,2686,en_2649_34855_1_1_1_1_37447,00.html for a comprehensive list of resources offered by the OECD on bribery in international business.

3 T.L. Carson, 'Bribery, Extortion, and the Foreign Corrupt Practices Act', *Philosophy and Public Affairs* (1984) pp. 66–90. See also www.usdoj.gov/criminal/fraud/fcpa.html for up-to-date information on the FCPA.

4 W. Bottiglieri, M. Marder and E. Paderon, 'The Foreign Corrupt Practices Act: Disclosure Requirements and Management Integrity', *SAM Advanced Journal,* Winter (1991), pp. 21–7.

5 www.oecd.org/topic/0,2686,en_2649_34859_1_1_1_1_37447,00.html.

6 For the most up-to-date TI Corruption Index consult the Internet at http:// www.transparency.org/.

7 W. Cascio, 'The High Cost of Low Wages', *Harvard Business Review,* Vol. 84, Issue 12 (2006), p. 23; W. Cascio, 'Decency Means More Than "Always Low Prices": A Comparison of Costco to Wal-Mart's Sam's Club', *Academy of Management Perspectives,* Vol. 20, No. 3 (2006), pp. 26–37; P. Ghemawat, 'Business, Society and the "Wal-Mart Effect"', *Academy of Management Perspectives,* Vol. 20, No. 3 (2006), pp. 41–3; A Harrison and M. McMillan, 'Dispelling Some Myths About Offshoring', *Academy of Management Perspectives,* Vol. 20, No. 4 (2006), pp. 6–22; and D. Farrell, M. Laboissiere and J. Rosenfeld, 'Sizing the Emerging Global Labor Market', *Academy of Management Perspectives,* Vol. 20, No. 4 (2006), pp. 23–34. See also websites such as www.walmartmovie.com and www.wakeupwalmart.com which are highly critical of Wal-Mart and www.walmartfacts.com where Wal-Mart responds to this criticism.

8 H. De Cieri and P. Dowling, 'Strategic International Human Resource Management in Multinational Enterprises: Developments and Directions', in G. Stahl and I Björkman (eds), *Handbook of Research in International Human Resource Management* (Cheltenham: Edward Edgar, 2006), pp. 15–35; P. Rosenzweig, 'The Dual Logics Behind International Human Resource Management: Pressures for Global Integration and Local Responsiveness', in G. Stahl and I. Björkman (eds), *Handbook of Research in International Human Resource Management* (Cheltenham: Edward Elgar, 2006), pp. 36–48; and P. Stiles and J. Trevor, 'The Human Resource Department: Roles, Coordination and Influence', in G. Stahl and I. Björkman (eds), *Handbook of Research in International Human Resource Management* (Cheltenham: Edward Elgar, 2006), pp. 49–67.

9 R. Schuler and I. Tarique, 'International Joint Venture System Complexity and Human Resource Management', in G. Stahl and I. Björkman (eds), *Handbook of Research in International Human Resource Management* (Cheltenham: Edward Elgar, 2006), pp. 385–404.

10 See www.bechtel.com/overview.htm for details of the Bechtel Corporation.

11 H.W.C. Yeung, 'Limits to the Growth of Family-Owned Business? The Case of Chinese Transnational Corporations from Hong Kong', *Family Business Review,* Vol. XIII, No. 1 (2000), pp. 55–70.

12 M. Fenwick, 'Extending Strategic International Human Resource Management Research and Pedagogy to the Non-Profit Multinational', *International Journal of Human Resource Management,* Vol. 16, No. 4 (2005), pp. 497–512.

13 M. Fenwick, 'Extending Strategic International Human Resource Management Research and Pedagogy to the Non-Profit Multinational', p. 508.

14 The authors would like to acknowledge the assistance of Tom Schneid, Professor of Loss Prevention and Safety, and Larry Collins, Associate Professor of Loss Prevention and Safety and Chair of the Department of Loss Prevention and Safety in the College of Justice and Safety at Eastern Kentucky University in Richmond, Kentucky, USA in the preparation of this section of Chapter 12.

15 Although much of this material is specific to national or industry regulations, see R. Mathis and J. Jackson, *Human Resource Management,* 11th edn (Mason, OH: South-Western/Thomson, 2006), Chapter 15 for a US perspective.

16 M. Schumann and T. Schneid, *Legal Liability: A Guide for Safety and Loss Prevention Professionals* (Gaithersburg, MD: Aspen Publishers, 1997).

17 For a review of the range of services available to firms, see '2007 Loss Prevention Resource Guide', *Loss Prevention: The Magazine for LP Professionals,* Vol. 6, No. 1 (2007), pp. 67–98.

18 Personal correspondence and interview with Tom Schneid, 12 February 2007. Also see T. Schneid and L. Collins, *Disaster Management and Preparedness* (Boca Raton, FA: Lewis Publishers/CRC Press, 2001). For a very similar discussion on the dimensions of risk management practices and the degree to which multinational enterprises are viewing security and terrorism as critical strategic issues, planning for these forms of risks and allocating resources for training and protocol enhancements, see D. Wernick, 'Terror Incognito: International Business in an Era of Heightened Geopolitical Risk', in G. Suder (ed.), *Corporate Strategies under International Terrorism and Adversity* (Cheltenham: Edward Elgar, 2006), pp. 59–82.

19 M. Czinkota, G. Knight and P. Liesch, 'Terrorism and International Business: Conceptual Foundations', in G. Suder (ed.), *Terrorism and the International Business Environment: The Security-Business Nexus* (Cheltenham: Edward Edgar, 2004), p. 48.

20 F. Dimanche, 'The Tourism Sector', in G. Suder (ed.), *Terrorism and the International Business Environment: The Security-Business Nexus* (Cheltenham: Edward Elgar, 2004), pp. 157–70.

21 Czinkota *et al.,* 'Terrorism and International Business: Conceptual Foundations', p. 55. For a very similar analysis specific to SARS, see W.-J. Tan and P. Enderwick, 'Managing Threats in the Global Era: The Impact and Responses to SARS', *Thunderbird International Business Review,* Vol. 48, No. 4 (2006), pp. 515–36. J. McIntyre and E. Travis provide a thorough albeit general discussion of MNE practices related to hardening global supply chains in 'Global Supply Chain Under Conditions of Uncertainty: Economic Impacts, Corporate Responses and Strategic Lessons', in G. Suder (ed.), *Corporate Strategies under International Terrorism and Adversity* (Cheltenham: Edward Elgar, 2006), pp. 128–60.

22 D. Wernick, 'Terror Incognito', p. 68.

23 G. Hulme, 'Under Attack', *Information Week,* www.informationweek.com/shared/printableArticle. jhtlm?articleID=22103493, 5 July 2004.; D. Wernick, 'Terror Incognito', pp. 68–9.

24 Czinkota *et al.,* 'Terrorism and International Business', p. 55.

25 D. Gillingham, 'Managing in an Era of Terrorism', in G. Suder (ed.), *Corporate Strategies under International Terrorism and Adversity* (Cheltenham: Edward Elgar, 2006), pp. 196–203, particularly Table 1.2, p. 199.

26 Czinkota *et al.,* 'Terrorism and International Business', pp. 55–6.

27 N. Adler, 'Cross-Cultural Management Research: The Ostrich and the Trend', *Academy of Management Review,* Vol. 8, No. 2 (1983), pp. 226–32.

28 See R.S. Bhagat and S.J. McQuaid, 'Role of Subjective Culture in Organizations: A Review and Directions for Future Research', *Journal of Applied Psychology,* Vol. 67 (1982), pp. 653–85; D.T. Campbell and J. Stanley, *Experimental and Quasi-Experimental Design for Research* (Chicago, IL: Rand-McNally, 1966); and R.S. Malpass, 'Theory and Method in Cross-Cultural Psychology', *American Psychologist,* Vol. 32 (1977), pp. 1069–79.

29 Malpass, 'Theory and Method', p. 1071.

30 See L. Kelly and R. Worthley, 'The Role of Culture in Comparative Management: A Cross-Cultural Perspective', *Academy of Management Journal,* Vol. 24, No. 1 (1981), pp. 164–73; and P.J. Dowling and T.W. Nagel, 'Nationality and Work Attitudes: A Study of Australian and American Business Majors', *Journal of Management,* Vol. 12, No. 1 (1986), pp. 121–8, for further discussion on this point.

31 H.C. Triandis and R.W. Brislin, 'Cross-Cultural Psychology', *American Psychologist,* Vol. 39 (1984), pp. 1006–16.

32 For a review and related articles, see M.A. Von Glinow, Guest Editor, 'Best Practices in IHRM: Lessons Learned from a Ten Country/Regional Analysis', *Asia Pacific Journal of Human Resources,* Vol. 40, No. 1 (2002). Special Issue.

33 M. Elvira and A. Davila (eds), *Managing Human Resources in Latin America* (London: Routledge, 2005).

34 M. Morley, N. Heraty and S. Michailova (eds), *Managing Human Resources in Central and Eastern Europe* (London: Routledge, 2007).

35 P. Budhwar and K. Mellahi (eds), *Managing Human Resources in the Middle-East* (London: Routledge, 2006).

36 H. Larsen and W. Mayrhofer (eds), *Managing Human Resources in Europe* (London: Routledge, 2006).

37 K. Kamoche, Y. Debrah, F. Horwitz and G. Nkombo Muuka (eds), *Managing Human Resources in Africa* (London: Routledge, 2003).

38 P. Budhwar (ed.), *Managing Human Resources in Asia-Pacific* (London: Routledge, 2004).

39 See P. Sparrow, 'Globalization of HR at Function Level: Exploring the Issues Through International Recruitment, Selection and Assessment Processes', International Programs, Visiting Fellow Working Papers, Cornell University (2006). (http://digitalcommonsilr.cornell.edu/intlvf/25); I. Björkman and J. Lervik, 'Transferring HRM Practices Within Multinational Corporations', Working Paper, September (2006); I. Björkman, A. Smale, J. Sumelius, V. Suutari and Y. Lu, 'Changes in Institutional Context and MNC Operations in China: Subsidiary HRM Practices in 1996 Versus 2006', Working Paper (2006); and P. Buckley, J. Clegg, N. Forsans and K. Reilly, 'Increasing the Size of the "Country": Regional Economic Integration and Foreign Direct Investment in a Globalised World Economy', *Management International Review,* Vol. 41, No. 3 (2001), pp. 251–74. For more on the nature and significance of an international HR perspective at various vertical levels in the MNE, see S. Gibb, 'Line Manager Involvement in Learning and Development: Small Beer or Big Deal?', *Employee Relations,* Vol. 25, No. 3 (2003), pp. 281–93; P. Magnusson and D. Boggs, 'International Experience and CEO Selection: An Empirical Study', *Journal of International Management,* Vol. 12, No. 1 (2006), pp. 107–25; and M. Svoboda and S. Schroder, 'Transforming Human Resources in the New Economy: Developing the Next Generation of Global HR Managers at Deutsche Bank AG', *Human Resource Management,* Vol. 40, No. 3 (2001), pp. 261–73.

40 C. Brewster, G. Wood, M. Brookes and J. Van Ommeren, 'What Determines the Size of the HR Function? A Cross-National Analysis', *Human Resource Management,* Vol. 45, No. 1 (2006), pp. 3–21.

41 *Ibid.,* pp. 13–16.

42 Z. Aycan, 'The Interplay Between Cultural and Institutional/Structural Contingencies in Human Resource Management Practices', *International Journal of Human Resource Management,* Vol. 16, No. 7 (2005), pp. 1083–119.; H. De Cieri and P. Dowling, 'Strategic International Human Resource Management in Multinational Enterprises: Developments and Directions'; S. Taylor and N. Napier, 'International HRM in the Twenty-First Century: Crossing Boundaries, Building Connections', in H. Scullion and M. Linehan (eds), *International Human Resource Management: A Critical Text* (Basingstoke: Palgrave/Macmillan, 2005), pp. 298–318; and C. Brewster, 'Comparing HRM Policies and Practices Across Geographical Borders', in G. Stahl and I. Björkman (eds), *Handbook of Research in International Human Resource Management* (Cheltenham: Edward Elgar, 2006), pp. 68–90.

43 M. Poole, 'Editorial: Human Resource Management in an International Perspective', *International Journal of Human Resource Management,* Vol. 1, No. 1 (1990), pp. 1–15.

Cases

Spanning the globe

Allen D. Engle, Sr. © 2004

Eric Christopher, Associate Director for Global HR Development at Tex-Mark, was sitting in his car in an early-morning traffic jam. He had thought that by leaving his home at 7:00 am he would have been ahead of the heavy commuter traffic into San Antonio's city center. The explanation for the long queue was announced by the radio traffic service. A large, portable crane, used to set up concrete barriers around road works, had overturned, and inbound and outbound traffic would be at a dead stop for at least an hour.

Eric had ended up at Tex-Mark, a computer input-output manufacturer and supplier, through an indirect career route. Brought up in the Hill Country Village district of San Antonio, Eric had graduated from Churchill High School and Baylor University in Waco, Texas with a major in History and a minor in Spanish. His maternal grandmother lived in Tennessee, but was born and grew up in Edinburgh, Scotland and Eric had spent several summers while in high school and at university backpacking around Europe.

His facility for languages was impressive and he had an excellent working use of Spanish, French, Italian and German. He could converse in Cantonese, as the result of working in a noodle restaurant during university and had started a tutorial course in Mandarin last fall.

Upon graduation, Eric backpacked around Europe and South America until his money ran out. Returning to Dallas he took a ticketing job with SouthWest Airlines and was quickly moved to the training unit. After four successful years at SouthWest, he was contacted by a headhunter about a position as Global Development Assistant with Tex-Mark. The promised combination of global travel, more money and a return to San Antonio proved irresistible, and Eric had been with Tex-Mark for five years now. His career progress to date was outstanding, despite the extra workload self-imposed by undertaking MBA studies at University of Texas at San Antonio as a part-time student.

Tex-Mark had started out as a 'spin off' firm from Dell Computers in the late 1970s. Patents combined with an excellence in engineering, an outstanding institutional sales staff, cost-sensitive production and pricing, all combined to make Tex-Mark a major force in the printer and optical scanner industry. Tex-Mark inherited a production facility in San Antonio from Dell, but the company also had international production facilities operating in three countries: Monterrey, Mexico, Leith, Scotland and more recently in Jaipur, India. A major new facility was scheduled to start production in Wuhu, China late next year.

Research and new product development activities were split between the home offices in San Antonio, a printer center in Durham, North Carolina and an optical research 'center of excellence' in Edinburgh, Scotland. Major sales, distribution and customer service centers had recently expanded into Asia and are now located in Rheims in France; in Memphis, Tennessee; in Sydney, Australia; in Rio de Janeiro, Brazil; in Hong Kong; and in Tel Aviv, Israel.

Faced with the long delay, Eric turned the radio volume down, turned up the air conditioning, and telephoned his office on his hands-free car phone to advise of his situation. Fortunately, his personal assistant was already at work so Eric was able to rearrange his schedule. He asked that the 10:30 meeting with Fred Banks, a Plant Engineer recently repatriated from Jaipur, be pushed back an hour. His major concern was a teleconference meeting at 2:00 with his Director who was currently visiting the sales center in Memphis, and the other four members of the executive career development team in San Antonio. The general topic was a review and evaluation of training and development strategies for expatriate professionals and managers resulting from Tex-Mark's growth and the new production shift to Asia. Eric had indirectly heard that Juanita Roberto, the Vice President for HR wanted costs cut and her delegates on the team would be pushing for streamlined (Eric had mentally translated that as cheaper) training programs, shorter expatriate assignments and a faster appointment of HCNs whenever possible. While Eric had prepared for this crucial meeting, he needed to incorporate some information from his office files.

The radio announcer broke into Eric's thoughts, commented that overextension or carrying too much weight probably caused the crane to overturn. 'I can identify with that', Eric thought to himself.

Eric's meeting with Fred Banks had not gone well. Fred was one of the last of the 'Dell legacies', a Dell engineer that had stayed on with Tex-Mark after the spin-off in 1978. Fred had been a bright and promising young engineer back then, and was one of the first people chosen to go to Scotland in 1983. He was so successful in bringing that facility on-line in an eleven-month assignment that he was made lead engineer of the team that went into Mexico in 1989. The three-year Mexican project did not go as smoothly. Certainly there were many unavoidable economic uncertainties during that period.

Reviewing the files, Eric felt a large part of the problem was that Fred's team did not relate well to their Mexican counterparts. Furthermore, the Tex-Mark team did not treat the local and national government agencies with enough respect and sensitivity. Eric noted that permits and authorizations that should have taken weeks instead took six months or more.

After the Mexican project Fred stayed in San Antonio with occasional trips to Durham, North Carolina. His assignment to India in 1999 was by sheer chance, as a last minute replacement for another engineer whose father was diagnosed with a serious cancer some two weeks before the family was to set off on assignment. Eric had helped design the pre-departure training program for the original candidate and had even included a one-week visit for the candidate and his wife.

Today Fred was angry and disappointed that an eighteen-month assignment in India had turned into a three-year assignment, and that a research position in Durham 'promised' to him by a previous VP (two VPs ago) was filled by a younger Durham resident employee. Eric bluntly countered that the eighteen-month assignment had become a three-year assignment largely due to Fred's unwillingness to train and hand over responsibilities to local engineers and his inability to work constructively with district and federal regulators in India.

The conversation took a hostile turn and although Eric did not lose his temper, he was troubled by Fred's final comment: 'If this is how you treat the people willing to go abroad, you'll never get your best engineers to leave San Antonio.'

Preparing for the 2:00 meeting, Eric reviewed the unofficial, yet 'standard' expatriate training program he had been instrumental in developing over the last three years (see Exhibit A below). Though Eric recommended that all pre-departure activities should be undertaken, it was not compulsory.

With the Chinese operation adding to the number of expatriate destinations, Eric realized Tex-Mark should have a more formal policy regarding international assignments. Feedback regarding the interviews and conversations with Tex-Mark employees with country experiences was mixed. Some had developed into longer term mentoring arrangements but other expatriates had found it not useful. Still, it was a lost cost way of providing information. Language courses were problematic. On too many occasions, there was not the time – employees left the country mid-way through their language courses. He recalled the idea of more 'extensive' assignments requiring more 'complete' and 'rigorous' preparation from an MBA course he took last year. Obviously China is a more challenging and difficult assignment than France, but can we differentiate treatment on the grounds of cultural difficulty?

More importantly, Eric asked himself, 'How can I suggest we make our training more rigorous given Juanita Roberto's focus on cost? Even if I win on this point, what will I answer when asked what methods or activities make up more "rigorous" training?' and 'What is the role of language training?' Eric knew not

---

Tex-Mark Corporation

Exhibit A

Policy for expatriate preparation and on-assignment support

Pre-departure activities

1 'Country briefings', outsourced to a consulting firm in San Antonio that had experience dealing with the countries in which Tex-Mark operated. Tex-Mark was prepared to pay for four sessions each lasting one hour.

2 'Reading Assignments'. Three to four books (depending on region of assignment) on national or regional culture and/or doing business in the focal region. Accompanying spouses/partners had access to a similar library.

3 'Interviews and conversations' with Tex-Mark employees with country experiences.

4 'Language courses'. Attendance at elective 'survival level' language classes. These courses last from eight to twelve weeks, with three course meetings a week. Tex-Mark will pay for spouses/partners as well.

In-country training and development

Upon arrival, Tex-Mark staff in the local operation will assist the accompanying spouse/partner with job search activities. They will assist with finding children acceptable schooling situations. Where possible, Tex-Mark staff will endeavour to provide a social support network.

Repatriation

Upon return all expatriates are required to go through a debriefing and career counselling session with HR staff. This should be held within two months of the person's re-entry to the home location.

everyone took to languages the way he did and that Mandarin is not Spanish. Finally, 'Is now the time to raise the issue of repatriation?' The meeting with Fred had been disturbing. Eric knew that the current debriefing and counselling sessions had a reputation for being more 'tell and sell' than a meaningful exchange of ideas and insights. Top management had recently signalled this as a growing 'problem'. Eric had planned to gather data on repatriate turnover. Perhaps this should be given a higher priority. After all, how could Tex-Mark decide to plan for international assignments, involving more TCN movements, and the transfer of HCNs into its US operations for training and development, without considering repatriation?

In the role of Eric

1 Summarize your thoughts on the problems at hand, alternative solutions and your strategy on how to proceed at the forthcoming meeting.

2 How will your proposal solve the problems you have defined?

3 How can you defend your solution from budgetary concerns? In what way is your approach both a solution to the problems of expatriates at Tex-Mark and a good economic investment?

Step back out of role and answer the following

1 Does Eric's personal background assist in his assessment of the problems he faces?

2 Would you have approached this situation differently? If so, what benefits would your different approach provide for Tex-Mark?

Quality compliance at the Hawthorn Arms

Allen D. Engle, Sr. © 2004

Sitting in his room at the Hawthorn Arms Hotel in Shannon, Ireland, waiting for a morning flight to London and then on to Marseilles, Alistair Mackay reflects on how uninspiring hotel rooms are. He had just completed a series of meetings with Irish officials in Limerick, concluding with a debriefing session over a Guinness with his Irish colleagues to plan their next move. Negotiations over a potential contract were proceeding well but there would certainly be labor implications that would require a formal response. Consequently, Alistair had missed the last evening flight out to London. 'Another night away from the family. Thank goodness I am not missing our wedding anniversary tomorrow. I must remember to find something really special in the duty-free shop.'

Six months ago, Alistair was appointed Director of Personnel Development, European Division, for Trianon, an Anglo-French avionics firm. Trianon had begun as a subcontractor for the Concorde, and gradually had gained a reputation in the 1970s and 1980s as a high-quality, if sometimes undependable, subcontractor for major French and British aerospace defence contractors. Attempts to expand into civilian markets by gaining contracts for the original European Airbus were unsuccessful, though today nearly 30 per cent of Trianon's sales are through civilian contracts. Now, under new executive management, Trianon is focused on major navigational display contracts for the next generation of Airbus production. Prior to joining Trianon, Alistair had worked in the legal department of a Scottish bank. European Union employment requirements had become his speciality, and provided a springboard into his current position.

His cell phone rings, and he receives an unexpected call from his colleague Henri Genadry, General Director of Joint Ventures, Mergers and Acquisitions, Display Division. Henri informs him that the expected outright purchase of a scanner-cathode ray tube production facility in Veceses, outside of Budapest, Hungary was not going ahead. Instead, the decision had been made at corporate headquarters in Marseilles for a ten-year joint venture with a Hungarian government-backed firm.

Henri goes on to explain that the Hungarian control and equity interests in this project are expected to make ministry officials in Budapest happy. Henri was hopeful the decision will make executives and administrators at Malev, the state supported airline, friendly to Trianon in the long term. 'We will now need a "Quality Compliance Manager" for a three-year assignment in Hungary. It is an important position as we will need to keep tight control on this joint venture operation. There will be some travel to France and Germany – at least in the first year – until we see how things are working out with these new partners.'

Alistair asks, 'When do you expect this Quality Compliance Manager to be available?' There is a pause on the other end of the line after which Henri blandly responds, 'Five or six weeks if we are to meet corporate timetables. We expect the person to be in on the ground floor so to speak. We will need a realistic assessment of current processes for a start. The person will need to be familiar with the joint venture's objectives and targets. We have some details through the due diligence process but skills audits were somewhat rushed.' Alistair then asks that details, including a job description, be emailed to his intranet address.

'Well', Henri admits, 'this is the first joint venture our firm has been involved in outside of the UK, Germany or France. The job description will be very precise on the technical – "quality" side, but vague on the administrative – "compliance" – side. You may need to fill in the missing pieces as you see fit.'

After a few more minutes of general chatting, Henri finishes the phone call. Alistair plugs his laptop into the telephone port on his room's desk, and after a few false starts, logs on to the secure corporate website and accesses three personnel files from a folder he had prepared some weeks ago in expectation that he would be asked for a decision. Of course, he had expected the position to be that of Project Engineer in an operation of which the firm would have 100 per cent ownership. Now he was looking for a Quality Compliance Manager in a joint venture.

Alistair doesn't like making these kinds of decisions when feeling so remote and 'disconnected' from the firm. He considers calling his friend and mentor, Gunther Heinrich in Frankfurt, Germany, and asking him about the Hungarian project, as the German-based divisions had more experience dealing with Hungarian issues. He looks at his watch. It was 22.30. 'Not a civilized time to call anyone, let alone Gunther.' Alistair knew that Gunther's wife Britt had presented them with a son three weeks ago, and they were having trouble getting the child to sleep through the night. 'I will call him from the airport and set up a meeting. I will have the job description by then.'

He is also feeling uncomfortable with the process he was going through. Surely we can do better than react like this after the event. Why were we not part of the decision-making process on the Hungarian venture?

1   Consider the three candidates in Exhibit A below. If forced to make a decision tomorrow, which candidate should Alistair choose for the job? What major factors should determine his choice?

2   We are told nothing of the process that Trianon uses to recruit candidates for this level of final selection. Given what you know about the firm from the case, outline a general recruitment and selection process for Trianon. Describe how your proposed process fits with 'best' selection practices as well as the strategic needs of this company.

3   Should HR staff be involved in strategic decisions relating to international business operations such as finalizing a joint venture agreement?

Alistair Mackay's short list of possible candidates

First candidate. Marie Erten-Loiseau. Born in Prague, her family moved to Toulon when Marie was twelve years old. Brought up in France, she was educated as an aeronautical engineer in France and Germany. Marie worked for Trianon for 13 years, in two divisions within France and Germany with increasing levels of project responsibility. Her leadership of two projects over the last three years in Lodz, Poland, and two sites in the Czech Republic has been marked by remarkable success. Married, her husband is semi-retired. They have one child in university.

Second candidate. Janos Gabor. Born in Gyor, Hungary, Janos was educated at University of Pecs, Hungary. He has a good background in the production of cathode ray tube and display systems technologies, albeit from the Central European perspective. He has worked at Trianon for nearly four years, and has just been transferred into the cathode ray tube division as a Senior Engineer. His family is reportedly very well connected with national government officials, particularly the old, ex-party members of multiple ministerial bureaucracies. Janos is single.

Third candidate. Sinead Marrinan-McGuire, a production engineer on loan to Trianon's London office for joint venture analyzes and 'due diligence' reviews on technical and legal grounds. She has spent three years in the R&D development team in Dublin and London, working on the very technologies to be applied in this Hungarian joint venture project. Alistair met and talked with her today in Limerick and was very impressed with her understanding of corporate level concerns and strategic issues. Most of her career has been in Ireland and around London, with only short, tactical trips to France. Married, her husband is a solicitor in Dublin. They have three children, ages 7, 9 and 13.

Jaguar or bluebird?
(A) Mark Chan's decision to stay overseas or return home after his expatriate assignment[1]

Günter K. Stahl (INSEAD Singapore), Chei Hwee Chua (University of South Carolina) and Rebekah France (INSEAD),

Sitting in a field filled with yellow buttercups, Mark Chan took in a deliberate deep breath of the fresh English country air and felt a sense of contentment as he basked in the warm summer sunshine. He and his family were having a Sunday picnic with their neighbors, the Howards, in their neighborhood park. Some distance away, his wife Linda was happily chatting with the Howards while his two children and the little Howards played with their dog.

Looking at them brought back fond memories of their time in England so far. Almost five years ago, Mark accepted an expatriate assignment and moved to England from Singapore with his family. Mark was glad that his family had settled down happily. They made new friends and assimilated well into the English culture and lifestyle.

Mark gave out a sigh. The thought of having to decide on his next career move hit him again. His international assignment in England was coming to an end in three months' time and he could either continue pursuing an international career or return back to Singapore. Mark felt that deciding on his next career move had never been so difficult. This time, he had a lot more to consider. He not only had to take into account his own career development needs, but also the needs of his wife and children. Mark knew that his company was expecting his answer within the next few days, but the numerous discussions he had with Linda in weighing the pros and cons of each career option could just never come to a decisive conclusion. The more Mark thought about it, the more confused and frustrated he got.

Mark's thoughts triggered his memory back to the critical career decisions that he had made in the past and the series of events that led to his current predicament.

A bachelor on the road: an initial string of international assignments

Mark started his career at the Singapore subsidiary of a Japanese consulting company and embarked on a string of international assignments that lasted about one year each. These international assignments brought him to Japan, Thailand, Indonesia, Vietnam and Malaysia. His job was to help foreign companies to scout and evaluate merger or acquisition opportunities in Asia, as well as the negotiations and closing of the deals. Deciding on taking up these international

assignments was easy. He had always liked the idea of living and working overseas and learning about new cultures. He was a bachelor and his parents were
not too old then and could take care of themselves. There was nothing to tie
him down.

Homeward bound: starting a new job and family

After working overseas for six years, Mark got married and decided that it was
time for him to settle down back in Singapore and start a family. He joined the
Singapore subsidiary of Energem,[2] a diversified, global company with market-
leading positions in a number of industries, including speciality chemicals, polymers, health care and gases and related products. Headquartered in the UK,
Energem employs over 60 000 people worldwide and has extensive operations in
Europe, North and South America and Asia Pacific. Joining Energem at mid-career,
Mark was offered a position as a marketing manager at its Speciality Chemicals division, with responsibilities for corporate accounts of multinational companies in
South-East Asia. Based on Energem's global management ranking structure,[3] it
was a level 4 middle-management position. Mark was attracted to Energem
because it offered international career prospects and had a well-known leadership development program for 'high potentials', including those who had been
recruited locally.

A year later, Mark had a job change and a promotion to level 3. He accepted
the offer by Energem's corporate unit, Group Mergers & Acquisitions (M&A),
to join its team as M&A manager and analyst for Asia Pacific. Energem was starting to embark on M&A activities in this region and Mark's past experience fit-
ted well with the requirements of the job. Mark reported directly to the global
M&A Vice-President who was based in the UK and Mark's responsibilities included scouting for M&A opportunities, conducting due diligence and negotiations and liaison with Energem's various country heads and global business
line heads.

An international assignment opportunity

At the end of his third year at Energem, Mark was offered a three-year international
assignment opportunity at the corporate headquarters in London by Energem's
Group Information Technology (IT) unit. Mark was very excited about the offer.
The job was to conduct M&A activities for the strategic IT needs of Energem's joint
ventures globally. Accepting the offer would mean another promotion for Mark
and he would enter Energem's senior management category. He would report
directly to the Chief Information Officer and would be close to the 'Gods' at
corporate headquarters. Mark also relished the challenge of living and working
overseas, and the salary and expatriate benefits package were very attractive. Mark
remembered that although making the decision to accept the assignment was not
as easy as it had been during his bachelor days, he did not find himself in a huge
dilemma. Although Linda would have to give up her job as a private banker to
follow him on the assignment and they had two children, they both agreed that it
was a small window of opportunity for them to go overseas since their children
were still very young and Linda could take a break from her career and spend more
time with the children.

An expatriate again

Mark recalled his first day at work in the London office. He felt comfortable and settled into his new office easily. Since he had been to the London office rather often in the past, he knew the place well and also knew a number of colleagues based there through past projects. By early evening, he was already having a beer with a few colleagues in the pub near the office.

Despite the initial friendliness, Mark soon realized that there were some colleagues who felt that he got the job because Energem needed a 'token Asian' in the team to show that it valued diversity. Since Energem's M&A activities in Asia were of a smaller scale compared with those in Europe and the USA, they did not think that someone from a subsidiary in Asia would have the knowledge and ability required for the job. Mark knew that there was nothing much that he could do about this perception, except to prove them wrong. Leveraging on his expertise in conducting due diligence and consummating M&As gained within Energem and through his six years as an M&A consultant prior to joining Energem, Mark learned quickly and performed well on the job. As time went by, he earned the respect of those colleagues who had their doubts initially. Mark also used the expatriate assignment opportunity to hone his cross-cultural skills and expand his network of contacts within and outside Energem. When his three-year contract came to an end, he was offered an extension of two years. He had a promotion to level 1 and was now responsible for special M&A projects within Group IT that were confidential and of a larger scale.

On the home front, Mark and his family had settled down in England happily and found the English lifestyle appealing. Energem provided them with a large house with a big garden in the countryside, less than an hour by train to Mark's office in London. They also bought an old English sheepdog – something which they had always wanted but were unable to do as their apartment in Singapore could not accommodate such a big dog. As Mark and his family were Christians, they got to know the people in their neighborhood quickly through attending church services and activities. Some colleagues also lived in the same neighborhood. Mark and his family found it relatively easy to integrate into the local community. They became close friends with several neighbors and often had dinner parties or Sunday picnics together.

After having been a working mum, Linda was thrilled at her new 'occupation' as a full-time home-maker. Linda found herself busier than when she was working. She had always felt guilty for not spending enough time with the children and was glad to make it up to them during their time in London. She felt that it was important to spend as much time as she could with them during their formative years. Linda made friends with the other home-makers in the neighborhood quickly and often met up with them for afternoon teas to exchange gardening tips and cooking recipes. Linda was fascinated by the gardens of their neighbors and became interested in gardening. Soon, their garden was as lovely as those of their neighbors and Linda was especially proud of her plot of red roses which bloomed beautifully in spring and summer.

As Mark continued to reminisce about how they had spent their time in England so far, he realized that the time they spent together as a family had been much more than when they were back home in Singapore and they had became more close-knit. Being away from relatives and friends in Singapore and having to travel a lot during the week, Mark made it a point not to work during the weekends and often brought the family out on weekend excursions and holidays. Back in

Singapore, Mark's family led a typical Singaporean lifestyle. When they went out, they would shop, eat and watch movies at the various large shopping malls found in the city. Hence they found the typical English countryside lifestyle a refreshing change and eagerly adopted it. They especially enjoyed the long walks in the parks nearby, the drives around the English countryside, visits to the castles and the horse rides on the hilly greens. The family also often went on weekend holidays to the neighboring countries. Moreover, compared with the year-round hot and humid climate in Singapore, they preferred the English temperate climate and were fascinated by the changes in seasons.

Being a car enthusiast, Mark was thrilled by the affordability of cars in England. Owing to the Singapore government's efforts at preventing traffic congestion in the small city state, even ordinary cars are luxury items. In Singapore, he could only afford a Nissan Bluebird. But in England, Mark had two cars and they were a Jaguar and a Triumph convertible. With an expatriate salary and benefit package, a temperate climate, a large house with a big garden in the countryside and two fancy cars, Mark's family found themselves living a life that they could only dream of in Singapore.

A bugle call for return

At the end of their fourth year in England, Linda's father passed away unexpectedly after a heart attack. After the funeral, Linda stayed back in Singapore with the children for a month to take care of her mother. The months after her return to England proved to be very difficult. Although she had a younger brother who could take care of their mother and she had always been happy and satisfied with life in England, she was often worried about her mother and felt the need to return to Singapore permanently to take care of her.

An international career or return home to Singapore?

Seeing that Linda was yearning to return home, Mark started to look for a position back at the Singapore subsidiary of Energem. After eight months of searching, Mark was beginning to lose hope when he learned that the Regional General Manager (Asia Pacific) for the Specialty Chemicals division had unexpectedly left for a job at one of their competitors, and Energem had to fill his position quickly with a manager who was familiar with the Asia-Pacific markets. Given his familiarity with the markets in this region and his extensive international experience, Mark thought that he was the natural candidate for this position. He was prepared to accept it on the spot.

Mark remembered clearly the Monday morning when he received the phone call from the Global Vice-President of the Specialty Chemicals division telling him that although nobody doubted his qualification, they had offered the job to one of his former colleagues who was based at Energem's Singapore subsidiary.

The memory of that phone conversation and the resulting emotions of anger, disbelief and betrayal all came back to him. 'It's ridiculous', he told Linda when he informed her about the bad news, 'they selected someone with zero international experience! What happened to all that talk about being a global player and the importance of international experience? It's all crap!'

Having the door closed on this option, Mark was left with the offer of a middle-management position in the Polymers Division to consider. The Global

Vice-President of the Polymers Division told Mark that he was impressed with his track record and that he valued his international experience. However, there were simply no senior management positions available at the moment and he could only offer Mark the position of regional marketing manager for its rubber and coatings business in Asia Pacific. He added that this would be a temporary position and that Mark would be given first priority consideration as soon as a senior management position became available at the Singapore organization.

The other option that Mark had was to continue pursuing his international career. Having proved his abilities in handling global M&A activities, Mark was offered a three-year international assignment at Energem's subsidiary in The Netherlands to where they were about to relocate the headquarters of the corporate unit, Group Mergers & Acquisitions, reflecting Energem's attempts to decentralize critical functions and units. Mark was offered the position of Global Strategy Manager for Energem's special M&A projects. This would mean a promotion to level D. Naturally, the promotion would also mean a higher salary and he would continue to enjoy the perks as an expatriate. On the other hand, taking up the regional marketing manager position in Singapore would essentially mean a demotion. He would have to accept a salary cut and would lose all the expatriate benefits.

The question that Mark continually wrestled with was: 'Does it make sense to give up an attractive international career and a good life in Europe for a return to Singapore at a lower rank position?' Career-wise, the answer was clearly 'No'. On the other hand, Linda had been pressuring him to return to Singapore. Moreover, looking at things on a long-term basis, Mark knew that moving back to Singapore now would be the best option for Linda and possibly also the children. If they stayed abroad too long, Linda would find it even more difficult to continue her banking career. As for the children, they had started to go to school. Unlike England's educational system, on which the Singapore's system is based, The Netherlands is Dutch-speaking and has a very different educational system. Mark thought, 'If we don't move back now, it will be even harder for everybody in the future. But I have worked so hard to be where I am now! I don't want to throw my career away.'

Having been absorbed in his thoughts for some time, Mark suddenly heard giggling and felt a tiny hug from behind. It was his younger son, John. 'Daddy! It's time to eat now! The shepherd's pie that Mrs Howard brought looks really delicious!' As Mark walked towards the rest of his family and the Howards, he felt torn between his career aspirations and the long-term needs of his family. Mark knew that whichever decision he made, either his career or family would suffer.

Notes

1   This case is intended for classroom discussion rather than to illustrate either effective or ineffective handling of an administrative situation.

2   This is a fictitious name.

3   Energem's global management ranking structure is as follows: levels 9, 8, 7, 6 and 5 are junior management positions, levels 4 and 3 are middle management positions and levels 2, 1, D, C, B and A are senior management positions.

Jaguar or bluebird?
(B) Mark Chan returns home after his expatriate assignment[1]

Günter K. Stahl (INSEAD Singapore), Chei Hwee Chua (University of South Carolina) and Rebekah France (INSEAD)

Home sweet home

After several more rounds of long discussions with Linda, they finally decided to move back to Singapore. The needs of his wife, children and mother-in-law were the overriding factors in his decision.

The following months were spent packing and shipping their things and bidding farewells. Other than that, they did not have much time to think about their return to Singapore until the day of the departure. In fact, it did not cross their mind that it was something that they had to be mentally prepared for. 'After all, Singapore is home', they thought.

Reality bites

It had been half a year since Mark and his family moved back to Singapore. To their surprise, adapting back to life in Singapore turned out to be not as easy as they had imagined. After getting used to living in a large house with a big garden in the countryside for five years, their apartment in Singapore seemed much smaller than before. Although they lived in a luxurious condominium complex with facilities such as swimming pools, jacuzzis, saunas, gym and tennis courts, they simply missed the vastness of the English countryside and the lifestyle that they led in England. Mark no longer had his fancy cars and drove a Nissan Bluebird, as he used to do five years ago, before he left Singapore. Linda had to give up her gardening. The children missed their teachers and friends at school. And they all missed their dog terribly. It was impossible to bring it back since it would have been too large for their apartment.

While the whole family was having dinner one evening, Mark's elder son, Jeremy, suddenly blurted out, 'I really *don't* want to go to school *any more*!' '*Me too*!' John, the younger one, followed.

Total silence fell upon the dining room. Tears started to trickle down Linda's face and she began sobbing uncontrollably. She, too, was unhappy. All the tensions and unhappiness that had built up over the past six months suddenly came out in the open. She could no longer pretend that it was great to move home. She knew that all of them were, in one way or another, unhappy with their new life back in Singapore.

Five months ago, Jeremy and John went to school on the first day with a bright and cheery face, but came back quiet and gloomy. Especially Jeremy; he hadn't been quite his usual chirpy self since then. Except for the weekends, the boys were either tired or felt ill every morning, and wanted to skip school. Mark and Linda found out that they did not like going to school because they felt out of place and were unable to make new friends. They said that very often, their teachers and classmates could not understand what they were saying and neither could they fully understand what their teachers and classmates were saying. Having lived in England since they were two and three years old, respectively, both boys grew up speaking English with a clear British accent. So, being in an environment where their new teachers and classmates spoke 'Singlish' – English with a Singaporean accent and Singaporean slang words – communication became a problem. Sometimes, their classmates made fun of their accent by imitating them. They also found Mandarin classes tough since they did not have Mandarin classes in England and they spoke English at home. Therefore, Linda engaged a private tutor to give the boys additional Mandarin classes. Linda and Mark consoled them and told them that they should give school a try and that things would get better. The sudden outburst at the dinner table showed that things obviously did not get better.

Linda and Mark could empathize with their children. Although Linda was happy to be back in Singapore so that she could take care of her mother, she found her life back in Singapore less satisfying than she had imagined while she was in England. In the beginning, her friends were glad to have her back and listened to her about her life in England with interest. However, this interest waned and they started switching topics whenever she mentioned England. Soon, Linda found it difficult to identify with her friends. Sometimes, she couldn't help feeling that some of them who had always lived in Singapore were rather myopic and uninteresting, whereas at other times, she felt left out when they talked about their jobs and office politics. Another problem was job search. Linda was keen to start working again, but with the economic downturn in Singapore, there were few suitable job openings. The application letters that Linda sent either had no replies or were rejected.

For Mark, he began to regret his decision to accept the job in Singapore. When he accepted the position, he knew that it would be a demotion in rank and the scope of his responsibilities would be less. However, he did not expect that he would be feeling bored with the job after just a few months.

Mark started asking the Global Vice-President of the division about more senior positions, but was told that such positions were not available at the moment and that he should be patient. With the downturn of the global economy, there was no growth in the Division's business, particularly in Asia Pacific. And nobody at the senior management level was leaving or retiring soon. Mark also got the same answer from the other Divisions. After six months, Mark realized that his 'temporary' position might not be 'temporary' after all, since senior management positions in Singapore would not be available for quite a while. He felt trapped.

The outbursts by his two children and his wife reminded Mark of his own frustration with his current job situation and his anger of being not offered the Regional General Manager position in the Specialty Chemicals Division. 'This is simply unfair! What's the point of getting international experience when it doesn't get you a decent job back home?', he thought, bitterly. 'How long am I supposed to wait? I've had enough! There must be companies out there that value international experience.'

After consoling his wife and children, Mark went to his home office and dialled the mobile phone number of his friend Nigel, who was head of the local office of an international executive search firm.

Note

1   This case is intended for classroom discussion rather than to illustrate either effective or ineffective handling of an administrative situation.

Wolfgang's balancing act: Rewarding *Healthcare* executives in a dispersed yet integrated firm[1]

Marion Festing and Allen D. Engle

Healthcare – a successful global player in the pharmaceutical market

Healthcare is one of the largest European pharmaceutical companies. The headquarters is situated in Hamburg, Germany, and today there are about 200 subsidiaries all over the world. In 2005, throughout the globe 30 000 people were working for *Healthcare*. Net sales amounted to €5.9 billion, with a net profit of €750m.

The company was founded more than 100 years ago. It started in a small shop in Elmshorn, a little town north of Hamburg. In the beginning, the main business was retailing with only a small part of the product range resulting from in-house production. The founder himself had a background in pharmaceutics. He was very dedicated to science and naturally interested in research and the development of new drugs.

Over the years in-house-production was expanded and soon the founder distributed his products all over Germany and later on in many European countries. Overseas, the activities started in the USA with a small affiliate in New York. Over time *Healthcare* acquired several local pharmaceutical companies, which later became 100 per cent subsidiaries. Today, the US market is one of the core markets for *Healthcare*. However, the first affiliate in the USA was only the beginning of the firm's globalization. After this initial success, *Healthcare* began to enter other lucrative markets of the world – such as Japan, China, Latin America and Australia.

Over time the headquarters in Germany grew dramatically. Headquarters' activities centered on research, and the production and distribution of pharmaceutical products that were now largely developed within the firm. While in the past the product range was highly differentiated, today *Healthcare* concentrates on a few business areas such as oncology or dermatology. Within these business areas the firm is now recognized globally as one of the industry's leaders. The firm intends to continue to build and extend this leading position in these worldwide specialized markets.

Discontinuous changes in the environment – such as increasing costs for research and development and increasing pressure on prices due to cost containment by national authorities, and generic competition – have forced innovative pharmaceutical companies such as *Healthcare* to operate their key business processes globally. The firm has developed a multi-centered company in order to ensure the effective utilization of the resources and provide nimble market penetration and product ramp up. Critical capabilities include corporate-wide R&D

processes, a concentration on a few production sites with worldwide supply responsibility and a fast penetration of the key markets. These capabilities will allow *Healthcare* to ensure the faster and more cost-effective development of innovative products, reduce production costs and thereby provide for significant sales growth and increased profitability.

In the past, *Healthcare*'s situation was characterized by worldwide activities but mainly local business processes (e.g., development and production focusing on local/regional markets). Local issues were aggregated to the four significant regions in which *Healthcare* has organized operations. These regions are Europe, USA/Canada, Latin America and Asia Pacific. Consequently, the human resource management (HRM) processes were adapted to country- or region-specific conditions, and global integration was not a major issue. For example, executives and high potentials were recruited, selected, assessed and compensated based on different regional standards. International human resource (HR) activities concentrated only on a few international managers that acted as coordination agents.

Wolfgang Hansen: the new HR manager

Wolfgang Hansen has been recruited as a new HR manager at *Healthcare*. Wolfgang holds a Master's degree in International Management from the University of Hamburg. During his studies he has participated in a study-abroad program spending a year in London. He has specialized in Human Resource Management and Compensation Strategies. Wolfgang's initial assignment upon graduation was in the HR department of a medium-sized German technical company. However, he missed the international dimension in this job and decided to pursue an executive MBA with a transnational orientation in order to prepare for this ideal career. His first job after having completed his transnational MBA program was at *Healthcare*.

For one year Wolfgang has been with *Healthcare,* beginning as an HR manager. Three months ago he was placed in charge of global compensation policies, with the newly created title of 'Personalreferent für globale Vergütungsstrategien'. His first project is reviewing existing policies and practices. He has been asked to make a series of recommendations on further coordination of global pay systems at the next meeting of the Board of Directors in Frankfurt in January. Preparing the Board meeting, Wolfgang reviews a series of documents such as recent annual reports, the Leadership Competency Set, the new Global Performance Management System and firm-internal strategic documents on the development of the corporate and HRM strategies. Each document set has been placed in its own folder. These six folders contain the following items:

Folder one: the *Healthcare* Group

In 2005, *Healthcare* again had a very successful year and reached records for key financial ratios (see Table 1). Thus, the firm was well prepared for reaching new ambitious targets for 2006. The *Healthcare* Group's very positive business development is based on the sustained growth of their top products in all important markets (see Table 2). Both the strategic reorientation and the improvement in operational efficiency have contributed to the growth of their business. *Healthcare*'s aim is to create a solid base in order to further improve the company's profitability by optimizing the cost structure.

Table 1	Key data on the *Healthcare* Group

Values expressed in €m	2005	2004	Change
Net sales	6,34	5,83	+ 8%
Gross profit	3,951	3,625	+ 9%
R&D costs	981	916	+ 7%
Operating profit	891	736	+ 21%
Net profit	750	577	+ 23%
Return on sales	12.5%	11.2%	+ 1.3%
Cash Flows from operating activities	982	702	+ 40%
Basic earnings per share (€)	3.33	2.52	+ 23%
Total equity	3,134	2,725	+ 15%
Equity ratio	52.6%	47.5%	+ 5.1%
Personnel costs	1,376	1,336	+ 3%
Number of employees (annual average)	30,680	29,875	+ 2,7%

Table 2	Net sales by region of the *Healthcare* Group

	in €m		% of total	
	2005	2004	2005	2004
Europe	2,512	2,394	42%	44%
USA/Canada	2,079	1,856	35%	34%
Asia Pacific	308	275	5%	5%
Latin America	667	565	11%	10%
Other Activities	365	326	6%	6%
Total	**5,931**	**5,416**	**100%**	**100%**

Folder two: personnel structure of the *Healthcare* Group

The *Healthcare* Group has employed 32 185 people worldwide as of 31 December, 2005, which is an increase of more than 10 per cent compared to the previous year (28 854). The number of employees working for the headquarters of *Healthcare* decreased by 232 and now accounts for roughly 33 per cent of the Group's worldwide personnel, while the number of employees worldwide increased by 3331 employees (see Table 3). Personnel costs have risen accordingly amounting to 1 699 €m in 2005 (see Table 4).

Folder three: the leadership competence set the *Healthcare* Group

The corporate leadership competency set defines the critical competencies managers need to possess to master the future challenges of the *Healthcare* Group.

Employees by region of the *Healthcare* Group in 2005		Table 3
	2005	*2004*
Healthcare Headquarters	9,853	9,621
Europe	8,732	7,956
USA/Canada	4,869	4,523
Asia Pacific	2,569	1,956
Latin America	3,706	2,944
Other employees	2,456	1,854
Total	**32,185**	**28,854**

Personnel costs of the *Healthcare* Group		Table 4
in €m	*2005*	*2004*
Wages and salaries	1,365	1,266
Social security and support payments	272	269
Pensions	62	61
Total	**1,699**	**1,596**

They have been developed based on an analysis of the business needs and by asking key players and HR people in nearly all locations of the company worldwide for their contributions. They are the basis for all HR practices and policies and are intended to ensure consistency across businesses and locations. They are comprised of business-related competencies, people-related competencies and personal competencies:

Business-related competencies include:

● Achievement orientation. Sets and works towards achieving challenging business objectives and targets and delivers outstanding results of the *Healthcare* Group.

● Innovation and change. Identifies the need for change and generates novel ideas to create or improve processes, systems, or products. Builds commitment to change.

● Decision making. Makes sound, timely and courageous decisions while balancing the risks and benefits to the *Healthcare* Group.

People-related competencies include:

● Team leadership. Inspires team members to maximize team output by providing clear direction, empowering them, establishing oneself as a leader and balancing team resources with assignments.

● Capability development. Develops people and the organization to ensure that the *Healthcare* Group has the capabilities needed for future success.

- Relationship building. Establishes mutually trusting relationships with people both inside and outside of the *Healthcare* Group in order to foster open communication and advance the goals and business.

- Impact and influence. Influences others to gain their support for driving the *Healthcare* Group's strategy and goals forward and enters conflicts if necessary.

Personal competencies include:

- Business understanding. Demonstrates an understanding of the implications of the *Healthcare* Group's strategies, industry dynamics, market trends, the competitive environment and one's function/profession in the accomplishment of business objectives.

- Analytical thinking. Approaches situations by identifying the best information available and systematically assessing it for meaning and impact.

- Self-development. Maintains a critical awareness of one's own working style and performance. Takes steps to build strengths and addresses development needs in line with the strategic objectives of the *Healthcare* Group.

Folder four: corporate human resource policies

The corporate human resource policies, which center around these leadership competencies are outlined in Table 5. These policies have triggered changes in the structures and processes of HR as practised across the firm's regions.

Table 5	HR policies of the *Healthcare* Group

HR area	Policy direction
Recruitment of key talents	Good recruitment practices
	Strategic workforce planning
Management development	Corporate management development
	system base on corporate leadership
	competency set
Transfer/mobility	Enhanced cross-functional mobility
	Well-balanced cross-regional mobility
Executive compensation	Attractive and competitive compensation
	Aligned bonus system
Pension system	Move to define contribution systems
Organizational development	Clear structures, efficient processes
	Corporate announcements on managerial
	and structural changes
Performance management	Balanced goal setting
	Measuring performance
	Clear feedback
	Linkage to variable pay

Folder five: the global performance system

Within the context of the new strategic orientation *Healthcare* has also implemented a *global performance system,* comprised of common standards for individual performance management, as well as a bonus system common to all executives. With this new global performance system *Healthcare* intends to strengthen the performance culture within the company and facilitate a common orientation for all managers.

The individual performance management system contains two elements:

1 *Goal setting and appraisal.* The new system ensures that every manager gets a precise orientation on expectations and priorities, clear feedback on individual achievements and contingent rewards.

2 *Leadership feedback.* In order to ensure a systematic development of each manager the system envisages a differentiated feedback on leadership behavior (based on the corporate leadership competencies), identification of development needs and a real consensus built for targeted development activities.

The individual performance management is based on consistent goal categories, a rating scale, a template, and a performance management cycle which is standardized at all sites, and coordinated to critical corporate processes. To ensure equal application, all managers belonging to the target group are trained on the system, its philosophy, procedures and goals.

Closely linked to the individual performance system is the *compensation policy* of the firm and the newly developed bonus system. The compensation policy is characterized by a balance of corporate standards and local applications for cash-related compensation. Fringe benefits are organized solely on a local or regional level.

The most centralized compensation element is *long-term incentives*. Following traditional industry practice, *Healthcare* grants share options to its managers. The size of the options is largely dependent on the level of management the position holds in the hierarchy. For every level a possible range of options is defined.

With respect to base pay and *short-term incentives* the situation is different. Global standards define an orientation for the level of total cash (fixed pay plus variable pay) to local/regional market standards. This means that the total cash a manager receives depends mainly on his or her local/regional compensation levels. Corporate standards define the market standards (based on target benchmark firms and target quartile positions). Pay level is largely defined according to local standards, while taking into consideration *Healthcare*'s industry-specific positioning targets.

The bonus of managers at *Healthcare* is based on three components:

- *Individual component.* Based on results of six to ten individual objectives in the respective area of responsibility. The weight of this component is 50 per cent.

- *'My unit'* component for regions, countries, global business units or regional business units. Reflects the performance of the organizational unit a manager is responsible for or working in. The weight of this component is 25 per cent. The goal achievement is measured by deviation between contribution margin and net sales goals and the actual numbers. Note that for Headquarter functions (e.g., controlling or HR), which have no profit and loss account the 'my unit' component is replaced by an additional individual component, which accounts for 25 per cent as well.

● *'Broader Context'* component. This reflects the joint responsibility for performance of a higher organizational level, i.e. the corporate level. The weight of this component is 25 per cent. The evaluation of goal achievement on corporate level is based on the degree of corporate goal achievement. Corporate goals are decided by the Board each year, the leading parameter is corporate contribution margin.

Both the 'broader context' and the 'my unit' components are leveraged. As a consequence, a goal achievement of, e.g., 120 per cent will lead to 200 per cent pay out for this component. On the other hand a goal achievement of less than 100 per cent will decrease the pay out for the respective component significantly. In this manner unit and broad context components have potential variance in payoffs and/or shortfall that are disproportionate to their simple weights. For every component a pay out is calculated, the sum of the three components is the total bonus a manager receives.

Folder six: an overview of the corporate and HRM strategy

As stated above, the competitive situation in the pharmaceutical industry has required *Healthcare* executives to redesign cross-border activities. While the company has always been active in a high number of foreign markets, business processes were traditionally locally oriented in the past. Wolfgang recalls a typology of international firms developed by Christopher Bartlett and the late Sumantra Ghoshal. Thinking in student terms, realigning or rebalancing *Healthcare*'s pay system means increasing global integration. In an abstract sense, *Healthcare* is attempting to develop a transnational strategy now by globally integrating certain activities while leaving room for local responsiveness. Figure 1 shows the developments in *Healthcare*'s cross-border strategy.

| **Figure 1** | Recent developments in the internationalization strategy of *Healthcare* |

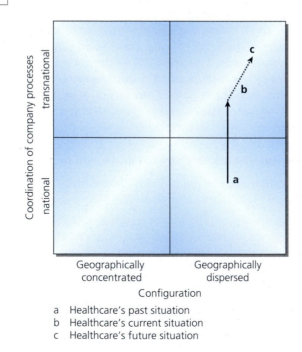

a Healthcare's past situation
b Healthcare's current situation
c Healthcare's future situation

This tendency is reflected in the HR strategy. While recruitment, selection, performance management and compensation policies for executives were designed according to local standards in the past, these processes are replaced by new solutions. These solutions focus on furthering global consistency of HR systems in order to respond to strategic changes on the corporate level. The overall goal is to strengthen an aligned performance orientation and to support global coordination, which is essential for globally integrated business processes. Elements indicating a stronger global integration include the above-mentioned common set of leadership competencies. This concept has been developed by the headquarters' HR department in cooperation with local HR representatives and managers from different regions and business units.

Bumps on the road to international coordination at *Healthcare* Group

Some of his colleagues in the HR department have told Wolfgang about problems with a standardized compensation model, which was supposed to be implemented two years ago. *Healthcare*'s aim was to have the same compensation system in each country. They wanted to have the highest possible degree of standardization in order to make transnational processes easier and more efficient. They planned to split the salary in two parts: 65 per cent fixed income and 35 per cent variable income depending on individual performance. The plan was to introduce this system not only for managers but for all employees.

Shortly after announcing the new plans, several of *Healthcare*'s regional HR managers and employees vocally opposed the new system. In France, managers even called for a strike. In Germany, the situation was difficult as well because the worker's council (Betriebsrat) did not agree to the new system and many negotiations followed. Many employees were frightened by the new 'risky' system as they had become dependent on a high percentage of fixed (guaranteed) income. They panicked at the thought of losing nearly half of their income and were afraid that they would never reach the 100 per cent they gained before.

As a consequence the implementation of this system was never realized. In designing the new compensation system, *Healthcare*'s management board had only considered economic issues, while disregarding existing, yet unspoken cultural frames of reference and perceptions. Wolfgang knew he had to be careful to avoid oversimplification and an overstandardization, and develop a more country-specific system which could be adjusted to local characteristics.

From his international background Wolfgang knew how important it is to include his HR counterparts from the different countries and regions in the process of further developing the HR policies and systems. This would allow him to more accurately understand the cultural and legal particularities at hand as well as ensure him a higher level of political support in *Healthcare*'s regions and countries.

For example, as a first step, Wolfgang has been in close contact with the HR representatives in the most important strategic markets, which currently are the USA and Japan. Here, he has negotiated exceptions for the standardized currency base of performance-based pay elements. He has learned that the local currency is most important because local managers are not used to considering a foreign currency and would not accept this as a major element of the compensation system.

Another issue for discussion was the percentage dedicated to fixed and variable pay. Wolfgang had problems understanding the Japanese opposition to the new global performance management system. During *Healthcare*'s yearly HR conference he felt that Mr Okubayashi, the Japanese head of HR at *Healthcare*, was not happy with the global performance system but did not really engage in discussions about how to improve or adapt the system. Thus, one evening Wolfgang invited him for dinner in a nice sushi bar in Düsseldorf where *Healthcare*'s yearly HR conference took place. Over innumerable cups of saki Okubayashi patiently outlined traditional compensation systems in Japan. Upon sobering up the next day, Wolfgang slowly realized that given culture and firm traditions it would be very difficult to introduce a high level of variable pay based on individual performance in Japan. He attributed this to a higher level of risk aversion characterizing the Japanese culture as compared to many other cultures. From his studies he knew about the Hofstede's dimensions describing cultural differences. As he recalled one of them was uncertainty avoidance. This points out the extent to which people are risk averse or are prepared to take risks. He thought that risk-taking managers were probably ready to accept large incentive payments while risk-averse managers were not prepared to accept a high income variability, which may be involved in performance-based pay. The latter may be the case in Japan.

When Wolfgang talked to the American head of HR at *Healthcare*, Thomas Miller, in a very late afternoon video conference, he received a different message. Miller loudly and repeatedly asserted that, from an American perspective, the global performance management system suggested by the headquarters was 'wimpy' and would not reward the outstanding achievements of 'franchise player' star managers. Compared to the big US pharmaceutical companies' percentage of variable pay for top managers, Thomas declared the monetary incentive system of *Healthcare* 'ridiculous' and demanded a higher proportion of variable pay. Wolfgang had to turn the video link sound down twice by the end of the web-enabled teleconference meeting. Was this a sign of a higher level of risk taking as a result of the underlying culture in the USA?

Step-by-step Wolfgang learned how important it is to ensure acceptance in the important strategic markets and to consider local labor market regulations. He came to realize that country-specific determinants such as cultural values or the legal environment of the firm must be considered if problems with cultural acceptance or legal conflicts are to be minimized. This newly acquired awareness made his mandate even more complicated. He had some general ideas about the contextual situation in some countries, yet he was unaware of the conditions in other countries. Implementing a new system always runs the risk of losing political support and insulting the perspectives of the local HR administrators and the business unit heads.

Thinking about the positive effects of the international HR conference as well as his individual discussions with Okubayashi and Miller, Wolfgang took the opportunity of visiting some of *Healthcare*'s subsidiaries and taking out the HR managers for lunch. He diligently tried to identify their relative positions as to the strengths and weaknesses of the current compensation system and collected ideas for his presentation to the board.

Conclusion: a not so happy Christmas

It is Christmas Eve. Wolfgang is sitting in a newly built ski hotel in Garmisch-Partenkirchen, overlooking the snowy mountains and preparing the final draft of his presentation for the management board meeting at the beginning of January. The six file folders lay spread out across the large blonde ash table and even across the oak floor as thick, heavy snowflakes silently fall outside. He is thinking about reorganizing *Healthcare*'s compensation system. His task is to find the right mixture of

Balancing global integration and local responsiveness in *Healthcare*'s compensation strategy

Figure 2

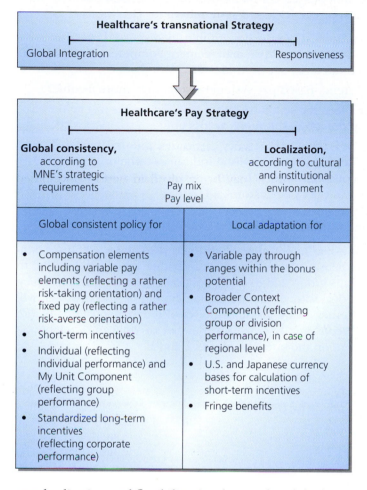

standardization and flexibility. On the one hand, he has to implement a new compensation system in order to reduce costs. On the other hand he has to take into account the traditional local HR practices. As he considers all he has learned at *Healthcare* over the last few months, he asks himself a series of questions. A visual learner, Wolfgang writes out a chart on a writing tablet that captures his sense of integration and local responsiveness at *Healthcare*. We present his sketch as Figure 2.

Question block A: standardization vs local responsiveness of compensation systems

Wolfgang reconsiders the degree of global standardization and local responsiveness of the current global compensation system.

1 Should he move some of the existing pay elements across the T account in Figure 2, shifting them from globally standardized to locally customized?

2 Should he add or delete some existing practices from the T account?

3 Should he change the weights or emphases (percentages) of existing elements of the pay system?

Question block B: job-based vs competency-based compensation

If *Healthcare*'s job-based pay dominated the existing system, while other approaches such as competency-based compensation have not been pursued, then what advantages might a competency based system have for Healthcare?

1 How can the firm communicate to the geographically dispersed executives the need to acquire and maintain those management competencies that have been defined in the competency set (in folder three)?

2 Would a purely competency-based pay system be somehow more flexible?

3 But then again, what about the standardization *Healthcare* has just achieved through standardizing the job descriptions across units?

4 How would he take these three competency categories and use them to develop a series of measurable, behavioral indicators to be used to assess an executive's contributions to *Healthcare?* In what sense should these new behavioral indicators be customized to local (regional) contexts? How can Wolfgang go about this process to ensure a balance of organizational standardization and local relevance?

Frustrated with the complexities he is facing, Wolfgang is planning a telephone conference with regional compensation administrators and other executives in order to expand his analysis with this group and to build political support for a new policy. Does he have the time to deal with all the inevitable differing perspectives that will emerge, and can they together create a systematic set of recommendations before his report is due to the *Healthcare* board? As a member of Wolfgang's telephone conference please comment on the question blocks A and B.

Note

1 The authors would like to thank Frank Kullak, Judith Eidems, Susanne Royer, Andrea Nägel and Sinnet Lorenzen for support.

Strategic forecasts and staffing formulation: Executive and managerial planning for Bosch-Kazakhstan[1]

Marion Festing, Professor of Human Resource Management and Intercultural Leadership, ESCP-EAP European School of Management, Berlin/Germany

Manfred Froehlecke, Vice President, Corporate Department Human Resources Management – Executives, Robert Bosch GmbH, Stuttgart/Germany

Introduction

Personnel planning and staffing issues are critical success factors in foreign subsidiaries of multinational enterprises. They must be designed in the context of corporate goals and issues and the specific situation in the host country. From a firm-internal perspective, personnel planning and staffing are related to a company's corporate strategy and embedded in the corporate human resource strategy. Thus, planning and staffing decisions must be coordinated with other HR activities within the MNE, such as human resource development. This perspective must then be balanced with a careful consideration of the particularities in the host-country context and the availability of qualified personnel within the external labor market.

In this case study, we will first outline the company background and then describe the situation in the country of interest, which is Kazakhstan. Based on this information it is your part to take the role of a Bosch corporate HR manager. You are asked to analyze both the company and country-specific context, and outline a proposed model for personnel planning and staffing of the Bosch subsidiary in Kazakhstan. If you should perceive any further information needs please explicitly define a realistic set of supporting assumptions.

Company background: Robert Bosch Group2

The Bosch Group is a leading global manufacturer of automotive and industrial technology, consumer goods and building technology. In fiscal 2006, some 260 000 employees generated sales of 43.7 billion euros. Set up in Stuttgart/Germany in 1886 by Robert Bosch (1861–1942) as 'Workshop of Precision Mechanics and Electrical Engineering', the Bosch Group today comprises a manufacturing, sales and after-sales service network of some 300 subsidiaries and more than 13 000 Bosch service centers in over 140 countries. One statement by the founder Robert Bosch is important to understand the HR philosophy characterizing this MNE: 'It is my intention, apart from the alleviation of all kinds of suffering, to promote the moral, physical and intellectual development of the people.'

Executive and managerial planning (EMP)

The international executive and managerial planning (EMP) at Bosch is part of the strategic planning process of the company. Once a year, the global executive staffing needs for selected countries are derived from each division's long-term strategic planning activities. Starting from the current local structure, the required number of managerial positions is determined within the parameters of an eight-year forecast. Various measures are taken to meet the managerial staffing needs. They can be short term (e.g. hiring of managerial staff from the external labor market, assignment of expatriates) or rather medium/long term (e.g. development of high-potential employees – see the employee development discussion below) or special programs like junior managers programs (JUMP).

The EMP is carried out using a standardized tool from the divisional HR department in cooperation with regional HR departments. Aggregated results are analyzed from division-, regional- and Robert Bosch World (corporate) levels. Continuous comparisons of the planned versus actual labor staffing situations provide feedback on those assignments which have to be initiated or redefined.

The planning period of eight years consists of two parts: the input for the first four years stems from business plans and succession planning. Forecast for the last four years is based on more global-macro assumptions, e.g. changes in the leadership projected at a figure of 5 per cent. Therefore, EMP is linked to instruments of employee development in the Bosch Group.

Employee development in the Bosch Group

Bosch understands employee development as a continuous process of maintaining and further developing employees' qualifications needed to cope with present and future challenges. A major principle in this respect is the promotion of employees from within Bosch rather than the acquisition of new hires from outside.

HR departments support employees and managers by providing tools and programs and giving guidance. The universally standardized systems and processes for employee development are depicted in Figure 1.

An important procedure for the development of employees is the management potential review (MED, see Figure 1),[3] which is conducted on a worldwide level. It pursues the following objectives:

- Full utilization of the company's reserves of high-potential employees without compromising on performance standards.
- Staffing requirements and development planning (middle and upper management) for the upcoming four years (succession planning – see EMP above).
- Consistency in planning and tracking of employee development and career advancement measures.
- Use of overseas assignments, project tasks, and cross-functional moves as common development measures.

Employees who show an above-average development potential with regard to specialist and management positions will be systematically prepared for the next management level by way of the 'manager development plan' (MDP). Besides outstanding performance, Bosch expects a task or role-relevant personality profile, preparedness to take on new tasks and greater responsibilities, mobility potential as well as willingness to take on international assignments. MDP is a prerequisite for promotion into managerial ranks.

Instruments of employee development

Figure 1

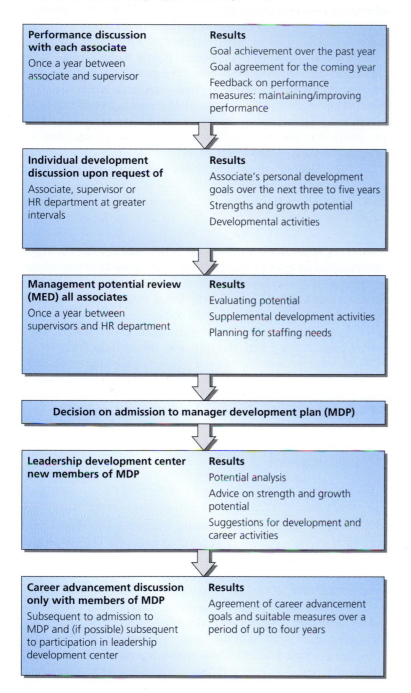

Performance discussion with each associate
Once a year between associate and supervisor

Results
Goal achievement over the past year
Goal agreement for the coming year
Feedback on performance measures: maintaining/improving performance

Individual development discussion upon request of
Associate, supervisor or HR department at greater intervals

Results
Associate's personal development goals over the next three to five years
Strengths and growth potential
Developmental activities

Management potential review (MED) all associates
Once a year between supervisors and HR department

Results
Evaluating potential
Supplemental development activities
Planning for staffing needs

Decision on admission to manager development plan (MDP)

Leadership development center new members of MDP

Results
Potential analysis
Advice on strength and growth potential
Suggestions for development and career activities

Career advancement discussion only with members of MDP
Subsequent to admission to MDP and (if possible) subsequent to participation in leadership development center

Results
Agreement of career advancement goals and suitable measures over a period of up to four years

The preparation of the MDP candidates is a mixture of on-the-job and off-the-job measures with the target to bring the employees into the next management level in no more than four years. In many cases the achievement of the career advancement objective is connected with the transfer to a new assignment.

Talent management

As stated before, Bosch mainly relies on hiring and developing talent from within the firm. Consequently, it is important to focus on the acquisition of qualified university graduates and professionals to meet a wider range of potential future managerial requirements. Besides direct entries and local programs, Bosch has a standardized Bosch-wide entry program for junior managers (JUMP).[4] The goal of the program is to recruit junior managers (master's degree with up to three years of professional experience) with the potential to assume a middle management position in 6–8 years.

The program lasts one and a half to two years and is comprised of three to four stages, including a six-month stay abroad as well as a cross-divisional assignment. This form of training emphasizes a common set of worldwide standards, experiences and activities, and is designed to permit more rigorous and systematic preparations for a range of management tasks.

Expatriates

Currently more than 2000 expatriates are working for Bosch worldwide. An expatriate, as defined by Bosch, is an employee working for more than 18 months outside his or her home country with special contractual conditions (contract in the host country for a limited period of time – normally three to five years – special allowances for hardship, cost of living etc.). Over 1100 Germans are working in more than 40 countries, approximately 500 employees from Bosch subsidiaries are working in Germany (inpatriates) and roughly 400 third-country nationals (TCNs) are assigned to locations outside their home countries for limited periods of time. A majority of these employees were assigned due to technical and process expertise, yet some assignments were made for career development or training reasons. Two-thirds of the expatriates are assigned in managerial ranks.

Bosch requires all top managers, beside their other experiences, to have at least two years international working experience. This international experience is an explicit prerequisite for promotion.

Country-specific features of Kazakhstan[5]

Kazakhstan is located in Central Asia with China, Russia, Kyrgyzstan, Turkmenistan and Uzbekistan as neighbor states (see Figure 2). It covers a total of 2 717 300 sq km. The climate is continental with cold winters and hot summers.

The population is 15 233 244 inhabitants (July 2006 est.) including a wide ethnic diversity (with 53.4 per cent Kazakhs, 30 per cent Russians, 3.7 per cent Ukrainians, 2.4 per cent Germans and some other ethnic minorities). Main religions are Islam (47 per cent) and Russian Orthodox (44 per cent). The state language is Kazakh but Russian is used in everyday business by most of the people. Kazakhstan became independent from the former Soviet Union in 1991 and is now is a republic characterized by an authoritarian presidential rule. The capital is Astana with 538 000 inhabitants.

The economic situation of the country can be described by a GDP real growth rate of 8.5 per cent (2006 est.), an unemployment rate of 7.4 per cent (2006 est.) and comparably low labor cost, averaging 0.86 US dollars per hour. Main exports include oil, ferrous and non-ferrous metals, machinery, chemicals, grain, wool, meat and coal.

The education system is one of the major concerns of the country. Public expenditure for education amounted to 2.4 per cent of GDP in 2006 but the education system is widely privatized. Nearly 4 per cent of the population holds a university degree. Due to a lack of public funding academic research is largely dependent on foreign aid.

Kazakhstan's geographic location | **Figure 2**

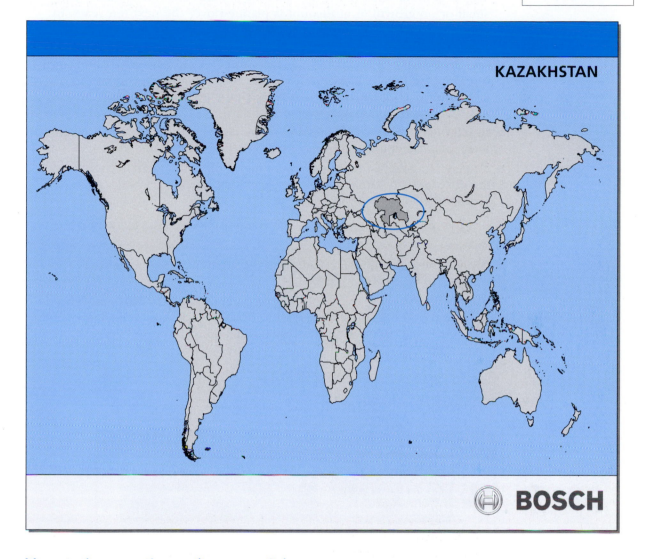

Your task: executive and managerial planning (EMP) for a subsidiary in Kazakhstan[6]

The board of management of the Bosch Group has requested an EMP for Kazakhstan in line with the yearly strategic long-term planning (eight years' forecast – see the third section above). The plan should predict the demand for executive staffing at all levels and for all divisions. It should also specify how the demand will be met, including staffing sources such as the use of expatriates, local management development plans (MDPs), special programs, e.g. JUMP, or external hires.

As seen from Bosch's corporate perspective, the situation in Kazakhstan is as follows:

● There are four production sites in different rural locations. Each one belongs to a different product division: gasoline, Bosch-Rexroth, security systems and diesel motors.

- Organizations are characterized by different market/product maturity stages: gasoline, Bosch-Rexroth, security systems are consolidated. Only small or no growth in headcount is planned over the next ten years. In contrast, diesel is still growing fast (headcount plus 30 per cent in the next three years).

- The labor market for qualified managers and specialists is very small. External hires in Kazakhstan will take much longer than equivalent processes in Germany. Local candidates have very little mobility and largely lack broader national or international experiences.

- Bosch's major production sites are by and large not attractive locations to most qualified employees.

- The high numbers of expatriates were the result of the rapid in-country growth especially for the diesel site. Higher management positions are currently solely filled by expatriates.

Taking the role of HR manager at Bosch you must address the following three issues:

1 Analyze the company and country-specific situation by using the steps outlined in Figure 3.

2 Plan the number and nature of short/medium-term (2007–2010) as well as long-term (2011–2014) staffing requirements on the basis of the figures in the chart on facing page and the described situation. Fill in your figures in the chart (Figure 4).

| **Figure 3** | Form for situation analysis |

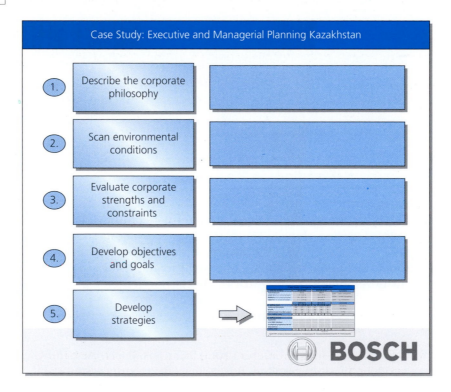

Planning chart

Figure 4

Case Study: Executive and Managerial Planning Kazakhstan

1. Personnel structure	Actual 2007	Forecast 2014	Comments
Total headcount	7632	8523	Lower = lower management
Lower (#/as % of total employees)	115/ 1,50 %	151/ 1,77 %	
Middle (#/as % of total employees)	54 / 0,71 %	70/ 0,82 %	Middle = middle management
Upper (#/as % of total employees)	3 / 0,04 %	3/ 0,04 %	Upper = top management

2. Staffing needs	2007-2010			2011-2014			Comments
	low	middle	upper	low	middle	upper	Further need because of growth
Headcount fluctuation	34	11	0	4	0	0	
Backfill	40	24	2	50	36	2	Replacement because of expatriate return, retirement
Additional needs from M&A projects	0	0	0	0	0	0	To simplify the case we left this point out
Total staffing needs	74	35	2	54	36	2	=203

3. Staffing sources	2007-2010			2011-2014			Comments
Expatriates							
Local MDP members							
Pogrammes, e.g., JUMP							
External hires							
Staffing total	74	35	2	54	36	2	=203

BOSCH

3 Finally, prepare an action plan describing how you will meet managerial staffing targets. Look especially at information provided in the 'employee development' and 'talent management' sections of the case for activities and timetables. Write down your action plan.[7]

List of Bosch-specific abbreviations and definitions

EMP: executive and managerial planning

MED: management potential review (MED is the German abbreviation for 'Mitarbeiterentwicklungs-Durchsprache')

MDP: manager development plan

Notes

1 The case study is imaginary. Bosch has no such activities in Kazakhstan. However, the described HR measures reflect current practices within this MNE.

2 See also www.bosch.com.

3 MED is the German abbreviation for 'Mitarbeiterentwicklungs-Durchsprache' or in English, 'Management Potential Review'.

4 The standardized entry program JUMP is still in the implementation phase. Other comparable programs, e.g., Management Trainee Programs, have been in place for some time.

5 This section is mainly based on https://www.cia.gov(cia/publications/factbook/geos/kz.html and http://service.spiegel.de/digas/servlet/jahrbuch?L=KAZ, 15 March 2007.

6 The case study is imaginary. Bosch has no such activities in Kazakhstan.

7 The case study is simplified. A detailed planning of functional areas is not our intention. The student should learn to ask the right questions about how to source manpower, what challenges the company faces in a difficult environment and what measures must be taken to meet future demands.

Norge Electronics (Portugal), SA

Stephen J.J. McGuire, PhD, is an associate professor of management and director of the CSULA Entrepreneurship Institute at California State University, Los Angeles. He taught at Georgetown University, the Catholic University of Portugal, Moscow University Touro, and the George Washington University, where he was awarded the Bender Prize for Teaching Excellence. He is a former partner of the Hay Group, where he worked as a management consultant for major organizations in 23 countries.
©2007 Reprinted with permission of John Wiley & Sons, Inc.

Executive summary

The case begins with the protagonist, João Silva, in Oslo for a meeting of personnel directors of the subsidiaries of a large Scandinavian multinational, Norge Electronics. Silva is the administrative director (finance and administration, HR, legal) of the division's smallest subsidiary – Norge Electronics Portugal. Silva had been asked by the vice president of human resources to present to the personnel directors what has been achieved in Portugal. The evening before his presentation, Silva received a fax from a consultant he hired in Portugal with the preliminary results of a climate study. The consultant's report is not what Silva expected and, in fact, raises questions about the effectiveness of a series of change actions implemented over the past two years. The case describes in detail the actions taken by Silva to 'professionalize' HR management in the Portuguese subsidiary. © 2007 Wiley Periodicals, Inc.

The annual meeting of personnel directors

In his hotel room in the city of Oslo, João Silva reviewed the presentation he would make the following day. Although he felt prepared, he was somewhat apprehensive. He had just received by fax from a consultant in Lisbon the preliminary results of a climate study of Norge Portugal. He had commissioned the consultant's study on the advice of Norge's vice president of human resources, with the understanding that the results would be included in his presentation, as initial evidence of the progress made in HR management in his country.

The next day, the annual meeting of Norge's personnel directors would take place. Silva would meet the personnel directors of the other Norge subsidiaries for the first time. He hadn't participated in the meeting before, mainly because Norge Portugal was a small subsidiary and Silva was not technically a personnel manager. His title was Administrative Director; he was accountable for finance, control and accounting, personnel, legal, and diverse administrative matters. In addition, the electronics division was one of the smallest divisions within the Norwegian multinational.

Each year, the personnel directors of the Norge subsidiaries met to hear the president of the conglomerate's vision of the company's future and the vice president for human resources' ideas for the HR function. Silva suspected that the VP of HR's speech might trigger a whole new stream of projects in some countries. After the speeches, there would be presentations by Silva and three other personnel directors about what had been done in their countries during the past year, issues encountered and results achieved. On the second day, the group would split up, with people going to different workshops. Silva had chosen the workshop on management development for the morning and pension plans for the afternoon.

Silva had been selected by the VP of HR to be one of the four directors presenting to the general audience. The VP had told many people, 'They do a lot of HR management in Portugal.' Silva had agreed with the VP of HR to provide an overview of the actions he had taken for the past two years and finish his presentation with the results of the climate study.

Norge electronics (Portugal), SA

Norge Portugal was founded nine years earlier, with headquarters in Lisbon. Its business purpose was the sale, installation and maintenance of sophisticated equipment for textile manufacturers. The Portuguese subsidiary endorsed a philosophy of 'total service' to its customers. Although its customer base was small, it was highly profitable and had an excellent reputation with the majority of its customers, many of whom were going through tough times. Norge's revenue came from four sources:

1 Sale of Norge equipment.
2 Fees from maintenance/service contracts.
3 Sale of spare parts (durable equipment as well as consumables).
4 Commissions on the sale of other equipment and spare parts from other manufacturers – mostly, but not exclusively, from other Norge companies.

Lars Jorgensen, the managing director, described the mission of the Portuguese firm the following way:

● 'Never sell to anyone who is not committed to increasing productivity.'

● 'Prove to the customer, and prove it again, that the textile industry, if well managed, can be profitable in Portugal.'

● 'Our prices should be a function of our added value to customers, not our costs.'

● 'Never hesitate to help a customer with a problem with a competitor's equipment . . . tomorrow the customer will remember who was there when help was needed.'

Jorgensen had an excellent reputation as a technician. An engineer, he also had a graduate degree in business administration from a leading international business school in Barcelona. The customers liked Jorgensen, who spent most of his time doing public relations and generating new sales. Silva also liked his boss very much, partly because Jorgensen rarely 'interfered' in the Administration Department.

The technicians at Norge Portugal liked to make their service calls accompanied by Jorgensen. They knew that he wouldn't hesitate to take off his jacket and tie (on those few occasions when he actually wore them) and get his hands dirty adjusting a machine or replacing a bit of wire. It was sometimes said that the best training that the firm had to offer was a service call with Jorgensen.

To service the maintenance contracts that nearly all customers had, the firm sent a team of technicians to the customer at least once per quarter to inspect the equipment and identify potential productivity problems. Technicians did preventive maintenance work, verified stock levels of spare parts and consumables, and so on. The team often spent time helping the factory's production manager with equipment that hadn't been sold by Norge. At first, Silva had thought that Norge went too far to satisfy a customer but gradually he changed his opinion. Customer loyalty was very high, and the commission that Norge earned on the sale of complementary equipment was one of the reasons that the Portuguese firm was so profitable.

Norge's unique selling proposition

Although many customers considered Norge's fees to be high, the monthly maintenance/service charge was generally accepted. The margin on the sale of equipment was high. The upcoming fiscal year promised to be good, since some customers expressed interest in upgrading equipment. Norge's unique selling proposition (USP) was its guaranteed increase in productivity. Before selling any equipment, Norge scrupulously studied current productivity levels at the customer. Although this was by no means an easy task, after nine years in the market, Norge had learned a great deal. Everything was documented carefully, and a complete report was prepared for the customer. Each semester, the customer controller produced a report on each customer's productivity level (per line of equipment) and compared it with a baseline, or starting point. Productivity was expressed as one number, the Norge Productivity Index (NPI). Naturally, the monthly report contained a breakdown of partial measures and a complete explanation, but Silva knew that the customers' general managers paid far more attention to the NPI number than anything else in the report. He also suspected they paid more attention to the NPI than to anything their own production managers might report.

This simple measurement approach had proven to be highly effective. GUIMTEX, for example, was a customer that followed Norge's advice scrupulously and was ready to add an additional line of equipment. GUIMTEX's current line had the following NPI evolution:

GUIMTEX		
Equipment: SA 4000; TXT 3.8: REV 47 (Model III)		
Installation: February 1999		
Baseline	2/99:	100
NPI	6/99:	83
NPI	12/99:	143
NPI	5/00:	161
NPI	11/00:	180
NPI	5/01:	199
NPI	11/01:	206
NPI	6/02:	219
NPI	12/02:	229
NPI	6/03 :	238
NPI	11/03:	244
NPI	5/04:	246
NPI	11/04:	269

Norge Portugal's structure

Norge Portugal had only 57 employees, although it did use technicians from other subsidiaries for major installation projects, usually from Norge Spain. Norge's departments were Sales, Service and Maintenance, Customer Control and Administration.

Sales department ('Departamento Comercial')

This department was accountable for the sale of new equipment and upgrades, pricing of products and services, and importing equipment and parts. The warehouse manager reported to the commercial director, Ole Halvorsen.

Service and maintenance teams ('Equipas')

Three intervention teams reported to the director, Henrique Fonseca. Lars Jorgensen considered the team concept to be strategic. Each team had between four and seven members: technicians and clerical employees. The North 1 Team was headed by Mario Pronto, North 2 Team by Ze Serra and Center/South Team by Pedro Paiva. In theory, each technician on the team could do all regular activities, although the team leader was the most experienced. Team members substituted each other often to ensure that each customer got 'total service', even on weekends and holidays, if needed. Rarely would a technician go alone to a customer, and quite frequently the whole team would descend on a customer, especially when a new line was installed.

Norge technicians had traditionally been classified in five categories, from Level I (the lowest) to Level V, basically according to their experience. Norge was not unionized (and thus had no collective bargaining agreement); however, the technicians found it practical to use these categories. It took between two and three years to train a good technician. Since technicians also sold, technical knowledge was necessary but insufficient. Customer relations, budgeting, teamwork skills and persuasion were all important aspects of the job.

Customers were assigned to teams based on geographic location and type of equipment. Fonseca tried to ensure that the amount of work done by the teams was similar. Some teams had to travel more than others did. Team N1, for example, concentrated more on the Greater Oporto area, although it also had one customer in the Lisbon area and GUIMTEX in Guimarães (between Oporto and Braga).

Team N2 had to travel somewhat more, servicing customers south of Oporto in Aveiro, near Braga, Guimarães, and Vila Nova de Famalicão, as well as customers near the Spanish border in Covilhã and Fundão. Team N2 had FEMIFA in V.N. Famalicão (north of Braga) but also TEXIWEAR in Aveiro (see Appendix A).

Team Center/South had customers in the greater Lisbon and Coimbra areas and still others scattered around the country, including one in the Azores Islands. This team also serviced two customers in Africa, although the maintenance agreement with African textile manufacturers was not identical to the agreements with domestic customers.

Customer controller department ('Depto. De Controlo De Clientes')

The customer controller was a young man, Nuno Abrantes, who had a special aptitude for this kind of work. According to Jorgensen, Abrantes was 'underpaid', but Silva knew that Abrantes wouldn't find any other work like this in Portugal. Abrantes' department had only four people, two of whom were administrative assistants. The fourth was a level III technician, who hoped to return to a service team but for now was happy to learn as much as he could with Abrantes. This department was accountable for invoicing, collection of receivables, documentation of customer productivity levels and preparation of NPIs based on information provided by technicians. Abrantes also played an important informal role in training technicians: Abrantes was Norge's IT troubleshooter, not because of his formal job duties, but rather because he was good with computers.

Administration department ('Departamento Administrativo')

Silva's department was accountable for finance management, treasury, general and cost accounting, legal and personnel. Outside counsel was retained to review all contracts and to provide general legal support.

The Norge family

According to Jorgensen, Norge's customers made up part of the 'Norge family'. Most were in the northern part of the country, which is why there were two teams for the North and only one for the South/Center. Silva saw no need to change the team structure or assignments, but Fonseca (director of 'Equipas') thought that another team was needed in the North. Team N2, according to Fonseca, traveled too much. Within the 'family', 18 customers contributed approximately 65 per cent of Norge's revenue, with the top four customers representing around 35 per cent of the business.

The current average NPI was 169 for all customers and not considering the year of installation. Jorgensen and Fonseca considered 169 to be 'good'. It was true that many Portuguese textile firms were 'behind' those in other European countries in terms of modern management. Silva felt that some of Norge Portugal's customers could compete in the global textile market, whereas others probably would not survive in the long term. Jorgensen was proud of his 'family' and prompted customers to expand their businesses. Although in theory all members of the 'Norge family' were supposed to get equal support, the technicians were more committed to some customers than others.

Silva was mostly worried about FEMIFA, an important customer in Vila Nova de Famalicão. FEMIFA's NPI (about 138) was not outstanding, but Silva knew that these things took time – and more time for some customers than for others. Because Silva had set up separate profit-and-loss accounts per customer, he knew that the FEMIFA account was highly profitable – if only Norge could collect its money in a timely and regular way. FEMIFA had one complete line installed but had also purchased supplementary equipment that brought high commissions to Norge. A good customer in all aspects except prompt payment, he thought.

Evolution of the personnel function at Norge Portugal

During his first year at Norge, Silva did little more than process pay. At this time, it had been important to establish basic procedures and routines and to 'legalize' the pay system. Before his arrival, some payments (for example, lunch subsidies and technicians' expense reimbursement) had been made in a disorganized way, and laws were being ignored; he had soon corrected that situation.

During his second year, Silva received Norge's VP of HR in Lisbon. The Electronics Division did not have a central HR staff. The VP of HR for the conglomerate directly took care of this division. During his visit, and through phone and written contact afterward, Silva developed an agreed upon set of priorities for the Personnel function in Portugal. Most of the ideas came from the VP of HR, but Silva implemented them without much support (or interference) from the MNC (multinational corporation) or from his managing director. Silva considered the VP of HR to be an 'ideas man' and Lars to be a 'customer man'. On the other hand, Silva considered himself to be a 'man of action', pragmatic, ready for any challenge, hardworking and business-minded. He approached the personnel function the same way he approached accounting: with an analytical mind and an orientation toward results.

Organization chart and job descriptions

Silva's first personnel project had been to put on paper the firm's organization chart. Although the company was small, Silva thought it necessary to document the structure. (See Appendix B.) The organization chart was presented to the directors, who agreed that it was an accurate depiction of the organization.

His second project was to obtain written descriptions of the tasks and responsibilities of all jobs. With Jorgensen's approval, he got each manager to describe the jobs of their subordinates on one side of a piece of paper. The next level of supervisors then described their subordinates' jobs, until all jobs below the directors were documented. To demonstrate that he took the matter seriously, Silva requested delivery of all documents by a certain date in December, and ensured that the deadline was achieved. He informed his colleagues that if documents were late, he would delay the payment of that month's expense reimbursement claims and the 14th salary.[1] Although there were a few complaints, he received all job descriptions within the deadline.

Job-evaluation project

With the job descriptions completed, Silva proceeded to job evaluation. He got from the VP of HR a manual with job-evaluation charts of an analytical point method of job evaluation used by firms in Scandinavia but unknown in Portugal. This method had been used by some of Norge's other subsidiaries, although references from these firms were not available. The system didn't seem very complex to Silva, who after a few phone calls to the VP of HR, managed to determine the points corresponding to each job description. He also evaluated the director-level jobs in the company, based on his knowledge of what they were accountable for, although job descriptions had not been prepared for directors.

When he had completed the exercise, he prepared a report for Lars and requested a meeting. They discussed this off-site over a long lunch at the *Clube de Empresários*[2] in order to maintain confidentiality. After explaining the methodology to Jorgensen, Silva showed him the points corresponding to the Norge jobs. Jorgensen made very few comments about the actual points that resulted but was concerned that there were too many job grades. He recommended fewer grades and fewer distinctions between jobs. Silva had argued that the *purpose* of the exercise was to differentiate the jobs! After some discussion, they agreed that instead of using the actual points corresponding to each job, they would 'round off' the numbers and use only one number (the midpoint) for all jobs in a given grade. They agreed to communicate to the directors only the grades – the points would not be disclosed. No information would be given to the employees at this point; it was 'too early'.

After the meeting, Silva prepared a 'map' showing the company's grading structure and the distribution of jobs in the grades. He wrote a memo to the other directors explaining that these grades had been approved by Jorgensen and should be used henceforth as guidelines in personnel decisions. The directors were instructed to discuss this matter only among themselves and not to communicate grades to the employees just yet (see Appendix F).

When new employees were admitted or when promotions occurred, Silva updated the grade 'map' and sent copies to the directors.

Dynamic human resources management

Silva's fourth area of concern was called 'dynamic HR'. The general idea had come from the VP of HR, who had asked Silva to think ahead about the HR needs of the firm in the years to come. In the job description project, Silva had come to the conclusion that certain functions were not really being taken care of by anyone in the company. It also seemed to him that some employees actually did very little. Silva described the long-term objective of this project as 'equipping the firm with the stocks of human resources needed to face the challenges ahead'.[3] To implement 'dynamic HR', he proceeded with two projects: staffing and pay-for-performance.

Staffing

Silva's first hire was Nuno Abrantes for the job of Client Controller. Previously, Fonseca had been accountable for this function. Although Fonseca had done a good job preparing the NPIs and reports, he had been overworked. Plus, Silva knew that Fonseca preferred to spend time with the customers, particularly some of the smaller customers – to show them that they were indeed part of the 'Norge family'. Fonseca didn't have a college degree but was an excellent technical engineer. Silva also hired an accountant, thus freeing his own time considerably. He hired secretaries for each director, so that they would have the support they needed to get the work done in a more orderly fashion. Although Jorgensen continued to claim that he didn't need a secretary, Silva knew that the increased size of the firm simply wouldn't permit that the directors continued to share one secretary. Upon Fonseca's insistence, more technical and clerical people were hired to fill out the teams.

Pay-for-performance

Silva knew that a staff increase would not necessarily lead to a more dynamic use of the company's human capital. Each employee, he felt, should be treated as an investment and therefore must provide an appropriate return. When he introduced the pay-for-performance system, he had four objectives in mind:

1 *To increase the pay of those employees with superior performance*. One thing that Jorgensen said sounded right to Silva: 'Good people are never expensive.'

2 *To reduce upward pressure on base salaries*. Without a system, salaries had tended to 'creep up' without any logic or justification. With a system, employees could look forward to increases as well as year-end bonuses in accordance with their performance.

3 *To detect those employees whose performance was unacceptable and take steps to remove them from the organization.* Firing in Portugal was a complex, messy affair to be avoided, except in extreme cases. However, Silva knew that if an employee did not receive any increase a couple of years in a row, then he or she would start reading the *Expresso*[4] very carefully.

4 *To rationalize the process of determining salary increases.* For many years, increases had been given for criteria that no one could explain logically.

Although it was true that very few employees had complained about pay, Silva felt that this was not necessarily a good sign. When the good performers complained, one needed to listen. When the poor performers *didn't* complain, one needed to listen even more carefully!

The results evaluation system

Because Silva had access to all the company's information on sales and profit margins per customer, it was possible for him to establish a system of remuneration for performance based on actual results – in other words, sales, profit margins per customer and so on. The accounting system allowed Silva to know exactly which employee sold what product or service, how many hours each technician had spent at each customer, and what margin each product or service provided. Silva called the new performance appraisal system the 'results evaluation system', which was implemented according to the following steps.

1 The administrative director reviewed the results of the year just completed, comparing actuals with the budget. For the Commercial Department, he calculated sales minus departmental cost of sales, not including any sales made by the service teams ('equipas'). This margin was compared against the budgeted figure. For the customer controller, he examined two aspects: days receivables and promptness in delivering NPI reports (percentage on time). For each equipa, he calculated the team's margin (revenues from sales, service, maintenance, spare parts and the like, minus product costs and cost of sales and service). All results were compared with the corresponding budget figures. This type of analysis was done for all departments, including his.

2 With the results of these analyzes prepared, he approached Jorgensen and asked the managing director to attribute a performance rating to each director. Jorgensen would review Silva's analyzes but was free to consider mitigating circumstances. Jorgensen met with each director to discuss how the year had gone. After these meetings, he informed Silva of his performance rating of each director.

3 Based on his own analyzes and the directors' performance ratings, Silva defined a 'recommended distribution' of ratings for each department. The idea was to allow the departments with better overall performance to have more 'excellent' and 'very good' performers and the departments with lower results to have fewer high evaluations. Silva informed each director of the expected distribution for his department. At first, there were some protests, but Silva explained that the director should use the recommended distribution as a guideline, and deviate from it if necessary.

4 The director of each department would then evaluate the performance of his department's employees. Because the firm was small, this was a manageable task. The director was free to use whatever system he felt appropriate; Silva asked only for the final results expressed in numerical form ('1' = poor; '5' = excellent).

5 Based on the best information he had, Silva prepared a theoretical performance score for each employee. Naturally, he didn't know the employees well enough to evaluate their performance, but he was able to get a good idea of each person's actual results. He was concerned that those employees who really added value to the company were not properly rewarded and that 'free riders' went undetected. For many employees, he

could calculate what he called a 'personal gross margin', an estimate of the value they added to the firm. The personal gross margin was calculated by revenue (sales, service fees, etc.) less salary, benefits costs and other personnel costs. This margin was then translated into a theoretical performance score on a 1 to 5 scale, according to the relative contribution of each person in the department. Silva's theoretical scores also took into account overall departmental performance – the number of '5's, '4's, '3's, '2's, and '1's corresponded to each department's 'recommended distribution' of ratings.

6   When Silva received the results from each director, he compared each person's performance score with the theoretical performance score. If the two scores did not match, Silva met with the evaluator to discuss the discrepancy. Well prepared with facts and numbers, Silva usually convinced the directors to change their evaluations, although this did not always happen. There were occasional disagreements with fellow directors and some tension with Fonseca.

7   With the final list of performance ratings, Silva simulated salary increases within the limits of the next year's budget. When calculating the new salary and benefits budget, Silva always left some 'fat' for unplanned merit increases during the year, although he disliked doing so. He recognized that both Jorgensen and Fonseca would pressure him for increases during the year and he wanted to make sure that there was some room within the budget to allow him to comply.

8   After he had simulated the salary increases, Silva calculated potential bonuses. The amounts would vary according to what money was available in the budget. For the current year, the system was designed to pay a bonus of about 20 per cent of base salary to the highest ('5') performers, about 10 per cent for 'very good' ('4') performers, 5 per cent to 7 per cent for 'good' ('3') performers, but no bonus for performance below 'good' ('2' or '1').

9   After numerous iterations, the administrative director would meet with the managing director to explain the proposed increases and bonuses, and get approval of the proposal. Typically, Jorgensen would make some minor changes to Silva's plan, but he accepted the overall framework (see Appendix E).

Based on this system, Silva had introduced some order into the salary administration process. Although personnel costs had increased significantly, some costs had become variable, which would provide the organization with greater flexibility in case of business downturn.

Pay market surveys

In order to understand how Norge Portugal paid its employees in relation to other firms in the country, Silva purchased two salary surveys. One survey provided data per function (sales, marketing, etc.) for 'typical' jobs in large, medium and small firms. This data contained no information on industry-sector differences. Silva believed that this survey was useful for comparing the salaries of Norge's directors, salespersons and secretaries with the general Portuguese pay market.

The second survey provided data for different job sizes, according to a certain job-evaluation method. Data were broken down by industry sector, firm size and ownership (foreign or Portuguese, state owned or private). To use the data, Silva correlated the Norge points that he had obtained in the job evaluation exercise with the benchmark jobs used as references in the survey. Thus, he obtained an estimate of comparable market pay for each Norge grade, aware that there was some margin for error. He chose as the reference point foreign-owned companies, which in Portugal tended to pay at a higher level than did domestic firms.

The climate survey

Based on a strong recommendation from the VP of HR, Silva hired a management consultant to carry out a study of Norge Portugal's climate. The VP of HR believed that Silva should present the study results at the Oslo meeting, thus providing some evidence of the progress that had been accomplished. Working together, the consultant, Silva, and Jorgensen had customized a questionnaire that the consultant had used successfully elsewhere. The questionnaire was distributed to all Norge Portugal's employees, along with a cover letter signed by Jorgensen and a pre-stamped envelope addressed to the consultant. Because of the small sample size, no demographic data on respondents were requested. All responses were strictly confidential. The consultant would report to Norge only the aggregate response. In addition, the consultant interviewed six Norge employees, in order to understand the firm better and be able to interpret the survey results (see Appendix C).

As Silva was about to leave for Oslo, the consultant informed him that 48 questionnaires had been returned. He promised to send Silva a preliminary report with the quantitative survey results as soon as possible. The consultant would also prepare a report with his conclusions after analysis of the results and interviews, but this report would only be available after Silva returned to Lisbon (see Appendix C).

Notes

1 According to Portuguese law, employees at all levels receive 14 monthly payments per year. The '13th' month is provided when the employee takes his or her vacation (usually one month in the summer) and the '14th' is paid before the Christmas holidays.
2 The Business Managers Club, a Lisbon upscale restaurant typically frequented by executives.
3 A somewhat literal translation of the original Portuguese.
4 The *Expresso* is the Lisbon newspaper with the largest job advertisement listings.

Appendix A. Map of Portugal

Appendix B. Organization chart, Norge Electronics (Portugal), SA

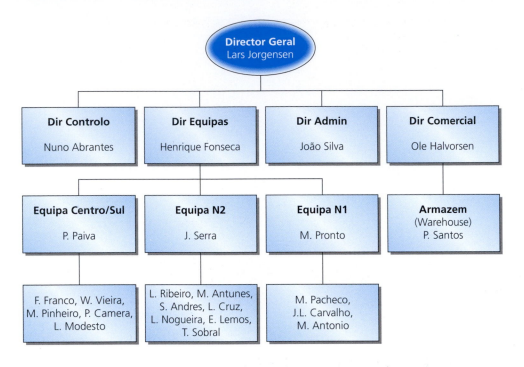

Appendix C. Climate study factors

SAT – JOB SATISFACTION
The degree to which employees are satisfied with their current jobs.

CLAR – CLARITY OF MISSION AND OBJECTIVES
The degree to which employees understand and accept the organization's mission and objectives.

ESTRUT – STRUCTURE
The degree to which the organizational structure supports, rather than interferes with, getting information, making decisions and getting the work done.

SIN – SYNERGY WITHIN THE ORGANIZATION
The degree to which people in different parts of the organization work together, support each other and do not duplicate activities.

AMB – BUSINESS AMBITIOUSNESS
The degree to which the mission and objectives are perceived as lofty and challenging.

ESTILO – MANAGEMENT STYLE
The degree to which managers' styles are supportive of employees and helpful in getting the work done.

REMUN – REMUNERATION
The degree to which remuneration is perceived as (a) internally equitable, (b) competitive with other organizations, and (c) supportive of individual and team performance.

IDENT – CORPORATE IDENTITY
The degree to which employees (a) perceive the organization as having a unique identity and (b) accept and support the identity.

EMPOW – EMPOWERMENT OF EMPLOYEES
The degree to which employees feel empowered to take the actions and decisions they need to take in order to get the job done. Also, the perception of how much the organization empowers, rather than controls, employees.

RH – HUMAN RESOURCE POLICIES
The degree to which human resource policies and practices are perceived as (a) supportive of getting the work done, (b) appropriate to employee needs, and (c) appropriate to prepare the organization for the future.

Appendix D. Preliminary results of the climate study

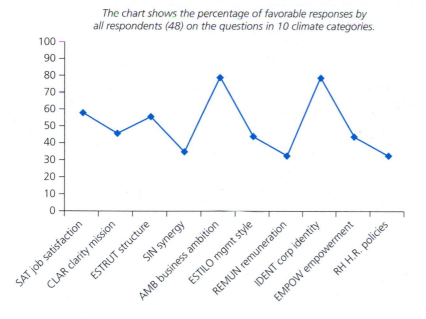

The chart shows the percentage of favorable responses by all respondents (48) on the questions in 10 climate categories.

Appendix E. Norge Portugal Grades

Grade 20 is the highest and corresponds to the managing director's job; grade 1 is the lowest.

Norge Grade	Grade Midpoint	Number of Employees
20	1500	1
19	1300	
18	1130	1
17	980	2
16	850	
15	740	
14	645	1
13	560	1
12	490	2
11	420	3
10	370	1
9	330	2
8	300	9
7	260	4
6	230	6
5	200	5
4	175	7
3	150	3
2	130	3
1	100	6
	Total	*57*

Appendix F. Job evaluations, Norge Electronics (Portugal), SA

Position	Incumbents	Grade	Grade Midpoint
Director Geral	L. Jorgensen	20	1500
Director Comercial	O. Halvorsen	18	1130
Director Administrativo	J. Silva	17	980
Director Equipas	H. Fonseca	17	980
Director Controlo Clientes	N. Abrantes	15	740
Accounting Supervisor	P. Pereira	13	560
Treasurer	A.P. Argento	12	490
Leader Equipa N2	J. Serra	11	420
Leader Equipa N1	M. Pronto	11	420
Leader Equipa C/S	P. Paiva	11	420
Tech Rep Level V	L. Ribeiro, M. Pacheco, F. Franco	8	300
Tech Rep Level IV	M. Antunes, J.L. Carvalho	8	300
Tech Rep Level III	L. Nogeira, S. Andres, W. Vieira, M. Pinheiro	8	300
Tech Rep Level II	T. Sobral	8	300
Import/Export Clerk	R. Ferreira	8	300
Tech Rep Level I	P. Camara, L. Modesto, M. Antonio, E. Lemos, J. Cruz	7	260
Bookkeeper	P. Costa	7	260
Senior Sales Clerk	S. Jesus	6	230
Warehouse Manager	P. Santos	6	230
Clerk (N1)	J.L. Reis, R. Coutinho	5	200
Clerk (N2)	H. Castelhano, C.J. Gouveia	5	200
Clerk (C/S)	P. Santos Silva	5	200

Appendix

Useful IHRM websites

http://www.shrm.org/
This is the (US) Society for Human Resource Management (SHRM) home page list of international HR websites.

http://www.shrmglobal.org/
Homepage of the Institute for International HR, a division of the Society for Human Resource Management (SHRM). This home page is valuable in details of the *International Human Resource Management Reference Guide,* mentioned later in this Appendix.

www.worldatwork.org
Home page of WorldatWork, a US-based total rewards professional association. This organization offers a certification for Global Remuneration Professional (GRP).

www.astd.org
Home page for the American Society for Training and Development (ASTD).

www.hrps.org
Home page for the (US) Human Resource Planning Society, based in New York City, New York.

http://www.aibworld.net/
The Academy of International Business home page.

www.emeraldinsight.com/
Emerald publishes a wide range of management and library and information services journals. The electronic databases allow instant access to the latest research and global thinking.

http://www.ihrim.org/
The International Association for Human Resource Information Management (IHRIM).

http://www.ipma-hr.org/
Home page of the International Personnel Management Association (IPMA), a professional association for public personnel professionals, primarily those who work in federal, state or local government. The page includes a list of useful HRM sites around the world.

www.cipd.co.uk/default.cipd
Home page of the Chartered Institute of Personnel and Development, UK.

http://www.workindex.com/
A search engine (based at Cornell University) targeting work and HR-related websites.

http://www.fedee.com/index.shtml
The Federation of European Employers.

http://www.eurunion.org/
The US site of the European Union.

http://ciber.msu.edu/
The World Wide Web server of the Center for International Business Education and Research (CIBER) at Michigan State University.

www.mgmt.purdue.edu/centers/ciber
Another of the Centers for International Business Education and Research.

http://www.ita.doc.gov
This site is produced and maintained by the International Trade Administration, US Department of Commerce.

http://www.windhamint.com/
GMAC Global Relocation Service provides information about international relocation and expatriate management.

http://www.meridianglobal.com
Meridian Resources website is designed to help pre-departure training for expatriates.

http://www.expat-repat.com/
ExpatRepat provides coaching for expatriate performace in international assignments.

http://www.ilo.org/
International Labour Organization.

http://www.ey.com/global/content.nsf/uk/institute_for_global_mobility
The Ernst & Young Institute for Global Mobility.

http://www.erc.org/
Employee Relocation Council's website provides information about international relocation and expatriate management.

http://www.fedworld.gov/
Fedworld information network hosted by the US Department of Commerce.

http://www.livingabroad.com/
Magazine for expatriates.

http://www.expatforum.com/
Site aimed at expatriates, with a chat line.

http://www.unctad.org/
United Nations Conference on Trade and Development.

http://www.transparency.org/
Transparency International's Corruption Index – ranks 102 countries on perceived level of corruption.

http://www.towers.com
Towers Perrin is a global human resource consulting and administration firm. It claims to help organizations manage their investment in people to achieve measurable financial performance improvements.

http://www.eiro.eurofound.ie/
The European Industrial Relations Observatory online.

http://www.eiu.com/
The Economist Intelligence Unit.

http://ethics.sandiego.edu
The site provides both simple and concept definitions and complex analysis of ethics, original treaties and sophisticated search engine capability; covers ethical theory and application.

http://commerce.depaul.edu/ethics/
Has many valuable ethics and professional resources.

http://www.eben-net.org
The European Business Ethics Network, EBEN, is an International network dedicated to the promotion of business ethics in European private industry, public sector, voluntary organizations and academia. It provides links to many other relevant websites.

Other resources

The Institute for International Human Resources, a division of the Society for Human Resource Management, produces a *Reference Guide* that is updated regularly. It lists resource organizations, expatriate policies, embassy listings and websites. It contains a glossary of terms used in IHRM, classified and alphabetically grouped into six major HRM functional areas: Management Practices, Employment, Training and Development, Employee and External Relations, Compensation and Benefits, and Other HRM (e.g. travel).

Index

Note: page numbers in bold refer to Figures, Tables and boxed material